JACK DANIELS IF YOU

JACK DANIELS
IF YOU PLEASE

Kelston Ross

Antony Rowe Publishing Services

*This book has been printed digitally and produced in a standard specification
in order to ensure its continuing availability*

Published by Antony Rowe Publishing Services 2004
2 Whittle Drive
Highfield Industrial Estate
Eastbourne
East Sussex
BN23 6QT
England

ISBN 1-905200-03-X

Printed and bound by Antony Rowe Ltd, Eastbourne

CONTENTS

Chapter		Page
1	Newton Heath 1949	1
2	Stateside	4
3	Hank Williams at Baton Rouge	10
4	Home Again	22
5	Scandinavia	30
6	The Drifters.	37
7	Mister Spaceman.	41
8	Truck Driving Man	47
9	Early Gigs	55
10	The Great Escape	64
11	Germany Calling	73
12	Welcome To France	89
13	Heartbreak Hotel	101
14	Back To The Bases	110
15	The Turkey Trot	119
16	The Playboy Club	149
17	Back To Europe Again	167
18	Hong Kong Blues	174
19	Good Morning, Vietnam	180
20	Thailand	210
21	The Land Of The Rising Sun	215
22	Taiwan	224
23	Malaysia	229
24	The Manchester Scene	237
25	Troubles And Tragedies	243
26	Cornwall	256
27	Stars And Bars	268
28	Johnny Bond Tour	281
29	North Of The Border	291
30	Television	299

Chapter		Page
31	A Blanket On The Ground	310
32	The Buffalo And The Arkansas Hacksaw	316
33	The Wembley Festival	320
34	Nashville West.	328
35	Kenya	332
36	San Remo.	340
37	Canada	345
38	The Tale Of Two Festivals	355
39	Viva! Espana	359
40	Brittany	370
41	Waltzing Matilda	383
42	Back To The Ramparts	396
43	The Jersey Lily	401
44	Beautiful Bath	418
45	Florida. We Love It!	423
46	Little England Beyond Wales	434
47	Oh No! Not Spain Again.	439
48	California Here We Come	444
49	Viva! Las Vegas	449
50	The Cherry On The Cake	455

ACKNOWLEDGMENTS

I sincerely doubt that this book would have ever appeared in print had it not been for the guidance, patience, and professional expertise of David Byram–Wigfield of Cappella Archive, who guided me through the mysteries of modern publishing and electronic editing with an amazing clarity and an ever–present word of encouragement. Such men are rare in these frantic times. I am deeply grateful to him and recommend his company to any aspiring writer marooned on the log–jam of the publishing world.

I offer a word of praise to Roy Ballantyne in explaining the mysteries of Adobe Photoshop and to the Bath Design Centre whose skills were invaluable in the restoration and production of the photographs in the book.

I am grateful to my wife, Kitty, who has been at my side throughout this Odyssey, encouraging me in the enterprise and spending long hours reading proofs, keeping me focused on the task in hand. I also owe a dept of gratitude to her mother, who believed in me when others had doubts, and the great entertainers from whom I learned my craft, men like Johnny Cash, Tex Williams, Lefty Frizzel, Willie Nelson, and many others.

To record producers Martin Grinham and Joe Stead, and respected journalists like Pete Smith, Tony Byworth, Alan Clacket, and Jean Mills, I give my special thanks, as well as to broadcasters Kelvin Henderson, Trevor Fry, and Joe Fish, for the air–play they gave to my work.

I also owe a debt of gratitude to the great Clinton Ford, who re–inspired me and showed me the path of destiny at a time when I was disillusioned and drifting.

Frank Yonco

INTRODUCTION

In a December issue of Country Music Round Up a few years ago, I suggested that we should honour the early pioneers of our music in the UK and asked the readers for some suggestions. The name that came up more than any other was Frank Yonco, who was one of the UK's first Country Stars and has remained one for more than four decades. The longevity of his career is quite remarkable and yet his induction into Country performing was even more so.

Today, it is a not hard for the would-be Country Music performer to learn his trade. There is a wealth of CDs, videos, Country shows on radio, television specials and regular tours from American artistes but back in the fifties when Yonco started, there were precious few sources to learn the Country Music trade from. If you were extremely lucky, you might have picked up the odd single left behind by the G.I.s or brought in from the States by some merchant seaman. So, as he saw it, there was only one way to learn and as fate played her hand, presenting him with an opportunity, he arrived on the Texas seaboard, where he began his career with the Galveston Splash band playing in the tough bars and oilrigs of the area.

Returning to Britain (care of US Immigration) Yonco immediately began to develop both his own career and the British country music scene by organising a band, starting the UK's first club dedicated solely to Country Music (as opposed to Folk music) and staging Britain's first country music festival, in Altrincham in 1962. Word drifted back across the Atlantic that at last there was a British band that could provide backing or support for top class American Country artistes.

Tommy Collins, a close friend of Merle Haggard, was the first in 1962 quickly followed by the Bluegrass legend Bill Clifton and then the doors opened, not only for Yonco, but also for the big Nashville names. Johnny Cash sought Yonco's backing in 1963 (and again in 1966) and following quickly Kay Adams, Bobby Bare, Johnny Bond, Skeeter Davis, Dave Dudley, Don Everly, Lefty Frizzell, George Hamilton IV, David Houston, Wanda Jackson, Roger Miller, Willie Nelson, Vernon Oxford, Carl Perkins, Red Simpson, Red Sovine, Billie Jo Spears, Billy Walker, Hank Williams Jnr, Tex Williams, Sheb Wooley and a host of others. A veritable "A to Z" of sixties American Country stars of the Golden Era

Soon, Kit Connors brought her singing talents to the band allowing Yonco to present the complete show. In a short time the Texas Drifters were in worldwide demand. In 1967 the show played in eastern Turkey and the following year, at the height of the hostilities, Vietnam, they were entertaining American and Australian troops. But it wasn't all war zones. Yonco and his troupe played some of the most prestigious cabaret clubs in Hong Kong, Japan, Malaysia, Taiwan and Thailand and it was whilst in Japan that Yonco met the legendary songwriter Harlan Howard and at his suggestion changed the band's name to the Everglades. Back home the Frank Yonco Show was the subject of a Granada TV documentary leading to numerous invitations for radio & TV work and he was kept extremely busy on the growing cabaret circuit. The demand for the act became so heavy in Europe that Yonco and Kit had to open a base in Frankfurt as well as their new home in Cornwall, a place they love and where they established the "Stars And Bars Club" and it was from there that the band made their many tours of Britain.

In 1977 the Everglades made successful appearances on the top rated television talent show "New Faces" and the "New Faces All Winners" shows which led to a contract with Westward Television for a nationally networked series called "Country Style". Appearances at the "International Festival of Country Music" at Wembley in 1978 and 1979 further consolidated the Everglade's position as the top country band in Europe but by 1980 the Yonco feet were itching again and so off to Canada and America he went. This was followed by shows in Italy, Nairobi and Mombassa, Kenya before further European commitments demanded a six year sojourn in France where summer seasons in St. Malo, Deauville and Dinard, supplemented by shows in Paris kept the Everglades extremely busy. This French connection was broken by a tour of Australia in 1983, then back to France for seasons at the "Mississippi Club" in Nice and the "Montelimar Hotel" in Monaco. The early nineties saw America beckoning again with shows at the "Cheyenne Saloon" in Orlando, Florida, "BB King's Club" in the Universal Studios in Hollywood, and guest appearances on the "Jumping Boots" television show transmitted from the "Excalibur Hotel" in Las Vegas. In 1997, back in Britain, HTV transmitted his show from the River Avon entitled "Frank Yonco's Bath Night".

Although now retired from life on the road, Yonco has turned his talents to acting and writing and is as busy today as he was throughout the years.

Forty plus years in the business, twenty–eight star tours in twenty–five countries, more than a dozen albums and five singles (including two chart entries), Yonco's remarkable achievements continued with twenty–five radio shows and five television series plus operating four night clubs, three pubs.

Frank Yonco is definitely a legend in his time.

So now it's time to enter the world of Frank Yonco, a world that takes the reader from post war Manchester and a teenager with stars in his eyes, to his homes in Bath and Nice, via many exotic, and some definitely dodgy destinations along the way. You will discover how the unknown teenaged dreamer became the world famous Frank Yonco in what the early fifties reviewers would have called "A Ripping Yarn".

Pete Smith 2004

PREFACE

This is the story of Frank Yonco, one of the great characters of the music business, of his personal experiences on the road and his refusal to accept any boundaries to either his music or to his life. This is a wonderful tale of travel, adventure and the music business, covering the period from his arrival in Texas to his last TV shows in Bath. It chronicles over forty years of world travel with all its ups and downs, from the desperate gambles and menial jobs to keep body and soul together to the great heights of performing at some of the world's top venues, from the tough 'Chicken Wire' joints of Galveston to the thrill of playing at Las Vegas, L.A. and on the French Riviera. Working with some real stars, and quite a few who were cheap, phoney and shallow.

Here are first hand experiences of the Cold War in Kurdistan and of a Real Hot one in 1968 Vietnam. The disillusion of Australia and the frisson of entertaining at some of the fabulous 'family' controlled casino clubs of Japan, Taiwan and Kenya. There is a lot of humour here but also tragedy and death. Experience a car wreck in the Anatolian desert and sample the manic world of Northern Clubland and a job designing astronauts' space suits. It's all here, with some tips for those who aspire to live by the Code of the Road from the *Little Red Book of Chairman Yonk*.

On the road with a travelling band finds you in the most unlikely places meeting the most unusual people and involved in some of the most fascinating and bizarre situations, some of them good, others not too pleasant. This Odyssey is seen through the eyes of Frank Yonco, a restless musician whose burning quest for adventure pushes him forever onwards to find out if the grass is really greener on the other side of the hill and it is a tale that will take you from the working class suburbs of Manchester, north to the Lands of the Midnight Sun. south to Sydney, east to Japan and Vietnam and west to Vancouver and we journey on to the plains of East Africa and the wilds of Anatolia and into the sophisticated culture of Western Europe and all stops between.

Worldly success comes his way but it is truly secondary to his love of the music and life's ever–changing kaleidoscope so come along and share these adventures.

We're leaving now. All Aboard.

*　*　*　*　*　*

1
NEWTON HEATH 1949
Crackin' Bovril, Grommit

I don't know if you have ever seen Manchester on a wet winter's evening. It doesn't look very good but a few years ago it was even worse.

I can clearly remember the scene as if it were yesterday. It was Tuesday and quite naturally it was raining. I was standing under the Failsworth Co–op store's clock which apparently had stopped at exactly three fifteen, about six years earlier. It was at the intersection of Church Street and Oldham Road in the shabby north eastern district of Newton Heath. The recently installed sodium street lights were reflected in the wet cobble-stones and I stood absorbed by the specter of a dirty, semi deserted, single bogie tramcar clanging and splashing its way down from Failsworth Pole—great.

I was a callow sixteen and dressed in the height of fashion of those far off pre Oxfam Days. The rain guttered off my cheap 'Attaboy' trilby hat, its imitation suede headband impregnated with the Brylcreem from my parted and quiffed short back and sides haircut. I was wearing my father's old gabardine raincoat, off which the rain ran down steadily to soak my twenty two inch wide, turned up gray flannels. It also seeped gently through a small hole in my dull yellow Freeman, Hardy & Willis crepe–soled brothel creepers. There I stood, a mass of teenage confusion, jangling my last one shilling and nine–pence (8p in new money), in the only pocket that did not have hole in it.

I was caught on the horns of a dilemma. What should I do? Go to the pictures or to Joe Hall's Temperance Bar? What I'd liked to have done was to join the French Foreign Legion, not that I wanted to shoot anybody, I liked the military music and wanted one of those caps with a cloth hanging down the back (Mad or wot). However, I was not old enough—and anyway, my Mum would have my supper ready. So how about going to the pictures then? Naw. That would take my entire one and nine pence and the thought of Jean Simmons and Anthony Steel did not really set me on fire. No, Joe Hall's it is. Yeah, that's what I'll do. I'll have hot beefy Bovril and sod the expense.

Joe's Missus, Fat Edna, served this Bovril in a sort of big eggcup with a handle on the side. The other side carried an advert telling you how the drink had sustained the British soldiers in the Boer War. (No wonder it took so long to get it sorted out). So turning up my grease–rimmed collar I squeegee'd across the cobbles, lost in my dream world, imagining I was a tall Humphrey Bogart or a thin Robert Mitchum. The Second World War was over. *And I'd missed it.*

In those days it seemed that I had missed everything but as I sat there, burning my mouth on the hot rim of my huge eggcup and watching the local girls having the vapours over the latest Van Johnson movie, I decided to do something about it.

Like many young men of my day I loved all things American. The bitter, resentful, brainwashed generation was not yet born and I was fascinated and will now admit, fooled by those wonderful college campus films where everybody had a car and the sun shone every day. Wouldn't it be great to be in one of those college bands. But how could such a dream come true? What could be done? By this time I only had a shilling (5p) left from my original one and nine so for the moment America was out of the question.

Although I was an only child I was never a lonely one, as I surrounded myself with reams of dreams and fantasies and in spite of my blistered lips and wet feet, I was not at all unhappy. You see I had a secret ambition—I wanted to be in showbiz. Late at night I would tune in my portable radio to AFN Frankfurt where I discovered a music that few British people knew about, American Country Music and vowed that one day I would have a band that played it but for the moment it had to stay secret because my Mum and Dad would not have understood my fantasies and having experienced at first hand the depression years of the thirties, they wanted me to have a secure job. So I kept my dreams to myself and on nights when I was alone at home, I experimented by putting a large copper pan on my head, which acted as a echo chamber. That way I sounded a bit like Bing Crosby, Dean Martin or my real favourite Buddy Clark. (Who?) It was all a bit hopeless really because I couldn't imagine anyone booking a singer with a pan on his head, still, it was an idea, wasn't it? (But one day my dreams did come true. The singing I mean, not the bit about the pan.*) A distant church bell struck the magic hour of ten o'clock. It was the time the pictures ended and soon the streets would be swarming with damp people wearing crumpled coats for about ten minutes and just maybe, a bit of talent might flop into Joe Halls by mistake. Ooh look—my Bovril's gone cold.

This burning desire was assuaged a couple of years later when the RAF unwittingly provided a conduit to my dreams with a radar fitter's training suitable for a job on one of the new supertankers. So I was off and running.

PICKER'S TIP 1

This is very important. Make up your mind at the outset. Are you going to run a Band or is it going to be a Group? Two very different codes of principles apply. Ignore them at your peril.

The Ballad of Clayton Vale

When I was nine and you were ten and we were both John Wayne
We'd hide in the Devils Archway from the drizzling northern rain
Then we'd climb the Cinder Mountains and ride the Medlock trail
To our land of adventure, we called it Clayton Vale

There was a river and two bridges and a singing waterfall
And a cave that you could hide in if you heard your mother call.
It was here we rode with Hop–along and Zorro was our King
And we could help Flash Gordon defeat the Emperor Ming

But Clayton Vale's gone away now it seems.
Gone forever is the land of my dreams
Childhood ghosts and memories wander through the new brick lands
And I wonder, will it ever be the same

When I was ten and he was nine and you were Randolph Scott
And I could swim like Buster Crabbe, believe it or not
Then we could chase those Clayton Kids across the Droylsden line
Oh yes we had ourselves a time

But the diggers and the dozers came and the planners had their way
And I doubt if what I sing about you'd find there today
But maybe on some summer's night as you walk the Medlock Trail
You might just hear the laughter that once rang in Clayton Vale.

*   *   *   *   *   *

2
STATESIDE
Galveston Island, Texas

Well, I couldn't wait to get off that stinking ship and my chance came when
we anchored off Galveston Island on the Texas Gulf Coast. It had been a
terrible trip: First from Liverpool in a dirty old freighter, wallowing across
the raging Bay of Biscay to St. Nazaire where we were hustled aboard a
huge freshly painted empty tanker for a nightmare passage to the port of
Caracas in Venezuela and with the captain stopping at every island in the
South Atlantic it took, over five weeks of bouncing about to get there. We
called in at Cape Verde and Madeira but none of the crew got a chance to
go ashore and when we did finally reach the Caracas Roads our Greek captain discovered that his floating dinosaur was far too big for the dock so we
had to spend another stifling fifteen days laid to in a haze of oil fumes ten
degrees north of the equator while our cargo was ferried out in lighters and
pumped aboard. The heat and the smell were appalling. Nobody was happy
not even the other two radar operators who were Spanish but I was more
desperate than anyone else and I had been looking for a chance to jump
ship since I realized that we were headed for the USA—I finally hit on a
scheme.

The following morning I went to the First Mate's cabin and said that I
was due for a malaria shot before we undertook the next leg of the trip. It
was not due for another ten days but I pointed out that the way things
were going it could be a month or more before we made our next landfall
and it was not wise to travel on without it, as it was putting the rest of the
crew at risk and if we got quarantined the owners wouldn't like that one
bit. With great reluctance our odious First Mate authorized my trip ashore
for the required booster shot and I mentioned that I also would have to pay
the doctors fee and drew $80 from my pay and as the inoculation had to be
recorded in my pay book I told him that I would need that as well. He was
loath to part with it but he handed it over, warning me to be back on board
before noon the next day or I would be fined a day's pay.

Little did he know that getting back on board did not figure in my plans.

The first thing I noticed about Galveston was the smell—jettisoned ships'
fuel and rotting fish gave the place a pungency that I will never forget but I
couldn't get off that bum boat quick enough and on that fuggy September
morning I first set my foot on Texas soil. *I had escaped.* It was almost like a
homecoming. From the moment I landed I felt I belonged there and, as I
walked up Mechanic Street, I could see the bulk of the tanker looming in
the bay and I swore that they would never get me back on board.

But wait a minute. If this was Texas where were all those Stetson wearing cowboys, the chuck wagons, the saddle horses and the vast cattle pens?
All I could see around me were old rust streaked ships, fishermen, oil tanks
and trucks? It was not a bit like the movies at all. At least not here on the
Gulf of Mexico but I loved it anyway.

I was as jumpy as a kitten and needless to say, I never went near the doctor's office but made my way to a back street café and checked out my situation. I had the clothes I stood up in, about eighty dollars in cash and my seaman's pay book, (a document that after tomorrow would be more of an embarrassment than an asset). At least I had enough cash to lie low for a few days if they came looking for me but I was banking on the ships sailing schedule. It was not likely that the captain would delay more than a couple of days or so because of one missing seaman but I could not risk looking for work until they had gone. In truth, I had no real idea of what I was going to do. I just wanted to get away from that ship and obviously getting out of town was the priority so I headed off to the bus depot.

The Coastlines Terminal turned out to be a large open space with a Quonset hut for an office and a trailer diner parked at the side. I checked the route map on the wall and bought a ticket to Freeport down the coast where I got a room at the YMCA. There was also a Seaman's Mission there but I steered clear of that because they usually asked a lot of questions and required ID. Food was another problem but I eked out my meagre cash reserve by limiting myself to one meal a day at a greasy spoon café and buying day-old rolls and baloney from the local baker. Three mornings later, feeling hungry and depressed I made my way down to the shore and looking east along the coast I saw that the tanker had sailed. Yes, now I could get moving, and two days later I was back in Galveston looking for a job. A guy I had met in the YMCA told me to try the fish market where they did not ask questions and were always looking for early morning porters so I made my way over to the fish dock on the Texas City side of the bay and as soon as I got there I knew where the smell had been coming from.

I found the crew boss who looked me over and said I could start at five a.m. the next day. I started to explain myself but he put up his hand and said that he did not want to know any more, telling me that he often used wetback labour and that what he didn't know he couldn't tell the police if questions were ever asked. However it would cost me five bucks a week for this indulgence. He also gave me the address of a rooming house where a few of his crew were lodging. The place was in a side street off Mechanic Street. It was a bit seedy but there was a Tex–Mex café, a mini–mart and a few honky–tonk bars on the same block. So what else did I need?

The work was hard and the early start even harder but I soon settled in, lugging boxes of fish and barrels of ice along the docks and loading trucks. The company withheld the first week's pay in case you did a runner which made things a bit tough for me until Jerry, one of the drivers, offered to loan me ten dollars which about kept me fed but was hardly enough for me to frequent the bars with my new workmates. When payday finally arrived and I emerged from the office, the foreman was there with his two big minders and his hand out for his five bucks—and not just mine. It seemed that half the crew were coughing up as well.

To celebrate my newfound affluence we all went out for a drink and that Friday night in that rough dockside saloon is forever etched in my memory because it was the first night in an obsessive love affair that lasted over thirty years. I first noticed him in the bar mirror and I knew right there and then that we were destined to spend the rest of our lives together. I tried to catch his eye but he coldly stared through me as though I wasn't there; but there was something about him that fascinated me. Was it the hat or the heavy black moustache? His distant stare perhaps? Or was it the fact that he was so popular and everyone seemed to crave his company and I knew that I would have to share him and that he could never, ever, be mine completely even though I would often take him to my lonely bed. He was dark, thick set and he dressed all in black or sometimes green but however he came I loved him faithfully his name was Jack Daniels. Ah, yes. A large one if you please.

Somehow the days passed quickly as the weather cooled and the cash money bonuses the skippers paid us for a quick turn round of their boats made life a little easier. I wrote a letter home to tell my family that I had found a job and would be staying on for a while and gave it to one of the drivers to mail for me in Nashville.

I made a few friends in the bar, mostly dockworkers plus a few of the other local blue–collar workers. My two main pals were a house painter from Memphis called Andy and a truck driver called Jerry from New Jersey, who were on the run, Andy from his virago wife and Jerry from the Draft Board who were trying to send him to Korea. We had some great times hanging out together. My tales of England and Europe fascinated them and I was full of questions about their world. Andy was a good guitar player and he would sometimes bring his Gibson flattop into the bar on Friday nights for a sing along. I liked singing and soon got into the swing of things and picked up an old Martin flat top in a pawnshop for $35. It was a bit scratched and the varnish was peeling in places but it had a good tone and a straight neck, Andy set it up for me and taught me a few chords and we spent many happy hours banging out the jukebox hits of the day, usually Hank Williams and Lefty Frizzel songs which at the time were quite looked down on by members of the Country Music old guard like Kitty Wells, Eddy Arnold and Roy Acuff who formed a powerful Nashville lobby dedicated to resisting change of any sort, particularly the polluting influences of rock 'n roll which they considered from black roots, which of course it was.

Oh yes, even back then there was friction and the same arguments of 'What is Country music?' are still raging on. These pompous, self appointed guardians were very suspicious of any attempt to broaden the appeal of the genre and looked askance when, early in 1951, Ray Price used drums on the Gran'Ole Opry stage, even though it was only a snare drum laying down a shuffle rhythm with the standing drummer using wire brushes: And what an outcry there was a few years later when Hank Thompson's

Brazos Valley Boys turned up with a full drum–kit. You could almost hear the outraged ghost of Scarlet O'Hara simpering.

"Weyal, Ah do declayer, Mary Lou. What is the deah Ole South a–comin' to?"

However, at that time Hank Thompson, the King of the State Fairs' was a big name across the South and his song 'Blackboard of my Heart' was making chart history and some serious money for the agents and the promoters, so in the end a kind of face–saving compromise was reached and the drums were played behind a curtain.

This cadre of purists ruled the Opry with an iron hand for may years, even refusing to let Bob Wills, the legendary King of Western Swing, use his brass section on the show. Would you believe it? Mind you, in spite of his virulent disapproval of the new trends, Roy Acuff, the fiddle–juggling singer of 'Wabash Cannonball', was astute enough to recognize the unique talents of Hank Williams and with Fred Rose, signed him up, in the process laying the financial foundations of the Acuff Rose Publishing Company.

But blissfully unaware of these undercurrents, we continued kicking a few songs around and had a good time in the bar, socking it to whoever would listen. Apart from our Country stock we were also doing quite a bit of Rhythm n'Blues and early Rock 'n' Roll, called Race Music back then. (Actually to Rock 'n' Roll was black slang for copulation—I won't tell you what a Salty Dog was, but you can guess).

I settled into the environment very easily. I never did have a strong English accent and so quickly adapted to the local patois and twang of the Gulf Coast but somehow retained the hard A and the rounded O of my North of England roots, with the result that people often mistook me for a Canadian, a mistake that occurs even today. However, due mainly to the gigs the band was doing, people began to ask who the front man was so the need for a new name became paramount. I did not want some zealous cop checking out the missing sailors list, did I? So in a fit of sheer devilment I took the name of that evil bastard of a First Mate on the tanker, Mr. John Coe and that is how the name YONCO came about. Later when I became a major cabaret artiste, recording companies and publicity agents, and even myself on occasions, would conjure up mysterious sources of my name, from Cajun antecedents to Native American folk lore but the bare truth is that most of the Mexican dock workers could not get their tongues around John Coe so they called me YON–CO and it stuck. It's as simple as that. Sorry I can't be more exotic.

In the bar one night Jerry told me that there was a driving job going. It was not on the road, just hauling trailers from the quays to the big selling sheds but at least it was better than dragging freezing boxes around all day, so I applied for it. The yard boss picked his teeth and spat out a stream of tobacco juice at my boots before asking me to drive the tractor unit around a few times and finally giving me the job. It paid more money so to keep things on an even keel he upped his weekly kick back to ten dollars. On the strength of this new promotion I decided to quit my fleapit and move in with Jerry and Andy who rented a big house near the beach and had a room available. It was a big improvement and at least it was quieter at night which made rolling out at 4.30 a.m. considerably easier. At my old place the din from the bars, the honking of car horns and the screeching of the hookers went all night. I even got a girl friend, a Mexican Chiquita called Juliana who worked behind the bar at a honky–tonk near the train depot but what with my early starts and her shift work, about the only time we could get together was in the afternoons.

The Galveston Splash Boys

We then decided to form a proper band. It was Andy's idea. I played rhythm guitar and did the singing, Andy picked electric guitar and we roped in a lunatic Cajun underwater welder called Jessie who smashed piano and sang back–up harmonies. Eric, the black crane driver was a natural on bass and somehow we dragged in Jerry the truck driver on drums. (Which he played like a truck driver). On steel guitar we had an older local guy called Tex (what else?). He was not very good but he was a gateman on the docks so it paid to keep him sweet. Pedal steel guitars were very rare back then and the basic slide or Hawaiian guitar was the instrument that provided the sustaining notes. Tex played the thing standing up with so many glissando runs it looked like he was polishing a table. He took a great shine to me and had a great empathy with all things British, having been stationed in Exeter with the US Army during World War Two. Apart from Andy, none of us knew much about music but we approached the bar owner where my girl friend worked and he said we could have a blow on Friday nights until around midnight, after which time the serious drinkers arrived and the jukebox took over. Up till then we had a lot of fun. It was never intended to be any more than that but several punters started asking us to play at weddings and things and began to offer us money. And that's how the notorious Galveston Splash Band was born.

Why Galveston Splash? Well it referred to Splash Day, a big 'Mardi Gras' type carnival held every year to commemorate the huge tidal wave in 1900 that virtually wiped out the town. It was a big occasion marked with gluttony, wild drinking and general debauchery and a big parade around town with people throwing water filled greased paper bags at each other. (Of course in time the bags were replaced by balloons and later by condoms).

Sitting around in the bar after the gig Tex told us all about it. Like most Texans I've met, he was very proud of the Lone Star State and knew its history like the back of his hand. He explained enthusiastically that the town was then entering yet another spasm of prosperity with the new Space Mission Control centre taking shape in Houston thirty two miles up river and the affluent government employees were buying condos down on the coast or heading to the beaches and clubs to let their hair down at weekends as both Galveston and Texas City had a hedonistic reputation and a relatively easy going police force.

To really appreciate this mood of excitement, Tex said that one needed to be aware of the constant cycle of the boom and bust economy of the region. Apparently after the big flood, with the help of Federal funds, the town recovered and developers moved in. A big fish cannery opened up, a refinery was built to handle crude oil from the Houston fields and there were plenty of construction jobs on the new docks. Things seemed to be going fine and the town was finding its feet but in 1917 another spanner was thrown into the works.

The City Fathers of New Orleans, in an effort to curb the violence and the growth of organised crime, decided to make the Vielle Carre brothel district off limits to the US Navy. The knock–on effect was that most ships, both merchant marine and Navy, began paying off their crews in Galveston, which whilst bringing a period of short–term affluence, put an end to any further commercial development. Once again the town was in the doldrums as the bad times of the Great Depression hit hard. The recovery was beginning again when one of President Franklin Delano Roosevelt's 'New Deal' public works projects began. Opened in 1940, the Houston Seaway was a canal and river scheme that would allow ocean–going freighters to nose all the way up to Houston to unload their cargos and completely bypass poor old Galveston again. Now, though, there seemed to be a light shining at the end of the tunnel with the arrival of the new space station.

I remember Tex's enthusiasm as he told us that at last they had a stake in the future and things could only get better. It appeared that at last, the hidden lair of the 17th century French buccaneer Jean Galves and one of the oldest cities in North America was at last moving towards the prosperity it richly deserved. But alas that light at the end of the tunnel proved to be a false dawn, for already plans were afoot and within ten years a new administration had moved all space research to the Atlantic seaboard of Florida at Canaveral (Later known as Cape Kennedy)

In the mid seventies I received a newspaper clipping from the Gulf Coast advertising superb apartments on Galveston Island on peppercorn rents to tenants who would pay the service charges and undertake to live there for at least five years. For such an historic and once vibrant city it was a sad destiny indeed.

PICKER'S TIP 2

When forming a band, first pick the best bass player you can find because if you are playing the right chords and singing in tune, a good bass man is all you need.

HANK WILLIAMS AT BATON ROUGE
Ray Price, Rose Maddox, Charlie Louvin, and Charlene Arthur

We started doing an early morning spot on radio at a small station serving the Texas City area. It was nothing great but it helped us blend better and we got paid for it. Unfortunately it was at 6.15 in the morning, which is not all that early if you are a farmer or a fisherman and that's what most of our listening audience were. Jerry, our drummer had only come back on a temporary basis and couldn't make the gig so the Station Manager Delbert Pinara laid down the rhythm by beating a big leather bound book with the result that everything came out like a Johnny Cash song. You know, like 'Boom chicka, Boom chicka Boom.'

Jerry was now seriously considering getting his own truck. His Dad had sent some cash down with a family friend. He could not make a bank transfer or mail a cheque because as far as the Draft Board was concerned Jerry was away in Honduras with the Peace Corps.(And what a racket that was. I knew one prominent Blue Grass artiste who spent over twenty five years living well and touring the world with his wife and kids at the government's expense on the slim pretext of presenting the ethnic music of the Appalachian Mountains). Jerry's windfall was not enough to buy a new vehicle and he certainly could not get finance for one but he did manage to find a fairly clean 1947 GM flatbed at a war surplus dealer's yard outside Pasadena. It was very basic no heaters or power steering but it did have a good multi fuel engine and servo brakes so he paid up and became its new owner. I clearly remember him parking out side the bar and leaning on the horn until we all came rushing out to see what the commotion was all about. He was so proud of it you'd think he had just bought a new Peterbilt.18–wheeler.

One muggy Tuesday evening we were sitting around on the sidewalk outside the bar when Andy came rushing round to tell us that he had heard on the radio that there was going to be a big open air show at a park in Baton Rouge that coming Sunday and that as well as the usual local talent, Ray Price and his new band were to do a guest spot—and it was rumoured that Hank Williams might be there too. Apparently he was re-cording at a studio somewhere outside New Orleans that weekend. We couldn't believe it. Our gig that Saturday night was at a roadhouse in Beaumont and from there it was only about six hours driving to Baton Rouge. We saw it as an opportunity to spread our wings and maybe get some gigs away from the usual local circuit also we might meet somebody who could help us career wise, so we decided to make the trip—and, who knows, we told each other excitedly, we might get to see the Great Man himself. Yeah.

However I think that I should make it clear that at the time, in spite of his huge success on radio and records Hank Williams was only one of the stars of the period. Lefty Frizzell was highly regarded as was Ray Price,

Faron Young and Webb Pierce. In the Gulf Coast area where we played, Billy Walker was making a big mark and we were beginning to hear about a couple of kids from Beaumont who were tipped for a big future locally, a part time carpet fitter called George Jones and a singing waitress that the world would later know as Billy Jo Spears. The 'Hawk from the West Virginia Hills' Hawkshaw Hawkins was pulling big crowds, while national network radio shows featured semi Country pop chart toppers like Tennessee Ernie Ford's '16 Tons, Eddy Arnold's 'Big Bouquet of Roses' and the great Tex Williams singing 'Smoke, smoke, smoke.'

We did the gig at Beaumont but didn't stay for the usual after show boozing. A guy from the club said he was going back to Galveston that night and offered to take Tex and Eric back with him because they were on early shift next day which left Andy, Jerry, Jessie and his cousin Bo'gar and me to handle the drive to Baton Rouge.

Around noon the next day found us trundling up to the gate where, making a big show of our instruments, we indicated that we were one of the back–up bands so they let us through to the back stage compound and into the Pickers Bar. It could not have been sweeter. We sat around in the sunshine and looked busy if anybody wearing a badge walked by, hiding our cans and bottles as we continued busily unloading our equipment, only to load it back aboard when the official had gone and then shuffling the bus to a new location and then repeating the performance.

The show itself was great. A local band kicked off and did a fine job of things before the M.C. brought on one of the main attractions, singer Charlene Arthur who was famous for her tear jerking songs and she certainly lived up to her reputation for dirges by singing her current hits 'Repenting' and the 'Waltz of the Angels'. It was a bit early in the day for such maudlin ballads and as the crowd began to drift off the organisers pushed on stage a group of wild Okie clog dancers who soon lifted the mood, readying the growing audience for Ray Price whose band certainly hit the spot. I think the song that impressed me most was his future biggy 'I Loved You So Much I Let You Go' which captured that mood of un–requited love so popular at the time. But the whole set was very good indeed if perhaps muted by Ray's monosyllabic comments. He never did seem to have much empathy with audiences, even in later years, as evidenced by his response to the news that he had been inducted into the Country Music Hall Of Fame. His brief speech of acceptance was just 'Thanks a lot. Its about time too.' Whether this was his little joke or not, nobody was quite sure but his superb singing could not be faulted. In many ways his stage behaviour was much like that of Roy Orbison who would stand in the spotlight and let his drummer introduce the songs. A superb version of his current hit 'Talk To Your Heart' rounded off the stellar performance but Ray did not do any encores, due, said the MC, to the fact that they had to be in the Nashville studios early the next day. (Later I discovered that Ray never, ever did encores).

I was not all that surprised to see Ray scurry off into the night before Hank Williams arrived. They had once been friends, not real friends like Waylon Jennings and Johnny Cash who once shared (and wrecked) a house in Nashville, but they got along o.k. and often worked together. In fact their singing styles were very similar but as Hank roared on his way to self–destruction, Ray's star was rising and the final crunch came in August 1952 when the Grand Ole Opry fired the troublesome Hank and replaced him with reliable Ray. After that they avoided contact whenever possible.

The local band did another short spot and then it was the turn of the Louvin Brothers Duo. Only there weren't two of them. Charley came on alone without Brother Ira, who was already famous for not showing up on gigs he didn't fancy. (A habit that later became known as the George Jones Syndrome). Little Charlie did a couple of numbers but they were nothing without his brother's high harmonies and inspired mandolin playing. This lacklustre performance was greeted with an equally lukewarm smattering of applause at which Charlie proceeded to cuss out his absent brother and stomped off stage in a huff.

By now it was getting late and the resident band were obviously tiring. They had started playing12 bar blues and ragged edged Rock 'n' Roll. (Always a sign that a band was running out of repertoire).So the organisers brought on their ace card in the shape of the vivacious Rose Maddox and her band. Rose was an Arizona girl but her family moved to Alabama where they formed a band. Her brothers Cal and Henry played guitar and mandolin respectively with Don playing rhythm guitar. They soon outgrew the rural circuit and were picked up as a regular act on the famous Louisiana Hayride in Shreveport, which was considered then to be one rung down on the ladder of fame from Nashville's Grand Ole Opry, the pinnacle of success for any aspiring Country performer. At twenty six Rose was a beauty, with a flashing smile, a superb figure and a terrific voice. To this day she is still one of my favourite female singers, leaving her con-temporaries like Jean Shepherd and Kitty Wells at the starting gate. What a performer and what a band. On electric guitar she had the legendary Joe Maphis and Moon Mullican on piano—and helping her out on bass was her brother Fred, who in the sixties became one of the leading Country com-edians. I came across him on the US Military club circuit in Germany and believe me, for the time his humour was very close to the bone and his delivery made Jim Davidson seem like a choirboy. (Although on this family occasion his jokes were a little muted). Early in the 1960s the family relocated to Bakersfield, California where Rose pursued a highly successful solo career winning a Cashbox Award for Best Female Vocalist of the Year in 1963. Rosie kicked off their set with her big hit 'Whoa Sailor' which fea-tured Joe's lightning runs on his custom built twin neck Gibson and in-cluded the old gospel song 'Tramp on the Street'.

It was a superb thirty–minute set but by now the buzz had gone around and everyone from cranky kids, frazzled mothers to ratty, drunken fathers was waiting for one thing only. To see Hank Williams. And finally about nine thirty there was a rumbling through the crowd and a battered Chevy station wagon with bull fiddle on the roof followed by what looked like a brand new green Cadillac nosed through the gates and rolled backstage.

The Great Man Had Arrived

The Drifting Cowboys opened up with 'Sally good un', a bright number featuring fiddle and a flash Don Helms steel guitar solo. Then Grant Edwards, a well known Louisiana promoter came on to announce his Big Star but before he could finish, a tall figure in a light grey suit and a white Stetson staggered out from behind the speakers and the crowd went wild. Over the noise the band kicked off with 'Happy Roving Cowboy 'and from then on Hank Williams was in charge.

I was quite shocked when I first saw him. He was much younger than I had expected. For some reason his songs and his voice seemed to belong to a much older, world weary, man and it was hard to associate this pale, hollow cheeked, lanky twenty nine year old with such profound and sad lyrics. His first song was 'Why Don't You Love Me Like You Used To Do?' being obviously slanted to his ex–wife Audrey. After that he sailed through a program of his hits, occasionally nipping behind the speakers for a shot from his hip flask during the solos but in spite of his boozing reputation he was always in control of the show. Now and then he would stumble and miss a few words but one look at those sad eyes and the flash of that boyish smile and you could forgive him anything. It was as if he was on some pre–destined journey to self–destruction over which he had no control and sensing this, the crowd went wild hoping that somehow the flood of our ap–plause would keep him with us a bit longer.

The sound that came from that open–air stage in the Dixie twilight was truly amazing in spite of the primitive amplification of those days. The blend was superb and at times it was hard to realize that there were only five musicians up there and when Moon Mullican joined them for 'The Devil's Train' it was breathtaking.

That was the first and only time I saw Hank Williams and it truly did start me off on that 'Lost Highway' and change my life forever.

But neither I nor anyone else in that crowd knew that we were watching one of his last shows because a few weeks later Hank died in the back of a Cadillac near Rutledge Tennessee from a combination of drugs and alcohol. They took him to Oak Hill Hospital West Virginia where on New Years Day 1953 he was listed DOA. An autopsy by Fayette County Officials recorded the cause of death as heart failure and there was no mention of drugs or booze in his blood—but there was a good chance that the coroner had been tacitly directed not to look too carefully for any. This after all was the early 1950s and they were dealing with a national celebrity. Today it would have been the first line of enquiry. Another doctor later did suggest that heart disease brought on by excessive alcohol intake over a long period of time may have been the cause but it was quickly pointed out to him that at the time of death the victim had not been out drinking and his opinion was swept under the carpet. No one mentioned Hank's silver hip flask.

Mass hysteria hit the South at the news and eulogies and tributes flooded in and the snooty Nashville establishment who had treated him so badly joined in the hype and paranoia. The funeral was in Montgomery Alabama on January 4th 1953 and the press from the Gulf to Montana put out special editions though it did not make a big mark in New York or LA. However throughout the South and the Mid–West there was a huge out pouring of grief the like of which was not seen again until the death of Martin Luther King fifteen years later. Even the mystery assassination of John F. Kennedy in Dallas did not have the same impact there. There is no real way of ever explaining such outpourings of spontaneous public emotion and it is timeless as we have witnessed in our own era with the tragic death of Princess Diana but this flood of emotion came mostly from the people who knew Hanks music, not the man himself. Those who worked on the road with him and had to put up with his wild antics and difficult mood swings had less flattering things to say about him, as shown when somebody said that 'There would never be another Hank Williams' and one well known sideman cryptically remarked. "Amen to that."

I still find it hard to reconcile the rural semi educated Alabama farm boy with some of the most emotive lyrics from the popular music scene of the past fifty years, an opinion expressed by such luminaries as Paul McCartney and Elton John, You only had to hear his articulate comments on live radio shows to realise that this was no back country hick. He really was the Hillbilly Shakespeare although there are a couple of fascinating anomalies about the career of such a prolific composer. For example, the song most associated with him, 'Lovesick Blues' was an old novelty from 1922 written by Irving Mills and Cliff Friend—and he did not live long enough to hear his self penned song of lost love 'Your Cheating Heart' become a massive hit in the charts world wide. This song went on to be recorded by over seventy five artistes as diverse as Fats Domino, Ray Charles, Frankie Avalon, Jo Stafford and Les Paul and Mary Ford—and finally became a US number one in April 1953, four months after Hank's demise. And jazz legend Tony Bennett's, first big hit 'Cold, Cold, Heart' was written by Hank Williams. However, for most pundits the real crossover breakthrough came when TV Star George Clooney's Auntie Rosemary, took Hank's 'Half As Much' to the number two spot in the pop charts.

PICKER'S TIP 3

Never, ever, turn your back on the audience. The simple act of turning to adjust equipment will lose you the attention of the crowd and wipe out any charisma you may have achieved.

The Fall Out

Of course, after the euphoria calmed and the dust settled a vicious range war broke out in the Country Music industry about who was going to fill Hank's boots. Now however it was a different ball game because Hank had broken the mould and taken the music to new heights of popularity, reaching out to a vast international audience and the potential pickings were huge and already had made his publishers very wealthy men indeed. Dozens of tribute albums were churned out and tasteless gimmicks were in evidence at every show. There was a rash of maudlin. 'In Memoriam' ballads like the Delmore Brother's 'Death is only a dream' whose opening lines were.

> In Montgomery, Alabama 'neath a beautiful white tomb
> The body of Hank Williams lies there in the gloom.
> Mourned by everybody since he left this earth
> But let me tell you friend, he's found a brand new birth.'
> —etc.etc.

And even the starchy Country Music Association made a big thing about his career and Ferlin Husky recorded 'Hank's Song' by stringing together the titles of some of his biggest hits. It was a clever idea but the result was a bit yucky. Here's a sample.

On stage he had a spotlight shining on a mike stand wearing a white Stetson.
'I just don't like this kind of living—(where) Nobody's lonesome for me.
I'm a rambling man—(on the)—Lost Highway. May you never be alone like me.

Waylon Jennings was certainly right on when, years later, he sang.
'Nashville is rough on the living but she really thinks well of the dead.

It was a dirty war with all the hype and false sentiment that came to typify the Nashville Establishment, even Hank's ex-wife Audrey joined in with the sharks, but in the end, much to the chagrin of the other contenders, it was the nasal tenor voice of the flamboyant Louisiana singer Webb Pierce that took the crown with a succession of number one hits. He was closely followed by Ray Price, Marty Robbins and Eddy Arnold who ruled the roost until the mid 1950s when the sensational talents emerging from Sam Phillips' Sun Records in Memphis like Elvis Presley, Carl Perkins, Johnny Cash, Jerry Lee Lewis and Roy Orbison kicked all the fences down, paving the way for Merle Haggard, George Jones and Waylon Jennings and Willie Nelson with. Chuck Berry and the Beatles leading a Pop Music revolution.

It had been a long haul since the first glimmerings of mainstream recorded Rock 'n' Roll when a black singer who idolised Bing Crosby called Roy Brown had recorded 'Good Rocking Tonight.' on De-Luxe Records in 1947.There had been earlier use of the phrase by Harlem singers in the early thirties. Of course the musical press didn't know what to do about it and hesitatingly dismissed it as just loud 'Race Music' but gradually had to accept its tidal wave of popularity and tactfully began to call it Rhythm and Blues, living up to their governing principle 'If there was a chance to make big bucks, prejudice was brushed under the carpet.' They were still trying to do that when Tamla Motown hit them.

Hit the road, Jack
Galveston Splash, George Morgan, Hardrock Gunther, the Carlisles

Coming back from that gig we got our first taste of real trouble in a truckstop diner outside a town called Edgerly deep in Klu Klux Klan country just short of the Texas line. It started with Bo'gar asking for the sugar from the next table where a group of rowdy farm workers and truck drivers were wolfing greasy hamburgers and lacing their coffee with whisky. I don't know how it all blew up but suddenly there was a shout from Bo'gar who reeled back holding his face before lunging back across the partition.

Next thing I saw was a big bottle of chilli sauce hurtling towards me. It hit me on the left side of the head and smashed, leaving a jagged splinter embedded above my left eye giving me a scar that I bear to this day. The pain from the chilli soaking into the open wound drove me mad and with the red sauce and blood steaming down my face I went ballistic, kicking away the table and hitting out at anything in range. One of the farm hands, a Mexican I think, turned towards me and his hand went behind his back, a favourite place to carry a knife but before he could draw it Jessie hit him across the throat with the edge of a plate and he dropped like a stone.

I was still squaring up an punching good but that was not the way to get the job done and the Cajuns and Andy showed me just how as boots, chairs, knees and elbows flew and blood spurted from broken glass shards and savage bites. Bo'gar nearly bit through a finger when a truck driver tried to fishhook him. (Grab him by the mouth and try to rip it open. A really vicious move).

It turned out that the place was a well–known trouble–spot and the police were soon there to apply their 'Attitude Adjustment Therapy' indiscriminately to shoulders and shins to all and sundry. Two very big dogs also turned up in the Sheriff's pick–up truck and started mistaking our legs for Pedigree Chum till everybody cooled down. At that point the owner appeared from behind the fridge and fingered a troublesome gang of itinerant fruit pickers who had been causing mayhem in the area since they arrived.

By the speed of the police response I suspected that they had been waiting for such a flash point before moving in and deporting the wetbacks, because they did not bring any charges against us and hustled us out without asking for any I.D, an oversight for which we were more than grateful, as such a request would have created serious difficulties for me and the Cajuns.

A few weeks later we played a club near Pasadena on Route 225. No, not the famous Gilley's Club, but Mickey Gilly who was Jerry Lee Lewis' cousin, did eventually open a club in the district and expand it to become one of the top venues in the South Texas. Mind you, a lot of its popularity might have had to with the fact that the area was beyond the jurisdiction of both the Houston Police and the Bay Area force—a No–Man's Land where anything could happen and often did. This was where I first came across the famous 'Chicken Wire' joints, rough strip clubs that employed a band for dancing and brought the girls on at regular intervals. As you can imagine things often got out of hand, so to keep the amorous drunks away from the strippers a roll of heavy duty chicken wire was kept on a pole above the small stage and when things started getting rough the manager would cut the rope and the wire curtain would fall protecting the band and the girls from ashtrays and bottles thrown at them and to stop the fights spilling over onto the bandstand. Of course you were expected to keep playing until they all cooled down and started dancing again.

Playing at one of these places I met up with an agent I had first en-countered at the Baton Rouge show. His name was Buddy Pyle, a short, fat, balding guy of about forty five who, when he was not sucking on his brown bag booze, (the cheap bastard never offered me a slug) was banging on about the trouble he was having in finding support acts and back–up bands for his Star tours. Sensing an opportunity, I gave him a line of busi-ness about how we had been booked as a reserve band at the Hank Williams Show and that we were available to step in if there were any 'No Shows'. I also stressed the truly international content of the band. Well, after all, a real Englishman, two Cajuns, a Jamaican, a Texan drifter and a New York Jew is pretty cosmopolitan isn't it? And that's got to be a good selling point. So Buddy became my friend and gave me his card. It was the first time he had met a Brit and asked me if I knew Winston Churchill. He never did pass that bottle but at least he promised to find us some work and a couple of months later he did.

It was not a Grand Old Opry tour it's true, but it was a step up and gave us a taste of life on the road with a 25–day trip into the depths of rural Oklahoma with such seasoned (and fading) pros. as Charlene Arthur, the 'Queen of the Weepies.' fresh from her triumph at Baton Rouge, (Oh yeah?)—a wild Rockabilly called Hardrock Gunther, the Sandy Grove Cloggers and the Carlisles, a husband and wife duo plus guitar wizard Terry Cahn, (who told us that Merle Travis had stolen all his licks) and us—the Galveston Splash Boys.

As I remember it, the tour kicked off in Vernon, hometown of singer Kay Adams, right up on the Oklahoma border where we were joined by our spe-cial guest Star, the great George Morgan who was still riding high on his monster pop hits 'Candy Kisses' and 'Roomful of Roses' and I also im-mediately realised why all George's publicity shots were profiles or in shadow. He had a severe cast in one eye, but he could write good songs and fathered a beautiful daughter, singer Lorrie Morgan, one of those talented ladies who spearheaded the 'New Country' movement of the 1980s. George died in July 1975 in a freak accident like the one that killed comedian Roy Hull (the Emu's keeper) who fell off the roof while fixing a TV antenna. George came and went throughout the tour playing only about four major gigs as the rest of us wandered aimlessly about the Amber Waves of Gold, (as Merle Haggard puts it) through a confusion of tin roof cinemas, High School gymnasia and National Guard drill halls. Small towns came and went, all of them the same. Sometimes we did two shows a day if the weather held. The main acts got motel rooms but we were expected to bed down anywhere we could, which, usually meant ending up legless in the tour bus unless you got lucky with some accommodating farmer's daughter and that was a bit risky out in the sticks where angry big brothers and shotguns were very common. We didn't get any billing but we were young and crazy and in spite of all the stress we felt like real big time troubadours. Well, I did.

After this first tour, as often happens, the band began to break up as the usual post tour depression set in and we took stock. Tex's wife finally found where he was and he had to do a quick shuffle down to Florida before the alimony bills arrived. The two Cajuns decided that they wanted to get back again to the bayous where life was less constricting and they wouldn't have to change their clothes occasionally or do boring things like washing. Eric our black drummer also quit, uncomfortable with the attitudes of the ignorant hick town redneck audiences we played to. So for the first time in my career I started looking round for replacements. It was a regular quest that I became conditioned to over the years.

PICKER'S TIP 4

When working a gig where you may be asked to do requests or are likely to have to vary your program, make sure the bass player is to your right. This way he can see your left hand on the fret–board of your guitar and knows what key you are in. (For Left handed pickers the reverse applies).

PICKER'S TIP 5

To facilitate quicker setting up colour–code your leads and their sockets. Eg. PA cables, Red. / Guitar leads, Blue. / Mic. Cables, Green./ Etc. And don't coil them too tightly. It will break the outer shield in co–axial cables.

Lone Star Road Stone

With the money I saved from the road tours I could afford to get a few bootleg identity papers and a quiet word with our Cajun buddies and a $100 provided me well thumbed drivers licence, complete with photo and weight violation stamps from the ITC, a Teamsters Union contribution book (All dues paid up to date), a ticket to the Lafayette, Louisiana public library (In French. My name was spelled Jeanceaux) and a dog–eared season ticket for the New Orleans football games.

Things were looking good and Jerry's trucking venture seemed to be coming together very well. It suited the Galveston Port Authorities who no longer had to be responsible for all the costly maintenance of their own vehicles and in spite of the mileages involved Jerry was very happy to be his own boss. So happy in fact that he asked me if I would like to join him. I pointed out that I had no money to buy a truck and that I was quite happy working on the docks and playing three nights a week and doing the occasional road tour but I did agree to help him out when things were slack so we began to travel together along the coast delivering boxed fish to vari- ous markets and rail yards.

After one gig at Baytown, Jerry told us that he was selling the flatbed and moving into dump trucks. He said that he could get a good contract, moving stone and gravel from the docks to some big new highway project on Route 290 about forty miles north of Sam's town (Truckers CB speak for Houston). It was a little out of our range but we made a deal with the local rep. from the Teamsters Union and in return for a special donation to their funds (Direct to the rep himself in cash, of course) we were allowed to operate in the area. Jerry then announced that he had now saved enough to persuade the bank to finance him on a couple of dump trucks and did I want to drive one for him full time. Wow. Did I? I jumped at the chance.

The following Saturday found us at the US Navy Disposal Depot at Port Arthur where vast stocks of war surplus equipment were coming up for auction at the end of the month. Most of it was in good condition, some of the units were brand new and unused. We talked to the gate man and he gave us a couple of identity tags and pointed us in the right direction for the sales office. The guy running the sales office was a real cigar chewing, miserable bastard but luckily he was from New Jersey so Jerry got on well with him and let him moan on about all the hillbillies and shit–kickers he had to deal with down here—but the ice didn't begin to melt until we put an envelope on his desk containing a hundred dollars, at which he mellowed a little and after sliding it into the desk drawer and locking it, said that he would show us where the best stuff was.

We piled into his jeep and muttering to himself all the while, he drove us along the long lines of vehicles, plant and equipment until we came to a collection of ex–Sea–Bee earth moving machines. Lined up were dozens of almost new Caterpillar bulldozers, bucket diggers, scrapers and draglines, even a trio of steam driven cranes of pre–war vintage. At the end of one line were six pristine Dodge Super six–wheel dumpers with Pacific Theatre of Operations paint jobs and we clambered all over them like two eager schoolboys fiddling with the levers and checking all the mechanisms.

Jerry and I put on a good show until the jeep left us at which point we slid between the front line to where we had noticed some units at the end of the row. They were also Dodges but in spite of being well used still stood well and looked good. Carefully looking round he selected two of them and reaching inside his leather jacket he brought out a small oilcan and crawling under the rear axle he squirted a puddle of oil on the dusty ground. After which he moved on to his second selection where he handed me a cold chisel and pointed to a rock on the ground. Following his signs I put the chisel at one corner of the windshield and hit it with the rock splitting the glass right across diagonally and making a starburst that covered the corner.

On the day of the auction we stood in the crowd as drivers and dealers made bids at lots that we had no interest in until we got the signal from the auctioneer that the heavy plant was coming up. The new trucks brought good prices but nobody was seriously interested in the two at the back. Who would be? One of them had a serious rear axle leak and the other one had a smashed windshield and by the look of that offside front wheel also a bad brake line problem. So we got 'em for a song.

We quickly paid the price and the commission and drove proudly out of the depot the proud proprietors of Lone Star Road Stone. A feisty new company with a fleet of two ex–US Navy trucks.

At another military surplus sale we bought a prime mover (tractor unit). It was an ex–Marine Corps heavy recovery Autocar which had been converted. The gear ratios had been changed and it had a blown Cummins two stroke diesel, powerful and fast, also the latest universal quick hook up fifth–wheel coupling, which meant we could haul any kind of trailer and it was not long before we were approached by some shady friends of Jerry in Houston to pick up a few loads for them.

They paid the going rate so we were quite satisfied until one day as we rolled into the yard the dispatcher told us that we had to call in at the office. Jerry's friend was there along with a big dark Mexican looking guy. There was no introduction and we nodded to the stranger. Jerry's friend said that the Mex had a deal for us and left the office. We said nothing but coolly waited for the next move. Making sure that the office door was closed he said that all we had to do was to hook up a trailer and take it to a certain destination.

"Well," We said. "That's just what we do. What's so special about this gig?"

Quietly he explained that this was a very special delivery and quoted a figure for the trip that made me gasp."Where did we have to go?" we asked but before he told us he asked if we were sure that we wanted the job as it had certain conditions. Well, this all sounded a bit mysterious but the stranger told us that it had to stay that way and not to enquire to closely about the load. So in the end we agreed and he said he would phone us and before he left he gave Jerry an envelope containing a third of the agreed fee, the balance payable when we delivered.

Three days later I got a call from Jerry to meet him at our usual bar that evening. When I got there he was sitting in a back booth looking round cautiously.

"He's called," he hissed

"Who has?" I asked, wondering why I was whispering too.

"The Spic," he murmured covering his mouth. "It's on. Tomorrow night. We gotta pick up a drag at a truck stop outside Jacinto City."

"Whoa. Hold it right there," I bridled. "I'm not so sure 'bout going out there."

In those days Jacinto City had something of a reputation. It was suburb of East Houston where many Latinos had chosen to settle but amongst the hard working field hands and domestics there was a hard core of opportunist villains who would do anything to turn a dollar.

"Naw. It'll be okay, stop worrying." Jerry dismissed my doubts. He was already counting the money. "Hombre says that the pick–up has to be made at exactly 4.30 am. The lading papers with details of the drop off will be in a canvas bag under the hook plate."

I was glad we did not have to hang around that barrio where gringos like us were not exactly welcome.

However, in the event it all went as smooth as silk. Dawn was breaking as we hauled off Highway 10 into the truck stop and found our trailer lurking near the rear fence. Trucks were hooting and snorting around the parking lot and nobody took any notice of us as we hooked up and pulled out. Feverishly I tore open the bag and found the instructions. Our destination was another truck stop parking lot outside Jackson, Mississippi some 400 miles away. All the documents seemed in order so off we went and early next afternoon we were unhooking the drag at its new home. Nothing appeared to be suspicious so we headed off to the freight depot in Vicksburg looking for a return load. Two days later we picked up the balance of the cash. We never did find out what we had been hauling but the money was good—so we did it again—several times.

We also did several trips up to Nashville, usually to a vast trailer exchange park on Route 65 near Berry Hill where the same mysterious drop–off and pick–up routine was followed. On these occasions we would stop overnight in a barrack block with chipboard cubicles containing a couple of army cots with blankets (but no sheets) a cane table, two chairs and a sink. Not much, I know but at $5 a throw, it did us.

On a couple of these occasions we caught the Gran' ole Opry show at the Ryman Auditorium. At the time, I was not all that impressed by the show. It all seemed a bit hayseed and messy but, as it was actually a radio show;

I suppose that the visual angle was not important. Acts I remember were Kitty Wells, Little Jimmy Dickens, Jim Ed Brown, Johnny & Jack Wright and of course, Roy Acuff whom I found humourless and over-rated. The spectre of Rock 'n' Roll had not yet reared its head and about the most modern sound around was Porter Waggoner. Red Foley was the MC and he was very patronising to first timers on the show. Mind you, he was in a position of power because even back then the Opry was important. An appearance there was a step up the ladder of fame.

Then things got moving for us on the music front. The band had plenty of bookings and a live radio link up from a club outside Harrisburg and more exposure from various County Fairs, dance halls and beach bars all along the Gulf. The line-up of the band changed as we began to expand the range of our gigs and it proved impossible for some of the boys to hold down a regular day job. However the early experience with the odd bigot made us cautious about taking on new musicians and we vetted them very carefully before taking them on. In the main we were lucky and managed to maintain the driving Country-Rock sound we had become known for. Everything in Texas was fine and I began to think I had found my Shangri-La. I had serious visions of a four-bedroom condo at Corpus Christi and a beautiful Chicano girl serving me rum and coke aboard a 40 foot Chris Kraft cruiser in the bay but alas, it was not to be. The Big Apple beckoned and destiny was at my right hand.

New York, New York. My kinda town
(Oh, really?)

One day when I finally got back from a boring resident gig in Del Rio, Jerry met me in the bar and told me that he had got a letter from his father saying that his sister Rachel was getting married and that it would be a nice gesture to come back to New Jersey for the wedding. He also mentioned that Jerry's mother was not too well and was due to go into hospital for some treatment.

Over a cup of coffee we discussed the trip. The Korean War was over so there would not be much risk of him being picked up by the Military Police and from my point of view it was most unlikely that there was a warrant out for a missing British seaman, so we decided to take the trip. Jerry's dad was over the moon at the decision and said that all the family were looking forward to seeing him again and meeting his 'Limey' partner, so we made plans for the visit.

Using Jerry's bright red Studebaker Commander we did the trip in easy stages and late in the afternoon four days later we turned off the turnpike and rolled into the pleasant small town of Teaneck. For me it was quite a buzz being in New Jersey as my great aunt Kate had moved to America in 1910 and had opened a trailer/diner for the workers near Lakehurst. The greasy spoon café had shot to fame in 1937 when the German airship Hindenburg blew up in the next field. After claiming the insurance money and with a good eye for publicity, her daughter Louise rebuilt the eatery and shrewdly changed its name to the New Airship Café. She married a local builder and the simple diner was developed into a motel and restaurant complex which prospered until 1945 when it too burned down during a wild World War 2 victory celebration.

Jerry's family greeted us like long lost relatives, which of course, Jerry was. His sister Rachel was particularly emotional about the reunion. Neighbours and friends came around and there was a big party that night at which we were the centre of attention as they all wanted to know about Jerry's time in Texas and about our trucking company, (road haulage not being a field of enterprise that boasted too many Jewish operators on the north eastern seaboard, usually being the domain of the Americans of Sicilian extraction) and yet, here was a good Yiddish boy dressed like Roy Rogers already, with a goy for a partner. And him not even an American yet. In fact they all regarded me as something of a curiosity. Their conception of an Englishman was somebody like Cary Grant or Noel Coward and as the conversation expanded they became more confused on discovering my penchant for Country Music, regarded at that time in New York with the same disdain that greeted Punk Rock thirty years later.

This wedding had apparently been a long time in coming and Rachel's mother was determined to make it the event of the season. A big synagogue in New York had been booked for the ceremony and the reception was to be held at Lateners one of the top kosher restaurants in Manhattan and we were all looking forward to the great occasion. However, there was the question of clothes for the big gig: Our Barnyard boots, Weather–All hats, leather saddle jackets and blue denim shirts would not be acceptable so we had to get properly kitted out. Jerry said he was going to hire an outfit and that he would fix me up too but I decided to buy myself a full formal rig. Things were going well and we were making good money, I also envisaged that as we prospered I would probably need some good clothes. But this time I made the wrong move. Oh yes. A very wrong move indeed.

* * * * * *

"Suits you, Sir"

Jewish weddings, particularly in New York, are very prestigious affairs and it was de rigueur to turn up in a formal dinner suit or Tuxedo as it was termed in the US. So where else should an affluent young man go to find one but the best shopping street in the USA, the famous 5th Avenue.

I found a top class store and strolled around the men's department stopping at a rack of shiny mohair tuxedos and commenced to go through them sorting out my size under the beady eye and tightly pursed lips of an elegantly attired salesman. I chose a nice midnight blue number with a shawl collar and held it up against myself to see in the mirror and the floorwalker moved in for the kill.

"Well, I must say that Sir certainly knows his formal wear. That is the very latest Sy Devore design, the style that is sweeping Hollywood today. Would Sir like to slip it on while I find the exact code?"

His schmaltzy, effeminate grovelling was irritating me but reluctantly I agreed to be escorted to a bank of mirrored fitting rooms.

"Oh yes indeed," he cooed, "Just the thing for a formal affair and I think that it would look wonderful with a 'Savile Row' brocade vest." He produced three colourful vests and bit his lip as he tried them against the dark jacket. "Ooh yes, Sir. Aren't they beautiful? We import them directly from England, you know."

"Oh yes? "I said casually. "That's where I come from too."

He paused, looking at me quizzically noting my cowboy boots and jeans.

"Oh, really? You certainly don't sound like a Brit. If you would have asked me I'd say that you came from Canada or somewhere out West."

I explained that I was in New York for a wedding and that I actually did live in Texas at which he went strangely silent and left me alone. Slipping into the suit I spent a few minutes admiring my new, distinguished reflection and then stepped outside to select another vest. The salesman was not alone. Standing by his side was a uniformed security guard and a bulky grey haired man in his late forties, obviously a retired cop.

Somehow, a creepy feeling stole over me and I sensed that perhaps things were not quite right but I kept my cool as the fussy salesman chimed in.

"How do you like it then, Sir? It really does look good on you."

"Great," I said, ignoring his companions. "I'll take it and a couple of those brocade vests as well, the blue and the green. Oh, yes and I'll need a bow tie and three shirts, size 16neck and some shoes and socks too."

He turned and smiled greasily "Do you have an account with us Sir?"

"No," I replied." like I told you, I'm just up for a wedding."

"Oh yes, I remember Sir," he smarmed on. "Well, if you are paying by check on an out of town bank we will require some form of ID. Is that okay, Sir?"

He pursed his lips again at the onlookers.

"No need." I smiled, hauling out a roll of bills. "I'll be paying cash. What's the bill?"

He looked shocked and then his eyes narrowed.

"Cash? Oh, I see. Er, that's a lot of money to be carrying around in this town. You must be very careful. Now, Sir, er, if you just wait here I'll see to the packing."

He bustled into the fitting room to collect the garments and then for the first time the grey haired man spoke.

"Er, I hear that you are a stranger in town, eh? Well I'm Gerry Flynn and I'm Head of Security here." He had a gravelly New York Irish accent and his breath smelled of whisky as he rambled on." Eric here just called me over to explain to you our new promotion scheme."

'Oh yeah?' I thought wondering why a security man was involved in a sales promotion matter. I kept my doubts quiet as he continued his spiel.

"You see, for our special new customers we run a lottery based on social security numbers every month. Who knows you might win $10,000 dollars. All y'gotta do is complete this here form an' you're in for this month's draw,Okay?"

He stood there looking at me and picking his teeth

I demurred "Er, No thanks. I'm not interested really. Dunno how long I'll be in town. Like I told, er, Eric, I'm only here for a wedding."

I was definitely feeling uneasy now as he maintained his prison yard stare at me and growled "Ah, yeah. Eric said sumpin' 'bout you wuz a Brit. Ya got ya passport?"

The hairs of the back of my neck were prickling as I reviewed my options.

"Passport? Naw I never carry it," I said coolly.

"Got any ID at all then?" He asked bluntly

"Well," I said cautiously, "Will this do?" and I handed him my seaman's pay book.

He looked at me coldly and thumbed through it until he stopped at one page.

"Well 'cordin'to this you ain't bin paid for quite a while. Whatcha bin doin'since then? Jes' how you bin gettin'by?"

I looked at him blankly as he rolled his shoulders again.

"Y'see, reason I'm askin', is that we been havin' a series of big cash heists here lately, an' I'd jes' like you to explain where you come by all that cash you're carryin'. Would you mind followin' me to the office, er, Sir?"

The uniformed man moved to my side and guided me towards the elev–ator.

And that was that.

They brought in the NYPD who interviewed me but I was trapped. I had no excuses. I could not tell them that Jerry and I had been operating an undercover trucking firm in Texas and had not paid any taxes or insurance for some time, (not counting a bit of shady dealing) could I? Apart from anything else, it would have put Jerry in a bad light and caused problems for his family. So I said that I had been bumming around playing guitar and gambling since I arrived, claiming that the ship had sailed without me. For their part, the police had no proof of my doing anything illegal and were somewhat annoyed at the store wasting their time. Finally, after much argument they decided to hand me over to Immigration Services who listened sceptically to my maudlin tale about my bad reaction to the jab, causing me to miss the ship's departure and classed me as an abandoned seaman. After which they moved me to a secure hotel to await passage back to Blighty.

I did not waste my one permitted phone call by calling a lawyer. There was no way out of this one, so I phoned Jerry and explained cryptically that I was helping the police and had been delayed. I think he got the message.

Six weeks later I stepped off a crabby old freighter at Liverpool docks.

I hope they all had a good time at that wedding without me.

PICKER'S TIP 6

Beware. Here are some examples of the Showbiz Publicity Hype.

What it says.	What it means.
Brilliant guitarist	Plays more that three chords.
Smart stage image	All wearing matching shirts
Very visual	Stands at the edge of the stage
Ex chart band	Got chucked out
Authentic	Complete copy of someone else
Amazing	Hard to credit it.
Got full date book	No pages missing
Professional	Signing on the dole
Semi–professional	Hanging on to the day job.
Top Country act	Along with about thirty others
Prepared to travel	Divorced
Very experienced	Still doing the pubs and workies.
Highly talented	Sings in tune
Versatile	Knows several songs.
All–rounder	No good at anything.
Few dates available	Desperate
Attractive	No visible scars. Own hair and teeth.
TV/Radio literate	Buys Radio and TV Times
Celebrity circuit act	Reads Hello magazine
Computer literate	Got a Nintendo Game Boy
Sensational	just above average

HOME AGAIN
Karl Denver, Clinton Ford, Johnny Duncan, Frank Ifield, Marvin Rainwater Mitchell Torok

Well, here I was again in Manchester. Back to dear old Cottonopolis. So what next? My parents now owned a nice pub so I moved in with them. That way, they said, they could keep an eye on me to check any more mad ideas I might have. They said they'd help me to return to a normal re-spectable lifestyle. (A well intentioned desire but quite impossible to achieve). I think that they were glad to see me but I was never quite sure. Oh yes, I knew they loved me and I loved them but I always felt that I was rather a disappointment to them, which no doubt I was. You see my mother wanted me to become a doctor and father had plans for me to become a clothing factory boss. So we did not exactly get off on the right foot.

I liked being called Frank and I wanted to be an entertainer, a profession that Mum felt was one step away from the gutter. She never did say whether it was up or down. I don't think my Dad was too concerned about it, as he had relatives on the boards. In fact, one of them, his Uncle Charlie had been a circus performer with travelling Wild West Show before the Great War and Dad would tell me how he once visited the family in full Red Indian regalia, (war paint, buckskins, beads, feathered headdress and moccasins, the lot) when he was playing the Oldham Empire. He came by tram and my Granddad Tommy took him to the pub. So you can see that there was already some eccentricity in my background.

Somehow the traumatic effect of my sudden and unexpected departure from the USA had left me numb so I stumbled blindly along wondering what was coming next. On reflexion, I don't think that I had returned at a very propitious moment for Mum and Dad. Their pub was doing well, the clientele being mainly middle class bourgeoisie and they had recently also got a catering contract from a snobby local golf club. So I was sworn to secrecy about my disgraceful deportation and requested not to socialise with the punters.

Let me tell you, it's not easy being the 'Black Sheep of the family' when you are an only child.

But things were about to change. Dad's friend got me a job as a trainee manager in a factory so I plodded along waiting for something to happen. And it did.

One evening I was invited to a factory party at the Beehive Inn in Pre-stwich and two things will always keep that evening in my mind. One was the girl who took me there. Ena was her name and she had beautiful big violet eyes and a very warm and passionate nature. Later in life she became a writer and an authority on classical music. The other was a chubby, pleasant young man with a guitar who was booked to provide the entertainment. His name was Ian but he later changed it to Clinton Ford, becoming the famous entertainer whose version of Hank Snows big weepie 'Old Shep' topped the Elvis Presley version on the British charts. Clinton started his career in Liverpool playing banjo and doing vocals with the Mersey City Jazz Band and apart from his Country hits, (which were very good indeed, just check em out) he really made his name with his unique versions of Old Tyme Music Hall ditties like those unforgettable classic hits, Fanlight Fanny and the Old bazaar in Cairo.'

That meeting was the catalyst that shocked me out of my zombie like state and put me back on track. His music recalled fond memories of my earlier life, rekindling my stifled ambition and getting me all fired up again and before I knew it I was up on stage with him banging out 'Wild side of life' and songs like 'Move it on over', 'Ivory Tower' and 'That's all right, Mama' and I began to see that raincoat factory getting smaller in my rear view mirror. But that was going to take some time yet.

Clint and I got on very well together, so much so that I invited him home for supper, a gesture that went down like a lead balloon with my folks, particularly as we both got drunk and he had to sleep over at the pub.

Little did Clinton realise that he had kick–started my stalled ambition that rainy night.

We arranged to meet the following week at the same pub and that's where I first made the acquaintance of such luminaries as Glasgow pub singer turned yodeller Karl Denver and USAF veteran Johnny Duncan (not to be confused with the deep voiced Nashville star of the 70's) This Johnny had a band called the Bluegrass Boys and they had already been featured on Radio Luxembourg in a mini series called 'Your Sunday Valentine' which started on September 8th.1957 (Your Valentine being a magazine for teenage girls). Also featured on this show was the South African pop idol, big band singer Denis Lotis. At that time however, Johnny Duncan's music was more a Country tinged skiffle than the real Bill Monroe style, with guitarist Denny Wright playing fussy lightening riffs whenever he got break. John's real Bluegrass period only came after he teamed up with talented banjo picker Pete Sayers in the early sixties when his Tennessee flat top guitar style and his 'High and lonesome' tenor fitted well with Peter's excellent five string picking. The Beehive soon became a regular watering hole for other acts that were beginning to make their mark on the developing circuit as the dull caterpillars of the old workingmen's clubs metamorphosed into the glamorous butterflies of the new cabaret clubs.

Karl Denver, (real name Angus McKenzie) who came from the Springburn area of Glasgow, took a great interest in my story, informing me that he too had been at sea but sailed mostly to the Orient, though later he claimed that he had worked in the USA. It was all rather vague but what was certain was that he had recently moved down from the Blackburn area where he had adopted his present stage name, although he occasionally worked under the name of Carl Leeman, and now shared a flat in Prestwich with Johnny Duncan.

His soaring falsetto voice certainly hit a chord with the public in that confused pre–Rock 'n' Roll era and he was seldom out of the pop charts. In fact, between the summer of 1961 and the spring of '62 he had four consecutive Top Ten hits including 'Rose Marie' and an unforgettable yodelling version of the South African tribal chant Mbube that as 'Wimoweh' entered the UK charts in January 1962 and stayed there for some 17 weeks, reaching the number 4 spot at one time.

Karl handled big money during his long career but somehow he did not manage to hang on to a lot of it due mainly to his love of the good life. He was always up for a laugh, delighting in driving his big American Plymouth through the Manchester city centre streets at night while lying across the front seat and peeping over the dashboard, making it look that it had no driver. His personal life unfortunately was dogged by tragedy. A succession of bad road accidents robbed him of his son and injured him seriously, and he had spent a spell in Strangeways Jail for maintenance default, but he always bounced back and we were good friends for over thirty years. The last time I saw him was in 1996 in St. Malo when he came over for a day from Jersey where he was working the season for agent Dick Ray. I found him a changed man due mainly to his caring partner Angie who had persuaded him to give up drinking.

In December1998 I was sad to read in 'The Times' of his death from a brain tumour.

Inspired and egged on by such talented company, I wrote to the BBC and asked for an audition. A couple of weeks later I got a reply and a form to fill in which led to a date for a radio audition at the old BBC Piccadilly studio in Manchester. Originally I contemplated forming a duo with the beautiful Ena but just in time I discovered that although she was very good at everything else a musician needs, Ena was no singer but she came down to the audition with me anyway. The song I had chosen was Eddy Fisher's current hit 'Cindy' but I think that my Country styling was somewhat alien to my accompanist, (a middle aged arty queen with a floppy floral bow tie). My performance was not exactly a wow and I was not about to become the new Dean Martin.

So it was "Thank you, Mr Jonkee (sic). Don't call us. We will be in touch with you soon. But don't give up your day job yet."

*   *   *   *   *   *

4
A SOJOURN IN SCANDINAVIA

Sometimes you can get by without your friends doing you a favour but I suppose that Karl was well intentioned when he introduced me to an old pal of his from Glasgow called Jimmy. (Yes, a real Glaswegian called Jimmy) who, like me was a singing guitar player—but his style was nearer to Sydney Devine than Johnny Cash. He joined us regularly for our Friday night jam at the pub where the idea of us working together was first mooted. He also played mandolin so we started doing local gigs together with an act based on the Louvin Brothers, you know, with songs like 'Blame me.' and 'My Baby' etc. We also did numbers by Earl and Bill Bolick. (A duo that soon realised that an act billed as the Bolick Brothers was inviting derision and quickly changed it to the Blue Sky Boys). Jimmy came up with an old rattletrap Ford van from somewhere and we started seeking the mother lode across the Pennines in Yorkshire where there was a vast and booming working men's club circuit.

Over those hills only the scallys and the snakes patronised the local pubs. Respectable folk usually went to 'Th'Institute,' which booked only top class 'turns' like us. And so it happened that while doing a classic Sunday noon and night gig in Grimsby we were buttonholed by a local agent who asked if we would like to do a trip entertaining on a cruise ship? A CRUISE SHIP? Wow.

He said that the passengers would probably want a bit of Rock 'n' Roll too so we decided to pack a couple of electric guitars as well. I already had a semi–acoustic Baldwin Virginian and he had a solid Burns Bison that was no problem. He seemed pleased and promised to contact us the following week. "Oh Great," we enthused and spent the drive home fanaticising about the warm beaches and bikini clad girls of the Caribbean but our euphoria was a bit dimmed when we got details of the trip a few days later. It was not sailing out of Miami as we had hoped, but aboard a North Sea ferry shuttling between Hull and Ejsberg in Denmark. Not ex-actly the Florida Keys but a better offer than our next booking which was a tour of the Cumbrian coast, kicking off at exciting Cleator Moor and ending ten days later at the sophisticated watering hole of Workington. There was no contest.

Regrettably they turned out to be a nightmare trips. The sea was choppy and the choice was to either stay in the fuggy smoked filled saloon playing to a lot of drunken rowdy booze cruisers or go out on deck and freeze—but the job proved to have a bright side. On our second trip across a Danish agent offered us two weeks in Copenhagen and having had quite enough of the wild North sea and the green gilled punters we were glad to take his offer and signed off the ferry in Ejsberg and made our way to the city of the Brothers Grimm and Danny Kaye.

* * * * * *

Jaws

Our booker met us warmly and fixed us up with digs in a row of old fishermen's cottages in the port area opposite the famous statue of the little mermaid, (which was much smaller than I had imagined, being only about a metre high). The gig turned out to be at the famous Tivoli Gardens, a big pleasure park in the heart of the city where we did afternoon performances at a lakeside café and the evenings in a huge bierkeller. We also took part in two big Folk and Rock festivals at the National Scala theatre. The agent was pleased with us and (for the moment) so were the bookers but I'm afraid that was soon to change. We were getting good responses and got a nice write up in the tourist brochures for the month but I could sense that 'Oor Jimmy' was getting restless: Success was not a condition that he was used to and it was not long before he made his move.

One evening we ran into some old friends of his who were working aboard a Scottish ship unloading timber there. We had a few drinks and as we all got along fine we invited them to meet us after our gig the following afternoon at the Tivoli Gardens. The café we had chosen for the rendezvous was on the edge of a big ornamental lake full of exotic fish where happy picnicking families could throw bits of bread into the lake to feed them. At about three o'clock Jimmy's mates turned up, obviously worse for wear and noisily made their way to where we were sitting lazily feeding the swarming white carp and exotic goldfish. I noticed that one of the lads was carrying a bright yellow oilcloth bag which I could have sworn contained some kind of liquid but nobody mentioned it so I presumed that they had been shopping. Beers were ordered and the usual flask of spirits surreptitiously passed around as we sat there swapping stories and drinking in the bright sunshine. Suddenly and without warning, the man with the bag stood up and with a fiendish grin, emptied the contents over the guardrail and into the swarming shoal. There was a loud splash and all the fish rushed towards it but quickly changed direction when they realised that the new arrival was a vicious two foot long pike who had spent the past few hours sloshing about in the yellow bag and was now desperate for his dinner. The lake exploded as terrified fish rushed everywhere, many of them jumping out of the lake to escape the attention of the vicious predator and onto the tables and the wooden deck where they squirmed and squiggled about, causing people to slip as they too struggled screaming and shouting to get clear of the carnage. The fish got into people's hair and into their food. Children started crying and two young girls started having hysterics trying to get rid of the goldfish that somehow got down the necks of their summer dresses.

Jimmy and his mates thought it was hilarious and were still prostrate with laughter when three bulky security guards forced their way through the crowd and grabbed them. I tried to slip away quietly but when the police arrived some of the girls with the fish invaded frocks fingered me, so we all spent the night in the cells at Klampenborg Police Station. Next morning we were thrown out on the streets and told to get out of town. It was the end of our Tivoli contract but fortunately they paid us what we were due so we decided to go to Norway and try our luck there.

In Berserker-Land

There was a ferry leaving next day for Oslo so we booked aboard and spent a very pleasant evening cruising up the Kattegat. It was a warm summer and we sat up most of the night with a couple of girls we had met and early next morning we were nosing up Oslo fjord to where the girls lived. One of them worked for the state railways and took us to a hotel where the crews would stay until their trains were ready. It was cheap and clean so we settled in and I started looking for work. And Jimmy started sniffing around the bars looking for deals. Finally I found an agent called Carl Gruss who had an office near the squat twin towered town hall that was looking for an act to take over from the Ray Ellington trio at a club by the harbour. We did a try out gig for him and he was impressed enough to give us a six week contract.

Having now got an advance on our wages, we picked up with the girls again and in spite of the monster cost of food and drink, we gave them a good time. The first gigs of the new contract were up at Holmenkollen where the 1948 Winter Olympics had been held and then at an open–air café in a city park full of erotic figures. Next came a few gigs at some fishermen's social clubs, which gave us the first inklings of what working in rural Norway was going to be like. They were wild and there seemed to be a permanent fight going on, shifting about the hall from corner to corner and in and out of the inebriated dancers: But that was nothing compared with what was to come when Carl sent us up to Stavanger, a pleasant coastal town where it seems to rain continually, and then on a two–hour boat trip to some kind of primitive settlement.

Now here were your real Vikings. Blond, bearded giants whose idea of dressing up for an evening out was to kick the reindeer shit off their boots, shake the fleas out of their fur lined parkas and drag a herring bone comb through their matted locks. The girls looked much the same. Big, blond, and full of life. Initially they were quite shy and they had the same social habits that I had seen in the Orkneys where the girls would sit down one side of the dance hall, giggling and generally dancing with each other until one of the local machos, who had necked enough moonshine, would ap– proach one of them and nod to the floor. Some bolder spirits would gradually join him until there were several couples wobbling or stomping around the hardwood floor. Other well–oiled Norse warriors would watch for a while, sneering at their mate's antics and cat–calling the dancers until some berserker threw a beer bottle and then it kicked off. It was like Texas City all over again as the tavern erupted into a spectacular bar room brawl that would have done John Wayne proud as it rolled from one end of the hall to the other. At one point a raving, raw–boned Rambo dashed out to his truck for a weapon and we all took cover behind the bar expecting him to come storming in with a hunting rifle but he crashed back swinging a big long handled snow shovel. For a moment everything stopped, but before he could get a good belt at anybody the bouncers were on him kicking him the full length of the hall and out into the pouring icy rain.

And this turned out to be the regular Friday night gig. Most other nights the same wild people sat morosely at the bar sucking on their beer bottles and waiting till Friday night came around again. Although who could blame them at those prices? Even back then, when a pint of bitter in England cost half a crown (25p) it would set you back more than a quid in Stavanger.

We lasted two weeks on that inclement littoral getting as far north as Bergen where it also rained a lot. We thought we had hit the pits in Stavanger but, compared to the next town they sent us to, it was like Menton. This was way up in the hills to play at a weekend Rock and Folk Festival at Voss. We were booked to play in a big soggy marquee to a crowd that had arrived drunk on Friday night. You can imagine what state they were in when it came our turn to play Music for Fighting at 11p.m. on Saturday.

As we had now come to expect, once again the place went berserk (now I know where the word came from) with everybody, men, women, children, husky dogs, and bear cubs, invoking their Norse Gods to revenge some obscure tribal vendetta from centuries ago. Finally, the distraught festival organisers had to bring in the Army to sort it all out. Yes, that's right, not the police—the Army.

PICKER'S TIP 7

Fix your guitar strap on the stud at the base of the neck (Where it joins the body) leaving the other end of it free to throw over your shoulder and fix to the stud at the base of the body. Saves all that fiddling about over your head.

Sexy Sweden

Next it was back to Oslo and the rain continued to follow us. We did two gigs in the capital, which weren't so bad and soon we were off south to Sweden and the moment we crossed the border bridge at Svinesund it stopped raining and the sun came out. The bus dropped us off outside Ud-devalla in a forest picnic area with many youth camps which was more our style, with young, cool, audiences who appreciated our raw rockabilly and American dustbowl ballads. From there we headed down to the city of Gothenburg where we were greeted by a sharp, enthusiastic, agent who was very excited from the reports he had received from his Norwegian colleague about our riotous gig at Voss. What had we got to do with it? Everybody was well canned when we arrived. But somehow we had gained the hard reputation for stirring up the crowds. Our first shows there were at some kind of college complex where we played for a Hank Williams ap-preciation society, which we enjoyed after all the crazy thrashing about in Norway. It was quite a surprise as at the time both Hank and Lefty were persona–non–grata in Nashville.

Gothenberg turned out to be a really nice city and I got the distinct im-pression that the Swedes had got things together much better than their Norwegian cousins. The public transport was good and the shops and parks elegant and well kept and it was in one of these shops, a big delicatessen, we met up with an English tourist who was overjoyed to find someone who spoke his native tongue and invited us to join him at a café. He explained that he and his brother owned a chain of chemist's shops in London and they each took off three months every year and he had chosen to sail his boat across to Gothenberg for his holiday. It was all very nice but the point of his story was that he had found a young Swedish sex goddess whom he had installed aboard his cruiser on the Gotha Canal where she catered en-thusiastically to his every sexual whim and fancy. To his chagrin there was no one around to whom he could boast about his good fortune and it was driving him mad. He wanted everybody to know what a lucky sod he was. (Everybody that is, except his wife in Chigwell). So he paid for all we could eat and drink while we listened to all the intimate details as he drooled and lived it all again. He became so excited that he invited us both to spend the night aboard the boat with them (I think he was looking for a performance of a different kind from us) but when we got there it turned out that his Svenska nympho had taken a hike with his spare Rolex, leav-ing him a 'Dear John' note on the binnacle. So we never did get to see her in action. However we helped him get over it by drinking the liquor locker dry and slipped off to sleep it off in the main cabin. What a nut.

The next few days were very pleasant at the seaside town of Falkenberg where the audiences were more mature and requested Tennessee Ernie and Eddy Arnold songs. At weekend we played at a couple of big public picnics in one of the city parks much like in the States. We had a great time but stayed out until two in the morning and found ourselves locked out of our hotel, so that night we slept in a workman's hut on what we thought was a quiet little copse. We woke to the roar of traffic passing close by and found that our grassy knoll was in fact a traffic island on the main highway.

But for Jimmy things were far too quiet and he got involved in a smug‐gling ring with the local low life. Cigarettes were their big thing and of course he got caught and was lucky to get off with a harsh warning but he was told to get out of Sweden immediately. He took his due share of the money and left that night on the ferry to Travelmunde. And that was the last time I saw him. (Although, that is not quiet true, I did see him one more time some time later when I did a show at Strangeways Jail. He was in the audience). I had to continue the tour on my own, a thing I never liked to do. Although it was not too bad as there were only three gigs to go, one at Helsingor and a couple in Malmo, a city I liked very much where I enjoyed the civilised atmosphere in what was then the finest shopping centre in Scandinavia.

A week later I was on the ferry home with a fistful of dollars. Mmm. Nice.

Sylvia

It was not long after getting back that I came across a stunning looking girl with finely chiselled features and large brown eyes working behind the tobacco counter in Lewis's department store. Her name was Sylvia and it wasn't long before we were going out together. Before my arrival on the scene she had been going out with a top sergeant in the USAF and also her departmental boss was trying to tempt her to move in with him. Looking back on it now, I can't help thinking that she would have been much better off with either of them than a dreamer like me. And no doubt her family would have agreed with me.

They were very conventional. Her father owned a small engineering firm and ruled his family with a firm Victorian hand, always referring to his wife as 'Mother' who usually wore a hairnet and a floral pinny and had a tongue like an adder. Sylvia also had a younger sister who spent most of her time at home getting ready for work the next day. They all thought that I was mad and dangerous. I wonder why? In time Sylvia modified her view of me but the others never did. The suspicion was mutual.

After a brief courtship we got married and in the early days were happy but my rebel Free Spirit views were at odds with her conventional upbringing. She held down a steady job but in spite of having had a good education, I was not looking to become a company man and was always trying to get something going on my own, though I did try to change.

At one time we lived in a damp flat in Stalybridge where I worked driv‐ing a dump truck in a hillside quarry there until the winter weather closed it down after which I got shift work at the Aerolite wire works, mixing tubs of powdered chemicals for the Calendar rolling mills and coming home at the end of each day covered in a carbon black film. I looked like Al Jolson. So you can see that the marriage did not get off to a very good start. The die was cast and after that experience I swore that the only person I would ever work for was going to be myself.

I also realized that I could earn a week's housekeeping money by doing one gig. So it was back to the music.

PICKER'S TIP 8
More Publicity Hype.

Has hit records	Collects Elvis Presley tapes.
Vibrant performer	Jumps about the stage.
Award winning	Has friends on the committee.
Close harmony group	Sing standing next to each other.
Evergreen	Over the hill.
Veteran	Past it.
Stalwart	Hanging on, but won't let go.
Enjoys touring	Willing to drive bus. Needs to get away.
Equipped for overseas	On the run from the C.S.A.
Got transport	Reliant Robin or bus pass.
Fantastic	Unbelievable.
Cruise experience	Weekend gig on the Ostend Ferry.
International star	Two gigs in Norway.
Trendy	Listens to Radio One.
Well known	Overexposed. Stale.
Self–contained	Nobody will work with him.
Fabulous	Not too bad.
Popular	Ordinary. Buys punters drinks.

PICKER'S TIP 9

More than any other profession entertainers suffer from periods of extreme euphoria and black depression. So when the blues hit you, just remind yourself that what goes around, comes around and don't do anything drastic. Remember too that this is the easiest job in the world to quit and the hardest to get back into.

The feeling of complete euphoria when you are up there performing well with a superb band behind you, is something that cannot be bought. No matter how much money you have. Realise this and you will never want to lose an opportunity.

5

THE DRIFTERS
It's Pickin' Time

One thing I did learn from that disastrous BBC audition was that if I was going to make it as a Country singer I would have to find some backing musicians who knew what the music was all about, not an easy commodity to find in the North of England in the late 1950's. I started looking around and came across a struggling skiffle group called the Kingfishers. I asked if they minded me sitting in, and three weeks later I was running it as a Country group called the Drifters, playing the local pubs and small clubs as a five piece. Two brothers, Roy and Malcolm Gaskill, played drums and bass respectively, Roy Farnell was on lead guitar, teenage Rod King played his home made lap top steel guitar, while I played rhythm on a gut string Spanish Estruch guitar (subsequently stolen, either by a fan—or a music lover) and did all the singing. It was a good clean sound, ideal for the Hank Williams, Johnny Cash and Webb Pierce numbers of the day and we even won a few talent contests.

Back then it seemed that everyone either played something or sang, and every street had its own skiffle group with a wash board, a tea chest bass, and a couple of cheap guitars. Amplification was in its infancy and the only sure sign of street cred was to have a Fender bass guitar in the group, but it was some time before we got round to that and in the meantime Roy had to tote around a massive double–bass fiddle. By far the best vocal amplifiers were the expensive Italian Miazzi or German Dynacords, which had built in echo units but, until British firms like Marshal and Vox started to make them in bulk, threadbare groups like us had to make do with whatever second–hand gear we could get our hands on.

Oh, yes. We were called Groups or Combos if you had any jazz aspirations, as opposed to Bands, which were run by tyrannical dance hall owners and used brass instruments like trumpet and saxophones where you had to be able read sheet music. Writing these memoirs now forty years on, fashions appear to have turned full circle when vocal groups using pre–recorded electronic backing tracks are now referred to as bands.

I suppose it was typical of me to be swimming against the tide. The skiffle boom was fading and the air was full of the new Rock 'n' Roll, yet here was I, trying to create a classic Country and Western band—but it was making a mark and we were getting bookings and took a step up onto the Sporting Club scene by winning a talent contest at the Devonshire Club in Prestwich and were rewarded with a week's engagement backing the newly returned immigrant from Australia, Coventry born Frank Ifield who was making a big mark with a yodelling version of the 1920's song 'I remember You'. Karl Denver also did a great comedy version too. but in a Glasgow accent which he called 'Ah remember yuh Jimmy, ya bastard.' A harbinger of fellow Scot's Billy Connolly's parodies years later.

Also around this time Carroll Levis brought his radio talent show to the

Ardwick Empire, then one of Manchester's premier theatres, so we applied for a place and got an audition. Carroll was a Canadian radio announcer from station CKWX Vancouver who had joined the BBC in 1936 and brought one of the first talent contests to British radio. Auditions were held at cinemas and theatres across the country and came up with such acts as 'The Two Laundry men from Peckham' and 'Bernard Flynn, the Singing Gas Collector'. These shows were such a success that Radio Luxembourg, then at the cutting edge of commercial broadcasting, presented the sponsored show as the 'Quaker Oats Half Hour.' The winners of the first 'Grand Cash Prize', something that the BBC could not offer, were the Crawford Brothers singing 'Ten Tiny Toes'. Levis' last run on started in July 1958 with 'The Carrol Levis Talent Show' a lunchtime show that he would introduce with his own unique catch phrase.

"The new and unknown artistes of today are truly the stars of tomorrow."

And in many cases he was right—along with fellow Canadian Bryan Michie, (pron. Mickey) Carroll was responsible for bringing the old seaside talent contest to national level and an appearance on one of the shows was a huge step up to fame and fortune These pioneers laid the foundation for shows like 'Opportunity Knocks' and 'New Faces' which did launch many showbiz legends. Bryan Michie took another route with a BBC production called 'Youth takes a bow.' which featured junior performers, his biggest discovery being Master Ernie Wise in 1939 who won his heat singing 'Let's all have a Tiddly at the Milk Bar'

But let's get back to the show. The number we had planned to do on the Ardwick Empire show was Hank Locklin's 'Geisha Girl', then riding high in the charts. It was a catchy tune and had a nice hook guitar riff between the verses that went Da–di Da–didi–di (G–A–G–A–G) and we decided to enhance the oriental effect of the opening with a spectacular cymbal splash. However Carol Levis' girl assistant on this occasion was none other than a very youthful Jackie Collins—yes, the very same lady who later found fame writing her steamy Hollywood novels. She must have been about seventeen and looked absolutely stunning with flowing dark hair and a superb figure. In fact our drummer was so entranced by her that when it came to our dramatic opening he missed his Zyljan cymbal altogether and knocked over his whole drum–kit, leaving us to straggle into our much rehearsed masterpiece. Needless to say we did not pass the audition. Well, you can't win 'em all can you?

The next time we played the Ardwick Empire was on a short tour supporting Mitchell Torok who was promoting his big hit 'Caribbean' and the almost identical 'When Mexico gave up the rumba'. We also did a few theatre dates with squaw man Marvin Rainwater (Old Starvin' Marvin') who was picking up a few bucks promoting his American chart toppers like 'Gonna find me a blue bird' and that wild rock classic 'Whole lotta woman.'

In general though the main source of income came from the smaller clubs and one of our regular gigs in the late '50s was Dargai Street Working

Men's Club in East Manchester. This was the venue for a weekly BBC radio show called 'Club Night' hosted by popular comedian Dave Morris that proved to be a pathfinder and an inspiration to many similar clubs. This show's producer was John Ammonds (the same man who was involved in booking our Far East tour some twelve years later) and featured the vivacious teenage singer Shiela Buxton. The shows compere was her then boyfriend, Roger Moffat, a plummy voiced staff announcer whose big party piece was taking the huff at some imagined insult and stomping off drunk into the night. He even did it when we were playing there and fell down some roped–off roadworks. Sheila's parents had a pub in Ashton–under–Lyne and we would sometimes drop in for a late night drink on our way home from Yorkshire. After negotiating that wild trans–Pennine route in a barely roadworthy old van you needed one.

In the end though, frustrated by the machinations of TV producers and the lack of proper exposure, she moved to Australia and built a highly successful career on the clubs out there. Shiela Buxton was a very talented singer with a bubbling stage presence, light–years ahead of her staid British contemporaries.

The Country Music Clubs

Around this time a strange phenomenon began to appear across the country that made me see that I was not alone. In the eye of the raging storm of Rock 'n' Roll the first clubs devoted to Country Music began to take shape. The two main catalysts were the merchant seamen returning from American trips who brought back with them records of this strange music and the social fall–out from the huge US military installations established here. Fans in ports like Liverpool, Bristol, and Southampton got together and devotees near the sites of the bases in East Anglia and around Oxford began to organize themselves. I started playing a regular gig at Barton airport where I met up with several Americans from the nearby giant staging post of Burtonwood who booked us for a regular Country Music night at the Starlight Club there.

Along with a friend of mine, Slim Traynor, who ran a group in Salford called the Hillbilly Bandits, we decided to open a club for Country fans in Manchester city centre, It was a like a New York floating crap game and never had a permanent home. We opened up in February 1958 at the Bodega on Cross Street and later at pubs like the Thatched House, the Fatted Calf (where the stage consisted of beer crates covered with a greasy old carpet) and at the old York Hotel.

As an indication of the current attitudes of the promoters, at the Hazel Grove AHS. Grand Gala at Stockport Town Hall on Boxing Night 1958 we were billed as a 'Rhythm Group' along with Arthur Brown's Orchestra. Incidentally we did the same gig a year later but this time, as Yonco's Texas Drifters (Country & Western).

Were they at last getting the message? But why the new name? Well, some of you may recall that Cliff Richard's original backing group were also called the Drifters but around this time the famous American black singing group of that name took out an injunction preventing anyone else using the name. So everybody had to make changes. And they became the Shadows and little tiddlers like us became the Texas Drifters.

Finally our floating club found a home at the Manchester Sports Guild (the MSG) a club run like one of Her Majesty's Shore Establishments by 'Jenks', an ex–Royal Navy martinet, who graciously allowed us to share the stage on his Folk Nights amongst all the scraggly beards, long neck banjos, worry beads and flowing muslin where our embroidered cowboy shirts stood out like a sore thumb. On our opening night there we met up with Bluegrass legend Bill Clifton, who, to the lip chewing chagrin of the hippy, ear–cupping folkies, said that he really liked what we were doing. These Country Music Clubs developed widely, becoming the major sources of employment for the many Country acts that developed but sadly in later years this vast network had been reduced to a shadow of its former self, due partly to the changing fashions of the time but also helped in no small measure by the petty jealousies and parochialism of the organisers. However, in spite of this improvement in the situation, work was not exactly flowing in and I was regularly and uncomfortably reminded by my long suffering wife and parents that it was about time I abandoned these juvenile ideas of a showbiz career and get a proper job. So I found one. Get this.

Welcome to Baskervilles.

PICKER'S TIP 10

Do NOT travel to a big gig in your stage clothes. Remember that people have come to see you. Not just to hear you. Show some respect. Don't straggle on stage in greasy jeans and a dirty T–shirt.
Don't be arrogant. You ain't that good.

6

MISTER SPACEMAN

The boring routine of the raincoat factory was driving me nuts, but I had to come up with the house keeping money somehow as my new band was not yet earning the big bucks I had been counting on. I began scouring the papers for a more interesting job and I found a really bizarre one. Let me tell you about it.

It was the late '50s and it was at a firm called Baskervilles; No, it had nothing to do with Conan Doyle or big hounds. It was a waterproof clothing factory that also did a nice sideline in rubber dinghies and life jackets for the RAF, but they also had a secret research facility devoted to the development of space suits.

Yes, *Real Space Suits*. That's right. Moon Walker's pyjamas.

I've never seen a set up like it. A classic case of the blind leading the blind with the government spin doctors pouring cash into it and the whole project was populated by the biggest team of oddballs sharks and misfits I have encountered.

The job advertised in the trade paper was very mysterious. It read.

SECRET GOVERNMENT CONTRACT
DESIGNER /PATTERN CUTTER REQUIRED
APPLY PO. BOX NO 666

Well, I had done a bit of pattern work at the old raincoat factory so I wrote and the reply came as quite a surprise to me. They invited me to visit their industrial development complex for an interview and aptitude test.

Cunningly disguised as a raincoat factory, this highly secret installation, was actually a ramshackle collection of dirty brick and tarred timber buildings on a pot holed cinder back road at the edge of a worked–out sand quarry in south east Lancashire, and the secret facility was in a big shed at the back. Even at this early stage I began to have my doubts about the set up. I had expected something like a state of the art underground complex with armed guards, not a wooden hut in the yard next to the canteen. The main part of the factory still made raincoats and was full of bustling and shouting women and thundering machines but the research facility was as silent as a grave and strictly off limits to those who had not been vetted and cleared by the Ministry—that is provided that they didn't drop in for a chat on the way to the canteen next door.

My interview was vague to say the least. I was led through the factory by a spotty office girl to where a sweating, heavily built man was arguing loudly with a very thin middle–aged woman. His name was John and I was gestured aside as he continued his battle with this screeching virago. It was all about seam allowances or something and he was having difficulty making his point due partly to his having a severe stammer which got worse as he became more excited, until he was virtually spitting all over the ratty forelady. Finally, feeling that she had won the day, she turned on

her heel and huffed off to the canteen leaving him open mouthed. Then he
noticed me and after finding out who I was and what I had come for, told
me to follow him to his office in the research and development department.
(i.e.the Shed).

John turned out to be the factory manager and asked me about my background and experience at which I presented him with a carefully prepared
CV of fibs, which he countered by giving me a glowing description of the
secret job which was about as far from the truth as my CV. Apparently
there was no real precedent for this job, as it had never been done before in
England. There were no designs or patterns to refer to. (Of course the
Russians and the Yanks had their own plans but we were not about to ask
them were we? After all we were British) and up to that point John had
been trying to do it himself, as well as run both the raincoat production
line and the research facility. Now it was all getting too much and he
needed some help.

In essence the task was to create flat, workable patterns from the three
dimensional models of space helmets, pressure suits, back packs etc. that
the other boffins, most of whom were bigger chancers than me, had
dreamed up or stolen from Dan Dare comics, after which they would be
made up in super strength nylon and tried out before being chucked in the
waste bin as failures. (Or Discontinued Projects as they were termed, for
the Ministry Reports).

'Well, I thought, that's not too hard. Nobody's going to tell me that I'm
doing it wrong, are they? They don't know any more than me.'

It was like making models, so that I said that I had no difficulty with the
concept and he pulled out some patterns of the standard production
raincoats and asked me to grade them up two sizes. He watched carefully
as I got stuck in. It was easy–peasy, just basic grading, but he announced
himself satisfied before I had finished. He then told me about the money,
which was more than I had expected, and after I accepted, he declared me
hired and took me off to meet the other elite members of this secret
development team. What a shock that was.

It was like walking onto the set of a 'Carry On' film.

First there was the Nutty Professor. He was a very thin bespectacled
young man in a wrinkled off–white laboratory coat called Adrian who
greeted me with a dead fish handshake and a nervous laugh. He had an
assistant called Tony, a large lad who had just come out of the armed
forces and still spit–shined his size 11 boots. He almost saluted when we
met but scuttled off after his mate at the first opportunity.

Then came Rag Bag Harold, the department's chief engineer. He was
about the scruffiest person I have ever met and wore a baggy ginger Harris
Tweed suit to match his greasy hair and a bright green Fair Isle pullover
and smelt like a charity shop. He greeted us with a thick Pennine foothills
accent and made his disapproval of my being inducted into his department
quite obvious. He was miffed at not being asked to vet my appointment

personally. It appeared that we were going to get on like oil and water. And we did.

Next up to bat was another misfit. He was called Eric, a f t, ruddy–faced Midlander, with a nicotine stained walrus moustache who, like Big Tony was ex–RAF and was the department's store man, who demanded three signatures for any item he was asked to provide. Eric was about forty–five and rather bitter that after doing twenty years' service he was no longer needed to guard the new Cold War V bombers and took his frustration out on anyone that crossed his path by being as pedantic and awkward as possible.

The two following characters were complete poseurs who somehow had bluffed their way onto the government payroll. First there was a horn–rimmed bespectacled upper crust Anglo–European with an unfathomable accent who claimed to be married to a Serbian countess and insisted an being called Mr (or Herr) Holtzberg. He had letters after his name claiming degrees in obscure subjects from colleges in places like Croatia and Es–tonia, All of them were deep behind the Iron Curtain, which was very handy because nobody could check them out. He spent most of his day in his office writing reams of recommendations or reviews of his complicated phantom experiments or booking tickets for his numerous overseas trips. Nobody knew what he actually did or even bothered to ask him.

The second con artiste was your classic North Cheshire suburban snob called Nigel. He arrived everyday in his Hillman Minx carrying an im–portant looking brief case and wearing his golf club blazer or a grey check suit complete with brown suede shoes and a Guards tie. (Home Guards that is, as Nigel had spent the war in a coal depot at Macclesfield). He was supposed to be our technical writer and could usually be found at any time of day in his office practicing his golf swing or having tea in Eric's stores talking about his house and garden. All the time I was there I never came across anything he had written.

Ensconced in an adjacent office was a real mad scientist called Henry where he operated a stress machine and whose day was punctuated by vio–lent bangs and rips as he tested something to destruction, at which point he would chuckle manically and stick his head out to grin evilly at every–body. He was, in short, a complete loony.

Now they were the foot soldiers. So what about the executives?

Well, we have already met the factory manager Spittin' John, but watch out, here comes the Head of Development—our main man. He is the guy that gets all that lovely government money and who keeps all those visit–ing MOD Inspectors sweet. Meet Old Joe Goldside. In late middle–age and as smooth as a puppy's first bowel movement, his white hair pomaded to perfection and his face a glowing mask of tonsorial perfection. He always appeared wearing a gleaming white on white shirt, a silver grey tie, and a black silk Italian suit above hand made crocodile moccasins. We see him about once a month when he shepherds a team of Ministry Men round the

department before whipping them off in chauffeured limos to some ex–
clusive Cheshire country club for lunch and kick–backs.

The last link in the chain is the current owner of the factory who is called
Marvin. He looks like a slob but is the grand nephew of the founder and
knows absolutely nothing about any facet of the clothing industry, having
inherited it all from his uncle. His main interest is hard pornography and
he often comes sniffing and shuffling into the technical writers office to
flash his latest collection of dirty snaps from his latest sex trip to Ibiza.

What a bunch of chancers. I felt quite at home.

My workplace was in one corner of the big shed where I was allocated a
huge cutting table about three metres square covered with sheets of
Formica and a rack holding big rolls of heavy brown pattern paper and thin
cardboard along with a large selection of shears, tape measures, rulers, set
squares and other oversized geometric instruments. Under my vast
platform were sturdy shelves holding sheets of wire mesh and several bolts
of cloth, and a big tub of modelling clay.

There was no stock check or inventory of any kind and I quickly caught
on to the reason why everyone carried a brief case and also why they con–
scientiously took home such a large amount of work when so much equip–
ment and gear went mysteriously missing. For instance, Eric the store man
seemed to have a brisk trade in resin and fibreglass fabric as so many cans
and packages would be stacked outside the back door with notes attached
declaring them to be out of date. Eric, of course, with his deep concern for
the planet's ecology volunteered to dispose of them safely. Usually via his
brother–in–law, who had a stall on Stockport Market.

Nigel, in whose office the duplicator lived, operated a thriving printing
and copying service from his Wilmslow home and also supplied his golf club
and its members and several of his brothers from his Masonic lodge with
headed stationary and other paper products from Eric's shelves. Herr
Holtzberg's fiddle was travel perks and he would be off with his aristocratic
wife to exotic locations for weeks on end on vague trips of research and
evaluation and conferences with equally obscure academics across the
globe. I recall one conference in Helsinki about the problems of the future
of the Borneo Dyak population. On his return he would scribble reams of
reports that nobody ever read. Adrian and Tony's big scam was in five
gallon cans of Araldite adhesive and technical books, which arrived crated
from the wholesalers and were moved on without even being opened. They
also had a nice line in electric tools. Rag Bag Harold, our immediate boss
was much more crafty and made his lolly in grateful considerations from
the myriad of small engineering firms he dished out sub contracts to for
unused spares. He also had a thing going with Janis the wages girl and
gave her a lift to the bus stop most nights in return for a quick blow job.
Janis was a tall girl with a strong Oldham accent and a severe glide in one
eye, which made talking to her difficult, as you didn't know which side of
her head to address. Still I don't think Rag Bag noticed it much, after all,

he found her at her most interesting when he was staring down at the back of her neck.

What me? Oh, I made the pleasant discovery of a bolt of fawn gabardine cloth under my work table which was just the right colour for shirts and pants for my newly formed band, so each night a length was snipped off and given a new home.

But all our little strokes faded into nothing when compared with Old Joe who was a real, heavy hitter in the rip–off game. He bought a tract of prime land at the side of the factory and had bulldozers and diggers working round the clock preparing the ground for a government–financed extension of our secret research unit that somehow turned out to be a small but select enclave of expensive executive homes. Oh yes, Old Joe showed us the way home all right. By the way, that estate is still there and if you knew exactly where I'm talking about, you could go there and see a street named after him.

Work? Ah yes, I had almost forgotten about that. Well, actually we did do some work and a lot of it serious stuff. America was going flat out on their space programme and if Joe was ever going to complete the monument to his memory we would have to produce some thing to keep the MOD coughing up the money. Our basic task was to come up with a space suit that really worked. The problem of the fabric had been solved by Courtaulds who produced a nylon–based cloth that weight for weight was stronger than steel. So strong in fact that it could not be cut by conventional shears but had to use a special heated wheel blade designed for the purpose. The root difficulty stemmed from the fact that the suit itself would have to be pressurised to operate outside any space vehicle, but if you simply inflated the thing it would become rigid and impossible to move in. So after several experiments and long discussions Spittin' John and I came up with the idea of convoluted joints; deep pleats at either side of the elbow, knees, ankles, hips and shoulders, which enabled the pressure to be displaced as the joint moved—and it worked superbly. So much so that Old Joe came down to congratulate us because the development allowed him to up his demand to the MOD for more funds and we got a write–up in a trade publication. This did not go down too well with the engineering lobby of Rag Bag Harold and the White Coat Twins who had always considered that groundbreaking ideas were their exclusive prerogative and for weeks had the sulks about it.

The net result of this new found prominence was a vicious range war led by Harold who particularly had the rats at me and started checking up on my somewhat erratic arrival times and finally caught me red–handed sneaking in the back door. I made some grovelling excuses like late buses and train derailments and got off with a good bollocking which must have made Harold feel great for a week and got me thinking about a way round this surveillance. So anytime I happened to be a little bit late I would head for the delivery gate of the canteen where I would stash my coat and brief case, grab a cup of coffee and stroll through the factory as though I had arrived much earlier. It worked very well but only for a while. Of course, it couldn't last and the odds were stacked against me. My American image did not go down too well with most of my fellow researchers who still believed that Dunkirk had been a great victory and said that Pearl Harbour was a big Hollywood hype—and that space exploration was their own private domain. (I think that some of them, the White Coats in particular, thought I was a CIA spy) and at some late night conclave they had decided to have a purge and get rid of us all.

Looking back at it now I can see how I must have rocked the boat by not knowing my place in the murky waters of Top Secret government scientific research where any gaffs can be covered up by the simple ploy of invoking the Official Secrets Act. They liked to imagine that they were at the cutting edge of progress but it did not hit me like that. Maybe I was too cynical (or observant) but all I could see was Joe Goldside's rip–off of the MOD and during my two years there I saw little progress as both America and Russia surged to the stars.

The end ironically came after another of my ideas for a totally convoluted shoulder joint was accepted by the Combined Space Agency and was featured in their quarterly review. It was the last straw for Rag Bag Harold as he saw power slipping away from him and suddenly the acrid smell of redundancy was in the air. Nigel, the writer, stock keeper Eric, Mad Henry and me were told that the project was finished and given three months pay and our contracts terminated. Herr Holtzberg was transferred to a rubber clothing subsidiary and Spittin' John took early retirement, leaving the field clear for Rag–Bag Harold and the White Coat Twins. Two weeks after I got the boot, my son Francis was born. How's that for timing?

PICKER'S TIP 11

On a flight take any acoustic instrument on board as hand luggage. Ask the cabin attendant to store it for you. If it is going in the hold it must be in an airtight rigid flight case and make sure you have it covered by the flight insurance, not just the case but the contents too.

7

TRUCK DRIVING MAN

Well, with the demise of my space suit job and the arrival of a son, the requirement to come up with the housekeeping money became pressing and I started the humiliating process of seeking a day job to supplement my musical career, but I did not want to get stuck in a clothing factory again, No Sir. I fancied a job that provided me with transport. Yes, so what are you going to do, become a deliveryman? Naa. I don't really fancy that. So what else? Well, I thought, why not become a car salesman?

So off I went knocking on doors and kicking up the cinders of every fluttering flagged banger pitch in the Manchester area—succeeding only in getting regular doses of scorn and humiliation every day from smart arse motor traders. It was a Catch 22 situation. You had to have experience but you couldn't get any experience without a job. But I did finally get taken on and quite near to home as it happened, at the local branch of Colliers Motors the main distributor for Austin and Morris vehicles in the North West. The sales manager there took pity on me and said that the only thing going was a trainee's job but it only paid £10 per week. Not much of a job for a family man but it was ten quid a week more than I was earning at the time and there was always the sales commission to be earned so I gritted my teeth and accepted it—a move that triggered off yet another chapter of wild adventures.

Colliers Motors

It was also a time of great kismet for me because a few days after I took up my position as trainee salesman. (A TRAINEE? ME? Aw, c'mon). An attractive young blond girl with an elfin face and a short petal haircut came down from the offices to take my personal details. It was her very first job and it was the first time we met. Her name was Patricia Connor and we were destined to spend a lot of time together. She came from Middleton, a small mill town just north of Manchester, the youngest of a large family of seven squabbling sisters and two brothers, all held together by her hard-working widowed mother, Elizabeth, with large doses of love and a ready clip around the ear when it was needed. The girls grew up fast into strong willed, attractive women, each of them beautiful in their own individual way.

Elizabeth was probably one of the first people who believed in me and she raised no objection to my seeing her daughter. In her younger days she had been a talented pianist and a good singer but the pressures of having children and an often absent, soldier husband, forced her to shelve her dreams and go in to the cotton mills. Pat also was a singer and often worked with a trio called the Three Jays so it was a natural progression for her to sing with my band. Our relationship developed deep roots and it proved to be a long running gig, because today, forty years later, we are still together, sharing all the ups and down of an adventurous life.

And it is quite true that if you have one person believe in you totally, you can achieve anything you set your mind to.

Ladies and Gentlemen—meet Miss Kit Connor

I was by nature a good hustler but was considered such an oddity and a threat by the other salesmen that they prevailed on the boss to move me, so instead of posturing around the shiny polished cars in the warm showroom I was posted down the road to the Elephants Graveyard (the Used Commercials Department), which was actually a cinder plot filled with decrepit old trucks and vans. The only cover was a small wooden hut containing two chairs, a desk, a box of tools, a trolley full of batteries, and some jump leads but I was happy and soon got a few good fiddles going. At least I had some transport, achieved by the simple expedient of waiting until the main showroom closed and everyone went home and then picking up the best of the bangers on my pitch to go home in. Nobody ever came over to check me out anyway and the main showroom closed down at weekend because they quickly sold out their quota of new vehicles every month and nobody at head office considered the sale of used cars important. They simply shipped them to the local car auction every second Thursday. Do you wonder they eventually bit the dust?

It dawned on me that if the managers did not miss me borrowing a van at weekends, they wouldn't notice my lending two or three out to associates, (and paying clients) who might have a problem hiring vehicles legitimately. So I let it be known in various quarters that such a service was available and it was not long before a few shady characters came calling.

One of the first was a con merchant called Billy who dealt in false stones. His scam was to take the Police Gazette where descriptions and photographs of stolen jewellery were shown. Billy would then get paste copies of the items made and sell them to the cash rich hoteliers and publicans around Blackpool, flashing the Police Gazette photos as proof of their authenticity and value. There is nothing like greed to catch a fool because these seaside posers daren't even get their stolen goodies valued. Another character called Vinnie was a sinister looking guy, with a broken nose and a livid scar from his jaw to his right eye, whose speciality was selling stolen US army equipment and supplies to Fleetwood fishermen. Actually Vinnie was not very sinister at all. He got all his facial damage falling off a coal cart when he was eight.

They were not exactly the pillars of society it's true, but they all needed transport, so they would select their preferred vehicles from my stock and after the showroom had closed at five thirty I would park them up outside the back gate with the keys hidden under the seat. Early next morning I would find them all back and simply shunted them into the cinder pitch, often finding a nice little bonus in the glove compartment if the evening had gone well.

Of course it couldn't last and it was a simple act of charity on my part that blew it when I lent an Austin van to a pal who got a skinful of Guinness and ran it into the side of the airport bus. I got off lightly with a warning to make sure everything was inside the compound before I locked up at night. For more about those days there is short story I wrote called *The Maverick*.

However, having so many used trucks to hand it was not long before that Stateside experience came in useful and I became a truck driver again moonlighting at weekends with an old ex–Army Bedford tipper from my stock, driving loads of rubble and hardcore from city demolition sites to the new M6 motorway projects out on the Cheshire Plain but soon another opportunity to make a few dollars more presented itself.

One rainy afternoon about six months later I met up with a rep from a new finance company who was interested in getting in with Colliers Motors and all that lovely new vehicle finance. But there was one big snag. Apparently, Colliers Motors held a major holding in a Birmingham finance company and was obligated to put all their new vehicle business through it. But one of the conditions was that no used vehicle over six years old was to be accepted, making most of the vehicles taken in part exchange unacceptable. Particularly the pack of bangers I had on my pitch, which, not even the auctions would take.

After a good lunch and a few drinks in a local pub where I introduced him to my friend Jack Daniels from my ever–present hip flask, I intimated to the ambitious finance rep. that if his company took on some of Collier's old stuff, they might get their foot in the door for the new vehicles. He jumped at the deal and through a friend who had a garage in Rochdale, which he imagined to be a Collins subsidiary. (And I must admit I did little to disabuse him of this idea). We soon had a nice little deal going down, which went like this.

A punter would come in and select one of the bangers, put down the deposit and sign the papers and would be told to come back a few days later after the finance was accepted. In the meantime I would approach my boss and tell him that I had a trade offer on one of our used vehicles to which he happily agreed. My Rochdale partner would get it for a clear–out price and a few days later the finance company would send him a cheque for the full price without questioning the deal, convinced that they were making inroads into a major national chain of motor traders. To my surprise the arrangement worked like a dream for several months but of course it couldn't last, as very few of these rubbish punters bothered to pay the instalments and it was left to the frantic finance company to try to find and repossess their motors.

*   *   *   *   *   *

Muck Shifting

Within a year I had given up the Colliers Motors job and was running three brand new Ford Thames Trader tippers and had three of my musicians working them with me, which enabled me to buy a small Ford Ten van with windows, sprayed a muddy grey to cover its origins. My first UK band bus. Mind you it was not all that reliable but the new tippers were. So on more than one occasion I used one of them as band transport and I have clear recollections of arriving at a couple of cross Pennine Sunday afternoon gigs with a Ford 7 ton tipper loaded with five musicians, a girl singer, three groupies and all our gear. Well, you've got to be a bit resourceful haven't you? Remember. 'The Show Must Go On' (a load of cobblers, that is) or to put a finer point on it. A dollar is always a dollar and if you don't show you don't get paid.

Licences? Oh yes you were supposed to have licences but there was not much chance of one being granted to any of my old donkeys so my usual authorisation was a muddied Guinness bottle label and an insurance cover note from a dodgy car dealer.

Under an assumed name I also bought two tippers for a knock down price, a '49 Guy Otter and an older Albion Clydesdale. Both were on their last legs but I thought they would be o.k. for short hauls. They both had smoking Perkins P6 diesels, which couldn't pull the skin off a rice pudding and were certainly not up to the truck wrecking work of muck shifting on the new motorway projects. I would put the drivers on the Thames Traders and I used the Otter until it flat refused to start one morning. The local DIY mechanic found it had a cracked cylinder head. So off it went to the knacker's yard and I changed over to the older Clydesdale, which turned out to be even worse than its geriatric cousin. I can vividly recall my last day out with it. An experience so traumatic that I decided to give the whole tipper business the elbow.

It was an early start at six a.m. on a cold and rainy November day. It took me about an hour to get everybody fuelled up and dispatched to a quarry job down in Disley and then, with the aid of copious injections of Easy Start into the air filter and a blowlamp on the block, I finally got the engine started, Then, like Fred Flintstone I climbed aboard my Jurassic dump truck and headed out to a job near Bolton where a select development of executive houses was planned and the site was being cleared. Apparently the loads were only rough cinders and hardcore from the demolished cotton mill that used to occupy the site. Easy–peazy and certainly well within the capacity of any modern dump truck and although my old Albion was not in that league, I decided to give it a go anyway.

The first shock was the fact that the site was at the excavation stage and a twenty feet deep pit had been dug to get firm foundations and there was a steep ramp out of the hole for us tipper drivers to negotiate. I edged Old Dobbin down the slope in a cloud of black diesel fumes and squeaking brakes and was rewarded by a disdainful smirk from the excavator driver who was doing the loading. Being a bit embarrassed by the other trucks, the pristine Seddons and Dodge Superpose 7s, I hung back, messing about in the cab with some paperwork before finally joining the end of the queue. Some indication of what kind of day was in store for me happened as I pulled into line behind a big Foden whose driver was yelling abuse at the excavator driver because he had loaded somebody before him. He cast aspersions on the man's parentage and the efficiency of his digger and moved under the Rushton Bucyrus' three–yard bucket. The digger's engine roared and the chains tightened as the operator dug his bucket deep in the earth to come up with a solid lump of clay that must have weighed the best part of a ton. The caterpillar tracks squealed under the strain as the load arced through the air above the shiny Foden, then as the cables slackened the bucket tipped and the huge meteor of clay hurtled down into the body of the tipper. There was a loud CRUNCH as the truck rocked under the impact and the welded aluminium body ruptured, the tailgate flew off and the rear wheels collapsed inwards as the half shafts stripped their splines.

"Oh Sorry, Mate," shouted the digger driver, "Terrible sticky this bloody clay is—but y' should be alright with th' insurance."

The Foden driver went berserk but there was nothing he could do but watch fuming as his beautiful new truck was unceremoniously dragged away by a bulldozer so that the loading could continue.

Content with his revenge, the digger driver took pity on me and my baby dinosaur and loaded us up with cinders and indicated I should take the ramp out of the excavation, which was easier said than done as my smoking Perkins P6 diesel struggled manfully to climb the gradient. Several times we almost got to the top but not quite. Finally, by holding the gear lever in first with my knee and pressing down on the red knob that activated the Eaton two–speed axle we had almost breasted the rise when the straining engine stalled and then suddenly it went Wwrroarrr. And *Reversed itself. Jesus!*

The exhaust had now become the intake and the air cleaner became the exhaust. The engine cover bucked at the roaring pressure before finally unclipping itself and filling the cab with fumes and hot oil. In a blind panic I grabbed for the engine isolator and somehow managed to stop the oily inferno while the digger driver and his mates stood by roaring with laughter at my fate. In the end, realising that unless they got the ramp clear there could be no more loading that day, the bulldozer rumbled up the ramp and with the blade shoved us to the top where I managed to get the engine started again, luckily this time the right way round, and rattled off down the Bolton Road.

The municipal tip was about six miles away and I got there without incident although there was a hairy moment outside Little Lever. As I topped a rise I saw in front of me a long steep two–lane road with an equally steep gradient on the other side. I realised that I would have to wind old Dobbin up if we were going to make the opposite hill and so I put the pedal to the metal and off we roared, wobbling down the hill flat out. But at that moment another tipper breasted the rise opposite. It was also an old Dobbin in about the same state as mine. Overloaded to the gills blowing black smoke and reeling madly all over the road it hurtled towards me as the driver frantically fought with the steering wheel, both of us white faced and staring as we desperately tried to avoid each other. At the floor of the valley we were about forty yards apart when he lurched in my direction. I desperately dragged the wheel over and felt the offside wheel go down a big pothole but somehow managed to miss the thundering death trap and shot up the slope Unfortunately the other driver had not managed to make such a lucky recovery and was now nosed into a farm gateway, engine roaring and his rear wheels spinning in the mud.

By now my engine was running well although the steering felt a bit funny but it normally steered like a Sherman tank anyway so I was not troubled much. At the tip they directed me to the edge and I backed up and engaged the ram. The body lifted but nothing came out. I got out to check it and found that when the bulldozer driver had helped me out of the pit he had damaged the tailgate hinges and it wouldn't open. So I got a crowbar and proceeded to loosen it and with a 'Whoosh' the load came free and poured down the tip face—taking the bloody tailgate with it. Oh No. There it was, thirty feet down sticking out of a pile of cinders and rubbish and as a tipper without a tailgate is about as useless as an Eskimo's lawnmower. I had to get it back, so I took the tow chain and fastening it round my shoulder like Spartacus the Gladiator scrambled down the muddy tip face and hooked it on the steel tailgate and clambered back up dragging it behind me. It took me about half an hour to get it to the top and fixed back on the body, by which time I was bleeding in three or four places and look- ing like one of Flash Gordon's Claymen. Thinking that things could not get worse I sat in the cab to eat my meat pie and finish off the Thermos coffee. 'Funny.' I thought. 'This seat does not seem quite level. Must be the rough ground.'

I thought nothing more of it until I started to move off again and as I lurched to the gate I realised that the steering was strange so I got down to check it and groaned. All the dragging about and the violent drop into that pothole at the bottom of the hill had loosened the U bolts that held the front spring and the axle had slipped back on one side, with the result that going to the left I could turn on a silver dollar but going to the right I needed a turning circle of twenty yards. As I stood there stunned and watching my life turning into a Heath Robinson cartoon I checked my watch and discovered that it was only 11.15am. What else was going to go wrong, I moaned? But there was more to come.

Like a crab I somehow managed to get through the gate and fortunately the road was straight for about forty yards and just before a curve I spied a lone telegraph pole at the roadside and rolled to that. Once again the ubiquitous tow chain came to the rescue. I wrapped one end round the telegraph pole and the other to the displaced axle and then slowly backed away Old Dobbin until I pulled the beam straight. Well, nearly straight but at least now my workhorse went roughly where I pointed it. Jumping down I threw the chain in the cab and with a big wrench tightened up the U bolts as best I could and headed back to the site where the next load went without incident, as did the next one but then I had to go to a different site. This one was like the Somme battlefield, knee deep in thick mud with bits of demolished building sticking out.

And it was here that Old Dobbin went to Great Truck Stop in the Sky. Trapped up to the hubs in the sticky clay, I tried to get out by rocking back and forth. You know, revving in first gear and jumping the clutch, and then doing the same thing in reverse. It worked first time and I lurched, roaring and smoking towards the road but after about ten yards I sank again. 'Well, I thought, you got out last time so just do it again.' So I tried, but this time, as I was struggling free there was an almighty bang and the gearbox blew up leaving bits of steaming iron casing sticking in the mud. Oh, No! That was it. Enough already. I got out, pocketed all my documents, picked up my thermos and headed to the bus stop. Old Dobbin is probably still there, covered in concrete and playing his part in the foundations of a vast tower block like some underworld informant. For me it was time to get on with my showbiz career and forget about the haulage business.

I finally realized the brutal nature of the work created massive repair and maintenance bills. An owner–driver could just about make a living but small companies like mine with half a dozen trucks and a bank loan went to the wall. Some manufacturers produced relatively cheap vehicles for the work that were only expected to have a short working life, such as versions of the TK Bedford, which was known by the drivers as the Three Threes. It cost £3000; it had a Bedford 300 diesel engine and depreciated to nil value in three years. Debts were mounting and the brown envelopes began tumbling through the letterbox. Truck re–possesion writs were taken out and bailiffs called, adding more stress to my already crumbling marriage. I appealed to my family for help but got the elbow from my affluent grand-father, who echoed my mother's line that I should get a decent wage–pay-ing job. So I had to get on with it my own way. I think the final crunch came when I staggered home exhausted one evening to find that my lovely Humber Hawk was gone. My wife had handed the keys to the finance com-pany re–possessors. What else could she do?

*   *   *   *   *   *

Flatbed Freight

I did have another stab at the haulage business however a year later when I persuaded my friend Derek, to form a partnership and his very reluctant parents underwrote an HP deal for a flatbed Commer TS3 for us. It was not the most reliable of trucks but we did a few jobs with it before it too gave up the ghost. One memorable trip was across the hills to Leeds with 8 tons of tinned meat pies. They were stacked eight feet high and wobbled dangerously on those steep Pennine gradients. It took us six hours to get there and then it took another hour for the engine to cool down before we could head back home but at least I managed to filch enough meat pies to keep us fed for a month

More nightmare experiences to followed. The exhaust blew again and then the starter packed up so I had to park it on a hill near my house and those shivering four–in–the–morning starts are forever branded in my memory. On a trip to a Smethwick scrap yard with a load of old railway lines, a front spring broke, and I had to rope the axle to the chassis to get there. I arrived just in time to get weighed but I could not get paid until the load was off and as by this time all the yard workers had gone home I had to lever the rails off alone. How I envied those going home with pay packets.

The old Commer finally bit the dust in a Gloucester village around four a.m. one winter's morning when, with ice building up on the INSIDE of the windscreen the engine oil warning light suddenly flared up. We pulled over to check it out and my fatigued partner mistook the oil filler for the dipstick hole and broke off the dipper, which mangled up the complex valve system. Well, after all it was a complicated engine, an air–cooled three–cylinder with six opposed pistons—and he was a bass player. It was at that moment I finally realised that I would never become a transport tycoon. Eddie Stobard had nothing to fear.

*   *   *   *   *   *

8

THE EARLY GIGS

By the end of the '50's the stiff–collared executives at the BBC were be–
coming vaguely aware of the momentous things happening in the world of
popular music, and tentatively began to dip a toe in the turbulent waters.
We did a number of BBC radio shows but it was not easy at all to break
through the glass barrier of the corporation careerist mentality. (Not much
changed there, eh?). After the years of Denis Lotis and Lita Roza these new
trends came as rather a shock. It seemed that our music made them a little
edgy and confused. They did not know quite how to bag it. The press
viewed country music fans and performers as eccentric musical anoraks to
be bunched together with Morris dancers and steam train enthusiasts. So
an executive decision on the top floor was made to classify it as US folk
music and invisible lines of battle were drawn. Jimmy Rogers' blue yodels
and the Old Tyme backwoods ballads of Jimmy Driftwood were acceptable
as quaint but still respectable ethnic folk music but Mitchell Torok's
'Caribbean', Ernie Ford's 'Sixteen Tons' or anything by Marty Robbins was
considered a little infra dig. The Corporation finally acknowledged the
genre by putting out a program called Country Meets Folk. (A recipe for a
bar room brawl if I ever heard one). It was a classic example of ignorance.
Much like the travel agent who advertised the Israeli resort of Elat as
being *A Mecca for Tourists*.

By now we had a much better venue for our music, the Club 43 near
Smithfield Market and we set up an arrangement with Liverpool's Black
Cat club and ourselvess to swap guest artists. Hank's Walters Dusty Road
Ramblers came over as did many other groups, but there were one or two
who failed to show, having found a gig nearer home, the usual excuse being
fog on the East Lancashire Road.

This tendency to fog on that East Lancs highway sometimes caused a
different kind of trouble though. One night after a gig in Salford one of my
musoes picked up a girl who lived near Haydock and offered to run her
home in his VW camper. All went well until they hit the fog, and around
Newton it became so bad that they decided to pull over and park up. Well it
was warm and cozy in the bus, so they put down the bed in the back and
naturally one thing led to another and before long they had stripped off
and were having a good time, after which they slipped off to sleep. When
they awoke it was six thirty in the morning, the fog had cleared and they
found that they were parked at a bus stop with a sniggering line of early
morning workers staring in at them.

My own backing unit was still not settled and I tried all sorts of com–
binations but there was always a conflict of ideas. I wanted to hit the road
seriously but most of the sidemen I found were either in regular day jobs or
were signing on the dole (Sometimes doing both) and were reluctant to be
away from home for more than a weekend. At one point I had my ex–
trucking partner Derek Clegg, on acoustic double–bass, and a milkman

called Pete Lewis on a home made lap steel guitar and cheap mandolin—
neither of whom could sing. It could not, by any stretch of imagination, be
called a full sound but we got by, (just) until I got a BBC audition in London and they both chickened out because it was on a Wednesday. So I went
down on my own and did some folk songs, like Foggy, Foggy Dew, and Tom
Dooley. (Originally a folk ballad called Tom Dula) and as expected, got
nowhere.

At one point I expanded to a seven piece band with piano, fiddle and
steel guitar but found it financially unsustainable and in 1961 took the
modern Swinging Country route (Much in the style of my idol Ray Price).
After that I formed a group called the Kingston Combo using Roy Farnell
on vibraphone, Rod King on pedal steel, Roy and Malcolm Gaskill on bass
and drums respectively, rounded off by the jazz guitar of Mike Latham. It
was a successful unit and the gigs were coming nicely, but fees were low
and it slowly dawned on me that, as most of our show was vocal, all I
needed was a good backing group, say bass, drums and guitar with some
back-up voices. At this stage people did not appreciate the subtleties of
pedal steels, twin fiddles, dobros or Cajun concertinas, and I had been letting my enthusiasm for the authentic sound run away with me.

Things did not settle down until I found a good guitarist from Scotland
called Pete Sweeny and brought in an old friend, Vince Evers on bass
guitar and support vocals. The vivacious singer, Kit Connor, joined the
band and off we went. It was a hard time because we were all trying to
hold down day jobs and weekends consisted of manic runs across the Pennines to perform at the affluent West Yorkshire clubs in a succession of
ramshackle old vans. There was no motorway network back then and
crossing those wild hills in mid winter for a noon and night gig at some
workingmen's club in Leeds or Bradford was a real nightmare. One
afternoon we came across Jimmy Saville on the Huddersfield road, sitting
on the bonnet of his broken-down Rolls Royce, smoking a cigar while waiting for the AA to get him to Manchester, where he was the manager of the
Plaza dance hall. We got him to put on a real Country night later. Back in
those days, Derek our bass player was quite a Lothario and, with his big
Ford Consul and his D.A. haircut, he looked like a blond Elvis, who always
had some good-looking chick on his arm. I remember at that show he excelled himself and brought as his guest a very outgoing full-figured young
lady from Heywood who had us all panting. Her name was Julie Goodyear,
later to become famous as Coronation Street's favourite barmaid Bet
Lynch.

*   *   *   *   *   *

The First Country Music Festival

Tommy Collins, Bill Clifton, Johnny Cash, June Carter, Slim Traynor,
Hank Walters, Ralph Denby, Paul Starr, Murray Kash, Pete Sayers,
Johnny Duncan

1963 turned out to be a quite influential year for me in several ways.
Early in the year Slim Traynor and I got the idea of doing a Country Music
Festival with the artistes from our club, and Jeff Bancroft, a guitar/singer
who worked under the name of Hank Beanfield, suggested the village hall
near where he lived in the pleasant Cheshire market town of Altrincham.
From the Liverpool area we booked Hank Walter's band, Ken Page and the
Sundowners, and from our area the Hillbilly Bandits, the Dunham Mountain Boys, and Rod King's trio. We had a specialty rope act called Jack Mc
Carton & Partner, and Canadian born Paul Starr organized a quick–draw
contest. (Remind me to tell you about these quick–draw contests later).
The whole thing was a great success and got good press coverage, even
though it was the local Dunham Massey newspaper, but it gave us a buzz
and we decided to do it all again next year. The date was May 18th 1963
and it was probably the first dedicated British Country Music Festival.

A spin–off from the visiting US entertainers came our way via Tommy
Collins who remembered me from his last visit. One night we were playing
at Barton Aero Club when an American guy came over and introduced
himself as the custodian of the Starlight Club at USAF Burtonwood, and
said that he had heard of me from Tommy and asked if could provide
back–up for visiting Country stars and maybe play for dancing after the
cabaret. Apparently, due to the current Cold War tension, visas for US
musicians were tightly controlled, putting a number of major star tours in
jeopardy. The money was good and the American ambience was like being
back home for me so I jumped at the chance. We did several shows at the
base and usually backed the 'Star' at other U.S. Military venues in the UK
as well. In the main, however, these stars were mostly second raters being
tried out by their agents.

But the real breakthrough began when Johnny Cash, June Carter and
the Tennessee three came over to do a short tour of the UK. The first show
was in October 1963 at the old Astoria Club on Plymouth Grove, Manchester and ended two weeks later at Colombia House, the American
Officers club in Hyde Park Gardens, London. We all got on well and the
shows were terrific. John's big number at the time was 'John Henry' and he
used two steel bars to simulate the sound of a railroad spiking hammer to
great effect against Luther Perkins's stark guitar styling. John, I remember, was very thin and although he wasn't drinking much he was taking an
awful lot of pills, though I never saw him snorting anything. Luther didn't
drink much either, usually only coffee but he seemed to have an aversion to
water in any other form, particularly if it was accompanied by soap. However he did chain smoke and as soon as he got off stage he lit up. A few

years later poor Luther died in a house fire, suspected of being caused by his smoking in bed.

Even at that point, my time on the road backing Nashville acts stood me in good stead as I found that I could convincingly imitate the styles and many of their voices and stage mannerisms, from Stonewall Jackson's pumping guitar to Johnny Cash's challenging posture. In fact on a later UK tour, at a club in Nottingham, when Johnny was incapacitated by a particularly bad batch of chemical stimulants, I actually did his show note by note and nobody noticed. (Mind you, he was not as well known back then).

They say everybody remembers where they were when John F. Kennedy was killed in Dallas on the 22nd November 1963 and I recall vividly arriving that night at the US. Airbase at Burtonwood for our regular gig to find the place closed down and being told about the assassination by the armed MPs at the main gate.

A few months later, in February 1964 we made our first recording at the old Eroica Studios in Altrincham. It was a four–track 45 rpm. EP and the band consisted of Bill Carton on acoustic double–bass, young Brian Matkin on harmony vocals, 4–string banjo and guitar and the eccentric Stan Stanley on fiddle and mandolin. The tracks were 'She thinks I still care', the George Jones chart topper from December 1959, and (Yes folks. The song is that old) then 'Railroad Engineer' a fast train song complete with 'Wahoo hoo' whistles, a song that I had learned from 'Country rocker Hardrock Gunther. Next came "If Teardrops were Pennies', a Carl Smith weepie I first heard sung when working a Freetown gig with Texas Bill Strength and we filled out the last track with a fiddle instrumental called 'Stan's Shuffle'. The disc was primitive but the music had a good authentic feel to it and we were on vinyl at last. I continued to use this line up for club gigs, occasionally adding John Harrison on drums if money ran to it. However it was not destined to last as Stan soon realized that he could get more money as a single act and Brian took a good job in London and Bill and John went back to their jazz roots.

I was still living at home (just) in Crumpsall, a once respectable gentle village on the River Irk, which had deteriorated into a collection of shabby bed–sits. It was not far away from where comedian Mike Harding lived, but I was miles away in musical and political terms from his folksy, Left Wing views. Like so many other trendies in those days of fashionable protest he made no bones about his dislike of Country Music in every form, which did not endear him to me. I find it ironic therefore that he got his break with George Formby style epic called 'The Rochdale Cowboy'. These days he goes to Nashville for the BBC.

There were many future celebrities living in that North Manchester area. Solomon King who recorded the hit 'She Wears My Ring' lived near the railway station and I would often come across a young teenager with a powerhouse voice having lessons at local musician Frank Maher's house, who shyly told me her name was Elaine Bookbinder—later to become the great Elkie Brooks.

Festival Number Two. 1964

In spite of the indifference of the Music Press, the success of last year's festival encouraged me to organize another one on a much bigger scale, and to help me organize things I took on board a sharp music shop salesman called Don Mc Donald. The venue was the Chorlton Sporting Club in Manchester and though that November night in 1964 was a foggy one, the place was packed and we actually made a few quid. We could have made more if my partner Don had not been caught up in the euphoria of the night and lost sight of the first principle of promotion—'Watch the door take'. At one point when I was on stage performing I noticed him at a table at the front enjoying the show, ignoring my frantic gestures to check the box office, but I must give him his due as a publicist and organizer.

We put together a most impressive line up with Pete Sayers and Johnny Duncan headlining. The Beverley Hillbillies was a popular TV show at the time so their Flatt & Scruggs act was doing well on the Northern Clubs. Pete was an excellent five–string banjo picker and he adequately supported Johnny's high and lonesome Tennessee Mountain tenor. Murray Kash the Canadian broadcaster did a great job presenting the show and awarding the trophies for best act, etc. We brought in acts from all across the North. From Liverpool we had Billy Cooper's fantastic Blue Mountain Boys and the Home Towners. Ralph Denby provided the comedy element and I held it all together with my band. Local acts like the Hillbilly Bandits, Pete Elliot's Hobos and Dougie Darby's Country Cousins plus the Double T Ramblers contributed to the authentic Country atmosphere.

Now for that quick–draw competition I mentioned earlier, always a favourite with the wannabe cowboys in the crowd. As for me I'd seen enough silly gun play in the US and I was destined a few years on to witness some serious fire–fights so I was not a fan of blank–firing guns. My old friend Paul Starr was a great singer–guitarist who had spent time in Canada and superbly portrayed the image of the Northern Plains Cowboy and his performance of the ballads of that genre was superb—but there was one small problem. In times of stress he had a speech impediment, which made his position as referee in a quick–draw competition rather hazardous. So having got the two well inebriated, contestants rigged up with six guns and holsters, he would put them in position and prepare to give them the start. All this stress in front of a crowd of drunks had wound him up somewhat and to add to this his vocal impediment suddenly locked in and the predictable result occurred as Paul spluttered "Wum—ttttwo—ff—fire." The blanks roared before he had finished, and to make matters worse he had loaded the revolvers with six cartridges each. Soon the stage was wreathed in white smoke as the guns and arguments banged on. We decided it was time for the finale and sent everybody home.

Mister Record Man
Johnny Cash, Hank Williams Jnr, Dave Dudley, Billy Walker,
The Hillsiders. Mel Haige, Tom Fricker, Johnny Batt

One afternoon I was in Godley's music shop in central Manchester, yakking with fellow musoes when a Pakistani guy came in hustling bootleg records and while we were sifting through his stock he asked me if I knew of
any Country Music sources he could use. Well, I told him that I had a big
collection of EP and LP American Country records, many of them un-
issued in the UK and his ears perked up and we adjourned to a local café
where after a coffee or two a deal was set up. It turned out that he had a
pressing plant in an old mill in Chadderton and in return for the use of my
collection to make master matrices he would supply me with records to sell
on the markets on a sale or return basis and so, for a while I became a
market trader and I really enjoyed it, on top of which things got better at
home because there was regular money coming in again. Kit joined me for
a while selling underwear until she took a job managing a local knitwear
shop as well as doing our regular gigs.

I met a lot of nice people on the markets and got deeply involved with a
beautiful Nordic–looking woman called Ann. She had a small factory making ladies lingerie and operated three or four direct outlets on local open–
air markets. She was quite wealthy but had taken up market life in
rebellion against her stifling middle class family. To her, our affaire which
started so casually, became very serious and she proposed that I move in
with her. She fascinated me and she seemed to be all I wanted at the time.
We had weekends away at good hotels in the Lakes and on the Fylde Coast
where she paid for everything. She was my own age, divorced, and had a
large house near Cheadle with her three sons and, here was the rub,
because the youngest one was the same age as my own son and whenever I
was tempted to take up her offer I would be reminded of him and held
back. Clay Feet? Well, yes, I guess so. But Ann and I did have a good time
together, each of us supplying the other with what was missing in our
lives. When the time came for the overseas tours she took it very badly,
and I learned later from her mother, who did not like me very much anyway, she was taken to Stockport General Hospital after an overdose of
sleeping pills.

In the following years our paths would cross now and then and although
the feeling was still strong, the passion had cooled. The last time I heard
from her was just after we got back from Vietnam in late 1968. We were
playing a gig at Mere Golf Club, Cheshire, when the manager came backstage and told me I had a phone call in the office. It turned out to be Ann.
She told me that she was now married again to a Hire Car proprietor and
her life was back on an even keel. We were both scarred by those wild days,
but that was all a long time ago.

My market venture did very well, but within a year my Pakistani friend fell foul of the PRS and MCPS watchdogs and was presented with a massive bill for royalties precipitating his immediate and complete disappearance and I was back looking for a day job. Then a friend showed me a vacancy in the Stockport Advertiser for a tyre salesman so I went for that. I got the job with a company called Tyresoles who had a factory in Heaton Moor restoring old tires. I was given a nice Ford van and an area where I had the double duty of selling the company's product and buying in old tyre casings for re-treading. Needless to say I did not do much work but the van came in very handy for a bandwagon. Most afternoons I would spend at Ann's house, after touring the local graveyards looking for names, and recording phantom visits to garages on my daily report sheet. It didn't last long and came to an abrupt end when, playing a Sunday lunchtime gig at Swinton British Legion Club, I ran into my boss who could not fail to miss one of his bright yellow Transit vans in the car park being unloaded by a bunch of scruffy musicians.

Early 1965 found us doing the Nashville Rooms circuit alongside groups like the Hillsiders, The Tumbleweeds and that superb Irish band the Kingpins who later somehow got embroiled in Ulster politics which resulted in the van containing all their gear being burned out one night. Apart from the Fuller's Brewery Circuit we also did a few of the bases in the area like Ruislip and Lakenheath, as support for Country Stars like Billy Walker, Hank Williams Jnr, (a rather surly blond young man back then before his almost fatal climbing accident) and the trucker's favourite role model Dave Dudley, who after opening up with 'Truck-driving Son of a Gun', did about forty minutes of hilarious truck driving jokes and rounded off the spot with his big hit 'Six days on the Road'. He was terrific. We also did the support spot with Hank Williams Jnr at the Columbia Club and the Douglas Hotel. I will always remember he did a song called 'I wouldn't change a Thing about You 'which I would love to have done on stage, but to this very day I have not been able to find a copy of it. I think it was issued as a single on the B-side of Hank's biggie 'Endless Sleep.'

If anybody comes across it give me a call.

A week after this show we were back there again with Johnny Cash. At the end of that trip John gave me one of his custom-made guitar straps and autographed the back of it and, when I went round to his hotel to say goodbye, he was busy packing. We chatted away and, when he finished packing the Samsonite case, he walked out on the first floor balcony and simply threw it down to the waiting van in the courtyard. It bounced around a bit and the driver waited until it stopped and threw it with equal abandon into the van. Luther, who was staying in the next room, watched what was going on and with a grin threw his case down too—but unfortunately it was not a Samsonite and didn't bounce. It landed with a loud plop and split completely asunder scattering dirty underwear, a bedside lamp, a couple of bath robes and the contents of the mini bar, all over the courtyard in front of the manager, who had been attracted by the noise of the bouncing Samsonite—Ooops. (I understand that he did the same thing in Germany too).

Unfortunately the guitar–strap was stolen some years later at a show in Mainz, along with a pair of alligator skin boots that Kit had bought me as a birthday present. I can't say for certain who took them, but the finger points at a band called Uncle Sam's People, who were sharing our dressing room on a show and whose lead singer was overheard in the bar of the Quellenhof Hotel in Wiesbaden trying to sell them to a German punter. The other big development of this tour was my first meeting with the Australian agent Jake Pearson. (Not his real name but some of his many victims will know whom I mean). However it proved to be a major step-ping–stone in my career.

Johnny went back home and I thought that was the end of it but several months later I got a letter from Pearson's office in Frankfurt inviting us to London where he was holding a showcase show for the US Military Clubs in Europe, and it is quite remarkable when you look back, to find out who was auditioning back in those hungry days. The much–underrated Mel Haige (Old Gravel Boots) turned up from Yorkshire. He was singing very well but was hampered by a poor band and a girl singer who looked great, but could not sing in tune. Wally Whyton was there, with a hippy skiffle group, and Johnny Regan also showed up with his Tumbleweeds from Kent. Tom Fricker's band Tomahawk arrived from the Isle of Sheppey, plus a couple of specialty acts, four or five comedians and a group of dancers, one of whom was Una Stubbs. In the car park we pulled up alongside a dark blue Mk10 Jaguar with sideboards advertising the Carrolls bolted to the roof-rack, two boys and a girl who sang and did some great im-pressions. Their real star was the young flame–haired girl with a show-stopping figure who was destined to become world famous on television as Faith Brown.

Our drummer Knobby Clarke could not get time off work for the trip so there were only four of us. Joe on guitar, Spud on bass and me playing rhythm and Kit singing back–up vocals. But we romped it and got full marks from the American bookers, so Jake signed us up right away on a two–year contract which should have been written on toilet paper because that was all it was useful for. Anything was better than nothing and I gratefully accepted before anybody could raise any objections. I knew it was going to cause big problems at home but I'd face them when it hap-pened. The family's response was exactly as I had expected, but I pressed on with trying to get enough money to make the German trip, Pearson having promised to reimburse us when we arrived in Frankfurt. Knobby had a good day–job and he didn't want to risk the trip, so we pulled in Dave Marks, who liked the music and sometimes stood in on drums at the Club 43. We worked feverishly and the clubs and pubs became a blur until every one of them looked the same, although one gig does stand out in my memory.

It was the last one of all, a double at the Salford Transport Club and St. Bernard's Catholic Club, but it was a double with a difference. As neither club had a late license, they had to close at 11p.m. Yeah, I know, impossible, but we needed the money to get away. So I said we'd do them. Even if it did mean loading and unloading our vehicle four times in an evening. The first gig was the Catholic Club, which had the added snag of having no stage door, so we dragged all our gear in through the club, got set up and kicked off at exactly 8 p.m. and left them happy 45 minutes later when we dragged everything out. The full drum–kit, amps, guitars, mike stands, speakers and an acoustic double–bass were loaded the van and rushed to the Transport Club on the other side of Salford where we arrived in time to hear the cry, "Quiet Please. Eyes down for a full house."

Yep. We had hit 'em at Bingo time. And we had to unload and set up the lot again. But this time in silence. the Bingo ended and off we went into 'Honky Tonkin' and 'Singin' the Blues' etc. and fifty minutes later we were off stage and loading again, before belting through the late evening traffic back to St Barneys Club, where we arrive in time for—yes, you've got it. *The Bingo again.* Only this time we have to silently weave our way through the audience to get on stage. (Remember, there is no back door here). By now we are dazed with fatigue and just about manage to churn out a show, but when I ask to be paid, the boozy Concert Secretary tells me to come back at closing time after everything is cashed up. Great!

So off we go to do the second show at the Transport Club where by now they are all drunk and keep shouting for more, with the net result that when we do get back to the first club for our money, the bloody place is closed and in darkness. Shit. Luckily there is a caretaker's phone number on the door, so we phone him to find where the Con. Sec. might be, and trace him to a late night shibbeen off Langworthy Road, where he pretends he doesn't know who we are. By this time, exhausted or not, I am prepared to put him through the wall and make my annoyance clear, which jogs his memory to the extent that he remembers us and hands over our pay packet.

What a night. Two days later we left for Germany.

PICKER'S TIP 12

To get more brightness from your rhythm guitar replace the G (third) string with a 9 gauge E and tune it to the 3rd fret of the 1st string. This octave higher note will give you that 12 String sound without all the usual tuning problems.

9

THE GREAT ESCAPE

"Its for you," my wife Sylvia spat coldly as she handed me the phone.

It was Spud phoning from Liverpool.

'Could I pick him up at the end of the East Lancashire Road at 9 p.m?'

I said it was o.k. and as I put down the phone I realized that she had overheard the brief conversation and had taken the news like Marie Antoinette being informed of the arrival time of the next tumbrel. With a snort of contempt, she turned on her heel and stomped off back to the kitchen. It was going to be another of those days, that much was obvious. To be fair; I suppose her attitude was quite justified. I was off on my first European contract as a professional singer, leaving behind my wife and child to get along without me. But regrettably, all thoughts of those responsibilities were swamped out of my mind by a wild ambition and a pathological dread of the endless, pointless, treadmill of a soul–killing regular day–job.

I missed lunch, or to put a finer point on it, I wasn't offered any. So I got on with the preparation of our transport for the trip. For once, it was not raining and the usual slate–coloured sky of Manchester was bright blue as I packed my guitar in the back and roped the Miazzi P.A. speakers onto the roof rack. I sang as I worked, trying to keep up an organised cool front, and my wife and son watched balefully from the front room window. I had told them that I would not be gone long and that a new life awaited us all after I had made a success of my chosen profession. Somehow I don't think they believed me.

Let me tell you something about this car. What a gem. A rather fitting description for something that looked as if it had been dug up. It was a big Morris Isis estate car, vintage 1953.You must have seen one, and it looked like a big Morris Minor Traveller with a headache. They were quite rare. I always had the impression that the factory had got the plans wrong and made the body inside out, with all the wooden frame on the outside. It had, YONCO'S TEXAS DRIFTERS stencilled across the back doors in big black letters and I was very proud of it. In fact, when I came across it again many years later that was the only way I recognized it. Not that I acknowledged having any interest in it, as the Huntingdon garage owner was anxious to trace a certain previous owner who, he claimed, had dropped it off for repair and never came back. Let's get on with describing it.

The best part of the Isis was its big six–cylinder engine of about three litres. It had bags of top end power and enough bottom–end torque to push over a bulldozer. True, it was not very economical, but in those days, with petrol costing less than one pound sterling for four gallons, that did not matter all that much. I had a great time with it. It could go like a rocket and I loved storming past those flash TR2 sports cars on the wide empty roads north of the city. However, looking at it objectively, I would have to admit that it was somewhat past its best after thirteen years of hard work.

(*above*) A very rare, early shot of The Drifters at Barton Aero Club *circa* 1958 left to right Roy Gaskill, Yonco, Malcolm Gaskill, Roy Farnell and Rod King.

(*below*) With Johnny Cash at the Astoria Club Manchester, October 1963

(*above*) Slim Traynor (with guitar), old friend and fellow Country Music Pioneer. *Saltford circa 1961*

(above) Vince Evers. *Salford 1962*

(*left*) Presenting an award to radio presenter Murray Kash at the second Country and Western show *1964*.

(*below*) With Sylvia at the York Club, Oxford Road Manchester *1962*. This was the third venue we moved our floating country music club to!

(left) Real Rhinestone Cowboys! Lavish, custom made Las Vegas style stage outfits, costumes for the USA club circuit overseas. 1966.

(below) Publicity shots for the first Tex Williams and Bobby Bare shows in Europe. *Frankfurt, Germany 1967*

Miss Kit Connor

(above) With Bob Morris and Faye Harding in Berlin. Bob was the co-writer of the big hit 'Tequilla'. *1967*

(above) The great Tex Williams, The complete showman. *Templehof AB. Berlin 1967*

Undercover at Checkpoint Charlie, the east Berlin border crossing at a tense time in the Cold War. Kit disguised as a hooker and myself as a window cleaner. *June 1967*

DİYARBAKIR

(left) After driving over 4000km from home, here we are at the edge of civilisation at Dyarbikir in Turkish Kurdistan.

Is this all there is?
What a Dump!
Wild and dangerous!

And we're booked for three months!

A breakdown in the Taurus Mountains at 3am.

(above) South of Zagreb in Yugoslavia, heading for Turkey. *March 1967*

(right) The big National Day parade Ataturk Square, Dyarbikir.

Top "Country & Western" Show Group

TEXAS DRIFTERS

Smoothly resplendent in our custom made mohair suits we found great success in the big Cabaret clubs of the north.

Backing was from:
Ady Edleston   Guitar
Spud Ward   Bass
Paul Richardson   Drums

Lyceum RAINBOW Club   BRADFORD tel 64987

PARADISE Club   GUISELEY tel 4682

★ NEXT WEEK ★ Tremendous entertainment with
Talented International
FRANK YONCO
and the TEXAS DRIFTERS

Tracy Davis

THIS WEEK   Comedian
THE STRANDSMEN   Paul Melba

Casino Open Nightly, 9 p.m.
CHEMI. STUD. DICE. Etc.

The RIVIERA NIGHT CLUB

MIDDLETON GRANGE LANE, HARTLEPOOL

ALL THIS WEEK
MIDNIGHT CABARET

FRANK YONCO
and THE TEXAS DRIFTERS

Restaurant, Grotto Room and Bars open till 2 a.m.
REG POWELL TRIO & Singer JULIE LEWIS

CLUB BA·BA

VIEW OF THE CLUB
FROM DINING BALCONY

★ Programme ★

23rd JULY Week	30th JULY Week	6th AUGUST Week	13th AUGUST Week
THE ONE & ONLY **ANNE SHELTON**	Europe's Top Country and Western Show Group **YONCO & THE TEXAS DRIFTERS**	Britain's Premier Show Group **JIMMY CRAWFORD FOUR**	T.V. & Recording Stars **DAVID & JOHNATHAN**
Musical Speciality ANEK DUO	VERSATILE DUO THE BEST MEN	Recording Star MARIAN ANGEL	Welsh Comedy IVOR OWEN
COMEDIAN N McBRIDE	Comedy Impressions VIC BLACKWELL	DANCING SPECIALITY THE SMART SET	ASHEME ZONDEK
ne Prize Singer AVE TTON	LYRICAL SINGER SYLVIA EAVES	OPPORTUNITY KNOCKS WINNER KIETH ANDREWS	Glamourous Singing Star KAREN RUSS

Kit recording in Frankfurt 1967

It had the strangest gear change, a copy of the old Bentley idea, using a complicated linkage from the box to a stubby lever in a cutout on the door side of the driver's seat. The fact that there were only two forward gears functioning in the box made it more interesting to drive. Originally it had been dove–gray but I decided to paint it white with Valspar quick–drying paint. Unfortunately, it was not quick–drying enough and the car ended up with a distinctive orange–peel finish because I had painted it on the street at our front door and an unexpected shower of rain had added the finishing touches.

The body was not bad, though there was a bit of dry–rot around the remaining hinges on the back doors. I did however go to a lot of trouble to get a good set of tyres for it; the result of moonlight commando raids into the local junkyard. (This was in the days before they invented Rottweilers). These new boots were not all the same make or tread but they were roughly the same size. Oh yes, I know what you're thinking. Just the sort of vehicle to undertake a thousand mile trip, loaded to the gills with five people and half a ton of gear. Well? What was the alternative? I was not about to stay in some dead–end job, but the thought that I was leaving the family behind did keep coming back to me. It was guilt, I suppose.

By six p.m. I had finished and was ready to roll to whatever fate had in store for me. I nodded sheepishly to my wife and son standing grimly on the doorstep of our neat little terraced house. They stared back, hoping the wheels would drop off or something. There were tears as I left, and a quick shimmering of lace curtains, as I drove out of our street with a distinct sound of tut–tutting in the air.

My first pick–up was the drummer Dave, who lived in Blackley, allowing plenty of time to pick up the others, but I had barely gone a mile, to the bottom of Crumpsall Vale in fact, when fate struck the first blow. As I stopped at some traffic lights, there was a loud clang from the engine compartment. In my haste to get away I had neglected to bolt down the air cleaner properly and it had slid from the top of the engine and hit the exposed cooling fan and started clattering and banging away. I stopped the engine and unhooked the wire coat hanger holding down the bonnet lid and as a group of office workers at the bus stop looked on curiously I untangled the red hot air cleaner and threw it into a privet hedge along with a couple of shattered fan blades. Soon after I was knocking at Dave's door, but there was no response so I went round the back, past the firewood, past the coal-filled old pram and a rusty bike to the back door. It was partly open so I gave it a shove. The TV was blasting away and David was coming out of the downstairs loo, zipping up his pants, the obligatory fag hanging from his lower lip.

"Oh s'you. Be right wid yuh, Dad. Just a mo."

He shot back and sticking two fingers in his mouth gave a piercing whistle to his partly–deaf mother who was glued to the TV and indicated that she should bring his drum–kit from under the stairs. His father, who was glued to the other side of the set, managed to drag himself away long enough to drop his son's bag on the doorstep. With a brief nod and a mumbled 'Ello' he shuffled back to Match of the Day. Eventually, with the aid of a plastic clothesline, we had most of the drums on the roof rack. David banged his cases inside and slammed the back doors before piling in beside me in a shower of cigarette ash.

"Right, Dad," He shouted. "Let's be off," and waved to his Mum. She did not seem to be quite clear about what was going on but she waved back and shuffled inside to the television. He lit another fag and coughed. "The old tub's runnin' well, innit Dad?"

"Oh yeah. No problems," I replied complacently, omitting to point out that since leaving his house we had been going downhill. As we slid into Victoria Avenue heading for Heaton Park, we began to hear a strange whistling sound from under the bonnet, but it was only the lonely twin choke carburettor calling forlornly for its lost mate, the air–cleaner. Even at that early stage I was having slight misgivings about our transport arrangements but diplomatically kept them to myself.

On we went, whistling our way through the village of Rhodes, once the proud possessor of the tallest factory chimney in Lancashire, and soon we were in the old mill town of Middleton. The whole area was in the throes of drastic re–development as the Town Hall venal vandals bulldozed away some historic and irreplaceable monuments of the Industrial Revolution to make way for more ugly concrete tower–blocks and breeding–kennels for delinquents. We rumbled, rattled, and whistled over the mud–smeared cobbles, past the sleeping diggers that had already gobbled up half the street, to where Kit was waiting at an open door with a bright smile on her face.

All her family were waiting to see us off on the Great Adventure and for one heart–stopping moment I thought that they were all coming with us. Everybody seemed to have a suitcase or bag of some kind.

Kit kissed her Mum goodbye as the family started slinging bags in the back

"Rattling' at bit innit?" She greeted us, wrinkling her nose at the car.

"What's all this bloody lot?" I retorted, eyeing the pile of luggage.

She looked indignant and rolled her eyes to her mother on the doorstep.

With a look of disdain, she spat back at me. "It's what I need. We're not off to Blackpool for the weekend y'know. Anyway, don't start moanin' already."

Well, I thought, that's a nice start to the trip, as she tossed her head and settled into a moody, as we churned back over the ruts and back onto the main road heading for Joe's house in Oldham. An argument had started between Kit and David about the mounds of plastic bags she had brought along, and David's non–stop smoking habits—I thought that the sooner we were out of town the better.

Whilst climbing up the steep hill to Oldham, another noise made itself heard. It seemed to come from the front, a sort of ticking? Maybe it was another vane falling off the cooling fan, but the noise did seem to be getting louder as we coughed and roared our way up the foothills of the Pennines but with our blown exhaust I could not be sure what it was. We shot the summit of Werneth Brew and stormed down the hill towards Watershed-dings where our own private Chet Atkins lived. Emily Street, I think it was called. All the streets looked the same up there. Long rows of neat terraced houses, small but very well kept, with bright curtains and crisp cream donkey–stoned doorsteps and windowsills. It looked lovely, a credit to the diligent house–proud residents, but there is always one that spoils the overall effect isn't there? And there it was, four doors from the end—Joe's house. Boasting streaked purple window–sills and grayish sagging cur-tains. The pale–green paint was flaking off the front door and there was a big dent in the bottom panels where heavy kicks had been delivered in an unsuccessful attempt to force it into the warped frame. There was an old brass knocker hanging crazily by one screw and a lop–sided letterbox stuffed with junk mail and old Racing Pinks to keep the draughts out.

David was out of the car like a shot and banged hard on the warped door which, after several tries, was eventually jerked open to reveal Joe, who waved us into his castle. Mumbling through the crumbs of a corned–beef butty, he told us to sit down and that he'd be ready in a few minutes. I groaned inwardly as I thought of Spud who would just about be arriving at the end of the East Lancashire Road expecting to find us waiting for him. In the kitchen, Joe's wife Marjory was throwing a wobbler and banging pots and pans around, ignoring the baby, who was having a good screech in its once–white carrycot. The television was doing its bit as well, belting out a pop music show loud enough to take the roof off. Joe shouted that the volume knob had fallen off somewhere and he couldn't turn it down and that it he couldn't turn it off because it was on the same plug as the sulk-ing one–bar electric fire that nestled in the littered hearth, surrounded by the cold cinders of some long forgotten fire. It was not easy to carry on any kind of conversation above the din, so I sat on a hard kitchen chair and took in the scene.

A bare bulb showed areas of greasy lino with old dog–eared rugs thrown here and there with their corners turned up like old railway buffet sandwiches. There were a couple of vinyl armchairs with the stuffing trickling out of them, and a tapestry settee in an intricate design of jam and snot. A drying rack of washing and a chipped and stained fireplace completed the whole effect of casual elegance. There was an all–pervading smell of wet nappies and burnt toast. No bloody wonder he wanted to go to Germany. I would have gone anywhere to get away from this lot. But when, at a later date, Dave started joking about his domestic set up, Joe said that he could see nothing wrong with it. He thought everybody should live like that. It was 'homely' he said. Who wanted to live in a furniture showroom? And he added pointedly, what was the point of getting married and having your own place if you couldn't do as you liked with it? I never did get Marjory's opinion on that score. She was far too busy wiping the baby's face and giving us all a cup of tea, very nice tea, as it happened, while Joe was getting his stuff together. This consisted of one Stratocaster copy guitar, one Watkins Dominator amplifier, one Copycat echo unit and several leads from under the settee, which he stuffed into a small plastic hold all. There was another small bag and it struck me that he did not have much luggage for such an extended trip. He had not bothered to shave and the only indication that he was going anywhere was a new piece of sticking–plaster holding his glasses together.

There was one awkward moment when Marjory foolishly asked for some house–keeping money for the two weeks he would be way. Two weeks? Two weeks! We all looked at the floor while he sorted things out with her in the kitchen. He'd obviously not told her that it was going to be a three–month contract and finally borrowed a tenner off me to make up the money and keep her off his back till we got away.

The ticking in the engine room now seemed a bit quieter as night fell, and we skirted the northern suburbs of Manchester to our rendezvous with Spud our bassist. It was now 10.30 p.m. and we should have been at the pick–up point at 9 p.m. Oh yes, he was going to be very pleased with me. En route, we passed within a quarter of a mile of my house that I had so painfully left four hours earlier. Spud was waiting across the road from the café where he had been until it finally closed at 10 o'clock. He was as happy as a donkey with a thistle under its tail and there was a lot of Scouse curs-ing as he jammed his stuff into the already packed estate car and tied his canvas covered double–bass fiddle on the roof alongside David's drums. He looked up in surprise when I revved the engine and I could tell, that like me, he had the slightest suspicion of a big end rattling somewhere, but there was no point in alarming everybody so I hurried him along and soon we were off and running.

The grand old clock in Manchester's Gothic Town Hall was chiming midnight as we scooted through Albert Square and took the main road south to the Cheshire Plain and the hills of the Peak District. Our destina-tion was Harwich, a difficult diagonal journey across England at the best of times and in those days a very twisting and turning one, leap–frogging from one main road to another. There were of course some motorways. There was a stretch that by–passed Preston and the M1 ran to some 70 miles north of London but, as our route lay basically South East, neither of these engineering marvels were of any use to us as we were routed via Stockport, Macclesfield, and the High Peak District. outside Derby the knock from the engine became quite pronounced and I could no longer kid myself that it was just a broken fan blade. Joe's pessimistic comments did not help my peace of mind much either. At an all–night garage I bought three gallons of oil, most of which the engine swallowed at one gulp and the noise subsided a bit.

By 3am. with eyeballs hanging out we had cleared the hills and picked up the A1. Somewhere north of Leicester we stopped a couple of times to get a cup of coffee and let the engine cool down. Things seemed to ease off as we crossed the flatlands of South Lincolnshire in the moonlight and rolled into Cambridgeshire as dawn was breaking. I drove blindly onwards, determinedly ignoring the odd engine noises, and the flaring arguments about which window should be opened, and where the smokers should sit, and why was the front seat littered with plastic bags full of shoes, make up and sandwiches. It was very cramped, but we were all too excited about our first trip abroad to let such things get us down.

Approaching Huntingdon things were becoming a bit desperate and we were laying such a smoke screen down the winding country roads it was a wonder we had not been pulled by the local constabulary. Suddenly there was a completely new set of rattles and bangs and I sensed that the end could not be far off, so I put the hammer down heading for the coast. The many diversions we had taken to avoid the worst hills and big towns caused us to take an odd route so that we were somewhere near the U.S. Airbase at Mildenhall when the crisis came. The quiet warm meadows echoed to our rattling big ends as we thundered to destruction. Suddenly there was a loud bang and a clatter as the crankshaft broke and a core plug shot out of the crankcase. Steam was hissing out from all over the front and there was a large slick of oil across the road with lumps of hot metal stuck out of it. Well, that was that. No doubt about it now. The car was indeed knackered. What a way to start our first overseas contract.

Thumbing It

This turn of events had varying effects on the group. Joe, who had not believed that anything good could ever happen to him anyway, had already given up and was at that very moment searching in his hidden money–belt for his train fare back to Oldham. David reacted in a manner that we would eventually become accustomed to. He sat down by the roadside and lit a fag, quite certain that somebody would soon sort the whole thing out and Spud showed for the first time, what a good man he was to have around in a crisis and started to check out what was left of the engine, suggesting ways of getting it in for a repair somewhere. Kit also brought out the sustaining practical qualities that made her so reliable in later crises by walking to the main road junction and trying to get a lift. As for me, I began to feverishly search my brain to find a way to continue our onward journey. There was no way I was going to give up this one chance to escape my life in Manchester and return to the deadening, demoralizing round of job searching and domestic strife. Oh no. This was an opportunity to change and I was determined to give it all I had

Kit came back with a big fish on the line, in the shape of a GM. pickup truck with an American sergeant at the wheel, prepared to help as best he could. Grateful of any assistance, I left the boys to look after the debris while I went with the GI to a local garage, hoping I could get a breakdown truck to tow in our sick vehicle. In its obviously distressed state, surrounded by a road full of destruction, no self–respecting garage would touch it, so I left instructions for the boys to push it to the main road and to clean it up as best they could.

The garage had just opened up and I can only assume that the manager had had a heavy night and was not quite with it because, after a brief chat, he dispatched the wrecker truck to pick up our Isis for repair. While we were talking about the repair I enquired about the possibility of hiring a van to take us to Colchester, hinting that we were playing at the nearby U.S. base. If I'd have let him know that we were about to leave the country for three months, I doubt if he would have let us unload it before we paid the bill for the tow in.

Yes, said the manager, they did have vans for hire but, even though I signed the Isis in for a full repair, he insisted that the money for a hire van would have to be paid up–front—and in cash. Ummm, difficult. It would be the best part of forty quid plus the deposit, a lot of lolly for those days, so I had to think again. We had breakfast in a local café and reviewed our options. Everyone's priorities were different. Joe wanted to know where the railway station was, David wanted to find a cigarette shop, Kit was worried about dirty mechanics sitting on her plastic bags and Spud was worried that his double–bass on the roof might get wet if it rained. Which it did.

Me? I was working how to split the load so we could hitch hike the rest of the way to the boat. When I told them this they went barmy.

"Wotcha mean?" yelped David. "Bleedin' 'itch 'ike. With all this lot?"

Joe wildly riffled through the dog–eared phone book looking for the local railway station, while the others sat gaping. I won the day however by reminding them what was waiting for us back up north. So they all reluctantly agreed to give it a go.

It stopped raining and the sun came out and 8.30 a.m. found us strung out on the main road outside the garage with all our gear, guitars, amps, speaker boxes, a full drum–kit, plus all our personal baggage and Spud's double–bass. We must have made an interesting picture to the passing commuters, standing there waving our thumbs and smiling hopefully, because after about half an hour a truck stopped. It was a big brick wagon and the driver said he could only take one of us but he could carry most of our gear on the back so, while Kit clambered into the cab, we loaded the junk onto the flatbed with Joe to guard it, planning to catch the next bus that came along and see them at the brickyard about nine miles down the road.

All the time I was on that bus I was working out the costs, which the agent insisted I pay up front, and now on top of the boat tickets, I had to find rail fares from the Hook of Holland to Frankfurt. As the Duke of Wellington had once commented at the Battle of Waterloo. It was going to be a close run thing.

I was wakened from my calculations by David's anxious cry.

"Eh, Dad. There's that bloody lorry. Over there, in that lay–by."

He pointed to the side of the road and sure enough it was our lorry all right with Joe and Kit sitting having tea with the driver. Something however was not quite right, as the wagon appeared to have developed a severe list to starboard due to a flat tyre.

With a scuffle we jumped off the slow–moving bus and ran back to the lay–by where Kit told us what had happened. It was a simple puncture and another wagon was already on the way with a spare wheel. When it finally arrived, we switched loads and went on towards Harwich on our second brick truck of the morning. Some eight miles short of the docks the driver told us that he was turning off to the new building site but pulled into a transport café and got us a further lift on a fish truck. Ugh. What a smell. To make matters worse, it started to rain again and we were forced to find shelter under the stinking tarpaulin all the way to the ferry terminal.

By this time, as you can imagine we were all very tired and hungry and our depression was made worse by the news that we had missed the ferry by one hour, and that the next one did not leave until midnight. Joe still had a few iron rations left such as cold toast and dripping butties, which he grudgingly shared, while Spud wolfed down a hidden Mars Bar before anyone could scrounge a bite off him. David had a bottle of Wilson's Pale Ale in his drum–case and a few Woodbines so he was all right and we settled down to wait for the night ferry. Joe then started moaning again. This time about his gear and swearing vengeance against the truck driver who helped him to unload it." He coulda bloody scratched it, or bust a valve or summat. Clumsy sod

In actual fact, I suspect that he was annoyed at everybody's reluctance to turn back but did not have the guts to do it on his own. David pointedly remarked that from the way he was going on anybody would think he had a Gibson 335 guitar and a Fender Twin Reverb amplifier instead of the load of second–hand crap he had picked up at Oldham Flea Market. Eventually the irritating arguing died down and we decided to look around Harwich town centre to pass the time until our departure overseas. It took the best part of fifty minutes to see everything of possible interest, but luckily by that time the ferry from Holland had arrived and by four that afternoon we were aboard and in our cabins for a much–needed sleep

Early next morning we arrived at the Hook of Holland. Most of us having had a good night's sleep, except David, who had been up most of the night keeping a wary eye out for any marauding U–boats or Stukas but he had not managed to spot any. The bloody war had been over for twenty years, but like he said, there might be the odd one left that did not know about it, like that Jap soldier on that Pacific island. I told him how relieved we felt that he was watching over us. He just nodded and murmured 'Bollocks'.

The trains at the Hook of Holland came right alongside the docks but there was no direct line with Frankfurt, so it looked like we would have to make a couple of changes en–route. I had enough money for train tickets but the freight charges for our equipment would have to be paid by the agency when we arrived in Germany. By now I was scratching and had barely sufficient cash to buy us all a meal at the station café. After that, we would have to survive on what we could pick up at the rail changes, which consisted of a bottle of lemonade and a sausage sandwich at Utrecht. The train rolled on through the flat Dutch countryside with David blaming me for the lack of windmills. "Well, where are they then? "S bleedin' 'olland innit?" He moaned. I explained that they were mostly on the coast, but I could see that he didn't believe me and kept watching in case one sneaked up on him unawares. Kit was in the corner fast asleep, exhausted, and in the other corner Spud was trying to nod off also, following the well–known musician's philosophy, that if one was asleep one did not have to spend any money. Joe sat in the middle of the seat opposite me, worrying about his gear, and trying to decide whether or not to have his first wash in two days. In the end he decided against it and to wait until we arrived in Frankfurt.

At the German frontier everyone woke up for passport control and, from then until dark, David sat glued to the carriage window looking for SS men and wondering how many people on board were Gestapo agents. As we clanked to a halt in the marshalling yards of Hamm, Joe suddenly decided that he could no longer trust the Germans and chose to finish the trip in the baggage car to keep an eye on his gear. There were several crates of pigeons in the caboose as well so Joe's B.O. did not disturb the conductor too much. It was 5 a.m. when they turfed us off at Frankfurt Bahnhof. The baggage office was not yet open and of course, it was far too early to call the agent's office. About the only place open was a Catholic Mission café under the station concourse, so we steamed in there. The manager was a nice old boy who, to David's suspicious surprise, did not seem to mind having lost the war. He gave us mugs of coffee and slices of thick toast and while Kit used the showers and washed her hair, the rest of us managed to get a kip on the hard pool table until the town woke up. Around 6 a.m. a group of noisy cleaners came in, and we were hustled out on the streets with all the other overnight shelter seekers, who were an assortment of East European refugees and derelict winos. It was cold in the dark cavernous main hall so we hurried out of the building into the warm morning sun. *We had made it.*

PICKER'S TIP 13

Put some colour in your program. Never play two consecutive numbers in the same key or at the same tempo, or even more importantly, at the same tempo. Eg. Follow a fast rocker with a gentle bit of Western Swing.

10

GERMANY CALLING
Mary Taylor, Don Hill, Tom Fricker,
George Hamilton IV. The Hometowners

Frankfurt, it appeared, never slept, for at a time when most people in England were yawning or slurping breakfast, the town was alive and shops, offices and cafés already in full operation. Smart office girls rushed by and crowds of businessmen pushed through the plate–glass doors of towering commercial buildings. Many of these men were wearing shorts which struck us as funny but after all, it was June, and Frankfurt summers can be very hot and muggy—so shorts were ideal—and in no way inhibited their business efficiency.

A little after 9am I phoned agent Jake Pearson's office and he sent a bus around to collect our gear and us. There was the expected wrangle about the freight charges but eventually everything was collected and I subbed a few marks to keep body and soul together until we got our first pay–check. The surly driver (Oh yes that was another thing. All these Germans looked surly, in fact most of the people looked serious all the time as though it was not done to be seen smiling. Very strange). Anyway, this driver took us round to a small hotel off the Echensheimer Langestrasse. A Hotel Garni. That meant that it had no restaurant attached to it, just somwhere to bed down. There was a coffee machine in the lobby and also a good cake shop on the corner where we stuffed ourselves with delicious cream torte.

The whole scene fascinated me. The tree–lined avenues, the bright yellow clanging tramcars. I got a buzz from listening to the people in the street talking. All was new and interesting, even the road signs. We quickly adapted to it all and were amazed at the vast difference between our life here and what we had left behind in the UK. Everything appeared to be neat and clean and the shops and cafés bursting with goodies. What we considered luxuries back home were everyday things out here. It was wonderful.

There was also a pleasant surprise awaiting me in the shape of an old friend from the Country Festivals, Paul Starr. He was also working the bases and still doing his quick–draw bit in his act. He did sometimes have a tough time when challenged by some Texas farm boy but generally he came off best. We had a few drinks in a nearby bar and he gave us a few tips about the best places to eat and which late night bars to avoid. When we got back to the hotel about ready to doss down for a few hours before going out on the town, there was a phone call waiting for us from the agency saying that we had to be at a rehearsal for 3 o'clock. Christ. We'd only been here ten minutes and Pearson was already talking about rehearsals.

just after 3 p.m. George, the Prussian Junker who doubled as our driver arrived and hurtled us down to Drake Edwards Caserne, 3rd U.S. Armored Division. HQ. It had two major claims to fame. The first was that Elvis

Presley had spent some time there during his army career and was reputed to have met his Priscilla there, and the other more recent event was that a former Custodian of the N.C.O. Club had done a runner with over sixty grand from the club safe. They picked him up two years later in Tahiti, drunk, broke, out of his head on Happy Grass.

Jake Pearson was at the rehearsal. It was the first time I'd seen him since he picked us up off the Johnny Cash Show in London a couple of months previously. He had not changed much, just as drunk as when I last saw him. He swaggered into the club with his 'Star of the Month'.

"Oh, yuh made it then, Yonco?" He sneered. His hard digger accent putting a sarcastic edge to everything he said and quickly got my back up.

"Yeah, 'course we're here. You sent a bloody van for us didn't you?" I growled back.

He ignored my obvious annoyance and with an exaggerated gesture introduced his clinging companion.

"Gentlemen," he announced, smarmily. "I'd like you to meet the Queen of the House. Miss Mary Taylor."

He was referring to Mary's minor hit record, a female version of Roger Miller's 'King of the Road', which had been written by Jodie Miller. In those days it was quite fashionable to write answer songs. As far back as the 50's Hank Locklin's 'Geisha Girl' was answered by Skeeter Davis' maudlin 'Lost to a Geisha Girl' and Kitty Wells quavering 'It wasn't God who made Honky Tonk Angels' riposted Hank Thompson's 'Wild side of Life'. Johnny Bond once told me that she sang it (several times) on every show. Not that everybody wanted to hear it. But SHE did. And Johnny said that she would stay on that damned stage until she got a standing ovation and only finally left when people started standing up to go to the toilet. I only met her once and found her one of the most boring female singers I have ever come across.

We all shook hands with Mary and said how glad we were to be backing her on her first trip to Germany. I don't think Jake had bothered to tell her that it was our first trip too. She seemed to like us but appeared to have a few reservations about her support artist, Don Hill, a Country singer from Alexandria, Louisiana, who sang well and included some good imitations in his act. I thought he was very good. He was an ex–GI who had married in Germany and settled in Kaiserslautern. Everybody called him Dokie and it was for me, an eventful meeting because I was to run into him all over the world in the next twenty–five years. For this contract he had brought along a buddy called Dick Burke, known as 'Wahoo' to his friends who played a nice guitar style and they often worked as a double act on the German off–base clubs around the Saarbruken area.

After setting up our gear we got into a run–through. Our program was strongly based on the material of Buck Owens, Hank Williams and Johnny Cash with a few of the currently popular Truck Driving songs thrown in, while Kit did a selection of country standards, mainly Jean Shepherd and

Brenda Lee ballads, spicing things up with some trendy Nancy Sinatra songs like 'These boots are made for walking' and 'Jackson'. It was a bright, happy show with a lot of presence about it. Joe was on a bit of a downer but his guitar playing was good and both Dave and Spud had a lot of flair in their stage manner. It all went together very well and Mary Taylor was happy with her backings, so that was a major relief. She had a lot of good patter and Las Vegas type showmanship and her show was good, bright and varied in style from the up–tempo 'Long Tall Texan' to the touching 'He called me baby, baby all night long'. In appearance she was a typical product of the West Coast, even though her billing was from Nashville and her management was by Jim Halsey out of Kansas City. She was tall with blonde hair and that open–air All–American Girl type of face. Much like Jane Fonda. Her grooming was superb, and her songs well selected and timed and, with the faintest hint of a Southern accent, she couldn't go wrong on those U.S. Military Clubs. (Well, most of 'em anyway).

Dokie's act was also well put together with a lot of good imitations of Country Stars like Marty Robbins and Hank Snow but he did have a moody side to him as well and would stomp off the stage in a huff if he was not being well received or if another act on the show got more applause. I once saw him tear his watch off his wrist and throw it out of the van window on to the autobahn because it had stopped and he was late for a gig. He was as 'Coon Assed 'as they come and would lapse into deep 'Cajun' moods, refusing to talk for days on end as his raw rural Louisiana back-ground came out. Strangely enough he made a good friend of Dave our drummer who was the complete opposite to him in temperament. Apart from doing support shows for visiting stars he often worked as Front Man with a G.I. outfit called the Hometowners, managed out of Kaiserslautern (known to us as K.Town) by the famous Pop Phillips, who was a legend in his own lifetime.

Pop had arrived on the scene after leaving Columbus, Georgia, under some kind of cloud but he soon established himself as a booker of semi–pro GI bands on the German circuit. A short, fat, hustler, much in the style of Elvis Presley's mentor 'Colonel' Tom Parker, his greatest coup had been in booking Charlie Pride onto the US bases in '65. It turned out to be a traumatic experience for Charlie, who was accepted by the Rednecks as just another entertainer with talent but ran into heavy flak from his Soul Brothers who either boycotted him or heckled his act. The 60's was a tense time on the overseas US bases, mainly due to the Black Panthers and other black militants, and the arrival of one of their own singing honky–music was like a red rag to a bull, but Charlie however, survived to become one of the most successful acts in Country Music, proving that old Pop Phillips had been right in his judgment.

These G.I. bands had things all their own way up to about 1965. They dominated the clubs in France and Germany, both for the 'House Band 'jobs and as support for visiting Stateside Stars but the difficulty of guaranteeing that musicians would be free from military duties for tours, and the emergence of good British country bands put an end to the monopoly. Apart from ourselves there was Tom Fricker's Tomahawk Band, the Hillsiders, Johnny Regan's Tumbleweeds which at one time included both Dave Peacock and Charlie Hodges, (later to become the famous Cockney rockers, Chas & Dave) plus the Muskrats, Phil Brady's Ranchers and many others who were more than ready and willing to take any kind of deal to get recognition, and it did not take the agencies long to get on to us. Pearson, Fitzgerald and Gisela Gunther in Frankfurt plus Charlie Klop and Ronnie Harris of G.A.A (German American Agency) in Wiesbaden were all offering deals that were far better than those on offer at home. Of course we did not realize the profits being made out of us. We were glad to be working.

Our first show was at Rhein Main Officer's Club on June 24th and it was a roaring success. Everything worked fine and although Dokie came close to throwing the expected wobblers, it was a good night and a great confidence–booster for us. Pearson clambered on stage at the close–out and announced grandly how pleased he was with the show and how proud he was to have found this terrific band and that 'FRANK YONCO and the TEXAS DRIFTERS' would be on all his future tours and that he was going to give us a long term contract and increase our salary every month. Wow. As it turned out, this was Jake's standard performance at the start of every tour and he made the same empty promises for every band that worked for him, from Mel Hag's Westonaires up to the Muskrats years later. Of course we never saw the increased salary, in fact on several occasions we had difficulty in getting the contract money due to us.

The sheer opulence of the clubs in those days took our breath away. In Vietnam, the war was escalating and the servicemen were needed, so every effort was being made to provide for their comfort and welfare. Government money was readily forthcoming for top–flight entertainment and there was a huge boost in income from the seemingly never–ending banks of slot machines that lined every hall and foyer. Add to this the superb food and drink plus Four Star service and you have an idea of the well run and beautifully furnished American servicemen's clubs of the circuit back then. However, on with our tale.

Next day, still on a euphoric high, we were off to Spengdahlen Air Base on the far side of the River Mosel. It was a delightful run which we became very familiar with, crossing the Rhine at Bingen and then across rolling farm land and rushing down the frightening gorge to Bernkastel and through the ancient Frankish capital of Charlemagne at Trier. Once again the show was a winner with Mary Taylor socking it to them and Kit showing more confidence as she sang, skipped, and danced her way round the vast kidney–shaped stage in her mini–skirt, banging away with her tambourine, pulling wild applause and wolf–whistles from the G.I crowd. On slow songs she held them in her hand, as her image was of the girl they had left back home. I think it was also the first time that we did 'Jackson' together. Anyway, I remember the whole show was a wow and we played for an hour's dancing when it was over.

The first serious hint of trouble showed from Dokie, with him throwing a moody sulk because at one part of the show I did a Webb Pierce imitation. The song was, I think 'Slowly I'm Fallin'. It went over very well, which did not suit Dokie at all and he refused to speak to anybody all the way home. The first thing next morning, he phoned Pearson saying that I was trying to steal his act. So I got warned off. There were to be no more imitations from me while Dokie was on the show. Ah well, that's showbiz, I suppose, though with that kind of brittle temperament he should have been working for the Bolshoi Ballet, not the US Military.

Arriving back at the Garni Hotel we found that we had been shifted around to make room for the American group 'The Fantastics'. They were a five–piece vocal harmony soul group and were absolutely superb, very well presented and great singers and movers, one of the best of those kinds of acts I've ever seen. At that moment however I was not exactly their number one fan, having been unceremoniously dumped into a ground floor room next to the continuously banging front door and all the comings and goings.

The Anker Hotel

At breakfast, the following morning we met up again with Paul Starr who told us more about this gem of a hotel he had found out of town. We were all a bit fed up of all the moving around at the Garni, so we decided to go there and have a look at it. Junker George from the Agency drove us out there and negotiated a deal for us. It was at Alt Sechbach, a quaint old village on the northeastern edge of Frankfurt, close to the select up–market suburb of Bergen Enkheim. Thinking back to it, I remember it as a winding main street lined with timber framed buildings, steep roofed houses and some good gasthouses. The hotel itself was called the Anker and was a conversion of a large farmhouse complete with cobbled courtyard and outbuildings with rooms on three stories.

There was no bar or restaurant but there was a breakfast room on the ground floor next to the kitchen. We got on well with the old boy who owned it and by four that afternoon we were well settled in. I think the reason we got on so well was probably due to the fact that we were the only guests, in fact, in all the time we stayed there I rarely saw another client. When we finally got a day off we used the time mooching round the village, which seemed to be under some very strict preservation order. It was like an illustration from a children's version of Hansel and Gretel, small shops and timbered houses with mullioned windows and stone steps up to the carved wooden doors. Bright green window boxes overflowed with bright flowers in the hot sunshine. And the whole atmosphere was charmingly old fashioned.

I had drawn some money from Pearson, having caught him in a moment of weakness at the bar of the NCO club, so that night we all adjourned to Schwann, a local boozer, where we got legless on good German lager and stuffed ourselves with those delicious fruit filled pancakes they called pfankuchen. No sooner had we become accustomed to our new home than we were informed that we would be leaving on a four day trip and to pack accordingly. The bus picked us up at 3.30.p.m. and we were being driven at breakneck speeds down the Third Reich's first stretch of autobahn to Mannheim to do two shows at Coleman Barracks.

Our bass player, Spud was fascinated by Mary Taylor and attended to her every whim and wish The rest of us were very impressed with her show and of course Kit was in a state of shock having to compete on stage with a woman who had years of Stateside experience under her belt, but she pulled through and her very inexperience and lack of schmaltz added to the 'Down Home' appeal for the young G.I.s.

To pick up on Mary Taylor's connection with one of her backing British musicians, I should point out that this was by no means rare, as most bands had experienced the syndrome. The touring American girl singers of this era suffered from a very confused outlook, the result of double stand-ard social mores of the USA. They went to great lengths to preserve their pure and wholesome 'All American Gal' image but at the same time longed to have a crack at the easy permissive life of the overseas servicemen, much like the Edwardian British who had distorted views of the wild Bohemian life of 'Gay Paree'.

The situation would usually go something like this. The Booking Agent would warn everybody involved that Miss X was a BIG STAR not some groupie bimbo and she was not to be approached without his say so. In other words, if anything was on offer, he wanted first crack at it. This was how the pantomime was played out. On the BIG STAR's arrival she greeted the back–up band coolly, while at the same time trying to sniff out a likely lad. The breaking–down period would take about a week or so, by which time she was being escorted by some club official or was in the per-manent company of the musician chosen to be her 'Musical Director' for the duration of the tour. I remember one Texas girl singer who collected NCOs by the dozen, all colors, ages and sizes. She was hard at it one night behind the side curtains at Ramstein NCO Club while we were playing her intro. She rushed on stage tucking in her blouse and wiping her chin.

Well, our experience of this species was not much different. Within days Mary had moved from her hotel in downtown Frankfurt to our little nest at Alt Sechbach. It was all very cozy and as her room was only two doors away from Spud's he spent many happy afternoons with her. He was not very worldly even though he was such an experienced musician. He had never married and his life was dominated by his mother, who, having steered her family through the German Blitz and the post war Liverpool Depression, thought that she could rule their lives forever. In fact it was

only with great reluctance she allowed him to get a passport. It was unfortunate therefore that Mary chose him to be her special friend. She was a
long way from home and was looking for a little fun. Spud, on the other
hand, fell heavily for her and bored us to a standstill with tales of future
trips to the States and all the jobs she was going to fix for him in the
Nashville studios when he was not on the road with her as her tour manager. Oh yeah?

It was all bullshit of course but he would not believe us. When Kit tried
to reason with him, he accused her of being jealous because Mary was so
good. I pointed out, as kindly as I could, that Jim Halsey, her manager in
Kansas City might have something to say about her promises and that
guitarist Roy Clarke who had helped her career so much, might also want
a word on the subject. When she left Germany three weeks later Spud was
shattered. After her last show at Ramstein he was almost in tears. He
would not go out and mooched around the hotel, sitting for hours in her
empty room and rushing out to meet the postman for his promised plane
ticket. It was all very sad, like 'Madame Butterfly' in reverse.

Speaking of Ramstein NCO club. It was the scene of one of the funniest
interludes I saw on the German club scene. This venue was probably the
most modern and best–equipped club on the circuit. The vast stage was
circular and revolved so that you would set up behind the curtains and as
one act finished, the stage revolved and brought you, playing your opening
number, to the audience. Which was great in theory but on this particular
night we were backing Sheb Wooley and were doing an early spot for dancing before the arrival of the big star. Things were going great, so much so
that for some reason Joe, who was playing guitar and singing harmony, got
carried away in the closing number of an Elvis tribute spot and moved his
microphone and amp forward off the moving apron. So the bass player did
the same—and then, as the audience went wild and curtains began to close
and the MC made an announcement, the stage began to revolve. The amps
and the mike stands stuck out front didn't move and ended up being
dragged round by their cables and they eventually fell off the edge of the
stage with a huge crash and a confusion of howling feed–back and
crumpled screeching metal as the mike stands got caught in the works.

Meanwhile back at Coleman barracks in Manheim the shows were not
going too well. The one at the NCO. Club was fine but there was a bit of
trouble at the Enlisted Men's Club where Mary's 'Southern Country' patter
did not sit easily on the high proportion of militant Soul Brothers in the
crowd who heckled the show to a standstill. In the end the M.P.s had to be
called in and the club cleared. After that incident the Mary Taylor Show
did not play many EM. Clubs. There was however, one notable incident,
which capped all the others.

Probably due to kickbacks from the Agency to the Club Custodian, slippy
Jake Pearson managed to book the show into the EM. Club at Baumholder,
a training area up in the wild moorlands around Idar Oberstein. The units

we played to were again mostly black, and had come in that day from a six day field exercise, sleeping in tents and living rough. And the last thing those tank crews wanted to hear was some ex–High School Queen WASP sing 'He called me Baby Baby' and Queen of the House. Once again the closing act was a routine club clearance by the M.P.s.

Up early and glad to be gone, we were on the autobahn by 7.30am and rocketing westward with George, our Uhlan driver working off last night's hangover by driving like a dervish, passing everything in sight from huge pantechnicons to Porsches determined to be the first one at the scene of an accident. Even if he had to cause one himself. I've met a few mad drivers in my time, but George took the biscuit. What a loony. I think he was the principal reason I decided to get our own bus. I know theoretically we still owned our own transport but that old Morris Isis was now forgotten, safely being taken care of by a Huntingdon Garage. Anyway I should have imagined that by now it would have become a very valuable vintage artifact that might make a nice few quid for the proprietor one day.

As it happened, we did see it again, about eight years later when I was working a nearby airbase and I pulled in for petrol before realizing where I was. Out of sheer devilment I asked about the rusting off–white Isis behind the shed. The proprietor said that he had inherited it when he took over the garage and that there was a considerable bill waiting for the owner when he collected it. We slipped quietly into first gear and slid off without waiting for our change. I wonder if it's still there?

There was then a small break and we spent time checking out Frankfurt and its attractions. First thing we needed were nosebags and soon we found ourselves in a Hanchen Haus, one of a chain of restaurants that specialised in roast chicken. Nothing new about that today, I know, but back in 1966 it was at the cutting edge of catering, and totally unknown in Britain. We became regular patrons. Naturally after eating we went looking for a few beers and where better than Meyer Gustels, a Bavarian bier Keller behind the Kaiser Strasse.

Gustels was a massive hall, decorated with leafy boughs hanging from the rafters while hunting horns and stuffed deer's heads, their spreading antlers draped with more greenery vied for 'Lebensraum' on the mock wooden walls, with brewery posters and tourist prints of the Tyrol. It was jam packed with bulky ruby faced, bellowing punters eating knuckles of pork and bratwurst bangers and quaffing huge steins of foaming lager. The place was absolutely bursting with atmosphere and bonhomie, urged on by an authentic eight–piece Bavarian Umpah–umpah band on a high stage that was trying to blow the roof off. Great. It became a regular off duty hang–out for us and one night we were in there when the football 1966 World Cup was being relayed over the radio. It was England versus West Germany and we were probably the only English folk in there but Dave Marks was not going to be put off by that and went to the station tourist shop where he bought a Union Jack flag and stuck it in a beer bottle on our table in the middle of all the Kraut hordes. It was like being at Dunkirk. Except that this time England WON.

Surprisingly, the Germans came over to congratulate us and sent a buxom fraulein over with armfuls of brimming lager steins. In response Kit offered to conduct the umpah band in a selection of boozing songs which she did magnificently, not losing a beat when one of the giants squatted down behind her and lifted her up on his shoulders while the beer continued to flow to our table. About the only downside was that I had to pay for a round of drinks for the band, and each one of the huge red faced Bavarian lederhosen wearers ordered big steins with chasers of Asbach brandy. (Which, by the way, is a great drink when taken with orange cordial). It was a superb unforgettable night. But next morning at 8am we were off again, scorching down the autobahn on another heart–stopping traffic blitzkrieg with Junker George to Stuttgart for a three–day trip. Oh no, working for Jake you didn't get many days off.

PICKER'S TIP 14

Do not tune up on stage if there is an audience watching. It makes you look a complete amateur and invites a lot of negative comments.

Red Simpson

Jake Pearson was very pleased with us and with the money he had made from the Mary Taylor tour, so he quickly got his next star out and earning. This was Red Simpson who had become one of the top exponents of the 'Truck Driving' songs, with hits like 'Roll truck, roll' and Nitro Express. His songs were bright and truly reflected contemporary blue Collar America but regrettably, one strand of the genre carried the seeds of its own destruction with acts like Red Sovine, whose maudlin tear–jerkers were often a source of embarrassment if you happened to be in the company of non–Country friends when one came on the radio. Remember Red Sovine's 'Little Rosa?'

I first came across this dreary eulogy being done by Hank Walters at the Black Cat club in Liverpool. It wasn't too bad because Hank was very good at monologues, but then a visiting 'Hat and Boots' act from Widnes heard it and chose it as his theme tune and did it to death. Liverpool concert secretaries often requested it towards the end of an evening because it was a sure–fire way to empty the club. I heard later that he had moved to Majorca. Wonder if he's still doing Little Rosa?

"Se llama Pequena Rosita," He olvidado las palabras.

Bakersfield in those days was serious rival to Nashville. It was the home base of Merle Haggard and Buck Owens, who opened a promotional agency there called OMACK. Its proximity to the Rock influences of Southern California produced some very good modern Country and Country–Rock music and Simpson was a product of this mélange of styles. On tour he did songs like' Jack–knife; Wolf Creek Pass, The Highwayman, and 'Black Smoke over 18 wheels.' All of it very good stuff, ideal songs for the time and place. He was an excellent guitarist in the classic open string Telecaster style, a fair piano player and a super songwriter, but being bred in the honky–tonk tradition did not know when to quit and had the unfortunate habit of staying late after the show, doing songs at the piano till four in the morning, to the accompaniment of the clinking Jack Daniels glee club, which resulted in him being left behind twice at Ramstein and Lahr

He was a nice, easy–going guy, but more of a recording artist than a cabaret performer, and on more than one occasion I had to stand behind him on stage and prompt him with the words of something he had only done in the studio, such as his big hit 'Forty Acres'. I can remember coming off the Frankfurt autobahn about 5.30 one morning and listening to a Country D.J. on A.F.N. introducing Red's latest hit from California, and envying his surfing lifestyle out there, while the subject of his envy was a dirty unshaven bundle in the back seat of the agency Volkswagen bus try–ing to grab a few winks.

Red never liked Europe and longed to be back in California, but he did like the working girls on the Kaiser Strasse in Frankfurt. There again, who didn't? They were very impressive, these Ladies of the Night, with their elegant clothes, expensive perfumes and Mercedes cars. A far cry from the harpies that used to haunt Lewiss Arcade in Manchester or the faded hookers of small town America. Most of them were very beautiful and they loved the free spending American servicemen. Quite a lot of the visiting cabaret stars used to patronize them. I especially remember one curious incident there.

A few months later we had brought one Nashville Star, well known for his serious gospel songs, to see this hooker's parade and he prevailed upon us to approach the lady of his choice and fix things up. The price being agreed, he was about to step into her Mercedes and be whisked up to her hotel room when he stopped to ask Kit if he could borrow her gold ring to slip it on the hooker's finger while they were making love. This way he said, he felt his conscience was clear and the Lord would forgive him. How's that for a bit of fundamental Bible–Belt philosophy?

As I said, Red Simpson was an easy–going guy but to be an easy–going guy when you're working for J.P. was like swimming with the sharks. The ruthless agent took advantage of him at every turn, often pulling three shows a night from him with sometimes 150 kilometres between each one. However, this time the Sydney Snake had picked the wrong man to mess with. Red was a hot number, riding high and making big bucks for a major management in California that handled all the business side of his career, song publishing, recordings, booking etc.

To them he was an asset, a commodity to be marketed to the top bidder and at the time there were plenty of promoters who wanted Red's services, so he could not be held to ransom like some smaller fish, and at the end of his contract he simply decided to go home. The tour ended on a Thursday and Jake tried to put the arm on him to do three more days by withholding his pay, but this time his ploy did not work. Red simply picked up his Tele–caster, booked out of his hotel and left Jake a note listing the shows he had done, including the infamous three–shows–a–night strokes, hopped on a Stateside bound military transport plane out of Rhein Main and left them all to sort it out.

Getting money out of Jake was often a matter of hitting him at the right moment, but at this time, smarting as he was from the experience with Red Simpson, it was doubly difficult. We were well overdue for a payment and I kept phoning the agency office but obviously his secretary had been given instructions, and she put me on hold until I got fed up and rang off or told me that Jake was out of town. Things were getting harder by the day. Drastic action was called for so we went to Frankfurt to confront him. As we were parking the van near the Echensheimer Turm I saw him sliding out of the office building. He had not seen us so after watching him drive off I went to a pay phone and rang the office. Erica, his German wife answered and putting on a strong Australian accent, I said.

"Oh Erica s'me. Jake, Yeah, Now listen. I jes' seen that bastard Yonco in town and I'd say he was comin' f'some money. Right? Now, make sure y'only pay 'im his contract up to date. Yeah? S'right. Just give him two thousand bucks. Gottit? Okay"

Erica said she understood and asked what time would he be back. I slammed the phone down and headed for the office. It went as smooth as silk.

We were sitting in a beer garden opposite the office when he got back and we could hear the curses from the open office window echoing right across the Marktplatz.

Cecelia

On the road with a girl singer in the band there are certain basic female goods and facilities that must be found, and high on this list of priorities is the hairdresser. So it was one Monday afternoon that I went with Kit to find one. There was not one in the village itself so we went to the tramway terminus where there was a row of shops, one of which was a hairdresser. Kit did not speak much German at that time, so I went in with her. It was the usual continental hair salon that did both men's and women's hair, a thing that you rarely came across at that time in the U.K. so I decided to have my hair cut at the same time. This was my first introduction to Frau Cecilia, the owner. She was in her early forties, (one of the real Whoring Forties, according to Dave) and was very chic in a neat Germanic way, slim–faced and a bit lanky, but superbly groomed and toting a fair selection of excellent jewellery. She had three daughters, two of whom worked in the salon with her.

The hairdresser's became a regular port of call for me on our days off and it was not too long before it was coffee in the back room and trips upstairs to inspect her flat or visits to her friend to show off her new admirer. We got on very well and it was a good opportunity for me to brush up my German. (Oh Yes, Yonk, we really believe that). In fact by today's standard it was quite a reserved platonic relationship—well, er, almost platonic. Her Old Man was in some kind of business in Hanau and as he only came home at weekends to their big villa in Bergen Enkheim, she was feeling a touch neglected and I must have been an interesting prospect in her eyes. I certainly had some interesting afternoons at that house in Bergen Enkheim.

She was a very nice lady and we got on well together but I began to get the impression that she had more serious plans for me, as she explained the finances of her business and began rearranging the furniture that I had commented on at her house. A few weeks passed pleasantly and we got on very well and she was very sympathetic to my moans about George's wild driving and the fact that I did not have transport of my own. As Sechbach was barely a mile away from Bergen Enkheim, she was nervous about meeting me or picking me up there. She was so sympathetic in fact, that she offered to stand as guarantor for me on a used Volkswagen bus.

Well, I thought that very nice of her, so one sunny August day we went to a dealer near the Henninger Brewery and, after signing a few totally incomprehensible documents at a nearby bank, I drove out in a shining green and cream bus of my own. (Provided of course that I kept up the payments) and I remember her saying that she thought she must be stupid to have arranged such a deal. I told her that she was talking arrant nonsense, but in the final analysis she turned out to be right. Of course, the arrangement entailed more frequent visits to the barbers and after a while I had a permanent smell of Bay Rum on me, but driving around in the hot sunshine in my very own bus was very nice and even the cloying coffee afternoons with my non–English speaking patron seemed more pleasant. Jake Pearson wanted to know if there were any more daft sods in Cecilia's family that he could have a go at? Oh Yes, Jake always did have a nice turn of phrase, something to do with him being Australian I think. After meeting him I came to the conclusion that Australians were the most balanced people on the Earth. They had a chip on both shoulders. And twenty years later playing dates in Sydney I found it quite true.

Everybody was quite pleased with the new development, though they all thought about it differently. At least we were all relieved to be free of the road stress from Junker George. To Dave, the new van meant an end to him having to bribe George to drop him off at the early morning market boozers, To Kit it meant also that she did not have to be nice to George anymore and an end to the cardiac arrest she felt coming down the Bernkastel Krues hairpin bends, although she was not very happy about my deeper involvement with Frau Cecilia. To Joe it meant that he would be driven all the way home at the end of the contract and to Spud it meant that he could save the train fare from Manchester to Liverpool.

Now that we had our own transport Dave decided that he had had enough of sharing rooms with Joe and having struck up a happy relationship with Gretel the hotel cleaner and chambermaid, moved into a small gatehouse in the yard with her. It suited his nocturnal habits and enabled him to get away from Spud's voice and Joe's feet. To Dave it was all a great adventure and he was determined not to miss a bit of it. On many occasions at, say, five or six in the morning getting back from Stuttgart or some soul destroying triple job. (Oh yes, that bastard agent now had us doing them as well). David would wake from his dozing as we approached Frankfurt, grab a handful of money off me and insist on being dropped off near the produce market where the bars would be open all night and start the day with a few steins of Henninger Turm. He'd come home about 2 p.m., in time to grab a kip before pick–up time.

Jake Pearson was also pleased that he did not have to provide transport for us anymore and, to keep us away from the other agents he sent us back down to work as a house–band at Bitburg NCO. Club, where we stayed for three weeks while waiting for our next star to arrive. The digs were terrible so we moved out to a small hotel in the village itself. We only worked four nights a week and so on the next evening off we drove across to Idar Oberstein, famous for its jewellery workshops, and caught the

Brook Benton Show at the Baumholder NCO club. Absolutely superb. It was while we were rehearsing on the following Monday afternoon that Jake showed up to tell us that due to his booking of Sammy Davis Jnr. (Oh Yeah?).

There had been a change of plans and we were sent to Ansbach NCO Club for a show with George Hamilton IV. George was completely out of his depth amongst all those tough, rough–arsed infantrymen, who were not quite attuned to subtleties of his 1950's bobbysoxer songs like 'A Rose and Baby Ruth, and 'Why don't they understand? (I thought the latter particu-larly apt in the circumstances). In later years I got to know and like George and did quite a few shows with him. Like Vernon Oxford, Billy Jo Spears, Slim Whitman and Hank Locklin, he made a bigger mark in Britain and Ireland than ever he did in his native America. (Not Canada, as many people seem to think. George was born in Winston Salem, North Carolina).

Pearson phoned to say that we were to stay on as the house band for the rest of the month. I pointed out that there were only ten days to go on our contract and that we had to get home. He didn't like it but he begged us to do the final weekend, four days over our stipulated time, and that we could come back a few days late for the second contract in September. Innocently we believed him but as far as he was concerned we were a spent force to be forgotten. How wrong he was.

Two weeks later we were on our way home after an emotional farewell at our home–from–home, the Anker Hotel in Alt Sechbach. Giesel was in tears and old Hans was down in the mouth as he considered the lost rev-enue, but he sparked up again when we said we would soon be coming back. The journey was very pleasant with everybody paid up and well fed as we rolled across Germany to the Channel Ports in our new bus. Nor-mally we embarked at Ostend in Belgium but Spud insisted that we pushed on to Calais in France because he said he could get a better ex-change rate there. So, to preserve the harmony of the band, we drove a couple of more hours to the French port. At that point after much heart-searching Spud decided to take a chance on the exchange rates in England and ended up changing only £6.50 in Europe.

As our new Volkswagen bus was left hand drive it was agreed that someone would always stay awake with the driver, as we would be driving on the wrong side of the road. It was a good idea, but regrettably did not always work as this next incident shows. Just off the ferry, we headed out of Dover towards London. I was driving and must admit was a bit tired, while all the rest were dozing in the hot sunshine, and nobody was doing more dozing than David, who was supposed to be keeping me awake. Blearily looking ahead I noticed less than a mile away that the dual carriageway we were on narrowed to a normal two lane highway and hurt-ling towards me over a rise was an old Morris Oxford wallowing all over the road about seventy miles an hour. I judged that we would pass just as the dual carriage narrowed, and I was more than a little disturbed at this lurching banger weaving towards me—In a flash of deja vu my mind shot back to my tipper driving experience.

My fears proved to be quite justified, because as I moved a little to the right to pick up the two lane highway. I caught the look of blind panic on the other driver's face, and there was a loud bang as the elderly saloon side swiped us, followed by the screeching of torn metal as the exposed steel hinges of our front door ripped a three inch wide strip from the bodywork of the other car, opening it up like a tin of salmon. I wildly struggled to keep our bus straight, and glanced in the mirror as the other driver tried desperately to stop the shaking mass that was now trailing a strip of twisted metal, like a maypole streamer, and sending up a bright shower of sparks Everybody woke up full of questions but I did not have time to answer and, considering discretion to be the better part of valour when one has rather dodgy insurance, I put my foot to the floor and shot over the rise and away.

"That was a near one Dad wosn'it?" chirped David, comfortingly, and tossed a shower of cigarette over the snoring form of Joe. After which he settled back in his seat to sleep again. Spud said that he had had a few experiences of this kind of thing in Liverpool and told us exactly what to do. So I stopped at the first Police Station we came to and reported the accident, all of us complaining loudly about the other car not stopping. It was just as well that we took the bass man's advice, because a few miles further on we were pulled over by a patrol car and questioned about the incident that had been reported by the sardine tin. On checking they found out that we had got our complaint in first. And there were four witnesses so nothing came of it.

Scalping Again

Encouraged by the success of our first tour, I decided to expand the band by adding a second lead instrument, possibly a pedal steel guitar. There were a few other changes as well. Due to family pressures and the fact that he had somehow built up a nice bit of boozing money, David said he would miss the next trip, so I brought in a superb drummer called Mel Dean. He was a very good musician and no trouble at all but only contracted to do one tour because he was already committed to return to Rochdale to run his own successful combo on the Tiffany's club circuit. The other addition I wanted was a good steel guitarist, but good steelies were thin on the ground. There were a few whose abilities varied from excellent to the pathetic. About the best back then was (and still is) Rod King, but he was aready booked for South Africa. Even at so early stage in his career, he was doing studio sessions and providing backing tracks for such luminaries as Rod Stewart and Eric Clapton, playing mood music behind readings by the Poet Laureate John Betjeman in the late 1970's.

Liverpool was the nearest source of good country pickers, so I contacted Billy Cooper, an old friend of mine from the Blue Mountain Boys, who put me on to Tony Coulston, who was a superb picker with a wonderful Scouse sense of humour. His playing was of the highest standard and he could make a standard C6th tuned six string lap steel do all the licks that later players could only obtain with an abundance of knee levers and foot pedals. Looking back at him, he was the least eccentric steel player I have ever known, which is saying something. At least Tony was funny.

There were no formal rehearsals for this tour. Everybody was more than competent and the program would be much the same as our previous tours. Our star this time was to be Buddy Cagle, a one–shot wonder who had made an American cover of Frank Ifield's chart hits 'I Remember You' and 'Lovesick Blues'. So backing Buddy was no big deal and being home for a while and having for once, a bit of money, things were fine. I had come back with a case full of goodies and was full of euphoria and the bright promise for the future. I also made arrangements with the bank to send regular money home and promised to find a place for us all out there, so the parting this time was not quite as fraught as it usually was.

PICKER'S TIP 15

If you are playing rhythm guitar position your own amplifier behind you to the right. Do not put your guitar through the PA system. All the other in–struments have their own on–stage sound source and so should you.

11

WELCOME TO FRANCE

With the spectre of our first traumatic departure hovering above, we loaded the bus and headed south and midnight found us aboard a cross Channel ferry to Calais in France. Not Ostend in Belgium. Oh NO. Clanger number one. Because our world fell apart as we rolled off the boat at 7am the next morning when a French customs officer innocently asked where we were heading and what we had in the back. Proudly I told him that we were a band and were off on a contract to play for the American Forces in Germany. His face froze and his eyes narrowed.

"Orchestre? Allemagne—Pour les salles Yanquis? Merde."

He turned to look sardonically at his mate who politely inquired

"Eh bien, Monsieur. Votre carnet, s'il vous plait?"

Carnet? Blank faces all around.

"Wots a carny" asked Tony.

The officer looked down his nose at our steel player." Carnet, Zur,? Eet eez a papeur for all your 'lectric goods from zee Ingleesh douane wiz all zee numbers of your equipment."

"Oh yeah," I said. "Of course, the carnet. Ah, er, No Colonel, We don't need one of them. It's all insured y'see."

I waved our contract at him but he turned his mouth down at the corners as I blustered on like Del Boy.

"I mean, come on, Marcel. We will only be in your country for a couple of hours.

This time he smiled, much as a tiger might smile at a tethered goat and shouting something to his mate waved us off the dockside and into a contraband compound.

We sat there confused and waiting until the offices opened at nine o'clock, when a clerk called me in to explain the situation in fractured English. It turned out that we had three options. One, go back to Dover on the next boat and obtain the carnet document from the British Customs and Excise people. Two, obtain a bank guarantee from Frankfurt or thirdly, as he suggested pointedly with a Gallic shrug, forget the whole thing and scuttle back home.

By the time I had left that office I had made my mind up which course to follow so there was no point telling the boys about the other possibilities. I was still confident that I could handle things at this late stage, so as the boys lay in the hot sunshine I got on the phone to Pearson's office in Frankfurt to explain the delay and our predicament. For once I got through first time and he was there. I heard the double ring of a German phone and the familiar voice of Erica, his wife, and I told her we were stuck in Calais and needed to talk to Jake urgently.

His Ozzie twang rasped through the earpiece.

"Oh—So, that's where yew are, eh Yonco?" He sneered. "Wotcha doin' in Frogland? Yew shoulda been 'ere a bloody week ago."

His belligerence took me aback.

"Whaddya mean, a week ago?" I gasped. " We worked an extra week for you on the last bloody contract so that we could get back a couple of days late. You said so yourself at Ansbach."

"Oh yeah? That's wot y' think is it? Well listen to me Yonco. I've got news fer yew. Y'r too bloody late so yew'd jes' better piss off back to Blighty."

I was getting all this verbal and I had not got round to explaining what had happened but I decided to ignore his rejection and continued with my spiel about the French customs, hoping he would understand, but he thought it was a huge joke and roared down the phone, laughing loudly until I told him that I wanted a bank guarantee from the agency. Then his voice went icy cold.

"Bank guarantee? Don't make me laugh. Listen you Limey twat. Yew are too bleedin' late. I've told you before. I've given Don Hill the job and I don' want to know about you or your bunch of five dollar pommie dick heads or any of ya troubles with the Frogs. Got it? Forget it. It's over."

I stood there dumfounded; the dead phone frozen in my hand. I could not believe that he had elbowed me but I should have known better. Enough people had warned me. Pop Phillips once said that if you were drowning Jake would be the first one to throw you a brick. But what was I to do? There had to be some way out of this dilemma. This was the second time that fate had tried to scupper my plans but there was no way that I was going to surrender now. Looking out of the window I saw my band lolling back in the sunshine drinking cans of lager and waiting for me to sort things out, and I knew that I had to do something and wracked my brain for a solution Then it came to me—Freddy Straub, the Nuremberg God-father, the licence man. Yes, I would call Freddy.

Let me explain about these Licence Men. You see, to avoid every Tom, Dick and Harry horning in on the entertainment scene for the US Military and to keep out the criminal influences, only a limited number of approved agents were appointed by the US Government. Apart from stringent vet-ting procedures, a large cash bond was required to guarantee that the acts were up to standard and were politically sound and not in any way anti-American. There were not many of these approved agents, maybe a dozen or so in Europe and they in turn passed down to sub-agents the opportunity to bring in entertainment to the bases. All payments by the Military were made directly to these approved agents and they of course deducted the due percentages as the money passed through their hands. Generally it was a very efficient system.

I knew two or three of these primary agents quite well and, in fact, we had become good friends. Al Zawadski in Wiesbaden was one and Freddy Straub in Nuremberg was another, and I don't think that either of them was over the moon about the strokes Jake had pulled on them in the past. There was already bad blood between them over the Sammy Davis Jnr. fiasco, when Jake had booked the show out at top dollar and then pulled the old chestnut of announcing that his big star had been unaccountably delayed and putting the Clarke Brothers as a replacement. The Provost Marshall's office threatened an inquiry into the agents involved and some awkward questions were being asked at headquarters. People's careers swung in the balance, not least the club bookers, who were often on a good kick back from the agents from whom they bought their shows. With this in mind I got on to Straub's office and explained the mess to his beautiful secretary Trudy. She listened sympathetically and arranged for Freddy to call me back, which he did within the hour to say that the bond I required would be waiting for me at the Dresdener Bank in Frankfurt where I had to sign certain papers to obtain it. Good Old Freddy.

I told the French customs what had been arranged and they replied.

"Very good. Now go and get it and then you can have your gear."

Oh yes. I could take the bus but not the equipment, which they would only release on actually seeing the bank document. Oh, Great. I argued passionately but they were adamant, so after an uncomfortable night in a Calais fleapit, we all piled back into our pretty Volkswagen and headed off to Frankfurt. We got as far as Bruges.

The journey was strongly reminiscent of our first trip and it has just struck me after all these years, that those anti–American French customs men might have knobbled our poor old bus while it was in their care. Anyway, across the Belgian frontier a slight familiar knocking began in the engine compartment and by the time we hit Bruges it was rattling its socks off. 'Oh no, I thought, not again.'

Luckily at that moment Kit spotted a VW dealer's sign by the roadside, so we clanked into get the bad news. Well, some of it was good, but there was quite a bit of bad as well. The good fortune was the fact that the garage owner was a Brit. Not only a Brit, but from the same area of Lancashire as Kit. He had stayed behind after the war and married a Belgian girl. He enjoyed being being able to talk to somebody in his native dialect and interspersed his examination of our bus with enquiries about the relative merits of Wilson's bitter and Holland's pies. Finally he got round to telling us that we had a broken piston and that it would cost forty or fifty quid to fix it, and, as he had nothing pressing he could get right on to it and hopefully do the repair in four hours. So it was time for a whip round and everybody chucked in what they could against my promise to pay them all back in Frankfurt. In the end we had enough to pay the garage man, buy a meal, and hope that a full tank and two spare gallon cans would get us to Alt Sechbach. Naturally there was a bit of moaning, but I blindly assured everybody that everything was fine and that we would be back earning as soon as we arrived.

That repair was something else and for the times amazing. Being used to the local back street garages at home, I was amazed at the cleanliness and equipment in this little Belgian repair shop. Once he was given the go-ahead, the mechanic and his apprentice jacked up the rear end of our bus and wheeled over a multi–layered tray with different shaped holes at each level. As they began to strip the engine each part was put in its respective storage hole and, as the first level became full, they moved onto the next one, and so on to the third and fourth levels. The shattered piston was found and renewed, and the sequence began in reverse until everything was back in place. The whole thing took over three hours from start to finish and by late afternoon we were back on the road again.

We picked up the main Brussels highway and crossed in to Germany near Aachen, heading through the early darkness into the unknown. Sometime after midnight on the Wiesbaden autobahn on the outskirts of Frankfurt, we coughed and spluttered into an all night–gas station where I managed to persuade the manager to take my transistor radio in exchange for ten marks worth of gas. This got us to our hotel in Sechbach, where our landlord Old Hans threw the big yard gate wide, and welcomed us back with a rare smile, showing us to our crisp clean rooms, little knowing that we did not have a pfennig between us. Going for broke we ordered bratwursts and beer on the account, and slept like babies, hoping tomorrow would take care of itself.

PICKER'S TIP 16

If your instrument is going to travel in the hold of a pressurised aircraft loosen the strings at least a full tone.

Herr Blintganger

Early next morning I was up and across to Cicilia's shop to tell her about the trip and borrow fifty marks to keep the band fed. Then it was down to the Dresdener Bank on Mainzer Langstrasse to pick up Freddy Straub's guarantee. Cecilia was very impressed with that and must have thought I was much more important than I really was, so when I told her that I had to go to Calais to pick up the impounded PA system and amplifiers she jumped at the chance. Why not go in her car? It was big enough to take all the stuff, she enthused excitedly. It would need two of us and would be an *Overnight Trip!*

Well, to tell you the truth, I wasn't that keen anymore. Somehow after being away from her for a bit, she did not seem to have the same appeal, but how could I refuse such an offer? The trip was set up for the coming Friday so that night I took everybody to the Schwann and told Big Hans that I would pay at the end of the week for whatever everyone had that night, beer, pfankuchen, shchnitzels, and more beer.

The trip was actually uneventful, much to Cicilia's chagrin, as she had envisioned a romantic elopement to some hidden hideaway, but it was not like that at all. We piled into her big Opel Admiral and headed for the French coast 400 miles away. We drove right through stopping only for coffee and petrol and arrived early the next morning. I handed in the documents at the French Customs office and received the clearance for our equipment, which fitted nicely in the trunk and back seat of the car. We had lunch at one of the best hotels in Calais, but I diplomatically sidestepped Cecelia's thinly veiled offers to spend the weekend there, pleading that the documents were only valid for a couple of days and that we had better get back to Germany as quickly as possible.

Of course she did not like it and kept nagging me to stop at every hotel we passed. Eventually I agreed to stop for a few hours near Cologne but the experience was a bit soggy, with her suddenly becoming coy and talking baby–talk, seeking to be wooed like a schoolgirl. So I got very drunk and when I woke up she was sitting in the corner of the room looking daggers at me and calling me all the bad names she could think of, accusing me of being a queer and a 'blintganger' (Literally a damp squib).

But I did not really care. I had got the gear and that's all I was interested in. We pushed on, with me driving and she eventually fell asleep, not waking till we hit the autobahn interchange at Rein–Main. Nobody looks very good in the morning so I fancied her even less when she suggested a sleepy leg–over at her shop before the first customers arrived. I have to say this for her, she was a real pusher and I thought I was trapped this time, but fortunately, as we approached her house at Enkheim, she saw her husband's car in the drive and, not wanting to risk losing her monthly pay check from him, she drove quickly by and booked in at the Frankfurter Hof, and bundled me and my goodies in a taxi to arrive in triumph to my waiting tribe at the Anker hotel.

My homecoming was a bit fraught because during my absence Kit, after a diligent and thorough search of my belongings, had accidentally come across my diary and in a fit of blind jealousy. (I wonder why?) had torn it to shreds because she had come across one or two little indiscretions of mine while working the northern clubs. Ooops. However the moment passed and we made up in a day or two and everybody felt easier having got their equipment back and ready to go to work. If and when we ever got some.

I phoned Pearson but all I got was a torrent of abuse from him but no jobs and neither Freddy Straub or Zawadski could find any contracts in their areas for at least a couple of months and agencies like German–American or Gisela Gunther would not touch us, thinking that we were on some kind of exclusive arrangement with Snaky Jake. It was yet another Catch 22 set up.

About this time a character called Woody Gosnell appeared back on the scene. He was another ex–serviceman who opted to stay on in Germany after completing his service tour of duty. He was a small, dark man from the Mid–West and his background had been in radio, in fact he had had his own program on A.F.N Munich called Stickbuddy Jamboree. He had joined us on the Red Simpson tour as a compere–comedian and I must say that he was good, and his monologues and comedy routines went down very well with the GI audiences. However, Jake, being Jake, realised that he was down on his luck and was paying him peanuts. He moved into the Anker with us bursting with ideas, but that did not help our work situation, which was as you can imagine now becoming stressed.

Truly the end was in sight. I heard on the grapevine that Cecilia had found another toy–boy and had temporarily given me the elbow, so there were no more free lunches there. The Anker provided breakfast of rolls and coffee and we could run up bills for goulash soup and kartoffel salat—and beer of course, but the situation was getting harder by the day. Things would have to change soon or we would be in trouble. The battle of nerves began.

The Buddy Cagle Show

Somehow we survived those early September days. Fortunately for us Old Hans went away on holiday, leaving the place in charge of the lady who did the cleaning and cooking. She was a good friend and although miffed at David's absence, (we told her that he had a passport problem and would be arriving in a couple of weeks), saw to it that we did not starve, though we did have to supplement our diet by scrumping in the local apple orchard. Some days she would boil up a big pan of soup and we would go round the rooms giving everybody a big bowl full with a lump of black bread. It was like being in San Quentin.

Kit went out to dinner a couple of times with Junker George, again mainly to pump out of him what was happening at the office and from one of these evenings out she brought back a copy of the US Army tabloid 'Stars and Stripes' and she pointed out what had caught her eye. It was an advert for:

THE BUDDY CAGLE SHOW
Direct from Nashville featuring
FRANK YONCO, KIT CONNOR & THE EVERGLADES

We were booked at Greenhouse N.C.O. Club in Hanau, a town north of Frankfurt that coming Saturday night. There it was in black and white. So a plan began to form in my mind.

The following Saturday afternoon everybody got cleaned up, even Joe looked quite presentable in a jacket borrowed off Tony and one of my shirts, and the band bus was given a good wash and with some money I had cadged off my blue–rinsed Fairy Godmother (who hinted that she would like things to be back as they were) we had just about enough for a drink each and enough fuel to get to Hanau and back. It was not all that far and the club manager Sgt Howie was a good friend of ours from the earlier shows we had done for him.

It was about 9 p.m. when we arrived there and Sgt.Howie was standing on the club steps anxiously chomping on a cigar and looked relieved and very pleased to see us again. He laid on drinks all round as I introduced him to the new members of the band and he greeted Spud, Joe and Kit as old friends, Out on the cabaret floor was a duo, Dokie and Wahoo (Dick Burke). They were doing a nice job playing 'Rocky Top' on two amplified flattop guitars. We all stood watching, Sgt.Howie with his arm round Kit saying how glad he was to see us all and how the show had been a sell out because he knew what a great night we were going to put on. (Oh yeah?). At that moment Dokie noticed us and looked anxiously at his partner. I gave him a little wave and delivered the coup–de–grace to Sgt. Howie.

"Well, Jerry," I said jovially. "Its very nice of you to make us so welcome, but unfortunately we won't be doing a show tonight. I only came over to explain the situation to you."

He stopped chomping his cigar, put his Jack Daniels on the bar and turned to me, his face getting redder by the second, "Waddya meanm Yonco? Y' won't be doin' my show? I've got a cast iron contract in my God dam office, it's signed and sealed, so don't think you can put the arm on me for more money or gimme any 'o' that bullshit about you not playin."

By this time he was as red as a beetroot and sweating like a bull. His voice was getting louder and a couple of club stewards came over to see what was going on. "Now, listen Jerry," I said, trying to calm him down "Don't get me wrong. My band is here as you can see, I'm ready to go, as is Kit, and the band bus is outside fully loaded with our gear, waiting to be set up."

"What's your problem then?" He demanded. "Get 'em in here. Get this damned show on the road." He turned to one of his assistants," Hey Billy, go to the office an' bring me that motherin' contract."

I put a hand on his arm, "Take it easy, Jerry, I know you have a contract. It's just that I don't. Pearson has fired us."

I recounted our adventures with the French Customs and Jake's response to our predicament, finishing off with a barbed reminder that we were ready, willing, able and fully equipped to do his gig. The Custodian's mouth went slack and his eyes searched wildly round the crowded clubroom, finally lighting on Dokie and Wahoo who were still twanging around the cabaret floor in white short sleeve shirts and blue jeans. He could barely speak but with a great effort managed to splutter. "Waal, who the fuck's that out there then? I thought they was jes' a fill–in 'fore the main event." I shrugged and looked at the Night Manager who was white–faced with stress and confusion. Howie whirled back to look at the cabaret floor. "Are yew a–tellin' me that they're Buddy Cagle's backing group? Christ. No wonder I was about to cancel the show, from the reports I'd been gettin'. Yew sayin' that y'ain't been on any of them shows, Yonco?"

I told him that we had not worked since arriving and we were having a tough time money–wise. Howie stood looking at me, chomping on his cigar, and then without another word, he stomped off to his office gesturing Kit and I to follow him. At the door he turned and told the Night Manager to fix the boys up with drinks and a good meal. We stood by sheepishly as he grabbed the phone and shouted at the operator to get Pearson on the line pronto. He was raging mad, so we said nothing and sipped our drinks. Outside in the clubroom the crowd was getting restless as the guitar duo went into their umpteenth song and loud conversations and catcalls began to drown out the twanging Gibsons and Dokie's brave attempts at imitations. The mood was getting ugly as the odd bottle was smashed and the bartenders began to look tense and check that their nightsticks were to hand.

Back in the office there was a tense silence until the phone jangled loudly. It was Pearson. Howie indicated the extension and we picked it up to listen–in. Without mentioning that we had arrived, Howie blew his top at Jeff about the support act and demanded to know what had happened to Yonco? Jake was at his slimy best as he went into his slippery eel act." Now Jerry, I know how y' must feel. But Christ man, I'm doin' me fuckin' best. Mate. That Limey bastard's let me down rotten," He wailed trying to smooth Howie's ruffled feathers. "That bum flat refused to come over unless I doubled his money—an' wot's more, he only told me a coupla days ago. Y'just can't trust them bastard Pommies. But no worries Jerry, I'll put you a coupla shows in at cost. Yew won't lose out. Stand on me, Mate."

So it went on for a good five minutes, while we listeners stood looking blankly at each other. Howie thundered back at him and the air turned blue with curses and threats until he said he was going down to Special Services at Manheim and that he was writing Freddy Straub about it. Pearson rose to the bait and said that he was coming over to the club to take charge of things personally. Howie, with a little grimace, told him that he thought that it would be a good idea if he did, and to get his ass down there as fast as possible, otherwise he was going to have a riot on his hands. Meanwhile out in the main room the duo took a break and ambled off the stage to a dribble of applause. The mood of the club brightened up considerably when the DJ put on a Merle Haggard record.

We had a few Jack Daniels with Howie and the Night Manager while we waited for Jake's arrival. We did not have to wait long and within half an hour he cruised in with Erica in tow. He was a big man and like myself, had been a boxer in his youth. In fact at one time he had been some kind of major contender in his native Australia, but rumor had it that he'd won a fortune on the fight by backing himself to lose. So you know what kind of man we were up against. He looked very smart that night, in a pale gray French mohair suit, his face was flushed with the awkwardness of the situation he had come to sort out. As usual, he felt confident that the situation could be rectified with the injection of a few dollars and a Masonic handshake but this time it was too late, because by now the buzz had gone all round the club and Dokie and Wahoo had come over to watch the proceedings.

Sgt. Howie met him at the door and as Jake started to unroll a long 'Old Pals' explanation the Custodian told him brusquely that he had a surprise for him and led the way into the office.

"Hello Jake. Evenin' Erica," I said pleasantly.

His eyes popped open in shock, and Erica looked like she had contracted dysentery. For a moment longer he gaped and then exploded. "What the bloody 'ell you doin' 'ere Yonco? Yer supposed to be in France. Thought I told you to piss off and to stay out of my manor." His eyes popped open wide and he gaped at me. He came swiftly across the room but stopped short when he saw I was ready for him. Still watching him carefully, I said. "Well, Jerry, There you have it, right from the horse's mouth. Listen, Pearson. If you had fired me, why are you still using my name on your posters? You chiseling cheap piece of shit. I brought five musicians over here on your say so and did the last weekend of the first contract for nothing to get you off the hook at Ansbach. And this is how you pay your dues. You're a fuckin' snake. No wonder Special Services are trying to get rid of you."

He blustered on cursing and blaming everybody involved; finally he turned on the trembling Erica. "Its your bleedin' fault, ya stupid kraut dingo," he raved viciously," Ya shoulda known he'd go to that fat Nuremberg toad. Freddy Straub has been waiting for somethin' like this to pull my licence."

Before Erica could strike back, he turned on Dokie who was standing in the doorway enjoying every minute of the verbal battle. "An' yew, Dokie, yew fuckin' hillbilly, why don't yew get some stage clothes and put a good act together. 'Aven't yew got any clobber? This is supposed to be a class show, not a bleedin' pig roast."

Finally he moved to the other side of the table and let me have both barrels.

"An' yew' y'pommie bastard," he yelled, "I'll fix yew, Yonco. S'welp me I will. You're finished. Hear me? FINISHED. Y'll not work another show in Europe. I'll have yew blacklisted on every club. Just fuckin' try me, G'wan try me."

All this fury was getting to me and I had to force myself to stand my ground.

"Bollocks," I shouted, realizing that there was no way back now, "It'll take more than you to stop me, you dingo's dick. I'm ready, willing and fully equipped with the best band on the circuit and you, you thick bastard, can't see it, can you? Well, let me tell you this, Digger, Gisela Gunther would welcome us with open arms tomorrow and cough up more money than you. So you can stick your contract up your arse."

It all sounded grand, full of hard-nosed bravado, but inside I was shaking like a leaf, wondering if my threadbare bluff would work. We were down to our last options. I did not even have the money to get us back to England. Pearson was supposed to reimburse me on our arrival but there was not much chance of that now. I'd burned my boats now so I dug my heels in.

By now, of course the club had become almost a riot, with everybody arguing with everybody else, and Wahoo and Dokie back on the floor picking like mad at full volume, desperately trying to get some attention for their star. The night manager compounded the confusion by unthinkingly announcing that the house would pay for a round of drinks and that for the next half hour 'Happy Hour' prices would apply. Waitresses cursed the shouting punters and the bar staff went mad resetting the tills, because though the prices were cut, certain charges had to be adjusted.

Pearson and I were still raging at each other when he finally stormed out of the club, cursing everybody from the American ambassador down, and pushing the bewildered Erica in front of him. Howie was equally mad, but was trying to calm me down with liberal doses of J.D. while the band was busy downing as much free food and drink as they could, blissfully unaware of the uproar in the custodian's office. Tony had the temerity to shout "Evening' Jake" as Pearson stormed by him.

Meanwhile, Buddy Cagle our neglected, ignored, 'star', was sitting backstage dressed in one of Carl Belew's old Nudie rhinestone suits, wondering why his agent had sent him out on this military tour. He'd been doing quite well out at Lake Tahoe, so what was it all about? How was this tour of one-night stands going to do him any good? Nobody of any possible influence was likely to see him here at Gelenhausen NCO Club. He shook his head and slurped another CC.7. Eventually he did take the stage, but by that time the club was almost half empty, and in desperation the manager brought him off stage after twenty minutes and cleared the club. What a wild night. But it had been a good evening as far as we were concerned, though I don't think Jake would remember the night with relish, and I was too far–gone on the old sour mash to care anyway, so Kit prevailed on Sgt Howie for a twenty–dollar loan and drove us all home.

*   *   *   *   *   *

Back at the Anker Hotel things were getting precarious. The end of the month was looming up and Old Hans kept dropping hints that he was quite willing to be paid in dollars if we wished while, down at the Schwann, the landlord mentioned that Joe and Spud were into him for quite a few quid. Oh yes, things were getting tight and so far there had been no re-sponse from our spoiling visit to Hanau NCO Club. To keep the wolf from the door I did manage to sell an old Vox Ac 30 amplifier to a local musician for about $100 but that did not go far between six of us. Junker George took Kit out to dinner now and then, so that we got the latest news on the war of nerves that existed between the Pearson office and us. Eventually George let slip that they were expecting another big star in before the end of the month and made the tentative suggestion that I call the office. I decided to stall a little longer and told Kit to let him know that I had made an appointment to see Special Services at Manheim the coming Wednes-day.

Of course no such appointment existed and in fact I had no idea where the Special Services Office was. It was something that I had heard about in Sgt. Howie's office, but Jake the Jolly Swagman did not know that and this time the bluff worked because three days later I got a phone call from the Pearson office. It was Jake, all, sweetness and light.

"Well, Frank, me old mate," he wheedled "What's it all about, eh?"

I was very suspicious. Jake only called me Frank when he wanted some-thing, so I acknowledged his opening play with a noncommittal grunt.

"Y'know," he continued in his Aussie whine "We don't need all this agro do we, you an' me? I mean, up to this little misunderstanding we've always got on fine aven't we. I'm sure we can sort it out. Why don't y come down to the office eh? Say t'morra afternoon?"

Well there it was. We were back on the rails. I went down to the office, and signed new contracts, got my fares paid and some advance money and the following morning we were off to Ulm near Stuttgart with Buddy Cagle. I even got Woody Gosnell a few gigs as well. Buddy was not a bad guy, but he was out of his depth on the Military Club Circuit. A little too naive for the rough audiences in the EM and NCO clubs, although he was a very good–looking lad and attracted a big following from the gays. But the word was out on the circuit and a week later he was gone.

The band settled down and things in the village returned to normal. I settled the hotel bill and everybody drew some money. I managed to make a couple of payments on the bus. Down at the Schwann our bills were paid and we all got stuck into the haxels, bratwursts and beer again. A famous German record producer and composer called Karl Goetz heard about us and paid Kit to put down some back–up vocals him at his studio in Bergen Enkheim. On the way to the studio we passed one of Cecilia's 'Safe Houses' and there was a nice green Oldsmobile with U.S plates parked in the drive. She had obviously replaced her Blintganger.

There was only one more incident that year when the bus broke down at Kassel one stormy night. At about 3am I got a lift in a Citroen 2CV driven by a Belgian lunatic back to Frankfurt where I hired another van and drove back to the band waiting in an all–night café. A quick transfer then we were off to Chambley in France.

* * * * * *

12

HEARTBREAK HOTEL

By this time, the latter part of 1966, the French were getting a bit resentful of the American presence in their country and were busy introducing all kinds of petty restrictions, particularly in regard to border crossings, so for some obscure reason known only to the agency, we headed a touch north to a back road used by local farmers and slid quietly into de Gaulle's republic instead of the regular crossing at Saarbruken

It was a strange time. The agreement had already been made for the evacuation of all American Bases by the end of the year, so these tours were visiting only the units left behind to wind up the U.S. camps and transfer the equipment to Germany. In hindsight it was a typically pragmatic French decision. The country was divided and reeling from the political chaos in Algeria and something was needed to bring the people together behind the President, and de Gaulle, appealing to certain traits in the French character, and their desire to find another Napoleon, decided to get rid of the disturbing presence of the Americans by withdrawing from NATO, virtually cutting off his long Gallic nose to spite his face. If he had been a little more far-sighted, the great economic miracle that had galvanized Germany could also have happened to France. However, obviously there was no way that Uncle Sam would invest in a country that was giving his G.I.s the old heave-ho. It took the French economy another fifteen years to catch up.

Taking secondary roads, we rolled through the outer districts of the city of Metz and on to the N.A.T.O. base at Toul Rosier. From here we were directed to another installation at Chambley. I had always imagined France to be a beautiful place, but this featureless, flat countryside was miserable. Dank empty, neglected villages drifted by in the rain and mist, all of them forlornly offering a war-museum of sorts to the few tourists who were passing through, most of whom were military history buffs curious to find the truth about the 1870 war and visit the battlefields of Rezonville, St. Denis Privat or Thonville, with their equally dank and neglected cemeteries and vandalized war memorials.

However, once inside the base a different world emerged. All was wild gaiety. These were the last few months in France for the service personnel and everything had to go. For months now, from every part of the country, convoy after convoy of trucks had been shipping out essential equipment to Germany and what was left behind would either have to be used up or given to the French, and nobody wanted to leave anything for the Frogs, whom most Americans considered the world's biggest rip-off artists. The result was abandoned eating and drinking and using the allocated entertainment budget to import the best shows to make the tedium of waiting for the close-down less boring. Parties went on all night and girls were brought in from Paris and Nancy, as well as the usual local hookers from Metz. It was just like the Gold Rush. There was an abundance of everything, booze, food, fridges, freezers, and other equipment. Club furniture, fittings and carpets were either being sold to local hotels or shipped to friends in England. Every weekend there were bar owners from all over the region hanging round looking for good pick–ups while the station M.P.s became afflicted with temporary myopia as their liquid assets increased enormously.

At one of the Canadian bases further south, a demolition team had been brought in and the Army sappers set charges in everything that was left— buildings, mobile homes, military vehicles, and storage tanks—after which they boarded helicopters and watched everything go up with a bang. However, before the smoke had cleared, the French scavengers were scrambling through the wrecked fence, grabbing anything left of value. Conditions at Chambley and Toul Rosier eventually got so bad that they were reported to the H.Q. at Fontainebleau and the Provost Marshal sent down extra Military Police to sort things out, but by that time things were well beyond repair and it made very little difference.

One thing did however change. The Provost Marshall issued an order forbidding Third Country Nationals from being on the base overnight. This was of course aimed at the hordes of visiting street girls, but in the interests of diplomacy this was not made clear and we were also classed in the same capacity, so we had to go too. The N.C.O. Club manager was very helpful though and said the club would pay for our accommodation, and gave us the address of a small hotel in the village.

"You'll love it," he said. "Sort of quaint, ya know wadda mean?"

It was quaint all right. I've been in some fleapits in my time but this was right out of a horror movie. They'd told us at the Base that it belonged to an ex–Provost Sergeant who had taken his retirement over there and married the local beauty queen, but they neglected to tell us how long ago this event had taken place. However, on the strength of the Club Manager's recommendation I thought it would do nicely and churned off the base to find this phantom hotel on the Chambley Road.

It was dark. Very dark—I don't like the dark, and it was raining cats and dogs. The village green looked as deserted and dead as only French villages can do on those flat, soggy, plains around Verdun. There was not a light to be seen anywhere as I turned into the only street. I checked the address again. 'Hotel Mignon. Grand Rue' it said. Tony shone the flashlight up and down the dirty masonry and we spotted a scrabby sign hanging on desperately to a rusty iron bracket like a man on a cliff edge, creaking and banging as the storm tossed it about. It read. 'Hot–l M–gn–n'.

"Bloody 'ell. Is that it?" Joe spluttered.

We didn't take much notice. It was just his natural reaction. If you'd taken him to the Paris Ritz he'd have asked for a dartboard. Everybody grumbled moodily as we got out and stood in the pouring rain while Joe gave the door a good kicking. (He was good at that. He could have Door-Kicked for England). There was no bell or knocker and Joe was used to handling doors like this, so I gave him the go ahead to obtain entry. Several minutes of thudding brought a response from an upstairs window and a big bald head was stuck out into the storm and quickly pulled back again only to reappear covered in an army poncho. It was the ex.–NCO.

"Waddya want? It's gone midnight. "He bellowed

"We're from the base," I yelled back. "We've got rooms booked with you."

"Y'r too friggin' late. Scram," he retorted and turned to slam the window. I gave Joe the nod and he went to work again on the door panels.

The window shot open again and the poncho stuck out again. This time he was waving a stick and shouting louder. "G'wan piss off. Ah done tol' yew once Boy. Yoh too friggin' layte."

"C'mon, you awkward bastard," I shouted back through the raging storm, getting even wetter. "Get this soddin' door open or you won't have a door left."

There was the crash of shutters and another light appeared in a nearby window.

". Right," he roared, "Get back from that door or I'll send the dog down."

"Oh yeah?" Shouted Tony waving a can of Mace in the air. "Then I'll give it a smell of this. That'll put Bonzo off 'is bleedin' Bonios, wont it?"

"Right," yelled the Poncho. "That's it, Buddy. I've gotta a twelve gauge up here. So get y'r asses offa ma property."

"Listen, you dickhead," I said, now fully soaked and completely pissed off. "We've got rooms booked here and if you don't let us in I'm going to the Gendarmes. Not the M.P.s, the bloody Flics. Gottit? An' they'll make you open up tonight and close you down tomorrow."

At that we all piled back into the van and revved up the engine, opened all the windows and turned the radio on as loud as it would go. In a couple of minute lights began to come on around the village green.

From the upstairs room came the sounds of a violent argument in pidgin American followed by a clattering and banging from the hotel and eventually a light went on in a window next to the door. This appeared to be some kind of shop window with dozens of plants in pots and a strange collection of dusty antique furniture. The door creaked open and a huge woman stood there holding a smoking oil lamp.

"That must be the dog he was talkin' about," muttered Mel.

She weighed every ounce of 250lbs and was wearing a long flannel nightgown and an old tweed coat that would not fasten. Her sparse hair was trapped in large tin curlers and her heavily lipstick'd mouth opened to reveal a toothless cavity. She stepped out in the rain to give us a splutter-ing cursing but retreated quickly as the water from a large pool at the door soaked through her worn carpet slippers. As calmly as possible, I explained to her in French why we were there but it all fell on deaf ears, until I men-tioned the local gendarmerie, at which she burst again into a torrent of local dialect, which I could not understand. At one point I think she was going to slam the door on us, but Kit conveniently turned the radio up again and Madame looked in panic round the square and feverishly ushered us inside.

Inside was as bad as outside. Shreds of carpets, old plant pots, shabby, worn furniture and a wobbly staircase with whole treads missing, but we were all glad to be out of the rain and gratefully looked round. "Not bad, is it?" Said Joe, smiling. I had forgotten, but by his standards it wasn't bad at all. He was quite used to this' Auction Rooms' Art Deco. In fact it made him quite homesick.

Elbowing us out of the way, Madame mumbled something and we followed this huge dumpling of a woman up the rickety, weaving, staircase and into a long passage, where she sat down heavily at a table and fished out the obligatory registration cards to fill in, and she brightened up considerably when I produced the voucher for our accommodation from the NCO. Club. It was easy to understand why. The space for how many persons had been left blank and the form simply read 'The Frank Yonco Band'. I'll bet Madame Monster was up all night filling out phoney registration cards. At this point her husband put in an appearance carrying a real dog, a mangy poodle, that looked like a burst tea cosy, and asked us if we wanted a drink or a coffee. He didn't look much better than his missus but I'll bet he had a real John Wayne charm when they first met, sometime in 1944. The year that Madame had won her first—and last beauty contest. I said that I'd like a Jack Daniels, so he dug out a bottle of Black Label and we all had a snort before being allocated to our rooms.

Kit and I were given (so we were informed) the best room in the hotel, on the first floor on the front. It was indescribable. Appalling. And it confirmed all our earlier suspicions about us being in a horror movie. First of all, it was huge and the floor sloped like a cinema towards the storm-lashed rattling shutters. There was a large puddle in one corner where rain had run down the inside of the wall and in another corner crouched huge cast iron kerosene stove big enough for a crematorium. Against the back wall was a massive wardrobe of carved oak tilting dangerously where one castor had come off and by the side of the splitting doorframe loomed a monster bed with a sagging middle. We peeled back the faded, frayed cover to reveal a spotted, stained, quilted counterpane and damp light gray sheets with rips and clumsy darns all over them. We looked at each other in despair. I tried to light the stove to dry the damp flock pillows but it stank and hissed and proceeded to fill the room with fumes. So that was out. However before we could make a decision there was a loud crash from somewhere.

A few seconds after that there was a knock at our door. It was Joe.

"The bloody kharzi's broke, "He whispered,

"Oh yes? "I asked, "How did you break it. Then?"

"Wot's up? "Hissed Kit.

"He's only wrecked the bloody toilet."

"S'not my fault," he gasped, "It come off th' wall when I pulled th' chain."

We all trooped down the passageway to inspect the damage. At the corner we tiptoed past the master bedroom where the two heavyweight proprietors were having a snoring competition. I peeked into the toilet and sure enough, as Joe had told us, there it was on the floor, the cast iron cistern on top of a crumpled mass of piping and a big pool of dirty water seeping through the floorboards onto the ceiling below. It was draughty in there and looking up I saw why. There was no roof. The toilet was in what could have only been at one time, a small church tower, the top of which had been blown away in some long forgotten gale. There was nothing we could do and, realizing that the crash had not awakened the owners, we decided to play dumb and let them think that the storm had done the damage. Kit and I got dressed in all we possessed and piled on top of the bed till the morning. Mel was in a cupboard under the stairs and Tony was also having trouble. Finding that there was one leg off his bed he decided to kip in the van rather than share a bed with Joe and his socks. That night still rates as one of the most traumatic I have ever spent, although a few years later I came close to it a couple of times at show–biz digs in Birmingham and at a friend's house in Cornwall.

The rest of that French tour was spent in Paris, where we stayed in the heart of 'Hookerville' at the Mont Jolie Hotel on the Pigalle, and worked the NATO HQ at Fontainebleau. The shows were good but the mileages were killing. For example, at the end of this French trip we drove straight from Paris to Frankfurt and then, after six hours sleep, we were off again like crazy road hogs down the autobahns to Grafenwhor on the Czech border to play to hundreds of rough soldiers training there. It was also a German infantry depot and the second night we played to a packed hall of conscripts, who probably did not understand a bloody word.

As expected, I had a couple of 'Palace Insurrections', usually led by Joe who harboured secret ambitions to become a barrack–room lawyer or a Union leader. The nearest he ever came was a job at the local DHSS office in Oldham, where he could stand in judgment on his fellow man and obstruct as many dole payments to fellow musicians as possible. This rebellion was the usual thing that all bandleaders have to cope with from time to time. In this case the problem was money, and they cornered me in my room wanting to know what the contract was worth and why was I getting more than them? I tried explaining about bookings, contracts etc. but they said that they could do just as well as a group. So, seeing that there was no swaying them, I offered to sell them the P.A. system and described where to buy a van and other equipment and that if they wanted it, I would work at an agreed figure and would take a flat 10 per cent for all the bookings I came up with. How about that? There was a lot of mumbling but nobody decided to pick up my offer.

I once read that the great bandleader Woody Herman said he never kept a musician for more than two years. At the time I felt outraged at this view but I can certainly understand it now.

Smoke, Smoke, Smoke!
Tex Williams. Bobby Bare

The great Tex Williams was our next star. He was billed as a Nashville Artist, but in fact was not a Grand Ole Opry performer, who had built his career in Las Vegas and Hollywood, both as a singer and an actor, much in the same vein as Johnny Bond and Jimmy Dean. He came from Ramsey, Ohio, where as a young man he had damaged his hip in a car accident, making him walk with a permanent limp, which had kept him out of the U.S. Army in World War 2. He told me that because of this limp most of his movie career was done on horseback. A few years later I saw one of his B. Westerns and it was quite true. In the whole film you only saw him singing on stage or on a nag, never walking. He was a wonderful artist, the completely dedicated professional. A cultured and an impeccably mannered musician and an all round entertainer. Truly a 'Star' in every sense of the word, who showed up some of the One–Hit Wonders for what they were, primitive hicks with little talent or style and too much money.

Tex's biggest hit was of course 'Smoke, Smoke, Smoke' in the late '40s' and was followed up with other biggies like 'Dark Town poker club 'and 'That's what I like about the South '. All of which became standards in the years that followed and are continually featured with Country Bands to this day. In the Fifties he had a superb band called the Western Caravan, which almost completely swamped the fading Bob Wills Texas Playboys and came close to pushing Hank Thompson off his pedestal as King of the State Fairs.

This Western Caravan was a really big band, sometimes twelve piece, which often included future stars like fiddle virtuoso Billy Armstrong, Glen Campbell, Denny Mathis and the ill–fated Spade Cooley who ended up with a life sentence in the State Prison for the murder of his wife. Tex and his own wife Dallas developed their own Western Village Theme Park near Lake Tahoe, which they ran successfully for many years before it was destroyed in one of the disastrous bush fires that often sweep through those tinder dry Californian valleys. Pearson introduced us at Baumholder one afternoon and we immediately hit it off as friends. It was one of the best tours I remember.

Of course, it had its odd moments of stress, for instance, one night at the Officer's Club at Ramstein and anybody who has had experience of the US Military Circuit will tell you that Officer's Clubs are notoriously hard. On this occasion we were required to play through a formal dinner before the show, you know 'Music to Eat By'. What, with this powerhouse line up? Well, we tried to do the kind of thing they wanted, slow Jim Reeves songs with the odd Ray Price smoothie but the Base Commander' wife kept waving her hand to quieten us down more. These Army wives were not my favourite people and the most obnoxious examples of the breed were the brittle shrews that had married into the Officer Class. Oh yes, there is such a thing in the U.S. Military, though most people seem to imagine that this privileged species existed only in the British Army.

We stuck it out for about half an hour with me singing in a whisper while trying to hold onto a fixed smile at the chattering diners, and I could see that the boys were getting pissed off about my transferred signals for them to play quieter, when finally Mel Dean, our usually mild mannered drummer, blew his lid. "Right," he bellowed. "Right. If its got to be that bloody quiet, you don't need a soddin 'drummer." With that he did a full round on his kit as loud as he could, threw his sticks in the air and walked off the stand. There was a stunned silence at the table for a moment and a few inquiring heads turned to glare at us balefully, but apart from that nothing changed and they all got their snouts back in the trough and continued grunting as though nothing had happened. As the clatter of cutlery recommenced we struck off into 'Take these chains from my heart' sans drummer. Nobody noticed the difference. They would have been better off with a record player. The strange thing was that when Tex came on they were very animated, but were still very careful to take their lead in applause from the C.O and his wife.

Tex's shows were a knockout everywhere he went. There was a lot of Western Swing in his act and this band were very good at that kind of four to the bar swinging country. He told jokes and did imitations and some vocal acrobatics you would not believe. I recall one song called 'Born in the Bottom of a Mountain' in which he would finish on a very low note and after the applause he would say:

"Hey, Boys, let's do that again, only this time a tone lower."

And he did it at the bottom of his register his voice it was almost a basso profundo, as deep as a bassoon—marvellous. Some time later I asked him how he got those low notes on his recordings and he said that he always insisted on recording very early in the morning, sometimes being at the studios as early as five am. And he would not speak all the way there so that his vocal chords would be completely relaxed when he started to sing. Very impressive, I can tell you. One night he took us all out to dinner at the revolving restaurant at the top of the Henninger Tower in Frankfurt. Truly a Star in every sense of the word.

Of course Jake tried to squeeze the extra dates out of him, even booking the show in a German Circus. That was a bloody joke, setting up on the sawdust, trying to avoid the zebra droppings and playing with two thirds of the audience looking at the backs of our heads not understanding a word. Great. Only Jake could've thought that one up. He flew us into Berlin for four days, landing at the old Templehof Airport, which is like trying to put a plane down in the middle of a high-rise city suburb. Whoaa.

* * * * * *

Bad Vilbel

It was time to move on from the dear old Anker Hotel. Old Hans had decided that he could not stand the stress of all these wild musicians, so we moved up the road to a small town called Bad Vilbel. It was very pleasant, with a few shops, a real castle with its own moat, and a nice open–air swimming pool. Kit got a flat over a butcher's shop and the boys moved into the annex at the back. Spud decided to return to Liverpool for a month to nurse his broken heart and await the transatlantic summons on the Cast Iron Shore, so I brought out a guitarist called Ady from Manchester. He was very good and Joe decided to go over on to bass and leave the lead–work to him. Which suited me fine. He added a new dimension to the music and his solid backings enabled Joe to sing more of the 50's Rock and Roll songs he loved. Well, he did look a bit like Buddy Holly.

Everybody liked living in Bad Vilbel and as Cecilia's house was en route to downtown Frankfurt, the old flames were rekindled. Tactfully I did not mention the Toronado and, as the relationship between us was now on a much more platonic basis, I assumed that she was still getting her new rations courtesy of the P.X. She seemed concerned about the slowness of my finance payments on the V.W. bus, so I took her to tea at Frankfurt Zoo to explain that the bloody thing kept breaking down and that I was behind on the 'Chukky' because I had to hire vehicles to replace it. She was very understanding and, at her suggestion, off we went of to Autohaage, the Frankurt Ford dealers. Since its mystery breakdown, the VW bus had been in a garage in Kassel waiting for some bits, so I did a deal with the Frank–furt garage that took it in part exchange for a brand new Ford Transit minibus. Apart from being the first new vehicle I had ever owned, it was one of the first Transits produced as it had the old Taunus V4.1300cc. en–gine. Later models had bigger engines but in such a big vehicle it was not too bad if you had a following wind. Once again I promised to keep up the payments and my friend signed the papers. Yes, Cecilia was very good to me.

*   *   *   *   *   *

Some Very Bad Times

The new truck's first duty was to go back to Manchester to pick up our dependants, my wife and son, and Joe's family and what a trip that was. We had a deadline to meet, so the whole thing had to be done in three days from Frankfurt to Manchester and back again. And to add to the complication, Joe did not drive. After a nightmare trip we arrived back at Bad Vilbel, where I had fixed up a flat for my family and got Joe a place out of town. Our flat was on the first floor of a modern but gloomy big house and, to be honest, none of us liked it very much. On the ground floor lived the owner, a widow and her son, a paranoid teenage loony who played Nazi records and bullied Francis whenever he got the chance. In a short time both Sylvia and I knew it was not going to work, and the rot began to set in when, in spite of my careful planning, we were sent down to do a house-band job at Ansbach, some 300 miles away, which meant that I could only get back home a couple of days a week. It was very difficult for them. There was enough money, but Sylvia did not speak German, and in a small town like Bad Vilbel the locals were not all that helpful. She did her best to make it work, as I did, but what with the out of town job and the requirement to keep the band working, I could not give them the attention necessary.

I did get back from Ansbach for Christmas with Syl and Francis, but it was not a good Christmas, the classic Xmas dinner not being part of the German festivities, but we did manage to get a meal of sorts at the Kurpark Hotel in Bad Vilbel. It was now quite clear that my Grand Scheme had misfired and the last straw came when I had to leave them again to go back down to Ansbach. Sylvia was very brave and made a supreme effort to adapt. She attempted to go shopping in Frankfurt only to get lost and end up in Mainze Kastel on the other bank of the river. In the end it all got too much for them and on one of the saddest nights I have known, I watched them pull away from Mainze Station heading for Ostend on the Trans European Express. After many problems they arrived back in the UK where Sylvia became very ill and had to spend time in hospital.

The whole episode was terrible and a matter of lasting regret to me.

PICKER'S TIP 17

On a long gig of say, 4 x 45 minute sets, if you find yourself short of songs do the first set again. Nobody will notice. And if they do tell them its a request.

13

BACK TO THE BASES
Bobby Bare, Don Gibson, Melba Montgomery, George Jones, Dave Dudley, Kay Adams, Bob Morris, and Faye Harden

After that Tex Williams tour, our drummer Mel left to pick up his Rochdale residency, so I got my mother to put an advert in the Melody Maker for a replacement. I phoned her a couple of weeks later and she said that a nice lady had answered on her son's behalf. She was a very refined lady my Mum said, from Sale in Cheshire. Very posh, Ohoo. So her son must be a nice boy and she had given him the job and all I had to do was pick him up at Frankfurt Bahnhof. So the following Wednesday we went to pick him up and, to put it mildly, he came as a bit of a shock. His name was Paul, about six foot four, thin as a rake with a shock of red curls to his shoulders, wearing very tight jeans and the biggest pair of yellow desert boots I've ever seen. Still, he was a very good drummer and sitting behind his kit he didn't look all that bad.

This 'Texas Drifters' line up was a particularly good one and the range of our music expanded to encompass Rock standards and Western Swing numbers. I did not have moody Dokie to contend with any more, so I could do a range of imitations and the boys put together some nice instrumentals. It was while we were on this house–band circuit that we met one band who had been working in France for Pearson and his partner Johnny Fitzgerald, on starvation wages for six months, and were now literally living in the stables of a hotel in Freiberg, still waiting to be paid. We did what we could to help them with a bit of spare cash to get food and booze, etc. The agency let enough money trickle through to keep the group ticking over and later we heard that in the process of squeezing the last drop out of them Jeff had sent them to do job in Luxembourg for a week. Because they had to cross the border, he had rented a nice new bus for them and given them the papers for it, so they did the gig, subbed $500 from the club manager and turned west and kept going till they were back home in Oldham, where they sold the bus for the outstanding pay due to them. Hooray.

It was from this band that we heard about Jake's final escapade in France

OK, Froggy. Jes' spin the wheel

When things were almost wound up there by the U.S. Military, the time came to make final payments to the suppliers and agents who had been providing entertainment on the bases. Jake got to know early, via a mole that worked at SHAEF HQ at Fontainebleau, and shot off to Paris to collect his outstanding money ahead of the competition. Nothing was heard from him for several days and down at the agency office they anxiously wondered what had happened. Finally at around 2 am. A week later Erica Pearson got a garbled phone call at their Frankfurt apartment. It was from Jake in Paris. He was calling from one of the city's top hotel casinos.

"'Ello. Ello. That yew Erica? Yeah, s'me. Jake."

Erica groaned as she recognized the signs.

"Ja, Jake, you okay? Ven you comin' back? Vere are you? Hef you got zee money?

Oh Jake, effer'body's vorried 'bout you. Ven you coming back?"

"Naw. Naw, Erica jes' listen. No friggin' worries eh? Ho, ho. Have I got the money? Let me tell ya. *Have I got the money?* Not 'arf.

Now, Erica, listen and jes' do what I tell ya, right? Get 'ere as quick as yer can. Charter a bloody plane outa Rhine Maine if yer have to. Anythin'. I've got 'em on the run 'ere. I'm over eighty–five grand up and on a roll. Eighty–five friggin' thousand. Wotcha think 'bout that, eh?. Wot? Naw, not francs, Erna, U.S. dollars. Green cabbage. So get out here quick."

Mrs. Pearson went white. She'd heard it all before and choked on her reply as Jeff said that he was going back to the tables now and he'd meet her taxi from the airport.

As soon as the line went dead she rang Junker George and ordered him to drive to Paris right away as fast as the Mercedes could go to pick up his boss and bring back whatever remained of their money. George got to Paris at eight in the morning to find Jeff sitting in the porter's lodge of the Casino Imperial. He'd lost the bloody lot, including his Crombie overcoat. One the way back to Frankfurt, he bribed George to silence and told his partner that he had not collected the three months' money the U.S Army owed them. His partner went to his grave eighteenth months later still frantically trying to find out what had happened to his cash.

'Oh, Lonesome Me'

Sensing how the wind lay, we changed agencies. One evening Gisela Gunther's office manager Leo Ferretti caught our show at an EM. Club at Guetleute Strasse, Frankfurt and offered us a nice deal with them at the end of our current contract. Gisela's was probably, at that time, the pre–mier agency in Germany, although Jake Pearson's set–up was a close second, with the other Wiesbaden based agencies bringing up the rear. I told Jake at the end of the month and I don't think he minded letting us go all that much. It had always been very much an up and down relationship between us anyway and he knew that I would work for him again if the offer was right. To be honest, I think also that the collapse of the 'Inter Bank' in Frankfurt around that time influenced me a little. Junker George told Kit that a good bit of Jake's loot went down with it, so I figured it would be prudent to make a move.

There then followed a number of short tours with people like George Jones, Melba Montgomery, and Don Gibson. All of them traumatic experi–ences. First George, out of his head on booze, smashed his Gibson Hum–mingbird guitar against a pillar on stage in the middle of his first number because it was out of tune and then sang 'Seasons of my Heart' three times on the run. Then foul–mouthed Melba was cussing out the band and changing her mind about her program as she walked on stage, throwing songs in that she had written on the plane coming over. But the real prize was the short time we spent with Don Gibson. What a banana he was.

The Don Gibson Show was combined Gunther–Pearson booking at the Topper Club, in Frankfurt. We had set up and started the opening spot at 9.30 p.m. expecting our star to be on stage at 11 p.m. Well, it was 12.45 a.m. and we were well into our third spot still playing when Don finally turned up, stoned out of his head with a Kaiser Strasse dolly on each arm. He was eventually pushed on stage wearing his sloppy green jacket with a guitar in one hand and his bow tie in the other. He stopped and stared in silence at the audience for a good two minutes before disposing of his bow tie by throwing it into the audience, rambling off into his current record called 'Lonesome Number One' which went down quite well, considering the crowd had been waiting since 8.30 to hear him. Then he grinned vacantly round at us and broke into 'Oh Lonesome Me ', his number one hit, which got the audience warming to him. Mouths dropped open however when at the end of the song, he gazed bemusedly at the packed clubroom, slurred. "G'night Folks," and lurched off, exiting stage left. That was it, two songs and then 'Goodnight Campers'.

We struck up our signature tune, Nashville West and trailed off after him while the audience looked on expectantly, thinking that this was part of the show. A regular bit of 'shtick' that performers indulge in to milk the applause—but this time the Star's departure was for real. The stage was empty and it was a good five minutes before the crowd became restive and the sound of stamping feet began to rumble through the auditorium. As we sat backstage sipping on Buds and yakking, we could hear the Club Custodian going bananas at our North Carolina star. He was yelling at Don to get back on stage and finish his act. He was being paid $3000 to do 30 minutes. What the fuck did he think he was playing at? Don looked confused and rolled his eyes skyward and then turned to the foaming official

"Oh yeah?" He slurred. "Didn't I do 'Oh Lonesome Me'?"

"Yeah, you did," replied the apoplectic manager "What the hell's that gotta do with it? Jess' get back out there an' finish your show."

Dazed and completely unconcerned Don replied. "Waal, Ole Buddy, Tha's what they come t' hear, ain't it? Tha's my last song. My number one, Man. That's the close out. Y'unnerstan'?" And then, with the two women hanging onto him, he stumbled down the metals steps at the rear of the club and off into the darkness, leaving the Club Custodian and the Night Managers to handle the turmoil.

As Chet Atkins once observed about him.

"After 'Oh, Lonesome Me', Don never looked back.

And after 'I Can't Stop Loving You', he never looked straight."

Chet always did have a way of putting things.

Once, at an awards ceremony in the sixties, the flamboyant chart topping Webb Pierce was holding forth about his new Nashville mansion and how he had a swimming pool shaped like a guitar. To which Chet replied,"That's nothing, I've got one shaped like an amplifier. Had it for years."

PICKER'S TIP 18

On the road when loading your van, pack the drum-kit last. It takes longer to set up than anything else; therefore it should be first bit of gear unloaded at the gig.

The German Circuit

As the winter of 1966-7 closed in we spent a lot of time with the American band, The Hometowners, led by a bass player called Pat Patterson who, like many County singers, held Ray Price in great esteem and did a lot of his material. It was one of those superb bands made up mostly from ex-G.I.s who had stayed on after their service and married German wives. Dokie was back with them as front man and the net result was musically superb, but the rest of it left a bit to be desired.

They were all wild. They had a big Chevrolet bandwagon, which was usually knee-deep in empty bottles, and beer cans and they took turns driving it as fast as possible. They used to let their drummer Blind Norman, who had only five per cent vision, take the wheel on the straight bits, with Billy Poe the steel player sitting beside him giving him directions, like:

"A bit to the left Norman. That's right, we've passed them trucks now. Bang the hammer down. Yeah that's it." And everybody would whoop and holler as the speedo needle hit 140 k ph. Talk about crazy.

On one long run, back from New Ulm, Dokie was at the wheel and, when he checked in the mirror, he noticed that everybody else was fast asleep. He too was tired and not a little bored at having no one to talk to so he pulled into a lay-by and gently stopped. To avoid waking anybody, he slipped the gearbox into neutral, jammed the gas pedal down with one of the ever-present beer bottles and snuggled down for a kip. After about half an hour, he awoke refreshed to find the band still sleeping soundly, so he eased the Chevy back onto the autobahn and headed north. They were all quite surprised to find how late it was when they pulled into Frankfurt.

They were touring at the time with Billy Walker, while we were playing support for Dave Dudley, who had brought with him his own four-piece band the Road Runners. Dave was a terrific entertainer and only did about a half a dozen songs in his 60-minute cabaret act, but the patter in between was superb, from anecdotes about Nashville to raunchy truck driver's jokes and imitations. He flat refused to pay homage to the Grand Ole Opry or the Old Nashville Establishment, who had some very reactionary views about the music. Dave had come up through the wide open honky–tonks and the dockside bars of the Great Lakes, where tough fishermen and lumberjacks let their hair down and had little time for the schmaltz and phony emotion of Music City USA. At one point in his act, he did a little take–off of Kitty Wells, calling her the 'Queen of Country Music', adding caustically that she had not always been 'The Queen', as Whispering Bill Anderson had also held the title for a couple of years. And Porter Waggoner had come in second.

Our Star attractions on the next tour were Bob Morris and his wife, Faye Hardin, who were a very good Las Vegas type Country duo. He was the co–writer of the hit 'Tequila' and she was a great singer. One of his stage tricks was with a Fender Stratocaster, where, by moving his wrists and working the tremelo arm, made it look as if he was bending the guitar neck. For some reason Ady hated them. He was probably a bit jealous of Bob's playing.

We moved our base to Wiesbaden, where we literally took over a hotel in the suburb of Sonnenburg. The owners were away and had left their son in charge. He was a music–mad 18 year old we had met in the Big Apple Club, who invited us to stay there for free in return for him and his girl friend travelling to the gigs with us.

The arrangement suited us fine, but it quickly degenerated into a complete bacchanal with all–night parties and everybody getting their own drinks from behind the bar and bringing along any old pals they came across. Of course it all ended in tears when Mutte und Papa Hoffman came home from Spain a few days earlier than expected and found their elegant biergarten littered with junk and drunken musicians and their son out of his head on marijuana.

On other nights off we would go to a hangout called the Vagabond's Club. It was a late–night bar near the Quellenhof Hotel, where the acts would congregate for a drink and a chat after their gigs. There was a notice board with messages from people all over the world which was used as an information exchange about international gigs. There were some great characters there like Jat Harad, a virtuoso violinist, turned comedian, who had a very nice lifestyle, spending his summers on the U.S. Military circuit in Europe and his winters on the cruise ships. It was great place, and the acts would often get up on stage and do a spot. The best ad–libber, by far, was Chuckles Walker, a black comic with a wicked sense of humour. We were with him on a package show at the Topper Club one night when he was being hassled by some cracker in the audience who kept interrupting his act. Finally, Chuckles stopped his patter and told the heckler to stand up if he had something to say and when he did, Chuckles had a spotlight pick him out and announced to the audience.

"Gentlemen. You've all felt one in the back of a car—that's what it looks like."

At which point the cursing heckler stomped out, to a chorus of laughter and catcalls.

Dee Donovan, too, was a great entertainer whom we did a few shows with at the beginning of 1967 in southern Germany. He was a top–class showman, who eventually went on to a great career in Australia. I shall be eternally grateful to him for the introduction to Bushmills single malt Irish whisky. What a wonderful drink. (Sadly proscribed for me these days). We had a few boozy skirt–chasing nights out together in the stews of Wiesbaden that I remember clearly. I don't actually recall who was involved or where we went, but I do know that we ended up at the Vagabond's Club and that we had a pretty good time.

British bands continued to arrive on the circuit, although not many country bands, its true, mostly they were 'Showbands' from the Northern Cabaret Club scene. Usually we met them at the monthly auditions held by Special Services to appraise, evaluate and check the entertainment on quality.

It was here we came across acts like 'The Performing Lees' a comedy band from Yorkshire, who later found fame as 'The Brothers Lee' on British TV in the 70's. My old friend Karl Denver came out with his trio, as did Lonnie Donegan, and from Scotland came superb acts like 'The Saracens' and 'Eck and the Echoes', who later changed their name to Scotch and Soda. This group combined solid rock n' roll with Scottish traditional music, featuring kilts, bagpipes and a sword dance. And many more came out to where the pickings were so good.

Quite a few British comedians arrived too, but it was not always a successful move, American humor being different than the British. Often comedians bred in the 'Clubland' tradition could not adapt to international audiences, as I found out to my cost a little later. The best of these British comedians was a Londoner called Dickie Bennett, whose act was fast and slick in that punchy Las Vegas style. He lived in great style in Majorca and flew in to do his tours.

As far as the regular house band scene was concerned, this was a mainly dominated by Balkan and East Europeans, who, if they were not actually cheaper, usually carried more personnel and could come up with a bigger sound. 'The Istanbul Five' from Turkey were doing great business back then around the Stuttgart area. The local German bands tended to follow the old tried and tested patterns of swing and jazz, but a few more progressive ones were into Soul and Tamla Motown, and some would pay big money for black girl singers. With typical Kraut efficiency they came up with the classic mix of organ, bass–guitar and miked–up drums for the back line, with brass, sax and electric guitar on the front. With the addition of a couple of singers augmented by taped harmony backings, the result was usually very good, producing bands like 'The Freddys' and 'Kontact', and laying down the foundations for the world famous bands of Klaus Wunderlicht and James Last.

An altogether different approach came from a German rock–soul outfit called 'Shotgun' led by a good–looking but tarty girl singer who took things to the limit, stripping down to her underwear and topping things off by giving the mike stand a good screwing, while rolling all over the stage moaning and gasping in a mock orgasm, which went down very well with the servicemen. If you were on the show with her, however, she was a right cow, doing all she could to wreck your act by coming onstage and gesturing at the audience. If all else failed she would kick out all your amp plugs in a fit of wild temper and frustration at somebody getting HER applause.

Usually, in those days the clubs had Country Music at least one night a week as well as the regular visiting Star Spectaculars. There were still a fair number of G.I. bands working but by now there was a big difference in the standard with many ex–servicemen forming professional bands that could travel and rehearse free of duty rosters. This was a far cry from the old G.I. groups that were usually just one good musician and four chancers. If you want to get an idea of what these early groups sounded like check out an album by the Statler Brothers called 'Lester Moron and the Cadillac Cowboys.' But the new bands were something else. Shell Bowling's band comes to mind. He was a huge guy who looked like Hoss Cartwright from TV's Bonanza. He sang well and did a hell of a show. He led his band on bass and that Fender Precision looked like a mandolin in his massive hands, but if you sing the songs and play bass in the band, you can't lose. Bob Maphis (brother of the famous guitarist Joe Maphis) and his family also had a band working for Pop Phillips out of Kaiserslautern, as did Buddy Jackson who claimed to be the elder brother of another famous re-cording artist Stonewall Jackson.

At that time Gisela Gunther did not have any major artists coming in and, knowing my reluctance to do house–band jobs, put us out on loan to German American Agency in Wiesbaden, a town we came to love. The agency had originally been run by Charlie Klop, but was now run as a joint venture by two British ex–performers—Charlie Woods, a black song–and–dance man from London, and Ronnie Harris, a former bass player and singer who had had a hit in the '50s with 'The story of Tina'. Unfortunately his promising career had been eclipsed by the arrival of Ronnie Hilton on the scene, a singer in the same style.

Charlie Woods was a real gentleman, whom I trusted implicitly, though I could not honestly say I felt the same about his partner, who was closer to Jake Pearson in reliability. They had a tour booked with Kay Adams, an ex–Buck Owens vocalist from Vernon in Northern Texas. She was an ex-cellent singer with the usual double standards associated with the species. This time, the chosen one was not a musician but a fair cross section of NCOs, custodians and night managers. Kay told Kit some horrific tales about the humiliations she suffered on the road with some of the bands. The boss's word was law. She either did exactly what she was told, with whom she was told, or it was 'On y'r bike', and she was regularly reminded, there were plenty of girls from hick towns waiting in line for such a high-flying band jobs. Fortunately, with Owen's Buckaroos, she found a protector in Don Rich, Buck's guitarist and fiddle player, but after his untimely death in a motor cycle accident, she was forced to move on and tried her luck as a single act. The current fashion for truck–driving songs enabled her to become 'The Truck Driver's Queen' and she made some good recordings, her biggest hits being 'Big Mack 'and 'The Girl In the Little Pink Mac'. She was very good, but little was heard of her after returning to the States, though she must have been very durable, for in the late 1980's she did a successful European tour.

The Good, the Bad and the Beautiful

Around this time a low budget movie by Serge Leone called 'The Good, the Bad, and the Ugly', took the film industry by storm and rocketed a supporting player from a soap called 'Rawhide' to international stardom. From that day forward the world would identify Clint Eastwood as King of the Spaghetti Westerns, so it seemed natural to put together a variety show called 'The Good, the Bad, and the Beautiful', with my old friend Reliable Ralph. The idea was a simple one, with me, Kit, and the band doing the music, Ralph doing the comedy and his stripper girlfriend, Tiffany Jones, doing her exotic dancing routine.

This was great, except for one important fact. Ralph had not bothered to tell her about it. I sent off the publicity (including photos) and Gisela Gunther booked it and the show was advertised in the club magazines. Everything seemed fine until about a week before our departure, when a sheepish Ralph admitted that he had only just mentioned it to Tiffany and she'd gone bananas. She was already booked for shows and did not want to leave her infant daughter and threatened to boot Ralph out if he went without her. So, some quick shuffling had to be done. Our bass player's girl friend, Jackie, was roped in to do the dancing and we went scouring the clubs for a replacement comic. At a Miner's Club in Wigan I found one who I thought might do. His material was a bit suspect but his singing close-out was an imitation of Norman Wisdom. So I decided to take a chance.

The first show was in Bremen and was a complete disaster.

It turned out Jackie's idea of exotic dancing was to cover herself with silk scarves and wobble about, and the comic's jokes were mainly scatological, talking about his wife's worms etc. and topping it off with his Norman Wisdom tribute. The silence was deafening. By the time we hit Frankfurt the news was out and the cancellations began. Club custodians were complaining about the toilet jokes and the wobbling well covered–up dancer, and they wanted to know who this fat guy wearing the tight suit and skew–whiffed cap was supposed to be, and who the hell was Mr Grimsdale? They had never heard of Norman Wisdom. What a mess.

In the end I cut the comic's spot to ten minutes and let Jackie do one number and we did our normal show. That ten–day trip felt like two months. The comic said he couldn't understand it. Everybody in Wigan thought he was terrific and they loved his Normam Wisdom. Bloody Yanks. They had no idea of comedy.

With my family gone, I went further off the rails. I was drinking heavily, half the time not knowing where I was, and if hadn't been for Kit I would have blown everything. I was making quite a bit of money, but my unruliness was also making waves at Manheim Special Services office. I got in a fight one night at Ansbach after the show, almost wrecking the backstage area of the NCO Club, and it was only the intervention of the custodian, Lee Lomas, who was a friend of Tex Williams, that prevented me from being slung in the stockade and barred from the circuit. It was time for a new deal and I started looking around.

About the only thing on offer was a trip to Turkey that nobody else seemed to want, so I decided to take a chance on that. This news was the last straw for Joe, who packed his gear and camped out on the steps of the British Consul in Frankfurt with all his family until they repatriated them back to Oldham. I tried using an ex–GI, but he was a disaster, so I contacted Spud in Liverpool, who seemed to have recovered from the Mary Taylor debacle, and after much umm–ing and aah–ing his Mum let him come out to join us again. I imagined the sensuous fleshpots of mysterious Istanbul and exotic Levantine nights, but it turned out to be different. Oh yes, a lot different.

PICKER'S TIP 19

When using monitor speakers make sure that the drummer can hear what is going on, particularly the lyrics. The drummer can add to the dynamics of a song by providing light and shade. He is not there only to bang out a beat. You can get a machine to do that. Monitor speakers are not just for the benefit of the singer. Listen to the top guys like Stavros Jackson, Peter Haige or especially Dave Marks playing on my 'Live at the Nashville' album and you'll hear what I mean.

14

THE TURKEY TROT

U.S. Early Warning Station Dyarbakir, Turkey. That's what it said on the contract but where the hell was Dyarbakir? Ronnie Harris was very confident and flippant about the whole deal, as though it was the kind of thing that he did everyday. "Just a bit farther on from Greece," he said—In fact it was a bloody long way from Greece and a long way back from the twentieth century.

At that time there was a big hustle on with the agents. Rumor had it that the lucrative club–booking market for the whole Middle East was coming up for grabs because of the current Persona Non–Grata status of the main booking agent for that region. This situation was all due to one of the Night Managers of the NCO. Club at Athena Air base, Athens, getting nervous about his pension and blowing the whistle on his boss to Special Services about the kick–backs (currently running at $200–$500 or more per show) being paid by the agents to the club bookers. Everybody knew that it was going on, in fact it had always been an accepted practice, but when somebody actually puts it in writing to the Provost Marshall's office, something has to be done. And naturally, at the first hint of the man's bad luck, all the other agents and fair–weather friends were in like a school of piranhas.

It was quite a big area, with bases stretching right across the North African coast from Tunis to the beachside casino and club at Weelus near Tripoli, and further afield to Ethiopia and Turkey, so the prize was well worth fighting over.

I had my first taste of Middle East procrastination when we visited the Turkish Consulate in Frankfurt for the required visas. It took four days coming and going and a few well–greased palms to get the paperwork in order, but eventually we were off down the autobahn towards the Austrian Tyrol. We had three days to get there, so it was a case of changing drivers and keeping moving. There were five of us on this trip, Ady, Paul, Spud, Kit, and myself. With the exception of Ady, we all drove, so it did not seem to be that big a challenge.

The route went south–east through Wutzburg, Nuremberg, Lintz and ever eastward to Graz. At Bad Gastein we took the mountain tunnel towards Italy. This was an experience in itself, as we drove onto a line of flat–bed wagons and stayed in the bus as it was chained down, and hurtled backwards through the rattling darkness. At the other end, high in the Austrian Alps near Spittal, we consulted our map and decided to avoid Trieste and the coast road and headed for Klagenfurt and the Yugoslavian border post at Maribor. This certainly was not tourist country but more like the old Balkan lands I'd read about. The border guards at Maribor directed us onto the motorway, the Autoput, as they called it, which turned out to be a two–lane strip of concrete across a muddy, featureless plain. Petrol stations were few and far between and we had our first mind–bending experience of oriental toilets—squatters with two footplates and a hole in the ground.

We pushed on through Zagreb and stopped for a few hours in Belgrade, where we had a meal in a self–service café. It was strange, because after we paid the cashier, a waiter picked up our tray of goulash and led us to a table where he smiled through his huge moustache waiting for a tip. I gave him a dollar and you'd think he'd won the lottery as he shuffled off bowing and beaming, to flash his new–found wealth to all his friends. None of the chairs in the café were the same, some old cane and others garish red plastic, and the tablecloths were a grayish–white with darns and patches, but the food was excellent, certainly the best Hungarian goulash I have ever had—better than in Hungary itself. It was as though they were stuck in some time–warp, a situation we rapidly became accustomed to. The town bristled with communist posters and slogans and quite a few grim-looking armed militiamen, but the ordinary people were warm and friendly towards us and formally polite to each other. While the State stores were empty of goods, the open air markets were busy and well stocked with everything from cabbages to second–hand shoes.

There was some delay at the Bulgarian frontier but soon we were out of Dimitrovgrad and cruising into Sofia, where we booked into a hotel. A very nice hotel it was too and very cheap. While drinking in the bar, we were approached by an official who asked us if we would like to do some shows for the State Circus. Not a lot of money, he said, but he could throw in some beautiful furs and wolf skin coats that we could sell in the West to supplement our pay. I would have liked to stay, but we had to push on to meet our contract start date. I was enjoying the trip. The fuel was all paid for and if we arrived late, well, we could always blame the border guards. Plovdiv came next with Ady doing his best to persuade us to take a long diversion north into the forbidding Carpathian Mountains to find Dracula's Castle, or the palace of Vlad the Impaler. Bulgaria was very beautiful, with mile after mile of majestic pine–covered mountains, with very good roads and some fascinating roadside inns. We picked up the river Dvina and followed the spectacular Sicevacka Gorge, with the highway ducking in and out of short tunnels as we followed the rivers twisting course, our road paralleled on the opposite bank by the State Railway. Six hours later, after skirting the Greek border, we arrived at Edirne, the Turkish frontier crossing. This was where we met our guide, a young Scotsman with reced-ing red hair and a bushy moustache, who turned out to be about as good a driver as Junker George. He booked us in at the town's main hotel, where we had to wait two days for some more paperwork to be completed, so we used the time mooching round the historic old town.

Situated where it was, right on the border, Edirne or Adrianopolis as it had been called, had constantly changed hands, at times Greek, Bulgarian, and Turkish, with the added disadvantage of being the route for invaders from both directions. It probably did not look much different when the

Crusaders passed through on their way to the Holy Land 600 years earlier. Only two of its main streets were paved, the rest being just tracks ankle deep with dust in summer and muddy quagmires in the winter. Down by the banks of the River Metic was a jumble of rickety shacks and open-fronted shops, where leather workers, blacksmiths and carpenters plied their trades, as their forefathers had done for generations. It was hard to believe that this was in twentieth century Europe.

That night we had a few beers with our new courier, who gave us the good news that we were now in Turkey and only had a further 1500 kilometres to go before we arrived at our gig, a US Early Warning Station deep in Kurdistan at Dyarbikir near Lake Van in East Anatolia, about 50 miles from the Soviet border. Oh lovely. Just what we needed. Another stretch of non-stop driving into a wild region riddled with blood-feuds and a semi-official but permanent civil war going on. We did a little show that evening in the hotel lounge and the following morning we were off to Istanbul. The road was quite good, much better than those in Yugoslavia, and very busy with huge heavy trucks and pick-ups loaded high with produce. By early evening we were rolling under the massive triple wall defences of Topkapi on the outskirts of the worlds most mysterious city.

The place was buzzing, with traffic rushing everywhere with a total disregard for the most basic traffic laws. The noise was deafening as police whistles fought with roaring diesels, honking klaxons, yelling street vendors and cursing 'Dormush' taxi drivers in their battered big American Fords and Chryslers. Nobody seemed to care as vehicles jostled for position banging into each other. At one point I saw a big Chrysler Impala shoot right behind a flatbed truck sadly misjudging his turn and ripping off an entire rear fin but nobody stopped. There was a lot of yelling and fist waving. We watched in amazement, but Rennie said that it was quite an everyday occurrence. He did however give us a warning about the 'Dormush' taxis. If you were in one of those chequered deathtraps and there was an accident, the only thing to do was to get out and run, because in the eyes of the Police and other parties involved you were to blame. To their Islamic reasoning, if you had not ordered the taxi it would not have been there to have a crash. Therefore you were the root cause of the accident. In'sh Allah.

There were more papers to be inspected and the usual two-day delay while bribes were demanded and haggled over, so we used the time to do all the tourist things. We saw the St. Sofia mosque and other famous buildings and the vast cisterns that held the fresh water in times of siege. In a pavement café near the City Hall in the Aksary district we had our first taste of Turkish food, which I liked very much, particularly the lamb kebabs, halva and those fragrant savory pancakes called lachmaljun. There was no Bosphorus Bridge in those days and we crossed the strait on one of the wallowing little ferryboats that plied between the dockside at Beyoglu to Uskadar on the Asian side.

Anatolia

It was dusk on March 2nd 1967 when we bumped up the ramp and began our journey across Anatolia, following almost exactly the route of Alexander the Great over two thousand years previously. This was the famous Conqueror's Road. The main road to Turkey's official capital started well but soon deteriorated into the pot-holed, rambling two-lane rock-strewn country road that we had come to expect. There was still snow on the Taurus Mountains and in parts the landscape looked a little like Switzerland with deep meadows, belled cattle and goats and steep roofed wooden chalets. We all took turns at the wheel, except Ady who did not drive and would not sleep, but sat there chain-smoking and wondering what was going to happen to him next. In the whole two-day journey he did not sleep once and, by the time we reached our destination, his eyes were bugged out like organ stops.

Sometime in the early morning as we topped a rise in the distance we caught sight of Ankara, a chain of lights nestled in the sinister black hills. An hour later we passed the City Limit signs, rolled by the Ataturk Dam and into the central district of Ulus. Rennie had a small flat there so we all bedded down as best we could., all except Ady who just sat in an armchair chain smoking and checking his guitar—Six hours later we were up and moving again for the next stage of the journey, south east to Adana and the Mediterranean coast, still following the Conquerors Road.

Here the landscape was different and it was much warmer, more like southern Italy, with lots of citrus groves and a very busy port. After that it was inland again, heading north east past the old ruined Crusader castle of Cephan and on into the barren Taurus Mountains, round hairpin bends with steep drops on one side and sheer cliffs on the other, climbing all the while. Time and time again we had to pull over to avoid being hit by massive trucks and overloaded buses with people hanging onto the outside and sheep, goats and chickens tied on the roof. There were no stops for coffee on this road and at times as it twisted and turned it was like being in a low-flying aircraft as we flicked nervous glances down the valleys and watched toy trucks and miniature people crawling up the distant winding road below. At one blind corner we ran into a cloud of smoke coming from a big car that was burning on a ledge twenty feet below, there was a big hole in the low wall where it had crashed through. Nobody was around and none of the traffic ahead had stopped, so we pushed on. On one bare the mountain road we were flagged down by a Turk who politely requested a lift to the next town for a spare fuel pump for his huge truck. He left his mate behind in the cab with a shotgun and a wad of bhang to guard the load till he got back. He was with us four hours before we came across a garage.

On another occasion, near Kaisiri, we came across a driver under his truck trying to weld a broken half-shaft with a lump hammer, while his mate kept the fire of wood and camel droppings roaring with a pair of old leather bellows.Oh no. There was no calling out the AA, on this road. Finally, we were on the plateau and the going got easier as both the vegetation and type of people changed. Here it was as it always had been in these isolated Anatolian villages. Kurdish and Mongol influences were everywhere and the only signs of Western culture were the big German trucks and the adverts for Coca Cola. The dreary towns of Urfa, Mylatia, and others with unpronounceable names came and went, and still the monotonous hills crowded the edges of the primitive roads strewn with rocks the size of coconuts.

So far everything had gone fine, but we did have one moment of anxiety however when, in the middle of nowhere, clouds of steam erupted from the engine and our hearts sank. As it happened, it was only a split radiator hose and Spud showed again how good he was in an emergency by jumping to my assistance as we bound it with adhesive tape. For me it seemed like a jinx trip, every time it was my turn to take a kip in the back something went wrong. Once it was a broken headlight, we heard a sharp pop and the off side light went out. Another time Spud ran off the road coming out of a gas station. We were mostly exhausted anyway, and I can remember one stint somewhere up on the bleak plateau late at night when I was so tired that I began seeing things. Looking ahead I saw a gas station about a mile away on the far side of the road, complete with pumps, forecourt and a brightly lit café and I was about to pull across the road into it when I came to my senses and found myself heading to an empty field. Paul too had his fair share of anxiety when, later that night, he ran into a large pack of gray wolves, killing one and injuring others as they leapt up at the cab. The following morning we found dried blood and fur on the bumpers.

We had to eat. The Turkish snacks and chocolate bars that we had been buying at roadside halts were not enough, so we decided to stop at Gazientep, the next town and get a proper meal. As we rolled into the main square it seemed that some kind of carnival was going on but Rennie explained that it was Friday night and it was the usual party night. Crowds were reeling arm in arm all over the place, singing, laughing and shouting and waving. Then I looked closer at the milling hand–holding crowd and realized that they were all men and boys. There was not a woman in sight.

I pulled up at what looked like a good café and we all piled out. A couple of us were wearing Stetsons and you can imagine the effect Kit had on all these wild Mountain Men with her blond hair, mini skirt, tights and high boots. The crowd stood back as we all entered the main room, except of course, Ady who decided to guard the bus, his wallet and his guitar. Rennie ordered a few things but the only thing I remember was a funny–looking very bony fish smoking on a bed of charcoal. In no time at all the café window was a mass of bulging eyes, gaping mouths, and drooping black moustaches, as they gazed at what they had only seen before in the movies. Ten minutes into our meal a police car rolled up and a team of shabby uni–

formed officers herded them all away and then sat in their car watching us themselves and pointing at Kit and waving bundles of Turkish Lira. It was not a comfortable meal, I can tell you, so we did not stay for the coffee and brandy.

The Final Frontier

In the early dawn the road had an eerie atmosphere with the ruts and boulders getting bigger all the time and the bare hills stretching away on either side to the distant snowline. The whole scene was reminiscent of Matthew Brady's photos of the American Civil War battlefields with lots of cannonballs strewn around. History was with us all the time as our primitive road was still continually crossed and re-crossed by the track of an even older one, the Conqueror's Road of Alexander the Great.

Late in the afternoon the next day we came across the base. The sign read:

```
No 167. ADVANCED SURVEILLANCE INSTALLATION
           DYARBIKIR. TURKEY. 23342.
             A.F.T. N.A.T.O. FACILITY.
```

Oh, shit! Was this really why we had driven two thousand kilometres? Just to play here? Naw, there must be somewhere else. We were contracted to play here ten weeks. This bloody place was in the middle of nowhere and anyway, where was Dyarbikir town, eh? It definitely existed, I'd seen it on the map, but this was only a high barbed-wire compound about half a mile square with some strange buildings in it and high wooden watch towers at each corner. At first glance it looked like a sinister Nazi concentration camp.

Over the main entrance flew the Stars and Stripes and the Red Crescent of Turkey and ominously, three short frayed ropes were blowing in the cold wind. In the middle of the road stood two Turkish military policemen in US Army surplus white helmets and ill-fitting green uniforms. They regarded us suspiciously and twirled their long white Billy clubs. They were, as we found out later, members of the Gendarma, a para-military militia who supported the civil police. Rennie exchanged a few guttural Turkish phrases with them and they indicated that we were to wait at the gate. After a few minutes a jeep rolled up, and a big fat Top Sergeant with a New York accent expansively welcomed us to Turkey. Then he ushered Rennie into the warm guardroom while we took in our surroundings and came to the obvious conclusion that this was some outpost and that the main camp with its big clubrooms, restaurant, and bowling alleys must be over the next hill. Rennie came out with the sergeant who gave us a big smile and spat a line of tobacco juice on our front tyre.

"Well," I said brightly. "Where are we staying and which clubs will we be doing first?" At this the sergeant looked at Rennie in surprise and then back at me. He handed me the copy contract that Rennie had given him, spat out another stream of tobacco juice and said:

"Hey, Boy, are you shittin' me, or what? Wotcha mean, which club? This is it."

He roared laughing and gestured to the jumble of buildings against the back fence:

"That's the N.C.O. club and that 'un there's the Officer's Club but mostly it's used by the civilian staff. An' you won't be stayin' here either. This 'ere is TCNR. Er' that means it's Third Country Nationals Restricted an' cos you're all Limeys, youre not allowed on the base overnight. So you've been booked in at the Touristik Pallas downtown DYK. S'bout twenty clicks down the turnpike."

He stopped suddenly and pulled the toothpick he'd been chewing out of his mouth and pointed at our headlight.

"Where'd you get that? That's a bullet hole. These bastards will shoot at anythin' on the road. Bring her round to the Motor Pool tomorrow. Y'gotta have good lights out here. Lots of 'em. Anyways, 'fore y' go downtown c'mon and eat with us."

Of course, everybody had a good moan about the news, but after an American steak dinner and a few whisky cokes we all felt a bit better. Then we unloaded our band gear into the N.C.O.Club, plonked ourselves back into the Transit and headed off to the lost city of Dyarbikir, the biblical Amida.

I had thought that Edirne was primitive but here in Kurdistan it was a wilderness. Dull, low, mud coloured hills ran away from the crumbling road, with the occasional caravan of camels winding through them. On the lower slopes flocks of scraggy sheep and scraggier horses wandered around, tended by young barefoot boys dressed in rags. Now and then, crossing the road, we saw the rare sight of groups of women in flowing black robes, veiled to the eyes, with high piled bundles on their heads. There seemed to be no trees, just a few bushes on the lee side of the hills, probably due to the constant wind that blew across these Anatolian mini–steppes. In the far distance, in every direction we could see high mountains, the ones to the east on the Russian border topped with snow. The air was cold and very clear and as we topped a rise in this apparent desolation we saw, before the outskirts of Dyarbikir, a flash of sunlight on Lake Van miles ahead of us.

The road flattened out for about two miles before we crossed a railroad line and turned off following the signs to the town centre, the railway run-ning alongside until it disappeared under the huge crumbling black basalt walls many feet thick, that had once protected this ancient city of the Hashamite kings two thousand five hundred years ago. Armed guards still patrolled these ramparts and here and there a tank or armoured car stuck its snub nose out of the old grain storage caves at the roadside, constantly on guard against the incursions of wild Kurdish bandits, high on hashish and oblivious of the military might ranged against them. After all these years the area was still regarded as an occupied zone. The violent collapse of the Caliphate and the emergence of the great Kamel Ataturk with all his modern reforms had not touched these ragged mountain communities, where vendettas and family wars raged on, as vicious as any in Sicily and had festered for generations.

The whole area was still very restive. Wild blood–feuds were ever–present in these wild hills, where there was the volatile mixture of Turks, Kurds and Armenians, all of whom had genuine or imagined grievances to settle. Of all of them, I would say that the Armenians got the rough end of the deal, due to successive attempts at their genocide by the Turks. Perhaps the fact that they were a Christian people exacerbated the problem. They had been attacked in 1906, again in 1917, and as late as 1926 by the otherwise enlightened Young Turks of Kamel Ataturk, after which most of Armenia was under the Soviet yoke so the poor sods didn't have a chance. The Turks were actually still trying to colonize and settle this area of Eastern Anatolia, but it was like Texas in the 1880's with range wars and family feuds running wild.

The Kurds were a different case altogether. They were at odds with all their neighbours and carried out the same kind of permanent guerrilla war as they had done for centuries, taking refuge in their inaccessible mountain villages when things got rough. The coming of air power had cowed them somewhat, but they still swooped down on any less–than–vigilant Turkish Army post at the slightest provocation. Some of them worked as cleaners and drivers at the base and generally they were very pleasant people, always ready with a smile and as helpful as possible, They looked different than the Turks as well, more European somehow, and if you did visit their villages you were struck by the cleanliness of things. The houses were neat and the women confident and cheerfully ran the house, the gardens, and their families, not at all cowed and dominated by their men folk as many Moslem women are.

Occasionally, in spite of the thin veneer of civilization however the wild roots showed through. For example, whilst we were there, a cleaner came to the orderly room with the station interpreter and requested time off to bury his father up in the hills. He requested a five–day leave, but the orderly officer consulted his book of standing orders and told him that he could only have the regulation two days off for the funeral. Why, then, did he want five days? Patiently the Kurdish cleaner explained, as though talking to a child, that the two days were truly to bury his father and the next three for his brothers and him to find and kill the men responsible for their father's death.

That was the immutable law of these hills.

*   *   *   *   *   *

Dyarbikir

Our first impression of Dyarbikir was that it was a pleasant regional town, looking more Russian than Turkish, but at that time we had no idea of the violent undercurrent of burgeoning Kurdish nationalism. There were a few villas and big houses with high walled fruit–filled gardens lining the main square, which was naturally called Ataturk Plaza. Although the city was only a remote provincial capital, the traffic was as frantic as in Istanbul. Ragged taxis smoked and thundered through the narrow streets and rattletrap pick–up trucks battled for elbow–room with hordes of high–stacked hand carts and staggering porters, who were so burdened that they appeared to be piles of bundles and boxes with bony brown legs. Everybody was shouting and cursing and the idlers outside the scrubby lean–to cafés loudly proffered their advice and opinions to anyone who would listen.

I pulled up at the Nebi Mosque and was proudly directed by a smiling beggar to the Touristic Pallas, which turned out to be an old hotel built around 1910 by the Germans, who back then had designs on British India and were cementing their relationships with the Caliphate. It proved to be a good move when Turkey became their ally in the First World War, but the Kaiser's grand imperial dreams never came true and India stayed British for another forty years. In any event, this Gothic pile was to be our home for the next three months. I don't think I will ever forget the aroma inside the Touristic Pallas. It was a muddy smell, like a dried–up river bed, not exactly unpleasant, but more like something that had been damp and dried out by a hot iron, kind of musty. The vast mosaic foyer was quite grand in its old colonial way and the smiling moustachioed manager, who had obviously been fore–warned of our arrival by the US base, bustled out to greet us in his fractured English, hoping that we would 'Hef good times' at his hotel. He smiled even wider at the note I gave him from the people at the camp and happily shuffled a wad of those U.S Military Accommodation chits that we had first come across in France, so it wasn't hard to tell why he was smiling.

I signed us all in and we were doled out our rooms which, although they were not exactly squeaky–clean, had the blessing of proper European toilets instead of the usual squatters, an unbelievable luxury out here. There was also a restaurant, very much like the one we had visited in Belgrade, complete with darned tablecloths and bored waiters, which I tried one morning, but the only thing they could come up with was runny fried eggs and soft doughy bread, so we only went there for coffee and a plate of hard biscuits. And of course, the traditional barber's shop, which seemed to be the social hub of the place, where heated political discussions went on all day, to the snipping of shears and the whoosh and snap of steaming towels. One disturbing aspect though was the hotel cleaning staff, all of them sinister, hard–faced local women swathed in colourful headscarves and shawls, and all wearing voluminous black trousers and hook–toed slippers. These shapeless spectres continually swept the tiled stairs and passageway floors with small bunches of twigs, shuffling like crabs endlessly up and down in complete silence.

With everybody settled in and the Transit locked up and parked in the hotel car park, it was time for a turn round town to see what was on offer. The permanently beaming manager informed us that Dyarbikir meant City of Copper and in the shops we certainly saw many fine examples of copper and leather. The shops were also surprisingly modern with glass windows and security grills. We took Mr. Rennie to the train station where a huge black German steam loco stood waiting to run the gauntlet through the lawless hills back to Ankara. Then we found a coffee shop, had a couple of rumbabas, and headed for the bazaar as the darkness closed in. Now this was fascinating. Strange shouts in a language we had never heard before and the smell and roaring of glaring white carbide lamps and the hiss of water on hot metal from the copper workers' booths. Lanes rambled aimlessly in all directions, lined with piled–up stalls of fruit, bread, old clothes, tools, and leather goods—and racks of guns and piled boxes of ammunition.

These guns are worthy of comment. They were not the usual army surplus stock you would expect, but homemade copies of early French Lebels, to the extent of having a thick copper wire installed under the barrel to appear like the regulation cleaning rod. The only part that was imported was the breech mechanism and there was only one calibre available, the local equivalent of the standard 12 bore shotgun. The cartridges were rather different. Instead of the usual load of shot it contained one big lead ball like the cartridge that the Swiss call a Brenniker. Later in our stay I had the opportunity to fire one of these monstrosities. It kicked like a mule and blew a hole in a metal road sign the size of a melon. I asked what they used the guns for and after looks of amazement at such a stupid question, they explained that they were for defending their homes, nodding meaningfully in the direction of a passing Turkish Army patrol, and if things got boring they could always go hunting wolves and wild goats.

Language was not a problem as most of the merchants and local officials were settlers from western provinces who spoke a little fractured English or passable German. None of the officials was Kurdish and it was only in the bazaar that that language was spoken

Next morning we were awakened by the crisp clip–clop of a mule train that came trotting past the hotel with a load of river driftwood for the charcoal burners on the other side of the market. Wood was a very precious commodity in a country that had so few trees. It was used for almost everything from fuel to the making of a children's play park. There was such a play park across the street from the cinema and it was a work of art, the swings, slides, and roundabouts all being made out of rough cut wood and branches, all roped together and working fine. The Kurds love their children and, whilst there was a side of their nature that enjoyed to play and gamble, centuries of isolation and persecution had also made them fierce and very hard–shelled when they were cornered. Another use of wood was in the traditional mode as scaffolding, but out here there was a difference. Hoists, cranes, and other mechanical building aids were very rare and I was fascinated one afternoon watching a big building going up. It was like an early Hollywood cartoon. A series of platforms were all joined by ladders snaking crazily up the side of the building, again, bits of wood and rough branches roped together, and on each level a man with a shovel was slinging loads of sand up to his neighbour above, until it reached the top where the builders were laying a concrete floor. They were all in time and happily singing some local ditty. I remember hearing the song later by Eartha Kit—it was a tale about a poor woman from Istanbul who dreamed of crossing the Bosphorus to her rich lover in Uskadar. "Uskadara geynit nur in gumlik. etc". (Or something like that—remember it?)

Around midday two days later, we piled back into our Transit and headed off to the base to do our opening stint. At the gate of the car park a well–dressed Turk waved us down and in impeccable English asked us if we would sell him our van. I explained that we needed it for at least the next three months and he smiled again, saying that he understood, but if the Effendi wished to part with it then he would willingly pay a good price for it. It would make an excellent dormush taxi he said and offered a cool £9000 for it. Wow. It had only cost just over two and I was quite tempted, until I found that he could only pay in Turkish Lira and that was no good. But it crossed my mind that there could be a good trade in shuttling used buses out here and selling them. The authorities seemed to put no controls on what came in, but they were right bastards when it came to getting anything out. We bumped onto the main road leaving the still smiling Mustapha at the gate to wait for the next foreign car to come out, and headed for the base twenty clicks away, a journey we were destined to do twice a day for the next seventy days.

The club itself was not very big, a long L–shaped room with a restaurant next door and the short arm of the L lined with the ever–present one–armed bandits and a long table where an Armenian, ostensibly a tobacco dealer, sat with his minders, ready to supply any narcotic that took your fancy. There were about three hundred military personnel and a civilian staff of technicians who undertook the highly secret functions of the base. They carried officer status and used the Officers' Club across the square. There was also a detachment of the Turkish Army, whose duty was to provide protection and security for us all, but God knows what they could have done with their 1907 Model Mauser rifles if the Russians had come to call. By the side of the main gate the flagpole bore both the Stars and Stripes and the Red Crescent of the Turkish Republic and, as I have mentioned, next to the camp sign, three ropes ends hanging from the gate crossbar. The camp interpreter informed us that these were the remains of a triple execution carried out a month previously by the Turkish comman-

der. Three deserters had been caught and in an abortive escape attempt
had stabbed and killed a guard. Unable to accurately place the blame, the
commander had all three hanged and left the bodies swinging there for a
week as a warning. Oh no, they don't mess about in Turkey.

The deal was for six evening shows a week at the NCO. Club plus one
Sunday afternoon session at the Officers' Club, for which we got a cash
bonus. It was a tight schedule but I felt confident we could cut it, even
though there was only Kit and me to do the singing. Although as it turned
out, both Spud and Paul did a couple of numbers and provided some
harmonies on things like 'Early Morning Rain', which became the camp
favourite. There was the regular shuffling around on stage until everyone
was satisfied as they could be on their allotted space. Ady as usual, was a
bit of a martinet about where his amplifier was going to go and spent a
good ten minutes pushing it around until he was happy about its placing. If
he'd had a joint or two he would talk to it as if it was a dog, patting it if it
performed well, or giving it a kick if it went wrong. One night in Venice he
kicked it so hard that it fell off the stage.

Spud was not so particular about amplification, but he was going
through the trauma of changing from upright double–bass to electric bass-
guitar and would drift off in a sulk if we had to play anything in the key of
F or Bb. As for Paul he was as frenetic as ever. Timing himself in the setting up of his kit. I have seen him have the whole lot set up, drums,
cymbals, stands, and pedals in less than three minutes flat from the opening of the van's doors. On one night stands he would be the same and could
strip it down just as quickly and he'd be at the bar waiting for someone to
buy him a drink (He never bought one himself) while we were still coiling
up the speaker cables. It was a work of art. He did have a flaw, however,
and could not resist buying extra cymbals and drums. Some nights it
looked like he was playing behind a nuclear reactor. Kit, of course was very
popular with the G.I.s and her songs, mainly Country standards plus a lot
of Carpenters and Ann Murray numbers were again just right for the
young Americans miles from home. For me 'Detroit City', 'Ruby' and Dave
Dudley's' Cowboy Boots' were big winners. The job itself was not very exciting, but little by little the word got around that there was a good band
on base and the once neglected club began to fill up again.

We made a lot of good friends at Dyarbikir. One in particular was the
camp jester Sgt.Hoppley, known as Hoppy to his mates. He was from the
heart of New York City and let you know it at every opportunity. He had a
profound regard for the rotgut whiskey sold on the Lower Bowery called
'Stillbrook' and an equally profound disrespect for the US. Army that had
dragged him halfway across the world, all because he had signed reserve
status forms when he had finished his compulsory military service, but he
had never expected anything like this. He'd picked up his bounty payment
for signing and had a couple of wild weekends on the money but then they
had called him back when the Cold War got warmer to fulfill his obliga-

tions. He thought that he would have been put on guard at the Hoboken Armory, where he could have gone home each weekend, but he'd not read the small print and so he ended up in Anatolia. He also professed contempt for Country Music calling us a bunch of 'Limey Farmers' and 'Turkeys' but he came to all the shows anyway. He was all hand signals and jive talk. A very popular guy with everybody but sometimes he went over the top with the result that, one night, we saw him get a severe chewing-out by a very Gung Ho Warrant Officer about his behavior. What did they expect? These guys were on detachment miles from anywhere and thrown together 24 hours a day and there was nowhere to go at night. Beyond the gate it was far too dangerous. There were several recorded sinister incidents of people disappearing without trace in Dyarbikir town after a night out.

Of Hoppy's friends, I remember a guy from Perth Amboy, New Jersey called Grimes, whose father was the local police chief and a black guy called Thomas who loved to dance. There was also a certain Sgt. Wilcox, a dedicated soak from San Francisco, whom we bumped into at various clubs all round the world. He had his own bar stool fitted with a safety belt. To liven things up we would often clown about for the show, sometimes dressing up as doctors and carrying Kit in on a stretcher. One night we dressed up as Turks but the waiters didn't think that was very funny. Boredom was our biggest enemy.

The town itself did not hold much attraction after the first few days and usually we were at the base for lunch or just after it. There was a small gym, a putting green and a P.X. There was also a Rod and Gun Club but it was almost defunct because the opportunities for either of these pastimes were strictly limited. If you went out with a gun there was a good chance that you 'd get shot back at. While we were there, the club actually did close down and sold off all the stock of superb fishing gear and guns. I wanted to buy a beautiful Austrian Steyr hunting rifle but I was informed that I would not be allowed out of Turkey with it, although I did buy a superb American electric train-set for Francis with lots of coaches, rails, stations, and locomotives, all for $40 dollars.

I learned a bit of Turkish, enough to order food and drinks and to get around the bazaar. Behind the Central Post Office there was a narrow street they called Gold Alley, which seemed to be bursting at the seams with gold and precious stones. Prices were much lower than in Europe and, with the added advantage of buying in US dollars, we could get some beautiful things. We got gold pendants; bracelets, and rings at knock-down prices. I also bought some rare Alexandrine jewellery, one ring with a breathtaking square cut stone that I got for Sylvia and some brooches and things for Kit, as well as extra rings as a hedge against the forever uncertain future. The boys also got gold and other goodies at the Rod and Gun sell-off. Spud bought a very good movie camera at a rock bottom price; something like £25. He took it home for his father's birthday—And SOLD it to him.

Some days, if I did not want to go down to the base early, Kit and the boys would take the workers' shuttle bus, which left about 11 am. They would get a meal and while Kit played the machines with some of her NCO friends, the boys would settle in to one of the huts and smoke a few of the abundant available joints. Usually everything was kept under control, and it helped to reduce the stress of our hard schedule of three forty–five minute sets six days a week and the cabaret cum booze–up on Sunday afternoons. Although now and then things went over the top, such as the night Ady turned up on the stage smoking four cigarettes at the same time, while playing what he imagined were lightening riffs on his Les Paul Gibson, but as I said, it helped the gig along

Thunderbirds Go

There was, of course a serious side to things. This place was the real thing, not merely a token NATO presence to keep the Turks happy. About three times a week a Russian spotter plane could be seen high in the blue sky, watching the base and by sheer chance I found out why when, towards the end of the contract, I had occasion to put a call through to Ronnie Harris in Wiesbaden, and had to wait for his call back. It was a Friday, and usually every second Friday, we were not allowed on the base before 5 p.m. but on this particular day I had arrived early to make my radio call to the agent in Wiesbaden, which was routed through Rein Main Air Base and on to the German civilian telephone network. I was about to witness the secret purpose of the unit.

About three fifteen a klaxon horn sounded and the Turkish conscripts of the garrison closed the gates and took up positions in the watchtowers and along the perimeter wire. Four jeeps took off to establish road blocks on the main road containing about a dozen U.S. Special Forces soldiers in green berets, packing heat and wearing flak jackets. Up to that time I had not realized that there were US regular troops there. Other Special Forces surrounded the innocent looking putting–green wearing white anti–blast hoods and trooped down an underground stairway in one corner. The radar scanners whirled round in every direction and, as another klaxon sounded, the entire centre part of the putting green began to come apart and open up like a gigantic book. When it was about halfway to the vertical, the two sides slid back and four large rocket launchers emerged from the ground, complete with red nosed missiles and a full crew in protective clothing at action stations. They then went through a series of battle exercises under the command of several officers holding stopwatches and wearing headphones, obviously connected to a Command centre above the Officer's Club. It was weird. Like a scene from a science–fiction movie, but here it was actually happening before my own eyes.

I realized then that this was more than a listening post. It was a front line defence unit against the Soviets less than 100 km. away, nothing in terms of today's guided missile technology, but it was quite a sobering experience in that long–ago spring of 1967. Luckily, I suppose, nobody had taken any notice of me watching quietly from the Duty Office window.

On the far side of Dyarbikir town on the bank of the River Dicle there was a B.P. oil installation and we got on very well with the British engineers when they came to the base for a bit of entertainment. Apart from us and frozen American steaks and good bourbon, the only diversion they had were the one–armed bandits in the alcoves. These bored, fed up, but highly paid ex–pat Brits were feeling the isolation, and pumped these machines all evening, pouring their winnings back in as fast as they collected them. Even the jackpots were no longer exciting. The dominant interest at the time was monitoring an intense and clumsily hidden illicit love–affair going on between one of the engineer's wives and a younger technician. Ah yes, there's nothing like a bit of intrigue is there?

Mind you, we all got a bit bored, and I must admit we started playing the gambling machines, but no one got the Las Vegas Fever more than Kit, who would spend the last hour of the evening glued to her favourite one–armed bandit, either gambling her own money or acting as a lucky mascot for some G.I. as she was supplied with an endless stream of whiskey cokes. I got into the Jack Daniels again and in the end a roster had to be made up for someone to stay sober enough to drive us back to the 'Sandbag Hilton'.

The people at the oil camp often invited us over for a barbecue or a birthday celebration, but the trip there was rather grotesque. Dyarbikir was on a high escarpment above the right bank of the upper reaches of the River Tigris, called the Dicle by the locals, and to get to the camp you had to bypass the town and cross by a bridge built by the Romans. It had been patched up and strengthened over the centuries, but the basic structure was still as it was when the Legions of Crassus tramped across it to their annihilation at the battle of Carrhae in 55 B.C. The road led below the escarpment to where the town cemetery was situated outside the black walls, but many years of erosion had washed away the cliff edges and now the white bones and skulls of long–dead inhabitants could be seen poking through the steep slopes. The return trip was sinister, with imagination playing havoc as the bright moonlight picked out the bleached bones, and packs of wild wolves howled in the surrounding hills. Brrr.

PICKER'S TIP 20

The Fender Telecaster is the best rhythm guitar in the world. In fact it is a super all round workhorse, comfortable to wear, with a great neck, simple electronics and machine heads that never go out of tune. No other guitar gives you that unique 'Country Twang.' Lou Fender got it right from the start.

My Turkey Dinner

One day, I was invited to dinner at the Officer's Mess at the Turkish Air Force base at the Dyarbikir Airport. The Colonel who'd invited me had done his training at the RAF College at Cranwell and had spent some time in the States, so he spoke good English. I met him as arranged and off we went to the Mess where he introduced me to his colleagues, a few of whom spoke very basic English and others spoke German, so we all got on fine. There was no whisky of course, although I must admit my lemonade tasted as though it had a shot of gin in it. And strangely enough raki, which has the same kick as Pernod, was considered just a digestive, so it was drunk quite openly. ("For health reasons, of course," said my friend the Colonel. Oh Yeah?).

We all went to the tables and the meal kicked off with much ceremony, lots of standing, clapping hands, and drinking toasts in the gin–laced lemonade. And what could only be described as hors d'oeuvres, olives, onions, sardines, and vine leaves stuffed with meat and herbs. Conversation flowed, and more toasts were drunk in a kind of Turkish absinthe and palate–burning Armenian brandy, mellowed by sweet soft drinks till the next course arrived. That turned out to be wooden bowels of clear beef broth, which was delicious. But there were no spoons. So it was a two handed slurping job. Then came my own particular favourite, the famous lachmaljun savory pancakes with dollops of thick sour cream. Tradition demanded that now the Guest of Honor (me) made a speech of thanks to the hosts before the main course was served. I got to my feet and made a brief address in German, which most of them followed, and sat down to a round of applause. The officers then stood up and toasted the Turkish President, after which they threw their glasses against the stone fireplace behind them. They then began to sing some kind of regimental song, banging their knife handles on the table top in rhythm, as a line of mess stewards paraded in with silver platters piled high with the ceremonial dish of the evening. A beaming black–bearded steward leaned over my shoulder and dumped two of these specialties on my oval wooden platter and gestured to the peppers and spices arrayed along the middle of the table. He then produced a bowl of what appeared to be oversized caviar and another of chopped hard boiled eggs and parsley.

I looked down at my platter. On it there nestled what appeared to be two medium–sized chickens without either wings or legs. They were a beautiful golden brown and their shape seemed rather familiar. I tried to cut into it but there did not appear to be a lot of meat on the bone? My host indicated that I should start and as I obviously did not know exactly what to do, he courteously proceeded to demonstrate what one did. It was at that moment that I realized that the lumps before me were roasted sheep's heads. And the 'Caviar' was sheep's eyes. Gulp. The colonel, still smiling warmly at me, grasped one of the heads and reversing the grip on his knife, smashed the handle down splitting the cranium neatly in half and scooped up a lit–tle of the exposed blue–grey brains with relish, pausing only to pop a few of the multi colored sheep's eyes in his mouth. Now, I am usually quite brave when it comes to culinary adventure but this time I messed about with my sheep's bonce and managed to drop a few slippery eyes under the table. Fortunately my fellow guests were now too busy smashing heads and swil–ling the ouzo to take any notice of me.

Suddenly in the next room a bazouki band opened up and we drifted in to watch the girl belly–dancers. I use the term girls reservedly, as the terpsichorean wobblers were at least forty–five years old, weighed–in at over 200 pounds and probably moonlighted as part–time Sumo wrestlers. After that the band played some Turkish pop tunes and the officers danced—with each other. Maybe that was their idea of Turkish delight.

Guest Artistes

Our shows continued to go well in spite of the captive audiences, but by far the best and wildest times were at the Sunday afternoon sessions at the Officer's Club. These events started off with a big buffet lunch at noon, and went on till about 7 p.m., at which time Kit and the boys repaired to the N.C.O.Club and I went to work at the Radio Station, AFRTS Dyarbikir, where I had a request program of Country Music called Down Home. I en–joyed being a D.J. and made plans to pursue a radio career when I got back to the U.K., but more about that later.

Now and then a travelling show came to the base, either from the USO or from one of the commercial agents. That meant we had the night off, but as there was nowhere else to go, we turned up at the club to watch. Some of them were good. Like Johnny Green and the Green Men, a five–piece cabaret, which included two trumpet–playing girls and a guitarist who did Trini Lopez numbers. They all had their hair dyed green. A good gimmick I suppose, but it always puzzled me. Why didn't they wear wigs for the show? That would have been the logical thing to do, but that's us show people. We're all crazy.

There were other shows, however, that had been thrown together and pushed out on the road, most of them totally unsuited to these isolated U.S. bases. God knows how they got through the auditions. Among them was one of the worst acts I had ever seen. A very bad female ventriloquist from Cheltenham, who spoke like Joyce Grenfell and had great difficulty being understood by the Americans. God knows what the Turks thought about her. I think that the bookers must have thought that it was some kind of alternative comedy and rather than appear to be out of touch, had given her a contract. Another night it was a family of trumpet players. That's right. A family. Mum, Dad and teenaged kids, all of 'em, budding Eddie Calverts, who had arrived courtesy of agent, Johnny Downs of Wiesbaden. They were terrible, but they went on and on, puffing out choked off ver–sions of Harry James hits. The nadir came when Mrs. X tried to do a bit of

Harry Mortimer style triple–tonguing and lost her embouchure in the last eight bars and ended the piece with the squeak of a dying tomcat. The grand finale was a four–part harmony version of 'Orpheus in the Under-world' but by this time the G.I.s had had enough and Hoppy's Gang per-suaded Kit to get up on the bar and do a can–can to the music. Everybody cheered and turned their backs on the red–faced trumpet puffers to watch the dancer.

Their leader, Ken something or other, was furious and reported us to Special Services for spoiling their show. Nothing ever came of it but some time later I ran into him at the Vagabond's Club and he snubbed me com-pletely. I can't say I blamed him.

Returning that night in a state of high euphoria, we almost forgot to halt at the exposed level crossing on the edge of the town. Just in time Paul remembered and stopped. We switched the engine off and wound down the windows but we could hear nothing but the howling of the wind so he banged the van in gear and shot across the lines and turned right heading for home. We had hardly gone thirty yards when a loud scream came out of the night and the glowing firebox of the unlit Mardin Mixed Freight roared past our side windows about ten yards away.

That certainly sobered everybody up double quick.

Welcome to the Scherhazade Club

At the hotel the boys said that they were not going to bed yet and made their way round the back of the Turistik Pallas to the nightclub called Scherhazade's Palace. I'd had enough and so had Kit, so we went up to bed leaving them to it. All went well until about 3 a.m. when the phone in my room started ringing. It was Spud.

"Yonk," he yelled, "Get down 'ere. We gorra birra trouble. Y'd berra get down 'ere."

I grabbed the spare metal bed–leg I kept for such emergencies, slipped on a sweater and a pair of pants and shot off downstairs. The whole foyer was packed with yelling Turks and in the middle of the mob, standing on the reception desk were the Hotel Night Manager and a thick set little man in a tight dinner suit, who it turned out was the boss of the nightclub plus our three white–faced lads. I stood on the stairs and banged my iron bed-leg on the banisters to get some attention.

"Alright. Alright," I shouted. "What's it all about then."

There was a chorus of yells and waved fists, this time in my direction. I pointed to the hotel manager and asked him in German what the problem was and he managed to shout across to me that it was a dispute about payment of the bill in the nightclub. According to the manager, the boys had used the club and its facilities but refused to pay up before leaving. Everybody was shouting and bellowing at the top of their voices and any moment I expected it to turn into a Holy War, and all us infidels would be strung up and gutted but money was the issue here so we got down to the nitty gritty. "How much is owing?" I asked.

"Fuckin' nuthin'," shouted Spud, "We never touched 'em."

"Wotcha mean, never touched who?" I asked.

"Them brass nails. Nowt t'do wi' us."

"What about these Brass Nails? You lot picked up the barflies did you?"

"Naw," chimed in Ady. "We only let 'em sit with us, that's all. We didn't ask 'em to have a drink or for a shag or anythin'."

"Yeah, an' anyway we only give 'em a bit of grope," blurted out Paul. "S'wot they're there for innit? Just a bunch o' tarts aren't they?"

My heart sank as the hotel manager rattled on loudly about the incident. In the end he broke off talking to me and embarked on a haggling discussion with the nightclub manager while the crowd got more excited and bigger. Finally he turned to me and smiled as he announced. "The charges eez two 'undred an' forty dollah, Effendi."

"Lyin' bastards," yelped Spud, "We never spent two 'undred bleedin' dollars. We only 'ad a few drinks and a sandwich or somethin'."

"Yeah, an' it were a load o' crap anyway," moaned Spud.

"Well," conceded Paul, "S'not as if we'd took 'em outside or anythin'."

"No? ". I pointed out as quietly as I could in the roaring mob, "But you did invite 'em to have a drink, didn't you? And you did give their arses a good feeling as well, right? What a load of boneheads. Don't you know what it's like out here? They'll cut your balls off. You just can't blow a bugle expecting the 7th Cavalry to show up. They're not bleedin' jokin' y' know."

Spud was really frightened now. Not of losing his balls, but of having to part with some money and shouted back desperately. "Well I'm not payin' 'em fuckin' nothin."

By now the Turks had settled down to watch the free cabaret of these Anglo Saxon loonies having a barney with each other. Some of them lit up bhang spliffs and squatted on the floor. There was the mention of calling in the Gendarma by the night manager of the hotel, at which the club manager started to roll round the floor shouting his head off. The boys stood open–mouthed and Ady said that he wished he'd never come to Turkey in the first place and that he knew that something like this would happen, etc, etc, until Spud gave him a clip and Paul had to step in to stop a fight developing between them.

It was obvious what was on the cards and I pointed it out clearly. They had certainly had a few drinks at the inflated nightclub prices, and had pulled a couple of the club's birds, and been messing around with them. So what could they expect? Furthermore, I pointed out that our only passport back to the civilized world was that bright blue, brand–new, Transit bus at the door, and if some gesture was not made to placate these poppy–seed soaked wild Kurds, it would not be there when we woke up. And even if it was, it would be a burned–out wreck and that it was a long walk back to Frankfurt. Finally, after much haggling, we got round to a settlement of the bill, which ended up with me paying the nightclub boss $150 U.S. there and then and docking the boys $50 each. They did not feel it, because it was spread over the entire contract and other, more serious, crises overcame us before we got back to Germany, but at least they did not bother going to Scherhazade's Pleasure Palace again.

Over breakfast next morning I got the full story, along with our runny eggs and bitter coffee, and it was much as we had imagined it and at least our bus was still in one piece. (For the time being at least). Paul told us that one of the girls at their table spoke a little English and said that she had just got out of the Karahani and that she was a shop assistant, but this night club job was all she could get. Paul asked her what this Karahani was, and she explained in halting English that it was a prison-cum-municipal brothel where women offenders could commute their sentences by becoming Town Hall hookers. She had been picked up for shoplifting and given two years in the poky, but had managed to work off her sentence by doing over seven months service in the Karahani. These girls were forced to wear metal shoes to show that they were working off their sentence. We had a drive round there later that day and it was all true. All these strange heavily made-up women beckoning from overhanging balconies. It was incredible, but it was an incredible place, with very basic values. Remembering those times I realize now how fragile the position of Western Nationals was out there. You had to be very careful about local laws and customs. The code was stringent and as the area was virtually under Turkish military occupation penalties were very strict. There were several well-documented cases of U.S. personnel being locked up for simple traffic offences. One guy got two years because his wing-mirror caught a woman whilst he was driving past the bazaar. A food truck was dispatched every day from the camp for him to Urfa Jail. Eventually he was smuggled out in a mail truck and flown to Cyprus.

April 5th was a National Day in Turkey, marked of course by parades and speeches and was the subject of one of the funniest episodes I have ever seen on a parade ground. It was like a scene from an old Charlie Chaplin silent movie. We were leaning out of the hotel window watching the procession of town dignitaries go by, when a band came into view. Now, I love military bands and so I got quite perked up at the sight of this fine big band, all dressed up for their special day in crisp khaki drill with white gaiters and white American M.P. helmets. The drums thundered away and the sparkling brass blared, scaring the birds from the overhead power lines and bringing cheers from the crowded sidewalks. The music also was a bit funny to our ears, sort of half-eastern, but still a recognizable march beat. The tramping of the following Gendarma was a bit flat-footed and ragged, but for all that, I was enjoying the spectacle. The big Drum Major proudly strutted past our window, twirling his big tinkling ribbon-bedecked baton and leading the two lines of throbbing brass kettle-drums, and it was just then that my eye caught a strange, out of time, bobbing about at the rear of band.

Here, a big sousaphone, with a huge brass bell and miles of tubing, was being played by a tall thin bandsman who had been umpah–ing along with the rest of his buddies, quite oblivious of the fact that one of his gaiters had come undone and was slipping down his leg. Drmm, Drmm, drm, drm, drm, on they marched until the sousaphone player felt something dragging at his ankle and looking down, to his horror he saw his gaiter dragging in the dust. He did a couple of hops to try and catch it but wearing this mass of coiled brass tubes made it a rather difficult manoeuver. At one time he did manage to get a hold of it but lost the beat of his Umpah–umpah–ing so he had to straighten up again and pick up his timing. The next time he grabbed for it, he missed and tripped up, bringing the bell of the sousaphone down on top of the helmet of flute player in front of him. Clang. The shocked musician blindly staggered sideways and crashed into the rest of the wind section with a screeching squeal. What a gas. The whole band lost time and started wandering all over the road, while the drum major marched firmly ahead to the throb of the kettle drums, totally unaware of the chaos behind him. Wonderful. I do love military bands.

Yonco's Last Stand

Speaking as someone who never quite managed the transition to adult–hood, I might as well tell you that apart from loving military parades, like Waylon Jennings, 'My Heroes have always been Cowboys'. In fact I once grew sideburns hoping to look like Clint Eastwood, but the result was more like Gabby Hayes. I suppose it was one of the factors that led me to choose this kind of music, although there is a difference between Country Music and Western Cowboy ballads, but I don't want to get involved in that minefield. Its an argument that's been going on for fifty years or more, As I saw it, if cowboys were good enough for Hank Williams, Willie Nelson, Johnny Cash, and many others, they were good enough for me, although, I might add, perhaps not for my musicians. So, in an effort to instill some enthusiasm for the ways of the Old West here in the Ancient East, I decided to take everybody horse riding.

There were a number of small villages nearby and I persuaded Sykes, one of the waiters, to negotiate a number of nags for us at a dollar an hour. Kit wisely declined to become a Calamity Jane, preferring to continue her attempt to win every jackpot in the machine alley at the club, where the stress could be lightened by the odd Bourbon and Coke. (Which only goes to show that women have more brains than us men). So one sunny afternoon, Sykes, who was a dead ringer for Manuel, the waiter in Fawlty Towers, came smiling into the club and announced that he had hired. "Many verra good, number one ossizes. Eez waitin' outside gate for 'fenndi. Chock guzel (Very Good)—Hokay Boss?"

Well, I think everyone of those 'ossizes' would have run away if they ever saw a brush or a currycomb. What a bunch of fleabags, and they were just as hard up for tack as well. I had not expected the Quorn Hunt, but this lot looked as though they'd have responded more to a ragman's bugle than the pink–coated master's View Halloo.

The one that Ady rode, or rather sat on, did not even have a saddle, just an old mattress slung over its sagging back, held in place by a wide web-bing strap with big enclosed Mexican looking stirrups. Paul's horse was not much better, and Spud's mare looked very pregnant. Mine had a saddle but only one stirrup, the other was a loop of rope and I had also a genuine rope bridle instead of reins. Hoppy and his gang had decided to join us, and squeezed a few more mounts from Sykes' villagers. Hoppy, Grimes, and Thomas, all from New York or New Jersey had also only seen horses on TV, though Thomas kept telling us that many of his soul–brother ancestors had been the real cowboys. He didn't sound very convincing, due to the stream of Tamla Motown street slang warnings he issued to his mount, like. "Now listen up. You mothf'yuh. Don' give me none o' dat jumpin up an' down shit. Right? Jes' straighten up an' fly right, you Central Park turkey. Oderwize, you gonna be dog meat."

Like General Custer leading the 7th Cavalry out to destroy the Sioux Nation, I raised my right arm and kicked my fleabag's ribs and headed for the hills. When you reflect on the fate of that fine body of delinquents, we were not so far off–target. I really did feel like John Wayne, as we walked at a cool stately pace past the camp gate and saluted the flag. Ho. Eyes Front. I could almost hear the trumpet's call and I turned to review my command. It was not a very inspiring sight. Although we had barely gone a quarter of a mile, Ady had already slumped into his mattress, causing it to poke up behind and in front of him looking like one of the illustrations from Chaucer's Canterbury Tales, with his feet dragging in the dust and bang-ing into big rocks as the horse just ambled, along oblivious to this shifting load of humanity on its back. My horse seemed to understand roughly what I wanted and plodded on resignedly on through the barren landscape, stopping, when it chose, to nuzzle the reeds at one of the many streams that trickled down from the low hills. I tried to kick it back into life, but it took no notice, and I had to smile smarmily as my troop jerked past in an equally uncontrollable caravan. Eventually, Dobbin had drunk his fill and took off in a totally different direction from the rest of his stable mates and gave me on a nice scenic trip round the hills. By now I had had enough of this Hippocratic insolence, and decided to show my power of command and freeing my right foot from the string stirrup I gave it one almighty kick in the ribs and unthinkingly jerked its head round—back towards the camp.

I could almost hear its gasp of relief as it tossed its mangy mane, seeking the fragrant smell of its warm stable and full nosebag far away, and then it was off, and I mean off. Like the wind, homeward bound. We thundered down the hill and across the flat rocky plain, flashing past the rest of my party, who thought I was showing off. They couldn't have been more wrong. I had nothing to do with it. I was like Flashman at Balaclava. I had no control at all and far from showing off, I was more concerned with get–

ting off. I was racing along while balancing precariously up on my one remaining stirrup, desperately trying to stop the monster by strangling it with my single fraying bridle rope, but that only frightened it more. I think by this time it was as scared as I was. I crouched as low as I could and hugged its smelly neck as it raced on. By now we were barrelling along the back of the perimeter fence of the camp on a narrow rocky path. As we flashed by a group of gaping–mouthed guards, I risked a glance ahead and saw to my horror a hard corner looming up; a quick mental calculation told me that there was no way that me and this horse were going to get round that corner together, so I steeled myself for our parting. Old Trigger slowed a little to a steady 85 mph as it approached the end of the fence and, taking my life in my hands, I closed my eyes and kicking the last stirrup free, slid off. It seemed ages before I hit the ground with a bone shaking CRUMP. I landed on my back and, as hooves and the mud stained belly shot above me, I skidded painfully for few yards until I came to stop in clump of gorse at the side of the path. I was groaning and bleeding in about six places and lay there numb and unable to move. My mount, happy to be relieved of its burden had now stopped and was contentedly munching on a bush about twenty yards away and I faded into oblivion.

I don't remember much else for a while but when I did come round it was to an accompaniment of my own groans. My head felt as though it was bursting and as I lifted my arm to stop the throbbing I felt the warm, sticky, slippery smear of blood. My back ached and I could see blood oozing out of my shirt. So far it was not so bad, I could turn my head and move one arm but when I attempted to move my legs nothing happened. A blind panic came over me. My legs did not work. After a few agonizing moments a shadow suddenly loomed over me.

I looked up and saw the strangest apparition. For a moment I thought I must be dead. Here was a most bizarre figure. As my eyes lifted, I took it all in with silent amazement. It was a huge Turk, dressed in baggy black cotton harem trousers, tucked into a pair of cracked red boots with curly toes, while the top half, above the thick leather belt with its massive brass buckle was encased in a greasy businessman's blue striped jacket and waistcoat over a collarless flannel shirt with a big brass collar stud. Then came a smiling brown face with a huge Joseph Stalin moustache and the final touch of a tweed flat cap. He carried a riding crop and held loosely onto the bridle of a horse about as shaggy as the one I had recently aban-doned. For a few moments he looked at me and after saying something in guttural Turkish, he strode away to grab my horse and without warning belted it full force on the nose. It reeled and stood there dazed as he tethered it to a thorn bush.

Then he came over to where I was lying and said something to me before grabbing my collar and dragging me to a large boulder by the side of the path. Here, he put me in a sitting position with my back against it. He smiled again, rubbed his huge hands together and stepped up onto the boulder, then he squatted and engulfed me with his massive arms and hugging me tight he slowly stood up with me hanging from his chest. He took a deep breath, flexed his knees and shook me up and down like a rag doll, until miraculously all the feeling returned to my legs. After a few minutes, he put me back down on the boulder and rummaged in his baggy pants and produced a small bottle of arrack, which he offered to me. Soon I could stand up and searched my pockets to give him something. Finally I persuaded him to take the only money I was carrying, a twenty dollar bill, which he accepted shyly, thanking me profusely. He went for my horse and, after unhitching it, smacked it again on the nose, and led it over to me telling me it was a very Choc Fanar (Very Bad) animal and that I must get rid of it. Then, with a smile and a wave he swung onto his own nag and jogged off down the track. Nervously I remounted and, keeping the wild mustang on a very short rein, walked it slowly back to the village, where the bastard promptly threw me again and contemptuously stomped off to its manure–strewn stable. I managed to get back to the camp on foot where a reception committee was waiting for me with a round of applause. Hoppy took some photos as I staggered through the main gates looking like a sur–vivor from the Indian Wars, covered in blood and bruises, with my shirt ripped to shreds and my pants covered in mud and horseshit. Well, I always wanted to be a cowboy, and I looked like the Indians had got me as I staggered back into the last frontier outpost at Fort Dyarbikir. After that I was not so keen on cowboy movies.

Spring time in the Mountains

Over Easter we were given a few days off from the base, which we spent in various ways, either around the town or over at the oil camp. It was a very welcome break. When it was time to get back, however, we had quite a shock. We picked up our old familiar route back to the base but everything seemed to be different—something had changed. Our road took us out of the town as usual and normally we ran through twenty kilometres of deserted dull–brown landscape, with nothing to see but a few low hills and rush–filled gullies, but this time, it appeared that low houses had been built by the dozen, with people moving between them, and mules, sheep, and camels were grazing nearby on the new grass. How could these people have arrived and created these settlements in the few days we'd been away? And then it dawned on us. The new grass. Of course. These people and animals had been there all the time, their buildings camouflaged by the dull brown earth they were made from. Now that same earth had come to life with a new crop of springtime grass and showed the occupants and their dwellings in sharp relief. It was a bit disturbing to realize that they had been there all the time, watching us go by everyday.

We slipped back into the old routine but, in spite of our efforts, the time was dragging and we began to count the days to the end of our contract. Psychologically, I suppose it has always been necessary for us showbiz people to keep moving on. No matter how good the gig is, most entertainers are constantly looking forward to the next venue, and it was the same for us. The agency in Wiesbaden had told us that we were due to go to the U.S. Navy base in Bari, Southern Italy, and we were supposed to go directly there from Turkey. In the meantime the last remaining weeks became boring, although somehow we managed to keep our captive audience happy. The big hitters of the time were Johnny Cash, Bobby Bare, and Hank Snow numbers, along with songs from the new boys, like Elvis Presley and Jerry Lee Lewis, who were making a big mark, while 50's Stars like Webb Pierce and Porter Waggoner were still hanging on. The biggest thing around were the truck-driving songs and all that CB radio jargon,10-4 Over and Out. Finally, it was time to go, and we were glad to pack our bags and load up for the trip home, but there were some problems that resulted in a totally unexpected crisis on the way home

The Wreck in the Wilderness

The Transit bus had three rows of seats, which were quite handy, but we rarely used the back seats except to carry some gear, but this time our drummer Paul was ill. He had a cold and went to see the medic on the base, who gave him a big box of pills and he wolfed the lot down and became almost comatose, as the reaction to the drugs he had been taking kicked in, leaving us with the choice of leaving him behind, or bedding him down on the back seat swathed in blankets. This we did, with the result that most of the gear, amps, drums, and guitars, had to be stashed behind the rear seat, making the steering very light but at the time it did not seem that bad.

Our replacement was a band from Liverpool, but we could not wait for them because of our deadline in Bari, Italy, four days hence, so, showered with good wishes and souvenirs we pulled out of the USAF Early warning station at Dyarbikir headed west through the wild mountains of Anatolia. Already we could feel the early chills of the changing season, and glimpsed once again the snow-capped mountains. To avoid the problems of stopping at the primitive Turkish truck-stops on the way back, we had packed sufficient victuals to get us back to civilization. Around Gazientep we stopped for a picnic with the sandwiches, chicken legs, and beer from the base, and pushed on, making good progress from the high plateau down to the Mediterranean coast at Adana. By now Paul was stirring and feeling a little better, but stayed in his blankets. At the next stop we changed drivers, Kit taking over from me and we gently cruised along the Turkish Mediterranean coast in the bright sunshine, passing orange groves and cultivated orchards towards biblical Tarsus, where we turned north-west and picked up the main highway that skirted the Taurus mountains heading to the Turkish capital. Here the vegetation changed; in fact, it virtually disappeared as we climbed gently up to the central plateau, where the landscape was almost lunar in its emptiness. For miles around there were rolling dusty plains, with the silence only broken by the whistling wind and the steady throb of our Dagenham Dustbin happy to be on its way to Italy.

It was true that the desert road was normally quiet, but this day there seemed to be quite a bit of traffic about and we were making good time. We were about three miles south of Aksaray and its lake, about midway between Adana and Ankara, when we hit a raised causeway that weaved its way over the empty scrubland. There were several vehicles approaching us, amongst them one of the huge buses that thunder through those regions. It appeared to be lurching this way and that, as its turbaned driver carried on a heated discussion with one of the passengers behind him and, suddenly, it swerved across the road towards us. Kit quickly pulled the Transit out of the path of the bus but unfortunately the soft earth at the very edge of the causeway gave way under our front wheels. Well, it was inevitable. Kit did not have a chance due to the light unresponsive steering.

The nose went down and over we went. It was all like one of those slow–motion movies. One minute I was on the seat, the next I was flying through the air as the Transit bucked and rolled over. Instinctively I reached out to steady myself on the windshield, but it had already gone, popped out of its rubber frame like a cork. Bodies were hurtling all around me and, through all the yells and bangs I distinctly remember Kit calmly saying. "It's going over boys. Its going," and switching the ignition off as we turned over. One of the big Vox amps came tumbling on top of me as the side panel next to me crumped in. It must have all been over in a few seconds, but it seemed ages before we all finally got out of the vehicle. The bus had gone over sort–of diagonally, first onto its front roof, which is probably how we lost the windshield and then onto its side before doing a full roll back onto its wheels.

We all sat there dazed, each one of us coping with the accident in our own way. I was raging mad about my brand–new bus, and started going on about it. Kit broke into tears from delayed shock and my tantrums. Paul was gone. He had only begun to come round from his crazy medication and did not seem to know exactly what had gone on or how lucky we were to get out unhurt. Ady sat on a rock and tried to light a cigarette. Spud got to him in time before we all disappeared in a roar of spilt petrol fumes. But there we sat in the middle of an Anatolian desert looking at our horribly bent bus and wondering what to do next

Spud was the first to react positively and showed again his great ability in a crisis. We inspected the damage. One wheel, the front offside, was completely buckled and the tyre ripped but the other three were o.k. except for the offside rear which was flat. The windshield was gone but we found it intact about thirty yards away but the body was very badly buckled. From the front, it looked as if the roof had been pushed sideways, with one front wing crushed and a headlight gone, but the radiator did not appear to be leaking. Only one of the doors would open, luckily no more windows were broken and, as Spud discovered, the engine still ran normally. Well, that was something but there did not appear any way to carry on with our journey. The spare wheel was o.k. so we wrestled the buckled wheel from under the crumpled wing and fitted on the spare, using a mike stand to beat the wing metal out of the way. I got in it and found that it drove properly and that the steering still worked.

Now, as I said, when the accident happened, we appeared to be in the middle of nowhere, not a soul to be seen anywhere around, and there were no mobile phones back then. Naturally the Turkish bus driver had put his sandal down when he saw the carnage he had caused in his cracked rear view mirror. By the time we had got out, he was a dust cloud on the eastern horizon. However, as we sat there assessing the damage, people began to appear from nowhere, like Cornish wreckers to see what could be picked up. Strange nomads with bright head–cloths and veiled women toting chubby, dirty children. The men had big black moustaches and smiled evilly with stained teeth, pointing at our incapacitated bus with thick sticks as though they had found a wounded dinosaur. Oh, goody. Dinnertime.

But, Hark. Tarra, tarrar tarrar. Here comes the cavalry. Well, not exactly tarrar, more like 'Honk–Honk' from a massive Volvo truck hissing to a stop above us. The driver jumped down and came to see what he could do. He was Finnish and taking his load through to Iraq and helped us get back on our way. First of all we got the windshield back in place and roped it in and also roped the one functioning door as closed as it would go. With his power winch he dragged us back onto the road and used his built–in compressor to blow up our flat tires. In short he was our Saviour.

As the hordes of Anatolian nomads began squabbling among themselves over the odd bits and pieces we had abandoned, we profusely thanked the driver, and took his address, promising to get in touch with him when we got back to Europe and rattled off again. And then it started raining and it gushed down all the way to the outskirts of Ankara.

Ankara

At the first cab rank I got out and after telling Spud to follow, got a taxi to take me to a good hotel, which turned out to be the old Hotel Berlin in the Ulus district below the citadel and its hillside shantytown of wood and tin shacks. Having got everybody booked in, I asked the driver if he knew a local garage that could sort out the bodywork, or at least make it more presentable. Even though it ran I doubted that the Greeks would let us through the frontier with the body in such a condition. In true Levantine fashion he assured me that his brother–in–law was the finest bodywork man in the city and took me to a street on the poorer side of the town. It seemed like the railway arches in any industrial British town. Here, there was a row of shops on each side of a cobbled street, all of them specializing in some form of auto–repairing There were engineers, coach–trimmers, spray shops, metal workers, and even specialists in re–cutting old tyres. Everybody came out to welcome us, while the taxi driver, who spoke a little German negotiated on my behalf for the bodywork repair.

Eventually it was all sorted out, and I was invited into one of the shop fronts and offered a glass of tea and a three–cornered discussion started between myself, the taxi driver, and the body man he had selected.

'How much for the full job and how soon would it be ready? I asked in German.

The driver frantically discussed the price with his cousin (they were all cousins, I think) finally coming back to me with a tentative offer.

"Zwei hundert dollah, 'Fenndi—Sehr gut preise." He smiled, obviously expecting an argument so I joined in the fun. At one point I suggested to my taxi driver that we try someone else, a prospect that caused panic in the shop and almost gave his cousin apoplexy. The price was dropping steadily, as I inquired what he thought he could do to make the bus pres-entable, and the bystanders joined in the heated explanations, obviously telling me what a good craftsman he was and how lucky I was to have found the very best bodywork man in Ankara. At this point I was checking the cab to see if we had left anything important behind.

There wasn't much, old guitar leads, cans of coke, old maps and magazines. One of these was an old dog–eared copy of Playboy and I threw it out. For a moment there was a stunned silence as it flopped onto the grubby floor, followed by a mad scramble for it, including the cab driver and my virtuoso panel–beater. When it was all over and the magazine in tatters they returned to the haggle, but by this time I realized I held two trump cards, U.S. Dollars and, more importantly, a dozen back issues of Playboy.

There was not much haggling after that, and in short order the price was settled at $100 in US Dollars and the magazines, and, here was the sur-prise, everything would be finished in two days' time at seven in the even-ing. I agreed, handing over the keys, and before I could finish my glass of arrack, men were swarming all over the bus, ripping out roof linings, and beating panels with small copper hammers and burning off paint with roaring blow torches.

Not expecting the work to be finished as quickly as they said, we settled into the Hotel Berlin for a few days and indulged ourselves. Paul was finally feeling better, so he and Spud went on a pub–crawl around the city, while Ady smoked his head off trying every kind of tobacco available. Kit and I went shopping and, as usual, we saw things that we would like to buy, including a beautiful Turkish copper coffee–set, but until we were sure of how much money we would have left when the bus was paid for, we couldn't commit ourselves. Needless to say, in the end we missed it.

The following day I went to the hotel barber shop and had the full works. It was great. They massaged my legs and shoulders and took off my shoes and pulled my toes until they all clicked. It was not in the least painful, and my feet felt so relaxed and warm, though' I did have moments of anxiety when it came to the shave.

One of the barbers (there were three of them working on me, as well as the girl who did the toe–pulling) swathed my face in hot towels, and the girl who had been on toe–pulling duty efficiently lathered my face. Then they all smiled respectfully as another large moustached man stood before me, stropping a large cut throat razor in his hand. He wore a fez, a white coat and DARK GLASSES. Out of the corner of my eye I caught a glance of an old polished brass shell–case near the door and nestling inside it, along with the umbrellas and walking sticks, was a stout red staff with a leather wrist strap holding small brass bells. It was the Kurdish equivalent of a white stick.

He gently reached for me and fluttered his soft fingers across my face. I froze in the chair. But without further ado Old Sweeney Todd got stuck in. It was the best shave I have ever had, as he felt his way over my face and removed every hint of stubble. It was the first and last time a blind man has ever shaved me. But it did teach me one thing. That you don't need a mirror to wet shave and to this very day I shave without one, although I don't use a cutthroat razor, just an ordinary Gillette.

At six–thirty on Thursday evening my taxi driver called at the hotel to take me to the garage. As we drove into the street, we were stopped at the end by our repairman, frantically waving his arms, and telling us that the bus would not be ready till 10.30 p.m. I had a sinking feeling and all my original doubts surfaced again, but there was nothing to do but go back to hotel and wait. At 10 o'clock I had the cab driver take me back to the body shop determined to pick up our vehicle, no matter what kind of botched job they had done. This time the little man smiled and waved us into the street with enthusiasm. We shook hands again and he led me proudly into his shop to show me his work—I couldn't believe my eyes.

There was our bus. It was just like new, with every bump and dent carefully beaten out, even the blemishes that had been there before the accident. I walked round it amazed. They had put little plastic Turkish flags on each wing. About the only indications of the accident were two slight creases on each side of the windscreen pillars and the fact that some parts of the body were still in primer paint, but overall it was a superb job. I was happy to hand him the hundred bucks I had promised, plus a little 25 dollar bonus and the pile of Playboys, which he shared avidly with the cabbie, thanking me effusively when I refused his offer of change. I did not then know that real U.S. greenback dollars were bringing over six times the normal exchange rate on the black market, and that the mild Playboy magazines were highly prized in a country where there was a severe crack–down on pornography, and would probably change hands for vast sums, before ending up in the waiting room of some local brothel.

There were only a couple of other incidents on our homeward journey. The first was an embarrassing moment as we were leaving the Hotel. The manager came fussing out to the car park saying that there was a big bath towel missing from one of our rooms and requested us to open up our cases. There was much objection to this, but in the end, indignantly, we did as he requested, and found the missing towel, which somehow had wormed its way into Spud's case, folded itself neatly in four and burrowed beneath his shirts. can't trust them Turkish towels can you?

The second incident occurred at the Edirne border crossing. The Turks were rather paranoid about losing valuable antiques U.S. servicemen had been buying and shipping back home. They were also hot on drugs, which were beginning to trickle out of Iran and Pakistan, so the border guards made us strip out the entire van. They inspected amplifiers, speakers, and took apart a set of toy trains I had bought for my son. We also had quite a bit of jewellery, gold and alexandrine rings and bracelets. Most of these we wrapped in masking tape and hung on the ignition key ring, which no one suspected. The whole border crossing took hours, but finally we were through and driving out of Edirne and into Macedonia.

There was a sequel however. In a café near Nis we met a band from Liverpool heading east for a gig at Trabazon. Twelve hours after leaving us they too had a bad accident at Uskadar. Those Anatolian roads were wild and dangerous places back in 1967. They probably still are.

PICKER'S TIP 21

In the band bus the best seat is the middle at the front. That way you get a nice view—and you don't have to drive or ask directions.

PICKER'S TIP 22

Get yourself a good pair of cowboy boots for stage work.

They come in handy if there is any trouble and you don't need a pair of socks: any two will do. They don't have to be the same colour because nobody ever sees 'em. But be warned. Don't ever wear cowboy boots without socks or you'll never get them off. Because as your feet warm up, they sweat and will stick to the insides.

Big Steve Turner once got stuck like that for three days and the only way we got them off was with a Stanley knife.

15

THE PLAYBOY CLUB. WOW!

The delay resulting from our accident in Turkey caused us to miss the next contract for Ronnie Harris in Bari, but I don't think that it bothered him overmuch because he simply sent down a British husband–and–wife team with a German band and called it the Western Drifters, figuring that none of the homesick good old boys on the bases would notice the difference. We pushed on to Frankfurt and arrived to find that Snaky Jake had left for Australia and Gisela was on holiday, but that Johnny Downs and Romano had founded a new agency, so we approached them for work. Terms were agreed and they did something that neither Jake nor Gisela did, in giving us a minimum fee per show. Of course it was not pure charity, but reflected the new tightening up of the rules after the Buddy Cagle debacle, and actually gave us no right to ask how much we were being sold for.

This eventuality was neatly covered by the small print in our contract, by giving them managerial rights to act on our behalf in the event of a dispute (even with our own agents, them). We did a few gigs in Frankfurt centre, including the notorious Guteluete Strasse E.M Club, (what a rat pit that was), until one day Johnny called me into the office to tell me he was dealing with an agent in England called Harry Rawden, who was seeking acts for the bustling Northern Clubland circuits. Great, I thought, it would be nice to visit Blighty again, but my heart dropped when he told us where this agency was based. Manchester. Right back where we had started from.

Well, reluctant as I was to return, there was no real alternative, so we packed our bags and drove to the cross–channel ferry (being careful of course to avoid Calais) and landed at Dover in June 1967. Was this the beginning of a new career, or was it a return to the dead–end pubs and workies? I was secretly very apprehensive. Billed as the New Texas Drifters (Nobody bothered to ask what had happened to the old ones so we accepted our new title) we did a few gigs en–route to the north at US bases like Alconbury and Ruislip. One of the shows was with Roy Clarke, which got Spud up–tight as the memory of Mary Taylor's empty promises came bubbling to the surface and ended up with him and Ady fighting.

Oh yes, it held the promise of being a great tour.

Being back in Manchester meant of course that I could stay at home, but this time things were different and I was not wholly welcome, especially when it was realised that I was not giving up the profession and there was a hidden agenda involving one of my ex–musicians who had stayed behind. Their love affair had not yet fully blossomed, but it did in time and they eventually married and were happy together, but Francis, our son, did not find the union easy and eventually joined us in Cornwall.

Harry Rawden was o.k; in fact he did not live far away from my house, in the faded but once elite Jewish district of Heaton park. His house doubled as his office, with a comfortably furnished front room where we discussed future contracts over a bottle of kosher rum. He was a nice man, one of the old school agents who looked upon his clients as part of his show–business family, and genuinely tried to get them the best deal possible. His son Derek eventually joined him in the business but he was a more modern hustling type and formed a partnership with another agent called Mossman and imported Frankie Davidson, an antipodean Frankie Vaughn. By chance, I met Frankie Davidson at the Bondi Diggers Club in Sydney in 1984 and he expressed fond memories of Old Harry and would not comment on Derek, but he did tell me a tale about his partner when he was trying to break into the lucrative US Military circuit.

Somehow Mossman got into a drinking session with Romano, Johnny Downs, Jake Pearson, Charley Klop, and a couple of American club custodians. The liquor was flowing and Mossman was watching carefully as he was very, very money conscious and hated having to buy people drinks. In fact, he made Ed Stewart look like Andrew Carnegie. He stalled as long as he could from ordering, but of course did not refuse his share of drinks, until late in the afternoon, when he figured that everybody had had enough and completely unaware of the German system of noting each client's drinks on their beer–mat, he grandly gestured to the waiter that he wished to pay for the table (meaning a round). So the Herr Ober simply picked up everybody's beer–mat, added them all up and presented this magnanimous Aussie with a bill for the equivalent of sixty quid. His fellow agents just sat there smiling and thanked him kindly. I can't personally vouch for the story but it certainly rang true to form.

Back at the house, Harry explained that we would have to do one or two gigs at new clubs to get established on the scene and the first one was a week at the Monte Carlo club in Birmingham The money was good, so the following Sunday morning we were off down the A5 to the Midlands.

The Monte Carlo Club turned out to be two big terraced houses knocked into one in the Hansworth district. The place seemed to be in a chaotic state of demolition and construction, all going on at the same time, and we appeared to be the only white people around for miles. Our type of music and the abundance of Dixie flags and slogans stuck all over our bus also added to our feelings of vulnerability. It was run by two very nice Greek guys, as were the staff and the resident trio. They had already booked digs for us down the road and our first week back in the UK went very well. They liked our Country Rock sound and paid us an extra £80 to play at somebody's birthday on Saturday afternoon. Kit went down a storm and was sent flowers on stage and the work was easy, usually only one forty–five minute spot a night, a pleasant change from the three or four hours a night we'd been doing on the bases. The basement area was a big casino where the mostly Greek patrons loved to gamble, but there was trouble on a couple of nights when somebody got knifed, and the police came in and swamped the place. We did an early evening TV spot at the Alpha Studios, about a mile away, to promote the club, probably arranged by the local Cypriot Mafia, and were given a bonus and allowed to fill up our tank for

free at one of the garages controlled by the mob. All in all it was a very nice
week.

On following Tuesday afternoon, I reported back to Harry, who had
already received a glowing report of our Monte Carlo week and was beaming like a cat that had eaten all the cream.

"Well, Yonco," He purred. "How would you like to play at the Playboy
Club then?"

I could not believe it. THE PLAYBOY CLUB. Wow. Images of big-
breasted Bunny Girls flooded my brain. as Harry casually dropped the
question on me. Would I like to play the Playboy Club. Would I? Is the
Pope a Catholic? I had always fancied playing in the West End.Great.

"Ah, well," demurred Old Harry "It's not exactly in London, Yonk."

"Oh. Where is it then?" I asked suspiciously. "Surrey, er, Bournemouth?"

"Err, No not exactly. It's at Seaham. A bit up north."

"Oh yeah? And just how far north is it, Harry?"

"Err, Yorkshire way. Y'know, just across the hills." He waved vaguely
towards the Pennine foothills and reached for his glass.

"But it is a Playboy Club? Yes?"

I was not very confident about his side–stepping, but he reassured me it
was.

"Listen, Yonk, don't worry. You'll be fine. Would I ever steer you wrong?
It's called the Playboy Club and it's at Seaham Harbour, a marina with lots
of boats. You'll love it there. You'll do a bomb. They have specially
requested you."

"Requested us eh?" I preened "Fancy that? Well, can't let them down
then, can we?"

I pictured this classy marina. Something like Porto Banus near Malaga.
Chris Craft and Princess cruisers gently rocking at anchor, while bikini-
clad beauties tempted us aboard with tinkling gin and tonics. Great. But it
wasn't quite like that.

There was a Force Nine gale blowing when we arrived at the derelict coal-
ing–port of Seaham Harbour, off the A9 south of Sunderland, on a pitch-
black Sunday night. Several fruitless enquiries of the Danish speaking
locals, (at least they sounded Danish—I tried German on a couple of them
but got no response) failed to reveal the location of this far–flung outpost of
Hugh Hefner's glamour empire, with its Bunny Girls, cool jazz, and rattling roulette tables. Eventually we met an English–speaking Welshman in
a chip shop, who directed us to a long corrugated iron Nissan hut on a wild
wind–swept cliff-top road which displayed on its rusting corrugated sides
a guttering neon sign which read:

SEA—AM ARBOUR PL—YBO. CLUB Ciu. .Affl.

We parked up and, more out of curiosity than anything else, battered our
way through the rough timber door in search of a quick game of baccarat
and maybe the odd slice or two of smoked salmon, but all we met was a
faded old coal miner in a cloth cap signing in three tarted–up, shrieking

women, and a doorman built like a brick shipyard who belligerently collared us.

"Hey—Hinney. Wotcha want lads? Divn't ye naw it's the cabaret neet? Naw Tee sherts or jeans t'neet—C'mon nah Lads. Ooot ye gan."

He cracked his knuckles and rolled his massive shoulders, but somehow I managed to explain to this monster that we actually were the cabaret, if this really was the Playboy Club, hoping it wasn't. He looked down at his list and smiled a gap toothed grin.

"Oh Aye—'Ere it is. The Drifters. Innit? Gan reet on thru lads. Stage door's at the back the bar—Ye canna miss it.

He opened the inner door for us and revealed a long hut, fugged up with tobacco fumes, heaving with big people crowding the bar, and overflowing the chipped orange Formica tables. Out on the dance floor a brigade of Amazon handbag guardians were bopping up and down to the obligatory organ and drums socking out their versions of the current hits of the day like 'Proud Mary' and 'The Land of a Thousand Dances.' (The song that was to get me in so much trouble later at that Naples NCO Club). The bar actually ran the full length of the room, with four barmen working flat out supplying pints of Federation Bitter, big bottles of Newcastle Brown Ale, and gin and tonics to the smoking yelling and guzzling mob—but there was no sign of Hugh Hefner and the Bunny Girls, and no caviar or smoked salmon.

Ady had already pressed the starter button on his moaning mechanism and Spud was searching his mind to find some new way of avoiding un-loading our gear. (By now we had all got wise to his 'Hanging up my coat.' routine so he was varying it with 'just looking at the stage.' and 'Gotta go to the kharzi.' escape plans).

Eventually however, we got on the stand and belted out 'Folsom Prison Blues' to the booze–soaked punters. During the guitar solo, I checked my watch and saw that it was only 8.30, and they were out of their skulls already. What was it going to be like at closing time? I did a couple more Buck Owen's type numbers and then Kit was next up on the auction block giving them 'These Boots Were Made For Walking.' to shouts of "Gerrem off, Gerrem off, Gerrem off." And not just from the lads at the bar either. Even the lassies were joining in as well. It was wild, so we went into solid Country Rock mode turning them into wild whirling Dervishes, and before you knew it, it was time for the main event; the reason the crowds had braved the howling tempest. Yes, folks, you've guessed it. The Bingo.

The microphone desk squealed from feedback as the caller bellowed out.

"Reet. Aal quiet noo, lads an'lassies. S'taym fer th' hoosey. Eyes doon noo. Hush up at the back theer. Ah canna 'ear mesel talk. Noo fer t'neets fylah."

We were wide–eyed. Bingo at the Playboy Club? Wait till I get hold of that agent. As we sat dazed in the dressing room, well supplied with a crate of Newcastle Brown and a bottle of gin, there was a knock on the door and the Concert Sec. poked his head in hoping for a quick flash of Kit getting changed.

"Err. Aye. Is the lass decent? Right, Ah wuz jest wundrin'. Could yez do some o' yore big hits? Ye naw, like 'Dock o'the bay.' an' Unner th' boardwalk.' Oor Lass' favorite, that is. Reet? Luverly. Howay Noo."

He actually thought that he had booked 'The Drifters', the world famous original black singing group from the States. He must not have noticed that our contract clearly stated that we were the New Texas Drifters or that we had white skins. Dumbfounded, we nodded and said we'd love to do his requests (Even if they were all Wilson Picket songs). I doubt if the official knew the difference. In the event it didn't matter anyway because nearly all the punters went home after the bingo and by 11.30 we were on our way to Sunderland and our digs at South Lodge.

PICKER'S TIP 23

Here's one we learned the hard way.

On tour don't be tempted to stay with fans or relatives. When offered, it might appear to be cheaper, but in the long run it's not. Furthermore, after a tough gig, you will be expected to stay up half the night listening to obscure recordings, while your boring hosts slag off other performers.

(Next week it'll be your turn).

The Cabaret Clubs—David Houston

Now, South Lodge was something else. It must rate as just about the best showbiz digs in the country at that time. It was a large, well–restored house in a Victorian terrace. that one time had been home to the families of senior shipyard executives. when business was booming in the shipyards of the River Wear. Now it had been converted into a very comfortable and well–appointed hotel for the theatrical profession and was run by an eccentric gay young man with bizarre tastes, his live–in boy friend and his mother, who was a friend of the Welsh singer Dorothy Squires. Derek her son, gay as he was did not let his sexual preferences affect the running of the digs, or the superb food served. A week there, including late breakfast, afternoon tea, a three course dinner at 5p.m., and a flask of coffee and sandwiches in your room when you got back in the wee small hours; all for around fifteen pounds a week. They were so obliging and friendly and being there was like being part of a big family. On one occasion we arrived very late, about 2am and Derek allowed us to stay in their private apartment rather than disturb his other guests.

Many now–famous names were grateful for digs like these on that demanding North Eastern circuit. Johnny More, a superb singer, and for my money one of the best Sinatra imitators in the business; knockout comedians like Dustin Gee and Paul Melba; plus Mike Yarwood and Benny

York, both impressionists supreme, all passed through the doors at one time or another. Of course, as in lots of showbiz digs, there was always light–hearted banter and horse–play between the acts, but there were plenty of bores as well. One or two forgot that they were in equally talented company, and insisted on doing their routines over and over again at meal times. Benny York, for instance, became so enamoured with his impressions, that he forgot the sound of his own voice, and you could end up passing the salt to John Wayne or Max Bygraves. And there was an Al. Jolson type singer called Jerry Valence, who insisted that he got a standing ovation every night, though Johnny More and Dustin caught his act one night and he almost emptied the club.

Gentle Derek and his fluffy pal Eric were often the butt of this good–humoured banter. For instance, one night at dinner, Derek cheekily let everybody know that he never wore underpants. "Oh, I can't be bothered y'know. an' they just keep gerrin' in the way," he simpered. So the following morning at breakfast Lynn Perrie (the future shrewish Ivy Brennan in Coronation street) and a great singer called Sheila Southern waited behind the dining room door for Gay Derek to deliver the breakfasts. And now came the moment of truth, for as he swanned gracefully into the room bearing a large tray of bacon and eggs, the girls pounced and, with a flick of his zipper and a swift tug, they de–bagged him. And there it was for all to see. But the ever–cool Derek still managed to place the tray on the table faultlessly. We all cheered and it proved that he was not lying—and that he did have something to boast about.

The New Texas Drifters made quite a mark on the Clubland circuit of that time. We were the first commercially–dedicated modern Country Music act to hit the clubs. It's true that Johnny Duncan and Pete Sayers had done a Flatt and Scruggs bluegrass act and although very good, it was more akin to skiffle than anything else, and they used the current popularity of the Beverly Hillbillies TV show to get across to the audiences. Elsewhere, there were borderline acts like the Karl Denver Trio and Joe Brown and the Bruvvers who would have loved to play our style of stone country music, but whose managements proved reluctant to stick their meal tickets with a C&W tag. About the only ones whom I remember, who stuck to their guns on that circuit and didn't run for cover to the folk clubs, were Scottish acts like Houston Wells, and whisky heir Big Pete Duchar—and of course, the much under–rated and neglected Cliff Leger Trio, from Redcar, was a major player indeed.

By now we had learned a lot about American showbiz from the many major American Country Stars we had worked with over the years, and would continue to do so. The net result was that we had developed a very polished and professional show, that could only be achieved on the hard–driving and demanding military club circuit and it proved to be a big attraction on the top–line UK Theatre Clubs.

Our next contract was our first escalation to the mainstream major league of Clubland. It was a week at the famous Ba–Ba Club, TV magician Peter Casson's place in Barnsley. Like so many of these venues it was a converted cinema and was situated in the town's marketplace. It was beautifully appointed and contained an elegant casino and a first–class restaurant as well as the big cabaret lounge. We lived out of town at a pub near another perhaps more prestigious venue the Batley Variety Club, which we played a couple of times in the coming year. This gig went well for the first days, until Ady had his standard weekly wobbler. On this occasion, he chose to have a go at the evening's compere, giving him a mouthful of abuse and claiming that his guitar amp had been moved around and scratched in the process. In the event the outburst proved to be a bit of a faux pas, as the compere that night happened to be the owner, Peter Casson himself, and it was only my humble and mealy–mouthed apology that saved us from being paid off. It's funny really. If you take on board all the stress and problems the man had given me, I should have fired him right there and then, but he was a good guitarist and I did not want to make major changes in the middle of a good run of work. So I let things slide (again).

The jewel in the crown of these theatre clubs was Sheffield Fiesta, a huge venue with a capacity of over two thousand paying patrons. It was beautiful with each quadrant of the auditorium furnished a different colour with its own maitre'd in radio contact with a central control room over-looking the whole scene. Highlights there were sharing the bill with such notables as raconteur/–comedian Dave Allen, and that superb song stylist Tony Christie. The high spot for me personally was on our second trip, when I did Kris Kristoffeson's great song 'Sunday Morning Coming Down.' on a blacked–out stage with a single spotlight on me sitting on a high stool. It was electric. And for a few seconds after I finished there was a silence before the whole place exploded with wild applause. I got a real buzz out of that. Such moments make all the hard nights on the road worthwhile. However, wonderful as it was, the Sheffield Fiesta did have one great flaw, there was no stage door. It had been adapted from a large building backing onto a multi–storey car park with the result that there was no back en-trance, and everybody, from big stars like Shirley Bassey and Tom Jones, to support acts like us with all our gear, had to come in at the front en-trance and negotiate a long series of twisting underground passages to get backstage.

Mind you not all Country acts got the appreciation they deserved or at least expected, as in the case of George Hamilton IV at Batley Variety Club, where his act was completely swamped by the slapstick comedy of Little and Large. Sid and Eddie had only been booked at the last minute as support, but they were solidly on their own ground and stole the show. And everybody knows what happened to them after that.

After a month in Yorkshire, it was back on the old A9 heading north to the swinging north–east coast, this time to the Riviera Club at West

Hartlepool. When we got there, the town seemed to be in its death–throes with big jawed yellow diggers and JCBs eating its heart out, while hard–hatted surveyors were laying down the outlines for a new metropolis, confident that the strong tide of progress and prosperity would go on for ever. In fact, I myself was so convinced of this, that at one time we seriously considered relocating our base from Manchester to Billingham. By some strange twist of fate (or perhaps some well–lubricated influence), the Riviera Club proved to be one of the few original buildings left standing.

It was owned by one of the affluent showmen with wide interests throughout the fairground scene. It turned out to be a much better than the Seaham Playboy Club, (well, that didn't take a lot of doing did it?) and the shows were the standard two 45 minute spots, one at 10 p.m. and the second at 1am. The real bright spot was the resident trio called Brighton Beach, who, I believe, eventually went to South Africa, where they had a very successful career. We had digs in Seaton Carew, about the only sea–side resort I know with an open–cast coal mine on the beach and it was quite apparent that the new renaissance did not extend this far. It was as if they were still in the depth of the 1930's depression. You could almost hear the tramp of the miner's boots as they passed by on that heart–rending Jarrow hunger march to a cold and indifferent Parliament in London.

During our stay at the Riviera we were featured on a special show at the Seaton Leisure Centre on the beach with US Country star David Houston. God knows what he thought about the location, but I suppose on reflection it was no worse than some of the harsh Kentucky mining towns he had played on his way to Nashville fame. His big hit was 'My Elusive Dreams', which he did with a local girl singer, who had no sense of timing or pitch whatever, who turned out to be the promoter's star–struck daughter. Judging by the look on David's face at the hotel afterwards, his 'Elusive Dream' must have seemed like a nightmare.

The people of that region are wonderful though. They are honest and truly appreciative of hard–working acts, but will not accept any second-rate talent. So many cocky or inexperienced acts have come unstuck by dismissing the gigs up there simply because of the bingo games, and thinking that the punters would not notice if they botched things up, or worse still, by mocking the local accents and customs. That's not to say that there weren't some bad clubs as well though, and I remember one quite clearly.

As a fill in, Frank Feeney sent us to do a Sunday noon gig at a club in Gateshead, that had such a bad reputation that some acts would stipulate a clause in their contracts to avoid it. We were new to the area, so didn't know what to expect, and when we arrived there at noon, a frantic Concert Secretary greeted us, saying that we were late and hustled us on stage. The place was heaving with 'The Lads', all slurping pints of Federation Bitter and St Luke's Brew (Newcastle Brown Ale) and shouting football slogans and generally having a riotous time. The last thing they wanted was entertainment, but having the acts was the price they had to pay for having a Bingo licence, and they made their contempt quite clear. We kicked off in style and the Sunday morning Rambos glowered at us for the first few songs until I brought Kit on, and then it was all "Gerrumoff. Gerrumoff," and all sorts of coarse jokes. She handled it very well and got on with her spot and to cool things down she went into Patsy Cline's touching, 'He called me Baby, Baby all Night long'.

This sudden switch left some of 'The Lads' looking ridiculous and they quietened down a little. But there's always one 'House Dragon' that feels threatened by a confident woman, and this one showed his mates that he was not going to be told what to do by a bloody tart. He pulled his cap down and smirking at the boozers, dragged his chair to the front and put his feet on the edge of the stage, got out a Racing Pink and buried his head in it. Kit struggled on, as he noisily rustled the pages and called out his selection. She was handling it well, but by now I had had enough of this plonker, so I borrowed a cigarette lighter from Ady and during the solo I casually edged towards him. He looked up and curled his lip then studiously ignoring me, he turned to look over his shoulder and preen at his mates. It was at this moment I pretended to drop my guitar pick, bent down and set fire to a corner of his paper. That made the ignorant bastard get his feet off the stage quick enough.

Needless to say, Frank didn't book us into that club again, ever.

August was not the peak time for the clubs, as a high proportion of the patrons were away on holiday, and most of the best acts had already found themselves summer seasons at premier resorts like Blackpool or Great Yarmouth, Mind you, there was always the other side of the coin, and you could end up in some tatty theatre in Hoylake or Jaywick. The late Colin Compton made a whole routine out of the fact that he was once the victim of a couple of such seasons in Morcambe. It was however a good time to launch young hopefuls and imported acts onto the circuit, and that is exactly how we came to be known on these bigger clubs. Usually it would be a double booking, like for instance, a week at the Rosegrove in Burnley and the Bolton Casino, but it wasn't all roses though. Some clubs could be rough like Wigan Casino, the home of 'Northern Soul Music', where they would throw meat pies at bad acts. They also had another tradition of throwing beer mats onstage if they liked you—which luckily they did with us.

In the August of that year, we were booked on a big double by Les Morgan's Agency, at that time the leading booker east of the Pennines. The venues were the Lyceum Theatre, Bradford, and the Starlight Club at Guisley. It was a double–top billing, us and impressionist, Paul Melba, with a good girl singer called Terry Savage as support—and what a week that was. On Saturday and Sunday both places were busy and the show was very well received, but for the early part of the week it was dead. We played the part of an audience for Paul and Terry, and they did the same for us, until, of course, Friday night came around and all the locals came out of the woodwork and got paralytic for the next three nights. Paul was excellent and his imitations were extraordinary, featuring people like James Mason, Noel Coward, and Patrick McGooghan, (whose 'The Prisoner' TV series was riding high at the time) while other impressionists were doing the dead easy ones like John Wayne, or James Stewart. I remember Terry Savage as a charismatic singer, who became one of the first top class entertainers on the cruise ships.

At the Starlight Club, we sometimes had the odd punter or work's outing that was heading back from Harry Ramsden's famous chip shop across the road, or just killing time until there was table available there. By the way, do not let that term 'Chip Shop' fool you. Harry's was actually a fish restaurant par excellence, it was the biggest in Britain. ('Though, not the first—that honour goes to Oldham back in the 1880s, but it was only fish back then, the chips came later, from the USA). Complete with crystal chandeliers and starched tablecloths, it could hold more than the Lyceum and the Starlight clubs put together—and it usually did. About the only other place I saw like it was years later in St. Helier, Jersey C.I. It too had chandeliers and private booths, and an elegant Victorian sign that proudly bore the message:

> ALBERT. J. RAMSBOTTOM
> Master Fish Fryer.
> The Fish Restaurant With A Touch Of Class.

We had a couple of great meals there. It was a super place, beautifully appointed, with real Lancashire lassies as waitresses, and great fish and seafood, plus the added bonus of French wine at sensible prices—but I digress. On with the tale.

The New Texas Drifters continued to work the top theatre clubs across the UK. Titos, Stockton, was the first venue on an extended stay in the Tyne–Tees area. Followed in quick succession by the Fiesta, Stockton, the Dolce Vita, South Shields, the La Ronde, Billingham, the Marimba, Middlesborough, and many others. Often there were doubles with CIU clubs or the bigger British Legions to start the evening and then, around midnight, a fifty–minute spot at one of the cabaret clubs, which stayed open till 2 or 3 am. It was hard work, with the usual headaches of broken–down vans and poor digs, but we were riding high, earning big bucks, and took it all in our stride. There was some tremendous talent on those clubs then and, as opposed to today, the profusion of clubs made it possible for young acts to get a start and learn the business. There were many great singers and comics up there and one that immediately springs to mind is old timer, Bobby Thompson, a Tyneside legend. The first time I saw him was at a Sunday lunchtime show in Middlesborough. The place was rocking with wild laughter but I couldn't understand a word of his Geordie patois. I thought he was a shipwrecked Scandinavian fisherman or something, but when I got used to his accent, I thought he was one of the most hilarious comedians I had ever seen.

Many of these highly–paid and popular acts were not tempted to move to the bright lights of London's West End, or any great desire for television exposure, as they found all the fame and fortune they wanted on the lavish cabaret club circuit of the North, with acts like Ronnie Dukes and Ricky Lee (with Ronnie's mother–in–law on the piano) playing to packed houses six nights a week, and getting home most nights. They were superb.

Our next stop was in the Rossendale Valley area of Lancashire, and one night Harry Rawden brought an agent from Blackpool to see us at the Rosegrove in Burnley. He must have liked what he saw, because he booked us for a week at the Planet Room at the Blackpool Winter Gardens. I remember one night in Burnley vividly, Max Wall was top of the bill and he was clearly not happy at this rather basic converted cinema club. I thought that he was wonderful and have always been an admirer of his unique and versatile talent, but this night he was so down.

We sat backstage and, sharing a bottle of Glenmorange, talked about his problems, and how his closest friends and the showbiz establishment had turned their backs on him because of the break–up of his marriage. By the time he was through, he was in tears and I was almost legless, but some-how managed to get through the show, though I think Kit and the boys did more than I did that night. But it was a forceful reminder of just how cruel and treacherous this business can be. It is like a jungle where the pred-ators turn on any unprotected members of the pack. Witness what hap-pened to Kathy Kirby.

There were quite a lot of acts working that circuit that later became household names. I remember one nervous Irish comedian called Mike Newman. (Can you ever imagine Mike being nervous?), Also there was a young ventriloquist called Keith Harris. I don't think that Orville was even an egg back then. But not everybody wanted the travelling life. With such a plethora of good venues in a relatively small area, it was possible to earn good money as a semi–pro.

We picked up on the Clubland circuits again, still billed as The New Texas Drifters, working full weeks with the usual change–over each Sunday. The first stop was a converted billiard hall in Blackburn called the Hot Spot Club. across the road from the oldest operating cinema in Great Britain, the Alexandra, which had opened in 1909, but was now showing only Asian films. A sign of the times perhaps. The moving pictures move-ment seemed to have made a great impact in the cotton towns of Lanca-shire, because the first purpose–built cinema in the UK strangely enough, was in the same region.

It was the Central Hall at Colne, near Burnley, opened by a certain Joshua Duckworth of the Premier Picture Company on February 22nd 1907 at a cost of £2000. It operated as a cinema until 1924 and was currently used as an engineering training establishment. While doing these clubs, our van broke down (again) so we went by a train that took all day to travel from Denos Club, Manchester to a club in Blackburn. The distance was about thirty miles and required three changes. Good old British Rail, eh? (Not that it is much better today, under its new set–up).

Another place that does stick in my mind about that period was an Irish club called the Tara in Wimbledon, where we were often booked on our way up to the ferry. Later, as the Tennessee Club, it became famous as a Country Music venue run by the imaginative Chris Ford, who was good at running clubs but not very good at all managing artists. The Tara was a very primitive place. It was not licensed for liquor, but back stage there were crates of Guinness and bottles of whiskey for the bands. The Irish Country scene was still in its infancy and the customs of the 'Ould Country' dance halls died hard, such as using two bands playing thirty minute sets each, with one band playing Irish traditional tunes and the other standard Country and Western numbers. But the strangest custom of all was that all the girls sat down one side of the hall (knees together, ladies) and all lads down the other side. The evening started off very laid–back, but after closing time at the local pubs it became bedlam. (It was like being back in Norway).

Scouse Land

I always loved working in Liverpool: Even after a long drag, say from Scotland or Cornwall, you would arrive knackered and jaded, but after half an hour in the company of those animated amusing Liverpudlians, you would be raring to go. The clubs too were great. Allinsons, Pickwicks, the Shakespeare, the Grafton Rooms, and the one I liked best, Terry Philips famous Wookey Hollow club in Croxteth. Back then it was quite a nice district of Liverpool but I wouldn't leave my car there now—or stop if I could avoid it.

I recall that one of those clubs burned down eventually. In fact it happened to quite a few clubs at the time, all accidentally, of course, but there did seem to be some correlation between falling audience figures and the increased fire–risk. Quite a few were destroyed and the resulting insurance pay–out more often financed a villa in Marbella rather than the reconstruction, which, strangely, seemed to be delayed by complex planning problems. In fact, I remember an enterprising family in the Speke area, who could supply this service on demand. Sometimes though, if the insurance company got suspicious, they would call in the police. In one case, they found a claim from a haulier for paintwork ruined when he had parked his truck in the club's car park on the night of the fire. Diligent work by the Claims Adjuster revealed that the truck had been carrying steel beams the exact size for the re–building of the premises and, due to some office mix–up, had arrived a week early at the site. The warm, scouse bonhomie could also backfire easily and be very uncomfortable. Here are a couple of examples.

A pal of mine, Carl Goldby, was a superb guitarist with the Blue Mountain Boys, one the top bands in Liverpool, and in a family unit with his brother, Johnny, and John's wife, Ann, who was a superb singer. From time to time, Carl would try his hand at promoting a show, but he seldom did more than break–even. Everybody admired his efforts and said what a good guy he was, until one night, when he put on a Country Music Festival at the Grafton Rooms. He booked some local Liverpool bands and us and it was highly successful, and he actually made a profit. At which point opinions about him suddenly changed. It was all right, while he was losing money, he was the classic Scouse Martyr. But now he was a snake. A racketeer, a rip–off merchant taking advantage of both the musicians and the fans. He couldn't win. A few years later, he called in at our club in Cornwall and told me that he planned to emigrate to South Africa. He'd had enough. The second incident occurred like this.

One afternoon, a day or so after this show, I was in a shop when two girls came clicking up to me on white stilettos. They looked like Dusty Springfield twins, with mini skirts, back–combed blond hair, and eyes like pandas. "Your that Frank Yonco aren't cha?" They chirruped. "We saw yuh at da Grafton de odder nigh'. We thought yuh waz great—but yuh not. Tarrar." Gulp. What could I say?

You don't stay on your high horse long in Liverpool; but it's still a great town.

In November '67, Harry Rawden fixed a contract with Andre Da Costa, now re–established in Athens, for a further stint in Turkey. These gigs were at some of the more civilised and less isolated bases like Karamusel and Adana, but alas, this was not to be, as the agency pulled out at the last moment, and took one of Snaky Jake's kickback acts instead, a not unusual occurrence. And there was nothing we could do about it, because we had no management to look after our career. Eventually, I did sign with a nice guy called Harry Gunn, who put a few good things our way. In general though, I was sceptical of managers who knew little about their clients. Before Harry Gunn, I had had three managers, and each one turned out to be rip–off merchants, who were busy feathering their nests at the artistes' expense. If you ever get a chance, talk to Bobby Ball about his long hard slog on the Northern Clubs with the Harper Brothers. In the end, it so discouraged my old friend, Wally Harper, that he gave it the elbow and took himself off to South Africa and a brand new career.

* * * * * *

In the Land of my Fathers

By now there were odd sinister murmurings from the front end of our Transit. We decided that it was probably our old Dagenham Dustbin suffering a bit of delayed shock from its Turkish experience, so we put our suspicions at the back of our minds as we packed up on the following Sunday morning and headed to South Wales for yet another week's booking. There must have been dozens of acts and bands shuffling across the British Isles on those Sunday mornings to fresh venues and the unknown perils of strange showbiz digs, some of which could be very cruddy indeed. Our gig for the coming week was at Titos Club in Cardiff as support for comedienne Kim Cordell, who was starring in the popular Stars and Garters TV show.

Unfortunately, before we hit the A1, it became obvious that we had some trouble. It sounded like a big end rattle and the spectre of our 1966 trip raised its dreaded head, but we decided that with careful driving and a minimum of stops we could make the 300-mile cross-country run.

Titos turned out to be a big multi-storied club in Greyfriars Road in the heart of the Welsh capital, owned by a local businessman of Arab extraction called Annis Abrams. He was waiting at the door as we spluttered up, filling the street with grey smoke, so he knew that we weren't kidding and accepted our apologies for arriving late. By 9 p.m. we were on stage and socking it to 'em, all us good old boys looking like Beau Brummels in our dark green mohair suits and Kit in a long jewelled evening dress. Our show went down very well and after the applause died down, a good speciality magician followed us on stage and then it was—Star Time.

"MISS KIM CORDELL," announced the compere and on stage stomped the buxom lady herself, waving a Union flag and singing old music hall songs like 'Goodbye Dolly I must leave You."

The songs were fine, but her East End hardcore humour created a lot of frozen smiles and embarrassed titters from the rather reserved Welsh audience, in fact when she told, and graphically demonstrated, the gag about the masturbating astronaut, the silence was deafening. But unperturbed, she pressed gaily on with such gutter gags as the fancy-dress ball where everybody had to come as a popular phrase or saying, the prize going to a man who had trapped his penis in the lid of a biscuit tin who came as 'Fucking Crackers.'

Ah! yes, Kids, all this in puritanical South Wales in 1967.

However, everything considered, the week went well and the club did a lot of good business, with Annis himself doing a stint of compering in his own inimitable style. I vividly recall the last night of the week when at the final curtain, he came on to announce the winner of the week's sweepstake in the casino and addressed the patrons in his sing-song Arab-Welsh accent.

"Oh, well now," he announced "Me, I'd like personally t'thank Frankie Yonka an Kit Connass an' the groop for a wonderful show. They waz marvellous, Eh wot? An' oh yess, I waz fergettin' 'bout Miss Kim Cordell—not a bad singer eh? Though I mus' say that I didn't unnnerstan' 'alf the bloody dirty jokes, tho' eh?"

The assembled Taffs cheered like they were at Cardiff Arms Park as he blew his nose on a big silk handkerchief before continuing.

"Oh yes, we've all had a bloody good week really, tho' the casino coulda done a bit better. Now let's 'ave a look at next week."

He scrabbled in the pocket of his dinner jacket to find a scrap of paper.

"Oh aye. There's goin' to be a bit of a change. Yes, we waz goin' to 'ave Bob Monk'ous, y'know, that comic from the telee, but I don't like 'is bloody jokes, an' he wanted three grand. An' I for one don't think that 'ees worth that kind of brass."

I couldn't believe it—a club owner slagging off an act in public on his own club's stage, but I didn't know old Annis. He shook his head and moved on.

"So I've decided to blow 'im out, but the only thing they could offer me was a Jewish cockney from Glasgow who sings skiffle—so I said we'd 'ave 'im instead, okay?"

They all cheered and slopped their pints all over the place.

"So next week, Ladies and Gentlemen we've go, err, Lonnie Donegan."

Wow. What a gig. No wonder Kim did the astronaut joke. I hadn't come across a club owner like him since I had worked for that paragon of tact and good taste, Bernard Manning, a few years previously. We did the gig again about a year later, but by this time Annis had moved on to bigger things.

I can honestly say that I liked working in South Wales. The people did enjoy themselves, much like the Geordies, and the clubs were very well-run and equipped with state-of-the-art equipment, even in the valleys where we went next. Up to the tough mining districts of Maesteg, Caerau, and Pontycymer, where the clubs were the centre and focus of the social life of the region, prosperous, and free from the corruption that tainted some big city clubs.

Max Boyce was king up there and he was very good—and his ethnic humour certainly endeared him to the crowds when we played a gig with him at Cardiff Arms Park. Things were going well for us now and perhaps I was becoming a victim of that creeping showbiz condition of egocentricity, but I was quickly brought to earth in the Valleys.

* * * * * *

Down in the Valley

Agent Arthur Owen from Briton Ferry sent us up to a club outside Merthyr Tydfil and that's where it happened. As part of our act I would bring out a bottle of whiskey and put it on stage as a prize for anyone who could find a country song that I didn't know. (Big headed or wot?) Yes, I know how pretentious it sounds nowadays, but back then Country Music wasn't all that well known in Britain, so I was usually on safe ground but not on this particular night.

The gauntlet was thrown down and the crowd responded.
"Your Cheating Heart"
"Will tell on you—" (Dead easy).
"China Doll"
"I'm tired of sighing. I'm tired of." (A Walkover).
"Cry, Cry, Cry,"
"Everybody knows where you go". (Simple).
"David of the White Rock"
"—What?" (Oh, shit).

It was an old boy at the front with a big tobacco–stained moustache and a blue pocked–marked face of an ex–miner, He stood up and shouted again as I tried to ignore him. I shifted my position away from the spotlight and this time I could see him clearly and I groaned. It was the same old bore that had cornered me at the bar during our break and rammed his opinion down my throat telling me that he knew Tom Jones as a boy. "An' you know wot?" He whined, "he couldn't sing a bloody note in tune. They wouldn't even'ave 'im in the choir." And then he went on to inform me that he had been on the committee the night they paid off Shirley Bassey. So I knew I had a problem.

I had heard of a classic folk ballad called David of the White Rock but the tune escaped me completely. In fact about the only Welsh song I knew was the Ash Grove, but I couldn't do that. And now this old goat was going for my jugular, egged on by his butties. (Mates).

"Oh, err, "I said," Well, that's not really what I meant—folk songs don't count."

There was a tense silence and pint pots were carefully placed on the tables and a sinister shifting of chairs commenced but—Tararr, Tararr. Here comes the cavalry in the form of the Bingo. A bell rang and the old boy's complaints were drowned in the stamping feet of the late ticket buyers and the clicking of the magic numbered balls. I thought nothing more of the incident. In fact our last spot went very well indeed. We left 'em cheering and I though the affair of the whiskey was all forgotten until it came time for us to leave.

As we emerged from the back door into the darkness behind the club we were confronted by a posse of big rough–arsed miners, all of them well pissed and out for trouble demanding that I gave the old man his whiskey.

"Bollocks," I answered, carefully reaching into the cab for my favourite tyre lever, "He asked for a Welsh song, not a Country song."

I could see the way it was going and it had never been in my nature to back away from trouble but these odds were a bit too heavy!—and in such circumstances my band were about as reliable as black belt origami experts. So I expected the worst.

"Oh, Yess?" said a big one threateningly, "and is Wales not a country then, eh?"

"Well, err. Yes, of course it is but—"

An even bigger tough stepped forward, his eyes blazing

"Well then, if you admit it's a country, 'es won fair an' square 'assen 'e? So you just give Albert 'is bottle. Right?"

It was Dyarbikir all over again. I could see the van minus tyres and us minus teeth, so, to the obvious relief of my band, I agreed with his reasoning and like a good old boy handed over the Famous Grouse and drove swiftly down the dark mountain road. Gulp. Well, you can't win 'em all can you.

Needless to say I did not use the Country Song Challenge again.

As '67 rolled to an end, there was one gig worth noting. On Christmas Eve of that year we played at Stockport County Football Club. One of the acts on the show that night was a smooth crooner called Will Torme, singing the songs of his idol Mel. Unfortunately the resident compere had a strong Denton accent and had no truck with all that Yankee rubbish and introduced him as Bill Tarmy. Yes, that's right the same Bill Tarmy who became Coronation Street's henpecked Jack Duckworth

I had Christmas at home as usual and for once it went very well. At least, I had enough money to justify my being away on the road so much, but it was not long before those two demons of a musician's life, boredom and wanderlust, began to reappear, and by early January 1968 I was on the move again to Italy and Spain.

PICKER'S TIP 24

Remember your show starts as soon as you walk on stage. Be cool. Arrive with grace and style. Don't charge on like a tornado. Let the audience get to know you, because their first reaction will be one of scepticism. You must win them over with your personality and ability, but let them warm to you. I know that Johnny Rotten didn't do it that way.

But you're not him, so be thankful for small mercies.

PICKER'S TIP 25

If you are starting up a band kick off with rhythm and blues. It's dead easy. Just learn the basic five Blues chords (Actually, you can get away with three). Then get yourself a capo so you can play them in any key and you're up and running, because basically that's all there is to it.

You can make up the lyrics as you go along.

'The 'World's Best Rock 'n' Roll Band' has been getting away with it for years.

PICKER'S TIP 26

Steer clear of 12 string guitars. In a band context their use is limited to open string runs and their constant need for fine–tuning is a nightmare.
They are o.k. for single performers like Roger Whittaker type pop-folkies with beards, glasses, and safari jackets. But if you feel you must have 'That Sound' first check out Picker's Tip No 12.

16

BACK TO EUROPE AGAIN

Sheb Wooley. Lefty Frizzel. Roger Miller. Molly Bee

As 1968 rolled around we were offered another contract in Europe. This time with Sheb Wooley, who was cashing in on his success as Pete Nolan, the scout in the TV series Rawhide. We got on very well and I had a lot of respect for him. Like Tex Williams, he was a product of Hollywood rather than Nashville, and was dedicated to his chosen profession and worked hard at it. In stark contrast to some of the so–called 'STARS' who had risen to prominence on the strength of one hit record and in no way could back it up with a credible stage act.

For this tour I wanted a more modern sound and decided to drop the steel guitar and add a piano to the standard guitar, bass and drums, line up. On bass I used Big David Nisbett, whom I'd met when he was working on the road with Eck and the Echos'. On guitar, in spite of my better judgement, I kept Ady and on percussion I pulled in an old friend, John Harrison, who had worked with me in my early days and, although his musical preference was for jazz, he was very adaptable. Well, adaptable musically at least, though as events turned out he was not so adapted to the travelling life. Back home in the small Cheshire town of Hyde he had been a real swinging 'Man about Town', a local James Bond, the 'Cool Dude' bachelor, living at home, with a good job and a nice car, popular in the local pubs and with the local girls. But he was sadly miscast for life on the road. He was a great pint of bitter man, but found German lager too strong for comfort, continually accusing us of spiking his ale with vodka when he wasn't looking. His prize performance was at Bad Canstatt Hospital when, after six big bottles of Lowenbrau, he hobbled down a stone staircase on his knees. He's probably still got the scars. I always enjoyed his company and admired his drumming talents and we had a good laugh about those days when we met up again a few years later.

The piano player though was something else. Slim Traynor put me on to him and I found him in a Salford pub pumping away on an old scarred up-right. He said his name was Lee (though everybody in the pub called him Clive) and his piano style was just what I was looking for. It was a hybrid of Floyd Cramer with a touch of Jerry Lee Lewis. Great. Like the drum-mer, he had never been on the road before, not even in the UK and couldn't handle the stress and did not have the self–dependency and discipline required for hard touring. I should have got some idea of what was to come when I went round to pick him up for the trip. Frantic gesticulating from his front room window indicated that we should wait for him at the pub round the corner where he turned up with a plastic bag containing his shaving kit and a spare pair of jeans. When we left he also insisted on a complicated detour to avoid any neighbours seeing his secret departure.

The tour did not set off all that well though. We did house–jobs for about four days, which enabled us to get the blend and the balance right, after which Gisela sent us to Torrojon Air Base near Madrid, Spain, where we were due to meet our star. We expected to fly but were sent by train, first to Paris, and then via Biarritz to the Spanish border at Irun, where we changed trains from the superb high speed S.N.C.F electric to a Spanish National Railways steam train. It was filthy and chugged slowly through the bleak miserable hills to the capital, where we were met by a van from the base. However, Mr. Wooley had not yet arrived, because he had run in to his old buddy Roger Miller in New York and they had taken off on a three–day binge, so we were ordered to do our show and try to hold things together. It was o.k. for the first night, but at lunchtime the next day, in the NCO Club Lee got so drunk he could not play a note that night, giving us a foretaste of what was to come. Luckily however the club decided to change the date of the Sheb Wooley show and, after two shows, at the US base at Sitges, they flew us back to Frankfurt to wait for him there.

Lefty Frizzell

We were still at Eisenblatter's Guest House when Gisela Gunther phoned and booked me to back–up one of Country Music's truly great legends, Lefty Frizzell, on a tour of Italy. By now this great icon, a contemporary of Hank Williams, and an inspiration to later legends like Merle Haggard and George Jones, was a sick man, a shadow of his former self, in the early stages of the illness that killed him a few short years later. Unfortunately, the drugs taken to control the condition often made him appear unstable, and could be easily misconstrued as his being drunk and, as you can imagine, quite a few bone–headed club managers gave him a hard time. He was not helped either by his record company's choice of company for him. They had sent over a virtually unknown mediocre singer called Tommy Gabler, whose attitude, lack of talent, and general behaviour did little to help the ailing star. He was a grossly over–weight character whose habit of performing in a bright yellow 'Nudie' suit resulted in him being given the title of 'The Singing Easter Egg'.

Lefty however rose above it all and gave a sterling performance of all his old favourites which went down very well and his closing number 'Saginaw Michigan' always brought a standing ovation. This tour took about thirty days and ended up at Pordenone in northern Italy, after which Lefty flew back to Germany for a much needed rest, and we were instructed to return to our base in Frankfurt by train The schedule gave us a few days off, so we took advantage of it to see Milan and Venice

I have always loved Italy and things Italian, (especially Sofia Loren) but I'm afraid that the band did not whole–heartedly share my enthusiasm, particularly our prickly guitar–picker who, in addition to his moody attitude, had a very short temper, which could be triggered off by the slightest thing, and all through the tour he had been building up to an explosion. He would alternatively sulk or spout off about what a bunch of wankers these American audiences were and how he could be doing much better somewhere else rather than schlepping round Europe with a bunch of no-hopers like us.

In short, he was not making any friends and was getting right up everybody's nose. But he got his come–uppance on the short train trip from Aviano to Venice, when he refused to share our compartment or entrust his amplifier to the baggage coach with all our gear, but insisted on taking it along with him. This would not have been so bad if it had been of normal size, say a Fender Twin or something like that, but just before the tour, he had swapped his normal one for a huge Ampeg Portaflex bass amp, which had a 15 inch speaker, was about a metre square and weighed the best part of 40 kilos. It also had the added problem of lacking castors. (Actually, it had had castors when he got it, but one night in Stuttgart it had rolled off the edge of a sloping stage in the middle of his solo and in anger he had ripped them off). To make matters worse, he was told by a pompous railway official that he had chosen a non–smoking coach, so he had to struggle into another with all his gear only to find that he was sharing it with a big Italian family.

Venice, as you may know, is on a kind of isthmus and on the mainland outside the town is the railway station of Venetzia Mestre, not Venezia Citta (Venice town) itself. When it stopped there, we looked down the train to see Ady emerge from his door cursing everybody in sight and struggling to drag out his monster amplifier. A couple of friendly locals tried to help but were rejected angrily.

"Piss off—I can manage without you lot," he yelled. Finally he wrestled his amp onto the platform and grabbing his guitar turned to us in a blind panic and shouted. "C'mon. Gerroff. Gerroff. It won't wait forever y' know. Bleeding Wops."

"Wrong station," I yelled back.

His face turned white and his mouth dropped open. "Y'wot? Wrong station, wotcha mean? It's bleedin' Venice innit?

"Naw," we all shouted. "This is Mestre. Venice is the next stop. You'd better get it all back on board again, quick."

Well, you can imagine the performance that followed, with Ady struggling to get everything back on board again. Our coach was nowhere near the platform so we could not help and the insulted locals ignored this sweating, cursing, Inglese, while the madly gesticulating Station Master frantically blew his whistle to get the train off the tracks before the Rome-Trieste express came screaming through the junction. What a gas.

In Venice he was still sulking and stomped ahead of us on a tour of the city. He refused to come in for a meal, though I offered to pay and bought a couple of sandwiches to eat as he walked around the Piazza San Marco. cursing the hordes of starving pigeons that followed him, dappling his boots with their droppings. Lee followed close behind, mischievously. tossing bits of bread at his feet to encourage the aerial scavengers, causing him to whirl round and kick out wildly at the cooing flock. No, I could not say that Ady was a happy man that afternoon in the City of Canals.

Next day we caught a local train to Milan to await the Brenner Express that would take us back to Frankfurt on Main. We arrived around 11p.m. and found that our connection was not until 2.30am. It was winter, and as we didn't have enough money to go into the few late–night bars still open, we mooched around the town until we suddenly found ourselves in front of a large round building that announced itself as La Scala. It was the world famous opera house and, as there was nobody around, we decided to have a bit of fun. In my brief–case I had a few self–adhesive flyers given to me by Gisela Gunther to stick across the Lefty Frizzell poster, so we found a notice board advertising forthcoming attractions and stuck a few across it, announcing to the world that the show would be:

LA TRAVIATA.
FEATURING FRANK YONCO & THE TEXAS DRIFTERS
I wonder if anybody bought tickets?

Ady was still nursing his wobbler and insisted on travelling with his gear in the unheated baggage car all the way through the Brenner Pass back to Germany, where we picked up the tour again with the well–rested Lefty. A few gigs around Stuttgart followed by a package show with Eck and the Echoes, who now had added two girl dancers and a keyboard player to their act. It was change–over time. They were just finishing the first part of a tour with Roger Miller and we were scheduled to take over after we finished with Lefty. Eck told me that on their last night with him in Man–heim, the King of the Road had given him a $500 tip. With that kind of wild generosity, it was no surprise that the millionaire composer went broke a few years later. Secretly I was hoping that his same largesse would extend to me, but my first meeting with him did not auger well.

Our last show was at an open day at Hahn airbase. We got there early and were pleased to meet old friends, Joe Butler and Kenny Johnson and the Hillsiders, (this was before they became the Fabulous Hillsiders) who were at the end of a tour with Molly Bee, and were about to pick up with Red Sovine (rather them than me). I had seen his show and already turned down the offer to back him, but I wished them luck. They were going to need it. Red was still doing the same act he had been doing for twenty years and maudlin monologues like 'Little Rosa' or 'The Drunken Driver' were not going to go down to well with the G.I.s. I enjoyed their spot, although Molly Bee seemed to be a bit of a Barbie doll joke. The Hillsiders were very good and I think that Kenny Johnson is still one of the best country singers on the domestic scene and Joe Butler's harmonies are legendary.

We were sitting in the dressing room with Lefty, relaxing before the show, when Roger stormed in with a bottle of Four Roses in his pocket, strumming a plastic ukulele and singing Lefty's big 50's hit 'If you got the money I got the time.' He obviously had had a few scoops already and in general he was a bit of a pain, boring everybody rigid with his lurid boasts of wild binges and erotic orgies with various Hollywood stars. There was a bright side, however, for us musical galley slaves, because playing guitar in his band was the famous session guitarist 'Thumbs' Carlisle. (So called because of his unique way of playing, left–handed with the guitar across his knees and played with banjo finger picks and his thumb). The other two musicians in Roger's band were not of any great worth; both of them well over the top.

The drummer was a clone of Louis Belson in boxing gloves with penchant for extended breaks, and usually ran about six bars over at the end of each number, and the bass player was under the apparent illusion that he was being paid by the note and played accordingly. I think Mr. Carlisle was as embarrassed as we were at Miller's antics and, to cover his discomfort, he took up the toy ukulele and played a high speed faultless version of J.S. Bach's 'Jesu Joy Of Man's Desiring'. At least he shut up Roger for a few minutes.

Towards the end of this tour, certainly the last one he did overseas, Lefty was looking in bad shape and flew back to the States with the Singing Egg and we headed back to Frankfurt. The proposed tour with Roger only lasted five scrappy shows before the word got out and the club custodians starting cancelling dates, so Roger retired to the Frankfurterhof Hotel for another three day bender before shipping out stateside, so I never did get a $500 tip like my friend Eck.

Sheb Wolley

News came from Gisela's office that Sheb Wooley had finally finished his bender in New York, (When Roger Miller had left he happened to bump into Glen Campbell at the airport, which delayed him another three days) and had now arrived in Frankfurt. Sheb's first claim to fame was in the fifties, when he topped the charts with a novelty rocker called 'The Flying Purple People Eater'. These days he was a highly successful comedy entertainer on the Las Vegas/ Reno circuit.

His act went down very well with the young GI's, who particularly liked his comic alter ego 'Ben Colder', who sang parodies of current hits like Conway Twitty's poignant 'Fifteen Years Ago', which Ben changed to a hilarious bar–room toilet ballad called 'Fifteen Beers Ago' and upbeat numbers like 'That's ma Pa'. We did the usual scoot around Southern Germany, Bavaria, and Northern Italy, after which we were sent again to play the gig that Sheb had missed in Spain. The most memorable part of that trip was our arrival at Madrid Airport.

Sheb and I, neither of us wild about flying, had diverted ourselves during the flight from Frankfurt by draining a bottle of Jack Daniels and, as we arrived at the airport, we could see big crowds waiting to greet us. "Great," we preened. Sheb said that 'Rawhide' must be showing on Spanish TV, and I thought that we had made such a good impression on our last visit that the news was out that we were returning.

As the plane rolled to a halt we could hardly wait to meet out fans, and lurched into the aisle as the passengers began to file off. There was a polite ripple of applause from the flight crew as we were shepherded past a group of athletic looking young men from the First Class area and staggered down the steps. The bright sun and warm air hit us as we stood, swaying slightly at the bottom of the metal steps and trying to take stock of our surroundings. As we started towards the terminal building, the big crowd surged towards us waving and cheering. It was wonderful as they immersed us in their joyous welcome, and then suddenly we were alone on the tarmac, as they all rushed by us to greet the victorious Real Madrid Football Team who had travelled on the same flight.

Twenty minutes later, a dark blue US Air force Chevrolet sedan and a GMC minibus arrived from the NCO club to pick us up, by which time the airport was deserted. But at least the club was full and Sheb's show went down a storm. He had the right mix of humour and irreverent comments that the homesick servicemen appreciated. On our arrival back at Frankfurt, we were immediately loaded in a van and shovelled off to an old Wermacht cavalry barracks up near Fulda. It was a foot deep in snow. Twelve hours previously we had been sweltering in the Spanish sun. I nearly froze to death.

One evening I was relaxing at our digs, when there was a loud pounding at the door and a red faced John Harrison breathlessly told me that Sheb was in trouble on the Kaiser Strasse. I grabbed my jacket and we shot off to see what we could do, but before we arrived it was all over. I found Sheb in an arcade doorway, mopping blood off his left ear and a cut on his head. Lying on the floor was an unconscious Italian ponce. Out on the pavement three policemen were questioning Lee. We patched Sheb up as best we could as he explained what had occurred.

By chance he had met Lee in a bar and together they went to review the usual parade of beautiful hookers on the street. Lee was like a dog with two tails. He had never seen so many good–looking women in his life, and wandered from car to car chatting them up and then walking off with smart remarks, until one of them called her minder, who had cornered him to ask him what he was playing at? Sheb went over to help Lee and, before you knew it, a brawl had developed with GIs and Italian and Turkish pimps all joining in. The next thing was the arrival of Frankfurt Polizei's Special Response Squad and three jeep loads of US Army Snowdrops, who soon put an end to things. But Lee's mischief was not yet finished. Oh no. Not by a long chalk.

Our contract was due to end, as they often did, after the Saturday night show, but as the offices did not open at weekend, Gisela Gunther paid me up on the Friday afternoon and, as I did not want to be toting such a large sum around with me, I paid everybody out before Friday night's show, intending to leave Germany on Sunday morning. The Friday night show went well, but the next morning our friend Lee was missing. He had taken off during the night paying his own fare back to Blighty. Homesick? Well maybe. But later that day two plain–clothes policeman came to arrest him. He'd been picked up allegedly shoplifting in a city department store and had failed to turn up for his court date on the previous Friday. Oh yes. If anyone came close to giving me ulcers, it was Lee.

We continued the round of military clubs, running into Johnny Batt and the Tumbleweeds at the Rocker Club in Wiesbaden. His band that year must have been at its best and included some super pickers like Steve Simpson on guitar, and Dave Peacock on bass and banjo, who later teamed up with another hard touring musician and session man, Charlie Hodges, to form the famous 'Rockney 'duo Chas and Dave.

I first came across Charlie on the Fuller's Brewery circuit, smashing piano at an after–hours drinking session laid on by Martin Grinham and Jessie Kent at the Red Cow in West Kensington. He was one of the great entertainers. Lonnie Donegan also came out to do a German Bierkellar tour and stayed in the same digs as us. Playing guitar he had Les Bennetts, whose regular breakfast consisted of pickled eggs and a bottle of Steinhager schnapps. Les was about the only guy I know, who could out–booze the legendary Adrian Legg, another super picker of that era, who used to arrive at gigs on a pushbike with his Telecaster slung over his shoulder and his Fender Twin amp strapped to the carrier. Both of them often ended up sleeping it off on the banquettes in the gig, too far gone to get home.

Not having any stars coming in and wanting to keep our services ex–clusive to her agency, Gisela Gunther persuaded me to take a three–week contract as the house band at Gaeta Naval Base north of Naples. It was not the best gig in the world and not the best location either, as Gaeta was the site of Italy's toughest jail. Every commercial enterprise in the town was under the benevolent protection of either the Camorra or the Sardinian Mafia, who conducted a savage never–ending range war. The gig was finally pulled out after we had played a concert aboard an aircraft–carrier in the US Sixth Fleet, that ended with a fire in the galley, apparently a regular occurrence. In fact, it happened so often that the ship became known as USS Zippo.

PICKER'S TIP 27

On the road, packing and storing cables and mike stands, etc. is always a pain, so try this.

Get an old car inner tube and cut it into 3cm (1.5 inch) sections to make strong wide elastic bands to pack all those awkward bits of gear.

To keep them off the floor get hold of some large butchers 'S' hooks and hang them on the inside frame of the your vehicle. Either in the back or below eye level.

17

HONG KONG BLUES

While we were away in Italy, our agent, Harry Rawden, got a call from the management of the Blackpool Winter Gardens offering us a summer season at the Planet Rooms, which was a very important gig in those days. I suppose that even today, a season at a major venue in Blackpool is still considered as a foot on the ladder of success. After the Winter Gardens, you were on target for one of the plum theatres on the Central or South Pier, leading hopefully to that elusive state called Stardom.

'Super', I thought and I was very excited about it, but as events turned out, something much more exciting came along and once again we were at a crossroads.

One morning, lurking amongst the pile of sinister brown official envelopes waiting in ambush behind our front door, I found a posh–looking missive with a West London postmark. It was a letter from an agency in London asking if I was interested in doing a Far Eastern tour and, if so, would I call in to see them. So I took a trip to see them and authorised them to negotiate on our behalf. I think that John Ammonds, then a BBC producer was also involved in some vague capacity. Anyway, within a couple of weeks I had confirmation from the agency in Hong Kong, and details of pay and conditions for a nine month tour of 'South East Asia' but no specific details of which actual countries that we would be visiting, but it was obvious, at least to me, that Vietnam might be included.

I had actually signed the Blackpool contract, but the exotic appeal of the Far East was too much for me so I passed up on the Fylde Coast opportunity, which did not please Harry over much, and he lost no time in letting me know it, and who could blame him? I apologised profusely and it was lucky that he didn't sue.

At that time, unknown to me, the showbiz piranhas were again on the prowl to grab a chunk of the big bucks on offer from the U.S. Special Services Division looking for acts to entertain the US troops in Vietnam. American acts would have been the best–suited, but many of the most popular artists suddenly found themselves in a dilemma. For the past few years, in fact since the very early sixties, they had been chasing the money on the lucrative folk–rock, 'Peace and Brown Rice', circuit, with its associated Protest Movement, so they could not go for the tempting military contracts without destroying their fragile credibility with the fickle young hippies There was also another dimension to the protesters that is seldom aired, it was the fear of doing military service, summed up in this Ogden Nash couplet.

I heave a proud and silent sigh, and think how tolerant am I.

And then I wonder which is mine? Tolerance or a rubber spine?

So the U.S. Government started trawling Europe and Australia for acts. I personally had no such hang–ups regarding the folk–rock scene or its much–vaunted protest movement. I had been fighting it since I started, hustling real Country Music in the teeth of the gale of pop and folk music swamping Great Britain throughout the late 50's and early 60's.You must remember, we began to get our breaks at approximately the same time as the British rockers like Billy Fury, Marty Wilde, and a whole host of Elvis clones. This was also a time for gentle, pretty people like Peter and Gordon and Mary Hopkin, and our image was hardly that. We were swimming against the tide, but we loved our music, and back in those days we felt like pioneers, true protesters, and a sense of destiny drove us on.

In the excitement of signing contracts and looking forward to the trip, I had almost forgotten that I did not at that moment have a full band to take with me. As I had more or less expected, the band broke up on our return to the UK. The first–timers like John and Lee obviously did not find what they were seeking on the road so the period was dominated by searching for replacements. Eventually Big Dave indicated that he still wanted to tour, as did the eccentric Ady. So that left a drummer and a steel player to find and, in spite of the problems he caused me, after Lee's playing, I still fancied a piano player in the band. Well, I had a girl singer and a half–hearted guitar player, who was liable to fly away at the first offer of a local gig, so I had to get a move on, and made a few enquiries about my ex–drummer Dave. He had become a bit disenchanted with the road back in '66 so he had taken a semi–pro gig and a day job, but my spies told me that he had recently been overheard in his local pub wishing that he was back in the saddle again. I thought I'd give him a call and that's just what I did, and it was almost a replay of his first trip abroad.

It was raining stair–rods when I got to his place and after rat–tatting on the front door, I was about to go away when I decided to try round the back. I threw some gravel up at his bedroom window.

"Oo is it?" Came a voice from the curtains.

"It's me, Yonk."

"Well, th' door's unlocked, just give it a boot an' come up."

As I pushed open the creaking door, I checked my watch. It was 4.15 on a Tuesday afternoon. Was he ill or what? Scrabbling through the deserted cluttered house I climbed the stairs to find David propped up in bed with a side–table full of bottles, beer bottles that is, not medicine. The rumpled bed was littered with cigarette packets and copies of the Daily Mirror and the Sporting Chronicle.

"'Ello, Dad," He sniffed. "Wot's up?"

"Nothing much. You ill or something?" I said, taking in the devastation.

He puffed on a Park Drive dog–end and coughed. "Naw, just fed up. Ah've nowt t'gerrup for. Got no poppy for th' pub, Yuh come to lend us a few bob, 'ave yuh?

"You can sod off," I returned. "just thought I'd drop round to see you."

"Oh aye? Wot else yuh got in mind? Yuh wouldn't come 'ere for nowt."

I admitted that I did have a reason and that there might be a little trip in the offing. I didn't have to ask if he still had his drum–kit. It was scattered all up the bloody stairs. "Right." I said, determined to get this thing over one way or another. "Do you want to go on another tour or not?"

He paused relight his dimp. "Where yuh goin' then?" He coughed.

"We're goin' to bloody Japan, that's where. Now, are you comin' or not?"

"When yuh leavin'?"

"Friday."

"Oh, okay then. Wot time?"

And that was all there was to it. He didn't even ask about the money, or how long we'd be away. What did I expect? That was Dave's way.

Now I had three. I needed one more, but not a steel guitarist this time: No, I fancied having a good electric piano player, but there was nobody in the area who was good enough, with the exception, of course, of the volatile Lee, and I didn't fancy going through that again, so I left him pumping his M.F.I. Bechstein in deepest Salford.

I mentioned the problem during a phone call to Big David in Edinburgh, and he mentioned his friend Roy, who was currently playing keyboards at the local football social club, and who would like to go on the road. I was a bit cautious. I'd had a few experiences with the boozing habits of our Celtic brothers so I made a point of asking David, about his mate's drinking habits.

"Oh Roy? Nae bother wi' Roy. Hardly ever touches the hard stuff. Couple o' pints o' heavy now an' then, but that's about all" He assured me.

It did not sound all that convincing, but with only ten days to go I took the chance and told David to bring him along and arranged to meet them at Heathrow.

Talk about buying blind.

So now the band was fixed and ready to go. It was a case of sewing up the final details. Midnight found us arriving at Manchester's London Road Station. Kit and I arrived first in a taxi, next came Dave, driven by his brother in a clapped–out van. Ady also came by taxi, wearing his band suit for the nine thousand mile journey to Hong Kong. It was his way of point-ing out that he was not wild about the trip. I let the incident pass without comment.

At Euston, a couple of black cabs took us with all our gear to Heathrow where, at 5 am, we met our new piano player, who turned out to be a pleasant tubby guy with thick glasses, a ready smile and an arm swollen from his recent typhoid injection.

Introductions were made all round and the baggage weighed in, which turned out to be some forty pounds overweight. I presented the contract to an airline official, pointing out the clause which required us to arrive fully equipped, and he agreed to take it up later with the agent, so it was simply a case of checking immigration and getting aboard. Then it was safety belts fastened and lift–off. As we crossed the south coast of Old England, I turned to check if everybody was o.k., and caught my new keyboard man dropping the remains of a Martell brandy bottle down his gullet. He saw me looking and, with a smile, he waved the bottle saying. "It's just for the jab, ye ken. Achin' a bit, it was."

I looked skywards. Was this the shape of things to come, I wondered?

Yes. You're right. It was.

The flight was great, the longest one we had ever done up to then. The first stop was at Frankfurt, then on to Rome, and after that it was straight through to Delhi passing over Dyarbikir en route. At Delhi we had an hour's break, and I thought that I was having hallucinations because as we walked towards the terminal building it appeared to be swaying or moving in the hot night under the airport floodlight. I mentioned this to the band, but by this time our piano man was solid gone and leaning heavily on his mate's arm, so he wouldn't have known the difference anyway, but the others did confirm my illusion. It did look as if it was moving, but when we got closer, we saw that it was covered with small green lizards continually moving about, seeking the warmest spots on the heat–soaked concrete, and giving the impression that the building itself was shaking. Was this our first introduction to the Mysterious East? The next stop was at Bangkok, where I bought a tropical shirt and the piano player bought some more beers. What a debacle it was going to be with him. And so far I had not heard him play a note.

At Kai Tek Airport in Hong Kong, Ralf, one of the partners in the agency that had booked us, greeted us. He was a heavily built man in his late forties, about six foot two, with greying hair and a large beer belly spoiling his otherwise impressive image. He said he was very glad to see us, relieved in fact, and booked us into the Sun Ya Hotel on Nathan Road, where he also had a suite of offices. I will never forget the first evening there when we stepped out of the air–conditioned hotel into the crowded street and were hit by a gust of furnace hot air. The noise was deafening, with everybody shouting in this strange language, and garish coloured neon signs every–where. It was nine in the evening and the busy shops and street vendors were going at it like madmen.

All of us were fascinated by Hong Kong. The constant din of the frenetic traffic, the glaring colours, and the strange noisy people all chattering away. Modern taxis jostled for road space with dull green tramcars, which looked like retired relics from Oldham (they were from Glasgow actually) that hurtled at suicidal speeds down to the harbour, packed inside and out with shouting Chinese. Most Europeans used the taxis that were very cheap. For example a trip from the ferry terminal to the Sun Ya in Mongkok, about a mile or so was 80HK.cents. (About 5p in today's money).

Ralf took me to meet his partner, an even bigger man called Fredo, who was something of a mystery man, even by Hong Kong standards. He was also well over six feet tall and must have tipped the scales around 18 stones, with the features of a old Sikh warrior, with dark pock marked skin, a large hooked nose, and a mass of black hair. He also possessed a big beer belly like his partner and I began to think that it was a requirement for the Gai–Jin (non–oriental) in the Colony. Maybe it had something to do with the old Cantonese proverb that said for a big nail you need a big ham- mer. Before their present excursion into the agency world, they had both been in the performing side of the game, Fredo had been a support actor and had featured in a number of films from the Indian sub–continent, as well as doing a stint as a cabaret singer. His partner Ralf had been a suc- cessful adagio dancer with his wife, so they obviously knew the business. At least at that time I thought so.

We had a brief discussion in the office and there was a shocked look on their faces when I presented the bill for the overweight freight. I pointed out they were the ones who insisted that we bring all the gear, so did not feel that it was my concern. (Later on this item was to become the subject of several bitter exchanges between Hong Kong and the agency in London). One thing I made clear was that we were not going to pay for it. Then there was also the problem of the electric piano that we had been told would be available. As it turned out there was none, so we ended up with a Farfisa electric organ and Yamaha amp, which, with a great deal of manipulation and imagination sounded a bit like a piano. We proved this by finally levering Roy away from the bar of the hotel to try it out. At least it showed that the man could actually play. And to be honest, play very well.

The following night, I was invited to dinner to discuss the itinerary, but when I got there I could feel a certain tension in the air and quick suspici- ous glances were flashing between my hosts.

"Well Ralf," I asked brightly. "Where's the first gig then? Somewhere ex- otic I hope." We were sitting in the main lounge of the Kingsland Restaurant, enjoying the top class food and watching the cabaret. Ralf paused with a fork–full of squid at his lips and glanced again across to his partner, who had been throwing a moody all evening, and obviously had something in his craw. Fredo also stopped for moment as though he was about to say something, but suddenly became obsessed with finding a waiter. Ralf put down his fork and with an air of resignation and hesitat- ingly said:

"Err, well, Yonco, you'll have a couple of days getting acclimatised, y' know, just relaxing and getting to know the region. The first three gigs will be here in the Colony, and then you'll be opening up at one of the top venues on the circuit. The Ben Hoa NCO. Club in, err, Saigon."

"Saigon?" I yelped, "BLOODY SAIGON? That's in Vietnam. There's a war going on there"

"Yes, we know that," said Ralf; trying to calm the situation "Didn't you know? It was all in the contract."

There's sod all about Vietnam in the contract," I said angrily. "All it said was Japan and other venues in the Far Eastern area."

Ralf, tried to calm the situation, by telling me that it should have been explained to me in London, and it was at this point that Fredo decided to put his oar in, and his attitude was very much different to that of his partner. It was as though his nerves had snapped, and he became so very belligerent I began to wonder why? I was the one who was being shafted here and I had every right to be annoyed, so what was he getting heavy for? The movie–actor in him took over, and I had the distinct impression that he thought he was playing in some tough gangster movie, but somehow his intended menace missed its target. He rolled his shoulders and fixing me with his most menacing prison–yard stare, he growled sarcastically.

"Listen Yonco. What makes you think that you are something special, eh? I tell you what, boy, I'm gettin' real sick of you kind of people. Now hear this and you might learn somethin' Country Boy. Vietnam is in the Far East. Gottit? Didn't they tell you that back in London, or wherever you come from?

(Ah, so that was it. He had probably been on the phone to the UK agents and they had told him that they weren't going to pay our freight bill).

By now the voice had lost its sing–song Indian cadence and had become a Humphrey Bogart snarl.

"So you're stuck Ol' Buddy. And if you break the contract you won't even get your fuckin' fare home."

By now several diners were looking up from their meals and the waiters were watching our table carefully as his partner attempted to pour oil on the troubled waters, by saying that it would only be a short trip and that we would be back on the top hotel circuit before we knew it. What could I do? As his partner had made so clear, they had me by the balls, but I swore that Fredo's insults would be paid for in full.

Personally, I didn't mind too much but, as I feared, telling the band was not easy and it provoked different reactions and lots of muttering when I did it. A few days later, another meeting was arranged for everybody at Ralf's house, where his Wakefield–born wife prepared a wonderful English dinner for us. Ralf was at pains to apologise for his friend's outburst, citing marital stress as the cause. Fredo himself was not there because he was at a meeting with his wife, who had taken a spot of leave from the War Zone where she worked the clubs as a very exotic dancer, travelling in her own jeep and arriving at the bases in jungle fatigues, toting a gold Rolex on her wrist and a Colt 45 pistol on her hip. As the evening passed pleasantly, everybody had a chance to ask the questions that were bugging them. In the end Ralf convinced us that the press reports of the situation in Vietnam had been much exaggerated and things were not bad. I realized that we were stuck with the situation, so I accepted it and, to be honest, was quite excited at the prospect, as were Little Dave and Kit, but Ady was definitely very dubious and the two Scots were concerned mainly about the supply of beer over there. Finally we decided to give it a go. As a parting question I asked how long we'd be in Saigon.

"Oh, just to the end of the month, couple of weeks at the most, " was the glib reply. Oh Yeah?

18

GOOD MORNING VIET-NAM
The Mekong Delta Blues
Tet. 1968

I never liked the Hippys much and Dylan left me cold
And looking back across the years, the truth shines out like gold
19 years old in the Delta swamps, just waiting for an order
A Leatherneck thinks of the boys that ran to the
NEAREST FOREIGN BORDER.
The AK 47s crash and the shrapnel whines above.
And he wonders now if Charlie believes that,
ALL YOU NEED IS LOVE.
OR THE TIMES THEY ARE A–CHANGING,
fast as you can draw a breath.
And the ANSWER BLOWING IN THE WIND
is known as sudden death.
WHERE HAVE ALL THE FLOWERS GONE?
Try that minefield over there.
But if you're aiming to go to
SAN FRANCISCO,
don't put 'em in your hair.
The medics drag in a screaming man.
You can see where the mud is grooved
It seems that Charlie's learned the words to
WE SHALL NOT BE MOVED.
A three–inch mortar opens up and the ground shakes like a drum,
And the Leatherneck wonders what it is, that
'WE SHALL OVERCOME'
Now, it's hard to light a Marlboro
'IN THE EARLY MORNING RAIN'
He thinks of the guy with the shattered thigh,
'LEAVING ON A BIG JET PLANE'
For when he's out of the Mekong stench and he knocks on the big
GREEN DOOR.
Will he find as he grips the wheelchair rim that
IT DON'T MATTER ANYMORE.
And that the hippy in the Afghan coat who greeted him 'Hey Man.'
Now wears a three–piece business suit to sell him a Pension Plan.
And the Worry Beads and the Jesus Boots and the love that was going free
Can be summed up in six short words "Thank God, they didn't get me."

Written by Frank Yonco, the Mekong Delta, South Vietnam. May 1968

*   *   *   *   *   *

Ton Son Hut

Three days later, we were over the South China Sea heading for the war zone. As we circled Saigon Airport, we could see the damage that had been done to the city, particularly in the Chinese district of Cholon across the Saigon River, and to the west in the Phu Tho section where remnants of the fifteen Viet Cong battalions, who had led the February attack had been holed up and shelled to destruction. Here and there were columns of smoke, and jeeps and armoured cars covered most major intersections. We had a couple of landing approaches, each one aborted at the last moment due to gunfire. The airport was under attack from hidden mortars by Viet Cong Charlie. Finally we were down and hustled across the tarmac to the pock-marked main building. I looked up as we entered and read the words Terminal Building, and it crossed my mind what an unfortunate title that was. At that moment it could have been the last stop for all of us. The date was Tuesday April 23 1968.

Over the PA speakers we heard this

ATTENTION ALL PERSONNEL — ATTENTION ALL PERSONNEL

INCOMING FIRE — INCOMING FIRE — INCOMING FIRE

IMMEDIATE VICINITY — MILITARY & CIVILIAN TERMINALS

THE AIRPORT IS NOW CONDITION RED — REPEAT — CONDITION RED

TAKE COVER AND DO NOT MOVE UNTIL CLEARANCE SIREN SOUNDS

DO NOT EXIT THE COMPLEX — OR DISCHARGE ANY WEAPONS

REPEAT — DO NOT DISCHARGE ANY WEAPONS

These were the first words that greeted us on our arrival at Ton Son Hut Airport, Saigon. Apparently we had arrived in time for the party. As part of the Chinese New Year celebrations, the Viet Cong had launched their big Tet Offensive on the night of January 30th. The anniversary of the great battle at Dong Da in 1789 when General Nguyen Hue had thrown off the yoke of the Manchus.

The pressure and guerilla actions had been constantly escalating since February, and two months on, the situation was far from clear. In spite of an agreement for a ceasefire during the Chinese New Year celebrations, which was due to be observed from 6.p.m. on the 29th January, the Viet Cong had struck simultaneously at bases across the country, and it was soon apparent that the explosions were not just celebratory fireworks, but military rockets and mortar bombs.

By the 4th of February, two regiments of the regular 5th Viet Cong Division were only about seven miles from the Delta and were arraying for attack in an arc north and north-west of the massive supply complex at Ben Hoa and Saigon itself. The airport at Ton Son Hut had already been under severe attack, as were many key installations, such as Pleiku in the central highlands, and Da Nang on the coast, and as far north as the old capital of Hue. Al of them places that we would come to know very well, and we were soon to experience this entire raging inferno at first hand.

God knows, it had been hard enough persuading the band to come here, and this was our welcome. However Dave was fascinated by all the military hardwear around him and, fortunately, our two Scots were well–oiled from the free booze on the flight and Kit stayed close by me and kept quiet, so it wasn't that bad. As for me, well, secretly I was looking forward to the excitement. At least I had not missed this war. (What a lunatic way of thinking). We had seen a little smoke and a few fires from the cabin of our Cathay Pacific DC.10 as we came in to land, but it did not look very sinister, but now, as we sheltered behind a pile of baggage in the corner of the arrival lounge, things looked very different indeed.

I peeped over the trunks and cases out of a small window and saw two Huey gunships hovering over the perimeter, raking the undergrowth with their Gatlings, while high above them, acting as a spotter, a small Bell chopper circled the parked aircraft on the dispersal apron. Two jeeps armed with twin 50 Browning machine guns rushed towards the action, while the steady crump–crump of incoming mortar bombs could be heard.

Through it all somewhere a transistor radio was playing 'The Andy Williams Show', while a noisy crap game continued in another corner, none of the sweating punters taking any notice of the emergency. There was another Crump. Closer this time, with the tinkle of broken glass but still Andy sang on. It was his big hit. 'Can't help falling in love', and that line that says 'Wise men say only fools rush in,' struck a nerve with me. This was the real thing, not the movies and I wasn't Robert Mitchum, so what were we doing here anyway? We could have been in Blackpool. So—
Always read the small print.

There was another blaring klaxon honk and the same Gung Ho voice came over the PA to assure us that,

THE AREA HAS NOW BEEN SECURED — CONDITION GREEN"

We cautiously emerged from behind our protective barrier and looked round. Now there was time to take in our circumstances. There had been none of the usual customs formalities or immigration procedures. The American M.P.s assuming that if you were a Round–Eye you couldn't be bad, hustled us through. I must admit that it was most unlikely that any-body would have sneaked into South Vietnam at that time. Although there was quite a few that would have got OUT if they got the chance—including us.

We looked round the big room and saw it was quite full and it appeared that we were the only ones who troubled to take cover, everybody else seemed too bored to bother. Naturally the vast majority of the crowd were G.I.s. with a sprinkling of hard–looking Koreans in their spotless and crisply starched green uniforms. Almost everybody was carrying some kind of weapon. Colt 45 pistols, Remington shotguns, M2 carbines, M29 grenade launchers and customized Wetherby sniper rifles, and several A.K.47s being taken home as a souvenir.

Over in the corner, a group of Marines were saying goodbye to a clutch of twittering Viet girl friends, wearing the long split skirt and black tight trousers known as ah–dohs, with their long shining black hair fanning out as they moved. They looked beautiful and were acting as though this moment of parting was the most tragic event of their young lives, but an hour later as we were leaving town, we saw the same four girls on the arms of their new GI boy friends heading into a bar on Hong Tap To Street, laughing and joking as though nothing had happened. By now I had become philosophical about things, trying to cheer everybody up by saying that the two weeks in Saigon would soon pass and then it would be on to the oriental fleshpots. They did not appear to be to convinced.

"Yew Frank Yonco? Ah'm Billy, yo' driver

It was a hard nasal Oregon voice and its owner, a fat balding man of about thirty five, stood looking at us, chewing on a cud of something that smelled like perfumed tobacco. I nodded in agreement and he told us to follow him

"What about the gear?" Asked David.

"Aw jus' leave it here," The man drawled. "Chuck'll send a couple o' gooks down for it but yuh'd better tote them thar geetars. C'mon"

We pushed through the crowded airport and clambered aboard a vintage V.W. bus reeking of body odor and stale beer. Billy, our guide, slammed the side loading door on us and lurched round to the driving seat. We looked at each other but said nothing. It was quite obvious that he had already had a few scoops while he was waiting for our arrival. Our suspicions were confirmed as he felt under the seat and came up with a bottle in a brown bag and took few quick gulps, his Adam's apple going like a fiddler's elbow.

We were all very quiet and more than a little tense after the attack on the terminal, Kit and Ady sat staring straight ahead, pretending it was not happening. Our two doughty Scots clung like drowning men to their last beer cans, while Dave was still oohing and aahing at the weaponry around us. I was still trying to get everybody to relax and attempted to carry on a conversation with our taciturn driver by asking relevant questions like "How long has this been going on, etc."

Billy could sense that we were a bit frightened, and enjoyed himself at our expense by rambling on as he swung the bus carelessly around, honking past bicycle taxis and shuffling pedestrians.

"Y'all see over there? That thar buildin'? Well Charlie bombed that last night. Killed about a dozen gooks—an' that 'un there, next to that burned-out bus. The M.P.s got three snipers there last night. A regl'ar firework display, that wuz. I reckon you'll see a bit for y'self 'fore yo're thru, Yonco."

"What?" I chortled," I don't think we'll see that much. You don't think the Cong will try it on again in Saigon do you? Anyway, we are only here for ten days."

The others looked relieved at my confidence.

"TEN DAYS," he roared. "Where'd ya'll git that bullshit from? You're here for fuckin' TWELVE WEEKS. I got my drivin' contract heah, wid yo name on it."

Oh Shit. I felt everybody's eyes boring into the back of my head, and I knew there was going to be trouble. I should've known that those Hong Kong bastards would pull something like this. God knows what they were charging the Saigon agency, for our time. I don't suppose that I had any complaint about the money, it was more than I had ever earned in my life, but I was not prepared for this stroke. The band had all overheard what Billy said, and Ady and Kit said there and then they wanted to be on the next plane out. Luckily Kit did come to terms with things, albeit with great reluctance, but Ady was a different case and was terrified most of the short time he stayed, eventually selling his gear for a ticket home.

Saigon

We were taken to a Vietnamese hotel on Hong Tap Tu, one of the main streets of this once beautiful city. It was called the Golden Building and was surrounded by a high security wall and the usual wire mesh over the balconies to prevent grenades being tossed in from the street. I still have this mental picture of Ady crawling along his balcony, and reaching up to hang his socks out to dry on these wire screens. Yep, that's right. His balcony, because as usual, he refused to share a room with anyone else. After we had been allocated rooms, the expected row occurred as soon as Billy left us. The less said about that the better. In the end most of us accepted the inevitable, with the exception of Ady who still insisted on get-ting out even if it meant going to the British Consulate.

Early the next day a driver came to take me to the booking office to pick up our work schedule. The agency was called Chuck Doherty Associates, (CDA) and was a sympathetic, well-organized set up. The office was in a large French colonial-style house off Yen Do Street and was where Chuck himself lived. He was chunky, with thinning fair hair, and had one of those jerky Chicago accents, making him sound like a twenties gangster and, in spite of his warm welcome, he came over as the kind of man one would not like to cross. By contrast, his right hand man was from London, and was as Golder's Green Jewish as you could be. He was a wonderful character called Arthur. A strange coupling, it was true, but they had been in action out here several years and it seemed to work very well. I met Arthur's father many years later in Hampstead, and he was more Yiddish than Arthur, and told me that his son had been on his way to Israel but must have lost his way. The agency provided the amps and P.A. equipment we used throughout the tour and also suggested that we used some of the guitars and gear that was stored in the cellar. They were very good guys and often advanced us money when we needed it.

Chuck told us that we would be doing an 'Appraisal Show' the following day at one of the clubs in Saigon, so that the price charged for our shows and our political attitudes could be approved by Special Services officers, and this struck me as strange. Fancy sending us all this way on the off chance that we would be acceptable to the US Government and not become a corrupting influence on their young servicemen. There was the usual gaggle of well-oiled club custodians and a table of Special Services brass hats, all making notes on the acts. When our turn came, they subjected us to a barrage of questions about the reasons why a bunch of British citizens should want to come out to the war-zone to entertain their troops? I gave them some mealy-mouthed patriotic bullshit about doing our bit to halt the Red Menace in South East Asia, and pointed out that there were Australian troops here too, and they were, well, practically family. What I didn't say was that we had been conned into coming here, and that the big money was also coming in very handy. There were quite a few acts there, mostly specialty acts, some Filipino bands, and one very good Soul band from Bangkok, but there was no contest, as we blew them all away with a driving rockabilly set. So our price per show was accepted. I never did find out how much we were actually earning. It is most surprising that with so much booze and ganja flowing that such secrets were kept from us but they were.

Our first serious job was the next night, out of town at the biggest military complex in the world at Bien Hoa north of Saigon. It was raining when we arrived, and there seemed to be guns everywhere and tanks on every corner. We were driven to the main NCO. Club, but altogether there were over twenty different clubs and concert halls on the complex and, on any given night, there could be a dozen acts and bands performing. Our show was good and, surprisingly, there were no wobblers from the band. Ady's guitar playing was very impressive and about the only downside was that the bloody Farfisa (which we didn't want anyway) went kaput, but we were made very welcome. Country Music was home music to the bored G.I.s and the fact that it was being played by 'Round Eyes' performers made it more effective, even if we were 'Limeys'. They were all getting fed up with oriental bands announcing songs like Webb Piece's current hit as 'Dare stran' de grass' (there stands the glass). Or the Marty Robbins big hit as 'Libbons o' dlaaknish', (Ribbon of Darkness). In fact we were the first, and probably the only, British band to visit the war zone of Vietnam. The numbers we featured in those days were West Coast Rock and standard Country songs with overtones of the good-times left behind and the hope of a safe return, like,'Detroit City', 'Silver Wings.' and 'In the Early Morning Rain'.

Back in Saigon, the Farfisa was repaired, (more about the repairman later) and Roy quickly picked up the style of music and Dave Nisbett's harmonies were very good. Ady's guitar playing was passable, though he could be great when the mood took him, but I suppose that was a bit too much to expect in his present frame of mind. Kit's great appeal were her clear uncomplicated songs and her warm 'Down Home' image.

Money was another thing. Drawing on the experiences of the Korean

War, the US Government banned the use of the American dollar in Vietnam, and the Treasury added its weight by issuing Military Payment Certificates (MPC) in an attempt to stem the flow of Green Dollars. It proved to be an exercise in futility by saving pennies and losing millions of dollars, whilst leaving the big underworld operators free to cream off as much as eight cents of every dollar going into the war–zone and, in spite of the government's actions, green dollars continued to flood into the country. Regular ocean–going freighters unloaded full cargos of luxury goods at Cholon, across the river from Saigon, throughout the war, while corrupt Vietnamese and US. officials turned a blind eye. I must admit that I felt very uneasy about leaving all our real money in the hands of those two bandits in Hong Kong, but there was nothing I could do about it at the time.

We were made very welcome by the club officials and well fed and watered. (Watered? I almost forgot what water tasted like out there). Which was just as well, because it was very difficult to get anything to eat if you were not on one of the bases. In Saigon itself there were only about five or six places where it was safe to eat. If you went into the wrong café, you could easily end up being dumped in the river with the kitchen waste. One of the approved restaurants was known as the 'Wal–hoo', a US Army cafeteria on the top floor of a building near the railway sidings, and the food was about the worst American fast food I've ever tasted. The staff and the cooks were probably selling off the best of the rations on the Black Market. Another place was downtown by the riverside run by the USO. This was a bit better, but very primitive, and run by a group of nice American lady ex–pats, who would not have been out of place at a church fete in the Cotswolds. Mind you, if you had the money you could always go to the Caravelle Hotel where a double Jack Daniels would set you back 25 green US dollars (MPC's were not accepted). I went there for dinner one night with the local agent and the dining room was superb. The decor was opulent with elegant French furnishing, the service impeccable, and the food and wine excellent. It was hard to realize that less than twelve miles up–country people were being killed and raw young G.I.s were living on K. Rations in damp tents.

There was one other place we used to go to get something to eat. It was a Soul Food restaurant in an alley behind the Golden Building, where we were made very welcome, though we were white, maybe because we were Brits or Third Country Nationals as the military so neatly branded us. The black G.I.s were fascinated by our accents, particularly David's. I doubt if they had ever heard an authentic Mancunian twang before. Lots of drug deals were going down there, but as we were musicians everybody presumed we were snorting, so there was no trouble. However, during our stay in Saigon, a couple of people were shot in there, which brought it to the attention of the 'White Mice '(Viet Military Police), who from then on demanded a cut to become as blind as their three brethren in the fairy tale.

The tension was constant and, contrary to the usual belief, it got worse the longer we stayed. It was not possible to get used to it, because the danger was everywhere. There was always the unexpected happening. We were doing up to three shows a day in and around Saigon at all sorts of hours. The inner city curfew was now 7p.m. to 7am. A few days later, we were driven up to do three shows for the Australian troops at a beachside rest area at Vung–Tau. The road was fine for about six miles out of Saigon and then we turned into the rough secondary road that ran through the jungle to the coast. The US Engineers had cut back the vegetation a couple of hundred yards from the road on either side but the dark sinister under–growth and black vine–strewn trees were still a bit sinister. An hour later, we arrived to a great welcome from the Aussies, and hustled into the bars, while the local Vietnamese unloaded our gear and set it up for the first show.

The clubs turned out to be very well–run and equipped, The Beachcomber was an open–air venue but the other two, the Crossroads and the Paradise, were in superb French buildings. Getting there had been relatively easy, but when it came time to head back, we found that the North Vietnamese Army had cut the road and they were launching a major attack on Saigon and had already infiltrated the Chinese district of Cholon. In the event they sent a C130 transport plane to pick up both us and the bus. We simply drove it up the loading ramp into the cavernous body where the loadmaster roped it down. On landing back at Tan son Hut airport, we were kept aboard the plane as the airport was under attack, which did not do a lot of good for the band's nerves, particularly to Ady and Kit. The others were by now up to their armpits in Budweiser and didn't care much about anything.

Ady was seriously scared and was talking about going to the British Consulate in an attempt to get away from the danger. I went to see Chuck about the situation, but he said that it was too late to change the contract and that I would have to sort it out with the agency in Hong Kong. So I decided to take Ady back there and re–negotiate the contract if I could. But before I could get round to it we were involved in a situation which completely ruled out any possibility of Ady changing his mind.

PICKER'S TIP 28

It is professional suicide to try and re–book yourself direct into a gig you have done for an agent. Word quickly gets around, and no agent will put bookings your way if you are not a team player. Remember everyone in this profession has a necessary function, the performer, the manager, the agent, and the booker. Try to short–circuit it at your peril

A Baptism of Fire

Well, I suppose, as the Hollywood starlet once said, it had to happen sooner or later. We had not been in Vietnam very long, when we encountered at first-hand an attack on a base where we were working. Up to that time we had done most of our shows on the big bases, or in heavily fortified areas, but this time we were sent down to a combined 7th Army-Navy unit in the disputed region of the Mekong Delta. The base was at the site of an old seminary in Dinh Tuong province on the north bank of the Tian Giang river, south-west of Saigon. It was under American control by day, but definitely a Viet Cong region after curfew.

Leaving Saigon about 2 p.m, after overcoming heavy resistance from our driver Billy, who wanted to hang around the bars on Yen Do Street., we rumbled south down Highway 4. He kept dismissing the warnings about the curfew, assuring us that he knew all the back roads, and that these curfew regulations were only to keep the locals in check. He sadly misjudged the situation and later was to pay with his life for his over-confidence. But that's another story. On this occasion we did arrive at the riverside post outside My Tho without incident. It was a fortified strong point, with small sandbagged cinder-block fort and a tall watch-tower to control river traffic up the Mekong. We were greeted warmly and the buzz went around the base that there was a Round-Eye band with a white girl-singer playing country music so the main club room was packed when we began.

The show went very well until towards the end of the evening. In the middle of one of Kit's songs, there was a terrific crash outside and sirens began to wail. It was a rocket attack from the opposite bank of the river and everybody scattered to the bunkers. An armored patrol boat moved out from the jetty with a searchlight seeking the attackers. A small sampan was caught in the beam and the twin 0.50 Brownings blew it out of the water. Nobody knew if it was the rocket carrier or not. It had got in the way. It was that kind of war, and we watched open-mouthed until somebody dragged us into a sandbagged shelter. A big sergeant told us that up-river, in the Plain of Reeds on the Cambodian border, there were some VC bases, but due to the swampy ground and lack of roads, there was no way of clearing them out. Air attacks did little to dislodge them, as the bombs buried themselves in the mud and even amphibious jeeps couldn't get through, so the US Navy patrolled the river to keep them bottled up.

"They do sometimes try to break out, tho'," he added, stating the bloody obvious. The crisis passed and we got down to a bit of sour-mash bashing with our hosts, and I was considering how free and easy everything seemed to be and that there was none of the starchy officiousness that one associated with the British Army, when something happened that proved to me that all armies are the same, controlled by the same inflexible protocols and red tape.

A report had come in that the road back to Saigon was now blocked by the Viet Cong, (Oh no. Not again). It was now impossible to get back that night, so we would have to stay on the base overnight. No problem, we were assured, until a red–faced Provost Sergeant hesitatingly explained to us that there was a standing order in Vietnam that no female third country nationals were allowed to stay overnight on any military installation and there was a problem as far as Kit was concerned. Suddenly, the senior NCOs, who half an hour earlier had been raving it up with us, were nowhere around to ask the CO. about obtaining special permission. So while the boys were to be bedded down in the safety of the bunkers, Kit would have to go to a hotel or something off the base. Crazy. And of course no way would I let her go on her own. Finally it was decided to take us across town to the house of a civilian veterinary adviser—and so began the nightmare.

By now it was around two am, and there was still a lot of action going on, but it seemed to be aimed at other targets, so a small convoy was put together in the courtyard outside the club. There were three jeeps and the vet's service van. Kit and I were in the third jeep with the vet's van bringing up the rear. There was a lull in the fire–fight and the gates were flung open and, under the covering fire of a machine gun from the watch–tower we shot out into the darkened roadway lit by the flashes of star shells and rockets and accompanied by the crump of mortar bombs and muffled explosions ahead of us. Driving our jeep was a Green Beret officer, a completely Gung Ho nut–case who thought he was in some John Wayne movie and was charging ashore at Guadalcanal. He was draped in cartridge belts with Special Forces badges all over him and carrying a Colt.45 on one hip and a bunch of fragmentation grenades on the other. Chomping on a big cigar and cursing everybody, he swung the jeep wildly from side to side of the narrow road going flat out.

Mortar rounds were now landing behind us as we shot through the main street where a couple of buildings were blazing. but we stormed on to the vet's house. Twice we were stopped by ARVIN (South Viet Army) patrols and redirected away from the hot spots, roaring with the pedal to the floor out into the suburbs.

In the back seat of the jeep we clung on for dear life, petrified. and hoping that this bloody crazy trip would soon be over. Old Chisom at the wheel cursed louder and roared after the other jeeps down a street full of wrecked and smoldering houses. We turned into what looked a quiet street of colonial bungalows with elegant, once cultivated lawns looking so placid in the moonlight. It was at this moment that the leading jeep of our convoy hit a land mine. It was not, thank God, a big one but it was big enough to turn the jeep over and throw the occupants out all over the road. The next vehicle jeep was following too close and ran into the wreck, and the front seat passenger hurtled over the windshield and into a stone garden wall. We screeched to a skidding stop and our driver jumped out. Drawing his pistol and still cursing the world, he ran towards the twisted figure crumpled against the wall and half–carried and half–dragged it to our jeep and dumped it on the front passenger seat. He glared into the darkness and fired two deafening shots at some shadow across the gardens, before peeling the vehicle wildly back into the road and shooting off in the opposite direction ignoring the shouts for help from the other crash victims.

"Holy Shit," he shouted above the din of the roaring engine and the loud explosions.

"This heah is ma sergeant, ma good buddy. Me'n him been heah since '62. Seen ever'thin' together, Ahn Ke, Dong Tap, the fuckin' lot, an' afore that we wuz with Special Forces in Loas. An' now, would ya believe it? He's gotta get caught up in this bit of shit. Here, Limey, grab a hold of him."

I reached for the figure in front of me and held on to him grimly. He was moaning and the blood pouring out of his ear was soaking into my thin tropical pants, as the crazy man at the wheel skidded and thundered his way through the crashing explosions and burning debris, steering with one hand and waving his pistol with the other. Suddenly the inert bleeding figure I was holding regained consciousness and sat bolt upright yelling in pain. Kit screamed for the Captain to stop but he pointed his gun at her and shouted for her to shut up and began a further bellowing recital about his buddy's misfortune. God knows what they did with people like him when the war ended.

After living like that for more than fifteen years, how do you fit into civilian life?

Kit was now white with fear and clung desperately to my arm while I tried my best to control the bleeding, delirious invalid. Once more we skidded to a stop and the sound of a helicopter could be heard. The driver spun the jeep, waited a moment and then shot off again through the deserted streets, weaving this way and that to avoid fallen masonry and coils of barbed wire, until we screeched to a halt at a riverside lift–off pad where a chattering Huey chopper was getting ready to take off. The side door was open and two paramedics were loading wounded civilians aboard. Shouting and yelling, our Gung Ho maniac pushed his gun into the pilot's face and demanded that his injured buddy be taken along as well. The young soldiers began to protest, but the Captain's bars and that all–persuasive Colt 45 pistol forced them to accept their new passenger. With a roar the helicopter took off and a strange silence came over the riverbank. The captain then sat back and lit himself a joint, before suddenly noticing us still frozen with shock and fear behind him.

"Oh yeah," he said lazily. "You Limeys. Ah almost forgot 'bout yuh."

He banged the jeep into gear and drove us easily to the accommodation we had been allocated, still giving us chapter and verse of his times in the Golden Triangle. How many gooks he had killed, and about all the things he and his buddy had been through. I was more convinced than ever of his mental state by the time we reached the vet's house. Any final doubts we may have been harboring were dismissed when, not finding anyone at home, he simply shot off the lock, and kicked the door in to allow us access, threw his buddy's M1 carbine at us, shouting that we might need it and roared away into the night. What a banana.

We stumbled inside and piled up furniture against the door and snuggled upon the rattan sofa to doze fitfully till dawn. The next day, we were picked up by the Veterinary Officer and returned to the base, where we found the boys tucking into a big breakfast. After a massive late night booze–up in one of the bunkers, even Ady looked a little less stressed. Raucous goodbyes were shouted, everybody piled aboard the bus with bottles of Jim Beam and boxes of Bud and we headed back to Saigon. It was a beautiful day; peaceful and quiet as though nothing had ever happened, but it struck me that the placid peasants tending the water buffaloes were probably the same goons that were trying to blow us up the night before.

Cholon

Unfortunately our Farfisa keyboard had suffered somewhat from being blown off the stage, so it had to go in for repair when we got back. There then followed one of the most bizarre incidents of the whole trip. In its own way, typical of the totally unreal world of wartime South Vietnam, and an example of how out of hand the situation had become.

In Cholon, the Chinese district of Saigon, there lived a young man called Lam Ho, who before the war, had been at Saigon University studying electronics, and now supported his family by repairing and rebuilding all kinds of electronic gear for both GI's and the Black Market operators. We were told that he was the best in town, so we ran the Farfisa round to him. His workshop was in two connected lock–up garages down by the river where, as well as repairing equipment, he also produced his own copies of Fender amplifiers, superb copies in fact.

All the soldering and assembly was done by a work–force of young kids of about ten or eleven years old under his careful supervision. They were super examples of his craft and the only way they could be distinguished from the real thing was by a small plate monogrammed L.H. on the rear control panel.

He inspected the Farfisa, and said that, although he did not have a schematic drawing of the circuit, he would be able to fix it. He said that it was an opportunity for him to see the latest electronic technology from Italy and would we mind if he took photographs of the circuits while he had it. This favour would be reflected in the price of the repair. I said okay and asked him when it would be ready, and without hesitating he said Tuesday afternoon, but not to try to collect it before Friday morning, as there was going to be a Viet Cong attack in Cholon on Wednesday. Apparently it was common knowledge in the Chinese community and everybody made allowances for the event in their business plans and golf games for the coming week.

By this time Kit had reluctantly come to terms with the gig, but Ady was becoming seriously paranoid and was scared, all the more so since the attack at My Tho, and no amount of cajoling was going to change his mind about getting out. He made life a misery for Dave, the drummer, moaning at him all the time, hoping to get him to leave with him, so he did not have to travel back to England on his own. Though it must be said that Dave did not always take it lying down. In fact he took a perverse delight in making Ady even more nervous. For instance, often on wild jungle roads he would bring talk round to the subject of Viet Cong ambushes, and at the moment he caught Ady looking round anxiously at the greenery, he would rap on the van's side paneling with a coin making a sound like an AK 47.

Ady would shout, "Look out," and throw himself to the floor yelling. "Get down."

At which point Dave would look at him and say.

"S'no use gerrin down there, Ady. If we hit a mine, yuh'll be th' first to cop it."

He pulled this stroke about three times in the period Ady was with us. Usually, after these incidents the rest of the journey would degenerate into one big slanging match between them. Ah, the exquisite cruelty of the Brotherhood of Musicians.

Don't you just love it?

*   *   *   *   *   *

PACIFIC
STARS STRIPES

AN AUTHORIZED PUBLICATION OF THE
U.S. ARMED FORCES IN THE FAR EAST

10¢

Vol. 24, No. 256   Saturday, Sept. 14, 1968

Yonco—the British Texan

By Elson Irwin

HE'S a well-dressed guy in a business suit and speaks with a clipped British accent with traces of a Texas twang he picked up around Galveston.

Frankie Yonco, after spending four months drifting the length and breadth of South Vietnam with three guys and a gal, spreading a kind of country-western joy to the troops, is now in Japan and intends to give the same kind of performances at the military clubs here.

Yonco's country-western is not the foot-stompin', shin-kickin' stuff from "cowboy-chaps" America, but a kind of sophisticated country built around guys who can sing and guys who can play.

He originally called his group "The Texas Drifters" but he's changing all that to "The Everglades."

He doesn't come out with a whoop and holler. He wears a string tie and a few rhinestones on his jacket at times, but there are other times when he steps into the spotlight in a subdued sax and makes like Dean Martin sans martini.

Yonco is just a little disturbed he comes into Tokyo as an unknown. He is a much traveled gent who has backed up the likes of such western stars as Johnny Cash, Hank Williams Jr., Kitty Wells, Tex Williams, Lefty Frizzell, Roger Miller and Don Gibson, to name a few.

He is a guy who has appeared on the concert stage, the sophisticated supper clubs of Europe, on television and on recordings.

He is well known in Europe . . . he is even well-known in Turkey. He was a disc-jockey in Turkey (and there's not many guys who can make that claim.)

In the group are two guys from England, two guys from Scotland and a young good-looking blonde gal from Ireland. And, if that isn't enough to make you interested, nothing's going to move you, man.

After Japan, Yonco will sweep through Okinawa, Taipei, Korea and the Philippines and returns to his native England in

The group was organized in England in 1962 and since that time Frank Yonco and his Texas Drifters have been in popular demand.

Above.
At a Montagnard village, up in the Central Highlands
of South Vietnam,
Pleiku. July 1968.

FRANK YONCO

KIT CONNOR

Part of a nice feature in the Tokyo edition of The pacific Stars and Stripes. September 1968

(*above*) Upon the Perfume River on the DMZ. They just dumped us from a Chinook and left u_
"Too dangerous for us." They said . . . What about us? An hour later a US navy boat picked us u_

(*below right*) Playing an early evening gig at typical primitive up country outpost in the Central Highlands.

(*below left*) A Montagnard Village Chief, one of the deadly marksmen of Pleiku

(above) Hong tap Tu Street in Central Saigon. 1968. Probably an undercover bomb delivery to a VC unit in Cholon. Note the cunningly disguised escort! These ladies were not above dropping a grenade through an open car window either!

(below) No. . . it's not a fashion accessory. It's the real thing, holding a .32 Frommer pistol, taken off a dead NVA. officer at Cu-Chi, which came in handy several times.

(right) Cutting a promotional album at the Sony Recording Studio, Rippongi, Tokyo for producer Tatsumi Nagashima

(above) With Bruno Brisco, the Cosa Nostra enforcer for the Asakusa district of Tokyo. . . The Real Thing! . . . A fully paid up Family Man!

AMERICAN FORCES VIETNAM NETWORK
Detachment #6
APO 96316

22 JULY 1968

SUBJECT: Letter of Appreciation

TO: Frank Yonco and the Texas Drifters

As the Officer-in-Charge of the American Forces Vietnam Television,
Detachment #6 at Tuy Hoa Air Base, Republic of Vietnam, I wish to
thank you and your group for the performance you gave during the
live telecast of your show.

With a minimum amout of notification, amid your very busy schedule,
you consented to take on the task of performing before our live
camera so that the forces unable to see your shows at the clubs
might have the opportunity to enjoy good Country Western music.

Your talent and professional know-how were invaluable in making the
broadcast one of the highlights of our normal programming. You can
take justifiable pride in knowing that your show was well received
and enjoyed by our viewers in the Channel Eleven area.

Special mention is made to Frank Yonco, for his selfless dedication
and stellar performance during the three live radio broadcasts he
participated in on the Base F.M. Radio station. His knowledge of
country western music, and his professional attitude on the air,
will long be remembered in the Tuy Hoa area.

I am confident that you will continue to do the same fine work whenever the opportunity is offered, and I wish you every success for
the future.

CHARLES R. SUITS
Captain   SigC
Officer-in-Charge
AFVN-TV   DET#6

The Malay Mail

MALAYSIAN EDITION

1896 ★   FRIDAY, OCTOBER 18, 1968   ★ ★   15 CENTS   K

KUALA LUMPUR Capital City of Malaysia

COUNTRY AND WESTERN SONGS THE BEST, SAYS YONCO

THE FRANKIE YONCO GROUP (FROM LEFT): KITTY CONNOR, DAVID NISBET, DAVID MARKS, RAY GOUDIE AND FRANKIE YONCO.

(above) Kuala Lumpur, Malaya. The Merlin Hotel was the final stop in the Far East. The shows were sold out long before we got there. Here we met Mr Chang.

(left) May 16th 1971 Leaving Weisbaden in a happy mood for the fateful trip home via Brussels. Vince Evers 3rd from left.

(above) Clubland comes to Cornwall

(right) Kit and I on a visit to see our Mums
in the North of England

(below) My son Francis and his family up
from Cornwall at our place in Bath
L to R: Felicity, Gill, Anthony and Francis.

(below) Everglades
Cornwall 1976

South China Sea Shuffle

This Ady affair was getting serious, and he insisted that I get him out of the war zone, so I had to make arrangements to get him back to Hong Kong. About the only man that could help in Saigon was agent Chuck Doherty. He was the man holding the return tickets. So I discussed the problem with the rest of the boys, and it was decided that Big Dave would move from bass onto guitar and the bass lines would be taken over on the organ keyboard by Roy. We demonstrated the sound to Chuck, and he was quite satisfied, so we got down to a fresh program, while Ady negotiated with Arthur for the sale of his gear, which included a rare Australian Maton guitar. Together with what pay he had to draw from me, he got enough money to pay for his passage back to the UK. I was also not very happy with the stroke that the agency there had pulled on us, so I wanted to go back to Hong Kong to get it sorted out, and Kit decided to come with me. It was clear that she needed a break too.

I had a serious talk with the boys to find out whether or not to continue. I had already realized that if the others elected to pack it in, I would obviously have to leave Vietnam myself, but I would not go back to England. Having got this far, I would have gone on to Australia put a new band together and easily pick up one of the US. Navy contracts for work on the South Pacific bases. However, Roy and the two Davids felt convinced that they could provide a solid musical back–up, so they decided to stay on. It is said that hindsight is 20/20 and, looking back, I consider that this was a missed opportunity, because with our Vietnam track record, getting a green card to work in the States would have been easy, and who knows what it could have led to? In the event, at the end of the Far East contracts, I went back to England. But I have always believed that to change one thing, changes everything leading from it. So I left it to fate and, there is not much I would have changed anyway.

A week later Kit, Ady and I landed in at Kai Tek airport in Hong Kong without telling the partners at Pan Pacific that we were coming, and we managed to book into the Sun Ya Hotel without being seen. We did not have much contact with Ady after that. He was booked into some hotel down by the ferry, and we met him for breakfast a couple of mornings, but most of his day was spent going round the shipping offices trying to get a passage home. At one point, he said he'd changed his mind and would come back to 'Nam with us but it was too late for all that. And anyway, if he had come back with us the same things would only happen again, so I turned him down. Eventually he did manage to get a cabin on a French freighter bound for Marseilles, but the journey took much longer than he planned, as the boat had a collision in the Singapore docks, and it was over a month before he got to the ship's home port in the South of France. There he was bundled onto a train, locked in with hundreds of Arab immigrants, and sent off to Paris. I never did get the full details, but I believe it was a bit of a nightmare trip, which turned him off anything French for the rest of his life except Gauloise cigarettes, that is.

It was good to be back in the bustle of the Colony and, after cleaning up, we did a bit of shopping up and down Nathan road, where we were amused to find a shopping–mall right opposite the hotel that contained the FUK YU shoe shop. If the pair you bought didn't fit, they could refuse to take them back by pointing to the shop sign.

The following day I watched Fredo's taxi drop him off so I gave it half an hour. I wanted to be sure they were both there when I called the office. Fredo picked up the phone when I rang. "Pan Pacific Attractions. Waddya want?" He used his macho Hollywood–extra voice. I made that hissing sound that you often used to hear on long distance calls in Hong Kong and then did a couple of muted clicks. "Hello Fredo,"I said cheerfully. "This is Frank Yonco. Glad I caught you."

I heard that dull plop that you get when a hand is placed across the phone. I could imagine him mouthing my call to his partner across the desk."Oh. Er, Hi, Yonco. What can we do for yuh? Wassa problem?" Still keeping up the happy–chappy approach, I continued. "Well, Fredo it's just that I think we should have a talk about this contract we're doin' out here, hiss, hiss, click, click. Hello. Fredo, are you still there?" At this he became very shitty about the whole thing. Mr. Hardnose himself, brusquely dictating terms from the safety of his 7th Floor citadel hundreds of miles away across the South China Sea, saying things like "Well, Yonco. You've been around. You know you shouldn't sign contracts unless you know the condition, etc. " Repeating with a snigger that, obviously, any Far Eastern contract could include Vietnam. What was I, chicken or somethin'? He was enjoying handing out abuse of that kind, obviously thinking I was calling from far away Saigon. Finally, he said that it was only for a couple of weeks anyway, so what was I yelping about? And, yes, sure, it could be all sorted out when I called in the office, etc., finishing off with a studded insult. "So now, if y' don't mind, you Limey Hillbilly Hank, we've got an office to run here. You're not the only act on our books, you know."

I was getting ready to blow his doors off. He must have felt as safe as houses, until I made my play. "Hiss—click, click.er, Wassat? You mean," I said slowly. "That you'll sort out my problems when I call in at the office? Oh good, that'll be great

"Yeah. Yeah," he agreed dismissively. "Now get off the friggin' phone, will ya. By the way," he said with a sardonic chuckle "Where you phonin' from? Must be costing old Chuck a bomb."

I played my ace. "It's not costing him a bean Fredo. It's all on my hotel bill. I'm here. Two floors above you and I'm coming down to see you NOW.

I heard him gasp and I was heading for the door before he could cradle the phone. I shot down the stairs and brushed past the protesting secretary in the outer office and burst into the room where Fredo and Ralf where sitting open-mouthed, gazing at each other. I was mad. There was no doubt–

ing that. What with the obvious rip–off that they were trying to pull, exacerbated by the Ady affair, I was about ready to explode and kick the office to pieces. Ralf, as usual kept out of things with a soft–looking grin on his face, while his partner tried to front it out, but he buckled when he realized that I was very, very serious, and was prepared to report the whole thing to Special Services, which would affect their operating license. (Actually I was bluffing, because on the evidence Special Services would have had nothing to do with it. After all, I had signed the contract).

After my ranting, Fredo sat down with a sigh completely deflated, and let his more diplomatic partner pour oil on the troubled waters. I stood my ground and by the time the Jack Daniels came out, I had got most of what I had come for. A new contract with more money, and a bonus if we completed the period without any more problems, and an extension of another month in Japan after Vietnam was finished. They paid the hotel bill and the return flight to Saigon, they were so relieved to get this paranoid lunatic off their doorstep. In the light of this result I did not think it diplomatic then to mention Ady was leaving, and that we were going to be one man short.

Whilst in Hong Kong, I also picked up a couple of suits and a fawn cashmere topcoat I had ordered when I was last there. They were superbly made and classically cut and very reasonably priced and certainly in the case of the topcoat, very long–lasting. It was another three days before we could get a flight and we spent the time as tourists. We went to a movie, and took in the Australian chip shop in Kowloon, where they sold Fosters lager as well as real fish and chips. We also took a boat across to Repulse Bay and had a picnic on Hong Kong Island, a most beautiful place indeed. But it was time to get back to work, so, reluctantly, in spite of the new deal and the satisfaction of getting my rocks off at the Pan Pacific Agency, we made our way back to the airport, and by two in the afternoon we were picked up at Ton Son Hut airport in Saigon by a CDA. Driver.

The Ambush

While we had been away, the boys had been rehearsing hard and, later that afternoon, we ran through the new re–vamped show in Chuck's garage. There were a few changes to be made and a couple of new numbers added. Kit did things like Patsy Cline's 'Crazy' and 'I fall to pieces', which actually sounded better now that Roy had more room to move, David's lead–guitar work being much cleaner and simpler than Ady's. In fact, most of our numbers came out with a more modern feel about them. We also now had a selection of instrumentals to pull on like 'The Shadow of your Smile' and 'Nights in White Satin'. Not exactly Country, I know, but still very popular. Chuck and Arthur said they preferred the new sound and engaged the boys to back Chuck's own stand–up comedy routine.

It was not long before we were back on the road again, but this time with one very important difference. This time I insisted on driving the van myself, instead of being at the whim of rum–soaked Billy, the agency driver. I knew where to go, or more important, where not to go, and could find my way round the bases and clubs. After a series of shows in and around Saigon, we were sent out to the Camp Holloway base in the Central Highlands around Pleiku, where we played several big NCO. Clubs. Unfortunately the stress caused by the excessive drinking of the boys, prevented the gigs being pleasant, in spite of the superb hospitality. Booze was plentiful and cheap; in fact it was almost free. For example, the brewers of Colt 45 Malt Liquor were trying to get the brand name launched, and it was handed out by the caseload to performers and, if it was free, our boys were going to drink it. And to be fair, it was not only them, as both Kit and I did our fair share of chug–a–lugging. Although in our case it was whiskey. CC7 & Coke for Kit, and for me it was "Jack Daniels, if you please."

By this time we had become an 'Accredited Act', which meant that we could stay overnight on the bases we played at. The large infantry base at Pleiku was very primitive, and we slept in tents under mosquito nets because of the heat. Washing and latrine facilities were also equally basic, so you can imagine some of the trauma Kit went through when she wanted to bathe or use the facilities. At such times we would first have to check that the shower block was empty and then stand guard at the door until she was finished.

Guns? Well, that was another thing. Officially, we were not supposed to carry them, but on the other hand we were not supposed to be shot at either. So it was just as well to be prepared to shoot back. Weapons were not hard to obtain from sympathetic G.I.s and soon we had a veritable armoury on board our bus. There was an M16 carbine, a sawn off 12 gauge Remington, and at the beginning, an AK.47 Russian assault rifle, but we were advised to get rid of this last one, as it was the standard weapon of the Viet Cong, and its unique distinguishing bark was likely to bring incoming fire from some nervous, trigger–happy grunt who might be in the vicinity. We also obtained a couple of hand–guns, a Hungarian 32 Frommer Stop that had been found on a dead N.V.A. officer for me, and a neat 22 Colt revolver for Kit's personal protection. We managed to bring both these handguns back home with us. Kit presented hers to Karl Denver as a birthday gift and, in one of those periods of financial famine that hit you in this business, I sold the Frommer to a well–known Manchester wrestler, who insisted on putting the cartridges in the wrong way round. I wonder if he lived very long or still has both hands.

You may think that with all the heavy military presence around, the chances of being shot were remote,but believe me the risks were quite real. Often, by the roadside, you would see the black uniformed bullet–riddled bodies of dead Vietcong awaiting collection. American casualties were always removed immediately. On one occasion we saw a group of dead Laotian villagers shot by the Viet for being US army scouts. They had been held prisoners by the Viet and had piano wire threaded through the palm of one hand, then passed through holes in their cheeks, and then through the other palm secured by pieces of bamboo. A medic estimated that they had been held like that for weeks, before being killed and dumped outside the gates of Ben Hoa base. Of course the boozing newshounds in Saigon never reported this incident. The world's press was thirsty for news of American atrocities, not Viet Cong ones. Let me tell you about another incident that happened whilst we were there.

Amongst the acts working the circuit at the time was an American pop group called 'Brandy Perry and the Bubble Machine'. They were a bunch of young musicians seeking fame and fortune like the rest of us who had accepted this contract to get some recognition Stateside. Arriving some weeks before us, they worked for an agency out of Da Nang, and were not familiar with conditions away from the coastal area, They blindly believed all that was told them by their driver, who was a friend and boozing partner of our ex–driver Billy, and had the same casual disregard for advice from the M.P.s. The group was booked at a club called the Mule-skinner's at Cu Chi about two hours along Highway One out of Saigon. It was close to an extremely dangerous area called the Iron Triangle, later famous for its network of Viet Cong supply tunnels. They were warned that the area was still swarming with heavily armed Viet, both Cong and NVA, who had been trapped there after the Tet Offensive, and the curfew code for that area was 'Condition Red' which meant, that wherever you were at three p.m. you headed for the nearest U.S. base, no matter what.

Their American driver Joe, had brought them down from Da Nang the night before, and was settled in a bar on Yen Do Street at the time he should have been picking them up. He was well–soaked in Jim Beam, so that by the time he got round to their hotel it was almost curfew time. At the big bridge on the way out of town, a city police jeep stopped them, but the drunken road–manager waved the patrol out of the way and headed off down Highway One to Cu Chi. The night came in with its usual tropical rapidity, and they were only about four miles from the camp when they were attacked. It was here that GI Joe committed one of the basic mistakes in the war zone, by insisting on taking what he described as a 'Short Cut' down a narrow secondary jungle road. As they rounded a blind bend they were waved down by what they thought was a South Vietnamese Army patrol but as the drunken driver braked they were riddled with machine gun fire.

Joe probably didn't feel a thing, as he was killed outright along with the seventeen–year–old bass player, and another band member was wounded. As the attackers disappeared into the dark jungle, the survivors, including Brandy Perry herself, tried desperately to get the bus going again, but its steering had been hit, and they had only moved a few hundred yards before it careered into a drainage ditch. Of the six people who had left Saigon, two were now dead and one seriously wounded in the chest. Nobody knew what to do or where they were and now, numbed with shock and fear, they decided to wait for daylight and then try to find the way back to the main road. The night passed slowly with the pitiful moaning of the wounded man, the frightening jungle noises, the shattered bodies sprawling on the floor and the clouds of insects brought by the smell of blood. They were parched with thirst but afraid to leave the safety of the crippled bus, and shared the chocolate bars and sticks of beef jerky they found in the drivers bag.

But worst was yet to come, because just before dawn the attackers returned with their friends to loot the bus, and as the terrified musicians cowered silently in the wreck it was sprayed again with bullets. This time a second round hit the wounded drummer killing him outright and one of the others was wounded in the head. Another round hit the steering wheel, and set off the horn, which made the bandits think that there might be people still alive in the bus, who may have radioed for back–up. So, after a few more shots and much shouting, they called off the looting and melted away again into the jungle, and the young musicians faced the lonely dawn and another anxious day. Nobody at the Cu Chi base questioned their non-arrival, putting it down to an administrative mix up, but luckily they were found early in the evening by a Thai Army patrol and taken to hospital in Saigon.

At a subsequent Provost Marshal's Inquiry, it turned out that Joe the driver, was in fact a deserter from the Marines, who had been working for Special Services since 1965, and that there was a grave suspicion that the attack may have been perpetrated by some South Vietnamese Army con-scripts, who had a base nearby. A theory supported by the fact that none of the spent cartridges found at the site of the ambush were of 9mm AK47 calibre, the standard Viet Cong weapon. The perpetrators were never found, but some of the more cynical journalists in Saigon viewed the official report of inquiry's findings as another attempt by the military to divert at-tention away from their flourishing protection rackets.

Les Montagnards

On days we were not working, there was not much to do around Pleiku, and the band's boozing was getting out of hand, mainly due to boredom. As a diversion I arranged a trip to the Montagnard country up in the Central Highlands, with a U.S. Army Veterinary officer. Kit did not want to go, so I took the boys out with me. The village was about an hour's drive out into the hills and contained a small advanced scouting unit in constant contact with HQ at Pleiku. about ten guys in a sandbagged stockade with a mortar pit and the standard twin 50 calibre Browning machine gun installation, surrounded by barbed–wire entanglements and booby–traps

The locals were not at all like the usual coastal Vietnamese. They were Montagnards, so called by the earlier French colonists, a mountain people, whose features were totally different from their jungle neighbours, whom they despised. Their culture was simple in the extreme, almost Stone Age in its concept. Isolated here in these almost impassable high valleys, they had been bypassed by the many waves of foreign invaders, who had coveted only the rich and fertile coastal plains. The French had mounted a couple of campaigns against them in the 'twenties but the terrain was so difficult, that even the Algerian trained Foreign Legion had abandoned the project. The Japanese in turn, had also despaired of controlling the area, and the village–burning tactics of the Viet Cong and N.V.A. troops had made no impression on them. After the regular discovery of sentries with cut throats, or pinned to trees with hardwood spears, they also decided it was too dangerous to stray into Montagnard territory.

The U.S. Army vet though, was very highly regarded by the Monts, and on our arrival they made us very welcome. We called at the small radio outpost and swapped stories with the young G.I.s there, giving them the mail we'd bought with us, while the smiling villagers crowded round look- ing for candy bars and cigarettes. Their houses were built on high stilts for protection against snakes and tigers. *Tigers! Wow!*

I had not realized that there were tigers out here, but later discovered that these killer cats were quite regular visitors, and contrary to popular imagination, were more than ready to pounce on any stray traveller for dinner, even in the daytime. On hearing this news, I made it a point not to stray too far from the truck. The vet got down to business treating a buffalo, which had been shot in the stomach. It was securely penned in a tight cage of thick bamboo and it bellowed loudly as the vet got to work. The wound he was treating was forward of its right rear leg, a hole big en- ough to take three fingers, and the Doc painted on some purple fluid and replaced the big penicillin–soaked poultice. He said that it was lucky it had been a female, because the wound was in the womb area, and if treated well would not be fatal. The natives crowded round anxiously asking the interpreter about its condition and how soon it could be put back to work.

After the chocolates and cigarettes had been distributed, a wiry, brown old man wearing only a colorful loin cloth, and smoking a corn cob pipe, was introduced to us as the village headman and proudly showed us the scars on his left forearm, each one announcing proudly that he had killed a man. Through one of his sons, who spoke a little English, we learned that he had killed his first man when he was twelve years old, a French soldier who was attacking his mother, and since that time nine or ten victims had tasted his thrown machete, barbed fish spear, knife, or bows–and–arrows. We were fascinated by the young man's stories about his father and asked to see a demonstration of his prowess. After translating our request to his approving father, the young man went off to get the required equipment, whilst the old man knocked out his pipe and unwound his small turban. The equipment, when it arrived, was at first sight a bit of an anti–climax. It was a short thick bow and a few small hardwood arrows, with a couple of cock's feathers bound to one end. They did not have metal tips, just a small burnt area at the point. The excited villagers began to gather round and the young G.I.s stopped digging their weapon pits to see what the old man would do.

He chattered some quiet instructions to his son, who hurried to bring the target, a board of wood about two inches thick, and maybe about six or seven inches wide, and about four feet long, with a dab of yellow ochre roughly in the middle. This he set up in the ground and moved back to his father's side. There was much whispering amongst the villagers, and it was obvious that bets were being taken, as the old man looked at the target for a moment before walking to the far side of the clearing some forty yards away, where he crouched down behind the bole of an old tree. At his son's signal everyone went quiet as the headman came forward at a bobbing, weaving shuffle, as though he was avoiding jungle obstacles until, about a third of the way across the clearing, he dived forward and rolled head over heels, ending up flat on his back with his feet pointing towards the target. Then with one smooth movement, he slammed his heels against the bow, and fitting one of the short arrows to the string drew it back with both hands. He lifted his head briefly to check his aim and released the string— Whoosh. There was a solid thud and the arrow hit the board. He repeated this twice more in quick succession, and the three arrows were embedded in yellow mark on the board, two of them projecting a good three inches on the other side. The whole village cheered and now we understood why people left the Montagnards strictly alone. We straggled happily back to the big hut, where we feasted on roasted pig and native honey beer, which our Montagnard hosts laced with Colt 45 liquor, while us Round Eyes demolished a couple of bottles of the ever–present Up Country tincture.

*   *   *   *   *   *

The Standing Ovation

We returned to Saigon to find that we had been moved to a small motel near the airport called the Bikini on Yen Do Street. I ordered some new band outfits, three sets each of blousons and pants in maroon, gray and blue, with contrasting outfits for Kit in red, green and gray. They were very well made and cooler than the European clothes we had been wearing. They only cost about $25 per set, custom–made from Diamond Tailors, round the corner from the Caravelle Hotel near the American war memorial. The North Vietnamese pulled it down with great ceremony when they finally captured the city, some time after we'd left, I'm glad to say. On the subject of leaving, I checked out our contract and depressingly found that we still had 88 days to go, and by now, little Dave and me were getting a bit anxious. Another 88 days was a bloody long time out here.

There were a lot of good acts in Vietnam. The best ones were from the States and sometimes we were booked on packages with them. One of the finest was a guy called Benny Mason whose act was much the standard 'Vegas' stand up routine. Quick–fire comedy with a good looking partner, who either sang or danced as he passed comments on her act, as she ignored him and talked to the audience. It was a very funny act indeed. Nick de Marco was also very good. Others however were not so good. At one venue we met up with an all–girl country band led by a lady called Annie James. They were appalling, the kind of act that gives Country Music such a hard time when it comes to mainstream musical acceptance. They were rougher than any hard boozing dockside band I had seen in Galveston, but the Club Manager assured me that they always got a standing ovation at the end of their act—later we found out why.

They did the exact opposite of all the things I had been taught by such luminaries as Tex Williams and Sheb Wooley, that I had tried so hard to instill in my band. These girls changed in the hotel and travelled through the tropical evening to the gig in their stage clothes, arriving looking like a bag of wrinkled and creased rags. They tuned up their instruments on stage at full volume, drank and smoked all through the show and talked loudly to each other across the introductions, and after their spot they wandered off the front of the stage to the bar. Their playing was atrocious and their attitude to the troops terrible, moaning all the time about non-existent advances from black GIs, most of whom would not have touched these redneck slappers with a barge pole. The bass player was the one possible exception. She was good and stayed on in the country after the others had left.

Their show kicked off in the old barroom style, without any announce-ment and them staggering into that old standby instrumental 'Steel Guitar Rag' which was played mushily standing up by a tall, bony girl in a long fringed skirt who looked like she was doing the ironing. Now and then she would suddenly break into a burst of clog dancing. The clacking of her turquoise cowboy boots helping the rest of the ensemble keep in time with the tempo she had in her head, which bore no relation to the actual sound, as she stormed on missing notes and making her amp howl with wandering glissando slides.

It was terrible. I thought she was tuning up. The big fat band leader who looked like some fading drag act, then took the stage and sang a few numbers, in a quavering Kitty Wells type voice accompanied by suggestive winks and undulating hips—Oh No. However, the agency was insistent that they always got a standing ovation. I failed to understand why—until one night at Cahm Ran Bay EM Club, where I caught the full show. They had been clumsily crashing through their program of well–worn Country standards towards the close out, when their middle–aged leader came to the front centre stage and began to take off her blouse and strutted about the stage with big floppy breasts bouncing at waist level, as the other girls sang 'God Bless America ".So naturally, everybody stood up, if only to get a better view. And that's a sure–fire way to get a standing ovation.

PICKER'S TIP 29

Working with Buck Owens in the early seventies I noticed that he was using a capo on his Telecaster and asked him why? He explained that it enabled him to get punchy, open string runs in keys like Ab, Bb, C#, F# etc. Give it a try.

R & R in Hong Kong

The different clubs merged one into the other until we lost count of the gigs. Travel by C.130. Hercules transport planes or chopper became as common as travel by bus or taxi, and we were glad to reach the halfway point of our contract when we could go back to Hong Kong for a few days rest and relaxation.

We got back to the Perfumed Harbour in mid June, the only bad point was that I had a swollen jaw from an infected tooth, but a course of penicillin tablets soon cleared that up. It was good to be back in Hong Kong, and to be able to mooch around without having to look over your shoulder all the time or avoid dangerous areas—that's not to say that there were not dangerous places in Hong Kong, because in Kowloon there were some areas that even the police thought twice about going, like the Walled City, an ancient crowded area where crooks of all kinds took refuge.

Kit and I did the rounds, visiting all the places we had been before, The Aussie chip shop, the brasserie in the Sun Ya Hotel, the evening street markets and the Kingsland Restaurant, where the manager was doubtful about letting me in because of the trouble I'd caused there on my last visit with the Hong Kong agents. Finally I reassured him that there would be no problems and he showed us to a table, and we passed a great evening in the company of some Australian tourists. The food was superb and the cabaret good, with a particularly great house band, Chinese of course, but playing both traditional and modern music.

As for the boys, well naturally they headed for the bars and the disco clubs and massage parlors down by the harbour. On one occasion they took a trip to Victoria Island where after the usual pub-crawl they missed the ferry back to Kowloon, and stole a boat and somehow paddled back across the bay by moonlight, ending up in Aberdeen Harbour with all the floating brothels. It was a wonder they didn't end up face down in the water with all the dead cats and offal. One afternoon we went on a combined shopping trip in the big open-air market. Little Dave bought some shirts and a sinister flick knife; Kit got some clothes and a beautiful fan as a present for her Mother. I bought a very nice Tiensin rug, which I sent back to the UK—and our two braw Scots laddies bought an anorak each. BLOODY ANORAKS. That you could buy at any street market at home for the same price.

Up Country

Three.days later the 11.am Cathay Pacific plane out of Kai Tek took us directly to Saigon Airport where we were hustled aboard a C.130 heading for Cam Rahn Bay where our gear was waiting for us. A bumpy truck ride to the US Marine complex on the other side of the airport, took us to an old DC3 Dakota that was waiting to take us further north to Ahn Ke. We arrived there, well knackered at 7.15 p.m. to face an 8 o'clock show for a bunch of bored Leather-necks. In contrast to most of the bases we visited, there was a general mood of discontent at Ahn-Ke. It was stiflingly hot and the accomodation was primitive, mainly big tents and wooden huts with canvas roofs and most unusually, the food was very poor.

On the first night Kit and I were put in one of these huts and about 2am the door burst open and drunken G.I reeled in looking for a bed. Kit shouted and I flashed on a light at the side of my bed, and brought out the Frommer pistol from under my pillow and pointed at him. He froze at the sight of the automatic and started to blubber about being lost and how he didn't mean any harm. I yelled at him to get out and find another place to sleep off the booze, but we did not sleep much that night because on top of everything, at around 4.30am there was a VC mortar attack. It was at that point I discovered that a rat had eaten the apple I was saving for breakfast, so that day started off early.

We saw our intruder about two days later, wandering round the camp showing everybody the cobra he had killed in his tent. Oh yes, and I had my boots stolen by a cleaner. I was as pissed off as could be, and it showed because the hit of the evening was a version of 'Life Gets Tedious', the old Carson Robinson hit, for which I had written a new set of words called 'Life in Vietnam sucks.'

'The canvas sags and the tent pole leans,
I'm sick of living' on pork an' beans
Charlie's mortars hit the ration trucks
and life in Vietnam sucks. Etc. etc.'

On most other bases they had gone out of their way to make us welcome
and nothing was too much trouble, but here, apart from when we were
doing the shows, we were left to our own devices and ignored. We were not
allowed to use the PX, and orders were given that nobody could buy things
on our behalf.

It was not a situation that I was prepared to accept so I set about changing it, and the first thing was to get us out of the basic accomodation.
Wandering around the base I found a small group of camping trailers for
visiting officers. They were unoccupied, so I took over two of them and
moved us all in, and in the process we discovered the main reason for the
discontent in the camp. It came in the shape of Warrant Officer Snoddy, a
skinny, shifty eyed, pugnacious Gung Ho type with a George Jones haircut,
wearing razor–creased starched fatigues covered in badges. He had been in
the military since a boy, and ran the place like an SS training camp, putting troops on punishment duty for the slightest infringement of camp discipline. So you can see that he and I we were not destined to become bosom
buddies. The first confrontation came when he sent round an orderly to tell
us to get out of the trailers, as we did not have his permission to leave the
tents. I sent a message back for him to piss off, and if he had any problems
to take it up with Special Services. He was raging, but there was nothing
he could do except cancel the shows, but if he did that he would not get
anymore, except those USO packages which were recruited from semi–
retired performers from the vaudeville era and more suited to a SAGA
coach tour than young, virile G.I.s a long way from home.

S.W.O. Snoddy and I crossed swords on several occasions during the time
we were there, and he tried to get Kit sent off base every night, and
threatened to have me sent back to Hong Kong for carrying a gun. I in turn
said that I would report his reign of terror on the camp to HQ in Saigon,
and to the baying pack of news hounds at the Caravelle Hotel. It was the
kind of thing they would seize on, and apart from denting the image of the
US Marine Corps, would not do his career any good at all. So it was a
stand–off and after five days there we were glad to get out.

Next day a chopper dropped us off for two shows at Camp Mahoney, the
oldest base in Vietnam, where there was an alert in progress: A false alarm
as it happened, but just as tragic in its own way. A bunch of GIs had
returned from patrol and were sitting in their tent tossing an old grenade
around, when it went off and badly wounded three of them. They had had
the bomb about two months and everybody thought it was a dud—but it
wasn't.

Yes, for us life in Vietnam was wearing thin, and we had it much better
than most. Nevertheless, there were those who liked the scene and who did

well there, the black marketeers, the drug dealers and brothel operators, though I do think that these things were sometimes blown out of proportion by the European press, in its quest to find the sensational and titillating items that help the all important circulation figures. It is true that the military conduct of the war was most inefficient and unimaginative, mostly in the upper echelons of the U.S. Viet command structure, which seemed to be completely out of touch with the situation on the ground, but the vice and corruption were endemic and did not arrive with the Americans or even with the years of French Occupation. A hundred years which produced only one single track coastal railway and a dozen Vietnamese doctors, is hardly a colonial record to be proud of. (But how can anyone be proud of any kind of colonial record). However there were times when we were glad of this French connection.

I mentioned earlier that we were staying in the Golden Building. It was Viet–owned but its major clientele was American Government employees and foreigners like us, but the trouble was food, or rather, the lack of food. The Golden Building did not have a restaurant and there was little point in going out because of the lack of suitable or safe eating places downtown, and any country area was very dangerous indeed so most of the time we were existing on K Rations and chocolate bars. The situation was also aggravated by the early shows that we were doing due to the strict curfew regulations. Very often we would do two shows a day, one at midday and the second at five p.m. and were confined to the hotel after 8 p.m. This left us with a lot of time on our hands in the evenings, and if the last gig had not got a canteen or snack bar,you were in for a hungry night.

Most of these evenings we would go up onto the roof of the hotel, one of the tallest in the city, with a bottle of J.D. and a few six packs of Bud, and watch the show as explosions rang across the river and streams of tracer bullets from some Huey gun ship's electric Gatlings, that indicated some raging firefight around the airport. It was like a huge firework show as colored flares lit up troubled sections of the city, and the bangs and crumps came echoing through the black velvet darkness. On the roof was a Viet Army observation post manned by conscripts, one of whom, an ex–student from the Lycee de Saigon (the University) spoke some French as I did, which made conversation easier.

The word soon got around among the hotel staff and one morning the pretty receptionist, whose father was one of the owners, asked me to explain some official U.S. document to her in French, which I did, and we were rewarded with the most beautiful omelette and home baked bread. It was as if a door had opened, just by speaking French. Thereafter I would translate a few documents each day for them, and we could order whatever food we wanted, excellent ham, fresh chicken or fish, all beautifully cooked.

Mid June found us again at Vung Tao, where we had played one of our first shows back in April. It was a strange place, a blunt peninsula on the coast north of Saigon, which in the French Empire days had been called

Cap St Jaques and it was a rest area, where US, Thai, and Australian troops could relax. The beach was breathtakingly beautiful and the restaurants, bars, discos, and hostesses were first class. The area was actually controlled and policed by the Australians who made us welcome, but asked us a few awkward questions about why the U.K. had not come in the war to help them as they had us in two World Wars.

Maybe I should qualify this rest area bit. Actually, only the south side of the peninsula was the Allied R&R zone. The other side, the north coast, was out of bounds because it was also a well known Viet Cong rest area. In fact, on two more occasions that we were playing there the road was cut, and we had to drive our bus on board a Chinook twin rotor chopper to get back to Saigon.

We had become used to the relaxed atmosphere on the big bases like Ben Hoa and at some of the Saigon clubs, so a trip to the Korean Base at Cam Rhan Bay came as quite a shock. There was a U.S. Transport unit there that had requested a show for someone's birthday. It was hot and humid when we landed, to find a R.O.K. (Republic of Korea) Army GMC.4x4 waiting for us. That was the first shock. Instead of the usual mud spattered junk that we usually travelled in, this truck was immaculate, even to the red painted wheel studs,. A chunky Korean driver saluted us and led us to the rear where the wooden slatted seats had been scrubbed white. He almost creaked, there was that much starch in his green denims, and his boot toecaps shone like glass. The base itself was more Gung Ho and would have put a Prussian Uhlan barracks to shame. A crisp flag snapped from a white painted flagpole, and squeaky–clean hard–faced guards stood stiffly to attention as we moved into the shade of the varnished timber entrance of the club to meet the manager.

Out on the glaring sunlit square a company of infantry was drilling in double time. They were still going at it an hour later when we left for the club. In another part of the barrack square a group was practicing hand to hand combat, and doing floor dips as bull–like NCOs barked orders. They were supremely fit and it came as another surprise to find how big they were. We had become used to the small stature of the ARVIN troops but these Orientals were very powerfully built, not particularly tall but very chunky and heavy.

Stories circulated about their extreme discipline and their ability to survive jungle conditions, for in training they were taught how to catch, kill, skin and eat snakes raw, and their reputation as merciless fighters took the heart out of any N.V.A. units opposing them. They took few prisoners and being relatively free from critical press surveillance were free to fight the war on the same terms as their enemy.

We were then sent about as far north as you could go, right up in fact to the D.M.Z. (Demilitarized Zone) above Hue, the ancient capital city of Vietnam. This was about as stressful as it could be, and we were hard pressed to keep up the old British tradition of the stiff upper lip. At Da

Nang we transferred to a Huey helicopter, and were taken to a meadow on the banks of the Perfumed River. This is the river, which divides the South (That's us), and the North (That's them) Vietnam—Gulp.

The chopper dropped us with our gear and said that someone from the River Patrol would pick us up by boat in ten minutes—and with that the pilot pulled the stick back and took off, saying it was a bit too dangerous for them to stay there. Bloody Great. Oh yeah, dangerous for them? What about us? We were sitting in a field with the N.V.A. across the river ready to blow the shit out of us, and there was nothing we could do but sit there and wait.

Almost an hour passed before a halftrack lumbered across the swampy field and took us to the River Squadron Base. They were real glad to see us but everybody was a bit jumpy. In fact, Red Alerts split the show into several parts. The last one was for real and we had to take to the bunkers. Quang Tri and Phu Bai were also on this part of the tour of an area called the 'Street Without Joy'. They did not get many shows up there. The Aussie bands refused to go North of Da Nang, and the Filipinos did not like going out of Saigon at all, but we, knowing no better, went where we were sent.

At the Phu Bai airstrip we saw something that a good comedy writer would have difficulty in topping. Whilst we were waiting for a C130 to take us back to Cam Rhan Bay, we saw a big four–engine Caravelle of Vietnam Air on the tarmac. Suddenly a bell rang, and out from the single storied terminal building trooped the passengers, dozens of them, men, women and kids wearing flat conical straw hats, short pants, sandals and elegant ah–doh dresses—but instead of climbing into the plane, they were ordered by a uniformed official to push it onto the runway. It was quite a sight, all these small people puffing and blowing as they pushed this huge plane along the runway until it was in place, after which they all clambered up the metal steps laughing and chattering. The locals told us that it was the usual practice. Seats were at a premium and the airstrip had no tractor, so if you did not push you did not get a seat. It was as simple as that.

We moved on to Phan Rang for a couple of gigs after which we spent four hours sitting on the metal floor of a C130, flying back to Saigon and then by truck on to Cu Chi, where we got some sad news that a good friend of ours, a Warrant Officer pilot called Randy Wering had been killed in a chopper crash. Those bloody Chinooks were always falling out of the sky— something to do with their twin rotors getting out of sync. It was sad because Randy had made us very welcome on our visits to the Muleskinner's Club there. We tended to accept things but the threat was always there. I vividly remember doing a midday show at a place up–country. I think it was at the Pink Palace. After the show we mingled with the young G.I.s and was shocked to find them so fatalistic about the war and you would overhear conversations like.

"Hey Mac, Why don't you move into our tent? Joey Roberts won't be coming back. Charlie got him this morning."

Joe Roberts from Vermont had just passed his 19th birthday.

It was while we were at Cu Chi that I met Lita Frizzel, Lefty's niece, singing with the Donny James Show. We had a nice evening talking about her uncle and it was from her I learned the true nature of his sickness.

In July we moved on to Tuy–Hoa where we did a number of TV Shows for the troops. It was from the C.O. here, that we got a citation thanking us for the shows and the radio request programs I did. We also did a number of shows at outlying units. One of them was at a Vung–Ho bay down the coast where the young G.I.s looked scared to death and with good reason, for only three weeks previously, there had been a massacre when a N.V.A. unit had slipped ashore at night, and been let in to the small base by a local worker. Up to that time it had been considered a safe posting, but that night the Viets slaughtered the unsuspecting garrison in their beds. After that it was given high alert status. We went there by truck and that two–hour trip in the back of an open GMC was very hairy indeed.

Back in Saigon the curfew was still very early so up at Ben Hoa a convoy system was instituted. On that huge base most of the shows would be over by 10.30, so every body would rendezvous at a certain point in the complex to be escorted back to the capital. This meeting point was always a scene of great jollity. Sometimes there would be as many as twenty acts with their vans and station wagons, waiting for the escort or some latecomers. There was always plenty of booze and marijuana around, and the entertainers would wander from vehicle to vehicle swapping drinks, clothes, guns and guitars or trying to pull one of those great–looking Korean and Filipino girls. The Aussie girls were best at that game and got the G.I.s heads spin-ning. They did very well for presents like watches, diamond rings, and the best goodies the Cholon black market could provide. And when everybody was ready, the convoy would move off on the twelve–mile trip back to Saigon, flanked by armored personnel carriers with tanks front and rear.

After a while the names and places became confusing as Quin–yon, Doc Tam, Phan–Rang, Pleiku and many others, from the Delta outposts to the DMZ. I reckon we'd seen it all and by August 1st we had had enough. We had been in Vietnam one hundred and eighteen days, and apart from the time in Hong Kong had worked most of them. We began to count the hours to our departure and sold our guns and the odd collection of other goodies we had collected, like four large tinned hams, which I sold to the hotel and a tiger skin rug that nobody wanted. Everybody was getting touchy and would flare up at the slightest thing, and Big Dave and Roy had got fed up with the ever–present booze. Finally there was only a week left.There were two shows at Da Nang and a final foolhardy trip back up to Phu Bai and then a charity show for the Red Cross on Yen Do Street in Saigon, all of which passed in a haze.

At last August 27th came around and saw us picking up the gear we had left in store at Chuck Doherty's garage, over four months previously. Some of the clothing was a bit mildewed, but the only real casualty was David's

'Beatle' bass guitar. The humidity had caused the arm to become unglued, and it fell apart when he opened the case. Back at the Golden Building we said our goodbyes and spent the last evening on the roof watching the nightly light show, and listening to the chattering gunships and slugging down Tiger beer. Searchlights from Bell and Huey choppers probed the dark corners of curfew shuttered Cholon, and the occasional jeep screamed through the dark streets, loaded with White Mice on the trail of some deserter, or looking for a brothel to raid.

The next day was probably the longest one we spent there. The bus was late picking us up and there was a bomb scare on the way to the airport causing us to make a detour of about four miles. Eventually we arrived, and with delight drove past the military installations to the far side of the airport, where the civilian terminal was located. There were still a few guns around but now at least the planes were all silver and bright colors, instead of the drab green and brown we had been conditioned to, and of course, the Bangkok flight had to be late. We had a further nail–biting two hours wait until everything was settled, passports checked, baggage inspected and gear loaded.

The Mekong Delta swirled below us as we unclipped our seats belts and were offered cool drinks by the delicate Thai hostesses. Looking down I saw two F.11 Phantoms zooming off on some mission or other, afterburners red in the closing dusk. Was it really over? Were we on our way at last? The South China Sea faded in to a Jack Daniels haze and my heavy eyelids slid down—zzz.zzz. G'bye Vietnam.

*   *   *   *   *   *

19

THAILAND

The contrast was a positive shock. Even the airport was calm. The plane touched lightly down at Bangkok—everything seemed like a gentle dream. Was this really a landing field? Where were all the guns? Where were the growling, prowling jeeps? Where were the ever–present guns and the fires, and columns of smoke around the perimeter and the ground shaking crump of mortar bombs? I can vividly remember looking out of the plane's window as we were on the approach to the runway, and seeing a large water buffalo plodding leisurely through a rice paddy, with a small brown–skinned boy sprawled across its broad back fast asleep

Still in a dream, we were whisked off to town in a bright yellow bus, and it was at that point we realized just what the big difference was. Everybody was smiling, even the traffic cops. The place seemed so prosperous and happy. past the town centre limits signs as we turned onto a broad boulevard called Rama Road, passing a number of impressive gilded pagodas and temples, Kit grabbed my arm and said

"Look at that. Isn't it superb?"

I followed her eyes and saw a magnificent building. It was a long low pagoda with a huge teak roof, glowing in the bright sun. Landscaped gardens ran down to the roadside overflowing with Bougainvillea and brilliant wild orchids and the manicured lawns glittered with rainbows from the arching sprinklers. We were still ooh–ing and aah–ing about this apparition when our grinning Thai driver turned into its driveway. This was the Siam Intercontinental Hotel, which was to be our home for this period of the tour. As soon as we stopped porters surrounded the bus, grabbing our cases and guitars and we were invited to go into the bar while our US Army Liaison N.C.O. attended to the booking in procedures.

As usual, they were not ready for us to go right out to the bases. The un–certainty of acts arriving from Saigon on time, made the club custodians cautious about booking too far ahead, so we had a good week looking round Bangkok while they got things organized.

In those days before the traffic and its horrendous pollution problems got out of hand, it was a fabulous city, laced with fragrant canals, floating markets and exotic buildings and even more exotic clubs. At this time it had not yet become a popular tourist attraction and our U.S. bucks brought a very good exchange rate for the local currency of Thai bahts.

Our days were spent lounging around the hotel pool waiting for the US Army to allocate our shows. Kit made good friends with an English girl called Judy who worked as a hostess for a Thai escort agency in the city. She told us that it really was a proper escort agency, not a euphemism for a call girl ring that it later became and explained how the system worked. In Bangkok, she said, there were many visiting businessman from Japan, Europe and the USA who wanted good looking girls to show them the town and this is what the agency provided. There was a fixed charged for a date extra if the client wished to go dancing, extra for dinner but if the girl allowed the client to take her to bed it was up to the girl to negotiate the arrangement privately. It was our first taste of Jet Set living. And it was great. We had the time and we had the money. As a delayed birthday present Kit bought me some real alligator skin cowboy boots and I had some dress shirts custom–made. Kit found a good dressmaker and we spent our first evenings at night clubs like the Café de Paris and the Sany Chateau where we saw superb acts, like the Tokyo Topless Ballet and world class specialty acts.

At the Palace of Joy, Taklee

The first jobs were not in Bangkok but a long way up country at Korat Air Base where for the first time I wore the white rhinestone embroidered 'Nudie' style suit that I had made in England. It looked good but was far too hot to work in and I soon dropped it in favor of thin Western style shirts. Another base was at Taklee and they were both more restricted to us than the bases in Vietnam. Certain runways and dispersal aprons were strictly off limits and though Thailand was not officially involved in the war, B29 bombers could be heard day and night straining to get their massive bomb loads off the ground and heading north to Hanoi and the Ho Chi Mhin Trail across the border. Kit did not play these remote bases so we got drunker than usual after the gigs.

One particular night I met up again with an old pal, Sergeant Cox from Dyarbikir (Remember him? He was the guy whose bar stool had a safety belt) and we all went on a trip to the local massage parlor. It was a large hut divided by eight–foot high partitions, leaving space for the air to circulate. Everybody was suitably installed and the girls were getting down to the business when David's gritty Manchester voice came echoing over the plywood.

"Eh.Yonco

"Oooh. Yes. Waddya want? Shut up!

"No Dad. Tell us summat, will yer?

"Wot?"

"Well, it's just, er. This massage lark."

He paused and everyone went very quiet waiting to hear what came next.

"Well, Ah were wunderin' like—Do they give you a wank first or after?"

The whole place exploded with hysterical laughter with the house–girls giggling nervously, looking dumbfounded and confused, It was a long time before they forgot our visit to that house of pleasure and a long time before the boys allowed Dave to forget the incident.

*   *   *   *   *   *

The Hilton Hotel, Bangkok

Most of the other shows were in Bangkok at local supply depots and at the Officer's Club out of town near the beach. They were much easier than the gigs in Vietnam and were better received, as real Country Music was quite a rarity. We also did several moonlighting jobs at private parties arranged by an enterprising Master Sergeant and at three hundred dollars a show they were very welcome. We moved back again into the Siam Intercontinental, which was great. On average we only worked three days a week but we were being paid on a time contract so it didn't matter, so Kit and I spent the days cruising around the shops and markets. In the evening we saw some of the super cabaret acts that worked that circuit. I think Diana Washington was one of them and another great act was Canadian Ronnie Fray and his group—the boys of course were off tom–catting around the clubs and cabarets usually coming back broke and subbing taxi money off the night clerk, assuring him that I would straighten things up the next day.

They were lovely people, these Thais, so gentle and polite. I recall one incident that really impressed me. Due to the difficulty of the Thai language, the hotel gave their guests cards for taxi drivers, telling them where the hotel was. Well, one time in town, near the painted bridge where Anna, the English governess met the King of Siam back in the 19th century, we picked up a cab and told him to take us back to the hotel, and gave him the card at which he glanced and threw down onto the seat beside him. And off we went.

An hour later we had visited the railway station, the docks, the Town Hall, several other hotels and the cattle market. At every stop he would turn in his seat and grin expectantly until we shook our heads, at which he would tear off in another direction—then I realized that he could not read anyway.

Finally by sheer accident we found ourselves on Rama Road and I spotted the teak pagoda roof of our hotel and got him to stop. Fearing the worst, I got the receptionist to ask him how much we owed him?—and why he had got lost? Smiling, the cab driver charged us the usual fare from the Painted Bridge and he denied being lost. He thought that we would like to see his town. What could you do? Nobody was in a hurry in Thailand.

On one trip around the shops I came across a gun shop. No licenses were required or any formalities whatsoever, so I bought a couple of boxes of ammunition .22 for Kit's Colt and .32 for my Frommer and a nice leather shoulder holster—but it was time to move on, so on the last night we went to the Hilton Hotel for dinner. The cabaret that night was Filipino singing star Carmen Patina who we'd seen in Hong Kong, and the famous Magician Paul Potassi.

We were greeted by the immaculate maitre d' at the velvet rope cordon that partitioned off the dining room from the bar. There were a few couples waiting, and we were very impressed by the way he greeted us individually in our own language. One minute he was speaking Dutch, then French or Spanish, and in our case English, so smoothly it was almost unbelievable. We were soon settled in at a table on the edge of the dance floor and tucking into a superb dinner. Suddenly there was a roll of drums and our immaculate head waiter announced that one of the lady guests had ordered the specialty of the house, the famous Hilton Bomb Alaska, and as it was the first time the lady had visited Bangkok, the management had decided that we should all share this delicacy. With that he clapped his hands and a dinner wagon carrying two large copper bowls came scooting out from the curtains covering the kitchen entrance, and as the band played a samba he pushed the trolley around the dance floor, dancing and breaking eggs in time to the music, pouring the whites in one bowl and the yolks in another. When he considered that he had enough, with a flourish, he shot the trolley back through the curtains—a few minutes passed as he sang a song and told us all about the city, and then a bell rang and the huge white mountain of the soufflé came rolling back into the dining-room and he started his samba again shuffling round the tables, giving everybody a portion of the delicious crisp ice-cream filled creation. What style.

The show started with Carmen Patina who did a great set of standard songs, much in the style of Ella Fitzgerald and then came the Star Spot, the man that most magicians rated as the world's best—Mr. Paul Potassi, someone I had heard a lot about. He was a round faced, dark haired, middle-aged European, sharply dressed in a full tail suit and the first surprise came when he pulled a small microphone from his top pocket and began to welcome everyone in various languages.

Now, I know that in this day and age, radio mikes are quite everyday things, but back in 1968 it was sensational to find a microphone without a cable. He then proceeded to go through a superb routine of illusions and everybody applauded enthusiastically. Well almost everybody, except for a party of drunk and loudmouthed Australians at a table behind us, who heckled and barracked him all the time in spite of the manager's requests to cool it.

"S' up y'r bloody sleeve, yew drongo," they shouted. "Why don't y' get a proper bleedin' job. We didn't pay t'see this kid's party stuff. Bring the tarts back on."

They roared and laughed loudly at their own comments until finally, Paul had had enough of their antics, and came over to ask them if they would help him out on stage. The party looked at each other suspiciously at first but eventually a big red-faced fellow got up and smirking at his mates, he lumbered onto the floor.

"And now. Ladies and Gentlemen," announced Paul, holding the man close. "I will remove this gentleman's wallet without him knowing."

"Wot? No way. Greaser," said the Aussie, pushing Paul away while his mates cheered him on.

Not in the least fazed, Paul said, "Really Sir, I think that perhaps you are a little late for that," and produced his victim's wallet from his pocket. As the man stood there dumbfounded, Paul continued—"and also, Sir, here is your wrist watch and your beautiful alligator skin belt—and tell your friend over there that he will find his wallet and passport under the cushion of the chair to his right. And now Sir, if you don't mind, may I continue?"

Five minutes after that the silenced Aussies paid the bill and left.

The following day we were on a late afternoon Cathay Pacific plane headed to Hong Kong again. A much more subdued and pleasant Fredo and Ralf, the Hong Kong Connection, were waiting for us at Kai Tek Airport and we got our old rooms back at the Sun Ya Hotel. We were only there for a couple of days, long enough to collect more of the clothes we had ordered and get visas for the Land of the Rising Sun. This time the terrible twin agents were very charming and could not get us on the plane to Tokyo quick enough. All very suspicious I thought. Mmm? Our arrival at Haneda Airport, confirmed my doubts.

PICKER'S TIP 30

Before you go on stage turn your watch round so the face shows on the inside of your left wrist so that you can time your spot as you play guitar without the audience knowing.

PICKER'S TIP 31

Use the time the audience is applauding to put right any minor problems on stage such as changing the positioning of a mike stand or swapping a bad guitar lead, etc. But remember to thank them when they have FINISHED clapping. And don't end every song by tagging "Thank you Ladies and Gentlemen," on to the last line. Give them a chance.

20

THE LAND OF THE RISING SUN
Harlan Howard, Rusty Draper, Del Wood, Bill Clifton, Pee Wee Harada

On a muggy September morning the big plane circled Tokyo Bay on its ap‐
proach to the runway, the cramped industrial districts seemed to swamp
the airport and a thick cloud of yellow pollution hung over the city. Was
this really Japan? The fabled Land of the Samurai, the home of a thousand
legends and the inspiration for Puccini's opera Madame Butterfly? It
looked more like Smethwick on a bad day. Where were the Shinto temples
and the paper lanterns? Was it all a fantasy?

The DC.10's tyres scuffed runway number two and soon we were stand‐
ing in the Arrival Hall waiting for our bags. A diminutive Japanese hurried
over to meet us and in halting English introduced himself. He was the local
liaison officer for the U.S. Agencies in Tokyo, and after a brief welcome to
his country, hustled us out of the building saying that our personal effects
would be taken care of by his people.

His people, eh? We looked doubtfully at each other but in the end
accepted his bland assurance, and followed him meekly into the main con‐
course of the terminal and aboard the much vaunted Tokyo Monorail—and
what a disappointment that turned out to be. I had expected to go thun‐
dering through the sky like some latter day Flash Gordon but this futur‐
istic silver and blue rocket ship trundled along its single elevated track at
about twenty miles an hour above the surrounding grimy industrial prop‐
erty, and the slums of the city before dumping us at the dull gray concrete
facade of the Haneda Airport Hotel, which was nowhere near the bloody
airport. Here we were told to order food or booze from room service—but
not go into the restaurant or answer any questions we may be asked. The
agency would cover our living expenses and would be in touch with further
instructions soon. We vegetated there for three days kicking our heels until
finally we were bundled into taxis and transported to the Yamato Hotel in
the Rippongi district of Tokyo.

At this hotel the agency representative was waiting for us. He was solid
gold Cosa Nostra. A big, heavily built Mafia soldier, with Sicilian features,
a mane of jet‐black greasy hair and speaking pure Brooklynese. His name
was Bunny Briosca. Yes, really. That was his real name and he told us that
he worked for his uncle Russo Carnna an ex Musician's Union enforcer
from Chicago who held the 'Family Franchise' for all the entertainment
services on the military bases in the Tokyo Bay Area. He was very nice to
us and took great pains to see that we were settled in properly and handed
me a bundle of money, but there was no mention of gigs. When I broached
the subject he mumbled on about work permits and said he would sort it
out in a day or two but in the meantime if we wanted anything to tell the
hotel manager and charge it to his office, but it was another week before
the first gigs began to trickle in. We really didn't mind. We had enough
money to tour the bars and the hotel was comfortable although the food

was a bit strange. The boys found the local bars and we all did the tourist bit, hitting the Ginza sushi bars and the nightclubs in the Asakusa district.

The Ginza was the main tourist street in central Tokyo and was a blaze of colour, noise and lights. Dominating one corner was a tall plate glass building with a vast car showroom on the fourth floor, way above the street, and there was a big pub specializing in serving genuine Guinness and real Scotch whiskey, although many of the bars used Johnny Walker bottles filled with the local Suntory brand. There were so many bars and saloons that we lost count. The Rippongi district was also the home of some great restaurants—French, Italian as well as Japanese. In fact Kit says that the first real Italian restaurant she ever visited was in Tokyo. I remember having superb meals at the Asakusa Fish Café and at the most surprising of them all, Ann Dinken's Kosher Diner which served up real chopped fish, blintzes, lox, chicken soup, bagels and salt beef. Great. It could have been Golders Green or Cheetham Hill. Most of the snack bars and restaurants had uncannily real colored plaster models of the dishes available on display in the windows; each one with its number on the menu. Music blasted out from club doorways and in a small square, a classic kabuki play was being performed. There was also a profusion of model gun shops. Yes, that's right, not cars or planes or ships—model pistols and sub–machine guns. On each corner were the ever present pachinko pinball kiosks with the rattling steel ball bearings whirling round behind the glass, the punters gasping or shouting wildly when they won.

Kobe Beef

In one of the free tourist magazines in the hotel we found a gourmet restaurant that specialized in Kobe beef, reputed to be the finest steak in the world so we decided to give it a try. This restaurant was in the Asakusa district, the main entertainment suburb, packed with discos, cafés, bars and clubs. The world famous Manos disco was here, where they had girls dancing topless in cages hung from the ceiling. The taxi, a big yellow Toyota with a thick Perspex screen hanging down to protect the driver from violent passengers, dropped us at the end of a crowded pedestrian precinct, and pointed down the street to a sign of a black bull's head swinging over a lantern lit doorway. Inside the restaurant however, it was quiet and peaceful with subdued background music and dark wood and light green paper screens. The waiter showed us to a T–shaped table with a square steel plate let into the centre of the shorter side, while we sat on either side of the long arm. We ordered Kobe beef and Tiger beer and we were then introduced to our personal chef, because our meal was to be cooked at our table.

With a slight bow the chef disappeared and returned with a big wicker basket and a teak tray covered with a white cloth, from under which he produced a blue porcelain flask of sake and two small cups and indicated that this was our aperitif. As we sipped tentatively at our warm rice wine, he started to prepare our meal. First he placed in front of us two squares of metal foil about ten inches square with a two–pronged fork and a sharp short knife, and then bent down to light the gas beneath the steel heater plate. Chatting all the while in broken American he took handfuls of green vegetables from his basket and then proceeded to chop them while telling us all about the wonderful qualities of Kobe beef. Apparently this special breed of Wagyu steers are pampered all their lives, have regular massages with sake, to keep the flesh supple, and follow a strict diet of beer and special cereals until the fateful day they are considered at their peak, taste wise, that is. Hence those very high prices

The chef then removed the snow–white napkin from his teak tray to smilingly display a most magnificent piece of beef. It wasn't that big, perhaps about two and a half pounds in weight, beautifully grained and some two inches thick, which he began to carve in thin strips. These he laid in criss–cross pattern on the steel plate and drizzled them with aromatic oil and a light mixture of Soya and special spices. As the meat began to sizzle he produced a large metal dome and placed it over the plate while he continued to prepare the vegetables. The ice cold Tiger beer arrived next and we caught the delightful waft of the cooking beef as he slipped the chopped greens under the dome—but so far there were no plates—and when we hinted at this our private chef simply pointed to our tin foil squares which he then filled with the crunchy vegetables, with the strips of beef draped across the top.

Well, it didn't look much for the price we were paying, and feeling slightly miffed we got stuck in, and what a revelation. It was absolutely the best beef I have ever tasted. Glorious. And although there did not seem to be a lot by our Western standards, this heap of food on our foil squares seemed never ending. The chef stood by awaiting our comments, and smiled widely when we praised the unique and subtle flavors of his creation. What an experience.

The 'Tokyo Glan-Oh Hop-ah-lee'

Just down the street behind the Yamato Hotel was the Tokyo office of the Pacific Stars and Stripes, the official U.S. Military newspaper of the South East Asia Region, and one day a reporter turned up at the hotel and asked me to do an interview. A Limey band playing the war zone of Vietnam was news, and the fact that we were now available in Japan got the club manager's phones buzzing. The resultant article and photos were very impressive, and rapidly extended both our reputation and workload throughout the region. I was described as 'Frank Yonco, the British Texan, equally at home in Las Vegas or Nashville etc.'

Praise indeed and I was very proud of my new title when we were invited to play at the Tokyo Grand Old Opry, a monthly Japanese TV show, held in the top floor cabaret room of a big hotel downtown, where we met up with quite a few Stars. MC of the show was Rusty Draper who had a big hit with

'The Auctioneer's song' and pianist Del Woods, Tennessee's own Mrs. Mills. (Remember her?). Del's real name was Adelaide Hazelwood and she hit the charts in 1951 with ragtime version of an old Gid Tanner clog dance, called Down Yonder. She was born in Nashville in 1920, but looked a good deal older as she mashed the keyboard like some demented leper, missing notes all over the place, but now somewhat recovered from the last time we saw her at an open air show at Vung Tau rest camp in 'Nam, where she earned a shower of empty beer cans and verbal abuse from the tough Aussie troops.

"G'wan y'ol tabby cat. Get off. Take off y'r hairnet. Etc."

Also at this show I met again Blue Grass singer Bill Clifton, who had worked with us at the MSG club in Manchester back in '64. He was on one of his never-ending cultural exchange world tours sponsored by the US Government, and I also met the great Nashville songwriter Harlan Howard. (Who lost a son in Vietnam) He introduced me to an arrangement of the old Floridian folk song "Everglades" he had done for Waylon Jennings. It was he who suggested that we change the name of the act, and so the New Texas Drifters became Frank Yonco and the Everglades. However for me, the real star of that show was Rose Maddox. I had long been an admirer of this lady since I first saw her with her family band in the'50s when she did some great songs like 'Whoa Sailor' and 'Tramp on the Street'.

Back at the show lounge we were greeted warmly by everybody, mainly due to the publicity blurbs and the article in the Tokyo press gleaned from the Pacific Stars and Stripes, and were given a good spot closing the first half of the show. We had deliberately themed our show towards the prospect of an early return to the States and hit a chord with the mostly GI audience. It was a great experience but there were a few bizarre moments. When we first arrived one act was warming up backstage, and I thought that Loretta Lynn was on the show, but it turned out to be a Japanese girl who had copied every twist and nuance of Loretta's voice, and had no idea what she was singing because she couldn't speak a word of English.

In fact, apart from the two Round Eye acts (Del Woods and us), this was the general trend. Rusty Draper would introduce some obscure Japanese act and out would come a rhinestone-covered figure with a Gibson J 200 flat-top guitar, singing exactly like George Jones or Buck Owens. The host act that evening was a band called The Tokyo Bay Cowboys led by the man who organized the show, a steel guitar player called Pee Wee Harada whose 'Piece de resistance' was a lifelike imitation of the Tokaido Express, whistling and moaning out of the main station. Well, I guess it was better than Steel Guitar Rag.

(I wonder if Pee Wee is Japanese for Brian?)

*   *   *   *   *   *

The Family Business

One afternoon I went to see Tatsuma Nagashima, an agent I had been corresponding with from Frankfurt. This was the legendary 'Tats'. He was the Number One (Ichibanshi) Agent in South East Asia, a tall, distinguished grey haired man in his sixties. He spoke good American English and said that he had heard of me, and would gladly book Kit and myself into the chain of large hotels he controlled throughout the South Pacific, but he did not want the band, though he did arrange for us to record an album for Sony in one of his studios. I explained that we did not have a lot of gigs in Japan and as far as I knew, we were only going to be there for a month, and to be honest I was not clear about what was going on.

For a moment he listened to what I was saying and then led the way into an inner office to explain the situation. Apparently for years now there had been a tense war raging between the Mafia and the Yakuza, its Japanese equivalent, to corner the services market for the U.S. Occupation Forces. The conflict finally settled down with the two gangster organizations splitting the spoils between them, with the Yakuza controlling the docks and the US Mafia the drug-trade and the street girls. It all went well until the escalation of the Vietnam War when suddenly things blew up out of all proportion, with thousands of combat troops and support personnel arriving from Vietnam on rest and recuperation visits.

Naha in Okinawa, an island in the Ryuku group south-east of Japan was the key to the whole picture. Its geographical position, straddling the sea lanes of the South China Sea made it a natural control centre and since the end of the Korean War the Cosa Nostra had been firmly ensconced there, fostering a huge Black Market in contraband goods, and during the Vietnam War, launched an equally vast currency laundering operation. Now, with half a million men in the theatre of action, money and services began to spread to the main Rest and Relaxation locations such as Japan, Taiwan, Bangkok and Singapore.The serpents of violence, corruption, and racketeering were close behind, most of it controlled by the Godfathers in Taipei and Naha, although few inroads were made into Macao and Hong Kong because of the opposition of the Chinese Triads.

Of course it was not long before the Mafia got into the booking of acts and the control of the GI Clubs, the kind of thing they had been doing in Las Vegas for thirty years or more, and we were one of the acts that they were all fighting about. Feverish telegrams were hustling back and forth from Okinawa to Hong Kong and Tokyo, heavy with threats and accusations of breaking hard-won business protocol arrangements. Who was booking the cabaret, and who was picking up the large fees before handing a bit on to the acts themselves. Not that it was a bit to us. It was more money than I had ever earned in my life, but it was only a smidgen of the cash actually changing hands. Eventually they got it sorted out. I don't know who won but I do know that we started working with a vengeance.

The first club was at Kyoto followed the next day by a US Navy club in Yokohama, and then a succession of clubs and theatres around the Tokyo area, which gave me a legitimate reason to claim some money from the office. Rather than phone, Kit and I decided to visit Russo at his office in the Askusa district. A cab took us there, but his house was difficult to find because Japanese buildings do not have street numbers, but are numbered by the date they were built. (The oldest house would be number one and so on to the latest office block. Yes, Very confusing).

Eventually we found the place and Russ and Bunny made us quite welcome with double gins and tumblers of Jim Beam. There was no trouble about cash. Russ handed me what I asked for. I couldn't believe it. He said that it was no problem, as he would charge it to the agents in Hong Kong.

As the afternoon rolled on, they explained one of the reasons for the delays. It was true, he said, that he had signed a contract for us to do a tour of Japan with Hong Kong back in March, but in May he had discovered that we were Brits and that it was not really practical to bring in Third Country Nationals, as the system established with the Stateside agents, by which the acts would be paid on the Mainland (USA) when they got back, would not work. There were also the American acts booked by the government agency USO. But this was a wishy-washy set-up dating from World War 2, and using rather mediocre acts who were scratching for work, either raw beginners or fading acts squeezing the last juice out of their careers although there were, of course, some good exceptions, but in practical terms commercially viable attractions were sponsored by various 'Family' factions.

Yamato Nights

By now our Pacific Stars and Stripes publicity was hitting the clubs and we were being requested by the club managers, so they had to come to some arrangement with our agents in Hong Kong. I never found out what it was but Bunny certainly got busy as the gigs came flooding in from all over Japan. Back at the hotel a few more acts arrived. I can remember a comedian called Phil Phillips and a girl singer from Scotland, who lost no time in telling us how good she was—her name was Jan Douglas and she would sit around the Yamato in her curlers, spouting off about her spark-ling career as a big band singer. Naturally we were all sceptical, thinking it was all showbiz bullshit, but after seeing her at a rehearsal when she rip-ped the Japanese house band to ribbons, stopping in full song to point out missed notes, crossed beats or split woodwind reeds, our respect for her began to grow.

When she hit the stage of the biggest nightclub in Asakusa we had no doubt at all about her talent, power and musical ability. She was terrific. In fact her version of the Sandy Shaw hit of the day 'Puppet on a String' was much better than the original. A great talent indeed. Years later, we met her again when we were doing the Glasgow Gran' Ole Opry. By then she had 'Gone Country' and fronted an all–girl band, but she was just as good.

We had some good times together on our nights off. Also nearby were some of the 'Bluebell Girls' we had met in Hong Kong, so Kit and Jan had a few girl's nights out with them. Drummer Dave and I found a great little bar down the street and made it our local until the money started to flow again, at which time he went off with the two Tartan Topers on their crazy nights out—they'd go out on the town and come rolling back around three in the morning, singing football songs and generally kicking up lots of noise. Naturally, some patrons complained, and the Yamato management got on to me about it and finally contacted Bunny Briosca, who gave me a tacit warning to sort it out or he would. Which cooled things down for a while.

For their next move the Haggis Brothers roped in Dave to demand their Vietnam bonuses. I had put it in the bank for safe keeping intending to pay it out when we got back to the U.K., but they wanted their cash to spend in Tokyo. I tried to reason with them but they insisted on having it there and then, with Big Dave saying that he had heard that I was going to rip everybody off and leave them stranded in the Far East. It was ludicrous so I arranged for them to pick up their cash at the Hong Kong and Shanghai Bank the next day, and left them to it.

Things were just as bad after they had got their cash, in fact every night it got worse, until the situation exploded about two o'clock one morning when they came reeling in with a big Canadian they had met in town. They began banging on all the doors along the hall with Roy yelling. "Come out, Yonco, ye bastard. Ah wish ye didna pay us at all, an'then we could really hate ye. How much money are ye makin' outa all this?" They all cheered him, banging and kicking more doors till I appeared.

Oho. Trouble again, Eh?

Now, experience had taught me that in such a situation one should never be caught barefoot, and I must have looked strange in a short bathrobe and cowboy boots. They wanted to come into the room but I blocked the way and closed it behind me as they crowded round shouting and breathing whisky fumes all over me.

Finally the big Canadian, I think his name was Duncan, pushed his way to the front and gave me a hard shove against the door, snarling, "So you're the bastard that's holdin' all their bread, are ya? Why don't ya pay 'em what you owe 'em?"

God knows what they had been telling him, but he was really wound up and pushed me again with the boys egging him on. Cursing me all the time, he swung a clumsy right, which I blocked, and then a left to the body that took the wind out of me. I staggered against the door and half turned gasping. I finally realized that he was serious. As he moved in for the kill, I shifted my weight and I hit him with a ramrod left heavily between the eyes and he went down like a pole–axed ox. A quick Tony Lama toe in his ribs and one to the head and it was all over. There was a brief and in-effectual scuffle from the others, at least from the two Davids. Somehow in the melee our fat keyboard man had slipped off to his room Anyway, once again the cowboy boots came in handy and it was finished—so I slammed the door, leaving them sprawled across the hall.

At breakfast next day I saw the Canuck still trying to focus his eyes, and he had a growing bruise on his right temple. He was not in anyway sorry and that if he had not been drunk, things would have been different, so "just wait until the next time."

I suggested that there and then would be as good a time as any. So how about it? He opted for a rain check instead and got stuck into his corn-flakes.

Osaka

Two days later we were at Tokyo station waiting for a train to take us south to play the U.S. Bases around Fukoka City and Osaka—well when I say a 'Train' I am understating the case. We were waiting in fact for the fabled Tokaido Express, the fastest train in the world. Right on time it came sliding into the station like a long silent snake and hissed to a stop. Automatic doors slid open and white–gloved train loaders with apologetic smiles, firmly pushed us clear of the sliding doors, ushered us inside, and the next thing I knew we were rushing silently through the Tokyo suburbs. It was uncanny. Apart from the hum of subdued conversation there was no noise or sensation of travel. It was a wonderful experience.

The only indication of our velocity being a large indicator on the wall showing a read–out of the +100 mph speed as we hurtled through the countryside. They had given us a handbook when we got the tickets, which described the train, and the journey. It was in four languages and informed us that at 3 p.m. precisely we would see the famous Mount Fuji. With the cynicism and suspicion that unfortunately runs through the travelling musician's character, I waited with eyes on my wrist–watch as the magic hour approached. At 2.57 p.m. we were still in a tunnel and I was already outlining my future complaint to Nippon Railways when we shot out of the gloom into the bright afternoon. It was now exactly 3 p.m. and there, a mile away, I saw the magnificent sight of Mount Fuji, a wisp of smoke curling from its snow–capped rim. It was breathtaking.

We left the train at Osaka but it had made such a mark on me. It was 1968 and here was a mode of transport brought almost to perfection, with showers on board, international tele–communications and computerized business aids. My only petty complaint was that the seats were a bit small for me—but apart from that it was perfect, and it was many years before I experienced again that same efficient, stress–free transportation, on a French TGV from Paris to Lyons.

There were about six shows in Osaka clubs, and then on by train through a long tunnel under the sea to Fukoka City for a big All Star show on the main USAF Base there. It was virtually the last gig in Japan and we were distressed to find out that no arrangements had been made to accommodate us or get us back to Tokyo. After the show the club manager hustled us out to the station and booked us through to Osaka, the limit of his jurisdiction. After that we were on our own. Around 11p.m. we arrived at Osaka station and I was raging mad. I phoned Tokyo but the agent elbowed us, telling us to find digs and call later. 'Right.' I thought. 'If that's the way they want it, okay, we will find digs'—and that's what we did. We loaded everything into four taxis and asked the driver to take us to the best hotel in town, which turned out to be the Osaka Royal where we booked in, charging everything to the agency in Tokyo. It was absolutely great using room service and all the four star facilities of this magnificent hotel. I phoned Briosca the next day and told him where we were, and he went bananas saying that we were due in Taiwan. I said we had no money and were staying here until somebody picked us up.

It was three days before an agitated associate of Bunny's arrived at the hotel. He shoved an envelope stuffed with Yen notes at me, paid the hotel bill and rushed us in taxis to the airport, where we caught the next flight to Tokyo and were hustled to the Taiwanese Embassy for our visas. After the incident at the Osaka Royal, the agents must have thought I was 'The Awkward Bastard of the Century' but four months of Vietnam crap had hardened our attitudes, and we had a good idea of the kind of money they were making from us. I insisted that we were treated right and they responded by getting us out of Japan as quickly as possible.

*　*　*　*　*　*

21

TAIWAN

Its original Chinese name had been the Island of Celestial Beauty but the Portuguese, the first Europeans to arrive, called it Formosa. Across the centuries it had been a favourite haunt of the ruthless South China Sea pirates, and by the time Chiang Kai Shek's Nationalist Army took refuge there in the late 1940's, it was known as Taiwan.

Its geographical position, straddling the sea lanes between China and Japan fostered a vast trade in contraband goods and during the Vietnam War it became another control centre for a huge Black Market, most of it controlled by the Godfathers in Taipei, and now we were going to work for them. Gulp.

The first example of their power was at the airport. As we came off the plane a little dazed and looked round at the milling passengers, we saw a big crowd at the Immigration Desk and another long line forming at the Customs Bench. Resignedly we shuffled over to the rotunda to collect our gear and meekly join the queue, when there was an announcement over the PA system asking for Mr Yonco and his party to make their way immediately to the V.I.P. Lounge. Four big Koreans were waiting for us wearing Club 63. T-shirts, and we were hustled through the waiting crowds, past Passport and Immigration controls and into a minibus. It took us straight to the club and almost directly on stage. I recall we landed at 9.15 p.m. and by 10.30 I was two verses into 'Folsom Prison Blues', with the audience of 'Good Ol' Boys and their women going wild. Although, to be honest we did most of the show on autopilot, but being so well rehearsed it came over well and none of the fatigue or stress showed through. Kit of course went like a bomb. Her sparkling personality and the fact that here was a real live blond 'Round Eye' girl singer, turned the place over. It was a live TV show and went out on U.S. South East Asia Network, which combined with the write up in the Pacific Stars and Stripes in Tokyo, generated a lot of interest, including an offer of a ten month contract from the US Navy to tour the Pacific bases, the very contract that had featured in my plans if the Vietnam deal had gone wrong. I often wonder what that might have led to? However just at that moment I was under strong pressure from various quarters, (but mostly from the band,)to get back to the U.K. It never crossed my mind to change the band.

After the show we were treated to a large meal and feted like Big Stars. The club was luxurious and the amenities superb. Bowling alleys, trap shooting pits, a superbly equipped gym with steam rooms and a nine-hole golf course. From the viewpoint of the US military it must have been the most desirable posting in the Pacific Zone. The weather was superb, the booze cheap and the women beautiful and only too willing to please. We were on the island about three weeks altogether, mostly living at a nice hotel in the city centre. There were several European acts there also, mostly specialty acts like conjurers and tumblers. About the only British acts were a girl singer called Dawn Lund, and Judy Moxton who did a foot juggling act with barrels. She was a really attractive girl and I believe eventually married the agent Al Heath. Oh yes, and there was also one guy from Wales who did a snake act and kept his three pythons in the bath. Ugh!

One day we were sent off to do a few shows in other parts of the island. It was V.I.P treatment all the way. We had a minibus and a driver and a stewardess to look after us, with cold drinks and warm cloths from a steamer to wipe our faces. I lost track of the bases we played, but I do remember playing a Chinese theatre in Taichen, as the featured act in a typical Chinese evening, jugglers, shadow dancers and acrobats and us. I don't suppose they understood a word but they clapped like mad.

The following Saturday night we were back in the lap of luxury again at the President Hotel in Taipei. After this it was two shows at Boston Base and then to the Club 63.

The real power behind the throne on the island was demonstrated to me on a couple of occasions. Most of the time 'The Family' 'kept a low profile and let their Chinese staff get on with the day–to–day management, but now and then they did present a bit of their awesome power, as shown in the following example.

The hard schedule and the constant change from the humid climate to the dry air conditioning played havoc with my throat, and by the time we returned to Taipei to finish the contract I was hoarse, and in real danger of losing my voice completely. I managed to tell the Club Custodian about my problem and he arranged for me to see the local 'Don'. He gave me a card that simply said 'Gary & Wong' at an address in downtown Taipei and pushed me into a taxi outside the club.

The driver dropped me at a shabby office block in a narrow side street. Without waiting to be paid he shot off, so I shrugged and mounted the bare wooden stairs to a small landing and a glass–panelled door. I knocked and was invited in to meet a small Chinese guy and a tall thin American with short–cropped grey hair. Both of them wore dark slacks, white short sleeve shirts and sandals but no socks. A brief introduction followed and Mr. Wong, who was apparently a medical man, gave my throat a probing examination and after asking a few questions, went over to the cluttered desk to write out a prescription of some sort. Ron Gary, the other half of the partnership, took me completely by surprise. I had heard stories of his legendary power and influence from the agent Tatsumi Nagashima in Japan, but the slim mild looking man standing in front of me was not what I had expected. Instead of a powerfully built, mumbling Sicilian padrone I was confronted by a man who looked like a mild–mannered Mid–Western lawyer or bank manager on holiday. His voice was soft and pleasant but a closer examination of his features revealed the well–hidden scars and some clumsy repairs from the violence of his wild youth.

Like many other prominent members of the Chicago mob, he said he was not from the city itself but was from one of the small towns further to the south, in this case Steubenville over the Illinois state line, home town of singer Dean Martin. In fact, he said he had known the Crocetti family quite well before their son found fame in Hollywood. He had been an Area Manager for 'The Company 'out here since the end of the Korean War and had not been back to the States for fifteen years, and had no desire to do so. At the time I judged him to be in his early fifties. He told me that the 'Company' was very pleased with our show, and if we wanted to play on the 'Mainland' they had certain connections, and that a Green Card US work permit would be no problem after our services in Viet Nam. I thanked him and said I would think about his offer but at that moment I was more concerned with getting the shows done and getting back to the U.K. (Although I later realized that I should have taken up their offer)—He smiled indulgently and I took the prescription slip from Mr Wong. Now came the steel hand in the velvet glove.

"Where do I get it filled?" I asked.

Ron Gary shrugged. "Oh, any pharmacy on the island will fill it. We own 'em all. Pick up a cab and just show him that card. We own them all too."

A paternal smile crossed his face at my amazed expression, but before I could comment he gave me a small hug and a gentle slap on the cheek.

"Don't sweat the small stuff, Yonco. We'll be looking after you from now on. Fact is we've been watching you since Bunny screwed you in Big T. (Tokyo). That kind of thing is not really our style, you know. We insist on a little respect for our artists,—and them two chisellin' Limey bastards in Hong Kong can forget about their cut on this trip as well. So don't you worry none. Now you go get that throat fixed and give them hicks at the club more of that good ol' shit kicking music. Okay?

For a brief moment the frightening raw power showed through his carefully cultivated gentle exterior.

The last four days went well and before we knew it, it was time for the final 'Saturday Night Spectacular' after which I went into the office to get paid. The Night Manager told me that Mr. Gary was in a poker game in one of the side rooms, and had left instructions that I was to be sent to him as soon as I was off stage. I found the room and as luck would have it, the players were taking a break. Ron saw me and gestured me over and introduced me to a few of his friends as his 'Favourite Limey Hillbilly'. They were all very complimentary and asked when we would be coming back. Ron said that it had been one of the most successful weeks they had had and for me to bear in mind his stateside offer. He did not normally like booking Country Music acts, as he often found them difficult to handle, but he thought we were something different. 'More Las Vegas than Nashville' as he put it, and that if ever I needed anything to get in touch. I thanked him and assured him that I had taken note of his offer but at that moment there was something else on my mind. We were flying out in the morning and I was still three thousand dollars short on my Taiwan contract and

could we possibly be paid up? To be honest I half expected some kind of ex‐
cuse or delay and up to that moment was still a little skeptical of his
'Family 'stories. What happened next convinced me that I was wrong. So
wrong.

At the mention of money his face froze and he eyed me coldly before
picking up a telephone to check what I said with the Night Manager. After
that he softened and invited me to join him in a glass of wine. We chatted
lightly until a waitress brought over a large gold trimmed leather brief
case. Ron thanked her and slipping it onto the table he flipped it open. It
was not locked and contained stacks of $100 bills. He tossed me three
bundles "Ok now Yonco? "He smiled. "All squared away?—No, there's no
need for you to sign anything. Just enjoy the cabbage."

He closed the lid and signaled the waitress to take it away. I was flab‐
bergasted.

"But you've not locked it Ron. There's thousands of dollars there. What if
gets stolen."

Again his face hardened and he said, "Listen Yonco, Lemme tell you a
story. Yep, you're right. There are thousands of dollars there, in fact to be
precise there is now twenty–five thousand less the three grand I paid you,
and that's normally what it carries and it's never locked. Now, Yonco, hear
this. A month ago, late one Thursday evening that case went missing from
the club, but by 11am. Monday mornin' it was back in my office, not a
dollar missing and containing two fingers from the man who stole it. How's
that grab ya? That's just the way it is out here. Okay?"

The serious faces of the other gamblers confirmed it to be the truth. I
was very impressed—and a little bit scared.

When I got backstage the others were all having a drink with the Night
Manager and I told them about Ron Gary's story. He confirmed the tale,
and told us about something that had happened at the club about a year
ago.

"We'll bury you here."

A well–known chart–topping black singing group were making a come‐
back tour backing their old lead singer's successful re–release of one of his
earlier hits. This new found fame had gone completely to the man's head
and he was giving grief to everybody from the members of his backing
group to the club staff.

Until he crossed Ron Gary.

Like us, this obnoxious 'Star' wanted to be paid, but he insisted on pick‐
ing up the hard cash BEFORE doing his show. He was being very forceful
about it, threatening everyone and boasting about his connections with the
militant Black Panthers. He was raving on, calling the Manager and the
Custodian a couple of guinea punks and that all this 'Family' shit did not
impress him one bit, ending his tirade with "So you Honky Wops better pay
up now, or there ain't gonna be no show. Right?"

Neither of the two club officials knew what to do with this awkward man. Normally they could handle most petty complaints, but this demand for money was out of their league so they called the 'Don', who happened to be in the poker room. Ron did not like Soul music any more than he did Country, but more to the point, he did not like being disturbed in a card game—or belligerent Afro–Americans. Particularly so, as a large number of black underworld gangs were deep into drug distribution and were be–ginning to threaten the Italian dominance in urban America.

Obviously very irritated at losing the good hand he had, he tossed in his cards and told his gambling friends that he would be back in fifteen minutes. He arrived at the singer's dressing room accompanied by three huge Koreans, his ever–present bodyguards, and demanded to know why his poker game was being disturbed. The Star was really hyped–up now, with traces of cocaine powder showing on his red stage shirt and upper lip, and launched into a vicious verbal attack on the Club 63, Ron himself, and Italians in general, expressing his contempt for 'The Family 'in particular.

One of the Koreans started to move but Ron held him back and listened silently before asking quietly exactly what the beef was? Again the singer sounded off, snarling that it was money up front or no show. In the long silence that followed, the undertone of the restless club patrons could be heard, as the house band continued playing dance music. Ron fixed the singer with a hard cold stare for a moment and for the first time the singer began to realize what he was up against.

Ron finally called for the briefcase. He asked the night manager how much was due and stacked the bills on the table. As the man moved to pick it up Ron grabbed his wrist and slammed it down on the table. He looked coldly into the singer's face and after a short pause said.

"Right, Soul Brother. Now ya got your money—an' that's for your full contract. Forget about your next two shows, I don't need 'em. But tonight we got a crowd out there—so listen very carefully to me. It's 10.30.now, and in thirty minutes you are due on stage and I want a good show. In fact, I want the best show you've ever done. You hearin' this, Boy?—'cos if you don't turn 'em over out there tonight, you won't leave the island—we'll bury you here. Gottit?"

Without waiting for a reaction he turned on his heel and left the room. Wow.

Can you imagine going on stage with a threat like that hanging over you?

News of the incident flashed back across the Pacific to the West Coast and the man never worked again in South East Asia, or any other venue controlled by the mob. About the only place I heard of him again was in the UK a few years later, where he was touring some shabby clubs in South Wales. We were not sorry to leave Taiwan.

*   *   *   *   *   *

22

MALAYSIA

Once again when we least expected it, the emotive subject of guns came to the fore. As I said, both Kit and I had pistols and in the dangerous and volatile atmosphere of war torn South East Asia we became quite used to the idea. Kit carried her Colt .22 in her handbag, it was small and fitted quite neatly, but whenever we travelled, I had to strip down my Frommer.32 and spread the parts round my luggage. I used to put the frame in the head of my guitar case under the machine heads of the guitar, and usually it was no problem, except when we flew into Kuala Lumpur in Malaysia. Here things were different. The country was well organized and a very efficient government and police force assured the country's economic development, and kept the crime barons out. Drug addicts were jailed and murderers were hanged or given life sentences that really meant life. The law was there to be enforced without prejudice to Black, White, Chinese or Malay, so this event was almost heart stopping.

We landed at Singapore airport and had passed through immigration and waiting for our luggage to be delivered at a long table in the customs hall. The porter slung our bags onto the table including my guitar case, which the customs officer accidentally knocked to the concrete floor. He apologized profusely and I picked it up to find that the stitching of the case had split at the end, and poking its nose out was the sinister barrel of my ex–Viet Cong pistol. I froze with fear. Bringing any weapon into Malaysia was a definite No–No. You could spend a couple of years in the pokey out there waiting for your case to come to court. Luckily the customs officer misconstrued my look of horror for one of concern for my instrument, and with an apologetic smile he banged the offending tube back into the case and chalked his mark on it. I was out of that terminal like a rocket I can tell you.

Our contract was at the Merlin Hotel in Kuala Lumpur, and waiting in the foyer for us were a reporter and a photographer from the 'Straits Times', who insisted that we change into stage clothes for the photo shoot. It was a bit of a bind but the resultant publicity was well worth it.

The Merlin turned out to be one of those half colonial, half oriental hotels that were found in so many places in South East Asia. It had been built in the heyday of the British Empire, and was the favourite watering–hole for visiting European and American businessmen, local big players, expensive hookers and British ex–pats, who were still operating the country's booming rubber and tea plantations. K.L, as it was called, was the last stop on our Far East tour and was a bit of a cheat in one sense for us. Let me explain.

For over seven months we had been living on US Army chow or Far Eastern fish and rice dishes, and we were really looking forward to getting home and having all the stodgy stuff we had grown up on, things like real Calne pork sausages, bacon and eggs, mushy peas, chips and roast beef.

229

Wonderful! However, here in K.L. with its tradition of the Imperial Past and the fact that there were so many affluent ex–pats demanding a touch of home, the hotel had imported a British Chef. Actually, he was a rather under–qualified ex–ships cook from Liverpool but he could provide what passed for the expected British cuisine. So our dreams were short circuited because here it all was, thousands of miles from Ye Olde England. Kippers, roast potatoes, marmalade, lamb chops and roast beef, even haggis and neeps for our Scots musicians, although roast pork was a bit hard to find as the kitchen staff were reluctant to handle pig meat. But we didn't mind a bit and tucked in to our newfound goodies like Billy Bunter.

The gig itself was very easy. The boys lived in staff accommodation on the top floor but Kit and I were allocated a room on the fourth floor. It was very nice and had two huge beds, a well–appointed bathroom, a mini–bar full of quality liquor and a balcony, although the view was a bit suspect as it overlooked the wall of the City Jail, but we found we could live with that. Our contract called for two forty–minute spots a night, the first in the Chinese Restaurant at 10.30 p.m. and the second one in the Savoy Grill Room at 12.30am. Everybody was accommodated within the hotel, so all we had to do was get ready and then take the elevator down to the ground floor complex. Even so, David was often late for the gig due to the many temptations of the hotel's four bars in the afternoon, and the beautiful Malay women—and it was at this hotel that I met one of those life characters that you never ever forget, a certain Mr.Chang.

PICKER'S TIP 32

Most Important. Remember. It is the Agent's job to provide his circuit of venues with suitable acts. The Manager's job is to find work for the artiste and guide their careers. Both of them make their money by charging the act commission at varying rates. Don't confuse the two functions.

Mr. Chang

About three nights into the contract we got a request for Ghost Riders in the Sky from a chubby middle aged Chinese guy with two gorgeous young Filipino girls at his table. This was our Mr.Chang. We played his request and he sent drinks over with a note inviting us to join him after the show, in the hotel's basement disco which was called 'Arthur's Cave' Yep. That's right. 'Arthur's Cave' here in deepest Malaya where most of the clients were Orientals? But this was just the first of the many surprises in store for us East of Suez, where according to Rudyard Kipling:

"There ain't no Ten Commandments and a man can raise a thirst."

Mr. Chang was there to meet us, with yet another beautiful girl, this time with Chinese features and a traffic–stopping figure. At the table everybody was formally introduced, and after the drinks arrived Mr.

Chang insisted that we try the hotel's famous aphrodisiac Chicken Porridge, a thick rice and chicken broth heavily laced with pepper and washed down with masses of ice cold Tiger beer. He accepted the fact that Kit and I were together, but he offered to hire lady companions, as he discreetly termed it, for all the boys but true to form, they declined the offer because they did not want to miss out on the free beer. We had a great evening in his company, and around two thirty his uniformed Korean chauffeur arrived to take him and his lady home. He shook hands with everybody and told the waiter to put all our drinks on his tab, and invited us to lunch the next day, which happened to be one of our days off.

Accordingly we were all assembled, washed and polished as required on the hotel steps the following midday, when two white Mercedes limos arrived to whisk us downtown. Marvellous. It was like a scene from a James Bond movie. Fifteen minutes later we saw Mr. Chang waiting at the majestic entrance of a big Chinese restaurant to greet us, smiling like an inscrutable and benign Buddha with the obligatory young beauty on his arm. We were ushered upstairs through the crowded noisy restaurant to a private suite on the first floor, where some twenty guests were waiting to greet us—'The Guests of Honour' as Mr. Chang put it. It was handshakes all round followed by large whisky sodas and gin slings, while all around us the conversation flowed in about six languages. Chinese, Malay, Dutch, Portuguese, English and some obscure Indonesian dialects I could not identify.

A gong boomed through the babble all around us and we were shown to the large T-shaped table in the dining room itself. Mr. Chang saw to it that we were all fixed up with more generous drinks before escorting Kit and I to join him at the top table while everybody else sorted themselves out into the correct pecking order. Once we were seated Mr. Chang took pains to explain to us that this was going to be a real genuine Chinese feast, not the pale Hong Kong imitation that we had come to expect in the U.K. And it certainly was.

There was a flurry of black bow ties and long white aprons, as waiters fluttered in to piped classical Chinese music and presented the dishes. The first course was very small sweet cakes filled with some kind of thick custard, to be followed by bowls of sharp savory crispy noodles that tasted of anchovy and peppery squid. There was a profusion of strangely scented drinks presented with platters of dried fish, pink roast Peking duck, cold spicy chicken, crisp roast pork, bowls of steaming beef and oyster stew, and masses of unknown vegetables and different colored noodles with fluffy light dumplings. It was a delicious gastronomic journey and the noise was deafening with everybody trying to carry on a conversation at the same time. At one point I was tucking into a dish of crystallized fruits in ginger sauce when the bowl was snatched from my grasp and a man sitting opposite began wolfing my goodies. I was about to grab it back when Mr. Chang touched my arm and explained that it actually was a compliment, and that the other guest was pleased to meet me and so admired my taste in the selection of the dishes that he wished to share my choice. At Mr. Chang's urging, I reluctantly took a piece of the guest's shark's fin, and noticed that all down the table everybody was doing the same, reaching over and taking food from other people's plates—It certainly helped to keep the party moving.

By now everybody was well oiled and had started smoking funny cigarettes and bhang–bhang roll ups. The piped music changed to Heavy Metal and three young strippers slid through the curtains of a low stage, and started doing their thing while we ogled and applauded. I thought that they were great, and I was quite surprised when Mr. Chang whispered to me that one of them was a boy. There was a break in the second part of the meal, (it went on for four hours), and I inquired of Mr. Chang who these other guests were? My host pushed a black Balkan Sobranie into his amber holder and after lighting it carefully with a pure jade table lighter told me the story.

These people, he said, were all his employees or business associates, and directly or indirectly they were all his dependants, and once a month he gave a lunch for them. It helped to keep them all in touch and preserved the family atmosphere. "How many businesses does your company own then?" I cautiously asked.

"Oh, I suppose about twenty," he said frankly. "But there are others that are financed by my bank."

"Ah, I see. You are a banker then?," I said politely.

"Ah, not exactly, Frank," He smiled, "Actually, I am a doctor. Yes, that's right, a Doctor of Medicine. Do you find that strange?"

I had to admit that I was rather confused. So he explained.

As a student in the late 1930s he had been sent to England to study at a well–known teaching hospital in London. His parents were quite wealthy and sent a servant along as well to look after him, providing him with en–ough money to rent a small flat near the college. In fact, everything was done to enable the young man to concentrate on his medical studies, but Lin–How–Chang had one great passion in life. He loved ballroom–dancing. In fact he spent almost every evening at Hammersmith Palais de Dance, fox–trotting and quick–stepping to the music of Roy Fox, Harry Roy and Al Bowley.

To indulge this passion, he evolved a unique life pattern. Instead of studying in the evening like his classmates, Chang went dancing and trained his body to accept five hours sleep a night. Every morning his servant would rouse him at 5 a.m. and it was at this period, before the college day began, that Chang would do his studying. The result was that he became the best student in his class, well ahead of his contemporaries. He graduated in 1941 and was all set to return to Malaya, when news came of the Japanese invasion. In the ensuing war he lost all his family, with the exception of one sister who disgraced the family name, by marry–

ing a Japanese officer and going to live in Okinawa. Stranded in London with time on his hands this qualified doctor began to take an interest in the fascinating world of finance and the stock market, where his self–discipline and concentration paid big dividends. By 1950 Chang was a millionaire living in Jersey, but tiring of the narrow parochial life of the Channel Islands, he returned to his homeland to help defeat the communist rebels, and do what he could in stabilizing the fragile new found independence of Malaysia. Now he was one of its leading citizens and owned a large chunk of commercial property in downtown Kuala Lumpur, and several harbour installations at Port Swetenham on the coast. A remarkable man indeed.

As he drove Kit and I back to the hotel that evening he pointed out some of his property. At the corner of one street he told the driver to stop and pointed to a long row of shops of all kinds, butchers, joiners, seed merchants, leather workers, and suchlike artisans, telling us that his bank financed them all. The system of finance was very interesting. If, for instance, a carpenter approached him for a loan, he would ask the man to bring his father or the head of his family to the bank. Then, after Mr. Chang had satisfied himself of the applicant's craftsmanship and business acumen, he would require the guarantor to give his 'Chop', literally his thumbprint on the loan agreement. From that moment on, the whole of his family became collectively responsible for the debt, so they all saw to it that the carpenter fulfilled his obligation to Mr. Chang.

Before he dropped us off at the Merlin Hotel I had one question for our host. How was it, I asked, that most of the businesses we had seen in Kuala Lumpur were operated by the Chinese who were actually a minority? That could all be explained by a simple folk proverb said Mr. Chang.

"When it rains, as it often does here, the Malay says. "Oh it is raining, let us seek shelter until it stops," while the Chinese say. 'Oh it is raining. That means it will be cooler and we can work harder.

The Batavians

The other dominant community out there was Dutch. They were amongst the earliest visitors to the Far East from Europe, arriving after the Portuguese. Unlike their fellow Europeans though, they were not so much interested in saving souls as trading in earthly goods, and in spite of the incursions of other nations like the Danes, Germans, British and the French, they had prospered. They were very strong in mining, rubber and shipping throughout the East Indies but due, I suppose, to the volatile state of things in Indonesia, they had made their headquarters in Singapore. Through the hotel manager we did quite a few private functions for them, either on the roof terraces of their office buildings or out at their luxurious estates. These parties were lavish, absolute luxury with worldly men and very beautiful women, usually either Dutch or upper class Indonesians who, except for shopping trips to Paris, Amsterdam or Milan, rarely left this oriental paradise. Money was certainly no problem. At a big society wedding in Malacca, they paid me the equivalent of £350 for a forty–minute cabaret spot, and provided rooms at a 5 star hotel. We found them charming and sophisticated, with none of the racial hang–ups of the British Raj. Some of the most powerful families were of mixed blood and their dealings were scrupulously honest.

Cruising around on our days off, a little jaded with our British cuisine at the hotel, we sought out a curry house but found it difficult, and about the only thing we found similar was a workman's food stand in the market. But even then it was not a taste we were seeking. Foraging UK musoes seek those battery acid vindaloos, not this light thin sauce perfumed and flavored with saffron. So it was back to the sausage and chips. Whilst in town though, I bought some more ammunition for our pistols, and a couple of ceremonial Malay swords, and Kit bought a beautiful small scale Fender bass guitar, which had a sad and sinister future when we provided it to an old friend who joined us later on a tour of Germany.

Homeward Bound

While we were away at Malacca our agent from Hong Kong, Fredo the Sinister Sikh, had snaked into Kuala Lumpur and dropped a note off, and a suitcase containing the clothes we had ordered from the Hong Kong tailor. The note said briefly that our schedule had been changed, and that we would not be returning via Hong Kong. There were air tickets but no money, only a note saying that the balance of our contract would be sent to us via the Eddie Rogers office, London. I think Fredo and Ralf were still smarting from the bill for the excess baggage on our original flight out. I was raging mad at this stroke and prowled the carpeted corridors of the Merlin Hotel looking for him but he had skipped. Fortunately I got on very well with the Merlin's Dutch manager who got a cut from the extra gigs he found for us, and he agreed to pay the Merlin's full contract price directly to us, which just about balanced up the amount outstanding to us. Regrettably the Food and Beverage Manager however was not so accom–modating, and insisted that we settle our drinks checks before we left, much to the chagrin of our boozy musoes who had run up monster bills.

There were no repercussions from Hong Kong or the London agents, who although anxious to keep booking acts out there, realized that they were out of their depth, and were wary of our patronage by the all–powerful 'Families'. Ahead of us lay Dubai and 32 hours of flying to London via Amsterdam, but there was one final twist to the story. We all parted at Heathrow: Roy and Dave decided to see friends in London before returning to Scotland, while Kit, David and I headed to the North.

It was the last Monday of October when our train finally pulled into London Road Station, Manchester. It was still raining and didn't look any cleaner than when we'd left it in February. As we each prepared to go our separate ways I noticed that David was stalling, which made me curious.

Away from my gaze as he helped Kit with her bags he asked if he could share her taxi, as they both lived in the same direction. She agreed but on the way to Middleton he asked to borrow twenty quid off her, as he was, quote. "A bit short for the Old Lady." After almost nine months earning big bucks in the Far East, which included his Vietnam bonus, the only thing he was taking home to his mother was a suitcase full of dirty washing and an American combat helmet. He'd spent the bloody lot. But he mollified his mother by telling her that his money had not come through yet, and I had not been paying him out there. I got a right earful off her three months later, for hanging onto her son's money so long. Still, I don't blame him that much. He was only about twenty–two and maybe that's the way it should be when you are young and wild

My homecoming too was somewhat different this time. Nobody, except perhaps Francis, was exactly ecstatic at seeing me again, although they went through the motions. I had brought home loads of presents and plenty of money, but Sylvia seemed very much calmer and unruffled, and when I saw the exotic underwear drying on the clothes–rack, I began to realize that something had happened while I had been away but I did not raise the subject, reluctant to disturb the fragile armistice we had achieved. Mind you, it did not last long. In fact we had our first row four days after I got back.

I hired a car and on the following Sunday lunchtime went to a big family 'do' over at my Auntie Annie's house. The party had nothing to do with my homecoming, but was to celebrate one of her kids passing for University, which had my Mum spitting feathers from the start. Eventually, after a few drinks my uncles got round to asking me about my Far Eastern adventures, and gradually everybody joined in with their own questions, while my mother looked on stony–faced at her waster of a son. Things were going quite well and I was regaling them with tales of jungle warfare, and exciting tree–top trips in helicopter gun ships, when my father put down his glass and said, "When did you say you got back?"

Everybody stopped talking and looked at me and I said. "Er, last Monday, why?"

"Oh," he said, shaking his head sadly, "You missed it. You should have been here on Saturday—Manchester United beat Everton."

And that was that. They all started talking about football and forgot about me.

PICKER'S TIP 33

Singer's with sore throats should avoid throat sweets. They have a mild anaesthetic effect, and you may strain your voice more without realising it. Gargle with warm sweet tea or slowly drink a glass of port wine. Dairy products also increase the amount of mucus and phlegm in the throat and reduce the clarity of the voice.

Postscript

After many months away from Europe it came as quite a shock to find the tabloid press so biased and misinformed about the war in Vietnam, seeking only sensational items and blaming every bad thing on the US. Forces. The basic truth was that the US was acting in support of the Republic of South Vietnam, who was being invaded by the Communist North supported by China. A peace treaty between the two countries had been agreed, but as soon as the Americans had left in 1976, the North Vietnamese had broken it and invaded the South. We saw it all at first hand, from the reporters of the International Press sipping their gins and tonic in the luxury of Saigon's Caravelle Hotel, to the endemic graft, treachery and corruption of Cholon, from the huge military bases, to the isolated jungle outposts up–country. In the end though, it all came to naught as the Communist dogma failed to produce the promised Nirvana, and today life in Ho Chi Minh City is much the same as it was back in 1968.

*   *   *   *   *   *

23

THE MANCHESTER SCENE
Bernard Manning, Hank Locklin

It was winter 1968–69—we'd just come back from all that excitement of touring the world and found ourselves once again bogged down back in Manchester.

By now things were improving a little, though an Old Guard of spivs and street girls from the post war boom times were still fighting a desperate rearguard action to keep their old haunts like the Cromford and Stage and Radio Club from going under, while fey ex–public school boys and sober suited businessmen continued to dance elegantly together at the openly gay Buckingham's Club in Spring Gardens, keeping all us show people busy—so everybody was happy and most tastes and persuasions were well served

In the working class inner city suburb of Blackley, Bernard Manning had persuaded his green–grocer father to back him in a showbiz venture, and had started laying the foundations of his prosperity at a converted Temperance Society snooker hall that was soon to become the famous Embassy Club, where we were booked on our second week back home.

Meanwhile Jack McCall, one of the true pioneers of the cabaret club scene, was still operating his own highly popular venue the Northern Sporting Club, about half a mile further down Rochdale Road and on the south side of the city, things were also stirring, as the almost inarticulate but financially astute wrestler Bill Benny, was pumping groan and grunt money into a chain of similar cabaret venues. The same exercise was being repeated across the Pennines and in the North East and Merseyside where affluent car dealers, scrap merchants, dry cleaners and other successful traders with cash to spare, sank their profits into the new clubs, seeking the glamour and local prestige of' Showbiz'

With the arrival of these new clubs some really superb acts developed. Cabaret singers like Tony Hulme, David Blakey and Pat O'Hare and Country/Folk performers like Paul Bailey, Bernie Shaw, and that pure Mancunian minstrel Pete Elliott.

In terms of earning big bucks the girl singers won hands down. Shiela Devereaux, Gilly Thomas, Shiela Southern, Helen Mack and others would often do three or four gigs a night as warm–up or link acts. It was usually four songs and then off to another club.

There were also outstanding musicians around like the eccentric fiddle player Stan Stanley, trombonist Eddy Warburton and guitar wizard Pete Cowap plus comics like Ralph Denby, and to complete the scene, that superbly topical comedian Jackie Carlton and his partner Eric Leroy, opened the notoriously gay Carlton Club (What else?) in an alley behind Market Street in central Manchester. So this might be a good time to tell you about Jackie.

Jackie Carlton

Most gay comedians I have met fit neatly into two brackets. First, there is the coarse, posing transvestite character like scouser Lily Savage (a.k.a. Paul O'Grady) or the veteran, more up–market, glamorous Danny La Rue type, bewigged, padded out and made over like Dolly Parton, pouting and slipping double entendres into his/her comments about homosexual sex or intimate female hygiene. (Like Queen Victoria, my mother would not accept this seamy side of homosexual relationships and said she just loved his frocks).

The second is the socially aware, cool, satirical commentator on modern life and attitudes. Years later this style was rediscovered by the so–called Angry Young Comics, who called it Alternative Comedy. (They were usually angry because nobody thought they were very funny).

Jackie Carlton was certainly the best of the latter kind. In fact he was almost the only guest artiste that Bernard Manning could not intimidate on his own turf at the Embassy Club. He was superb and completely open about his homosexuality, a rare quality even in the Swinging Sixties. I can vividly remember the first time I came across him. We were topping the bill at the old Luxor Club in Manchester where he was the compere. There was also a singer on the bill called Sheena Smyth whom he introduced by announcing to the packed club that apart from her singing, she had other alleged talents.

"Oh.Yiss. Our Sheena'll make you 'appy. worrever y'want. She's had en–ough cock to make a handrail from 'ere to Piccadilly, 'aven't you love."

There was no one on the Northern Club circuit who could touch him and his shows were always a sell out—and in spite of Johnny Hamp consider–ing him too risqué to be included in Granada TV's ground–breaking 'The Comedians' show, he was at one time, actually lined up to take over as compere of a plum TV show of the period, 'Sunday Night at the London Palladium', but it never really came together. The story doing the rounds of Clubland was that he made the mistake of inviting a researcher to visit him at home, where his collection of Nazi memorabilia and his enthusiasm for Oswald Mosley's fascist politics undoubtedly crabbed his chances with the controlling Bernstein dynasty, who replaced him with the saccharine Englebert Humperdink.

The Manning Myth

While we are still in Clubland, perhaps a word about the hard facts behind the old Bernard Manning myth might not go amiss. First off, let me say that I consider him to be a true One–Off, a Northern Comic Genius in the mould of the great Frank Randle, and one who was not only very aware of current trends and fashions, but also superbly quick–witted. He was also a good singer of standard ballads, and though his voice lacked any dis–tinctive defining quality, it was certainly good enough to get him out of trouble if his gags were not hitting, (a rare event indeed). It was only many years later, after a period of great personal loss and family tragedy that he became the bigoted racist dinosaur of the 1990's. He was a Mancunian Alf Garnett, but make no mistake about it, this man has a great talent.

Back then we used to work his club regularly. It was nothing special, just another venue on the Northern Club circuit, cramped, cheaply appointed, and barely a step above the rough local workingmen's clubs. Careful reading of Jonathan Margolis' excellent biography of the man, reveals that he was not much liked by his fellow performers, a fact that I can confirm. This was not, as Bernard often spouted, due to envy, but was down to his unprincipled actions and bullying tactics. Although he was very good with embarrassing one–liners at the audience's expense, (an easy ploy when you have a microphone and your victim doesn't) he blatantly stole other comedian's material. In fact he boasted that he kept a tape recorder behind the bar, so that he could play back the previous night's performances and steal the best gags. He did it to everyone, Little and Large, Cannon and Ball, Ken Dodd, Jimmy Tarbuck, and Mike Yarwood, along with many others. He tried it with us one night but was not very convincing, and after the second night he realized that he was out of his depth, as he couldn't grasp the phrasing or the timing of our music. (Mind you, he was not as bad as Vera Lynn when she tried to do it. That was a waste of air tickets to Nashville if I ever saw one. The results of that session were buried and forgotten to save the veteran Force's Sweetheart's face), even so, he had to try some spoiling tactics. This is a typical example. Our usual opening was for the band to play a number and then Kit would come on and say something like.

"Good evening everybody and welcome to the show. My name is Kit Connor. The name of the band is the Everglades and now here is the boss man himself. Mr. FRANK YONCO."

But on our second night after the introduction Bernard blustered on the stage and coarsely shouted.

"Oh—no, lass, you're wrong. There's only one bleedin' boss man 'ere an' it's me. So don't you forget whose paying the bleedin' wages."

It might seem strange to describe Bernard being insecure, but it is quite true. Abroad or outside his own narrow environment he is uncomfortable, and carefully avoids areas with strong regional characteristics like Merseyside or the North East. He did get a singing job with Oscar Rabin's band in the '50's, but the pressure of constant travel got to him and he soon returned to the damp terraces of Harpurhey, but his tales of poverty and deprivation are nonsense. I lived through the same period about a mile away across the Irk Valley and witnessed the struggle of real working people.

Some years later when he visited Las Vegas for a few days to feature in a Granada Television documentary, he surrounded himself with his family and some of his local fans. An old friend of mine Fred Carusio, who was a booker in Vegas around that time, recalls Bernard's performance there. It was an early afternoon spot and about 400 punters trickled into the vast lounge of the MGM Grand to catch the free show. The audience, with high Jewish content, had actually come to see kosher comic, Shecky Green, but Shecky had to go to court that afternoon, and Joan Rivers was rushed in to introduce someone she didn't know from Adam. Bernard gave it his best shot and some of his gags got a good response in spite of the American's difficulty in understanding his coarse North Manchester accent and jerky delivery. They presumed he was some kind of Scandinavian settler from Minnesota, much as they did when the beautiful Marti Caine played there some years later—but the bald fact remains. Bernard Manning did play in Las Vegas.

He is still a great comedian even if his material is a little flawed by today's P.C. standards, probably due to the loss of the guiding influences of his life, his mother, his wife, and brother Frank, but perhaps more from mischievous tabloid journalists, who could always goad him into an outrageous comment or two. In the end he fell into the same journalist's trap that exposed the flaws of Freddy Starr, Paul Daniels, Keith Harris, Rod Hull and others who, reluctant to accept that time had passed and fashions had changed, insisted that they could still cut it and took up the poisoned chalice of a live show on national television to prove it.

Bernard's humiliation came when, after boasting that he could entertain any kind of an audience, he was challenged to take his club act to Bombay in June 2003, where he played to a selected audience of affluent middle-class Indians at their exclusive club. He would have stood more chance at Frinton–on–Sea.

After being abused by fifteen minutes of profane Mancunian raving, the sophisticated Indian yuppies gaped in shock, as this racist untouchable in their midst continued his rambling monologue of obscenities, and they watched in silent disgust as he walked off stage, cursing everything oriental, from the microphone to the climate. The closing shots showed a muffled up Bernard being buffeted along Blackpool Promenade, waxing lyrical about how happy he was to be back among his own kind of folk again. Oh, yes, it's definitely 'Horses for courses.'

These days any criticism is met by Bernard's stock reply that he is a self–made millionaire, and so he must have been right all along. This may impress the punters at his Embassy Club, but does not make much of a mark in today's showbiz world. He was certainly a Man of his Time, but that time has passed.

But maybe I am being a little unfair because, whereas Bernard loved his rainy North Manchester fiefdom and never wanted to leave it, I spent the first seventeen years of my life desperately trying to get away from Cor-onation Street.

Hank Locklin came over to tour the Irish clubs and dance halls, and we backed him and played for dancing at the Ardri Club in South Manchester. He was a nice guy with the most amazing bouffant hair–do. I think it was a rug, because it kept slipping about. Somehow he had forgotten his guitar and for the show he borrowed mine and I played mandolin. The guitar was not a very good one, it was a blond Big Timer which looked impressive but had no acoustic ring at all, which didn't really matter because I'd mounted a De Armone pick-up on it and played through the bass player's amp. After the show which went very well, Hank handed me back the guitar and apologized for the spattered blood across the face of it from a cut finger, which fortunately I did not wipe off, because at the club a week later a rabid Hank Locklin fan offered me twice what I had paid for it, because it carried his hero's bloodstains. I took the money and bought a Levin Goliath, one of the best guitars I have ever owned. I lost it in one of those frantic scurries for housekeeping money that is endemic in the music business. Later when things had improved I tried to buy it back but the new owner flatly refused to part with it though I offered him a very good price.

They really were great guitars, those Levin Jumbos. I personally think they were far better than some Gibsons and Martins. A few years later I bought a Martin D28E electric acoustic off Karl Denver, but it was not a patch on that Swedish Levin. But I think that by far the best acoustic guitar I came across was Pete Sayer's superb Guild, although today's Takamine flat-tops are very good indeed, and while we are talking about music I must confess that it was around this time that I assembled what were some of the worst bands I ever put together.

Scraping the Barrel

After such an extended tour of the Far East it was not surprising that the band broke up so I decided to seek out new blood, and had the idea to infuse it with young musicians, to give it some youthful energy and drive (That's an oxymoron if there ever was one). Accordingly I got hold of a student on a gap year, a trainee doctor, and an escapee from a Catholic seminary, an apprentice plumber, a Polynesian refugee and a window cleaner. The result was mind blowing and how we got away with it I'll never know.

To start with we had a frantic hyperactive drummer who really wanted to be a comedian, which in a strange way he was. He certainly wasn't a drummer. He would start out brilliantly, doing great fills and ripples and then spoil it all by running two or three bars over in the solos, at which time he would stand up to apologize and tell the audience a joke. Wow. Later he did try becoming a stand-up comic but it was not successful. I think in the end he emigrated to Australia.

The guitar player was an Irish medical student who played 'Tiddly Aye dye dye' Celtic runs all the time, no matter what the song was. It could be anything from a rippling Blue Grass to a Hank William's weepie but you could be sure that those 'Hi diddle dee dump' licks would come plinking through.

The steel player came from Bolton and claimed to be from the South Sea

Islands, but looked and sounded Pakistani. He found country licks a bit strange and eventually gave the job up to form his own Hawaiian band, complete with bright flowered shirts and leis. He even offered Kit a job as hula singer in a grass skirt.

Playing bass we had a complete lunatic who made being the eccentric musician into a fetish. I suppose his playing was all right but not very perceptive, as he demonstrated by stopping halfway through 'Jambalaya' to ask the drummer what the chords were. (There are only two).

His off stage behavior was also bizarre in the extreme. We used his van that nobody but him was allowed to drive, and he also insisted on loading himself in a certain set sequence. It was an obsession with him, so much so, that on a return trip from Frankfurt he stopped the van on the autobahn to reload it, because we had done it wrong in wanting to get home quicker. Also if it was raining he would turn off the windshield wipers when we went under a bridge, and kept the tyre pressures up to 60psi.with the expected result of stripping the tread off two of them outside Ostend. What a loony. Eventually I bought it from him and to be brutally honest, that van was the only reason he got the job in the first place. Later I heard he joined a band called the Specialists.

Specialist what, I wondered?—Rat catchers?

Some time later on a subsequent tour of the North East, this Transit van set itself on fire in the Tyne Tunnel. Slamming my foot down I cleared the exit of the tunnel and managed to get the bonnet open and throw a blanket over the flames, which I then soaked with the spare water we always carried. I sent the boys on in a taxi and Kit and I waited for the AA. Eventually the damage was repaired by a back street mechanic in Sunderland, but he did not do a very good job, and the bloody thing set on fire again on the way back to Manchester.

The bass player's revenge, perhaps?

*   *   *   *   *   *

24

TROUBLES AND TRAGEDIES
Bobby Bare, Willie Nelson, Buck Owens, Wes Buchanan, Tex Withers

1970 proved to be a very busy year. Gigs were averaging at about twenty-two to twenty–seven a month, mostly one night stands, with the exception of a couple of European tours. In January, a contract arrived from Gordon Smith, to make an LP for Pye Records on their new imprint Lucky Records. (Oh yeah, lucky for who?). The actual session was recorded at a basement studio in the Orange Music shop, off Charing Cross Road in London. The personnel included Ady on various guitars, and that superb piano player Tom Parker. The disc also had tracks from a couple of guest singers, Brian Hatt and Brian Goldby, whose voice always reminds me of the 1930's singer Frank Crumit,—you know, the guy who sang songs like 'Abdul a Bulbul Amir'.

Yeah, that's right, Brians. And here there were two of 'em. It seems that I've always had trouble with Brians (or Bryans)—right from my first faltering step into the jungle of the music game, it's been a name that has haunted me. I never could get on with anyone called Brian. However, there was one exception. (Yes, Brian X—it might have been you). How's that for tact? It even happened abroad. I recall one particularly obnoxious Brian in Australia and a couple in France. I'm not saying that they were all bad. It's just we did not gel. Maybe it's me.

By the way, I have also known a few dodgy Daves as well.

Around this time I also made a single of a Tom T.Hall song called 'Ballad of Forty Dollars', that hit the British Country Music charts and held a number one spot for Lucky Records. I thought the production was a bit frantic but it sold well, although I much preferred the B Side, which was a great, emotive, Waylon Jennings number called 'The Choking Kind.'

The British scene was busy, due mainly to Pat Jones's very efficient Jigsaw Agency in classy Harrogate, and most of the overseas work was based in the Frankfurt–Wiesbaden–Mainz region for German–American Promotions. This was the first time we toured with Bobby Bare, and I have lasting memories of him at the Hotel de France in Wiesbaden, blowing his nose on the table–cloth and relieving his bladder all over the radiator in our hotel room, too far gone to find the bathroom. We did a couple more tours with him in the Seventies including the Wembley Festival, and I found him a very pleasant guy when he was on the planet, but he was seriously hooked into booze and chemicals and if you came across him then you might have a problem. But I guess when you are a Star you can do what you want on an overseas tour. Last time I met up with him was at the Cheyenne Saloon in Orlando with George Jones around 1996—and he seemed very much together which is more than I can say for George.

Whilst in Wiesbaden we met up with the riotous Linda Leyton Show. What a gas that was. It was one of those superb comedy groups from the North of England—Leeds, I think in this case—and our meeting up with them itself was startling to say the least. We were living at the Hotel de France and late one night there was a terrific commotion in the room next door. Furniture was being flung around and two people were screaming obscenities at each other in English. Suddenly a set of French windows crashed open onto the shared balcony and two figures came struggling and cursing through the debris. This was our first acquaintance with Morris and Linda Leyton, and by all accounts this was one of their little tiffs, but we thought at that moment that it might be serious, because at that moment he was trying to throw her over the balustrade, and five floors down to the traffic on Taunus Strasse, but somehow she managed to kick him in the crotch and they reeled back into the wrecked room.

"Er, Anything wrong?" We asked sheepishly.

"Naw," shouted back Linda, "It's our fookin' Morris. 'E's pissed again. No bother."—Crash. Bang. "See yuh at breakfast, eh Luv?"

And that's how it went on. It seemed that every time we met them they had a barney. But their show was great and the musicians were very good. Their bass player Kenny Gee became a good friend of ours in Jersey in the 80's. Morris played guitar and Linda sang, and there was a drummer but I don't recall his name, and collectively they did great comedy, both vocal and visual. Linda was one of the first singers I knew to use a radio mike, and she would create havoc by running off stage in the middle of a song, and rushing into the gents toilet to give the audience a running commentary of what was going on in there.

Another very funny part of their act was called "The Great Escapo", when one of the musicians appeared on stage in a leopard skin and pink tights, and with much ceremony and a commentary from Linda, he would be chained up and pushed into a big sack, which would then be tied at the neck. With a drum roll Linda would announce that the Great Escapo would now extricate himself from his bonds and the sack in 30 seconds. The figure would then begin to wriggle and shout—the required thirty seconds passed with no result, except the jerking and muffled cursing from the sack. At this point, accepting his obvious failure, the band would strike up and Linda would go into a song while someone dragged the Great Escapo behind the drums, where he would continue to struggle and curse till the end of the act, completely ignored by the others. As the panic overcame him the Great Escapo's Balkan accent disappeared and became pure Leeds, going from,

"Laydees an' Genamen. In only t'irty seconds I, the Great Escapo shall be free."

To. "Eh oop. Aw, Bloody 'ell, Lads coom on. Gerrus out of 'ere. C'mon you bloody rotten sods. Ah'm fookin' gaggin' in 'ere."

It was hilarious—and anyway if it didn't work, there was always the regular on-stage row between Morris and Linda.

We stayed in Germany for most of that year playing the bases, lodging again at Heinrich Eisenblatter's Guest House, and I bought an Opel

Kapitan car from his son in law, which we brought back to England. An ex–drummer of mine fell in love with it and asked me to sell it to him, so I did—at a nice profit too.

Back in the UK again we scrabbled around the North Yorkshire social clubs. At the Steels Club in Sunderland, Kit made the national papers by almost getting electrocuted by a shorting plug. Her hand was badly burned but fortunately they had fitted a fail–safe device to the system, which probably saved her life, even if it did black out the club and all the houses for miles around. There was a shuffling of musicians again with a pleasant young man from Bury called Barry Hogan coming in on guitar and teenager Paul Armstrong taking the bass job. And Dave Marks came back to replace Dope Head Barney on drums who, one afternoon simple disap-peared off the scene—I last saw him on TV as an extra in a Spaghetti Western. We all got on very well, the only flaw being the fact that none of them could drive so it was left to Kit and myself to do it all, and there were many hard miles to cover in those days before a comprehensive motorway network was in place, so we were continually shuffling from one end of the country to the other. The ex–bass player's Transit van blew a gearbox (as they usually do) and our transport then became a fine Austin A60 saloon with a big trailer for the gear. It went like a rocket and due to the weight of the trailer stuck to the road like glue.

Our favourite gig in those days was at the Blayden Club in Ironbridge run by two brothers, Ivor and Clive Sothern. We seemed to do it nearly every month. The quaint little town of Brossley with its odd shaped cottages and winding streets and all those wonderful meat pies and cakes fascinated Kit and me. We thought of moving to live there. Mind you that was before the arrival of the West Midlands overspill estates so perhaps, in hindsight, it was as well we did not make the move There was a lot of work in that area—Hereford's Crystal Rooms was one of our regular gigs, and nearby on the river there was the Bridge Inn, one of those quaint old pubs where they made their own moonshine. A single malt whiskey called Pigs Eye and a blended one called Sheep Dip, both of 'em' very good. I wonder if they still do?

In fact all across the Welsh Marches there were some super country pubs that featured music. One of the major gigs in there was a pub at Craven Arms beyond the Brecon Beacons where the manager ('Mummy' owned the place). was a complete control freak. He would make people queue up in the snow before he would open the doors and kept a tame fox in the yard. At least he said it was tame, but he always kept it chained up. I'd bet the bloody animal would have been off to the hills like a shot if it ever got free. And no matter how good your show had been or how many punters you attracted, you were always pointedly told about an act that was there last month that absolutely packed the place, and did a really wonderful show. What a lovely guy. At Telford too there was an impressive and well–man-aged venue called the Anstice Club. The last I heard was that Ivor Sothern and his family still live in Brossely where they operate the comfortable Cumberland Hotel.

Willie Nelson came over to do a tour and we did a few road gigs with his show. This was not the Outlaw Willie that we all know and love today, but a neat, shorthaired youthful figure wearing white silk polo neck shirts and Sta-Pressed pants, and picking a pristine Telecaster while modestly introducing his songs. The great talent was there but the image was much smoother and conventional—but still very impressive. The man who got my vote on that tour was guitarist Wes Buchanan, quite the best country picker I had seen. Well, that's not counting Jim Hornsby.

That same year we also did a couple of shows with Buck Owens and his band, on the US bases. We also witnessed a horrendous show in London where the BBC tried to record as a live broadcast, and almost masked out the band with sound baffle plates, so the audience only saw half the show and the fussy producer (I think it was Ian Grant) kept insisting on retakes, which produced nothing but confusion. I saw him later in the Clarendon Hotel, busy telling his cronies what a huge success it had been when in everybody's opinion it had been complete crap.

But in those days BBC Country Music producers were an elitist clique who wallowed in an ethos of self-satisfaction and were totally out of touch with the commercial music world in general and avoided involving British country talent whenever possible ('tho they did have their favorites, but to quote the late Sam Goldwyn 'they included me out.'). I was not exactly flavour of the month with the journalists either.

Dave Sharpe wrote in 'OPRY' magazine in February 1970:

Frank Yonco

'I said earlier that we in Britain lack personalities; Frank Yonco is a gentleman who has perhaps too much personality. Revelling in the title of the bad boy of British Country Music, Frank goes from one controversy to another with gay abandon. Actually Frank is a great character who naturally gets into hot water. One thing though: Frank Yonko (sic) and the Everglades are one of the most professional acts in Country Music and the most travelled. Now on the Decca label, they recently recorded a live album at the Nashville Rooms.'

With write-ups like that was it any wonder I kept travelling?

He couldn't even spell Yonco right.

In all honesty though, it did not bother me that much. I've always been optimistic

In fact, if I woke upon Christmas morning to find my room full of horse dung I'd think somebody had bought me a pony.

But that is not to say there were not some, more open-minded journalists around. Pete Smith, Joe Fish, Jean Mills, Alan Clacket, Bob Powell and the authoritive Tony Byworth all gave me some nice write-ups.

Our happy band held together for about five months, but then yet another tour with Bobby Bare was offered in Germany, and we had to make changes again due to domestic commitments. Dave the Drummer became entangled emotionally and gave up the road, and we added a steel player from Yorkshire called Brian. (Brian? Oh, no! not another Brian). At least this one was very good at his job but he still had a few Brian–ish qualities. Our association was not destined to be a long one, as he was intent on emigrating to South Africa or Australia. He picked us up in Munich and got on well with Bobby Bare and the rest of the boys, particularly Charlie our guitarist, who found a soul mate who also had a great reluctance to spend anything at all. As an example, on a tour in Scotland we were given a house in Grangemouth to live in for two weeks, and to provide regular sustenance we decided to collectively buy milk, tea, bread and butter and after that it was down to everybody personally to provide their own main meals—with the predictable result that Brian and Charlie lived for the whole week on cups of tea and buttered toast.

Back in Wiesbaden, Charlie Wood's charming son Ray was the tour manager this time and it was from him I bought my first Mercedes car, a grey 220s saloon. It was wonderful and I became a life long convert to the Stuttgart legend that says.

'There are only two kind of cars in the world. The Mercedes and all the others'

There were several tense but funny incidents with him in the Nuremberg clubs. Ray was black but he was from Clapham, London, and he copped a lot of flak from the American black militants for handling 'Honky' acts like us. At one of the clubs a bunch of 'Brothers' cornered him and asked him all about it, trying to put him down with their Philly street talk so, in return, Ray gave them a full basinful of eels and mash cockney rhyming slang, and they walked away confused. However it did get a bit heavy now and then, so Charlie sent an old wrestler pal of his along as a minder.

Once more we were sent south on a second Bobby Bare tour that ground to a finish with a double at the Rocker Club Wiesbaden on December 13th, so we managed to get back home for Christmas, and rounded off 1970 with our regular New Year's Eve show at the US Columbia Club in London. Luckily by then I had replaced our bass player with a real good old friend from my early days, Vince Evers. He had been having a hard time with his wife and was feeling particularly low, so we gave him the Fender bass which Kit had bought in Kuala Lumpur and got him playing again—little knowing what cruel fate had in store.

We moved up to the North East again and were approached by an agent who offered to become our manager. He came round to the digs in Roker Park to thrash out the details. Anyway, to cut a long story short, we signed up and for several months we worked steadily for him, often visiting his office, a beautiful old coach house in the country behind Sunderland.

* * * * * *

Tex Withers

In March we moved to London and did our first tour of Fuller's pubs in West London, which were known by the bands as Paulton's Palaces, because the brewery's Entertainment Manager was the irrepressible Ted Paulton. He was a wonderful character that always appeared to be terribly confused, but in fact was very, very much in charge of things. There was a constant running battle between him and his wife who would phone him at all hours, even when he was at some gig or other. The chain of pubs was always packed and very well run. There was the Red Lion in Brentford, the Roebuck, Lewisham, the Adam & Eve, Hayes, the Red Cow, Hammersmith and several others, the flagship of the circuit being of course the famous Nashville Rooms in West Kensington, run by another great character, Charlie Stephenson.

The Nashville Rooms really was a super venue. A lot of thought had been put into the conversion of this big pub and the atmosphere was terrific and the place was always crowded, but we managed to get a table for Kit's glamorous sister Frances and her family for the show, and they enjoyed it immensely, particularly their young daughters Anne Marie and Denise, who were open mouthed at the 'Elvis' tribute we did that night. We often stayed at their place en route to the cross channel ferry and I would convince them that I was a Martian and could turn off the radio by looking at it. Actually Kit was next to the wall plug in the hall. On these gigs we were accommodated, if you could call it that, in a building behind some railway hoardings at the side of the Clarendon Hotel in Hammersmith, and the cost of this was deducted from our contract. Also, believe it or not, Ted collected 10% commission for getting us the gigs. This was the famous Paulton Hilton, a four-storey, crumbling slum, semi-furnished in what could only be described as Boot Sale Art Deco. In the basement lived a timid young woman called Mary with her baby, who acted as a kind of housekeeper for the visiting bands on the circuit.

On the first floor lived one of the great characters of the British Country Music scene, the famous Tex Withers. He was a man I admired greatly both as a singer and as a man, who had overcome an abused childhood and physical deformity to become a giant in his chosen profession, and I think it is one of the most damning indictments of the British Country Music Establishment that the agents, the managers and the promoters allowed this massive talent go to waste. Tex spent most of his time stuck in the seedy Irish clubs of South London. Club owner Chris Ford eventually moved to help him by taking him to Nashville, where he visited his long time idols Johnny Cash and Tex Ritter who received him warmly, which contrasted with his meeting with Charlie Pride, who was very snotty and patronizing indeed. I've met Charlie a couple of times and found him much the same. Nothing ever came from the trip except a period of time in Ireland, which only served to exacerbate his drinking problems.

Returning to the UK he met a young woman whom he married. She was a good influence and accepted his eccentric ways. Tex was very sympathetic to the plight of the Native American and their wedding ceremony was in full Red Indian costume. They even had a papoose. His squaw truly loved him and happily shared the tepee that he sometimes lived in but only when the 'Great White Spirit' moved him. This ex–army bell tent, (for that's what it really was) was erected in a closed down beer garden behind a suburban pub and I remember going to find him one time. I got to the pub and they told me where he had pitched his tepee and as I approached it, Tex, fringed, beaded and buckskinned, came out, raised his right hand and greeted me with a solemn stare.

"How. Welcome Yonco White Eyes to my Lodge

I admired the blanketed and decorated interior but as I sat cross–legged on the floor drinking 'Firewater' from a leather cup, I noticed a thick cable snaking from the pub.

"What's that for Tex?" I asked.

For a moment the inscrutable mask of 'Chief Grey Otter' slipped and he said in broad cockney. "Oh, that? That's for our electric blanket."

Ah well, even the most dedicated Sioux brave used to take advantage of the white man's trading post. His magnetic presence dominated every stage he stepped onto, and I am proud to say he was the compere at The Nashville Rooms when we made that live album for Decca from there. A Great Character and a wonderful man.

And what a party animal. Or to be more precise, what a giver of parties for animals. Just read on.

PICKER'S TIP 34

If your gig has a reputation for trouble, make sure that you have a professional size heavy–duty canister of hairspray to hand. It is very effective in diverting an attacker. Mind you, overseas CS gas is available which does the job perfectly—but remember, it is currently illegal in the UK.

Tex's Party

Fullers Brewery had really gone to town on the Nashville Rooms con-verting the pub to a real authentic looking Western saloon complete with a big stage, changing rooms and a good sound system, not that the last was all that important as most performers insisted on using their own P.A. It soon became THE PLACE to play. If you played the Nashville Rooms, then you were on the way to the Wembley Festival. George Hamilton 1V and the Hillsiders played on the opening night and the resident compere, for a while, was our old friend from the Mary Taylor tour in Germany, Don Hill.

It was quite usual for the bands to have a farewell party after a week at the Nashville Rooms and we were no exception, so after the last show on Saturday night we all headed back to Paulton's Palace where it was all happening in the cellars. Jessie Kent, who was at that time an agent or promoter of some sort had organized the party. Actually it was rather hard to define Jessie's function but she was always somewhere around the Country Music scene. Last time I heard of her she was working as a P.R. for the Mervyn Conn office, and I remember her visiting us in Cornwall with Canadian fiddle player Roy Warhurst (Roy who? Yes, exactly).

I could tell from the outset that this was not going to be a fun night because as Dave Fidler, Kit and I arrived at the door, there were two guys on the door demanding entrance money. TO OUR OWN PARTY. I told him who we were and made to go past, but one of them, a tattooed heavy with a Mohican haircut pushed me back menacingly, so by sheer reflex action I grabbed him by the throat and slammed him against the door and was about to smack him one, when the door opened and the gracious Jessie arrived to sort things out. Well, lots of people from the London scene were there including Tony Rocco from the Kingpins and Johnny Reagan who ran the Tumbleweeds—Tex Withers was well gone on the Jack Daniels, and the rest of my band were already there with an odd assortment of com-panions of both sexes, one of whom knew Dave very well from his days with Phil Brady. She was a real loony, dancing by herself and popping pills all night along with the booze.

All went well until about 2.30am when Jessie suddenly announced that somebody had nicked her purse. There were fervent denials from all and sundry, and Tex took umbrage that such a thing should happen in his 'Lodge House' and stood at the door with a bloody big hunting knife, yelling that nobody should leave until the money was found and his honor as a 'Southern G'enmun' was restored.

Jessie started wailing and saying that all her money was in the purse including forty quid sent from her mother in Scotland. She said the last place she'd had it was in the back room with a big mirror, that the girls used as a cloakroom. So Kit suggested that the girls went in there one by one and Jessie could search them.

Well, there was no sign of the missing cash until the lunatic one was called in and it all came tumbling out of her bra. It was her money, she cried. "Then why were all these fivers from the Bank of Scotland?" asked Kit. At which she went absolutely berserk, kicking and fighting and cursing everyone in sight. She grabbed hold of Kit's hair and started pulling it, so Kit gave her a few kicks and grabbed a handful of hair herself. They came rolling out of the room into the crowd shouting and screaming.

Tex, well out of his skull, now deserted his post at the door and staggered over, threatening to cut the girl to pieces with his Bowie knife, for attacking 'His Princess' as he called Kit, and Jessie was by now a wobbling jelly of tears. Everybody was about to take sides when the girl's boy friend said that she was ill and should not have been on drugs, though he had been supplying her all night. I suppose he could see which way it was going and wanted to get out before someone called the Police.

We all tried to free Kit's hair but this junkie was by now out of her head and insensitive to pain. I eventually got Kit free by bending the girl's fingers back, when somebody belted her on the nose. Her pusher hurriedly dragged her out dripping blood on the stone cellar steps. Kit was in a bad way; her hands and arms bruised and had patches of hair missing. We wrapped her head in a damp towel and I took her upstairs and put her to bed. Going back to pick up her coat I met the doorman, a wrestler called Johnny Two Rivers who apologized for letting the lunatic junkie in. She was a well-known 'Tea Leaf' he said, but he didn't expect her to perform like that. Gipsy Delbert said that she had blown it now and nobody would want to know her.

They all loved Kit, especially Tex and Del, who said that his job was a car burglar and he specialized in stealing radios. His only tools were a length of wire and a tyre lever, both innocent items, if the Old Bill stopped him. The wire was for hooking up door locks and the tyre lever for smacking people across the shins if they tried to chase him. Being a true Romany he would not give you anything, but would hand over the most valuable presents and insist that he had something in exchange, if it was only a 5p piece. They were a fascinatingly strange bunch of shadow–land characters.

When I got back upstairs Kit was moaning in her fitful sleep so I gave her a couple of tablets, which relieved the nagging pain and sent her off properly. I'd just got on the bed to rest when I heard a banging outside and rushed to the window to check what it was. There below in the street was this crazy woman again, clothes all over the place, beating hell out of our bus, swearing at the top of her voice. At that precise moment she was attacking the mirrors with one of her high heel shoes. I went crackers and flipped right over the edge. I dashed down just as she was transferring her attention to our windscreen. But by that time Delbert and Tex were out of the door and grabbing her.

"Y'wanna hear it break, do you?" Yelled Delbert. "Well, try this way."

He smashed her head against the van, and the banging, screaming and shouting must have wakened up all the neighbours, and lights began to appear in nearby bedrooms. By this time, more late drinkers came pouring out of the door, just as they were dumping her in a waste skip, and dragged them off. We'd only got back inside when two police cars came flashing round the corner—God, what a night.

Goodbye, Old Friend

I first met up with Vince Evers 1960. In those days he was playing bass around the South Manchester area with guitarist Dougie Darby, and occasionally with Pete Elliot's Hobos. When Dougie left for the States around 1962 he joined us on bass with Scotsman Pete Sweeney playing guitar, working the British Legions and social clubs around the North of England, but when I started travelling seriously, we lost touch for a while but now and then we met up at Country Music clubs.

Early in 1971 Vince told us that he was having a tough time with his wife and was really depressed. We had a vacancy for a bass player and we asked him if he would like the job. He had no gear so we fixed him up with Kit's short scale Fender bass, and persuaded him to join us on the ill fated 'The Good, the Bad, and the Beautiful.' show. His new girl friend, you may remember, was the replacement dancer.

Vince liked being back on the road and both Kit and I liked him, and thought that we had finally got a bass player who was 100% happy being with us, and came on our second trip to Germany in the May of that year. It was a good tour, the shows impressive, and the weather perfect. We played the Canadian base at Baden–Baden on the last night and it was an absolute sensation, as I included a special Canadian section with Kit singing Ann Murray's songs and me doing tributes to Hank Snow, Orville Prophet, Ian Tyson, and Gordon Lightfoot. After that it was free drinks and food all night and bottles of JD and goodie bags to go.

Two days later, we left Wiesbaden early for the Luxembourg border to do our final lunchtime gig at Bitburg NCO Club. As we rolled through the gates, the MPs informed us that for some security reason, the club was closed, so we sat around in the afternoon sun, resting up for the trip to the ferry, and left the base that evening intending to take an easy drive through the night to Ostend. It was not familiar country, as usually we left from Frankfurt, but I worked out a cross–country route that would get us there in good time. I have always had this belief that no matter how well things are planned, there was always the fickle Hand of Fate ready to strike, and this night it seemed we had such an appointment with destiny, because every time I dozed off the van would somehow find its way back to the old route. When I took over the driving I would bring us back on course, but when anyone else took over we would hit various road works and detours until we found ourselves in the outskirts of Brussels. It was pouring rain and blowing a gale and around 3am we saw the lights of an all–night café and being well ahead of our schedule, pulled up in a lay–by opposite.

We spent about half an hour in that café and Kit and I went back to the Transit to sleep, while the boys, Vince, Jed, Charlie and Bryan stayed playing pool. Next thing we heard was the café door slam and the boys come out. They were laughing and messing about as they ran through the storm across the road to the van. Jed had just got to the side door, when we heard a loud bang, and saw the taillights of car speeding by, and a figure being thrown in the air and into the gutter forty yards up the road. It was Vince. We rushed out into the rain and ran to him but he was unconscious. He was barely breathing, so I reached into his mouth to clear his windpipe and pull out his palate, but when I lifted his head it was like a broken egg. The Police and the Belgian Ambulance Service were quickly on the scene, but he was dead on arrival at the hospital. It was a terrible shock to us all. I had to phone the British Consulate where a very bored, 'Hooray Henry' Duty Officer asked me for the details, and said he would inform the Cheshire Police who would contact the victim's family. We took the hovercraft back across the channel and, as you can imagine it was a very solemn and sad homecoming. Many of his old friends from the Country Music scene came to the funeral in Altrincham and, of course, we cancelled all our gigs until we decided what to do next

Vince Evers was only 32 and a real good friend, on the threshold of a new career—and as to that chilling Hand of Fate? Well, listen to this. The accident was on May 17th 1971 and the district of Brussels where the tradgedy happened?

It was called. EVERS.

PICKER'S TIP 35

Posters are also useful with a space for your picture. Send a couple to the venue (More than two will be a waste), and send a few to the local shops well before the gig. Believe me, the returns are well worth the expense involved.

Rip-Off

Eventually, we got things back on track and realized that we had to keep working. I put an advert for a bassist in the Country Music People magazine and from the many replies, I chose a young picker from Liss in Hampshire who worked under the stage name of Karl Benson. He had a wide knowledge of our music, played well, and had good gear, added to which he had also been in the Ivy League pop group, so his vocal abilities would be useful as well

We headed back to the Clyde Valley area of Scotland and Cumbria. There were no high spots on this tour, just low spots, like bad digs in Lanark and St Bees, where the beach chalets had no electricity, and all cooking had to be done on the open hearth. The latest Transit blew its radiator and our new bass–player insisted on bringing along his girl friend who, on meeting our guitarist Charlie, changed horses and married him instead. Oh yes, it was a short tour but a bad one.

There followed a series of weeks on the major cabaret clubs starting at the Fiesta, Sheffield, playing support to Irish comedian, Dave Allen, with a late double at the Ace of Clubs, Leeds. July found us at Saracen Park in Glasgow followed by a week at the EXEL Bowl Middlesbrough, where Karl took one of the office girls out for a late night drink, during which she hinted that our new manager might be ripping us off. When Karl told me, I just brushed off the suggestion. I wished later that I had listened to him. Another BBC Radio session in London, more Yorkshire cabaret clubs followed, and finally back to South Wales for a week at the fabulous Double Diamond Club at Caerphilly, where a week previously, the British singer Dickie Valentine had been killed when his car hit a railway bridge outside the club.

Tragedy also struck on a personal level when I received news that my father was desperately ill in Manchester. After the show that night, Kit and I drove up there but we arrived too late. He had passed away in the night. My mother was very distraught, particularly so with the casual, off-hand, attitude of the Asian doctor she called. He briefly examined him and asked my mother how old her husband was, and on being told that he was 71, he shrugged his shoulders and remarked that he had had a good life, and he was now dying. There was nothing he could do for him, it was just fate. Callous bastard. I was glad to see that the next year he was struck off for molesting one of his female patients. We spent most of that week driving to Manchester after the show and getting back to Caerphilly in time for the evening.

It was while we were on this tour of South Wales that I found out that the Middlesbrough office girl had been right, and that our new manager really was ripping us off. Bloody managers. Why could I never find an honest one? On this occasion we were playing a week at the Townsman Club in Swansea. The club had two cabaret rooms on different floors and we did a ten o'clock show downstairs and a later show around 1 am in the upstairs lounge. It was a good gig and they were an appreciative crowd, but on Friday evening the manager called me in the office and said that he would not be there on Saturday night, so he would pay us some of our contract money now and we were to pick up the balance from his secretary after the last show. 'Okay,' I said, 'fine,' and he opened the safe and handed me a wad of notes saying that he was pleased with our show and they had had a record week. Well I was surprised to say the very least.

My contract stated a fee less 15%. And here he was giving me over a hundred quid more as an interim payment, with more to come, so I asked to see his contract. And there it was. The Frank Yonco Show, an invoice for a direct payment to the management. This guy was robbing us of over a hundred quid a week and had been buying and selling us and charging commission as well, which was totally illegal. I got on to him the next day and demanded an explanation. The net result was that he coughed up some money but only a token of what he had actually taken and the contract was scrapped, but it didn't stop the skimming scam because I heard from another act that he was still at it a year later.

However there was one good thing to come out of the debacle. While we were at the Townsman an old friend of mine, a Liverpool bandleader called Phil Brady, dropped in to see me. His band was working the miner's clubs up in the valleys on their way home from Cornwall. They had been doing a kind of working holiday gig at a big pub on the beach at Hayle for a mutual friend Ronnie Whitford, who was looking for more Country style acts. Phil gave me the name of the agency down there and so began our long association with the Sunset Country.

PICKER'S TIP 36
STAR SYNDROMES
or how to behave like your role models

Hank Williams
Turn up drunk.
George Jones
Do not turn up at all.
Kitty Wells
Do not get off the stage without a standing ovation
David Alan Coe
Challenge the audience to a fight.
Don Gibson
Forget the words to your own songs

Skeeter Davis.
Tell the folks about your recent medical history
Jerry Naylor
Don't tell the band what songs you intend to do.
Hank Snow
Don't employ anybody taller than five foot two.
Jerry Lee Lewis
Carry a gun and don't marry anybody under 13

25

CORNWALL
Red Rocks and White Water

Did you visit Mevagissey? Did you see the boats leave Par?
Did you ever sit on Gribbon Head and nearly touch a star?
Did you cross the Bodmin Moor, where the grouse and tern fly free?
Then you've seen this land where red rocks & white waters reach the sea
just to see the lights of Newquay or Falmouth's busy quay.
Though' I wandered cross the Tamar, I'm home at last and free
From the demon called ambition and the phantom called success.
And a way of life I knew was not for me.
And though I wasn't born here, its home at last to me.
I love this land where red rocks and white waters greet the sea.
Did you see Looe and Polperro, or Perran's rolling sand?
See the dreamy creeks of Helford or the Lizard's stormy strand?
See the old tin mines on Camborne Hill or Truro' shining spires?
Tintagel and St. Mawgan, the White Hills and Pentire?
Did you see Luxilyan Valley on a sparkling summers day?
Or the beauty of Polkerris, as the sea mist rolls away?
I have sailed the Carrick Roads, seen the Helston Flora Dance
Seen Mylor and Hayle Towans, Marazion and Penzance.

Frank Yonco. Lloret de Mar 1975

Kernow

There is absolutely no place in the British Isles like Cornwall. It is a unique magic land, full of legend and history, where the names reflect the mystery and tell of black times long gone. Where else would you find towns with names like Truro, Lostwithiel, or Fowey? Or families with pre–British names like Hobba and Carrow?

Here on wild nights with clouds scudding past in the moonlight, you can almost feel the presence of witches and druids. All of it crammed into a peninsula less than 60 miles long. but where a journey from Par on the south coast to Newquay on the north coast, a distance of perhaps sixteen miles, will take the visitor an hour by car, even longer in the summer season. Speeding on the narrow, twisting high–hedged lanes between Trewoon and Summercourt can be very dangerous indeed.

I had been there before but always as a holidaymaker; an emmet (ant) as the Cornish would call me, but I always wanted to return to spend more time there. Everything about it fascinated me. In fact, in some of my lowest moments, when debts and emotional crises beset me, I would pore over a map searching for a place to hide from my problems. Somewhere nobody could find me, and I wondered what life would be like in the peace of the far southwest around the Helford River. And with these thoughts in mind I got in touch with the agent Phil had mentioned.

Eclipse Promotions was the agency, a very apt title as it happened,

Kishorn and Star Gazey Pie.

The oil platform at Loch Kishorn in the Scottish Highlands. *1976*
It became a regular winter gig! At the upper left is the old Italian liner we used as digs Il Pensione Stronso.

(below) Here's Kit, socking it to 'em on the Star Gazey Pie Show Westward Television. *1977*
With top class pickers Steve Turner on guitar Tim Collingwood on banjo.

STAR GAZEY PIE

FRANK YONCO and KIT CONNORS

Picture taken during ATV'S NEW FACES Television show.
Contact: Rainbow Club, St. Blazey, Cornwall. 072 681 229?

walker

Presenting a new image on the New Faces All Winners Show. *October 1976*

The Wembley Festival *1979*

INTERNATIONAL COUNTRY MUSIC STAR

Frank Yonco

Photo taken at the International Casino, Nairobi, Kenya,
during East African tour, November 1980.

CARL PERKINS. London 1980

SAINT-MALO

Saint-Malo

Justice et Liberté

Jeudi
30 juin 1983

Nº 11 764   2,60 F

Normandie - Bretagne
Pays de Loire

Fondateur :
Paul Hutin-Desgrées
Président : Louis Estrangin
Rennes - Tél. (99) 03.62.22

ouest france

Franck Yonco et son orchestre au casino: rythmes et nostalgies du Texas

Le chapeau texan rivé sur le crâne, ce n'est pas « J.R. », c'est Franck Yonco, et si ce dernier ne vient pas de Dallas, c'est tout comme puisqu'il arrive de Galveston, au Texas. Lui, son épouse Kitty qui est la chanteuse du groupe et ses musiciens sont pour trois mois sur la Côte d'Emeraude. Après avoir animé en juin le casino de Dinard, ils seront en juillet et août sur la place Chateaubriand à Saint-Malo. On a tout dit sur la « country music » qui a son temple à Nashville et ses adorateurs partout dans le monde. Encore faut-il savoir qu'il y a autant de nuances

dans la « folk-song » qu'il y en a dans le jazz :

« Nous chantons le monde tel qu'il est, précise Yonco, et non tel qu'il devrait être : avec ses problèmes de boulot, d'alcool, de solitude et de violence. Si notre musique est teintée d'une certaine nostalgie, c'est que le Texas est malgré tout notre « sweet home ». Et puis, même si on est sans illusions sur la société actuelle, on se souvient que ce sont les vraies valeurs qui ont permis de bâtir l'Amérique : le travail, l'honnêteté et la foi dans son dieu et dans son pays. »

Cet ancien boxeur et conducteur de poids lourds qui fut aussi un vétéran du Viet Nam connaît bien la France pour y revenir fréquemment. Il court aussi le monde, de l'Angleterre à l'Australie, en passant par l'Espagne et le Japon. Baladins du monde occidental, lui et ses musiciens sont autant de messagers du grand rêve américain : quand il restait dans l'Ouest des terres à conquérir, le pistolet à la ceinture et la guitare dans le dos.

Jean-Claude WEISZ.

Chaque soir, au restaurant du Casino.

1983 Our second welcome to france.
A clipping from The Ouest France announcing our show at
Dinard Casino.
(Certainly a better welcome than the first one back in 1966)

Frank Yonco and Kit Connor

J.D. and DALLAS
EARLY SUNDAY MORNING
Frank Yonco and Kit Connor

J.D. and DALLAS

because in terms of commission charges, deductions, and expenses they charged both the sun and moon, and were as slow in paying due fees. This vast Cornish 'Coast to Coast' network was run from the front room of a bungalow in Trelisk by a young, energetic young man called Peter. He was as smooth and slippery as an eel but, in spite of his constant wheeling and dealing, I liked him and I got the impression that one day he would make real big bucks. A contract was arranged and we made our plans.

After finishing the South Wales tour and the gigs set up by the Jigsaw Agency in Harrogate and North Yorkshire, we returned to our base in Manchester. Dave the drummer left the band for the umpteenth time and was replaced by a moody–looking young man from Rochdale called Martin Brewster, who fitted in very well with our new West Coast image. (California, I mean. not Blackpool.)

Serious car troubles then began. The Mercedes started to show back axle wear, mainly due to the constant high speed runs to the high paying clubs in South Yorkshire. These were the days before the construction of the M62 Motorway and that cross–Pennine route was a killer, so I put the car in for repair. Our Transit was also acting up and yet another sodding gearbox jammed. The transmission on these early models was a constant weak point, either the half shafts would shear, or more often it was the gearbox that seized up. It seemed as though we were buying a fresh vehicle every year, although it must be said that we were doing terrific mileages carry– ing heavy loads. By this time I had learned how to recognize the early symptoms and, when the gear box began to stiffen, I knew it was time to make a change and true to form, I left it to the last minute, in this case the Saturday morning we were leaving for Cornwall.

At a garage on Cheetham Hill Road I had found a beautiful white Bedford Ambulance. Oh Yes, it was beautiful indeed, but unknown to me at the time it was completely knackered. The body was fine but on opening the hood I found the engine marked B.E.R. in white paint. The salesman said that it probably meant Bedford Engine Replacement. (He was a very good salesman). I found out later that it actually stood for Beyond Economical Repair. And it was. However in my traditional 'Bull in a China Shop' way I charged ahead and did a deal. The papers were signed, a little money changed hands and the smarmy salesman ushered me into my new possession, smiling to himself as he gently reversed our freshly washed part–exchange Transit into line. As I eased out into the main road, I caught a glimpse of him, red faced, trying to get it in first gear. Mind you, I did not see him too clearly as I appeared to be being followed by a cloud of black smoke. Umm, Curious?

This cloud followed me all the way back to Kit's house, where the band was waiting for the next adventure to begin. And how did they welcome our new chariot? Er—Well, sort of mixed really. It looked nice but as there was no time to convert it, our gear was bundled into the back and everybody crowded aboard, either lying down on the built–in stretchers or in the cab, and we were off to the great unknown. By the time we were rolling down Princess Parkway, six miles into Cheshire, there was a loud banging on the back panels of the cab so I pulled over and the musicians came spluttering and coughing out of the back.

"The bloody thing's full of fumes!" they gasped. "We can't soddin' breathe in there!"

By now the black cloud had gone but a film of oil and dirt covered both back doors and on the dashboard the oil light was a bright blue dot confirming that the engine was burning oil. Quite a lot of oil in fact. That journey to Cornwall required twelve gallons of it. Yes, that's right a full Twelve Gallons of Castrol GTX.

We opened all the windows and forced open the roof ventilators and changed them round to become air scoops, which improved conditions inside somewhat. The trip to the Sunset County then continued with a choice of three travel options. Either drive, crush up into the cab or lie down in the relative comfort of the back and fight for breath. There was always of course the fourth option: To call the whole thing off, but nobody mentioned that. (Ain't life on the road just great?). In spite of its astronomic oil consumption our shiny new acquisition was quite a flyer and its big wheels and long nose made it feel much safer than our earlier 'Dagenham Dustbins' and, by the early evening of October 23rd 1971, we were across the Tamar Bridge and into Cornwall and a new set of adventures began.

The Driftwood Spars

Our first show was to be at Mount Charles Social Club in St. Austell. Negotiating the narrow dog's leg lane leading to the clubroom was a feat in itself, but the reception more than compensated for our difficult journey. The place was packed with fat jolly people slugging down pint after pint of the local ale and having noisy conversations in accents I had never heard before, while in one corner friendly, fussy, buxom ladies were doling out mountains of Cornish pasties and ham sandwiches. The most incongruous thing of all was the affable Concert Secretary, who turned out to be a Geordie. This man really knew his stuff and soon had everything organized, directing a bunch of muscular young Cornishmen to help us unload. It also appeared that our reputation of being a hard–drinking band had arrived ahead of us, because as soon as we were set up, the stage was lined with pints and Kit and I were given a bottle of Jack Daniels and a crate of cokes. Yeah, I thought, just my kind of people.

The show went well. Good music, free drinks, a crowded dance floor and plenty to eat, all contributed to the great evening. So that by the time midnight came everybody was happy and Geordie was badgering me for a return date. So far it had been an outstanding night but there was more to come. It was time to move along. I banged yet another gallon of oil in the engine, while the customers helped the lads load up, laughing and joking and singing traditional Cornish songs in superb harmony.

"Going' up Camborne 'ill, comin' down."

And another gentle ballad devoted to a local beauty who was just a bit thick.

"Woit stockin's, woit stockins' she wore, but she couldn't tell sugar from shite"

They were having a great time, oohin' and aarrin' at the top of their voices all round us. It sounded like a TV commercial for Country Life butter. Another jolly wave, and we were off bumping up the dog's–leg lane again, then over the hump backed railway bridge and down the winding hill into sleepy St. Austell town centre.

"Where are we staying tonight, then?" Asked Karl.

I was driving so Kit rummaged in her bag to check our itinerary.

"The Driftwood Spars Hotel" She replied. "Wherever that is."

Karl reached for the map and after checking it, told me to head for Truro.

In all my years on the road, Karl was by far the best navigator I ever had. His eyesight was unbelievable and he could clearly read road signs that most of us could barely see. He would've made a great sniper. He planned all our travel schedules and, barring accidents, we would arrive at our destination within minutes of his estimated time. He proved to be an excellent bass player as well as a great pathfinder.

By now it was pitch black, and the euphoria of our first evening was beginning to wear off. The night was wild and stormy, no moon yet, with gusting rain and a strong wind howling across the empty farmland all around us. The bright lights of Truro came and went and the farms and bungalows thinned out until we were driving across wild gorse moorland. We stopped to read the signs at the Redruth to Bodmin road and then headed straight on to our destination. Mount Hawk was to our left and at last, as the pale moon broke from its cloud cover, we passed the abandoned railway station at Goonbell and skittered round the bend into St Agnes.

Nothing moved. Every window was shuttered; every door barred and by now a steady rain was cascading from the stone gutters. We pushed on, past the closed up St. Agnes Hotel, and down past some flint cottages to a small square where several roads met. I stopped the bus and switched off the engine and the true ferocity of the storm hit us. The wind howled while not far away was the deep sound of roaring breakers and the delayed answering echoes from nearby granite cliffs.

Here there was no sign of life, not even a stray dog or cat, only the dreadful roaring of the wind and the wild sea. There was something though. On the far side of the square was an unlit phone box so I decided to try that. Head down and collar up I splashed across the road and took shelter inside the kiosk and dialed. 'O'. There was a brr–brr and then a soft female voice with a gentle Cornish lilt came on the line.

"Yes, c'noi 'elp yew then?"

I told her where we were and that we were looking for the Driftwood Spars Hotel.

"Oh, Zurr!" She gasped, "Yew'm agoin' there now? Tis a bit late y'know."

I said that we were booked in there and were expected.

"Waal, me 'andsom," she burred. "Tis easy to find from where yew'm to now. Yew jus' turn left. No, no 'tis roite, yes roite. An' then y'go down far as yew can go. Almost to the beach an' there 'tis. Yew'm can't miss un." Then she added wistfully. "Tis luverley in zummer down there. G'noit, Zurr."

A little dazed by her fascinating accent I climbed back aboard and pointed the Bedford's nose downhill, let in the clutch and prayed that I had got the instructions right. The road narrowed and descended steeply twisting and turning all the way, with the waves getting louder all the time, and the wind rocking the big vehicle. Finally we rounded a tight bend and there it was—the Driftwood Spars Hotel.

Was I dreaming? The whole place was ablaze with lights. Music was thundering out of the windows and the open doors. Cars were parked on both sides of the road and people were dancing in the rain, eating pasties and guzzling beer and gin from the bottle. It was like a mad Mardi Gras carnival. I really thought I must be hallucinating and began to wonder if someone had spiked my drinks at the club with marijuana. I checked my watch. It was 1.45am. Was this really St. Agnes in sleepy tranquil Cornwall? Open–mouthed and dazed, we staggered out into the now–forgotten storm and lurched inside with people cheering and shaking our hands like some long lost expedition, thumping our backs, giving us gap–toothed grins and waving pint pots. It was packed to the gills. A pleasant young man with a huge handlebar moustache pushed through the crowds to greet us.

"Hello!" He yelled above the din. "I'm Robin the manager. Welcome to the Driftwood Spars. Get your bags in and the girls will see you to your rooms." (Girls? Rooms? We began to think we'd like it here) "and then you can come down and meet all our other guests."

"They all guests, then?" I asked dumbly.

Robin gave me a funny look and coughed, "Well, they are all booked in for the night. Got to be to make it legal."

Over his shoulder I saw the local Police Sergeant and a massive constable in the kitchen, each with foaming jugs of Devenish Bitter, so I did not ask any more silly questions. Everybody seemed to know everybody else and we met several other bands and acts that were also touring Cornwall. Johnny and the Sunsets, Dave and June Taylor, plus a couple of local acts I did not know, and some old friends from Paddy Kelly's band who had decided to stay on when Paddy had gone back to Liverpool. There was even a group of marathon revelers who had followed us from Mount Charles.

The wild party went on till dawn, by which time people were sleeping all over the place, on the banquettes under the tables, in the kitchen and the wine cellars, not counting the lucky ones who had taken over the bedrooms. I don't remember where I slept, but next morning I was in the kitchen sipping sweet coffee and nibbling an aspirin omelet when Robin, genial as ever, came rolling in, swirling his ever–present brandy goblet and introduced us to our agent from Truro. I thought it was a bit early for an agent to be up and around, but it turned out that he had been there all night, and everybody had been too drunk to make the introductions. He was a very polite young guy and, most unusual for an agent, he asked me if we wanted any money. Then he gave us a new revised list of venues for the tour. A couple of nights were actually at the Driftwood Spars and most of the others were relatively nearby, the most distant being the Carlton ballroom in Liskeard about thirty miles away. This Carlton gig was also destined to be a regular booking, though it really only came about by accident.

The Carlton, Liskeard

Up to our arrival in Cornwall the most popular big show bands were Trad Jazz bands. In fact the county produced some really top–class musicians in that field, like trumpeter Rod Mason, clarinetist Ian Wheeler, and the talented artist and accordion piano player Morley Westcombe, who played regularly with the county's top band the Clay City Stompers from Mevagissey. In fact, Liskeard's Carlton Suite was actually advertised as a Trad Jazz venue. It was a large cinema, which had been cleverly converted into a social club complete with two bars, a restaurant, a nice dance floor, and a big, fully–equipped stage with lighting, curtains and a good sound system. The place was always busy because, situated in East Cornwall, it drew its patrons from Plymouth as well as central Cornwall. In fact the owners had opened their first club in that city and, as they prospered, many of their clients had followed them to Liskeard. Our first contact came about in a somewhat bizarre way.

One evening we were sitting in the Driftwood Spars Hotel wondering how to spend our evening off when a phone call came in from Peter Bawden. 'Could we get up to the Carlton as quickly as possible?' It was an emergency and he said craftily 'It could lead to a few good gigs.'

"How much? "I asked.

"Oh, about a ton n'arf (£150) "He said, qualifying the paltry fee by going on about the prospects of regular bookings at one of the top Cornish venues. I looked around the bar of the empty hotel and thought that a hundred and fifty quid was better than nothing, so we took the job.

The owner greeted us enthusiastically on our arrival and hustled us on stage. We did a great show and the dance floor was crowded and, as is normal at Country Music gigs, the bars did record business. The owner coughed up the money and flushed with the success of the evening, told us the reason for the call. He had booked and advertised the Syd Phillips Band, but they had had some kind of emergency on the way down from Birmingham and in a panic he had phoned our agent in Truro, to see if anyone was available at short notice. He was very grateful for our un-precedented appearance and the fine show we had put on, and gave us an extra fifteen quid. He bought us a drink. A VERY RARE event indeed. This got me thinking but it was only on the way back that I realized that he had kept the place full by paying us £165. (less 10% commission to Eclipse of course) instead of the £500 plus he would have had to pay out to Syd Phillips.

However on the good side, we did get a lot of gigs at the Carlton at a fair price, and we did make a lot of money for them, but that's what promotion is all about I suppose. Really, I mark this gig as being the beginning of our deep relationship with Cornwall and the start of a connection that is still strong. During the following ten years, we established a whole community of entertainers and musicians down there, many of whom are still resident in Cornwall, enjoying the laid-back lifestyle of the Sunset County.

As this first tour came to an end, we began to put the final touches to the live show album we were scheduled to make for Decca Records. Everybody was psyched up for it, and by now we had sorted out the problems with our new band-wagon. The interior had been gutted, new seats fitted, and I had a brand new engine installed by a local garage in St Agnes. They did the job in three days and it proved to be the best £350 investment I ever made. Actually for all of us, this tour could not have happened at better time, as I was concerned that we were becoming a bit jaded playing the blasé Northern Club Circuit, where the audiences were used to at least one top-line cabaret act every week. The honest enthusiasm of these Far Western punters was a pleasant surprise, and we began to sharpen up and take a greater interest in our performances.

By far the weirdest gig on this circuit was at a converted cinema in a small village on the main coastal road to St Austell. It was a most bizarre venue. There was no booze. And—wait for it—No electricity. (Probably due to an unpaid bill).

Fortunately there was a pub across the car park, which was doing a roaring trade in carry-outs As we rolled up to the front door, we almost crashed into a mobile electric generator that had been borrowed from the local quarry, along with its semi-inebriated operator, to provide current for our equipment and the temporary lighting. Inside the place, it was all damp and dismal, the owners working to the principle that it was cheaper to put red bulbs in the toilets rather than employ a cleaner.

The show itself went well and though we did not pick up any money there, the well-inebriated punters and the bickering owners treated us very well. (More about them later)

In the meantime, let's go to London. It's time we made another record.

* * * * * *

Frank Yonco & the Everglades
Live at the Nashville Rooms

After three great weeks in Cornwall, we packed up the bus again and made for London and our recording date at Decca Records. The band I put together for this session were road–hardened experienced top professionals. Dave Marks was on drums, Karl Benson on bass, the brilliant Jim Hornsby on guitar, and Tom 'Smiley' Bowker playing dobro and five string banjo, adding a bright new dimension to our solid basic country–rock sound. The other session men would be waiting for us in London

Ted Poulton and Charlie Stevenson, the irrepressible manager of the Nashville Rooms theme pub, had somehow persuaded the Decca people to make our album at their venue during a week's tour of the Fuller pub circuit. Martin Grinham, who at that time was still with Decca, was there producing along with a brilliant sound engineer called Martin Smith and, of course, the ever present Jessie Kent. I never did work out exactly what she did. The recording unit itself was a bit late in arriving, as they had been in Vienna recording the Boys Choir from that city, so we did not really get under way until the Wednesday. In the meantime Rod King arrived to play pedal steel, and a pal of Smiley's came in to play a bit of fiddle. Rod King was certainly at that time, and probably still is, one of the best steel players in the UK. He was my first slide guitarist back in 1958 and he is still up there, along with greats like Bob Dixon, Pete Heywood, BJ Cole and Derek Thurlby

The session was great, thanks to superb engineering from Smithy and first class imaginative production from Martin, who selected most of the tracks. It wasn't easy for them, because the only place for a control room was in an upstairs guest bedroom, so most production was done by closed circuit TV. The taping was done over four sessions, two of them live shows, and two afternoon closed sessions, but Martin's clever editing made the finished product sound like one live concert. The wonderful Tex Withers was the resident compere and added to the atmosphere with his deep Dixie tones. I can hear him now wishing the wild audience.

"Safe home, Folks. An' don' fergit yo' sang–widges frum the baowr."

The musicians excelled themselves. Karl Benson playing bass guitar with a pick to get a clicking toppy sound, punctuating the solid bass beat. Dave Marks, ever–inventive, used a technique he had learned from the American session drummers of using two sticks in the right hand to play cymbals, giving that running effect often heard on Nashville records. Smiley Bowker, of course was astounding on dobro and banjo, while Jimmy Hornsby left us all breathless with his fantastic performance on Telecaster, swapping licks with Rod King's lightening steel guitar work. Absolutely superb. Looking back over the years I've been in this business world wide, I consider Jim Hornsby as the finest exponent of the Fender Telecaster I have ever heard, and that includes Buck Owens and Albert Lee. Kit and I split the vocals with Karl and Smiley Bowker providing back–up harmony. About the only person who was not happy was the girl photographer. who shot off a dozen rolls in the smoke filled Nashville Rooms before she got an album cover shot that pleased her.

The finished product was very good, the precursor of a decade of good Country records in Great Britain and it became a benchmark in live show recording. Regrettably, petty squabbles and jealousy spoiled the potential. Martin Grinham left Decca to join his former boss at Valentine Music, while the Decca project was handed over to Louis Rogers' son Frank, who had other ideas, and the result was a succession of below par productions, which were in the deleted racks almost as soon has they hit the shops.

Decca certainly made a bold move in trying to gain respect for the music and get it accepted as genre but the attempt was not successful at that time. It is true that Pye had made an earlier stab at it with its Lucky label, but the target then had been the dedicated fan. The series did not sell well on general release and found most of its buyers in the Country Music clubs. In fact it took another fifteen years before the music was grudgingly accepted as 'Easy Listening.' Why did it take so long? Who knows? Was it just a fashion of the times? Maybe it was too American. In fact, as far back as 1968 Buck Owens tried to get it classified as American Music, or maybe it was too blunt in its message and its factual revelation of real life situations, who knows?

As for sales and distribution, well that's a different tale and the market–ing men are always wary about things they don't fully understand. As an example, take a quote I read in one of the music papers in the sixties from that mail–order teacher of all things musical Maurice Berman, who said:

'The mumbling, out of time, style of Elvis Presley will soon pass and be forgotten.'

A lot he knew. He was also the man who in the early fifties forecast that singer Jo Stafford had no future in the music business as her voice lacked vibrato.

Grinding On

Soon the heady days of recording were over and we were back on the hard grind of the road. First stop was to play a circuit of seedy clubs around York, and then up to Bonny Scotland. Digs were at a damp neglected house near the oil refinery at Grangemouth, hardly the Bonny Scotland we'd been expecting. So the usual rounds began—clubs with early finishes and half the audiences running out at the end of the Bingo, so that the third spot of the evening was played out to the sounds of the club steward cashing up and the waiters keeping time by banging chairs on the tables for the cleaners. Wednesday night the clubs were closed so, having a night off, we wandered down to the local pub called the Charlotte Dundas, named after the first steam–powered ship on the Clyde. It was a nice little place with one disadvantage. It closed at 9.30 p.m. The boys ran to form of course. David getting canned every night, Karl falling in love with the landlady's daughter (married, of course) and the others grim–faced and sulking. At that time it was considered un–cool to be caught smiling if you were a professional musician.

We visited the throbbing metropolis of Falkirk, doing the standard club artiste's tour of cafés and music shops. At one of them I traded my Baldwin Virginian guitar for a beautiful Fender Newporter which I still own. The Newporter was a very rare mahogany–faced acoustic with a Telecaster neck that Fender produced as a venture into the burgeoning Country–Folk market. They only produced about five hundred of them but, finding pro-duction costs too high, changed the format to cheaper timber and adding an acoustic truss rod that ran through the body to produce the Palomino range, including a 12–string version called the Shenandoah.

At the time, however, entertainers were not all that welcome, because the town had been rocked by a scandal when pop singer Danny Williams had been caught puffing a joint in one of the big hotels. What with him being black as well, the air was thick with rumors of drug pushers and white slavery. It was really nothing by today's standards, but back then in the bigoted Kirk–dominated lowlands of Scotland, it was considered very serious indeed. I think Danny was lucky to get away with only a fine. The way things were up there, he could easily have spent Christmas in Barlin-nie.

At this juncture we were floating, that is to say, not being booked by one exclusive agent so we had a few problems. A taxi operator and part time agent called Bogie had booked this particular portion of our time and I remember having a bit of trouble with him. After the last show we spent most of the following day haunting his office and various clubs for our money. Finally we caught up with him at his house late in the afternoon when he was recovering from his lunchtime booze up. Luckily his minders were equally ineffective. There was a bit of stalling but I was carrying a tyre lever and when I proposed to plant him alongside one of his garden gnomes he came up with the cash. I really don't understand why he was cursing us when we left. After all we'd earned it. Nobody robbed him

Cornish Cream and Devon Dumplings

By 1972 were well established now on the Devon and Cornwall circuit so we decided to promote an open–air Country Music Festival at the St. Austell Speedway Arena. It was a scorching Sunday in July and we hired a big stage and all sorts of attractions, including side shows, fortune tellers, hot dog stands, ice cream vendors and a whole children's play park with bouncy castles and clowns. Music–wise we had quite a few local acts and a number of touring bands including Pat Kelly's band, and the great Tex Withers came down to perform and MC the show, making a tremendous impact on the fans.

But a week previously it had all been in the balance, when the Lord's Day Observance Society stepped in to say that we could not charge entrance fees on a Sunday. It all seemed like a no-go until Kit and I got thinking it out and came up with a solution. Entrance would be free but we requested that the fans each bought a program, which entitled them to take part in a prize draw. So between that income and the concession charges from the vendors we cleared our costs and kept everybody happy. We even made a few bob.

After that long hot season in the West Country we took off again on the road. There was the usual winter tours of the North of England and Scotland, we got as far North as Scrabster and Thurso, with the obligatory visit to Barrow and the Lake district on the way back and then across the country to play at the US Bases on the Suffolk coast and clubs in Essex.

Later in the year when we were back in Manchester, my cousin contacted me about doing a TV show. Her husband, David Henshaw was a producer at Granada, and had a three times a week spot to fill after the local news around 7 p.m. They had seen our touring show when they had both been at Anglia Television a couple of years previously, and David thought that the fact that a British band had been in Vietnam was unique enough to warrant a feature spot. It was to be our first UK TV exposure so I grabbed at the chance.

We were booked for a week at the Duke of Wellington pub in Swinton, so it was decided to do an Outside Broadcast (OB) from there on October 18th. We did a couple of afternoon rehearsals and sound and vision checks and, as Karl had commitments in Cornwall, Martin's mate, Ian Gilliat came in on bass. We had a great week, with the place packed to the gills every night.

The TV show was an absolute blockbuster and when it went out a week later. Sadly, in spite of recent lengthy enquiries I could find no video record of this show in the Granada archives.

There was a promise of more to come with preliminary discussions about a series, but it all came to nothing, as did David and Judy's marriage. They divorced and he returned to other parts of the media, while Judy stayed at Granada and reclaimed her family name of Finnegan, and after marrying a local presenter called Richard Madely, fronted a very successful US style TV daytime magazine show.

We played Christmas week in Manchester and finished the year with a week at Pickwicks Club in Liverpool. Yes it was hard going.

1973 kicked off with my being a sponsor on Hughie Green's Opportunity Knocks TV Show for my old friend Reliable Ralph, the comedian. (When will I ever learn?). He did very well, but I don't know what became of it, 'though I did meet Hughie again sometime later at our own disastrous audition in Bristol.

About the best thing that came out of that trip was that I got to see the Nitty Gritty Dirt Band at the Nashville Rooms and became a fan forever.

What a sound! I loved the way Jeff Hanna and the boys switched styles from classics like 'Old Dog Blue' to modern hits like 'The House at Poo Corner'. Superb.

Cornwall was still pulling so we decided to head back and consolidate our early success there. The crowds were glad to see us again and we worked to the limit. The summer seasons were long and the good weather brought holidaymakers in the thousands. Mr. Leggett's fairground on Carlyon Bay Beach came up for sale and was bought by the McNallys, an enterprising family from the Midlands, who converted it to become one of the most modern big venues on the concert circuit. It was superb, with a massive concert hall boasting the longest bar in the UK, with several smaller suites, one of which became a regular Saturday night gig plus the most spectacular disco on the Cornish Riviera.

However, at the prospect of another long season in Cornwall the band changed again, with Johnny Laing coming in on drums and Trevor Couchman taking the steel guitar spot. They both fitted very nicely with Karl on bass, and one of their first jobs was backing Kit and I on a record-ing session with Tony Waldron's label. 'West of England Sound' in Torquay. The result was a clean but bouncy album called 'If you don't like Hank Williams,' which, I am reliably informed, has now become a sought–after cult pressing, bringing big money from serious collectors.

In the early years our visits to Cornwall had been organized by the Eclipse Agency, and we had been based at the Driftwood Spars in St. Agnes. As the seasons extended and the manager, Robin, had more friction with his boss, who wanted him to run a pub in Newquay as well, it became obvious that we needed to find a new base. The owners of a club offered us accommodation at good rates in their big house in St. Austell. It was a good central location, which was essential because at the time we were doing six or seven gigs a week, from St. Germans to Penzance. In fact at that time the scene was developing rapidly and continued to do so right through the Seventies. The acts in the Cornwall, South Devon areas were keeping very busy and making good money. I think that the record for gigs per week reached its peak with a duo from Wales called Bicycle in the summer of 1975 with eleven full gigs in seven days.

But now it was time for another adventure. How about opening a nightclub?

*   *   *   *   *   *

26

THE STARS AND BARS
Alice, Bob and Tommy

Within the first week of our stay at the big house it became obvious that the two owners of the club were not quite in agreement how it should be run. They were nice people but neither of them had been in the hard world of club operation before. Previously they had both been involved in the more refined world of air travel, Bob as an office manager and Alice had been some kind of courier, when such occupations still had glamour and charisma.

I was curious as to how they had become club owners, so I began to ask around at a busy pub in Par where the innkeeper knew all the local gossip. His name was Richard and he was a very outgoing jolly figure, who enjoyed being Mine Host, offering drinks to all and sundry and using any excuse to have a party. He blatantly left all the business worries to his harassed wife, who got her own back by never missing an opportunity to pull him up in front of his assembled boozing pals—so much so that the pub soon became known as the Dick and Dragon. This is the story he told me.

Apparently a few years previously, a shadowy figure arrived in the village and bought the old building, and proceeded to convert it into a nightclub. It had previously been a wool warehouse, a local jail, an auction hall and most recently a cinema. Local gossip had it that he was very slippery, a fast mover from 'Somewhere up Country 'who had built a reputation for being a ruthless operator, and in the innocent Bob and Alice he saw another golden chance. A few things were now closing in on him and he was ready to drop his latest venture on somebody's toes, and who better than this naïve couple. For the purpose of this narrative we will call him Tommy.

'Tommy the Taker' as the locals knew him, was not a Cornishman. As a child he had been evacuated to the county from the Midlands at the beginning of the Second World War, and he had stayed on. The old couple that took him in became fond of him and came to regard him as the son they never had. When his real parents separated Tommy grew to maturity in the Cornish house, and in time he influenced the old people to sign over the family home to him as a tax dodge. This done, Tommy simply banged them both in an old people's home and sold the house, lock, stock and barrel, the cash providing a power base for several shady property deals, and several suspect retirement homes across the county.

'Clubland' was still booming in the North but the necessary expertise to operate such an establishment had not yet penetrated into the deep South West. Tommy soon realized that unless he invested some cash and brought in specialized staff he would have a loser on his hands and would soon be calling the place the White Elephant, so his evil genius got to work.

Alice and her friend had rented a small shop at the side of the club as a local craft centre, and she was soon involved in doing little jobs for Tommy, like picking up the mail and letting the cleaners in. On his almost daily contact with this rather bored lady he remarked how busy the club was, and told her of his grandiose plans for a rosy future of a big network of cabaret clubs throughout Devon and Cornwall, and a booking agency that would bring in the best acts in the country, but he needed some help to activate these ambitions, so 'Could she come in a couple of nights a week, just to help out with the bar and keep an eye on things for him? He would pay her for her time etc.' Alice was flattered and enthusiastically agreed— this was the chance she had been seeking to rub shoulders with showbiz stars and return to the glamorous life. Tommy was very pleased and saw to it that she did the quiet nights like Tuesdays and Thursdays.

It was not long before husband Bob became jealous; especially when Alice started rolling home worse for wear at two in the morning. She mentioned this to her new found friend Tommy who suggested that if her Bob would like a piece of the action as well, he could help out by doing the books. Like his wife, Bob jumped at the chance. He prided himself on his book keeping and at the same time he could keep his eye on swinging Alice. Tommy's plan was working like a charm as they both became mesmerized by his showbiz plans. Alice loved the buzz of it all while Bob became very self–important as the official bookkeeper and cashier. Tommy, craftily only used them on the off–peak nights, but every time Bob came in Tommy gave him a big bunch of notes and coin to sort out, saying it was the previous night's takings, which really impressed Bob as he duly checked it all and paid it into the local bank. Tommy was equally pleased when he went down to the bank the following day to draw it all out again and repeat the pantomime.

One morning, over an intimate coffee in the upstairs office away from the prying eyes of the cleaners, Tommy mentioned to Alice that he was on the lookout for a buyer for the club. Bigger opportunities had now presented themselves in St Ives where he had been invited to join a syndicate planning to develop a theme park there. "Did she know anybody who might be interested?," he asked innocently.

His dart hit the mark. Alice could hardly wait to pass on the news of this fantastic opportunity to Bob. He pushed his glasses to the end of his nose and warned her not to be hasty but he was already hooked. After all, who better to assess the true potential than himself? He was already doing the books. And to think of all that free booze.

Six weeks later the deal was done and by raising a mortgage on their big house they paid Tommy's price and became proud owners of their first (and last) nightclub. Tommy of course, cashed the cheque and took a long holiday in Italy, the phantom St Ives theme park forgotten. Within a month Bob and Alice were at each other's throats about the running of the club. He was putting whisky away wholesale and she was getting the flat–tering attentions of the male patrons:—and that was the state of play when we arrived back in Cornwall from a tour of the North of England.

There were eight of us now, Kit and I, Johnny our drummer, on the run from Salford with his impressive girl friend Big Dee, and steel guitarist Trevor who also brought along his elegant wife–to–be, plus bassist Karl with a beautiful Manchester girl called Diane in tow, although at this point Karl's arm was still in plaster, due to an accident involving the earlier than expected return from sea of a certain lady's husband at St. Agnes.

It was a big house and we were very comfortable there, working every evening and sunbathing every afternoon in the vast garden. Alice would sit with us discussing her problems with her husband, and their difficulties in running the club, while Bob would sulk in his office with a bottle of single malt. She would ask us questions and we would answer her queries with ease. The lavish cabaret clubs of the north were where we had got our first breaks, so it was natural for us and eventually she got round to asking if Kit and I were interested in joining her and Bob in running the place. Her reason was that she would like to go into the showbiz digs business in a big way, and that she was worried that Bob's excessive drinking was under-mining his health.

Kit and I were cautious about the proposal but said we might be inter-ested in leasing it from them for a fixed period, complete as it was and that she could involve herself if she wanted. After that things moved very quickly and we signed a lease on October 16 1973.and named the new club 'The Stars and Bars'.

The days became hectic. We moved to a small chalet at Tredenham House near the club where I was now heavily involved in the conversion. Kit supervised the layout of kitchen and fitted out and stocked the new bars I built. We also built a new stage and dressing rooms. Peter Dew helped me and he was an indispensable human dynamo and seemingly, an expert on everything, electrics, cooking, carpentry, and putting in a com-plete new sound system.

Johnny, our drummer, became involved in a nominal capacity and did most of the art work for the posters and signs, but the other members of the band were not interested. It was agreed that we would accept gigs until Christmas, after which the band would break up and I could concentrate on the running of the Stars and Bars. As the club took shape we moved into the flat at the side of the building, and had a door knocked through so that we need not leave the building at all, and we could have some great parties when all the punters had left.

In the middle of all this I was getting heavy pressure from Alice and Bob for money. Originally they had agreed to wait until we opened up but for some reason changed their minds. I went to Lloyds Bank in Plymouth and true to all their adverts they listened, but that is all they did. Finally, by signing my life away for the next ten years, I got financial support from a brewery in Redruth and all the time somehow doing five or six gigs a week.

I met some great people though; a big Cockney ex–sailor called Ted Schroff came in as House Manager. He was absolutely superb. A great personality who had had such an interesting and varied life as a Royal Navy first mate, Merchant seaman, policeman, butcher, cook, taxi driver, pro-wrestler, London underground train driver and a publican. What a character. He had three sons who later formed the successful pop group Birth and he also managed that. Then I found a knockout compere/comedian called Al Jackson who, as it happened, also came from London. And by 30th November 1973 we were ready to open up.

Curtain up.

It was a great opening night, packed to full capacity and the acts booked for the weekend were Al Jackson, folk group Rivondell and comedy magician Peter Kane, and our band playing for dancing. The kitchen service worked like a dream but Kit found it hard overseeing both the bar and the food service, so we brought in the elegant ex–air hostess Jill Oliver and a perky Cornish girl called Mo to keep the bar crowd happy, and one of the musicians volunteered to become bar manager. We also advertised for waitresses and recruited some real good–looking beauties, including a couple of dark–haired full figured Cornish girls, a big brash blonde from London, a warm hearted northern girl and two Devon dumplings from Ply-mouth. So there was something for everybody.

It also didn't take us long to realize that paying the band just for dancing was not really viable, so we got hold of a DJ and once again the ubiquitous Peter Dew took on the job. Was there anything that this guy couldn't do? On the door we had the husband of one of our waitresses. He was the tough quarryman who had provided the generator on our first trip to the club. A perky, bright girl from the local bank ran the box–office and they blended very well. (In more ways than one, as it happened).

The first crisis was not long in arriving. Billy Fury was booked for the Sunday show but he did not arrive and Al Jackson went missing as well, but somehow we got through the night and when Billy finally showed up at 9 p.m. on Tuesday we had a good show. I had sub–contracted him out to other clubs but that proved to be a disaster as well, with a club at Penryn paying me short and Billy doing another No Show at Plymouth. He was proving to be about as reliable as George Jones. Apart from that one hitch we did real good business by combining imported acts with local talent until the end of the year.

There were a few wreckers of course. A visiting comedian friend of mine from Manchester (yes, that's right. Mr. Reliable) came down to see us and bought a sailing dinghy from a local butcher but forgot to pay for it, and two of our regular punters got caught pulling a fire insurance scam in St. Austell. The second and more serious crisis arrived when I finally had to tell Sylvia that I would not be coming home for Xmas, which proved to be the last nail in the coffin of our marriage. Who could blame her? She and Derek had plans of their own by now.

The Christmas Show was a wow and featured a group that I booked from

Blackpool called Alias, which included two musicians who stayed on in the Duchy and are still there. One was the virtuoso guitarist Steve Turner and the other a very talented but somewhat unstable drummer called Gary (Or El Loco Normales as he preferred to be known, due to the reduced level of blood in his coke-stream)—Unstable? You bet. He had done the lot—as Bobby Bare once said about one of his sidemen. "There was nothing he wouldn't drink, smoke or shoot up." For example, on one gig his girl friend arrived and Gary asked who was minding their baby?

"Oh, he's all right. He's fast asleep," she shrugged. At which point Gary went berserk, dragged her home and cut off lumps of her hair for neglecting his son.

Oh yes he was a real Main Line Man, was our Gary.

Arriving during the same holiday period were two young men from South Wales who called themselves Bicycle. Only guitar, drums and vocals but they were great. One of them, Howard, settled in the Duchy and became a talented children's entertainer as well. It really was the start of big influx of talent into Cornwall where up-country entertainers found a very busy season available in the growing profusion of hotels and holiday camps, and soon the word was out.

Dave Wayne returned to Cornwall with Paddy Kelly's Tennessee Four after which he formed a band called Hobo and virtually cornered the Rock 'n' Roll market, until the emergence of Colin Price Jones' band 'Shades' in the mid 70's. Musically it was a great time and the club was booming, but there were the usual operating troubles. Noise problems mainly, and parking complaints from the villagers, who got up a petition to have us closed, but in court the case was thrown out, when the chief complainant asked the magistrate to speak up because he was very deaf.

Of course there was the odd bit of unpleasantness. We began to suspect that there was some pilfering going on, when Kit noticed that the till did not quite balance on a number of occasions. It was never down; but sometimes the cash was a small amount over, which aroused her suspicions. In the past she had managed cash-flow businesses and made a shrewd guess about what was going on and decided to get it sorted out. On the next big night Kit prepared two floats for the till and about half an hour after opening, without any warning, she took the till drawer out, emptied it into a bag, took a reading, replacing the float with the prepared one. The bag turned out to be £15 down. The theft entailed taking an amount from the drawer at the very beginning of the evening and gradually by short-changing or ringing in the wrong prices to replace the missing sum. It was a fine scam but one that required constant monitoring of exactly how much has to be replaced and this is how we caught one of the part time barmaids. She was handed her coat and barred from the club. Around this time too I had suspicions that our bar manager was being a bit too lavish with the free drinks. After the first month a brewery stock check found that he was £250 down—so he had to go as well.

By this time a weekly pattern had emerged, with general cabaret each weekend, Country Music on Thursdays, Jazz on Fridays. Wednesdays were usually function nights and we ran a kid's disco on Tuesdays from six p.m. to nine. We also launched one of the first discos in Cornwall when we turned the old garage into a creepy cavern called Miller's Cave. In the end it took more money than the main club. It was proving so profitable that we sought a good pro D.J. and were lucky enough to find John Barry a New Zealander from Radio Otago visiting the U.K. He must have liked the gig because he stayed with us almost a year, though I think it was more the good–looking women thronging the club that held him, rather than the scenery. Another notable event was the arrival of the group Saraband from which three of them, Alan Knight, Jizz Brookes and Tim Collingwood, found Cornwall to their liking and settled there.

One morning in the mail was a poster of a chubby young man standing by an old time railroad engine, accompanied by a letter from Plymouth agent Robbie Hart telling me that this was a British Folk/Country singer, who had returned from Sweden where he had built a solid reputation, and was coming to the South West on tour, so I took one of the dates. It turned out to be my first meeting with Kelvin Henderson who became well known as a respected bandleader and very informative Country Music broad–caster, with one of the distinctive voices on the British scene. We became good friends and the next thirty years would see our paths cross on many occasions.

PICKER'S TIP 37

On the road you need your nourishment, but be careful. Over the years Kit and I have run several restaurants, so here's a couple of insider tips.

Don't ever order the Chef's Special. It might sound exotic but it's usually something made from leftovers or from ingredients bought cheap.

But don't order the fish on Monday. It's probably been in the fridge all weekend. Happy Eating.

PICKER'S TIP 38

If you are buying a used guitar, check that the neck is straight by looking along it from the level of the bridge, but check it also for turning or warp–ing. If it is a little curved you MAY be able to tighten the truss rod but if it is warped just forget it. The tuning problems will never end.

Francis and Danny Dog arrive

Another important event was the arrival of my son Francis and Danny Dog our big Labrador. Francis had finished school that March so Sylvia packed him off to me along with the dog. Realizing that it was over between us she wanted a clean break and get on with her life. Francis was not really wild about the idea—he was not very fond of Kit and objected to most of the things she wanted him to do, like having baths etc. but in time the moods passed. I thought foolishly, that he would help me develop the club, but it was not to his liking so I got him a job with a local coach painter. So that he could get around we bought him a Puch motorbike and later a Riley car. He was not wild about the paint shop job, and we prevailed on a friend of ours Dave Cooke to take him on at his carpet shop near the club, but he did not really settle until he met a pretty girl called Gill Hobba. He found in her tight–knit pure Cornish family, the stability he had been seeking and they set up home in Bodmin. It proved to be a good union and they married at Lanhydroc on April 7th 1979. They had two children, Felicity Jane and Anthony Ross and still live in Bodmin. We were happy to see them settled in such a nice place and although we had close connections in the 90's and we keep in touch by phone we don't see much of them these days.

Danny Dog however, was a totally different case and became like a child to us. That was one happy relationship that did work. He was a big yellow Labrador, about five years old, bursting with energy and he did sterling work as a guard dog at the club. The tales about him are manifold and in the years that followed we were inseparable. Only Kit, Danny Dog and me. When he died in France we buried him in the orchard of the Manoir de la Rance complete with his own headstone.

We had lots of visitors to the club, mainly from people who were on holiday in Cornwall. My cousin Cal and wife Rochine dropped in, as did Kit's sister Margaret and her strange husband Ron (He insisted on sitting on the floor) also Dokey Hill, our moody singer from our first German tour in '66 dropped by. I hardly recognized him, as he had grown fat, and sported a huge ginger beard. He brought along his new English wife and now lived in Ramsgate. Kit's three nieces Barbara, Christine and Maggie also came on holiday, and made quite a mark on the local lads working a few nights behind the bar in the club.

Goodnight Mick

Mind you, things were not always rosy and we had our fair share of troubles as any club expects, so I took on a couple of so–called bouncers, both of whom proved to be useless, leaving a lot of clearing up for me to do. I arrived one night to find one of the punters I had barred, boozing at the bar, out of his tree and causing all sorts of trouble with the bar staff. He was a big guy known as Wild Mick and had tattoos all over his body, in–

cluding a Union Jack on his neck. I told Arthur, our body builder bouncer to get him out, but Arthur stood there arguing and flexing his pecs. He finally came back to tell me that 'Mick was as good as gold and that every-thing was going to be all right now. There'd be no trouble. He'd just got out of Exeter Jail and was celebrating.

"'Not in here, he ain't," I said. "just get him out."

At which point I looked across in time to see Mick whip out his penis and urinate all over the bar. We rushed over and Arthur started arguing with him again. He was obviously very afraid of this guy, so I grabbed them both in a bear hug and rushed them down a short flight of stairs at the side of the bar and slammed them into the emergency door bar. Wild Mick cursed us both and made all kinds of threats, while Muscleman Arthur tried to mollify him by saying he was only doing his job. I told them both to piss off and threw Arthur his leather coat and told him to forget about coming back, and slammed the door on them.

Mick however did come back half an hour later raving and kicking the front door of the club demanding that I come out. Roy our doorman came running to tell me and I went down to listen to the tantrums—In one of the pauses I said.

"Yeah, Mickey it's me—Waddya want? I told you before. You're barred."

"Oh yeah?" He raved on. "Come on out 'ere Yonco, an' we'll see who's barred."

I told Roy to put the door on the long chain (Always put two chains on a door. A short one to take the shock of the charge and a long one to prevent it being kicked in. A trick I learned in the chicken wire bars of Galves-ton)—and sure enough, Mickey charged the door and came up short as the second chain held—and then the idiot stuck his head through.

Well, it was a gift wasn't it? What else did he expect, SMACK!

And that was the last we heard of Mickey—or Eric the bodybuilder.

Cap'n Yonk

Then I decided that I wanted a boat (Well? If you own a nightclub you've got to have all the baubles haven't you? What's the use of having bad taste if you don't show it off by buying loads of brash, vulgar, goodies?) And I found one down at Charlestown Harbour. The very harbour that some years later was the setting for the Michael Caine film 'The Eagle Has Landed'. This boat wasn't actually in the water, it was on a trailer outside a boatyard and at that point it was not really for sale. I got to know John the boat builder there on my visits to the harbour and finally got round to asking him about it. Apparently this vessel had had an interesting provenance.

It had been constructed in Poole about twenty years previously from the plans of an Australian shark fishing boat, and was now part of the estate of a very wealthy man who had spent the last of his eighty eight years getting rid of as much money as he could, by buying all sorts of things to prevent his squabbling progeny from inheriting anything. He bought luxury cars. (Including two Porsches), property (A whole estate of post–war pre-fabricated houses on a derelict sight in Coventry), acres of useless brownfield wasteland, a number of caravan sites in North Wales and some boats, including the one I was interested in. This man was certainly one of the classic English eccentrics. He was once arrested for speeding down the newly opened Redruth bypass at 95 mph, with one arm round his girl friend. She was fifty–six and at the time he was seventy–eight years old.

It was a nice boat with a Ford Corsair four–cylinder engine and a Z Drive both of which were well worn but the wooden, fibre sheathed, hull was in good condition. I got in touch with the solicitors of the deceased and after a bit of haggling got the thing for £800. It had a nice cabin and plenty of space on board. Oh yes, and they threw in the trailer as well, so it was a simple thing to get it towed to the club, where aided by my son Francis, who now lived with us, and Johnny Lang, I began to renovate it in the back courtyard of the club. Eventually it was ready, fitted with new strakes and control panels, everything painted and all the metal work burnished bright. We got the engine running but it sounded a bit rough and reluctant to start, but we soon sorted that out by doubling up the batteries and banging 24 volts through the glowing starter. The Z Drive also rattled a bit so we rigged up oil drip–feed which reduced the noise of the sloppy cogs.

October that year was lovely, so the final touches were done on the quayside at Charlestown and we scheduled a launch date for a warm Sunday. When the time came we were very excited and watched with pride as a dock crane lifted 'TEXAS DRIFTER' and swung her over the oily dock and then slowly down. There was a gentle splash as she touched down and we jumped aboard to unhitch the sling. Watching the jib swing clear we failed to notice that the boat was still going down and that water was coming in from the hull drain plugs, which we had forgotten to put back. Ooops! Francis was the first to realize what was going on and dived over the side with a big spanner and two bungs, which he managed to hammer home and stop the leak. After that we all spent some happy autumn afternoons chugging around the little dock until the Harbour Master began to hint that some mooring fees would shortly be due. Accordingly we decided that is was time to put to sea and moor up at Golant near Fowey where it was free.

And so another day was burned deep in my memory.

It was Friday, November 1st. 1974 and Emile Ford was booked at the club for a special show. We first made careful preparations for the move from Charlestown to the Fowey River by parking up a car at Golant so that we could get back after finding a new mooring. About three in the afternoon we got aboard and prepared to leave but Cap'n Birdseye would not open the dock gate without us coughing up our mooring dues, so we waited until there was a ship due in and planned to slip out before the gate was closed again—but it was close to 5.30 before a rusty coaster nosed in and we braved the choppy waters of St Austell bay. The first thing we noticed apart from the unexpected wallowing and pitching was that it was getting rather dark. There was a small cabin light but apart from that we had no navigation lights at all. Francis had a cycle lamp so we put him in the bows to let the shipping know that we were there. Johnny was at the wheel and I was by the side of the engine trying to keep it going, because the control cable from the cabin had got snagged on something and it would only run at full throttle, roaring away with the grating worn gears of the Z drive throwing oil everywhere as we banged and buffeted our way through the changing tide. Francis kept shouting how far we were from the rocks of Polkerris as we hugged the Gribbon headland round to the mouth of the busy River Fowey.

By now it was really dark, and great freighters kept looming up heading up river to the English China Clays landing stages. We'd steer away from them but they kept hooting at us as we bobbed around like a glowworm. Finally we found the mouth of the river by following in the phosphorescent wake of a big fishing boat, and edged past Ready Money Cove and the Fowey quays up to Bodinnick. By this time our nerves were stretched to breaking point. Meanwhile while back at the club Emile Ford had arrived and Kit was calling out the Fowey Coastguards.

Eventually, cold and soaking wet, after about an hour wallowing around in the moonlight, we found the village of Golant on the west bank but then a further crisis presented itself. We had been towing a little fiberglass dingy behind us to get ashore and as we couldn't find a rope we had used a piece of electric cable, and as we slowed a little, this wire got tangled round the propeller and the Z Drive screeched to a tortured stop. We were well short of our intended mooring with the boat drifting free and the dinghy with its stern in the air and its bow almost under our boat, so there was nothing for it, but to chuck out the anchor, so we would not be swept back out to sea and wait for somebody to rescue us.

With a lot of straining and splashing about we managed to cut the wire, and were about to climb into the dinghy when Jonny slipped into the water, and we discovered that it was only three feet deep, so we left every-thing where it was and waded ashore to the car we had parked earlier, just in time to meet the Coastguard's Land Rover and get a king-sized chewing out for breaking every sea law in the book—but that was nothing compared to the treatment we got when we arrived at the busy club from a raging, distraught Miss Kitty.

After its eventful maiden voyage Texas Drifter remained moored up at Golant being systematically stripped by the local drunks. The battery was first to go followed by the steering wheel and the wipers. Eventually I found another dreamer, dumber than I was, who wanted to buy it and it went to a new home further up river at Lerryn. At least I learned a few lessons from that trip. The first was that the water in Cornwall is very cold and that there are two great moments in the life of every weekend sailor.

The day you buy your first boat
and the day you sell the boody thing.

We kept the club for a couple of years but in the end it got to be too much. I was itching to get on the road again and Kit wanted to spend more time looking for a house for our ever–expanding family. Then Bob and Alice, with the help of a crafty brewery manager know as Tricky Dickie, managed to wheedle their way back in as partners and it became un–comfortably messy, with far too many Chiefs and not enough Indians; so in the end we sold out to them. They ran the place as a disco for a short while but soon the old frictions arose. They would row in public and she would storm out while he would top up his glass again with single malt, until one night they were mugged on the way home and were robbed of the takings. This proved to be the last straw and they closed the operation down, sold the house and retired to the coast.

Financially we did o.k. out of the venture and Kit did a deal with the local council, buying a very nice repossessed house off them. It was a detached pink dormer bungalow with three bedrooms on a big triangular plot in Par Moor, quite near the beach. We also bought a nice Citroen Dyane and drove it to Loret de Mar in Spain for a little holiday. It was while we there that I wrote the haunting 'Red Rocks and White Waters' and sent our old Mercedes a birthday card because it had been at a garage in St Austell exactly a year waiting for new injectors.

There was however, a sequel to the tale. Somehow Tommy the Taker got his nose back in the door and opened the building up, as a cut–price fabric warehouse. And—surprise, surprise. Two months later he had a fire. The insurance coughed up and he disappeared abroad. The last time I saw the building it was only a burnt out shell. On the wall, next to the door some wag had written: *Frying Tonight.*

Elvis Costello

Just as a footnote let me tell you about another bizarre event of 1975, when I was present at the birth of Elvis Costello. Weird eh?

Well, one warm April afternoon I was sitting on the beach at Ready Money Cove in Fowey, having a beer with Russ McManus, one of the singers from Joe Loss' band, when the talk, quite naturally, got round to showbiz and I mentioned that my son had no interest in the business at all. He said that his boy Declan was just the opposite, always clowning around and making up songs and he definitely wanted to be a pop singer, but Ross didn't think that Declan Mc Manus had much billboard appeal and decided that he would have more impact if he had an unusual name. So he named him after his two favourite American characters Elvis Presley and slapstick comedian Lou Costello—and that's when Elvis Costello was born.

*   *   *   *   *   *

Country Music Trends

I have always liked to keep abreast of the constantly shifting moods of the music and by the mid 70's there was a great restlessness in the air.

Some writers and artistes were becoming disenchanted by the schmaltzy 'Nashville Sound' of Kenny Rogers, Tammy Wynette et al. and led by Willie Nelson, many musicians had moved to Austin Texas, where a new fresh wind was blowing the tinsel away. Western Swing took on a new lease of life as the old songs of Bob Wills and Hank Thompson were revived, while in the southern part of the state Doug Sahn was making the D.Js sit up with his Texas Tornados band, reviving Frogman Henry numbers and songs of social comment like 'Cowboy Peyton Place' and 'Country Groove', plus a strong helping of Delta Blues. It was around this time that another pure Texan George Strait, began to be noticed for his uncompromising stand for classic Stone Country music.

Beyond the reach of the Nashville Establishment, Waylon Jennings, Billy Joe Shaver and others were stirring things up, particularly Waylon with his distinctive 4 beat Country–rock and cynical lyrics as typified in 'Are you sure Hank done it this way?' He also had a fascinating way of changing the mood of a song by switching from a 3/4 waltz to a throbbing 4/4 rhythm as he did with Hank Williams' 'Darling' let's turn back the years.' and Earnest Tubb's 'Waltz across Texas.' And who can ever forget his unique treatment of the Kenny Roger's weepie 'Lucille', as he dragged it kicking and screaming into the melting pot of the future. This originality endeared him to the modern Country pickers like me who still had a love of the Golden Age classics. I particularly liked his version of 'Crazy Arms', which was a superb production with Ralph Mooney swapping steel guitar licks with a brilliant fiddle man, all of it under–laid by a Soul bass guitar and Waylon's Telecaster. Sheer magic.

Tex–Mex influences were also coming to the fore through Freddy Fender and Flaco Jimenez and these styles were absorbed and modernised by the young students from the University of Texas. Willie also tried to persuade Jennings to make the move back to the West Texas Plains but old Waylon turned him down flat. He said that he had seen enough of the Lubbock area, as it had taken him the best part of twenty years to get away from his hard beginnings and he was certainly not going back now. A sentiment I can well understand.

It truly was a time of great change and I was all for it. I was still bas–ically a performer of classic Country music but felt that the chart chasing puppet masters in Nashville had strayed too far from the true roots with its banks of strings and layered tracking. Our own show also now showed strong Texas influences and songs like Red Stegall's 'Tight Levis and Yellow Ribbons' and 'Texas Silver Zephyr 'began to appear on our new play list. On the back of the so called Outlaw Movement, a fresh wind was blowing as Waylon & Willie were joined by Hank Williams Jnr, Jerry Jeff

Walker, David Allen Coe, (a real outlaw) and Dwight Yoakum laid the foundation of this New Renaissance, spearheaded by what K.T Oslin termed 'The '80's Ladies', a crop of beautiful, seriously talented young women who kicked off the gingham and the 'Charlies Angels' hair–dos, shortened their skirts and started to 'Kick Ass' with attitude. Susie Bogus, Mary Chaplin Carpenter, Lorrie Morgan, Reba McIntyre, and the superb Paulette Carlson all made their impressive marks.

PICKER'S TIP 39

It is illegal for a manager to buy and sell an act and charge commission as well. Mark Twain once wrote, "Feed a starving dog and he won't bite you."

That is the difference between bad managers and bad dogs. Watch 'em.

PICKER'S TIP 40

When people request their favourite song they like to hear it sung as close to the original as possible and over the years I have developed this ability so here are a few tips I have found useful.

Hank Williams. Key E.

Willie Nelson. Key C.

Haggard and Jones. Key F. (Open string chords capo 3rd and play D shape).

Cash and Waylon. Key Bb (Open string chords capo 3rd and play G shape).

Webb Pierce? Oh, any key will do, just put a peg on your nose.

And a most impressive trick is to do one Star's song using another's voice.

27

THE JOHNNY BOND TOUR

Refreshed and raring to go again we started looking around for the next move, not quite sure what we wanted to do. I was well established as a Country name, so it was a natural move to rebuild the band and get back out on the road, so I was soon out scalping the local scene for pickers. Luckily there were still a few around, though most of my old sidemen had gone their separate ways, so a concert was set up at Carlyon Bay, including the Plymouth based Medicine Bow and a few local single acts, where I did a spot fronting a mixture of refugees from various Country groups. It was just a session of standards but it gelled very well, so I now had my band.

After we disposed of the club, my scheme was to keep my hand in by playing the local pubs and holiday camps, I had no idea how big it was to become. To me, it was just a bit of fun and a way of making a living. There was plenty of work around back then. It was the middle 70's and the Cornish Leisure industry was booming and in a short time we were back doing seven gigs a week. We actually did three consecutive nights a week at Perran Sands Holiday Camp,

This is where we first met the Cornish comedian Geoff Rowe (Jethro, to you), and over the years we became good friends. I thought he was terrific and he still is a truly original comic, so refreshing in these days when cheap mockery, schadenfreude and irony masquerade as comedy. So much so, that we would stay behind after our show to listen time and time again, to his wonderfully hilarious stories of Cornish life. He has had TV offers by the score after guesting with such comedy legends as Jim Davidson and Des O'Connor but, like the great Bob Hope, his attitude to television was and still is, wary. He was offered a series but turned it down to continue his never ending tours of his one-man shows, still playing to packed houses and his live show videos sell very well too, both in the UK and worldwide. I'm proud to say that he features my song Red Rocks and White Waters on his latest one. By the mid-nineties his hard work and unique talent had made him a millionaire property owner and entertainer to the Royals. One of his regular gigs is at Highgrove House for HRH.

For a short while I retained Mike Blackborough, a superb bass player and singer from Bodmin. Alan Knight played guitar and Dave Wayne was on drums. On pedal steel I used Sandy Horn, an ex-pat northerner living in Plymouth. All in all it was a really good band, its main strength being its blend. In those early days none of them were outstanding musicians, but they all had a natural ability to gel, at least musically if not socially. At the end of the season, which in those days ran from May to September, decisions had to be made about the future. Various news items about the band had appeared in the music press, and there were some good offers of work coming in but it meant travelling, in other words total professional commitment. From my point of view there was no contest, I was glad to be back on the road and considering that there was nothing else on offer, Kit agreed to come along as well, though she wanted to get on restoring our new house but Mike said that he did not want to travel outside Cornwall. It was understandable really, he had a good job, a wife and a new baby so Sandy suggested a friend of his for the job, an excellent bassist called Keith, who soon became known as Dormouse due to his quiet retiring ways, and was bullied unmercifully by Dave the Drummer whenever he thought I wasn't watching.

A week or two into this travelling life I was contacted by the agent Louis Rogers, a man I came to like and respect, in spite of a few flankers he pulled on us. Louis was a well known manager and had been a major impresario in his native Ulster, being responsible for bringing Jim Reeves to Europe and for guiding the career of the vivacious Alma Cogan. He was also the father of chart pop singer Clodagh Rogers, and his son Frank was an executive at Decca Records. Lou told me that he was bringing over the old cowboy movie actor and songwriter Johnny Bond from the States, and would like us to do a showcase tour with him, that is, working as a support act and backing him. The money was good so I accepted and three weeks later we kicked off the tour at the Pope John Hall, Heston, West London.

Johnny Bond himself was a charming and humorous man. His song writing abilities were beyond question having included such hits as 'Cimarron' and 'I wonder where you are tonight' as well as some funny duets with his contemporaries Tex Ritter and Jimmy Dean, but he had a great tongue–in–cheek sense of humor. I once asked him if he'd written any more songs and he said.

"Oh yeah. I've written lots of songs for Johnny Cash, Merle Haggard and Charlie Pride—they don't sing 'em—but I still write 'em."

For the first part of the tour he travelled with Kit and I and sometimes with Lou Rogers as well, in our rather cramped Volkswagen 411 estate car, while Mrs. Bond stayed in London to do some shopping. The rest of the band was transported by Terry Dean whom I had first met playing bass with the Haz Elliott Band when they worked the club. He had hit one of those low spots in life when nothing seemed to be going right. The band had broken up and he had some heavy family troubles, a situation that most pro–entertainers have to cope with at sometime in their lives. It happens to some performers over and over again, until the idea of a long–term stable relationship becomes just a dream. (Or in some cases an impediment on the road to other dreams) In Terry's case, Louis had come to his rescue and helped him out financially, and as Terry had a huge Austin Vanden Plas 110 saloon, gave him the combined jobs of Transport and Road Manager.

The mileages were enormous with Louis grabbing gigs all over the UK. One night we would be in Plymouth, the next in Carlisle and the third one at Grays in Essex, where Uncle Lou disappeared without telling us he had forgotten to book any digs. Thank God we did not do the Emerald Isle, as Louis would probably have had us rowing across the Irish Sea. I began to think that he had some private arrangement with the Pope because every second gig seemed to be at some Catholic social club.

Johnny Bond's health was also suspect and he was really not in any condition for such a grueling schedule. He was about sixty–four years old at the time and had been making Hollywood 'B 'movies as far back as the mid thirties and was a leading light in the days of the Singing Cowboy films, working with Spade Cooley's band and Tex Williams' Western Caravan in the forties, but now his health was not so good and he looked old and tired. The British end of the tour was hard going but the crunch came when we had to go to Italy.

Louis and Mrs. Bond did not come on this part of the tour either, which I suppose was just as well, as she would have had Johnny on the first flight out if she'd seen the confusion and stress. Terry Dean was supposed to be in charge of the trip but he seemed overcome by the responsibility of it all, probably due to his emotional problems back home. Most of the time he stood around like a lost sheep. He did not speak a word of Italian or any other European language and Louis, who at times could make Colonel Gadaffi look like Mother Theresa, had left him bereft of money and paperwork. In short, it had all the makings of a cock up.

When I told friends about the proposed trip to Italy, a local farmer friend and good drinking buddy of mine called John asked if he could come along. I checked it out with Louis who said that it was okay with him as long as John paid his own expenses so I fixed it up. I felt I owed him one anyway, because some months previously he had taken me to the Smithfield Show in London on the Farmers Special from Cornwall—which is a story in its own right. I have never seen a group of people who could eat and drink as much as these Oggy Yeomen. In fact, the special train from Truro ran out of booze at Reading and had to be re–stocked before going on to Paddington. Up to that trip I thought myself quite a bon–viveur and trencherman but I was not in their league. By the Sunday night I had to put up the white flag and leave.

Bella Napoli.

But let's go back to Italy. The travel arrangements were up to normal agency standards, resulting a 24–hour wait at Heathrow, and Kit was looking decidedly off–colour. We all thought that it was a cold but it proved to be something much more serious, and Johnny Bond was pale and drawn and coughing like a good 'un. The stress factor was also heightened by the disclosure from a very nervous Sandy Horn, that this was going to be his first flight EVER. Also the constant squabbling from the bass player and the drummer shredded everybody's patience. And, if that was not enough, Terry mislaid the air tickets, adding to the sense of impending doom.

Eventually the plane took off about midnight and landed safely in Rome over two hours later, which was fine, except for the fact we should have been touching down in NAPLES. Frantic phone calls to the US Navy Base at Gaeta (Not easy on the Italian phone system at any time but particularly difficult in English) eventually brought forth a convoy of one car and two baby Fiat 650 vans to carry the twelve people in our party and all our gear, on a wild overnight drive to Napoli. Oh yes, and it gets worse, because when we got to the city there was further confusion as nobody knew where the hotel was, and we spent another hour roaring round the inner city slums, where hordes of lunatic Italian kids played football in the misty dawn.

By the time we finally got to bed at 6 a.m. everybody was well knackered. Johnny and Kit getting steadily worse and Sandy being brittle, withdrawn and absolutely useless, his nerves shot to pieces by the flight. Dave and Alan Knight did their best to cool him down but all they got for their trouble were bills for meals he'd ordered then refused to eat, and loud complaints about everything European. It was really the tension and after the first show he was okay, at least until it came time to fly home.

Our first show was actually at the naval base. It went well—but the sailors were young and were not really appreciative of Johnny's humorous monologues or even knew who he was, but they treated him with grudging respect. Kit did about four songs but was not really up to it. Fortunately the band was on good form and we did a rock 'n 'roll set with Sandy playing great tenor saxophone, which got the crowd going. By sheer coincidence while we were there the aircraft carrier Guadalcanal came into port. This was the same ship that kept setting itself on fire back in '67 when we were in Venice with Lefty Frizzell, and I began to think that the 'USS ZIPPO' was following us around the Med.

Apart from the civilian gigs, which were confusing to say the least, (the subtleties of Johnny's jokes being more puzzling to the Italian patrons than they were to the GIs) we played at two completely contrasting military clubs. The Flamingo, at the top of a hill overlooking the beautiful bay of Naples, was a lush, luxurious, top class venue on a par with the best clubs in Germany such as Ramstein or Spengdhalen and here we were treated very well indeed, and another which was just the opposite—but more about that later.

The first show was at the Officer's Club. Johnny and Kit did this one but were not really well enough to do the second one at the combined NCO/EM Club the following night. Which as it turned out, was just as well. We did our usual show with a few near the knuckle jokes thrown in and some imitations of the big stars of the day like Webb Pierce, Hank Williams, Johnny Cash etc. but about the best number of the night was Johnny Russell's 'Red Necks, White socks & Blue Ribbon Beer' which went an absolute storm and had to be reprised twice with the audience bellowing along. It was like wildfire in there. During a break the Custodian explained the rapturous reception.

Apparently, as in Germany, there was a heavy 'Black Power' thing going down on the bases here, and there was a move to stifle Country Music because it represented Southern 'Honky' views, and Soul shows were being pushed wherever possible. So a wildly Redneck song like 'White Socks' was what they all wanted to hear—but not everybody, because during this break, as I was going back on stage, a couple of the militant Brothers cornered me saying that they did not like my attitude and that Country Music was not their bag, and they wanted to hear a bit of Tamla or Soul. So I asked them why they had come to the show? It had been well advertised and if they didn't like what they'd chosen to come to see, that was just tough shit.

It was like Rhein Main NCO Club all over again and my hackles rose. If somebody takes a confrontational line with me something impels me to return the compliment, which might account for me switching from Johnny Cash's 'Folsom Prison Blues' to Otis Reading's 'Land of a Thousand Dances. (You know the one that goes "La, lala, la, la.lala, la, lala la la, etc") and announcing that it was a track from my latest album called 'Soul Sucks'. There was an angry outburst from a group of black activists at the back of the club and they loudly demanded some 'Roots Music"—so I offered to do Bluegrass version of a James Brown's 'I Feel Good.' but that didn't help much either.

My reaction was nothing to do with skin colour. I would have taken the same stand if it had been a bunch of white football hooligans. Oh yes! I was a right awkward sod back in those days. After the show a group of very nice M.P.s escorted us to the bus.

Driving back to the hotel we found the roadside dotted at intervals with 'Ladies of the night'. Their micro mini skirts and low cut blouses on full display in the lurid light of burning truck tyres in the gutters. It was the regular pick–up run, much like Frankfurt's Kaiser Strasse but with nowhere near the same class. The boys had a lot of fun with them, Dormouse and Dave running up and down asking prices—the girls responded using the few American phrases they had learned from the G.I.s

"Eh Boy! You wanna party? Ten tousan' lire? "

"Hey Joe! 'Ow 'bouta da blowjob? Y'wanna da besta 'ead in Napoli?"

"Eh Fella, 'ow 'bout forty dollah short time?

"Naw. Well–a Fuck–a offa den."

This was a very dangerous practice as most of these girls were run by the Camorra, a Neapolitan equivalent of the Mafia, and remembering the trouble caused by Lee James in Frankfurt, I warned the boys that they could easily end up in the Bay of Naples if they persisted in tormenting these girls.

There is one final comment however on the Flamingo Club and it might serve as advice for any entertainers considering the life as a full time pro. The house band there was called Pandora's Box, an English four piece group that I had first met on the US Military circuit in 1966 and they had been fully employed on the circuit ever since. It was true that they were virtually unknown outside these US Clubs and had not pursued the usual things like TV, radio or recording contracts, hoping for that one big break as we had done. Instead they had cleverly geared their act to these U.S. clubs and the regular highly paid work had brought them the good life. They all had nice apartments, Porsches and summer homes in Majorca with the kids at private schools in Switzerland. I'll bet they're still making mega bucks. So who was right?

Now for that other club I mentioned. It was a complete garbage can, rough as a bear's arse, in a back street right in the heart of Naples. I remember stopping the bus opposite the entrance and seeing big rats running up and down the steps. Yes, real rats. Johnny Bond was very ill by this time so he was confined to bed back at the hotel and the place was considered so tough that Kit was also advised to give it a miss. The air was thick with marijuana smoke and there were tarts, dealers and pimps lining the foyer. There was a stage door in the alley behind but one of the bouncers advised us against using it—"just stay in the light, Buddy!" was all he said so we lugged everything through the whore's palace in the foyer.

The show started about 10 p.m. and we gave them both barrels, a solid full-bore Country Rock session, all Eagles, Outlaws, Dr Hook and Jerry Lee Lewis, with all the amps blaring. It was loud but the drunken punters kept shouting for us to turn up, so we did. At which a couple of the local chippies started dancing and ended up stripping, causing the despairing Night Manager to call in the M.P.s who started turfing the girls out to the accompaniment of loud booing.

As soon as they left a fight started in the corner but nobody took any notice of it. Most of these E.M.s were zonked out anyway on a combination of drugs and Jack Daniels so that by the time we got into some Western Swing the place was going crazy. This time the Snowdrops (M.P.s) stood at the doors and watched. The pale Custodian came over and told us to cool it, so towards the end of the night we played "Faded Love" and as we hit the bridge second time around, I went into a narration as Sandy played a gentle backing on steel guitar.

It went like this:

"Well folks, we are nearing the end of our show and we'd like to thank you for having us at your place tonight. We have been very impressed by your welcome, your abundant booze and warm appreciation of our music. So much so, that when I get that big Number One Hit and all the money that goes with it, well, I'm going to come back and buy this fine club— *And burn it to the fuckin' ground.*

At that the place really erupted with rebel yells, cheering, stomping, and bottles and chairs started flying through the air, the private feuds came to an end and everyone started fighting everybody else. And as we switched to a storming version of 'Take me back to Tulsa.' the riot police came rushing back in again, whistles shrilling and the white nightsticks hitting everything in sight. They never booked us back there again. Can't think why.

The following day Farmer John and I went down to get some medication for the prostrated Johnny Bond, who looked about ready to pop his clogs and head for that great rodeo in the sky. Terry was supposed to look after him but he could not get any co–operation from any of the US Clubs and of course Louis's phone was off the hook, so he spent most of his time in his room playing cards with Johnny and waiting for divine intervention. Farmer John was the perfect tourist and a street trader's dream. In the broiling Naples heat he wore his best Harris Tweed jacket, Fair Isle sweater, Bedford cord pants and his thick–soled dung spreading brown Veldtschoen, complete of course, with a woolen shirt and tartan tie—oh yes, and his camera on a short strap that was almost strangling him. The further he got from Cornwall, the more Cornish he became. When we went to one of the most famous pizza restaurants in Italy he kept asking for Ginsters pasties. He brightened up however in Zeno Square. Here he was cornered by a couple of spivs hustling watches. But they didn't fool my friend John.

"Aaargh no, me 'ansome," he told me later over a gin and tonic on the plane. "They greasy buggers, they'm come up agin Roche Rock this toime, Matey. There ain't no flies on this Oggie."

He showed 'em the way home all right as he haggled and argued as though he was at Liskeard Cattle Market and in the end succeeded knock–ing down the price of the offered Rolex Oyster Datemaster from £120 down to £55 quid. He was as pleased as punch as he flashed it to us all with a sly knowing smile. Well, anyway it said Rolex on the face but its plastic strap made it a bit suspect and it had a tick like a time bomb. I was surprised that they allowed him on board the plane to London.

Back in the UK the tour ground on and as Johnny Bond's health im–proved the reports in the Country Music press became favorable. Looking back at that tour I am left with the impression of his superb professional–ism. His stage presence was immaculate and the years he had spent in Hollywood gave him that rare polish of the complete entertainer. He was in short, a Great Country Gentleman.

Sweet Folk All

One of the spin–offs from the Johnny Bond Show was the offer of a re–cording contract from folk singer and promoter Joe Stead, who had a label called Sweet Folk All (which just about summed up what we got out of the deal). It could hardly be described as an efficient operation. On one occa–sion I received two hundred records from Joe, all in my covers but contain–ing Shag Connors records. The first album for them was called 'Old Greyhound' and the second, about a year later was a much better produc–tion, called 'Drinking a beer and singing a Country song.' The studios were deep in the beautiful country of central Wales at Llanfair Caerinion in a converted farmhouse, and in theory it was an ideal tranquil location for re–cording.

The sound equipment was state–of–the art and Joe himself was very dedicated to folk and Country music and a good producer but the end product, in my opinion, suffered from the ego and constant interference of the resident engineer (and part owner) who would not confine himself to technical matters, and his tactless criticisms and forceful opinions upset many musicians. I remember some fabulous session men there like guitarist Phil Beer and super steelie Ken Byng. Oh yes, and two great girl back–up vocalists Mai Jones and Beryl Watkins but all in all, I could not say that the sessions in Mid Wales produced anything earth shattering, but there were a couple of tracks like "Drinking A Beer" and "Let No Man Tell Me What To Do" that were good enough to be included in later compilations.

After Italy Kit gave up the road for a short while, and was fully occupied at home attending to things in Cornwall and the complications of various family problems. The house at Par was nice and apart from the odd crisis like Danny Dog insisting on running back to his old home at the club where he could often be found on the steps, waiting for the doors to open up, life was fine. There was more work than we could handle and money was good. One of the high spots was when I returned tired and weary from an extended tour about five o'clock one morning, I found a surprise birthday present from Kit waiting for me in the drive. A beautiful dark blue Mercedes 250 tied up with a big ribbon. Wonderful!

Gypsy George

Things were going along quite nicely but you are never quite ready for the unexpected twists of fate, and this one came in the shape of Gypsy George.

As I remember it, the first time I came into contact with him was around 1974. It was a few weeks after we opened the club. Our steel player Trevor told me he was leaving to get married and returning to Kent, and the word went out that we might be looking for a replacement. Trevor made his move and we got by for the remaining gigs by using a local guitar player, until the time came to open the club when I gave up life on the road. It was therefore with some surprise that I got a long distance call from what I first thought was some kind of an Arab refugee called El Imber inquiring about the position of steel guitarist with my band. He told me that he had been pushing pedals with a band out Colchester way but felt like he needed a change of scene. I told him quite clearly that things were at a standstill at the moment, music–wise, and that due to my committments with the club I had broken up my band but he did not seem to believe me and rang off in a bit of a huff.

Nothing further happened for a year or so and then, right out of the blue, he turned up at our flat next door to the club. I had never seen him before and had no idea who this stocky man with wild eyes and short beard was.

Yes?" I said, confused. "What can I do for you?"

"I'm El and I've come for the job," he announced belligerently.

"Oh yes? What job's that then?" I asked, thinking that he was a waiter or something. His eyes glazed over and his jaw hardened.

"The steelie's job. That one you promised me on the phone. I've come for it. Got all my gear here in the car," he growled, pointing to a battered mud stained Mini at the bottom of the club steps, and stating pointedly that he could start right away.

Painstakingly I pointed out that there was no job and that I had not promised him anything—and anyway, it was at least twelve months since I had heard from him.

He seemed most put out and told me that he had driven all the way from Essex on my say so. What could I say? I'd never seen the man before and now he was blasting me about a non–existent job.

I was astounded but I later learned that this situation was par for the course with Gipsy George. Time and time again he would pick up on the most casual suggestion and then considered it a solid commitment. I saw him do it in Kenya and several times in the UK. But at that moment I must admit that I felt a bit guilty, as I could not recall clearly what I had said on the phone, so his attack left me rather confused. Finally he stomped off to his car saying that I had really let him down. It was a most uncomfortable encounter—stranger still was the fact that, in time he became a good friend and helped me out on many occasions.

Some time later the real truth came out. For an unknown reason he had left the East Coast and had moved to his mother's house in St. Agnes: The trip had nothing to do with me. Some days later I got another call from a girl singer in the band he'd suddenly left, asking if I had seen him? Life was getting very complicated with George. After that I heard that he had got a job with a group in Falmouth, but it was some time before he did any gigs with us. In the meantime other things developed and we were off on the Johnny Bond tour and I had little to do with Gipsy George. Even though I was away from home, odd stories about him trickled through about the trouble that seemed to follow him around.

One night we played in Norwich at the Talk of the East Club where we shared the gig with a band from Essex, and during the break the band gave me the wider background on this volatile musician and perhaps a reason for his strange behavior. Apparently for several years he had been a firefighter until one day while attending the blaze in a caravan, he had been blown up when a gas bottle exploded. He was thrown twenty feet in the air and suffered severe concussion, with the result that he was in-valided out of the service on a good pension, which enabled him to pursue the career of a professional musician with out the specter of poverty, which constantly haunts the rest of us. The effect of this accident however was probably the cause of his wild mood swings, changing from a gentle humorous calm to raging temper in the passage of an evening. With George you never knew.

I would meet him from time to time and we got on very well. He was an avid Hank Williams fan and had visited Hank's grave in Alabama, and also an exceptionally good steel player who knew the music well, and most of the time was good fun. As we became more acquainted he revealed that he came from an old and much respected Romany family, the Imbers. Yes they were real Gypsies, he claimed, not merely your travelling tinkers. So after that, I called him Gipsy George.

I heard from friends at the Driftwood Spars in St Agnes that he was putting together a band called Misty Dream and was looking for pickers and it wasn't long before two of my boys, Terry and Dave joined him. They started off fine, honking around the clubs in West Cornwall. Terry was a good front man and bassist, and Dave sang harmony and played clean drum licks and George provided nice backing, so they decided to take a trip abroad. It proved to be an experience better forgotten.

Terry somehow persuaded Louis Rogers to put together a tour of Germany for them, backing a woman who described herself as an Alternative Country singer. She was a six foot black Amazon with a soulful voice (And you can't get more 'Alternative' than that, can you?). The tour included Christmas at Baumholder, a garrison town and the main battle-training area for the US Army, in an area that looked like the far side of the moon. For transport they had four mini vans and after chasing Louis all along the South Coast of England to get some expenses money, they headed off across the Channel. To add a further complication, some of them took their girl friends with them. David's lady, Debbie, was convinced that she was going to spend the Christmas in some romantic Tyrolean ski lodge. Instead they ended up at Baumholder E.M. Club trying to play 'Me and Bobby M'Gee' to an 80% black tank battalion, all of them homesick and drunk.

So it was not quite the success it might have been and they headed for the ferry home. There were disputes all round but in the end they blamed it all on Lou and like most musicians, it was soon forgotten and everybody became pals again.

PICKER'S TIP 41

To clean the inside of an acoustic guitar put about a half a pound of uncooked rice in it and shake it around. When you pour it out you will find that it has gone dark grey and the tone of your instrument has improved immensely.

28

NORTH OF THE BORDER
Loch Kishorn

The winter of 1976 was a severe one; so quiet naturally, we were touring
the wilder regions of the Scottish Highlands. I think the agent was Alec
Bailey who had seen us first at a show in Grangemouth. Unfortunately,
this time I couldn't blame anyone else for this one because I had contacted
him. We played the Police Club in Glasgow and then the Saracen Park Social Club, both of them good gigs and then on up the western shore of Loch
Lomond and beyond Fort William to the work camp at Lake Kishorn where
they were constructing, what was back then, the biggest oil production
platform in the world. It was a wild and isolated place and I have no doubt
that when the heather was in bloom and the skies were clear, it must have
been a beautiful and awesome place but in the depths of winter it looked
like Afghanistan.

Our accomodation was aboard a de–commissioned Italian cruise ship
moored in the Loch itself, which would not have been so bad if it had
moved about a bit, because obviously its sanitation system dumped un–
treated waste overboard, and as it had been parked up for over a year (I
was going to say motionless, but would hardly have been true, would it?) it
had built up quite a residue of, shall we say, silt, making it smell like a
slave galley returning from a long haul. In fact its Italian crew called it Il
Pensione Strozo (the Turd Hotel) and it got so bad that I moved the band
into a couple of portacabins on shore. There was the usual wrangle about
women staying overnight on the camp, but we got round it by dressing Kit
up in a donkey jacket and a yellow helmet. So it was all right in the end
but you could still smell that ship all over the camp.

Was there any trouble at Kishorn? Well, I'll admit that the place had all
the ingredients for a riot every day, but security was taken care of by a
corps of big, dour, Hebridean Site Police, very hard sinister men who never
smiled and stared silently at the roistering mob, conversing in quiet Gaelic.

They were all hard ex–policemen from the Hebrides, very capable of
handling any problem that might arise. At the first sign of any confrontation they moved straight in and dragged the trouble makers bodily out to
the back of the club, where a mobile site–patrol would be parked in their
dog vans, ready to relieve the boredom by kicking a few drunks around. On
top of which, persistent offenders could be thrown off the contract, losing
not only their wages but also their end–of–contract bonus dependent of
good behavior, a severe penalty indeed.

In spite of the apparent wild bonhomie in the club, there was a lot of
misery around. There were illegal bookmakers taking bets, and dealers in
drugs milking the high earners. And there was no welching on bets. On
such dangerous projects accidents could easily be arranged. A bigger
deterrent however was the place itself and its isolation. At worst, one could
be barred from the club and condemned to the misery of an area where

there were no pubs cafés or anything else for miles around.

The amenities on the camp were very good considering its isolated location. There was a small but well–equiped gym and sauna, a big comfortable TV lounge with a huge screen showing sports programmes, and three superb food halls serving top quality meals round the clock but one particular incident, small as it was, summed up the situation for a lot of the lonely men at Loch Kishorn. It happened like this.

Our gig was a strange one, tailored to fit the shift patterns with one show at 10.30 a.m. and another at 9 p.m., both of 'em packed to the gills with hard–drinking riggers and labourers. Wild shouts filled the crowded clubroom as Celtic war cries and football chants competed with the sound of crashing glass, and good natured shouts and taunts, that at times almost drowned out our powerful Country–Rock. It was at one of these 10.30 a.m. shows, with the heavy drapes at the windows tightly drawn against the pale Highland sun, that we came across an example of the trauma and misery that working on such projects can cause.

This was the night shift. They had come off the rig two hours ago, and after a huge breakfast, got down to the serious business of drinking the morning away before stumbling through the mud and slush to their portacabins, to sleep all afternoon. They were on back to back shifts, over four thousand of them working flat out to complete the biggest oil rig ever built, and racing against a tide of encroaching technology that was threatening to overtake them, and already some features of the platform were becoming obsolete.

The tables were littered with dirty ashtrays, soggy beer mats and pint glasses, many of them half full of whisky. At the side of the tables were nests of bottles rattling in their crates, some full, others empty. In the midst of the din several boisterous card games were in progress but at least the first ten rows of scarred tables were hooked on the music, and enthusiastically applauded us as I did a parody of the old Johnny Cash hit 'San Quentin'. This version boldly stated everybody's mood and loud roars of approval greeted the lines. "Kishorn, I hate every inch of you."

The band stormed through the cheers with a driving version of Chuck Berry's 'Promised Land' to the sound of rhythmic banging on the rocking tables. The yells and din got louder as Kit skipped onto the stage and flashed her eyes at the rough, whiskey–soaked riggers, and then hit them with the opening staccato bars of John D. Loudermilk's 'Break my Mind'. She followed this with a gentle Country Standard to try to calm the atmosphere a little. It had the intended effect and the catcalls and shouts gradually diminished as her clear voice rang through the club and sentiments of the lyrics struck home. At a table to the right of the stage, maudlin tears began to course down the rough cheeks of a swarthy rigger and elsewhere in this jungle of noise, expressions of concern crossed more than a few booze flushed faces. Nobody commented on this new feeling of deep emotion or appeared to be in anyway concerned—such troughs of melancholy depression were everyday occurrences on these isolated work camps.

In the case of the rigger, the approaching Christmas was on his mind. His wife and bairns were at home in Glasgow looking forward to his coming home loaded down with goodies, and to the wild nights out at Hogmanay, but the prospect filled him with dread. The gambling and heavy boozing brought on by boredom had become compulsive, swallowing up most of his pay in the vicious circle of trying to break even by doubling up his bets. He had petitioned the Company to send some of his money direct to his wife, but they flatly refused to do anything as they had found from bitter experience that such arrangements often misfired, causing much trouble with the workforce and disputes with their men's families. All that had been abandoned and now everyone got paid in cash on the site, every second week., that way there was no argument. He shook his head and took another gulp of whisky from his half–pint glass. As the song finished he rubbed his stubbled chin, sighed with resignation and dried his face on the rough canvas of his work shirt. What was the use in caring? What could he do? This bloody job ended the first week in January. What then? Maybe he could switch contracts and maybe stay on here as a laborer or a machine driver. Most riggers kept a good reserve fund to allow them to pursue the best jobs but he had blown most of his cash away. Right now, he had about ninety quid left from his last payday and around £350 in the Camp Post Office—and Christmas and his family were about six weeks away. There was of course his Christmas Bonus. The Company paid a double packet then, but most of that was already pledged to the camp shylocks who would have no compunction at all in maiming a debtor who welched on them. As the tears filled his eyes again he stuck his nose deeper into the glass hoping that some good fortune would change his dismal future. I often wonder what happened to him.

Mind you not everybody took it so philosophically. The building we were presently playing in had originally been the canteen. The first club had been a prefabricated structure erected at the edge of the camp but now it was gone. It was wrecked one night by a drunken Irish digger driver, who disgruntled at some grievance or other, had broken into the vehicle park, stole a Caterpillar D8 bulldozer and drove it straight through the building pushing the wreckage into a deep bog, losing the digger as well in the swamp.

Not content with all this cross country shuttling, the agent then sent us up to the barren Shetland Islands to play at some of the most northern clubs in the British Isles at RAF Solom Voe, and an oil camp at Saxavoe. I'll tell you, we earned every penny on those gruelling, lonely tours.

* * * * * *

Up in the Tundra

Only an idiot would attempt to cross the Pentland Firth in a small fishing boat in Force Seven winter gale, especially if he wasn't forced to. But I did. However in defence of my common sense, let me say I would not do it again—but please read on.

It was in that icy January of '77 that I left Cornwall to do yet another tour of Scotland and I took with me a back–up trio of first class talent. Big Steve Turner was on guitar, Alan Knight on bass and Alan Rideout on drums. We put in some rehearsal time at Carlyon Bay and by the time we were due to leave we had put a nice solid sound together. All three musicians had strong Country–Rock 'n' Roll backgrounds, and their driving beat were ideally suited to my singing style. Everybody got on very well and we looked set fair for a somewhat extended but comfortable tour. The Transit had passed its M.O.T. and I had invested in some new fog lights. Everybody was geared up for the trip and everything checked out o.k.—nothing could go wrong, or so we thought. In the event we got as far as Exeter where the gearbox jammed (Yes, again), and to complicate things more, it was a Friday. Urgent phone calls to Par brought Kit out with enough money to pay for a new one, and the garage worked well into the night to fix it. We booked in at a local hotel and it was 11.30 on Saturday morning before we got moving again.

It was now snowing and it got worse as we headed north, but we arrived at Biggar in Lanarkshire about seven–thirty that evening, and at the Minto Hotel we met up with the tour's promoter, who turned out to be a cocky, unpleasant little man. He was waiting for us with our schedule and he was quite unsympathetic about our £200 repair bill, brushing it aside as he moaned on about us missing Friday night's gig. (What Friday night gig?). I was annoyed at the time, but on reflection I accepted that it was the standard reaction of that particular breed of small time entrepreneurs—I had heard rumours from other travelling acts that there was some doubt about the legitimacy of his parentage—and our first meeting with the Poison Dwarf, as he was known by the acts, confirmed the suspicion. He booked us into a local club and at the end of the night refused to pay us, saying that we should have arrived in Scotland on Friday—though our contract did not begin until the Saturday, but when you are 300 miles from home and at the start of a tour, any argument is both academic and useless with a booker determined to squeeze the last bawbee out of everything. So we had to swallow it and got on with the job.

The tour was an absolute monster, the Scottish equivalent of the Johnny Bond tour schedule. The same crazy distances, the same lack of co–ordination and poor digs, on top of which it was still snowing heavily. Straight from Biggar we headed northwest along the banks of Loch Lomond to Fort William and then up through the wild glens, past Glencoe and the Eileen Doonan castle to a hotel at Ullapool in the far northwest. The landscape on this journey was starkly beautiful, the hills covered with snow and the smaller lochs frozen over. On the slopes of the glens, herds of wild deer scraped for moss and stunted grass, while hairy Highland cattle would lumber across the hoar frosted fields to stare curiously at us whenever we stopped. The inland roads were not good and some of them were already blocked by drifting snow so wherever possible we hugged the coast, cutting inland at Loch Torridon, following the wild river through the glens and then westward along the southern shore of Loch Maree to Gairloch. We passed Loch Ewe, its desolate snow–topped island looking more lonely than ever in the pale late afternoon sun, its sister island in Guinard Bay looking even lonelier.

At this point, as the crow flies, we were not that far from our next destination. but it took another hour and a half along Little Loch Broom before we hit the frozen headwaters of the River Broom, and we started the descent towards Ullapool. Gradually there was a change—the frozen waters became a trickle and the snowline receded, as the lights of the town were reflected in the distant open sea. It became warmer and at the outskirts of the town palm–trees appeared in the streets. Fishing boats churned busily about the small harbour and wild ducks dipped and pad- dled in the shallows. The change was quite amazing and it was explained to us at the hotel where we were gigging, that a strange diversion of the Gulf Stream brushed this exposed coastline, and kept the climate mellow and the harbour was free from ice most of the year. It was a remarkable oasis to find in this hard frozen region.

With his customary immaculate planning, the Poison Dwarf had booked the next segment of the tour in the Orkney Islands. Well, it might have been just possible to make the ferry in time if it had been summer with no snow, traffic or road–works to cope with but right then, from where we were on the west coat, with the only route open being the one through In- verness on the east coast, it was bordering on the impossible. We made an early start but it was well past midday as we left Golspie, on the last leg heading for Thurso, and it was no surprise that we arrived at the ferry of Scrabster half an hour too late. The car ferry had sailed and there was not another one until the next day—Shit!

An Orkadian Nightmare

So what now? We sat on the almost deserted wind–swept quay and con- sidered the options. By now all the terminal buildings were closed and the staff from the ferry offices had all gone home, and about the only sign of life was a tatty caravan serving cups of tea—Ah. But wait a minute. Further along the dock there was a small fishing boat loading timber. I got an idea that might work. I decided to give it a go. Sending the lads to the snack bar I approached the boat and got talking to the skipper. He was a big pleasant man; in fact all three of the crew were and soon a deal was struck. They were going to their homeport of St. Margaret's Hope on South

Ronaldsway and for £50 agreed to take us with them. They knew who we were because they had seen the posters on the island; in fact they had one of our tapes playing on their cassette player. Aglow with my success, I told the boys about the new arrangements and was somewhat surprised at their lack of enthusiasm. In fact, I myself soon had cause to regret my resourcefulness.

The crew was not at all secretive or dour; totally different from the Hebrideans we had met in Kishorn. They were also really very strong and tough. For example, we were using a couple of Marshall 4 x 12 speaker boxes for the P.A. and one for the bass. These things had Goodman speakers in them and each one weighed over sixty pounds and was cumbersome with it, as anyone who has handled these monsters on the road will confirm, but these Orcadian fishermen tossed them to each other as though they were nothing. Finally all the gear was stowed and we locked up the van and jumped aboard. Ok, Kirkwall, here we come. The boat made a little toot and we headed out towards the open sea. Everything was fine until we cleared the breakwater and then it hit us. The trawler suddenly bucked and heeled over as the gale struck. The Skipper slammed the wheelhouse window shut and wrestled us back on an even keel and into the teeth of the howling wind.

Well, let me tell you. Those big commercial ferry boats take about an hour and a half to traverse the Pentland Firth. It took us over five hours. Yes, FIVE HOURS of bouncing up and down like a cork across the roughest stretch of water in Northern Europe, where the angry waves of the Irish Sea, the Atlantic and the North Sea all fight for mastery of the straits—and we were in the middle of it all. The wind was howling and the rain coming down in sheets. At times we were almost standing still as the roaring diesel fought the crashing waves and the shrieking wind, as the boat nosed this way and that to make headway.

The crew thought nothing of it. To them it was just another day, a bit rougher than usual perhaps, but nothing to get stressed about. In the rocking wheelhouse they laughed and joked together and one of them went below decks to make lunch. LUNCH? Oh No! It turned out to be thick pea soup and greasy bacon sandwiches. Alan Knight and Big Steve did not seem to be bothered and happily wolfed everything on offer, but Alan Rideout and I couldn't handle the fug below deck, and had to get out. I can see us now, sitting on the afterdeck roped to a big steel pipe, Alan staring wildly, seeking a sight of land, while I was alternatively being sick all over my binoculars and being washed as clean as a new born babe by the lashing waves and spray. Oh yes. We had a great time. Was I ever glad when that old tub lurched into St Margaret's Hope? I know now what she had been hoping for—but there were more shocks to come.

The proud skipper had radioed ahead to tell the harbour master about his cargo and the local agent was on the quayside waiting for us in his Jag, and a van for our gear. Alan Knight and Steve oversaw the loading while the drummer and I were trying to find our land legs. Soon everything was done and I piled into the Jag, while the boys climbed into the cab of the van and in the gentle gloaming off we shot along the deserted roads at high speed, until at one point we turned towards the seaweed strewn beach, and shot down a sloping ramp RIGHT INTO THE SEA. Oh, What now?

My eyes popped open but before I could say anything we were in the water but it seemed that our car was floating. We appeared to be skimming across the bay and soon we were climbing another ramp back onto dry land.

These were the so-called Churchill Barriers; concrete causeways built just below the surface, to link the islands and secure the Royal Navy's Scapa Flow anchorages in World War 2, and were now used at certain times of the day as short cuts by the locals. They had been Churchill's idea when he was at the Admiralty (A much better plan than his idea of storming the Dardanelle's in the first World War)—but the old Navy Establishment was against the idea and considered the fleet's anchorage impregnable until they got a shocking wake-up call.

On October 14th 1939, barely a month after the war began, the German submarine U 47 commanded by Lt. Prien, sneaked into the fleet and sank the 29,000 ton battleship Royal Oak, killing 786 British sailors. This daring strike had a telling effect on British Naval prestige as it took place in the very waters where the impounded German Grand Fleet was scuttled after the first world war in 1919—As the U-boat slid out back into the North Sea the old fogies changed their minds, and hundreds of Italian POWs were later detailed to do the shovel work.

Our shows were very well received and took about ten days to complete but it was a trip I will never forget. Also on the island at the time, was that talented singer John Aston who was hustling his new song, a very nice re-working of the Bing Crosby classic 'The Old Lamplighter'. Backing him was super steelie Pete Heywood (still carrying his Fender amp in the cardboard box it came in, Peter being the careful kind when it came to money). It was an example of why things never got better. On such a small island, two rival promoters were importing acts at the same time, splitting the already limited number of fans. I saw the same thing happen in Jersey too. How stupid can you get?

All subsequent tours I did to the Orkneys and Shetlands were by air usually from Dyce Airport, Aberdeen. No more Pentland Firth Ferries for me. In fact it was at Dyce that we met up again with Dangerous Dan our promoter again, at the end of our tour. With a crafty smile and a couple of heavy minders behind him he paid us off £150 short, saying that the job we did for him at Lanark was included in our contract, which it certainly was not.

Quite obviously we did not do any more tours for this joker who continued to enhance his reputation so well that in the end most of the English bands gave up touring for him. He still did all right though by booking

Boxcar Willie. Some time later at Reading I was having a drink with Boxie, when he confided to me that the promoter was paying him a grand a week. "Guaranteed, every week," he said happily. At that time he was doing six shows a week for this promoter at around £850 per night. Oh yes. There's no business like show business.

However, it was while we were away on this tour that a crisis arose in Kit's family. We heard that her niece Chris and her child were having a hard time in Manchester. Her partner had done a runner and left her living on the edge with money troubles, just existing from day to day. Her mother was in the throes of a new relationship, and was not really interested in sorting things out, but it was an appalling situation, so we told them they could come to live with us in Cornwall.

Francis picked them up at Par Station and installed them at the bungalow that soon became home to our new extended family. Me, Kit, Francis, Chris, Michelle and Danny Dog. They settled well in Cornwall and the house was always full of visiting friends for barbeques and parties. In short it was a very happy period. I remember taking Michelle horse–riding for the first time and how relaxed she was in my company, completely confident that if anything went wrong 'Daddy Wank' (sic) would sort it all out.

PICKER'S TIP 42

Take an unorthodox approach to your publicity. In spite of these days of the Internet, fax, texting, e–mail etc, you will find that a well–written letter arriving by conventional mail (especially one bearing foreign stamps) will get more attention than all the IT.

Particularly if it is written on tastefully coloured headed notepaper—try yellow. That way it will be easy to find.

PICKER'S TIP 43

Thinking about making a come–back tour? *Think very carefully.*

And consider this. It's a difficult call, because if you are still as good as you once were, well, that's what everybody expects. So, no medals there.

But if you are not quite as sharp as you were, you are confirming what the doubters said, that— *You are past it.*

I did it a couple of times and came out on top because I made sure that I had the best pickers behind me, rehearsed the show, and I carefully chose a familiar set of songs. It's not a time for experiments. Don't make the same mistake Harry Connick Jnr did by including a totally different programme to what the punters were expecting.

Remember, it's supposed to be a 'Come Back' show—y'know, Old Memories.

29

TELEVISION

As I mentioned earlier, our first musical TV exposure in the UK came in October 1972 with a show for Granada TV in Manchester. The feedback was very good, so much so, that I hoped that something would come from it, but in the event it proved to be a one–off and it was to be another four years before we got a national show. In the meantime I did take the odd stab at various TV auditions and kept the mail flowing but with no results, until I heard on the grapevine that auditions were being held for a TV talent show called 'Opportunity Knocks' so I made it my business to get on the show. I knew the producer Barney Colehan from my days in the North, and had a very tenuous connection with the host Hughie Green, having been on his show a year earlier as a sponsor for comedian Ralph Denby. Fortunately he did remember me and we were selected for the regional heats being held at Bristol and that turned out to be a complete disaster.

On the run up from Cornwall everybody was tense and squabbling over the slightest thing, on top of which we arrived late, so we were well down on the list, the delay adding to our tension. The net result was that we ended up churning out Merle Haggard's 'Daddy Frank' about three times faster than it should have been and I suspect, in the wrong key. Hughie gave us a sickly smile and Barney, flushing somewhat, told me he would be in touch. (I'm still waiting for that call).

However Opportunity did knock again though, but from a totally un-expected direction about six months later while working for an agency in Devon, who put us up for an audition for a discovery TV show called New Faces.

New Faces

This time I decided to keep it under wraps. Again the auditions were being held in Bristol at the old Empire Theatre, and to avoid another severe attack of panic I simply told the band that we had an afternoon show at Clifton, and it was not until we actually arrived at the Empire that I broke the news to them. It was too late now for any nerves and we put on a great performance of the title track from my third SFA album 'Drinking A Beer And Singing A Country Song'. It knocked 'em out and we were booked on to a New Faces show from Birmingham later that year. Strangely enough the agency did not bother to sign us to any kind of man-agement contract, which would have been the obvious move, putting them up for the 20% commission due that could have amounted to a considerable sum. I heard later that they had folded. With such an obvious lack of busi-ness acumen I was not too surprised.

In the event it was April 1976 before we got the call to present ourselves at the studios of Associated Television in Birmingham.

This New Faces tour was to be a four–day trip with all expenses paid, but I don't think that this 'Expenses Paid' bit sank in with me. I was prob-ably too excited to realize that we could have booked in any where, the

Albany, the Hilton, or even at the exclusive La Reserve in Sutton Coldfield, but mesmerized by the thought of TV exposure, I booked us into the usual showbiz digs we used when touring in the Midlands, known to all and sundry as Debbie's Den. This was a converted four–bedroom semi in the crummy part of Digbeth, where Debbie's DIY husband had converted the outhouse to a visitor's canteen or Guest Dining Room, as she so genteelly termed it. It was neatly paneled out in pine printed hardboard which had probably fallen off the back of a lorry, and covered with lots of victims (Sorry, I mean guest's) photos where Debbie dished up steaming heaps of stewed something, and greasy chips and asked for more signed pictures. I often wished that her husband would come across a knocked off load of washing powder, so that the sheets might be a bit cleaner, but as Debbie once said, too much washing wore them out. These digs were about two miles out of town and on our arrival at the TV station we discovered that the more wide–awake acts had booked into a four star hotel next door to the studios but the die was cast and so we made the best of things.

Complications did arrive however over the choice of song we had intended to do. Originally it was intended, quite naturally, that we should do the number that we did at the audition but when seeking clearance from the American publishers we discovered that they wanted $2000 for a single performance, and ATV declined to pay out such a sum for inclusion in a discovery program, so we had to do some quick thinking, and in the end we did a Waylon Jennings song called 'Ladies Love Outlaws'. As we were essentially a live cabaret act the first rehearsal on an empty studio did not sound so good, but on the night of the show with a big live studio audience, we really hit some form and came over in a really big way. Everything fitted together perfectly. Voices, musicians, costumes and routines.

We did not win however, but came in second to a bunch of fresh–faced twelve year olds from Liverpool. Well, they do say in this business that you should never work with kids or animals. To be honest though, I must say that they were very good. I think it is wonderful to see such young talent like that emerging. I wish them every success. (And that I'll kill the little sods if they ever cross my path again).

Wotcha mean, jealous? Moi? Never. Grrrrr!

The cloying cult of Political Correctness had not yet arrived, and the judging panels could be scathing and very harsh in their criticisms, and Mickey Most in particular was noted for his vitriolic comments, but in spite of his built in prejudice against what he called 'White Southern Music' he was quite kind to us, saying that he really liked what he had heard and that we sounded fresh and authentic, commenting favourably on Kit's stage presence and my voice and visual image. Other judges including Shaw Taylor, Jimmy Henny were most complimentary about our show and Lionel Blair was very enthusiastic about Kit's dancing and said we were great. One thing that does stay in my mind was the superb job the compere did. This was Derek Hobson and he really kept things rolling smoothly along, Not an easy thing with all us nervous artistes around. For once there was no anti–climax after the show as we had a full diary and we were on the road under pressure most of the time. However, a couple of months later we were happy to hear that we had been selected for a special guest spot on the All Winners Show.

During the intervening period there had been a number of changes in the personnel of the band. Sandy Horn who was having health problems left, and Alan Knight moved onto pedal steel guitar. Terry Dean came in on bass, Steve Turner played lead guitar and Dave Wayne stayed on drums. It was a superb sound, much cleaner than the earlier Everglades. We had new costumes made and this time the song was our own arrangement of a Chip Taylor number called 'I Wasn't Born In Tennessee'. It was a Wow. And the studio audience went crazy. I recall that the Eurovision Song Contest winners 'Brotherhood of Man' were in the audience and they came excitedly rushing down to congratulate us. Once more the panel of judges were very impressed and once again, Mickey Most had good words for us.

"Yeah," he said. "I think they're the best. Great stage presence. A little more Rock in the act and I think they've got it made."

Which was high praise indeed from the caustic record producer.

Another judge, song publisher Alan Freeman, said enthusiastically that we certainly ought to be on the Wembley Country Music Festival and that the promoters should book us, but it was another two years before this came to pass.

However when the final scores were totalled up we came in second again, but we did get a special award. This time the winner was a glamorous black girl singer called Simone whose frantic manager did a lot of back–stage lobbying and she went on to pick up some nice contracts on the cruise ships. Gig–wise the 'New Faces 'show did not initially make much difference to us as most shows had been booked many months in advance, so the main advantage lay with the promoters who got their venues full—and naturally they did not up our fees. But once inside the TV world a number of things did begin to happen.

One was the arrest of our lead guitarist for defaulted alimony payments. His ex–wife had been looking for him for years and finally spotted him on TV. The police made an attempt to nab him at a club near Chard, but he heard them asking questions in the bar and we managed to smuggle him out under a coat on the back seat of my car. We were too well known, and they caught up with him at Mount Charles Club in St Austell. I went down to the Police Station the following morning and magnanimously offered to pay his outstanding warrant to keep the band on the road. However I quickly changed my mind when the Inspector told me how much was involved, and contented myself with a few good wishes as he boarded the train to London handcuffed to a policeman.

*   *   *   *   *   *

Star Gazey Pie

Another development was a series called 'Sounds of Britain'. The idea was that each Independent TV region was commissioned to produce a representative program of its own area. Our nearest station was Westward Television in Plymouth, and producer Paul Bernard invited enquiries from interested acts. He was not a staff producer but had been brought in specifically to do this series. He had been a producer at Granada and his credits included some dangerous and impressive documentaries in Ulster. He was also a very talented artist, and I am the proud owner of one of his Cornish landscapes, a study he sketched while staying at our house. The buzz went around the region like wildfire, and I quickly realized that in spite of our success on New Faces, that every act in the West Country would be banging in an application, so I decided to take an oblique approach and wrote to Westward TV as the manager of the band, inviting Paul to come and see the act in action. The experiment worked, and he responded by coming to see us at a gig at the Harbour Lights Hotel in Padstow with his PA, and he must have liked what he saw because a week later I got a contract from Westward TV for a show to be called *Star Gazey Pie*.

I can hear you asking what a Star Gazey Pie is, so I'll explain. In the days when the staple diet of the Cornish miner was the ubiquitous pasty, usually a hard–baked pastry envelope of meat and vegetables, there was sometimes a desire to produce something different and a fish filling was the obvious alternative, and in Cornwall the mackerel was the most available fish. But the mackerel is quite a big fish, so the pasty was made with the tail and head hanging outside the pastry covering, the tail limp but the eyes gazing hopefully at the stars—hence, Star Gazey Pie.

The show was made partly in the Westward Television studios at Drake Circus in Plymouth, and a number of outside locations such as the Tamar Bridge, Exeter, and at Porthtowan, Cornwall. Other acts involved were a trio from deepest Devon called the Broken String Band who did some very good original numbers. I thought they were great and two of their self–penned songs were most impressive. 'West Atlantic Border', the story of a frustrated holiday romance and 'The Western Motorway', a ballad about the return of the ghosts of Brunel's labourers to build the new M5. Motorway.

There were a couple of other acts too. One was a very pretentious English Folk–Rock unit called the Albion Band who turned out to be your typical 'Blue Denim Heroes'. Classic 'Finger in the ear' folksy posers, doggedly determined to push their 19th century working man image. Even off–stage they seemed to be wallowing in a time–warp of their own and had little to do with us mere mortals. Their contribution was a dull, rambling ballad about the bungled hanging of a murderer called John Lee at Exeter Jail in the 19th Century, and the Dorset farmer's accent droned on and on. We thought it would never finish and the floor manager's eyes were rolling skywards by the time it stumbled to a straggly end. The only thing good was Dave Swarbrick's inspired fiddle playing. Later on, some of my folksy friends berated me for my opinions, telling me that the Albion Band was quite famous in folk circles, but on that show their entertainment content was absolutely nil and left me unmoved.

I had written a couple of songs about Cornwall for the show, one of which was the haunting 'Red rocks and white waters', about the lure of the Duchy, and the mystic charm that holds people there and constantly calls them back. Other numbers suggested by the producer were standard Country & western songs, (Oh, how I hate that connotation) which we reluctantly did. However soon the rehearsals and camera timings were complete, and the show was recorded in late September 1977 and was screened in the Westward region in November, and on national TV on December 28th 1977 putting the final touch to a great Xmas. Martin Grinham and his girl friend Meg came down to Cornwall, and we had all the usual crew around to party at our place. The only shadow was Kit's growing thyroid problem, although at that time we did not know exactly what was wrong. She had been chronically ill since we got back from Italy, but the local GP put it down to just a heavy cold and the stress of moving house. In fact it was not until a locum doctor took over the local health centre, that the real reason for her condition was discovered and treatment started. It took a full year to get truly better and on a final visit to Trelisk Hospital on 15th December she had direct treatment to the thyroid gland in the form of a radioactive fluid drink, and thereafter kept the flow under control by thyroxin tablets. It was an immediate improvement although to this day she still has to take medication to prevent any re–occurrence of those debilitating symptoms,

As the New Year rolled around we did a BBC radio show in London, and after that carried on touring all over the UK doing the usual one night stands. Our old Transit finally collapsed from road stress (as they usually did) and gave up, so we bought another one. This time it was bright yellow, as it happened quite a good colour for a lemon, and a right lemon it turned out to be! Within a month it needed a new gearbox, and a fortnight later another engine. Those Ford Transit vans might have got a good reputation as getaway vehicles for warehouse robbers, but they were no good as bandwagons.

* * * * * *

The BCMA Dinner

This event turned out to be the usual sycophantic parade of record in-dustry big-wigs, has-beens and wannabees, paying tribute to the pro-moters and their great expertise in finding suitable (or gullible?) sponsors. Also there were the usual suspects from the Nashville Establishment pay-ing homage to the Great Money Hunter, and one or two British Country Music parasites were busy brown-nosing around, hoping that someone would send them to Nashville. There were also a clutch of Country Music journalists recording VIP interviews, and studiously ignoring the British performers, but as usual, any representatives of the mainstream musical press were conspicuously absent.

It really was amazing to find even at this late stage, with over twelve thousand people a day attending the week long Wembley Country Music Festival, that music tabloids like Melody Maker and NME still stubbornly refused to accept that Country Music had arrived. Yet when I hosted a Country TV series later, both the Daily Express and the Mirror sent reporters and a photographer to interview me, and later published a warm review of the shows. One thing that did impress me that night, was the business acumen and sense of timing of Britain's biggest Country Music promoter, Mervyn Conn—I admired his serious commitment to our music.

I kept in touch with Paul Bernard and brought him along that night as our guest,, and took the opportunity of introducing him to Mervyn. To-gether we explored the possibility of further television shows, and the idea of collaborating on a major Country Music series later in the year with me co-producing the shows, and Mervyn providing us with American guest artistes. From my point of view this was a major break. Finally, a show was going to be screened on the national network TV featuring our music, with me as the host. Great! Such a thing had not been done since Canadian Gordon Lightfoot was featured in a series almost twenty years previously.

Another thing I remember very clearly about that night, was the fact that there were no places set for Kit and me in the dining room. The B.C.M.A's Girl Friday, that night wearing her public relations hat and concerned that I might make waves, lamely explained that all the tables had been allocated alphabetically and as my name began with a Y there were no places left—but we could have our dinner upstairs in the bar. Lovely! We told her where she could stick her Poussin et Frites. Thanks a lot, Jessie. Kitty really appreciated it. What a nice way to treat someone who nearly got scalped fighting for Your Money at Tex Withers mad party in Hammersmith.

*   *   *   *   *   *

The Superglades

Why the 'Superglades'? Well, let's get one thing straight from the start. It was not my idea. It was Mervyn Conn's and was suggested by him at a lunch we were having in Soho to discuss the forthcoming Billy Jo Spears tour. To be honest I preferred the old name of the 'Everglades', a title conferred on us by the legendary songwriter Harlan Howard whom we had met in Tokyo during the Vietnam War, but right at that moment I was walking on eggshells wanting to get on the Wembley Festival, and was very susceptible to anything the promoter suggested. So 'SUPERGLADES' it was and I can see now that it must have seemed a natural progression, because the band had actually been getting bigger over the years, sometimes numbering as many as seven musicians.

But before I go on, perhaps I should tell you more about this band that was giving me a permanent headache. It was an enigma. The combined sound was superb and the individual talents of those concerned were beyond reproach. Everybody was so good at what they did but the contrasting personalities were a nightmare. I suppose the basic fault was my obsessive search for authentic sounds, and was a classic case of overkill on my part, not recognizing when I had a good thing going and trying to improve something that was already very good.

It was an excellent unit but sadly Sandy was the weak link, not musically you understand, but health wise. Sandy Horen was in fact a very good musician, playing guitar, piano and sax but he was at his best on the pedal steel guitar. His style was unique due mainly in his tuning to a D major chord instead of the traditional E 9th or C 6th, which gave him an almost authentic, Dobro sound. However he was not very robust and physically was not really up to the hard nights on the road, but he never once complained about the tough conditions and poor digs. Finally, at the end of one particularly gruelling winter tour of Scotland, his wife Cathy met up with us in Stockport, and after taking one look at him insisted that he quit the tour and come home to see his doctor. After that things really began to unravel. His replacement arrived, and then I came across a really topclass fiddle and mandolin player and that was all that was needed to destroy the fine balance we had achieved.

Sandy's wife was a very attractive woman and a superbly expressive big band singer, who had successfully made the difficult change to Country, and as Cathy Ann Porter made quite a name for herself on the club circuits. This transition from easy listening ballads was not easy because so many of the rules of strict tempo vocalizing did not really apply to an art form where emotion and expression are paramount

*   *   *   *   *   *

Stone Ginger

Look out. Here comes the wrecking ball.

We were in the North East at the start of an extended tour when we hit a period of uncertainty. Sandy did not show up at the first club. We got by somehow, and on returning to our digs at Cliff Leger's house in Redcar, there was a message from Kit who was still in Cornwall sorting out some family problems. Cathy had called to say that Sandy was ill again and had been ordered to take a rest. So really that was that, but Kit said that there was a steel player advertising in the musical press for a job, and she had spoken to him and that he was prepared to travel right away. I told her to contact him again with the terms and conditions and get him to join us in Redcar.

For the purpose of this narrative I will call him Ginger.

He arrived one afternoon while we were out rehearsing at a nearby club, and Cliff's wife Delores made him welcome and showed him his room and got him settled in. We got back around five and got down to discussing the job at the dinner table., He was of medium height with a shock of spiky red hair, of stocky build but carrying a lot of flesh around the midriff and spoke with a rich Birmingham accent. He seemed well informed about the music and said that he had finished a tour with a visiting Texas singer. His steel playing was excellent and he could also sing and play a little basic guitar, so on the surface everything seemed fine but for some reason I felt uneasy about the man—why had I not heard about him before now?—I had been around for some time but this was the first time I had come across his name and I thought I knew most steel guitar players on the scene. It was only a vague unease I felt but I finally dismissed it, putting it down to tour fatigue.

The boys did their best to make him feel at home and we were all pleased with his stylish playing, but in spite of his willingness to get his hand down at the bar, one or two of them expressed feelings of doubt about him. After the first gig I phoned Kit and gave her a glowing report of her find, and settled down to the rest of the tour, but I rate the fifteen months he spent with us as one of the most stressful and unpleasant periods in my career.

It all started with his sudden obsession to get fit and slim, and the resulting jogging and dieting brought about a complete change in his warm personality. Gone was the jolly, easy–going, pudgy man, and Ginger became very picky and belligerent, and generally upsetting the delicate balance of the band with his forceful unsolicited opinions, but as we were all earning good money we put up with it.

However it got worse when we discovered that women and booze were his other problems. In the main the band were not skirt chasers, being more into the charms of sweet sensimilla weed and magic mushrooms, but because nobody except the drummer would go with him on these dog hunting forays, he accused us of all being gay. One of the first rows I had with him was because of my refusal to wait an hour outside a flat in a sink estate in Stockton after the show, while he got his leg over.

He began to criticize everything around him, my singing style and choice of material, Big Steve's style of playing, which he said clashed with his own, and he so intimidated Stavros on drums that he became reluctant to put in any fills at all in case he upset Ginger. On tour I ended up sharing a room with him because nobody else would, due to his constant moaning. He then began to say he was leaving whenever things didn't suit him. All in all he threatened to walk out over nine times in the period he was with us. Every time he felt that he had an edge, he would play his moody ulti-matum card, like at the beginning of a TV series or before the Wembley Festival, or while waiting to board the cross channel ferry for a German tour—and two days before kicking off a long summer season in Cornwall.

And still I put up with it. I must have been mad.

The situation was exacerbated when I took on a brilliant fiddle player from Leamington Spa. When he joined us the personalities were split even deeper. The music was superb, but the six vastly differing life styles and attitudes were becoming impossible to handle. One gig in particular was at Newquay British Legion where there was an argument every time we came off stage. (Later developments showed that this was actually triggered by Ginger getting knocked back by the Manager's pretty daughter.)

It was much the same at other Cornish gigs like Perran Sands Holiday Village and the big Hendra Complex, where he would kick off at the slightest excuse, and he made the subsequent Jerry Naylor tour an absolute nightmare. I think his role models were Ken Livingston, Tony Benn and union boss Red Robbo.

As for the fiddle player, he was a well-educated young man from a talented middle-class family but his social attitudes were fashionably anti-Establishment and hippy orientated, anti-American in general, and anti-Yonco in particular. I really don't know why he wanted to join our Country band anyway. He knew what we were about musically, but would alternatively paint his fiddle IRA green or Che Guevara red just to wind me up. However he and Tim the bass player got on famously, due to a shared love of modern English electric folk music, and they would spend hours on board the bus talking about the mind numbing Albion Band and Fairport Convention or Maddy Prior's charms.

Country Music Television

Eventually the plans that Paul Bernard and I made at the BCMA dinner did come to fruition in April '78 when Westward Television got the go ahead from the ITA, and I started seeking a title for the shows that would make a big mark and draw all the fans together—regrettably however the option was taken out of my hands and Paul came up with the inspired title of, wait for it—COUNTRY STYLE Traaarr (Oh no). He wanted wagon wheels and bales of hay on the set. I was surprised that we didn't have

Doris Day singing 'The Black Hills of Dakota' running over the credits, and Big Bill Campbell giving us pearls of homespun wisdom.

In fact, Paul and I had a covert running battle throughout that series. We both had differing views of what the content and message of the programmes should be. To me it seemed to make sense if each of us pursued those facets of the industry we understood best. Paul should do the studio production and the direction of the shows, and I would look after the artistic and musical content including the guest artists, but that was not the way it worked out. Paul was a great believer in the hands–on approach and insisted on personally vetting the acts. (Particularly the female ones.) Of course it was all done in the very best 'Luvvy 'tradition but there were tantrums and tears before bedtime, and more backstabbing than on the Ides of March.

Another stress factor came into the equation around that time because Peter Cadbury, the then boss of Westward TV was locked into some financial battle with Mr. Bryce the chief of Brymon Airways, a bitter dispute that contributed to the sad demise of Westward TV a few years later. There were some great people working there back then. We made many friends with such great characters as that superb anchorman Ken McLeod, and that very attractive and cookie presenter Judy Spiers with her famous rabbit Gus Honeybun.

The technicians were lovely people too, very helpful and co–operative with us, but I got the distinct impression that they were not exactly wild about the way Paul did things. Technically I thought that he did a great job, but to my mind the shows seemed crowded with too many guest artists, and that perhaps camera work and the sound quality could have been better. The fact that the two gay audio engineers were having lovers spat every day made the latter problem worse. One facet of the show however was great. Paul decided to use a live studio audience and lots of our friends from Cornwall were there. Checking videos of the shows today it is fascinating to see how we all looked back then, and these images certainly trigger off a lot of happy memories

We made an arrangement with Mervyn' to supply some US guest artists and he came up with a few goodies like Carl Perkins, Don Everley, George Hamilton IV, Skeeter Davis and a few lesser known artistes like Texas rocker Roy Head and New Yorker Randy Gurley (Was that her name or her condition?) plus a selection of totally unknown performers recommended by certain Nashville agents but not necessarily for their musical abilities.

I did manage to get my way with some of the UK. talent, including The Kelvin Henderson Band, Raymond Froggat and the White Rose herself, Jeanie Denver, but my co–producer insisted in second guessing me, and chopped out quite a few of my recommendations. I remember coming in one morning and as I was passing Paul's office he called, "Hey Yonk, just listen to this. Its great."

I had to agree, it certainly was. A great version of 'Oh, Las Vegas.'

"It's just come in," he burbled. "It's a girl singer from London. She's worked all over the world and what a looker. Just check that publicity pack."

I rifled through the publicity pages until I came to a glossy soft focus 8x10 photo of a pretty woman in her thirties whom I knew well from the British Country Music clubs. "Oh, I know her," I said, "that's Jane Smith (not her real name) but that's not her singing. That's Emmylou Harris and that guitarist is James Burton. I've got the LP.

"Oh no, its not," he insisted. "You are getting really paranoid about these guest artistes Yonco. If she is that good, she's on the show."

So that was that. Jane had simply taped off that Emmylou number and sent it in as herself—and it had worked. Of course she did not do that song on the show so no direct comparisons could be made and she got away with it.

Actually this was a time of great stress for us too. Kit was ill with her thyroid problem, but she managed to be supportive and put on a good show, and the Superglades were at the height of their temperamental extremes. Ginger the steelie was sniffing the continuity girl's skirts, and the violin player wasted so much studio time, sulking or throwing wobblers and threatening to walk off the set, that the camera crew called him 'The Fiddler on the Hoof.' Eventually though, it all came together nicely and soon all six studio sessions were in the can, plus a number of outside location settings including a nice children's Western dance routine on Plymouth Hoe, and we did a nice segment at Montecute House, a rambling stately pile where I featured the title track of our new album called 'Old Greyhound', in a vintage car that could just about run and had to be pushed over the humpbacked bridges on the estate.

About four shows were filmed at the Moving Picture Studios in Soho, with a taciturn Don Everly and Carl Perkins who was off his head on chemicals, and kept mistaking me for Johnny Cash. At one point he wandered off the set on the middle of a take to ask Albert Lee what was going on and where were they? I also recall with dread an excruciating duet I had to do with Skeeter Davis. Brr!

The other outside broadcasts were done in Cornwall and the whole thing was completed in less than three weeks. The series was shown on Westward TV in August, and then on the national network on six consecutive Fridays from 14th September 1978. It got good reports from the critics and a warm response from the viewers, and the usual flutter of broken promises of more TV work.

*   *   *   *   *   *

30

THE BLANKET ON THE GROUND
Billy Jo Spears, Lloyd Green, Vernon Oxford, Merle Haggard, Mo Bandy

In March '78 we played another Country Music banquet at London's Grosvenor House. Kenny Rogers was the guest of honour and we were the resident band. The high spot of the evening for me was meeting up with two old friends from Germany, American agents, Fred Carusio and Harry Kriner who offered me a month's work on the bases backing Tommy Overstreet, a smaltzy singer who was currently Flavour of the Month in Nashville. But more about Tommy later

The Wembley Festival came around as usual at Easter and Mervyn Conn invited Kit and I to present a 'Best Of British' show at the Conference centre there. It was a super show and showed that British acts were very good, but certainly in need of better mainstream press support and radio time. I met Rod King again and we had a good time shooting the breeze with old friends. We also met Kenny Rogers again, and I had a desultory conversation with a very moody Merle Haggard who confided that he thought London sucked. Don Gibson also turned up, wearing a Stetson hat two sizes too small for him and just as pissed as the last time I saw him in Germany nine years earlier. Also there balancing on a barstool, was a rather confused Mo Bandy, who was out of his head on something, and kept standing up to give us all a twirl in his tartan jacket which had a pleated skirt.

The place was full of loonies and moodies. In fact, I felt quite at home.

In the spring of that year, American Country diva Billy Jo Spears made her big breakthrough into the British pop scene with a succession of very similar but catchy pop songs like 'Blanket on the Ground, '57 Chevrolet' and 'I will survive.'.

(I still think that her version of this old drag queen anthem is the best.). It was only natural then, that she should do a big UK tour and also naturally, Mervyn Conn was the one who put it together and we were booked to play support and back her. It was quite a big production with Billy Jo sharing top spot with steel guitarist Lloyd Green and supported by Ronnie Prophet, Vernon Oxford and Frank Yonco with the Superglades

On October 26th we were all assembled for rehearsals or rather, run-throughs at the Royal Garden Hotel, London, and the tour managers were Rob Zawafdski and Warren Davis. There was a lot of talent on the show so it didn't take long to get things together, I think a couple of afternoons were sufficient to get the running order right, and Zawadski and Davis were experienced tour managers who diplomatically ironed out any snags, about the only complaints came from Ronnie Prophet, but as the tour went on we came to expect that this was his normal behavior. We sorted out our rooms and I shared one with Tim Collingwood our bass player. He was a great guy but quite fond of the booze and on the first night there, while I was out having dinner with Martin Grinham, the Mervyn Conn Office sent round a magnum of champagne as a send–off for the tour. Not realizing (perhaps) that it was intended for the whole band Tim simply opened it and drank it all himself. When I arrived back he was sprawled stark naked across both beds mumbling incoherently and hanging onto the empty bottle. The following day he moved in with the fiddle player down the hall and I ended up sharing with moaning Ginger the steel guitarist.

Billy Jo Spears was from Beaumont County, the same area of South East Texas that spawned the great George Jones, and had had a chequered career in the business, starting as a singing waitress when she was just sixteen. The usual pattern of grinding tours followed as a support singer on those seeming interminable tours of the of America's Middle West, until she got a break at an age when most people would be thinking seriously of kicking it all into touch. In Billy Jo's case middle age turned out to be the Golden Age, as her music hit the button with the BBC Radio Two audiences and under an enlightened producer she came up with a succession of middle of the road hits. Even though her voice was pure Texas Country with a charming huskiness, the most receptive public were not real country fans, but mainly 'Easy Listening' audiences, the kind of people who bought the synthetic Nashville Glitz of Tammy Wynette, Kenny Rogers, John Denver and Dotty West.

At the time we met her at the Royal Garden Hotel she was in her late forties but still looked good, with a full figure and a pretty elfin, heart shaped face. She was accompanied by someone she described as her manager, an odd looking guy with frizzy hair and glasses. He did not know much about the music business and generally did not have much to say but as a dedicated boozer, he became a great pal of Vernon Oxford.

Vernon was still in the full flood of his British success, the result of heavy pushing on the Country Music Club circuit. His act was based on the Hank Williams image and he portrayed that basic kind of Country Music very well, though he was virtually ignored in the USA, being regarded as too 'Country' by the record executives. I got on well with him. We both shared a passion for the music of Hank Williams and Jack Daniels Sour Mash whiskies of which we drank a full bottle one afternoon in the sauna at the Peterborough Hilton. In time he almost followed his hero's footsteps by nearly boozing himself to oblivion before turning to Jesus in the time honored way of fading Country singers and hitting the Gospel Circuit.

*   *   *   *   *   *

The Belfast Booze Cruise

The tour dragged on and at one point we were sent to Northern Ireland where we did about six shows, two in Belfast, two in Londonderry, one at a seaside resort and a very scary one at some kind of Para–military base. We flew into Aldergrove Airport and were booked into the most bombed hotel in the world, the Europa Hotel in Great Victoria Street, Belfast, where we got our first experience of the high profile security situation. British Army armored cars and RUC Land Rovers prowled the streets and steel barred gates controlled pedestrian access to the shopping precinct with armed policemen wearing flak jackets in constant attendance. The shows were always early usually starting about six p.m. and were usually very well attended particularly in Derry. The venues were strange though, mostly disused cinemas or public halls, not theatres and always with a strong security presence.

About the most bizarre gig was somewhere in the outskirts of Belfast. We travelled in convoy with Police vehicles front and back, (It was just like Vietnam all over again) until we came to some tall corrugated iron gates where our escort departed. After several minutes the gates scraped open and we were directed into a large compound. The walls were about twelve feet high, roughly built of old bricks, concrete filled plastic beer cases and roughly laid breeze blocks, with sandbagged watchtowers at each corner. In the middle, was an old cinema that had been converted to some kind of club with more sandbags at the entrance. We were ushered inside and found a complete bacchanal in progress. The place was packed with shouting and laughing hard–looking men and women, slugging back as much booze as they could drink. The air heavy with tobacco smoke and marijuana fumes. Sweating waiters and barmen were struggling to keep up with the loud demands for Guinness for the lads and whiskies for the women, that were always drunk in tall tumblers topped up with sweet lemonade. No money changing hands at all except for handfuls of change for the servers. At the side of the stage a fat DJ wound the crowd up with screaming Rock 'n' Roll and Irish songs.

Somehow or other we got set up, refusing the booze that was being forced on us until everything was ready, and the show went absolutely great. We couldn't do a thing wrong. They were all well oiled before we arrived but by the time we left they were completely crazy. and insisted we stay on for a few drinks which we did until well past midnight. Everything was available. Booze? Any kind you wanted. Drugs? Wotcha want? Horse, Freebase, Ganja? No problem. And there were plenty of willing women if required in the upstairs office complex. And for us it was all for free. But of course the Code of the Road prevents me from listing the temptations further.

I made cautious enquiries about this availability of everything and was warned quite firmly not to ask too many questions. Apparently they (whoever They were) simply phoned up the local brewery or drug baron and ordered what they wanted. Any refusal could result in a serious bomb attack on the offending company's property or a kneecapping of the supplier. It was a great night but I was relieved to get out of those corrugated iron gates I can tell you.

Back in Belfast before the last show of the trip, Big Steve and I decided to take a look around the city and visit one or two of the bars, which were open all day. We were getting back to the Europa Hotel about three in the afternoon when we met Vernon and Billy Jo's manager, heading out for a liquid lunch. We reminded them that the first show was at 6.30 p.m., but Vernon waived us aside and assured us that they'd be back in time. However when 6.30 came and the show began, there was no sign of Vernon.

We kicked off as usual and as we were approaching the end of our spot a note was passed to me saying that Vernon had been delayed, and to do another two numbers. And then I got signals from off stage to do another one, and caught a glimpse of a glassy eyed Vernon leaning against the wall. Finally we got off and one of the road managers came on with a tall stool, and announced that Vernon Oxford had fallen and badly strained his back, but being the trouper he was he would not let his fans down, and do his spot on the stool. And to add authenticity to the Star's condition, they asked if there was a doctor or a nurse in the audience who would come backstage later?' Vernon was then helped on stage, playing the invalid to perfection and plonked reeling, onto the stool for his spot, which, considering his condition, he did very well, even if he had to be almost carried off at the end of it.

The sequel was a hoot. Half an hour later he was stretched out on a billiard table with two nurses pulling and pushing him painfully around, trying to mend his non–existent back injury. Finally he was hauled off to Belfast General Hospital for X Rays and traction treatment, missing the next three shows and losing the money. He finally caught up with us four days later at the Floral Hall, Southport, and admitted later that it was one of the most expensive pub–crawls he had ever been on. Mind you, I didn't have much sympathy for him financially because, due to his Nashville roots he was getting more per show than we were getting for the whole band. But Vernon was fun and was not a bad guy, which is more than I can say for the other support act Ronnie Prophet. He was really bad news and did his best to make everybody feel as uncomfortable as possible. I never heard him say a good word about any other artiste, even his fellow Canadians like Ann Murray. However he was a good guitarist and did some clever comedy numbers but he not a nice guy at all.

* * * * * *

Lloyd's Highland Horror

Lloyd Green, one of the top steel guitarists in the world, was also featured on the show. He was a pleasant, quiet man and a renowned member
of MENSA who spent most of his time on the bus reading books about his
latest passion Ancient Egypt. Mind you, it was rumored that the Land of
the Pharoes wasn't his only passion, which was one reason that Mrs.Green
was also on the tour. She had heard about all these pushy European
women and she was determined to save her husband from any temptations
that might be put in his path. After all, that kind of thing never happens in
Nashville, does it? (I wonder if Glen and Tania would agree with her?)

Lloyd was not noted for his sense of humor either so we did not have
much to do with him. However, musicians and road crews are not easy
people to ignore and his superior attitude built up a bit of resentment,
which manifested itself on the last night at the Eden Theatre, Inverness.

The tour had been a long one and due to poor logistic planning we spent
lots of boring hours in the coach, which for some reason was rather slow, so
on the last night in Scotland everybody came in for a bit of stick from the
stage crew. For my part of the show they had a skeleton on a string, which
kept bobbing up and down behind the drums all through one of my
tearjerkers, completely wrecking the mood of the song of course, but that's
what you expect on the last night of a tour. In Ronnie Prophet's spot, a
rubber chicken was tossed on stage and with Vernon, all the stage lights
started flickering to ruin the tempo of his songs, but the piece-de-resist-
ance was reserved for stuffy Lloyd who insisted on closing the first half,
and locked himself in his dressing room to avoid being involved in the last-
night horseplay, until it was his time to go on stage, but the road crew
decided that he was not going to get off that lightly.

When they positioned his steel guitar on stage, they taped down the
volume control pedal, smeared soft soap on his playing bar and attached
nylon fishing-lines to the two knee levers controlling the change of tuning,
leading them off to the side. The compere, who that night happened to be
me, introduced him to the audience, but delayed his sitting down with a
few questions, and a flowery welcome to Inverness, so that by the time he
got to his instrument there was no time to check anything. He was obviously ruffled and after a false smile and a grim 'Good evening ', he
launched into his own special version of 'Tammy's in Love'.

Well, you've never heard such a row. As he hit the first chord the soapy
steel bar slipped out of his hand and clanged against the strings, causing
the amplifier to screech out a hideous feed back from the taped volume
control. Lloyd went white and scrabbled to rip off the gaffer tape and dry
his bar on a cloth. The audience sat in astonishment at his wild antics until
the laughter began. After a few moments he regained his composure and
launched into the tune again. This time the stage crew let him get through
the first verse, but as he moved into the middle eight bars they began to

pull the nylon lines, causing the guitar to play out of tune. Lloyd looked as though the roof had fallen in and stared around desperately for help, but somehow or other everyone backstage was busy. At the end of the number there was a smattering of applause and a lot of stifled laughter. After that the crew let him get on with it, but he would not speak to anyone when he came off stage, not even B.J.S. and spent the long trip to the Lake District in a sulk.

PICKER'S TIP 44

To remove those stubborn plastic labels and stickers (decals) spray some WD.40 on a bit of cotton wool and rub the offending object and leave it a few minutes and it will peel off easily.

PICKER'S TIP 45

Always carry at least two spare guitar picks on stage and keep them somewhere convenient like a shirt pocket. Not in your pants.

31

THE BUFFALO AND THE ARKANSAS HACKSAW
Jerry Naylor, Tommy Overstreet

After the Billy Jo Spears tour the band began to break up. One by one the musicians left. The Cuba Libra fiddle player joined an obscure, short-lived Country Rock outfit. And guitarist Steve Turner and Tim Collingwood the bass player, decided that they too had finally had enough of Ginger's moaning and confrontational attitudes, and packed their gear and left, leaving me with the job of having to rebuild the band around the drummer and Ginger. Not an easy task. In fact during that period I did some of the worst shows of my career. At any other time I would have let them all go, but I'd got confirmation of the Wembley Festival. The prize gig that everybody wanted. The one that gave you the prestige to move into the top line of Country Music and into the Big Money, but don't hold your breath—it might be just another mirage. Oh yes, the Superglades was a wonderful sound but what a bloody nightmare.

First thing I needed was a bass player and I was lucky in getting one of the best pure bass players in the business Big Stuart Duncan, formerly of the Midland band Tennessee Stud (aka Chevvy). Stuart did not sing, play guitar or any other instrument but was an absolutely superb rhythmic bass player, solid as a rock and with tremendous feeling in his playing. He came down to Cornwall and moved into a house I rented in Lostwithiel with Ginger and Steve, and we spent a few cold afternoons rehearsing at the St. Blazey Football Club. The result was very thin but we made a brave show at the gigs anyway. We did the Riviera, Carlyon Bay, the Companions Hotel in Plymouth and a disastrous show at the Carlton in Liskeard, the same venue where we had been such a sensation seven years previously.

One thing was certain, we needed a good lead guitar player too, so I began to make a few scalping trips, checking out other bands for discontented pickers. It was a tall order to find a replacement for Steve Turner. He was a great musician and superb stylist and under his influence the band had adopted a cool 'West Coast 'sound, as he was an avid fan of L.A. groups like Seatrain and Little Feat. In the event it was Stuart who came to the rescue, saying he knew somebody who would be ideal, an Irish guitarist he had worked with a couple of times who was looking for a job. As an added bonus he also sang, played fiddle and blew a good blues harmonica.

I told Stuart to go ahead and contact him about an audition. About the nearest we would get to his Swindon home in the next few weeks was the Wheelwright's Club in Gloucester so we arranged to meet him there. His name was Denis but he used the stage name of Danny Kirwan. A small but well muscled man with a ready smile, a really happy outgoing personality and an air of constant harassment, but he could play guitar very well and do all the other things, so I gave him the job. Ginger was fuming about my decision and threw his usual wobbler in the van. True to form, throughout

316

the whole time Denis was with us he never missed a chance to bring him down and criticize every aspect of his playing. By contrast he trod very carefully when it came to Stuart who would have had no hesitation in putting him through the wall if he got too smart.

I really liked Denis's guitar work. He had a unique style that later became known as 'Chicken Picking'. A staccato riff against the fret board which you can hear clearly in his backing on 'Jukebox Cinderella', a track from a CD I made later. He did some tasty harmonica work as well, although I'd have to admit that his fiddle playing was a little bit frantic, hence the title.' The Arkansas Hacksaw' bestowed on him by Kelvin Henderson, but he settled in nicely with us and soon we were off to the North East and then along the South Coast, ending up in London.

Stuart and Dennis got on surprisingly well. They could not have been more different. Stuart was massive, tall and heavy, with that slow burning, intimidating presence that one sees in the television portrayal of a Victorian policeman. Dennis on the other hand was small and wiry but just as tough and gutsy. The one thing they had in common was that they were both great musicians but there was also a vast personality difference, each one being typical of their respective backgrounds.

Stuart was your cautious Midlander, very careful with his money who had perfected the art of getting the punters (or anyone else who was dumb enough) to buy his booze, while Dennis was the open handed Irishman who spent money whether he had it or not. For many weeks he would often be subbing wages two or three days after pay day.

Kit came up from Cornwall and for her birthday Martin Grinham and his girl friend Meg took us to see the show 'Evita' in the West End. After that it was back to the snowbound North again. I bought a new guitar in Birmingham. It was a blond Marlin flatop which I eventually sold to Carl Heatley, and when the trip ended I headed home to pack for a tour of Germany and Holland with Jerry Naylor,, one of Buddy Holly's ex-Crickets, which prompted Ginger to state that he would not go, followed by the usual blackmail for a few more quid.

The Jerry Naylor tour was a real drag with Naylor boring the arse off all and sundry with his political posturing, and slugging wine by the bottle on stage and like Red Simpson, staying on stage till all hours. Sometimes he ran over an hour and a half over time. He did not play guitar and although a fair singer and teller of tales, he had no idea of tempo or what key he was in.

He traded shamelessly on his time in the Crickets, Buddy Holly's backing group, but in actual fact he did not spend that much time with them and that was after Holly had been killed, but he could really turn on the sentimental mood with his 'Tribute to Buddy' numbers. On another occasion we were booked into Fulda Officer's Club, where the Custodian complained that we were playing too much Country Music. What else did they expect?

Tommy Overstreet was also touring the bases at this time and unfortunately was also booked in to the Forum Hotel in Wiesbaden with us. He was riding high in the chart with a schmaltzy number called 'My woman, my woman, my wife' and held an inquest every morning at the breakfast table, demanding to know exactly where his band had gone after the show and who they had been with etc? He tried to do it with us but got very short shrift indeed.

Earlier I mentioned Denis' big spending ways and in Germany he really went to town. On one particular occasion, during that Jerry Naylor German tour, I saw him go through $300 in a single day, and bought nothing he could not eat or drink. It was a day off and it was payday so I gave him a lift to Frankfurt, advancing him another $100 in case he hit some emergency, only to have him phone me at three in the morning from the hotel front desk, asking me to o.k. an advance from the night clerk, to pay a taxi and his bill at the BIG APPLE disco in Wiesbaden.

And would it be alright for him to give the taxi driver a whack for overcharging him?

I pointed out that it was almost dawn and that the cabbie was within his rights to charge a bit more than at lunchtime.

On top of everything, when I got back I found that because he had not made arrangements at home, his wife Sandy had been drawing on his pay from Kit as well, with the net result that it took nearly six months for Dennis to level off his debt.

Denis the Destroyer

During the '79 season in Cornwall, Stuart and Dennis shared a caravan on Par Beach. It was hilarious. They shared the cooking. At one time Stuart accused Dennis of serving himself more beans than him so at the next meal Dennis counted them out one by one. There were many funny situations but by far the most hilarious occurred at our bungalow in Par.

We had been on an extended tour and got back to Cornwall about two am. Kit had already gone to bed but had left a note for Stuart and Dennis to sleep in our spare room across the landing from us. I had a couple of beers with them and then went upstairs. They were laughing and giggling in the kitchen and making such a din, that Kit banged on the floor to tell them to get to bed. All went quiet and after a few minutes we heard them coming up stairs and getting to their beds and everybody settled down for the night.

At this point, I should perhaps mention two important facts. Firstly, that the door to the second bedroom was a sliding one and that while we had been away, Kit had bought a large Victorian mirror from the Par Auction Rooms—it was very tall and she had left it leaning against the wall of their bedroom.

Suddenly, around four in the morning a terrific crash echoed through the house, followed by a string of Irish curses and a second ripping crash. We jumped out of bed and Danny Dog started barking his head off. Rushing out of our room we saw Dennis, wearing only his Y fronts, struggling to climb over the crazily hanging door, heading to the toilet downstairs. "Oh Jesus!" He yelped. "Sorry but Ah've gotta go!"

We gaped at the wrecked bedroom. The sliding door was hanging off its runners, its guide rail torn from the wall, while the carpet was covered in broken glass and plaster molding. In the corner Stuart's bed was rocking, as he tried to stifle his laughter under the duvet, and the shattered mirror frame lay twisted and splintered on the floor. What mess. It looked as if a bomb had hit it. Dennis had by this time climbed sheepishly back upstairs and began to explain what had happened as we tried to clear up the debris. Apparently he awoke wanting to go to the toilet, but due to all the booze he was confused and disorientated. He could not find the light but he saw the mirror in the moonlight and thought that it was the door so in desperation he grabbed it and as he pulled, it fell away from the wall and almost crashed on top of him. He yelped with shock and then saw the real door but forgetting it was a slide door, managed to pull it off its runners.—Crash!

Naturally Kit was not best pleased by this incident, and told us we'd better get it all cleaned up in the morning while she was out at the shops, which we did as best we could, but the incident did not end there. After we'd finished sorting out the broken glass, the splintered wood and the crushed plaster, we were sitting in the kitchen having a well-deserved coffee, when Dennis said that he would seize the opportunity of doing some of his laundry in the washing machine. It was soon obvious that Dennis did not know a lot about washing machines, put too many clothes in it, and used too much detergent, because after about five minutes it had stopped revolving and started making funny noises. Umm? Then Dennis, without switching it off, opened the door. WRrraannnng. Wrrranngg. it roared— and commenced to spew washing all over the kitchen floor and floods of dirty soapy water went everywhere.

And at that moment Kitty pulled up in the car—Oh Dear!

Needless to say, Dennis and Stuart never stayed at our place again.

PICKER'S TIP 46

When re-stringing your guitar strings thread them through the machine heads and leave about six inches over. Don't cut it off but thread it back to form loops about one inch diameter. It provides a convenient location for a capo (Dunlop model).

32

THE WEMBLEY FESTIVAL

The Venue. WEMBLEY STADIUM, LONDON, ENGLAND.
The Event. 11th INTERNATIONAL COUNTRY MUSIC FESTIVAL.
The Date. SUNDAY APRIL 15 1979

At 9 p.m. compere Ronnie Prophet comes onstage and announces:

Ladies and Gentlemen, we would now like you to welcome on stage one of the great pioneers of British Country Music. International Country Entertainer — FRANK YONCO and his band THE SUPERGLADES

The applause was thunderous. This was the moment I had been dreaming about.

To play at what was then the premier Country Music Festival in the world, every bit as prestigious as the Grand Ole Opry in Nashville, (which was going through a very traumatic state at that time). I had been trying to get on the show for years, in fact since the first festival, and this was the eleventh. I got so hung up about it that at one point I had taken an advert in the Country Music press to announce that.

'For the 8th year running FRANK YONCO will not be appearing at Wembley.'

Well, it should have been one of the highlights of my career and I suppose actually it was, but I was so stressed with the band that I don't think I enjoyed it as much as I could have done. The Wembley Festival show itself was very exciting and the band personnel involved were Denis on guitar, harmonica, fiddle, Stuart on Bass, Stavros on drums and Ginger on steel guitar, and I managed to persuade Big Steve Turner to join us for this one show, to add his own unique guitar styling to the band.

But I don't feel that I picked the best material for the show. Again influenced by Ginger's moans about trying anything new. I think 'Crazy Arms' and 'The Battle of New Orleans' were our best numbers and of course the song I had written about Cornwall 'Red Rocks and White Waters'. When I opened up with this one there was a tremendous roar of Oggie, Oggie' Oggie, from the massed Cornish contingent and a majestic Peller (A Cornish white witch) in full costume came bustling down the centre aisle of the hall carrying a huge tray of home made pasties for us.

They'm great people, they Cornish.

Backstage was a real gas, with everybody slugging back the booze as fast as possible? I met up again with Bobby Bare, which was great, and with Ronnie Prophet which was not. He was floating on cloud nine from some chemical or other, and was as obnoxious as he had been on the Billy Joe Spears tour, effing and blinding at everyone in general until Boxcar Willy gave him a warning, after which he sat sulking in a corner with some tart he'd smuggled in. Loose tongues were flapping at one table where George Hamilton IV was having his ear bent by a well-known small time agent, who was listing all the fiddles that went on in the promotion business, so I

320

plonked myself down next to George with a Jack Daniels and a silly smile and listened in.

"There's nothing I like better," said the agent smugly, "Than spending O.P.M."

"What's O.P.M.?" Slurred George, putting on a real good drunk act for a guy who said he never touched the stuff—you could've fooled me, George.

"Other People's Money," said the agent."

I thought about asking the promoter more about it, but before I could get round to it he was off sniffing around that luscious fiddle player Jeanna Jae, one of Buck Owens' many ex–wives.

Earlier that day I had introduced the British section of the festival at the smaller auditorium, and met a lot of old friends. It was really a competition, set up I think by the British Country Music Association to find the best British talent. Free Spirit. (Jon Adkin & Mike Mills) won the duo prize with a great version of 'the Fox on the Run' and it was good to see a young man from Oldham, who used to haunt my every show in the North West, asking questions and desperately wanting to become a full time professional country singer, win the solo singer prize with one of his own songs called 'Roses in the snow'. This was Ben Lee Rivers who went on to such success both in the UK and Australia.

Regrettably however that Achilles heel of British Country Music, petty jealousy again was in evidence, when a frustrated songwriter requested a moment on stage to make an important announcement. I said it was o.k. and introduced him to the crowd, whereupon he launched into a tirade about the injustice of the music industry and how it should have been him introducing this show and not ME.

I thought that the array of British talent at that show was very good, but as usual the mainstream showbiz press ignored it, and everybody trooped back to the small clubs to scratch out a marginal living while a gaggle of third rate American acts were given the hero worship treatment.

On the other hand there were some real greats at this 1979 (11th) International Country Music Festival. I think it was probably the best collection of talent of all the festivals, with stars like Marty Robbins, Billy Jo Spears, Don Gibson, Bobby Bare, Conway Twitty, Crystal Gayle and many others. The sensation however was the Texan singer Marty Martin who created the charismatic character Boxcar Willie. He was right on target for the British crowd and they took him to their hearts. He really was the Man of the Match that night.

Apart from us other British acts on the show were Lonnie Donegan, Jeannie Denver, Raymond Froggatt, The Duffy Brothers. Ken and Billy Ford, Al Doherty, Poacher and Nancy Peppers and not really unexpectedly, we all got slated by the sycophantic British Country Music press who were busy flattering the U.S artistes managers, still hoping to get that elusive free trip to Nashville.

Stung to respond, I wrote a vitriolic article to 'Country Music Round Up'

(July 1979)—and I got criticized for that. One critic saying that entertainers should accept their judgment and not presume to reply and one
bitter, twisted, club singer wrote into say that the only way to get on the
show was to rent one of the display stands from Mervyn Conn, which was
totally untrue. Is it any wonder that things never got better on the
domestic Country Music scene with all these petty squabbles and bad vibes
floating around? That weekend at Wembley had a great climax too. Martin
Grinham from Valentine Music, hosted a big champagne party for us at the
hotel and we had a riotous night before getting back on the road again.

Prison Visitors

It was time for the road again working our way to the North. We did a
few gigs around Exeter and then into the Home Counties with the atmosphere in the band getting worse all the time due to Ginger's continual
complaints. The crunch came at a gig in Milton Keynes where he predictably went into his routine performance before any big tour, and tried to
put the arm on me again by demanding more money, or he was not going to
continue on the tour. By this time I had had enough of these blackmailing
games and refused to cough up any more cash, at which point he said he
was leaving that night. I said that was fine. Denis and Stuart were overjoyed at the news, but the drummer was not too pleased as he got on well
with Ginger, and was the only one who would go out with him. So
lightheartedly, we parted with our steelie at Mrs. Bigg's digs, and headed
for the booming clubs of the North East and on to Scotland. It felt good to
be finally rid of him.

Kit had put this tour together for us so we were not involved with the
Poison Dwarf, and did some nice places. At a club outside Glasgow I picked
up another steel player I knew called Donny Johnson, so we didn't miss
Ginger one bit and the humor came back into the tour, in fact, it was a
great relief to be free from his constant carping. Donny was a good steelie
and a natural comic who got on with everybody.

He wore a hairpiece and had no hang ups with it, sometimes putting it
on sideways for a laugh or taking it off at the breakfast table and pretending to feed it biscuits. Later on he took to doing comedy full time, and built
a big reputation in the Lowlands and the Clyde Valley. He was a great guy
on the road and a very funny man.

It was a big tour, mainly in the North East of Scotland taking in Elgin,
Nairn, Inverness, Scrabster, Thurso and Sandy Paul's club in Aberdeen on
the way back. Then it was back across the Firth road bridge for the jobs in
the Clyde Valley, before ending up at Carnwath Mental Hospital near Big-
gar.The place was a Scottish Broadmoor housing some of Scotland's most
dangerous mentally disturbed criminals. Normally we only did the Ward-
er's Club, run by a good friend of ours Jim Beverage who later retired, and
with his family, opened a very successful restaurant at Forth. This time
however it was a two–night stay with one of the shows being for the

patients (Patients? Actually he meant mentally sick killers and rapists.).
Yes, scary.

We followed the Chief Warders car through the high wire mesh gates
into a secure holding area. The inner gates were not opened until the outer
ones were locked shut. Then we slowly cruised through the vast hospital
grounds to the dining–hall where the 'Patients' were waiting impatiently,
banging on the tables and shouting all sorts of obscenities. One of the first
surprises was that there were women in the crowd. This turned out to be a
MIXED top security mental hospital. Wow! Anyway we got set up and
socked it to 'em. The pornographic Rodeo Song was a great favourite. They
demanded three encores and when your audience includes people who have
thrown their wives out of tenement windows and kicked folk to death in a
drunken rage, you do your best to please them. Jim Beverage and the club
committee were very happy and the patients (?) presented me with a
painted bed sheet advertising THE FRANK YONCO SHOW in blood–red
ink (At least I hope it was ink) We used it as a backcloth on our shows in
France until some cleaners in St. Malo ruined it. It was a great memento of
that show and it certainly lasted longer than the six bottles of Glenmoran-
gie they gave us.

Goodbye Superglades

A month later we were booked at the Gaiety Theatre, Douglas in the Isle
of Man. I brought in Johnny Spencer on piano and the sound was very good
indeed. It turned out to be a nice venue and was busy most nights but we
had lousy digs and a nightmare run back from Liverpool Docks to Cornwall
at the end of it, arriving at Hendra Club near Newquay, almost an hour
late, with a distraught Kitty somehow holding the show together with a
few songs backed by Spike Hooper the guitarist from Shades, until we
arrived.

In July we did the Brighton Festival again and on the way back did a gig
at one of our regular venues, the Lamb and Flag pub at Ottery St Mary in
Devon, and who should I meet there but the great Clinton Ford, the man
who had kick–started me back on the road all those years ago. It was great
to see him again and we insisted that he sang a couple of songs. Memories
for me came flooding back as he sang 'The Wild Side of Life' and his inimitable version of 'Marie' and 'Ivory Tower'. We talked about the Manchester days and our recent Isle of Man trip. He told me all about his Manx
residency and the way the Inland Revenue had almost stripped him bare,
but being the trooper he was he was now back on the cabaret scene presenting Old Time Music Hall shows—I wonder what he's doing these days?

In August guitarist Clancy d'Angelo joined us from the Hank Wangford
band and stayed until the end of the year. He was about the only person I
met who was as money conscious as Stuart. I can see them both now, sitting at the bar of a hotel when we did the Harlow Festival. Each one had
about half an inch of beer in his glass and they sat there talking rubbish

and studiously avoiding finishing their drinks so they wouldn't have to buy another one. Every time anyone came in the bar their heads would swivel in unison, hoping it would be somebody they could bum a drink off.

Oh yes, when it came to scrounging they both had Olympic potential. And it was not only drinks. Free food was also a great attraction to them both. Clancy's favourite ploy was at the motorway cafés where he would hang back at the counter, letting everyone go before him. Then as the line moved slowly forward Clancy would help himself to glasses of milk and anything else on show, consuming them before he arrived at the check out with a packet of cheese biscuits and a cup of tea. However, he did come unstuck late one night at Frankley Services on the M5, where he eyed a half-eaten meal on the next table. Presuming it to be abandoned he grabbed it and was in the process of wolfing it down when its owner, a huge trucker returned with the ketchup he had forgotten, and Clancy had to cough up for a complete trucker's fry-up—classic justice indeed.

Back in Cornwall there was some good news when on April 7th 1979. Francis and his girl friend Gill got married at a very old church in Lanhydroc. We put on a big reception for them at Carlyon Bay. I think that there were about ninety guests, and we knew about eleven of 'em. But we were happy to see them settled to a peaceful life in Bodmin, which must have suited them fine as they are still there over twenty five years later. We kept contact when the children were younger; in fact they often stayed with us but by the turn of the century, as Anthony Ross and Felicity Jane became teenagers and had their own life and interests we did not see as much of the family as we would have wished.

There was one other high spot of this period however—and I count it as one of those lost opportunities. It was meeting an Irish builder called Frank Atkins at a gig in Stafford, who offered to act as my manager. He was a nice guy and very sincere and we got on well together. Unlike most of the so-called managers I had come across, he had the money and the contacts in Ireland to back up his proposal, but at the time I was preoccupied with the band's internal problems and stressed by the heavy touring schedule, so I did not pursue the idea. If I had been thinking clearly I should have ditched the band and made my move—but I didn't

The long year ran slowly to an end and despite all the success I was exhausted, and feeling disenchanted with the constant travelling. It had been 25 years since those wild, head jarring, grinding tours of the Middle West, but back then I had been a young buck, tough as a hickory bough, and now I was ready for a new experience. Finally the last gig of the 70's arrived at Teddington's Social Club, Holmbush on New Years Eve. The place was packed to the gills and we put on a great show with the finale being a great flash of fancy underwear, as our niece Christine did cartwheels along the whole length of the dance floor. It was a great evening, but to me the real high spot was paying off the band at the end of it and watching them leave for the last time.

And that was the end of the SUPERGLADES: The relief was quite wonderful.

The Curse of Paladin

Well, did he do it?—or was it only coincidence? Well, from his track record I'd say that it was at least possible.

It was the early eighties, just before we opened the shop and I was wind‐ing up our music commitments in Cornwall. Quite obviously our musicians began shuffling around looking for gigs for the coming season, and it was then that Paladin, one of my former sidemen, came up with the startling news that he had a contract for Japan in his pocket, from Ronnie Harris's office in Germany. I personally thought it was a bit strange when Clive the drummer told me about it, because I knew that Ronnie Harris had long given up his agency in Wiesbaden and had moved to Florida. However Clive was convinced that he was on to a good thing and it wasn't for me to spoil his dreams of geisha girls and cheap electronic gear. Maybe Paladin had something going I did not know about! He certainly had the musicians excited.

He also recruited one of the best guitar players in Cornwall, a nice, gentle man called Jim Forrest who at that time was managing a music shop in Newquay. Clive was so much taken by the prospect that he even allowed Paladin to move in to his house while he took his family on holiday to Butlins for a couple of weeks. While he was away Paladin really laced into the phone, running up enormous bills by phoning all over the world, quite confident that by the time the bills arrived he'd be long gone. But of course the time for departure to the Land of the Rising Sun was creeping ever nearer. The drummer came back from Minehead to be assured that everything was fine, and it was merely a matter of picking up the air tickets at Heathrow and they would be Tokyo bound.

Paladin was by far the best con artist I have ever met and odd trickles of information I had heard showed him to be a man to be wary of. He would come up with wild tales of how he had once been flown out to Gibraltar by the Royal Navy to open a safe containing highly confidential papers after the combination codes had been lost (Apparently he was one of the few people in the world who could do this sort of thing) and later, when he said he had been mistakenly arrested for alleged alimony arrears, he had only to show his special passport to the senior police officer and his friend at the Admiralty had the whole thing dropped. This begs the question—what was such a uniquely talented, important undercover agent doing playing guitar for me?

One night on the way back from a gig in Devon I fell asleep and he must have forgotten I was there, As I awoke from my dozing, I heard him telling the others all about his hard times in Vietnam, and repeating almost word for word things I had told him. There were also odd phone‐calls from the States enquiring about his whereabouts, and rumours about an affair with a female American Army officer in Europe. Much closer to home however, was his asset–stripping of a close friend of ours, who almost lost her Bodmin house because of him. Foolishly, she let him move in and relied on him to pay in the Council rent cheques she gave him, while she was at work. Instead, Paladin cashed them and could be found most afternoons at the bar of the White Hart with his open–mouthed cronies, telling them about his worldwide exploits. He was still bull–shitting to the arrival of the eviction notice and he talked his way out of that as well.

About a month after this his long–time girl friend turned up at our door demanding to know where he was? I waffled around saying I was not sure but I thought he was with the drummer. She was wiser than I anticipated and after making a few enquiries presented herself at the Bodmin house where she went berserk at the sight of all her engagement presents on display. Our friend also had hysterics but somehow Paladin's Cheshire Cat smile cooled the crisis and he smoothed his fiance's ruffled feathers by installing her in an isolated semi–derelict house in the heart of Bodmin Moor, where even the buses hibernate in winter. Two weeks later he was back again at the house in Bodmin.

To outsiders, the Cornish often appear to be a bit slow to react to situations but this is a false assessment. They like to stop to consider their actions and when they do move it is swift and serious. We liked the people and our respect was reciprocated. To this very day Kit and I have a solid band of supporters down there who make us welcome every time we return, but against such an accomplished and ruthless trickster like Paladin the local lads were not really sure what to do. It's the old rabbit and fox syndrome, the paralysis of insecurity.

I remember one incident and the scene is still indelibly impressed on my mind. Imagine this. It is a rainy night in St. Austell and in a phone box outside the Band Club, Paladin is pretending to talk to agent Ronnie Harris in Germany while the mesmerized drummer stands outside the booth waiting for the good news of their departure date. A full ten minutes passes as Paladin nods knowingly, with the phone clamped firmly to his ear, and asks important questions to the talking clock on the other end of the line. He finally emerges with a broad smile and tells the drummer that everything is now in place, and they will be leaving on Monday morning.

But, what is he going to do? Monday is getting closer. The guitar player has cancelled all his gigs and given in his notice to the music shop. The bass player is on his way from Torquay and Clive the drummer has spent Friday saying goodbye to all his boozing pals—and there were a lot of them, I can tell you. Then he recruits them to help clean his van that is to take them to the airport. So it is all coming to a head. And so, the lemmings gather themselves for the leap over the cliff.

The crunch came on one of my last gigs in Cornwall at the Garrison Club in Bodmin. Everything went as normal except that during the last break, Paladin went missing for a few minutes. We all presumed that he had met up with an old flame and had gone out for a quick, er, talk (?) and thought nothing more of it. At the end of the evening I wished Paladin and the drummer all the best for their new venture and we all began to pack our gear. That night they had come in Clive's Bedford while everybody else had come in their own cars, so we picked up our money and split.

The following morning we had just finished breakfast when Clive and Jim turned up at our house. The guitarist was raging mad and the drummer almost in tears. "We can't go," he wailed, "My van's packed up."

"Oh yes? What happened then?" I asked suspiciously.

"Last night, on the way back from the club the bloody engine seized. We can't go. We've missed the flight, the contract, everything."

"And where's Paladin?" I enquired calmly.

"Oh, him," spat the guitarist. "He's gone to London to try to sort it all out. What a mess! I'll bet he's gutted too. He had people waiting to see him in Japan, U.S. Navy bookers for the Pacific Fleet, contracts signed and everything. Bloody Yanks!"

They sat there, slurping their tea, looking shattered and I began to wonder how gullible people could be, especially hard–shell pro musicians, but Paladin had cast his spell over them easily

Did you ever actually see this contract?" I enquired.

They looked at each other before answering. "Er, no, not exactly."

"But did you ever talk to Ronnie Harris?"

"Well, no—but Paladin will sort it out. He'll fly to Wiesbaden" They assured me.

I mentioned that I thought Ronnie Harris now lived in Florida, but I was assured that I was mistaken as Paladin had been phoning him regularly. Clive had heard him.

In the face of such self–delusion there was nothing I could say except that they should try to get their old jobs back until their Messiah returned, but not hold their breath till he did.

After they had left I shot up to the Garrison Club and there, on the concrete parking apron where the Bedford van had rested the previous night, was a pool of oil and in a nearby gutter I found a sump drain plug.—I wonder how it got there?

Needless to say they never got to Japan. Like a phoenix Paladin rose from the ashes and was back in Cornwall. The last I heard he had latched on to a prominent Cornish comedian as some kind of Man Friday. He was indestructible.

PICKER'S TIP 47

Be generous and supportive to street entertainers. They are only trying to make a living, and believe me, it's a tough life. Also remember, if things had not gone right that could have easily been you. Or, would you have just scuttled back to the day job?

So show some respect. These people are Buskers not Beggars.

33

NASHVILLE WEST
Freddy Starr, Marty Robbins

"NASHVILLE WEST". What a marvellous name.

It was the title of a track on an early album by the BYRDS, and for many years I used it as a signature tune. You can hear it on the opening track of our Decca album 'Live at the Nashville Rooms'. It's a great tune and Jim Hornsby's raw Fender Telecaster sounds superb on it—so I thought why not call our shop 'NASHVILLE WEST'. It sounded just right.

The music was popular, booming in fact, particularly so down in the far South West, and people at our shows were always asking where the band got their duds from and I'd been buying western shirts and boots for some time from a shop in East London, Ken's Western Store on Romford Road, and he agreed to supply us at wholesale rates, so we now had a reliable source. A place came up for sale in Mount Charles, a secondary shopping area on the outskirts of St. Austell. It was a nice big shop with excellent living accomodation and a big garden, perfect for our project, so we went for it.

The amplifiers were bought brand new from the Music Man Company, who at that time were making a heavy sales drive to get in on the music scene, but the guitars, dobros, banjos and other instruments were mostly second hand. In addition we carried a selection of the fringe products of the Country and Western scene, including the illegal (at the time) C.B. radios and cowboy paraphernalia like Stetsons, stock whips, belts, yellow slicker capes and reluctantly, replica guns and rigs. I sacrificed my collection of Country Music People magazines, using cover photographs of celebrities to add an authentic touch to the decor.

We did good business from the outset but of course we got our fair share of loonies and eccentrics, usually the John Wayne/Clint Eastwood fanatics, who bought blank firing replica revolvers and indulged in mock quick-draw competitions at gigs. They were the bane of most performers lives and invariably they would blast off in the middle of songs. In fact you could guarantee it in Folsom Prison Blues. You know, at that line that says. "I shot a man in Reno, just to see him die." Then it was Bang! Bang! Bang! And if you played 'Dixie' you could also expect a huge fusillade at the end of it. In fact up in the North East of the country there was a club called the Gunfighters that devoted itself to the World of the Cowboy. They had gunfights, quick-draw contests with electronic timers, and re-enacted full scenarios from old Western B movies, complete with bar room fights and lynch mob trials. All good fun really I suppose, but nothing whatever to do with the music. In the end it got so that the audiences were more dressed up than the performers who were mostly happy enough in jeans.

Some three weeks after we opened one of the locals came into the shop. He was a clay worker and had called in on his way home from the pit, and told us that his mother had recently died and left him and his sister £500 each, and he wanted to get himself a full western rig. He was going home to get cleaned up and said he would call down later to make his selection.

About four–thirty he turned up, not a lot cleaner but without his clay covered overalls. He plonked a bunch of notes on the counter and started his selection. Three H bar C shirts, a selection of bandanas, two replica guns and holsters, two pairs of jeans, one blue, one black, two belts, two Stetson hats one white, one black, a grey Confederate Army cap, two pairs of boots, one brown and one black with spurs, a full Western style suit in brown gabardine, a harmonica and a C.B. radio. (His call sign was the White Mountain Ranger.). He carefully selected what he was going to wear and got changed while we bundled up his old clothes and other purchases.

"Do you want a lift home?" I asked him.

"Oh, no thankee," he said. "I got me boike outside."

So there he was in full cowboy regalia, mounted on his 125cc Puch moped with his parcels strapped to his carrier and what remained of the £500 in his fringed leather waistcoat, riding off into the St Austell sunset. With head held high and the brim of his Stetson turned up in front from the prairie breeze blowing in from Brown Willy, he guided his trusty mount the Palomino Puch round the tumbling tumbleweeds (runaway bin liners actually) and up the wild mountain passes, before stopping for a shot of Red Eye at the Lone Pine Saloon, (aka the Penwithick Social Club) where unfortunately, a posse of the members got jealous of his new duds and gave him a bit of a duffing up. They also had the rats at him, because they thought he should have spent his legacy on buying them drinks like his sister had.

There were some quiet times though at the shop when things really dragged. Jon and Linda used to come down from their caravan at Penwithick and hang around in the shop or schlep across the road to the Duke of Cornwall, but there was not much else to do. April was really cold that year and business was slow, but as spring broke through we began to get a few tourists, both British and European. The Germans in particular were very enthusiastic about all the Western gear and bought boots, hats and belts aplenty.

We did some promotions at the cinemas in town,, whenever there was a movie with a Western theme, and hustled the shop on all our gigs on the road. Lots of visiting musicians and acts called in for something as the season began, and we started a hire service of equipment, mainly PA speakers and guitar amps. In a fit of enthusiasm at the opening of the shop I had ordered the full range of Music Man amps—eight of them. And so far we had sold only two. So they came in handy for this hire service. We finally managed to sell the last one, a big 4x12 combo, in France six years later, after toting it all round Europe.

Marty Robbins and Freddy Starr were two of the stars that used the service on their big shows at the Cornwall Coliseum. I found Starr to be a complete megalomaniac who lived in a fantasy world. He considered him-self a great singer and slagged off everybody from Tom Jones to Frank Sinatra—and considered himself a second Elvis Presley. He tried his hand at Country Music but like so many others, he had no idea about phrasing or timing.

He was anxious to come over as a hard man and always had a minder at his side as he regaled me with tales of his delinquent youth. He was a very funny comedian but as his paranoia increased, his act became more profane and coarse. Some years later in Liverpool I was on a show with some of his ex-mates from his original group The Delmonts who said that they were relieved when he got his break and left the band—they had a party to celebrate.

Not that Marty Robbins was any less obnoxious than Freddy. At Heathrow Airport, where he arrived late for a UK tour, he refused to let the waiting British backing band share his 52 seat coach on the trip to Cornwall, and they had to hire two cars to follow him. Speaking of coaches, I'd like you to meet—

Old Greyhound

After the trauma of the Superglades, I put together another band and I was determined to keep it small. Having made peace with Gipsy George again, I brought him in on steel, Jon on bass and Clive on drums to make a very clean flexible unit. Also having become totally disenchanted with Ford Transits we bought a blue Commer van that proved to be about as useless as the Ford. On a run to Exeter a wheel fell off near Ivybridge and a week later the engine blew up, as did a second one that Jon and I labored to in-stall in the car park of the shop, so it had to go. But luckily I found exactly the kind of vehicle I had been seeking. Standing forlornly on a filling sta-tion forecourt in St. Blazey with a hand written' For Sale' notice in the windscreen, was a Bedford Duple 21 seat diesel engined coach, which with a bit of customizing would be perfect for the job. However I was a bit short on the price as I was waiting for money from the club settlement and had just paid the house deposit, so George, ever unpredictable, offered to lend me some.

You see, in spite of his mood swings, he was a very helpful and reliable guy.

Jon and I got to work with a vengeance, stripping out seats and altering the interior layout, re-flooring the luggage compartment and finally repainting the body green and silver. We mounted a big pair of cow horns above the cab, put on some US number plates on the front bumper, and named it Old Greyhound after one of my an early albums. Its first outing was to one of our regular gigs in Newton Abbott and apart from a little fuel pipe vibration problem, it ran like a dream and felt so much safer than our old vans.

To help move things along I then went back on the road and Kit ran the shop for a couple of months and when I came back we decided we would like to expand the operation by moving to Plymouth. We both liked the place and particularly the old Barbican area where the Council had gone to great lengths to preserve the area as a tourist attraction, and had encouraged a very sympathetic development of flats and shops on the cobbled roads round the harbour. Amongst the older property was a large detached building facing the fishing port that was currently a curio–cum–junk shop that we had heard was coming up for lease, so I went round to check it out. Apparently the owners were having some family trouble and wanted to get back to Falmouth, so they were prepared to lease it to us, after which we started looking for somewhere to live and found a very nice apartment on Southside Street. A deal for our shop was set up with a guy in St Austell who was looking for a carpet showroom, and we started selling off stock and fittings, but about a week before we were due to leave the carpet man pulled out on health grounds, so our Plymouth plan had to be put on hold. It was a shame really because we were geared up for the change and neither of us felt like reopening the Nashville West shop again in Mount Charles. It would have meant restocking and doing a lot of advertising so we decided to close the shop as planned and re–think our next move. And here comes that Hand of Fate again.

PICKER'S TIP 48

Avoid giving strangers a lift; particularly abroad and never take a stranger or any of their baggage across a foreign border in your vehicle. If they do get caught with anything illegal you will be presumed to be involved too.

34
KENYA

It was on one of those grinding tours of North East England; you know the kind, one Working Men's Club or British Legion after another, that I had my first contact with the Italian agent Piero Massari from Milan. I was in agent Frank Feeney's office to pick up some cash from the tour when he tossed a letter across to me.

"What d'y think of that, Yonk?" He snorted, "Askin' me for acts for th' Middle East and Africa. There's enough work round here for bloody years yet. Who the 'ell wants to go out there?"

"Oh yes, Frank," I replied blankly. "Who needs it?"

I groaned inwardly. Who indeed? Well, me for one. I'd had about enough of the faceless masses and the adverts for Newcastle Brown Ale and Federation Bitter to last me a lifetime, so I made a mental note of Signor Massari's vital statistics.

I stumbled down the stairs counting my gig money, mentally deducting transport costs, wages, digs money, and wondering what the bloody hell I was doing here? Like Peggy Lee I wanted to know "Is that all there is?" Was this really the best there was after the heady glories of the Wembley Festival? Was this what all the TV exposure had been about? To end up back here on these social clubs again, just providing the two slices of music on a bingo sandwich? Don't get me wrong, I loved the North East, particularly the warm honest people and we had had great success on the clubs up there; but that had been back in 1972, so what was I doing here now? First time around it had been on the main cabaret circuit, and now we were a major attraction on the Country Music club circuit, and I wondered if that was progress or not? About the only difference I could see was that instead of bouffant hair–dos and flares, the audiences wore ill–fitting Stetsons and shot at each other with blank firing Navy Colts.

Away from the North Sea Blizzard Coast I contacted the Milan Mystery Man and got a nice letter in response, so I moved to Stage Two and sent him tapes and a publicity package. A few weeks passed and just after Easter I received an offer of a contract for a month at the International Casino Nairobi, Kenya, later that year. There was plenty of time to sort out a good band so I gladly accepted Signor Massari's offer.

Gypsy George was in the throes of building a recording studio in his house, but ageeed to put the project on hold till he got back, and I realized that for such a prestige gig the trio I had put together would not be versatile enough, so I added a teenage banjo virtuoso from Helston called Carl Heatley to complete the line up, which then became the Texas City Dance Band that I took to East Africa. Carl also played guitar and more importantly, pedal steel, which would come in handy if there were any problems.

You may ask why take two lead players for what was essentially a vocal act, but I knew all to well the danger of being dependent on one lead musician, particularly when you are a long way from home—sooner or later they begin to think they are indispensable, and start throwing moodies and causing stress, as demonstrated by the early days in Germany and with the recently departed Ginger. In the event, it was as well that I had made contingency plans, as once again, the experience paid off.

The dates were fixed with Milan, and we were scheduled to be in Africa for five weeks in November and early December 1980. Documents arrived, passport details sent off and equipment prepared. I did some gigs with the new band and a good program was put together, although I had sneaking doubts about pedal steel taking the place of the normal electric guitar, particularly on up–tempo numbers. For slow ballads there is no problem, but it is very difficult for pedal steel to drive a band along, unless you are an absolute genius like Buddy Emmons. (Some time later I discussed this problem with such great steelies as Rod King and Pete Heywood, and they both said that vamped blocks with linking runs is the most one can do with fast rhythms). I hoped that the electric five–string banjo of Carl would give me the punch required but to be on the safe side, I decided to use a Tele-caster for this gig instead of my usual Newporter Fender flat top.

We did a gig at Hungerford Football Club on the way to Heathrow. It was our fourth gig at the club and had a great time there, so much so that we did not finish until 2am by which time there seemed no point in booking into a hotel so we pushed on to the Passenger Lounge at Terminal Two. Of course we were late. My son Francis, who was running us to the gig and the airport, kept telling me that I had got the wrong date. And he was right. On phoning Kit to say that we had arrived safely in London, it turned out that Massari had been going frantic, phoning all round the world to find out why we had not caught the flight he had booked us on. It was a simple case of over organization. In all my meticulous planning I had failed to notice that the flight was at 12.15am not 12.15 p.m. Gulp!

Unfortunately there was nobody else I could blame for this cock up.

Nairobi.

Eventually we were shuffled aboard the Jumbo and we all got stuck into our individual versions of the Good Life, with me and Jon trying to con-sume the plane's stock of sour mash whiskey, Carl and Clive trying to look down the front of the air hostess's blouse, and Gipsy George checking the seats every twenty minutes for secret agents. (He had once had his passport stolen in Cairo and since then was convinced that spies were everywhere.) Several hours and probably a bottle of Black Label later, we zonked into Mombassa and transferred to a smaller plane for the last leg (In our case that should read 'Last Legs') of our safari into the wild interior and on to 'The Place of Cool Waters'—or if you prefer Swahili, Nairobi.

As we stepped down from the plane the heat hit us like an open furnace door, a real shock after the cold British winter. I could hardly breathe because apart from a thick H–C embroidered cowboy shirt, I was wearing a

heavy, fringed buckskin jacket and a felt Stetson hat. I felt about as comfortable as an alligator in a handbag factory.

There was a guy waiting for us who was obviously Italian. I must admit I
was a bit surprised—Italians? Here in Kenya? I thought it was still a very
English place in spite of the newfound independence. Maybe we were at
the wrong airport, or had I made another cock up and got the wrong plane.
Or maybe it was the Jack Daniels, eh? I voiced my fears but with a bright
smile our guide explained that the Italians had been in East Africa for
many years, maybe not in Kenya but certainly in the Horn of Africa.

I knew that they'd had a couple of goes at trying to colonize Eritrea and
Abyssinia, coming badly unstuck first time round in 1896 at Adowa when
their army got chopped to dog meat but in 1936 with the help of tanks and
mustard gas, Mussolini had managed to get a foothold, only to be booted
out again by the Allies in 1942, with the result that many 'Colonas' were
relocated as POW's to the more secure British parts, where they quickly
discovered that the local Kikuyu and Masai tribesmen were much more
amenable to settlers than the proud unpredictable Somalis, and after the
war many of them stayed on to open businesses establishing quite a big
community.

Picking up my guitar, Giovanni led us through the main concourse,
where a beefy black police sergeant was slapping shit out of an unfortunate
drug courier that had been stopped by the Customs. The sergeant stopped
his beating as we passed, saluted smartly and wished our guide 'A very
good day. Sah.' Giovanni responded with a casual lifting of my guitar case
and swaggered on through the main booking hall hoping somebody would
mistake him for a rock star

"Eez orlrigh'. Meester Yonco," he assured me. "Don'a worry, Signor
Massari—'ee feex ever'tin'. We runa da Casino 'ere an' da one in Mombassa
as well. Anytink you wan'. You gottit. Okay? So don'a you worry.

Through my whisky haze I thought how welcoming he was. It was like
being part of a big family—then I realized what FAMILY IT WAS—the
same one I'd worked for in Taiwan.

There was the usual pushing and shoving at the terminal exit as we
strove to get our gear onto a Toyota pick–up truck, and ourselves into a
Fiat 1500, and in no time at all we were roaring down the wide new Uhuru
Highway towards the distant Kenyetta Tower and the city of Nairobi.
There was a delay of some sort on the road so with the customary impati-
ence of his race, our excitable, cursing macho Italian driver shot off up
some dirt track at 70 mph to find a detour. We ended up in Eastlands, a
dusty, sad shantytown behind the railway tracks. Row upon row of un-
sanitary rusting tin roofed shacks, the narrow garbage strewn alleys
between them teeming with sad looking women and half naked black kids.
Some of them were eating out of cans, most of them with purple scalps
where gentian violet ointment was being used to hold infection at bay. It
certainly was a far cry from the spectacular travel agent's posters that

loudly touted Kenya, as the new showpiece of emerging independent Africa. The few men there were stood about in sullen groups with resentful eyes waiting to snatch at our baggage from the following pick–up truck, as our snarling wop threw the car into a dust–storming 180 degree turn, and shot away across the railroad tracks, past the mosques and into town.

Suddenly the surroundings changed. Now, this was more like it. Modern hotels, well–stocked shops, office blocks and restaurants, crowded streets and dozens of bars jammed to overflowing with happy Nairobians guzzling Tusker beer. We were whisked through the wide streets, past the elegant Norfolk Hotel, with its old trek wagon in the archway of the main entrance, and with Gipsy George keeping a sharp lookout all the while for any agents that might have trailed us from the airport, (in the event, I found out later that we were being shadowed by the Kenyan secret police, so George might have been right all along), we found our new temporary home, the Devon Hotel.

In our innocence we had naturally presumed that it would be the sister hotel to the Norfolk.—we could not have been more off target. It was a collection of wooden huts and at one time had been a British Army barracks. Cosmetic attempts had been made to turn it into a hotel but it still looked like a transit camp. It was laid out around three sides of a square threadbare lawn that obviously had once been the parade ground. The fourth side consisted of an office block, a restaurant and a bar packed with more guzzling Tusker Beer fanatics. We were greeted warmly by the office staff who were also Italian and shown to our respective huts. Carl and Clive shared one, Gipsy George and Jon another, and I had one to my-self. Next thing was lunch, taken in what once had been the Officers Mess and was still very colonial. Smiling African waiters, this time in off–white badly ironed mess jackets, served thin mulligatawny soup on chipped plates and though the hotel was Italian owned, the menu was extremely British, very pukka indeed. There was Toad in the Hole, crumpets, Carr's wafer biscuits, and Lipton's tea bags. It was like a Noel Coward play and it was almost as though the Mau Mau thing had never happened. Being treated like sahibs was just up Carl and Clive's street and our Brave Trelawny Oggies wolfed down everything in sight, snapping their fingers at the black waiters and trying to converse in pidgin English.

"Eh there, Sambo. You bring um plenty choc–choc cake, Imshi. Damn Quick."

To which one slim young waiter replied in faultless Oxford tones.

"Oh, don't be a Dickhead, Bwana: You'll give yourself the wind."

After that, everyone knew where they stood. Even so, them Good Ol' Cornish boys could see off a plate of bread rolls before the scraping of dinner chair legs finished.

The casino club itself was beautiful and the Bruno Picano Italian House Band was superb. They had a fine Swedish girl singer, who also doubled as the comere. Our show went well and up to a point everybody got on fine.

We did one 45-minute spot an evening in the week and two on Saturdays. The most requested songs were 'Is this all there is to a Honky-Tonk?' and that great Gatlin Brothers number 'I don't want to cry.' Bruno liked it so much that he translated it into Italian, presenting it as romantic Neapolitan serenade. There was also another superb song popular at the time, which I liked very much, a Kenyan folk song called 'Malaika'.

Featured along with us was a trick rope specialist from Southend-on-Sea called Vince Bruce. He was a remarkable young man who, when still only a teenager, had gone west to California and beaten some of the their best rodeo stars at rope spinning and quarter horse racing. He won many prizes and silver buckles and then became a specialty act on the international circuit. We have stayed good friends ever since and corresponded from odd corners of the world. Last time I heard from him, he had just finished a world tour with the Harlem Globtrotters Show and settled down in Sarasota, Florida.

I hired a car and we took a few trips into the countryside, of course being very careful to avoid Eastlands this time—It was all very nice but there was an underlying uneasiness, especially in the city itself. It was not exactly a Black versus White thing. (Although nobody really went out of his or her way to make us honkies welcome.)

It was a vague feeling of tension and insecurity everywhere. On the odd occasion when we were in the bars, violent and noisy arguments seemed to be raging all the time between the different tribal and political factions. Later on I met a number of the major players in this volatile, violent political scene; people like Dr Juragi Mungai, a powerful force in one of the country's most important families and a relative of the late Jomo Kenyetta, the leader of the Mau Mau revolt and the first president of Independent Kenya. There was suspicion in many quarters that Mungai had been involved in the plot to overthrow the great leader during a visit to the Rift Valley, but nothing was ever proved, although he was concerned in the squabble over Kenyetta's will with Jomo's daughter. It must be remembered that at the time of his death in Mombassa Jomo Kenyetta was one of the richest men in Africa.

Of course, our two young oggies were off like randy rabbits as soon as the show was over. Across the hotel lawn was the Bacchus Club, where there were plenty of local girls ready and willing to perform for a few quid and an evening's boozing. Jon and I usually headed downtown to the clubs there or the late night bar at the Hilton, while Gypsy George would borrow my car and, sometimes very early in the morning, he would shoot out to the airport to await the arrival of his girl friend but somehow she never turned up. About three times a week he would phone her up in Newquay and give her a chewing out for not coming out to Nairobi.

The long-awaited wobbler finally arrived about two weeks into the contract. The pressure of being watched day and night by the secret services and the non-appearance of his lady finally made him flip his lid. That was it, he was off back to the UK on the next plane out. Bollocks to the job. He was Gone.

I stayed out and let Jon and Carl handle it, which they did very well, Jon moving onto guitar and Carl switching to bass, so I still had a back-up unit and, with a bit of program trimming, things were going to be alright In the event. I think George took one evening off and, after realizing that we could get on quite well without him, he calmed down and started picking again, but he still haunted the airport terminal. One night when I was having a late night drink in the bar up there, I spotted him prowling the concourse and checking the arrival board.

An old friend, Dave Parsons, turned up one afternoon at the Devon Hotel. He had grown up in Kenya and was on an extended holiday, making quite an impact with his white hunter outfit. Short shorts, with legs like tree trunks hanging out of them, (Giving the mem-sahibs the vapours.) knee socks, safari jacket and a bush hat, and of course driving the regulation Range Rover. It was good to see him and he invited us to a dance at the local flying club on our night off. The place was full of the kind of people I disliked intensely, wealthy young Hooray Henrys. The sons of the once privileged white settlers who, unfortunately, still behaved like their colonial fathers, bossing the black club workers about and generally becoming more obnoxious as the evening progressed. We did not go back there.

Mombassa

After Nairobi we did a week at Oceanic Hotel in Mombassa. It was a vast contrast to Nairobi. For one thing it was very much hotter, being on the low-lying coast. It was also a favourite holiday spot for blue collar German workers with as many as six flights a day arriving from Frankfurt's Rein Main airport bulging with sun-seeking Krauts. Many of them stayed at the Oceanic and it was quite a sight watching them stripping the breakfast buffet tables for the beach, shovelling ham, bananas, bread rolls, and hard boiled eggs into the striped beach bags that would sustain them during a hard day on the pure white sands of Diani Beach. A beautiful palm fringed strand, unfortunately marred by the rusting wreck of an old tramp steamer on a sandbank half a mile out to sea.

Most of our shows in Mombassa were in the open air and Gypsy George was quite a sensation there, the clients and staff never having seen or heard a pedal steel guitar before, although they were quite keen on Country Music. Charlie Pride and of all people, Skeeter Davis, were their favorites.

One party of tourists were from an isolated region of Switzerland called Graubunden, who spoke a language I had never heard before. It was a strange, jerky, mélange of Latin, Old German and coarse French called Romansch and was reputedly the Lingua Franca of the Roman Legions. These Swiss clients were not very popular, either with their fellow guests or the staff, as they never bought anyone a drink or ever left a tip of any kind, and at the end of the holiday went to unbelievable lengths to change every single Kenyan coin back to Swiss francs.

Meanwhile back at room 407 in the Oceanic Hotel, the heat and frustration was sending George into 'Stress Factor Warp 9' again, as he stared out to sea from his balcony and noted that some of the coastal shipping had quite clearly slowed down to take telephotos of his room as they passed, before beaming them up to a satellite for onward transmission to Cheltenham, Moscow, Tel Aviv or Langley, Virginia. He could plainly see the flash of the camera lenses.

He told us all about it at breakfast and warned us to be careful whom we talked to. He also complained loudly about the heat and turned his air conditioning up full. When he returned to his room an hour later it was like the inside of a cold storage plant, the curtains stiff as boards and the sink lined with ice

I made a good friend of one of the Kenyan guards at the casino called Joseph Irungi, who invited me to his home in the hills above Nairobi. It was simply a mud and corrugated–iron shack with beaten earth floors but it was scrupulously clean. His wife and two kids were charming, and proudly showed me pictures of the Royal Family they had cut out of magazines and pinned on the wall. They gave me a present of sugar cane from their own garden as a leaving present. They were very poor, but also very proud and hospitable. Lovely people. After meeting them all I realized even more how obnoxious the arrogant young colonials at the Aero Club were and how they were recklessly building their future troubles.

As though to confirm my forebodings, one night I was invited to the table of a group of Kenyan politicians including a justice Minister called Albert Jet, with his German mistress, and the sinister Dr. J. Mungai. The talk was seething about the latest machinations of the President Daniel Moi.

The appointment of Moi actually was a clever political ploy to keep the balance of power between the Masai and Kikuyu tribal groupings, as he was not a member of either ethnic group. In the event Daniel Moi eventually became the country's despotic leader, transforming the fragile tribal truce into a one party police state where any dissent was ruthlessly put down. In fact the whole atmosphere seemed to be getting more sinister day by day.

Even Dave Parson's friends in the posh district of Westlands engaged a couple of 24 hour a day guards for their house and everybody was getting jumpy and took serious security measures, including barbed wire and steel toothed bear–traps in the gardens. Some of the backstage staff at the casino also warned us diplomatically to cut down on our visits to the discos downtown after the shows and to make sure our rooms were locked at night. The gossip in the hotel bar blamed the heightened tensions on an influx of Nigerians and there were often violent arguments late into the night.

However our shows were good and visiting American tourists gave us a
boost and, although most of the white patrons were British and had been
in Kenya for years, I could not escape the feeling of trouble below the surface, and we were all glad when we got on the plane home. All, that is except Gipsy George of course, who now wanted to stay in Nairobi and get all
his recording equipment shipped out to get a studio off the ground. He told
us that he had met a financier who was prepared to back him. I think that
somehow he blamed us for forcing him to come home. When we arrived at
Heathrow he told me where I could stick the job—but he was always saying that. However, this time he seemed serious, so I paid him his money
and let him go. He actually did go back to Kenya later but nothing came of
it, somehow his phantom backer had disappeared and, although we had
never met the man, I heard later that George blamed us for that as well.

PICKER'S TIP 49

Tune up to a piano or electric keyboard. Tune to A. 440 hertz. (Vibes per
min. In the USA its 442 hertz).

Do not attempt to tune up to a fretless bass guitar, a Dobro, a pedal steel
guitar or a mandolin, or a trombone.

35

SAN REMO

Massari must have got a good report from our tour in Kenya because in the following January he phoned me to ask if I could do a one night gig in San Remo on the Italian Riviera. Apparently the Municipal Casino was opening a new American gambling room with Black jack. Craps, Five card stud, and they wanted a major Country Music act for the opening night spectacular.

"How much, " I asked.

"Er. You name–a da price. its a town hall job."

"Ok, then, I want a grand. Thirteen hundred, if you are taking a bite— pounds sterling or dollars—not lira.

"I tell you wot, Yonco,. I put you in for two tousan' dollah an' I take 15%, okay?"

I did a quick calculation and gave him the go–ahead. Two days later he phoned me to say that the deal was on. "What about our gear?" I asked.

"Eez hokay. Jes' charge it to Casino Municipale San Remo," he said jovially, "An'make a sure you bring evertin' you need for the show on 14 February. Tickets gonna be waitin' Heathrow. You fly Friday, an' dona missa da plane dis time Hokay?" I thought a minute—fly out on *Friday the Thirteenth?*

Never Happen, G.I. "Listen Piero," I hedged," not Friday! I never fly on Friday the 13th. Anywhere."

He wasn't fazed and said. "Hokay. Come out onna da Thursday. I don' care."

So that was it—and Kit's birthday was on the 12th. What a nice birthday treat. However, putting a band together proved not as easy as accepting the gig. I had Jon on bass and Clive on drums but the other two were not easy to find. I cast around for a good lead guitarist but no one seemed to be available. Finally I tracked down Clancy d'Angelo, who was now back with Hank Wangford's band and he said he could get away for a few days and came down to Cornwall for rehearsals. Young Carl Heatley, who was about to leave for Norway, agreed to delay his trip and came along too. Carl could play anything with strings from pedal steel to five–string banjo and he knew my program from his Kenya trip, so he was well worth having on board.

A few days before we were due to leave, I got down to putting a show to–gether, trying out the line–up on local gigs and rehearsing in the back room of a nearby pub where Carl and Clancy were staying and around this time we started getting cryptic phone calls from Gypsy George's lady, who had obviously heard about the San Remo gig. She informed me that George would be back from Kenya any time now and he would be available for San Remo. I pointed out that last time we parted he had told me to stick the job and that had been months ago, and that I was fixed up nicely now, but thanks for calling. I would have loved to have him aboard, but we were too far down the line to change, as the air tickets and accomodation etc, had already been arranged. However that was not the end of it, because he trailed us on try–out gigs and often ensconced himself in the bar of the pub where we were rehearsing. Even after we had left Cornwall he phoned the bass player's wife, trying to find out the time of our flight to Nice. Oh yes, Gypsy George was a good old boy, but a bit strange.

Mind you he was not the only oddball. When the time came to leave and we piled aboard the bus for Heathrow, Clancy turned up with his clothes in a brown paper potato sack. Yep. That's right, A POTATO SACK. And in case it got lost, it had Wangford Nurseries, Norfolk, printed on the side. Guaranteed to raise an eyebrow or two in chic San Remo, but with Clancy what would you expect?

The arrival at Nice airport will be forever in my memory. As we wheeled over the Bay of Angels and turned to the Riviera coast my mouth dropped open. What a beautiful sight. It was absolutely breathtaking. The bright beach and the beautiful white buildings, and tree shaded parks, bright green and bursting with flowers. In the harbour, magnificent motor yachts rocked gently at their moorings, and two large white cruise liners stood off shore. In the soaring hills behind the bustling coastal strip, little clusters of terracotta roofs marked out villages where time stood still. All of it glowing in the bright warm sunshine. And it was only February.

Oh yes, just my kind of place.

We were escorted through the customs area by four cool characters in dark glasses and superb mohair suits and led out to where two big Fiat cars with Italian plates were waiting. I asked about our gear and one of the Italians pointed to a white van and indicated that it was all being taken care of, although the driver almost threw Clancy's potato sack away. I was still punch–drunk from the beauty of it all. I was in love with the place, didn't want to leave it ever and swore one day we would come back (and one day we did). Reluctantly we were hustled aboard and the Nice–San Remo Grand Prix commenced as the three vehicles hit the Autoroute— Jesus!

They must have been doing 85 mph all the way; even the van was keep- ing up with us. Approaching the Italian Frontier at Ventimiglia the van shot ahead and pulled in at the customs post and as we reduced speed to a respectable seventy we were flagged through leaving the others to complete whatever border formalities that might be required.

Massari was waiting with his son at the Hotel Nacionale in San Remo and made us very welcome, telling us to charge the hotel for anything we needed, and that there was rehearsal the following afternoon for the show but on Saturday morning I had to do a promotional TV film in the new salon. Kit and I settled into our rooms and gave room service a whirl for a couple of gin and tonics, then got changed and went for a stroll round the town. The sea front was beautiful, very modern and clean, even the little railway station had a marble foyer and the shops were very classy and well stocked. The more interesting part was the old town. Here, dusty, dull yellow, balconied buildings four or more stories high lined the winding, twisting streets that opened into a succession of cobbled squares where the day's market stalls were being dismantled. It was fascinating. Little shops sold provisions, electric goods, and elaborate chocolate creations, and out of this world ice creams. Corner bars were full of chattering smiling people and we saw our first chicken rotisserie there. In fact we bought a chicken to eat as we strolled along, which the man cut into pieces for us. In one square we bought some pieces of onyx, a telephone, a jewel box and two table lamps, all of which we sold later when we hit some hard times in France.

Then it was time for dinner so we toddled back to the hotel—and what a dinner that was. You could hear the buzz as we got off the lift on the fifth floor and as we made our way to the restaurant where every diner was talking at once. A smiling headwaiter greeted us and seemed to know us as he guided us to our table. The boys were already there, Clive and Carl well into their cups, each one with a massive seafood risotto in front of them. Clancy and Jon had steaks and we ordered rack of lamb and it was magnificent. As we appeared to be unsure about wine the waiter placed several bottles of both red and white in front of us and in short we were given the VIP treatment—and it was all on the house.

The following morning we wandered to the show room for the rehearsal, guided by what we thought was a jukebox playing the latest chart numbers but imagine our surprise when we walked in and found that it was the ten–piece house band playing live. This was serious talent. Somewhat nervously we did our sound check and ran through a couple of numbers and sorted out stage positions etc, and then sat back to watch the others go through their paces. A magician and his assistant turned up with cages of white doves and a couple of floppy eared rabbits. He was a Balkan dwarf in a fur coat, who lost his rag at the slightest thing and yelled at his gipsy helper who had a bust like a pouter pigeon and a face so wrinkled that it looked like a map of Southern Finland. They mimed their way through their act and then got stuck into a wild shouting match until the lighting and sound crew threw them off the stage,

Next came the dancers and I must say they looked a real motley crew. Young girls of every nationality, in curlers, ripped jeans, old cardigans, leg warmers and Doc Marten boots but they could really dance. The flagrantly gay dance master took them through their paces by chalking out numbers on the metre square glass tiles that made up the stage, then he gave them all a numbered sheet and they followed the chart. Almost dancing by numbers but it worked well.

On the morning of the day of the show Carl, Kit, and I did our promotional TV stint in the Black Jack Room. Exquisitely groomed male and female models were draped round the craps table as I sang 'Roving Gambler' and threw dice around and Carl and Kit joined in. The models looked superb but one girl told Kit that they had been on the road from Rome since 5 am.

By 11.30 p.m. that night the big room was packed to the gills with beautiful women and expensively tailored men. Crystal glasses clinked and cigar smoke wreathed round the snow–white tablecloths and sparkling silver as black–suited waiters discreetly bustled about. Massari came backstage to tell us that a lot of important clients were there, including the Mayor of Genoa and the Police Chief from Portofino, down the coast, who had heard a lot about us from the Nairobi faction of the 'Family'—"So give 'em yo' best, Yonco."

The girls opened up with an electrifying Hollywood routine and they were terrific. Every movement was perfectly coordinated. Where had all those dowdy scrubbers gone? Here were sixteen absolute beauties, all dancing topless, with their bodies sprayed with some kind of body varnish that glowed. Marvellous. Then came an Italian comedian whom we couldn't understand, but he had the place rocking and stayed on to work as a compere to introduce the magic act. Here again it was a transformation, with him in an immaculate tuxedo and her looking stunning in a long lace dress. Their act was also very good with animals and doves appearing and disappearing everywhere. Then there was a short break before we came on for the star spot.

It was superb. Everybody gave their all to the show. Kit was really on form and her catchy songs and bright bubbly personality had the men cheering and shouting for more, while their elegantly attired women smiled tightly and drummed the tablemats with their perfectly manicured fingers, speculatively eyeing our tight jeans and cowboy boots. Clancy played a delicate and very touching version of 'Somewhere over the Rainbow' on guitar, while the speed and accuracy of Carl's banjo playing had them open–mouthed. With this kind of support I couldn't lose and really socked it to them. Jon was on form and his harmonies were strong and Clive drove it all along solidly. It was just what I loved, a Nashville show in a Las Vegas setting.

Jet Set Country. Who said it was only Blue Collar music?

We were on a winner and so was Massari, who came rushing backstage after the show full of congratulations and introducing me to several very smooth characters in dark suits whom, he assured me, (sotto voce), were very influential.

Behind the scenes though it was really chaotic, and by the time we got through a war had broken out backstage. Rows were raging all over the place with the stage–hands loudly arguing and noisily dragging props around; the dancers were screeching in a dozen languages and throwing clothes and shoes at each other. Doors were slamming, and when I glanced in at the magician' dressing room the gipsy lady was sitting in a corner crying her eyes out while the mad Serb stomped around shouting and emptying his hat and cloak of dead rabbits and crushed doves dripping blood and feathers. Ugh! Talk about volatile. They wouldn't have got any medals from the RSPCA. Being a Serbian magician's dove or rabbit is the animal equivalent of becoming a Kamikaze pilot.

Later I was at the bar enjoying a nice Black Label Jack Daniels when a deferential waiter told me that Signor Massari wished to see me in his room. He was due to leave early in the morning for Milan, so I went up half expecting some trouble, but he handed me an envelope full of dollars. It was my fee, less his percentage. What a fantastic trip. I was in a daze all the way back to Heathrow.

Then we had a rude awakening—the next gig was a huge pub in Deptford.

But waiting in the mail at home was a contract for Canada's Pacific Coast.

PACIFIC COAST LINES

Willie, they say you're down in Santa Barbara.
Playing in that bright warm sunshine.
I'm stuck here in the cold rains of Vancouver,
Dreaming about the Napa Valley wine.
Seems so long since I've been to California,
Picking with those happy friends of mine.
When my gig's through, Seattle, Sunday morning,
I'll be riding down those Pacific Coast Lines.
Heading south towards Sierra Madre.
The shadows of the Rockies at my back.
Roll a smoke and dream about the morning,
Did you see the way this Greyhound passed that Mac?
Waylon's on the jukebox in this truck stop.
Won't be long before I'm feeling fine.
San Joaquin and Bakersfield roll by us.
Seems this bus is getting there on time.
Home again at last, the chilly rains have passed
Riding down those Pacific Coast Lines.

Frank Yonco, Vancouver BC. June 1981

*   *   *   *   *   *

36

CANADA
First Impressions

CANADA — Modern Clean, Progressive Everythin' Australia ain't.

QUEBEC — A pretty town. Pas tellement mal, si vous etes Francais.

TORONTO — All hustle. Looks like a cleaned up version of New York.

BANFF — Not quite sure what it wants to be, Edinburgh or Dallas.

LAKE LOUISE — A big lake.

LAKE ALBERT — Another lake.

CALGARY — Definitely plastic Dodge City with cowboys and rodeos.

VANCOUVER — Captain Cook was right when he named it after his duff navigator (who told him it was an estuary.) Rains a lot.

VICTORIA — Ooh! Now Ya talkin'. A superb city with the best mix of British and American influences—A Great Place.

In spring 1981 I was invited to do a short tour of Canada by an agent I had met at the R.C.A.F base at Lahr in Germany. I went over with Bernie, a German friend who was interested in the prospect of emigrating to Canada. He had given up a pub in England and was seriously contemplating a change of life style. As an added bonus he sang harmony well and played guitar.

We landed in Toronto in the late afternoon and contacted the booking agent for the eastern part of the tour, which turned out to be six gigs in and around the city. He turned out to be German. He had arrived in Canada as a Prisoner of War and never gone back home to Dresden. After all, as he pointed out, after the R.A.F. had finished with it there wasn't much left to go back to. However he still had a trace of his Bohemian accent, a soft floating sibilant sound like Swiss German or perhaps a lazy Bavarian.

The first gigs were at the Eaton centre in downtown Toronto, which was actually a huge shopping mall, a complex of shops, bars, cafés and hotels. It even had its own bus station. A five–piece session band from the Canadian Broadcasting Corporation was already set up in the main hall, a vast high glazed dome with open elevators and escalators to the upper levels. The centrepiece of this area was a beautifully sculpted flight of mallards and wild geese, swooping down from the top of the dome. It was an afternoon session and I was expected to do only a thirty–minute set with a further hour in the evening. The band was good as most Canadian bands are, but their fees were surprisingly low, about the same as British sidemen, around $75 dollars a gig. (Approx £40) at that time, but they supplemented this by having a very broad repertoire to cope with the many requests and dedications from the crowd, usually accompanied by five or ten dollar bills. One great luxury for me was that they were bang up to date in their knowledge of current Nashville hits so that I could confidently do things like Willie Nelson's 'Yesterday's Wine' and a lot of those superb Waylon Jennings songs. It was wonderful. They could do anything I threw at them.

The whole thing was very well received by the hordes of shoppers, and I noticed that the band spent their breaks hustling their latest cassette.

After the session we decided to stay downtown until the evening gig and have a look round. Further down the mall we came across a large open piazza. It had eight sides and in each of these was a restaurant, each one of them offering a different international cuisine. There was Japanese sushi, German wurstchen, Italian pasta, Peking duck, French cuisine, American hamburgers, Scandinavian smorgasbord, in fact everything except British cooking. Ah no, not exactly, because there was a fish and chip shop, but it did not have vinegar and salt, only tomato ketchup so you couldn't really call it authentic. I am sure that Harry Ramsden or Middleton's Tommy Thompson would have done a much better job. However there was one saving grace. On the first floor there was Ye Olde English Pub called the Pig and Whistle (What else?) but when we tried to get in the doorman said that they were full up. There was plenty of room at the bar and I pointed out the fact but he told us that drinking while standing at the bar was not allowed, and there were no seats vacant at the moment. As an afterthought he told us that in Canada the pubs did not even open on Sundays. Weird eh? I'll tell you more about that when we get to British Columbia. The other clubs were very good as well. They were usually big lounges in major hotels, much like the US Military clubs in Europe, a mixture of restaurant, bar and dance hall, certainly a far cry from the wild honky-tonks of the rural America that I had experienced. In one of the clubs I met British Jazz singer Mark Murphy whom I had not seen for ten years or more. I hardly recognized him. He had adopted a complete change of image, all long hair, flares and a heavy Mongol moustache, but he was singing as well as ever.

I was booked into a modern hotel near the airport for a week. The venue was the big cocktail lounge and it was only the resident keyboard player and myself: It was dead easy really. The keyboard had a big false top shaped like a concert grand and it was ringed with high stools for the punters who wanted to be part of the act. Mostly it was Willie Nelson or Kristoffeson stuff and there were plenty of $5 and $10 tips. While I was busy doing this my travelling companion was prowling the downstairs bar beating all comers at darts. I don't know who picked up the most money him or me.

All the time I was with him in Canada I never saw him lose a game and it was down in this bar that the strippers did their thing. The customers in here were mostly young blue-collar workers, rowdy and wild but no real trouble. The room was big with a cold lunch counter at the back, and long bar down one side complete with a red plastic top and fixed barstools. Here again, there was no standing drinking, seats were a must. Bright young waitresses served the tables mostly with gallon jugs of beer (Plastic jugs, not glass.) that cost about five dollars each. Around midday the place began to fill up with construction workers, truckers, reps and office workers and everybody got down to some serious boozing.

Exactly at 1 p.m., on came the girls. Tarrarr. Canned rock music filled the air as the room dimmed and the stage lights glowed, shedding a new found glory on the tatty mauve curtains, and here comes number one. She's a tall girl with a full body that in Victorian days might have been described as buxom, but today just looks fat, and she does not have much idea about dancing, but these customers hadn't come here for Cyd Charisse. They wanted flesh and they got it. In spades. Old Tubby threw her knickers in the air and departed to the sound of Tina Turner and then on came the next one. In fact there was a different stripper every half hour until 5.30 p.m. when there was a break until 8 p.m., at which time it all began again till closing time.

There were ladies to suit all tastes. Tattooed Hell's Angels, blonde Baby Dolls, black Jungle Queens, French Maids, Red Indian squaws, veiled harem slaves, St. Trinian's School Girls in gymslips and blue serge knickers, Barbarellas from Outer Space and an English Countess, who stripped completely to the music of 'Greensleeves'. It was unbelievable. And it was here that I first saw a pair of silicone breasts. They were sticking out pertly like sixteen year old's on the sagging and stretch marked body of a faded old hooker, who was lolloping around the stage like a confused carthorse. Later on we got talking to one of the girls, a French Canadian, and she told us that she worked five or six hotels a day in Toronto at $50 a show. Her daughter was at a top finishing school in Montreal and had no idea what her Momma did for a living. Shades of Bernard Shaw's story *Mrs Warren's Profession*.

I was then sent on a short tour by bus and plane to gigs in the lakes area of Manitoba, before returning to Montreal and Toronto. All these gigs were in classic Honky-Tonk mode and were mostly all the same. The second part of my contract was in British Colombia, but as I had some spare time we thought we'd see a bit of the country. First we tried to book on the famous Canadian Pacific but found that it no longer took passengers from Toronto, and that we would have to fly to Banff for a scenic trip through the Rockies so that was off. Obviously that old George Hamilton IV, number had been written in the 50's.

Next we heard of an agency that delivered cars to the West Coast. It's a long way, some three thousand miles and many re-locating Canadians did not want to drive that distance, and used these specialized bonded agencies to provide a service. There was no shortage of people who were seeking a cheap way across country who would act as delivery drivers. If you were accepted you got $250 and fuel, accommodation vouchers and a further $200 and probably a tip, if all was in order when you delivered the vehicle undamaged to the owner at his new address in British Columbia. The only thing was that their insurance company would only accept Canadian driving licenses. So, for us it was out. In the end we took Braniff Airlines flight out to the British Colombia coast, the journey time taking longer than our flight from London.

Vancouver, BC

Arriving at Vancouver Airport the first surprise was that all the signs were in two languages. Not English and French as in Quebec but English and Chinese.

And the second was that that the cheapest thing on the menus was fresh salmon.

An old friend from Cornwall, Phil Coulter who now, after much wandering, had settled in North Vancouver, picked us up and we stayed with him and his family for about four days. Phil enjoyed talking about the old days and doing a bit of picking. He was really a good guitarist but said that he did not do much playing any more. I did some gigs at roadhouses in the Vancouver area, the strangest being at a self–service restaurant called Kelly's Kitchen, with an Irish folk group which ran from 4.30 p.m. to 7p.m.The next gig was a few days in one of those piano bars. Easy–peazy really, merely requests from the punters round the bar. We got good tips, a massive meal and plenty of free drinks. Great!

In Vancouver of course, it rained. Apparently it rains a lot out there but it didn't dampen the nightlife, which centred on a district called Gas Town, famous for its steam driven clock and its Red Indian hookers from up-country. These Native Americans were not allowed to buy booze there, but there were always a few white winos around to get it for them. The clubs were strictly ethnic. Polish revelers never went to the Irish clubs or vice versa and the growing Japanese and Indian, (Real Indians this time from Delhi etc) communities also kept very much to themselves so in most of the clubs I played, the audiences were strictly redneck, wild but cheerful.

Of course you always got the bores, usually drunks bumming for drinks and sometimes they were difficult to get rid of. One night Bernie and I went for a drink in a small bar near the harbour, and got cornered by a guy who insisted he was a war hero, and that he had fought in Europe. He kept pestering us for drinks and saying how much he disliked the British and why didn't we get out of Ireland, and what were we doing there in any case? To get rid of him we started talking in German, which only made him even more inquisitive. Finally Bernie put him up against the wall and whispered that we were a couple of hit men from Chicago on a contract, and that our mark was due in the bar anytime and to "Shut up and stay out of the line of fire." The guy went white and scuttled off glancing over his shoulder, and the barman, who was in on our scam, laughed saying that he had been trying to get rid of that bore for six months. And now, with a bit of luck, he would not come back to such a dangerous watering hole again.

*   *   *   *   *   *

Fort Knox, Nanaimo

Two days after this incident we took the ferry across to the town of Nanaimo on Vancouver Island. We had another four days to kill before I started my contract in Victoria, so we decided to visit some friends of one of Bernie's pub patrons from Torrington who lived there. It was certainly a remarkable experience.

Having landed at Nanaimo docks we phoned the friend, and after a wait of about two hours a guy turned up in a mud spattered Ford Bronco and got out cautiously carrying a shotgun. He was tall and lanky with a square–cut Abraham Lincoln beard, and dressed for the backwoods in oil stained jeans, big yellow boots and a heavy windbreaker. He half smiled and enquired who we were. Introductions were made and he gestured into his wagon where three big tail–wagging hounds greeted us. Apparently he was the son of the man we had come to see. He didn't talk much, just mumbled that he didn't meet many people, and that his Daddy had told him to feed us on the way to the house. After about half an hour driving on almost deserted roads, he pulled into a diner where we were treated to some of the best chicken curry that I have ever tasted. Probably the last thing we would have expected in such a wild and deserted place.

Another forty minutes brought us to the house where we met our hosts Edward and Mary, a charming couple who were the head of the clan. Edward was a big man; heavily set and very fit for his seventy eight years, and his wife was in her mid sixties. She was the real reason for our visit and greeted us in the same cultured classic English accent she had had when, as a sixteen–year–old girl had arrived in Canada on a school–exchange trip from Bideford. On her second day in the Dominion she met and was swept off her feet by this charismatic Canadian woodsman. Within a month they were living together, and on her seventeenth birthday they married and moved out to British Colombia. Thereafter their life had been one adventure after another and now they were very wealthy with interests in property, land and timber all over British Colombia.

Although, it had not all been milk and honey, he had been wounded in Europe with the Canadian Army, and after the war in his fifties they had moved to New Zealand with their growing family to try their hand at sheep farming and lost every penny. He returned to Vancouver and borrowing from friends, he started a timber company with his sons, and six years hard work put them back on top. Now he took life easy while his Mary, his gentle English Rose controlled their vast business empire with a steel hand in her delicate velvet glove.

We spent a nice evening in their huge cedar bungalow, redolent with the fresh smell resin, and strange creaks. They told us that the house was never still as the logs expanded and contracted with the seasons. Mary asked Bernie a lot of questions about friends and relatives in Devon, and Edward told us all about British Colombia, and how wide open it was for money–making. I asked about their timber business and Mary insisted that we went to see one of their operations. The following day found us back in the Bronco churning up Route 19 from Nanaimo, north to Lanzville.

Another of their sons was driving and after about an hour we picked up a two–lane blacktop, almost opposite Departure Bay, and headed deep into the country. Four miles on, we scrunched into four–wheel drive and turned into the woods. Here it was all–quiet except for a faint humming, which got gradually louder. It was like a flight of model airplanes in some Sunday park. We bumped along through the underbrush with the dogs in the back scratching, and Ed. Junior silently chewing on a tobacco plug until we debouched onto a narrow dirt track, hemmed in by gouged and scarred tree trunks. At a crossing marked by red poles, a huge yellow dump truck lumbered by and our mud bespattered Bronco lurched along in the wake of this roaring, groaning, leviathan and we soon discovered the source of the humming, which was now underpinned by the throb of several big static diesels.

It was a stockade. That's the only way to describe it. Pointed logs rearing fifteen feet into the cloudless sky were embedded firmly into a trench, forming an impenetrable wall perhaps a mile in circumference, with two gateways. The main entrance looked like a Hollywood film set, with its massive gates and two high watch towers, and the big red painted sign announcing THE NANAIMO LUMBER CO. Ed Junior got out and we followed him through the gate, ankle deep in mud, to an old rambling wooden shack which was obviously the site office. Here he introduced us to another brother called Colin who looked very much the same as he did, boots, heavy coat and the same kind of Abraham Lincoln beard. Coffee was brought in big tin mugs and a bottle of Canadian Club broached, as Colin gave us the run down on the company's operation. The figures quoted took my breath away. They were so used to big numbers that the estimates and prices were in units of 10K (ten thousand dollars.)

Apparently on his return from the disastrous New Zealand venture, their father had picked up a 99–year lease on this woodland from the B.C. Government. It was wild timber, tangled and unworkable, but contained a good growth of cedar, however due to its isolated situation nobody wanted it and the ecology conscious B.C. Land Dept. were only too glad to give this eccentric loony a peppercorn lease on the area.

"Then HE would have to worry about the wildlife there. And HE could have the battles with those crazy Green–Peace people." (Quote from an official)

But old Edward had learned something from his trip to New Zealand. Out there he had witnessed the extent and efficiency of Japanese industry and the huge market in South East Asia for timber building materials, an observation that would earn him more money than he had ever seen and make every one of his family millionaires.

Having got the lease he contacted a Victoria timber company and sold all the standing timber, but as there was a royalty payable to the B.C. Government on each tree felled there was not much profit there. The real gold lay in the spaces, the underbrush, and this was Edward's ace card, because under the terms of the logger's contract they could only take trees with a base diameter of three feet, and they sub–contracted to Edward's company the responsibility of clearing the work roads through the undergrowth for their heavy felling machinery, and of course anything he cut under this minimum diameter was his. And that's how Fort Knox, Nanaimo, was born.

I had often heard the phrase 'A license to print money.' but this was the first time I'd actually seen it in action. Twenty four hours a day, seven days a week, the massive bulldozers and dump trucks would be out crashing through the brush, and the felled timber would roll into the floodlit stockade to be processed. Log after log of good cedar would be sawn into 18 inch sections to be split into roofing shingles, the rest was shredded into one inch flakes, pressure–packed into containers and shipped off to Japan or the Philippines, where it would be made into chipboard and some of it re–exported to the States. The system was breathtakingly simple and astoundingly profitable—the lumber company even paid them for keeping the loading areas clear.

Inside the stockade it was like a Heath Robinson cartoon. Huge unfenced saw–wheels whined as they spun wildly, some of them eight feet in diameter. Further over, a line of open–toothed shredders chomped away, all of them hand fed by local Native Americans. On a high platform primitive log splitters consisting of an exposed axe–head on a hydraulic piston thumped away. These were also fed by hand. The operator simply held the log section in place and then pressed a foot switch that triggered the axe and hoped that his hand didn't get in the way.

"Dangerous? "I asked

"Naw, ya soon get used to it," replied the seven–fingered Indian.

In the middle of the stockade there were three massive ex–railroad diesels roaring away, and from their drive–wheels sagging power belts stretching every which way round the site powering all kinds of machinery, the huge open saws, cutters and choppers making a constant screaming, ripping, deafening din—one machine they showed us was like a giant meat grinder into which logs were fed, to be chewed into pieces and packed into the containers thirty seconds later. Colin said that the machine had been imported from Germany costing over half a million dollars, and within two years it had been paid for.

Every second Thursday a Brinks armoured car arrived from Victoria with the payroll, and every second Friday morning all workers, dependants and loan sharks would set up camp outside the gates, to grab their relative's pay packets before it was boozed away in the cat houses and saloons up in Ladysmith and Chemaimus. What an operation.

The Ferry Boat Serenade

Two days later we left and I met up with the KOWZ band for my first gigs at a dance hall in Port Albertini, and it was on this show I first used 'On the Road Again' as a signature tune. I had first heard it on the plane from Toronto and I was knocked out by it, so much so that on that same flight I wrote the basic part of 'Pacific Coast Lines', and started the as yet unfinished, 'Victoria Rains'. The KOWZ turned out to be a truly wonderful band. A melange of Rock and Roll, Pure country, and Sixties Pop, very much like the early Nitty Gritty Dirt Band—and it was from the KOWZ I learned that masterpiece of musical pornography, the infamous 'Rodeo Song'.

It was a strange facet of Canadian music that much of their pop and easy listening numbers were far more permissive and profane than was acceptable in either the UK or the States at that time. For example in May 1981, one of the chart successes there was a steamy number about sexual variations by, of all people, Mick Jagger's old girl friend, convent girl Marianne Faithful, and there were several near–the–knuckle songs around by Anne Murray and Denise Foray that were never heard outside Canada.

The show moved on to Victoria at the southern tip of Vancouver Island, a city that I thought was wonderful. It was certainly the most British of Canadian cities, complete with its ivy covered buildings and red London double–decker buses. For me it seemed to combine the very best facets of American and British lifestyles. The huge harbour was full of motor cruisers, yachts and fishing boats and the fishing was reputed to be some of the finest in the world.

"Them steelheads just jump into the damned boat", one old salt told us.

The agency had booked us into the Harbour Crest Hotel just by the marina, where we met the owner, a very wealthy man called Murray Gam- mon who took a shine to us, and insisted on showing us round the town. He seemed to own most of it. The Gammon Empire encompassed at least three Four Star hotels, a number of cruise liners, actually floating casinos, that took tourists up to Alaska, an auto museum featuring the worlds biggest collection of classic Cadillac convertibles, and several shops.

I stayed about ten days in Victoria, doing various venues and it was a magical experience. Great music, superb musicians and very enthusiastic audiences but one incident really threw me. It was on our first Saturday night (If you remember, back then Canadian pubs were closed on Sunday) and we were about in the middle of the last set. It would be about 11.15 p.m., and I had just launched into 'Panama Red' when I noticed that the band had cut out their solos and two songs from my set.

"What's going on?" I whispered to Larry Mc Gallivery, the bassist.

"It's Saturday night, " he said, gesturing me to finish the song. "We gotta get movin. The boat leaves at midnight. C'mon!"

"What boat? What's a boat got to do with us?"

He grimaced and out of the corner of his mouth hissed. "The Seattle Ferry. We gotta finish early: Cut it short. Right?"

I shrugged and went into "Life of a rodeo cowboy "which was my finisher and almost before the last note faded, the road crew were up on stage stripping the gear and coiling cables. Then one of the roadies grabbed my guitar and hustled me outside and into one of the waiting taxis, which rushed us down to the docks where the huge white Seattle Ferry was moored, and we were hustled up the gangplank.

In the vast main saloon the road crew were already setting up the gear on a corner stage and our appearance roused a cheer from the already well–oiled crowd, who sent up several tumblers of sour mash and two pitchers of beer. By this stage I didn't care what was going on and rolled with the flow. Although I didn't realize that we had such a large road crew, who were actually fans of the KOWZ who had sneaked aboard carrying any old piece of band gear. By twelve thirty we were picking and roaring away with the dance floor crowded. I suppose that the ship must have set sail sometime while we were playing, because at our first break an hour later all you could see of British Colombia, were the distant shore lights. We must have played until about three am, by which time everybody was spaced out and kipping all over the place. I had been given a cabin but was too drunk to find it, and woke up on a banquette in the restaurant, daylight was streaming in and we were tying up in Seattle. I found my cabin, took a shower and changed shirts before meeting the rest of the boys on deck. I thought that Seattle looked like Plymouth, Devon. It was almost the same layout. A cliff surrounded the harbour with a big green space behind it, and then three parallel streets of shops; it even had a big river bridge. That lunchtime we played at a hotel in town where we were fed like kings, and I made $140 in tips. Then it was back on board for a kip before we set up for the evening session on the return trip, arriving dazed and hung over at Victoria around 7 am, at which point most of the passengers went directly to their offices and jobs. While I was watching them go Larry came in and gave me my share of the takings, a very nice $350. Yeah.

What a trip. And these people did this every weekend.

*   *   *   *   *   *

Shuffle off to Buffalo

A club at Horseshoe Bay followed, and the next weekend I was aboard another ferry back to the mainland. The Kowz took off on a tour of the Rockies, so a local band backed me at a club near the Burrad Inlet, and at a Red Light club in Gas Town where all the brass nails looked like Eskimos, and the manager tried to pay us in pussy. The remaining gigs were uneventful and eventually I ended up back in Toronto. Here I played the Eaton centre again, preceded by an early evening set (4.30 to 7.30 again) at a restaurant in China Town.

That weekend I was in Niagara Falls with a local band, but the Sunday night gig was across the border in New York State, somewhere in the sub-urbs of Buffalo.

As we rolled through the inner city my mouth was aghast. Let me tell you, in my time on the road I've seen some shit heaps, but for sheer dereliction and neglect Buffalo, New York takes the biscuit. What a dump. It appeared to be one huge ghetto slum. It was like TV newsreel footage from Beirut. There was garbage everywhere, the streets littered with burnt out cars and waste skips. Acres of empty boarded-up buildings were splat-tered with ornate graffiti, while sinister groups of shabby characters hung around the alleys and bars eyeing our band bus with covetous eyes, as black and white police patrol cars, riot guns at the ready, cruised the streets. I should have known what to expect from the huge sign we had en-countered at the City Limits. It read.

ATTENTION. ATTENTION. ATTENTION.
YOU ARE NOW ENTERING THE CITY LIMITS OF BUFFALO. N.Y.
IN THE EVENT OF A VEHICLE MALFUNCTION FOLLOW THESE DIRECTIONS
FOR YOUR OWN SAFETY AND SECURITY.
LOCK ALL DOORS AND WINDOWS. SWITCH ON HEADLIGHTS AND ANY
EMERGENCY LIGHTS. SOUND HORN INTERMITTENTLY.
WAIT FOR POLICE ASSISTANCE. DO NOT LEAVE YOUR VEHICLE OR OPEN
DOORS UNTIL RESPONDING UNIT ARRIVES.
INSIST OFFICERS SHOW I.D. WHETHER IN UNIFORM OR NOT.
FOR YOUR OWN SAFETY OBSERVE THESE INSTRUCTIONS. NIGHT AND DAY.
STAY ALERT — STAY AWARE — STAY ALIVE.

The show that night was at a big club surrounded by a ten-foot high razor wire fence, with armed guards and dog handlers at the gate, but in-side the buzz was fantastic. Most of the two thousand people there were Southerners who had moved up to Detroit and Buffalo area to earn big bucks in the car plants. They went crazy, screaming for Johnny Cash, Merle Haggard and Waylon Jennings numbers, and crowding the dance floor. It was after 2.30 a.m. by the time we got off stage. The entire band was zonked out on free drinks and pills. In spite of the invitations to call into one of the all night bars, the driver didn't stop the bus until we heard the roaring of Niagara Falls and we were back across the Canadian border.

*   *   *   *   *   *

37

A TALE OF TWO FESTIVALS

The music business has always had its fair share of chancers but some of them are even chancier than others. And Robert Ross Balmoral was a fine example of the breed. A con-man par excellence, approaching the talents of Paladin himself. (Remember him?).

We first met him at a pub in Golant, Cornwall. He was visiting an old friend who lived in Lostwithiel and seemed to be a very nice fellow, as most of these chancers do at first contact. He looked about thirty-five, a biggish chap with thick glasses and thinning hair, and a colonial accent which was difficult to pin point. He said that he had recently returned from Hong Kong and expressed an interest in managing us, but I said I wasn't interested. However in general we all got on quite well, and saw him from time to time over the next year or so at various gigs in the Home Counties. He turned up at the Brighton Country Music Festival where I introduced him to radio presenter Neil Coppendale, who organized a yearly festival of British Country Music, which I think, gave Robert the idea of promoting a regular festival in Cornwall.

A few months later he had somehow horned in on one of the premier Country promotion agencies, and fooled a lot of people with his big talk of Arab money and his contacts in the City. He had big ideas about a Nashville TV spectacular with George Jones and Tammy Wynette, but the project predictably foundered when it came time to do the accounts, and the Arabs wanted to know what they were getting for their money. Somehow greasy Bob avoided losing his legs, and dropped out of sight for the best part of a year, so it was quite a surprise when he contacted me about organizing a festival show at Carlyon Bay. It seemed to be a great idea, about the only fly in the ointment being that the only date the venue was available was the last weekend in August, which clashed with our booking at another major festival at Peterborough the next day, but with a bit of juggling I thought we could do both gigs.

Bob did a good job putting the show together, booking headliners such as Frank Ifield, the Wurzels, with support from comedians Jethro and Slim Pickens and the modern bands of Kelvin Henderson and Roger Humphries providing a musical contrast to the superb Blue Grass Revival. Frank Ifield was backed by Barbary Coast who, to be honest, were a bit over the top, particularly their drummer who had a kit that looked like a North Sea oilrig complete with a huge Chinese gong. It was finally decided that it was going to be a two-day affair running from Friday night, through Saturday afternoon and finishing with the main attraction on Saturday night. (After which we would have to make an overnight 200-mile cross-country run, to be on stage for an afternoon show at Peterborough). I was contracted as compere and stage director and the Everglades as the resident band. There was a pre-show dance on the Friday night and a talent show on the Saturday afternoon, which was won by the sensational 17 year old, Sandy

Delane, who in those days looked like Lynda Carter (Superwoman) and sang like Emmylou Harris—quite a combination.

Saturday night, the show went very well and the place was packed with Country Music nuts from all over the West Country having a great time. About the only point of friction was with our drummer Clive, who had too many lagers and got upset about the band's comments on his jeans, which were wrinkled and grease stained. He thought they made him look cool and trendy, but somebody was tactless enough to mention that he looked like an industrial window cleaner, (you know how warm and gentle musicians can be). Anyway, it must have touched a nerve causing him to storm off to pack his kit and go home, saying we could stuff the job. There was no time for wobblers. We had to pack our gear and drive 200 miles through the night to get to the Fen Country for the next gig. This time we did not have to worry about the drum–kit. On the down–side however, was our new guitar player Peter, who as usual was legless by this time, and had to be loaded onto the back seat of the coach. He was a superb guitar picker, but was not worth all the trouble, being heavily addicted to the booze and cer-tainly not reliable at any time. He had some really beautiful gear including a rare Gretsch White Falcon guitar, which he kept leaving behind on gigs and somehow survived without being wrecked or stolen. At about 12.45 a.m. we were ready and Jon got behind the wheel, and Gypsy George and I piled aboard and off we headed into the night.

Running Wild

Old Greyhound seemed in fine fettle and fairly romped along as far as the Exeter Services on the M.5 where Jon mentioned that there was some-thing wrong with the gas pedal, which seemed to be sticking down. I took over and realized that the problem was with the fuel pump, and removing the engine cover showed us that the control valve had stripped a thread, and was jammed wide open.

It was decision time and there were two alternatives, either call off the trip or head back to Ashburton, and switch to George's car. We were all on a high from the success of the Carlyon Bay show, so the idea of canceling was not really an option, and as Peter was in no position to object, we decided to push on. I kicked the starter and before the big diesel roared to its peak revs I carefully slipped in the clutch and with judicious and heavy stabs on the brakes, we managed to negotiate our way out of the parking lot and back onto the motorway—and then we let it rip.

It was about two in the morning and fortunately traffic was light as we roared on through the night. The engine was running flat out and there was no controlling it, and the speed was now up in the seventies as the huge bus hurtled like a comet towards Plymouth, rocking and bucking like a wild horse. At one point I tried to shut the engine down only to find that the fuel cut–out valve was also broken. Then we could not get the engine cover back properly and fumes started coming into the cab. All we needed.

There was nothing for it but to keep going, lurching round curves and flying past the scattered night travellers.

After what seemed a lifetime the signs for Ashburton began to appear,
and some serious thought had to be given about stopping the monster
which by now was hitting eighty miles an hour. About a half a mile from
the slip road, I put in the clutch and began stabbing the brakes. Gradually
I got the thing slowed to manageable speed although the noise from the
screaming motor was horrendous. With squealing brakes and tyres we
skittered onto the exit road, and bumped over the bridge into the sleepy
little Devon town. Lights appeared in bedroom windows as, with the engine
roaring, radiator hissing, jets of steam and clouds of smoke coming from
the roasting brake drums, we jerked down the main street and into the
yard behind George's house. I was holding it back on the brakes, but there
was no way of stopping the engine and by now the whole bus was full of
carbon monoxide fumes. The only way was to stall it so finally I put the
front bumper up against a low granite wall, slammed it in gear and let the
clutch out, which after some demented jerking stopped the lunatic motor.

We staggered out into the deafening silence and stood looking at the
vehicle settling in a cloud of steam. There was an ominous pool of oil under
the front axle getting bigger by the minute, and the smell from the burnt–
out clutch and brakes wafted by on the warm summer air. In the new
silence came a series of creaking and minor bangs from the engine compartment, which led us to believe that it was probably knackered.—which
it was. But, time was of the essence. We had to get to the second festival, so
we left the steaming wreck where it was and transferred our gear to the
car. Then, after a cup of tea to calm our nerves, we shot off to complete our
marathon drive across the breadth of England. We arrived at the Crest
Hotel in Peterborough around 8am and just dropped into our beds. All, that
is, except Peter who had not really been aware of what had occurred and
could not understand why we did not want to spend the morning in the
hotel bar.

Jon borrowed a bass guitar from somewhere and I collared the drummer
from another band and paid him £25 to do the gig with us. The show itself
went very well indeed, although our inclusion of the Rodeo Song I had
brought back from Vancouver with its profane lyrics was a bit controversial. Some people caught the infectious rhythm and began to join in
before they realized what they where singing.

"Oh, it's forty below an' I don't give a fuck—etc. "

And of course we got a slating for it in the next month's Country Press.

Paralytic Peter was true to form, playing very well but flaked out in the
car and had to be carried to bed. Unfortunately he woke up about three in
the morning and wrecked the TV, which required a quick switch to another
room before the maids spotted it.

The journey back was almost as stressful, with Jon and Peter arguing all
the way, as George and I switched the driving. By the time we reached St

Austell, Peter was asleep again so I dropped him off at the Four Lords pub and told him that our relationship was over. I don't think he cared one way or the other. Shortly after this I believe that he left Cornwall and went back to his native South Wales.

As for Old Greyhound, I had a reconditioned six cylinder Bedford 300 diesel fitted and had a general check over. After that it was magnificent. Smooth, fast, safe, comfortable and economic to run and for the rest of my career in the UK it gave excellent service. But it was a little too late. In less than a year we decided to move to Spain and left the magnificent coach in the tender care of a friend.

PICKER'S TIP 50

To boost your image (and your income) get seen out and about in popular places and have a definite image, don't just follow current trends. Be somebody people will notice and remember, *If faces fit, fortunes follow.*

PICKER'S TIP 51

Beware advice from the Foreign Office or any diplomats. These people are featherbedded against life's storms and live in an alien world. They have a totally different set of priorities to travelling minstrels like us.

PICKER'S TIP 52

Two weeks before your gig contact the local newspaper in the area. Send a picture and a little background information about yourself.

These journals are always looking for stories and an article will often boost your audience.

Also, inform the local radio station and send them a tape or C.D. of your music.

38

VIVA! ESPANA

By 1981 we had done most of the things that one could expect to do on the Country Music scene in Britain, and could see no further progress on the horizon. I'd been in the business long enough to know what was needed was a good manager. A difficult species to find, especially in the world of Country Music, a branch of the business which seems to attract a vast fringe of self seeking hangers on, all of whom think that they are experts in the field of promotion and record criticism.

We vacillated this way and that but the die was cast on Christmas Eve 1981. A year previously we had played at the Cornwall Coliseum at Carlyon Bay, to a big, good–time audience for a very tasty fee. This year the best I could manage was a gig out of Shirley, at the Duke of Cornwall opposite our shop, for less than half last years fee with free drinks thrown in, and playing to a chattering, drunken mob of about fifty faithful fans and local drunks.

On Christmas Day my mind was made up and we set the date for our departure. As far as I was concerned our race in the Sunset County had been run. It had been ten great years but it looked as if it was over and I did not want to stay until I became part of the local musical wallpaper. It was time to go.

At the time I was coughing really badly, and I had a three–bottle–a–week whisky habit that I blamed on the damp Cornish winters, but a lot of it was down to boredom, so something had to change and Spain sounded fine. It was warm and a lot of British people went there on holiday, so there had to be some gigs. My old friend Frank Feeney the agent, talked a lot about it and had bought a house there so I called him. He was very nice and told me a lot of do's and don'ts about the place, impressing this piece of important advice on me.

"Whatever you do, Yonk," he said. "Get somewhere down on the Costa Del Sol in the deep south—don't go to the Costa Blanca. It's full of retired Dutch plumbers, German ex–S.S. men and British lager louts, and what's more the cabaret scene is shot through with East European acts who work for peanuts. The place for a guy like you is around Marbella."

It was solid advice and if we had taken it we would probably be still living in Spain but somehow we ended up on the Costa Blanca. In the shade of a huge rock called the Penon de Ifach. Well, it wasn't altogether our fault. The idea was really fostered by a couple that used to come to our shows in the north of England, Sam and Brenda. They both had had enough of the cold British winters and when the opportunity of a good redundancy package presented itself Sam decided to take it and move to Spain. We saw them off at Plymouth and thereafter Brenda bombarded us with cards and letters saying how good things were, and how their new villa was coming on great—and how cheap the booze was. (We did not realize the deep significance of this last point).

It all sounded good to us so we got all the paperwork ready, leased off the shop to Anglian Windows and stored some of our goods with Francis and Jill in Bodmin. Then we packed the car, gave Danny Dog his dinner and took off for a new life.

The first call was at the Spanish Embassy in Southampton to get Danny Dog's documents authorized, where we ran into a dog–hating official who then insisted on more injections and papers from the Central Veterinary office. So we had a mad day running round South Hampshire, which by the way, is a really beautiful place. I know that because I saw most of it trying to find that bloody animal hospital. Finally we got everything right and drove aboard the cross channel ferry to Le Harve.

As I mentioned earlier we had left my Bedford band bus and a magnificent Shure P.A. system in the safe keeping of a fellow musician, but I should've known then that I'd never get either item back—in fact, some years later when I saw what had happened to them I no longer wanted them. The PA system had been sawn up for installing in a recording studio, and the bus gutted to make a mobile shop, a sad end for such a magnificent vehicle. In hindsight I should have left the Mercedes behind and took that coach. It certainly would have made things a lot easier in Spain.

The first overnight stop was at Poitiers and the next day we reached the Spanish frontier. The Falklands War was raging and we were rather apprehensive about the border crossing, particularly about our dog's papers, but the guard waved us through without asking for our passports. The sudden change of atmosphere and surroundings was quite a shock. The last town we had visited was Biarritz, an elegant, if rather faded, classic French casino resort, but suddenly we were in Spain at the shabby frontier town of Irun and we couldn't get out quick enough.

Barbed–wire lined the main road, and as we headed out to Bilboa we were stopped at more roadblocks by iron–faced soldiers. I was getting very paranoid thinking that it was because of our car's British registration, or something to do with the Falklands, but we were assured that in this part of Spain where the Basque terrorists (ETA) were active, it was quite normal.

Somehow I had never associated Spain with being dirty, but Bilbao changed my mind very quickly. It was filthy. Piles of plastic rubbish bags dumped on every corner, and the scabby peeling bars were overflowing with surly people in dusty black clothes and floppy berets, who shouted and spat at our car when they saw the GB plates, more evidence of their attitude to La Guerra Malvinas. There were drunken brawls in the alleys and side streets, while all the time, political agitators yelled at the volatile mobs in the small parks and plazas. The Police and Garda Civil, all armed to the teeth, stood idly by and watched, but did nothing to cool things down. At one point I stopped to ask directions, and fortunately the traffic cop spoke a little English and warned us to keep moving, and not to stay overnight in the city.

Some time later I met a Dutchman in Benidorm, who told me of an experience he had in this Basque Area. On the outskirts of Santander while held up at some road works, he had seen a car lose all its baggage to some local thieves who had obviously perfected the system. As this Volvo estate car pulled up in the line of waiting traffic, the gang rushed out. Two of them had rolls of wide strong adhesive tape while two others were armed with sharp knives. In a flash, lengths of tape were run down the sides of the car, effectively sealing the doors, while the others slashed the holding ropes and stole everything on the roof rack and ran—this was in a built up area. Nobody did a thing. When the police arrived about half an hour later no witnesses could be found in the grinning crowd of bystanders.

Glad to be out of such dangerous country we headed off towards the glories of the Mediterranean Costas. At Zaragoza we cut off the main motorway, and headed due south on the mountain roads through the Corderlllos of central Spain. It was a barren–baked landscape, a very poor land indeed, shimmering in the heat and dust of summer, in fact one of the hottest summers for many years. The few villages we saw were shuttered and deserted in the fierce glare of the sun, but as the evening grew cooler groups of poor peasants would cluster on doorsteps or on hard kitchen chairs, the men drinking rough local brandy and arguing passionately about crops, politics or more importantly, football. The older women formed a 'Duenna' bodyguard round the young women of marriageable age who had to cover their hair and sit with their backs to the road, so that no passing stranger could tempt or molest them. Here, deep inland, time stood still. Nothing had changed for ages, except perhaps that now they could curse and criticize the government openly, as Franco's secret police were no longer feared.

Calpe

Another night in a mountain motel, and a long haul brought us through to Valencia, and on down through the empty Costa Del Azahar to the buzzing Costa Blanca. It was around midnight when we arrived at the small fishing village of Calpe Penon de Ifach. The town seemed to be deserted and somehow very confusing. I can usually get my bearings quickly on a strange town, but I couldn't make head or tail of this place. Only half the town had street lighting, but after cruising around for half an hour or so, eventually we discovered the local police station only to find it closed for the night and not a patrol car in sight. It was stiflingly hot, but there was nothing for it but to bed down in the car for the night. Well, we tried to get some sleep but it was like a verse from that Peter Lind Hayes song 'Life Gets Tedious'. (Remember Vietnam?)

> I open the door and the flies swarm in.
> I close the door and I'm sweatin' agin."
> I move too fast and I bark ma shin.
> Life gets tedious, don't it?"

It was very uncomfortable indeed. I thought we were by the beach. By the few dim streetlights I could see some shimmering water and parked the car close by. By three in the morning it was unbearable, so we spent what was left of the night in a bar where I sold some tapes to pay for our drinks. In basic Spanish I asked some local patrons where the Penon de Ifach Estate was? Nobody knew. Time after time we were told that the Penon de Ifach was the huge rock that dominated the Bay, and about six new developments had been named after it. This did not give us much help so we had to go back to the car and wait for daylight, at which time we discovered that we were parked on the edge of a salt marsh, the perfect breeding ground for mosquitoes.

There were no cafés open, so after breakfasting on a packet of Ritz crackers and a bottle of lukewarm Perrier we set out in earnest to find Brenda's phantom villa by shooting up into the hills around the bay. After a couple of hours fruitless trundling up half–made roads and assorted building sites we were hot, dirty and tired and no nearer our target. Luckily, by the time we got back into Calpe, the police station had opened up. Enquiries there led us to the Post Office who after tediously checking their lists gave us vague directions leading to a development about a mile inland.

The farther we proceeded away from the seashore the more the quality of properties gradually declined. At first there were smooth asphalt avenues lined by large balconied villas, with either Dutch or German plated Porsches and Mercedes parked in shady double garages, but as the gradient increased the scene changed dramatically, as the asphalt disappeared, and was replaced by a rutted track to an estate of small houses.

"An Ecstatic Welcome"

These red–roofed, white little boxes housed tanned British families who were trying hard to create English Country gardens, and getting by on cheap wine and canned beans, and it was in one of these dead ends we finally found Sam and Brenda's 'Villa'.It was not quite what we had expected, in fact in Smethwick it would have been called a pre–fab.There was a jumble of big rocks and broken concrete slabs that perhaps one day would become a garden, and the chomp–chomp of an axe coming from the back of the building. We rang the bell and waited, but the only thing that happened was that all the noise coming from the half finished house ceased. We began to feel as though we were a pathfinder group for the Black Death, and the greeting added to my doubts about spirit of Northern Hospitality. We rang again and this time we heard a stage whisper from behind the door. It was Brenda's flat East Lancashire whine.

"Oh, Sam. It's them. An' they've brought the bloody dog as well."

I couldn't honestly say that the welcome was ecstatic. It was clear that this was going to be nearer to Belsen than Butlins. The door creaked open and with fixed false smiles the usual formal insincere greetings were ex–

changed, and we were reluctantly invited inside. They asked about our journey, but they were so busy flashing coded looks to each other, I don't think they heard a word that we said. It turned out that a friend was staying with them, using the only spare bed, so after a cup of tea we flopped out on the settee while they all went out for a meal. We were not invited to come along.

"There's tea in' th' cupboard. See you later Luv, Tarrarr," being their parting remark. We flaked out on the chairs and dozed fitfully until they came steaming back in the late afternoon, and got stuck into the gin and tonics on the balcony, after which Brenda dragged herself into the kitchen. Refusing help from anyone and in a boozy haze she made a brave attempt to cook the evening meal.

Well, it was 'Close but no cigar.' There were nice hard spuds, soggy mushy beans and a piece of meat on the border of putrefaction, with that strange sweet taste that even the greasy OXO gravy could not disguise. Just the thing for our first meal on a hot night on the Costa Blanca. This sumptuous repast was followed by a hard night on the Fundador, and a domestic row between our hosts before one of them sulked or stormed off to bed and we piled back onto our lumpy settee. Next morning, as their friend was leaving for the airport in a taxi she looked pityingly at us and rolled her weary eyes skywards. Apparently, this was the regular nightly performance.

This routine went on for a couple of days, and we wondered when they were going to put into action the plans we had discussed back in England. They seemed to have forgotten that it was their enthusiasm and encouragement that had decided us to come to Calpe. In fact on one occasion Sam burst out that he didn't know why we had come there anyway. Nobody had invited us. At that point I produced one of Brenda's gushing letters insisting that we join them as soon as possible, and that there was plenty of room and we 'd be most welcome. This of course, triggered off another row. By this time we'd found a supermarket so Kit would cook something for everyone's dinner, usually chicken or pork chops, it was time for the cabaret. The Sam and Brenda Show. Wow! what a way to live.

It really was time to go and we started looking around for alternative accommodation, having had enough of all this domestic stress and Brenda's King Alfred cooking style.

Originally, our intention had been to use Calpe as a staging post, somewhere I could leave Kit and Danny while I tried to get together with a Spanish real estate agent to develop a Western theme–park further down the coast around Almeria. I already had a letter of introduction to a land agent called Valesco in Benidorm via a contact in Truro, but there was no way I could leave Kit and Danny in this volatile atmosphere, but quite obviously our master plan was out of the window.

On one of my many walks with Danny Dog I got to know a German called Ernst, who had been an officer in the German Navy during the war.

Now he was retired and owned a block of small bungalows down by the beach. I explained our situation and he offered to rent us one until we found something more permanent.

We moved in that same afternoon, overjoyed to get away from the War Zone. It was a nice little place, two bedrooms, a bathroom, a large kitchen-diner with tiled patios front and back. It was adequately but simple furnished and quite near the shops. There was a communal club and about thirty other bungalows on the site, a few mobile homes, a nice swimming-pool and a short cut through to the harbour for Danny's early morning swims. Danny actually needed a lot of careful looking after because of the heat. It was in fact the hottest summer for ten years on the Costa Blanca. Some nights if he was panting, we would lay cold wet towels on him or put him in a lukewarm bath, and towelled him dry. Apart from swimming and eating he spent most of the day sleeping. Well, he was getting on a bit and to be honest he didn't do much else back in Cornwall.

Our little love-nest was not far away from Brenda and Sam's but we did not visit them very much, nor did they visit us. We did go over one evening to their Dutch neighbours for dinner, when Brenda arrived as the meal started, and because she felt somehow slighted sat silently in the big stone fireplace with a lampshade on her head, and slurping from a gin bottle all evening until it was time to go home. However a friend of theirs was a regular caller. She was in the property business, hustling Brits hoping to settle in Spain, and tried very hard to move us into one of her places. Some of them were quite attractive villas with swimming pools, but others were atrocious slums in Calpe town. In any case we were happy in Ernst's bungalow but she was not easy to get rid of. Another one we gave the elbow to was the British snack bar in Calpe. It was a real 'Greasy Spoon' café, run by a retired British Army NCO. (who had obviously been drummed out of the Army Catering Corps.) His wife was also a devotee of the flamethrower school of cookery, and there was always a devoted group of aging ex-pats hanging around, banging on about how good things had been in the 'Good Old Days.'

El Rancho Yonco

We appeared to be settled at last, so I decided to look up the contact given me by the Truro accountant. I phoned the man and made an appointment, and the following day called at his office in Benidorm. The Cornish insurance man had already lined up some finance in the UK, and other people I knew in Europe had promised investment if I could come up with a viable feasibility study, and this is what I hoped to put together with Senor Maresco

This Western Theme-Park idea came to me after a visit to one of those medieval nights in Loret de mar some years previously, and after going into the logistics and the profits involved, I was astounded. A thousand people a night at £9 per head. (Kids a fiver). Cheering wildly as knights in plastic armour riding mangy cart horses crashed into each other, while dark eyed buxom girls in low cut peasant blouses loaded the tables with free sangria and roast chicken. Good value for money at the first glance but the catch came later. The show, and free food and drink ended at 11.p.m., but the coaches did not return from town until 2am and in the meantime the bars were open and the disco roaring, so you can imagine the cash–flow involved. I had seen 'Dude Ranches' in Western Canada and the big dance halls in Texas, and I figured that a combination of these ideas would be a big tourist attraction to Europeans.

It was a sticky hot day when I parked up, and found my Spanish contact's office building in a narrow cul-de-sac near the centre of Benidorm. The young girl receptionist spoke good English and brought me a cold drink, and told me that Senor Maresco would be available soon, as he was with a client. A few minutes later a good–looking Arab girl came out patting her hair and clicking her high heels on the marble floor. The receptionist watched her leave, and giving me a knowing look told me that her boss was ready to see me now. Snr. Maresco turned out to be as shabby as his office. He was a puffy–faced man in his late thirties, of middle height with sandy hair and a shifty smile, who greeted me effusively, telling me in his fractured English that he had received a letter from my contact in Truro and already had located a number of properties that were perfect for my purposes. He had no idea that I spoke some Spanish and could well understand what was going on around me so I let him think that I did not speak a word. That was unusual for me. Normally I liked showing off my love of languages, but for some reason on this occasion I kept quiet.

In the cool of the evening he took me on a trip round town looking at his selected venues. The one I remember best was a large ex–carpet showroom on the corner of a main street. I stood back looking pleasantly stupid as Senor Maresco went into his sales pitch.

"Oh no," he assured the doubting shop owner. "El Ingles would not be selling liquor and there would be no music and of course, he would not be requiring the terrace." (The terrace was two thirds of the bloody property.)

"Oh yes," he continued, "It would be no problem, in fact El Ingles would only be too pleased to pay a years rent up front, and would not need any living accomodation."

"Really?" I thought, "Who is this guy working for?" But the next one was the clincher when I heard him say that we would be closing at 11.30 each night.

Maresco kept nodding and smiling at me while making his own translations of what was being discussed, assuring me all the time that everything was "Hokey–dokey. " I shook hands with the beaming shop owner who really thought he'd hooked a live one, and then headed out to the hills to look at some more rural locations that my Spanish wolf had found. On the drive to the hills he told me that the man was amenable to all my proposals. The liquor licence, late opening, terrace service and the man–

agers flat, but that there might be the remotest chance of a hitch at the Town Hall about the change of use etc. But such natural impediments were normally overcome in the time–honored way—you know, wheels might need lubricating? And of course there would be a fifteen per cent charge for his services as negotiator, and get this. Could he have a £1000 advance? We parted with a handshake and agreed to meet at the Benidorm Palace the next day. He's probably still waiting there.

I began to make enquiries off my own bat and in the process came across some of the pitfalls of buying property in Spain, particularly if you were not a Spanish national. There were some very strange laws relating to freehold land. Titles were vague and contained obscure and conditional clauses. It was not unknown for instance, for a developer to be halfway through the construction of, say a block of holiday flats, to be suddenly confronted by a lawyer, representing someone claiming to be the true owner of the site being built on, the title passing to him from an ancient land grant from some long dead ancestor. At that point the lawyer would demand a further large payment before allowing building to continue, hence the large number of half finished steel skeletons dotting the Costa Blanca skyline, and from what I hear it is not much different today.

Inland from Altea I came across what I was seeking. An old abandoned corrida. Apart from the bullring itself, with its seating and central open space, there were a number of outbuildings and plenty of car and coach parking space. I thought it would be perfect for my project , so I started making enquiries. I found the land agent, who in turn, put me onto the Bank of Bilbao to sort out the financial side of things. The price was about £190,000 for a nine–year lease, not out of the way for the size of the en-visaged development, and I had that level of financing available from a consortium in Belgium, but the project foundered on a peculiar facet of the Spanish banking system. The previous leasee, a promoter of bullfights, was still in debt to the bank and the lease had been used as collateral to the tune of another ninety grand plus charges—and they insisted on having their money back before agreeing to any further use of the place. At over £280,000 it was a non–starter and rather than lose face with the moneymen I reluctantly abandoned the whole scheme.

*   *   *   *   *   *

Disenchantment

I did a few cabaret spots in the tourist pubs and a couple of weekends at the Benidorm Palace but really; there was no place for my kind of music except strangely enough, in the German and Dutch bars where they were truly interested in American music. Benidorm itself was full of discos from the UK or live bands from Southern Italy and the Balkans, who were working for buttons and leg–overs with holidaying British girls. At one point it crossed our minds to buy a bar or something but after two weeks in the town we scotched the idea completely. Scotched seemed a good word to use in this context as all the side streets seemed to be infested with open front shops selling McEwan's Export to hordes of paralytic Scots and Liverpudlian yobs. By chance we happened to say in passing that we might be interested in buying something and were inundated with British people trying to sell us bars, garages, taxis, cafés, etc, etc. It seemed that after a couple of years of constant sunshine, most people had had enough and wanted to get back home to rainy Britain.

As the hottest summer for twenty years on the Costa Blanca ground on, the frustration and heat got to us, we began bickering and for the first time our relationship faltered. Kit had had enough. She was adamant and wanted to go back to the UK while I wanted to head further south to the Costa del Sol, where I thought that there might be more opportunities, but it was clutching at straws and I think deep inside I knew it. There was also a feeling of great vulnerability being in Spain at that time. The passions roused by the Falklands War did not help either. On top of which England had beaten one of the Latin American countries in the Football World Cup, so it really was time to get out of it.

We stayed a few more weeks becoming more bored and brittle. At one time we met up with Kit's sister who was on holiday in Calpe, but we did not see much of Brenda and Sam or the other tedious ex–pats. We became more and more frustrated trying to find gigs or something to invest in. To make matters worse, our dozy solicitor in Mevagissey was dragging his feet completing our lease agreement with Anglian Windows, which did not help the situation. Also, his first move, when he finally got round to sorting it out, was to send our money to the wrong French bank. We had selected him to handle the deal because he was a Londoner and I thought he would be on the ball. But consider this. A London lawyer who decides to move to Mevagissey is not likely to be a Perry Mason is he?

As the Beatles put it 'I shoulda known better'.

* * * * * *

Homeward Bound

Somehow we achieved some kind of compromise and moved up to Lloret de Mar, where we had stayed on our first visit to Spain in 1976. In those days it had been a nice quiet town with a beach and a few cafés. In fact back then, one of the best floor shows in town was at a chip shop run by a Birmingham family, who were in a continual state of war with each other, and would curse each other loudly and profanely in front of the customers.

Regularly burning himself with the hot fat, the tall thin father would yelp and shout. "Oh shite, not again. I fookin' 'ate this job. I didn't wanna fookin' come 'ere in the ferst plyce. It was all yore fookin' idea."

At which his fat wife and daughter would shout back "Oh fookin' shuttit, yer daft twat, an' gerron wi the bleedin' fryin'. Theer's folk fookin'gaggin ere."

Most of the customers were German and couldn't understand the Brummy accent but to the few Brits there, it was a gas because you didn't often hear that kind of language in public. However, those genteel days had gone and now it was horrible. High–rise blocks everywhere and the streets crowded with lager louts. and discos flashing and thundering out all night. We could not get out quick enough. The next stop was at a small hotel on the outskirts of Barcelona. Here we met an American couple and under their influence the atmosphere between us began to soften a little.

We crossed back into France near Perpignion and headed to the Brittany Coast via Carcassonne and Bordeaux, arriving at Roscoff where new prob- lems arose. We had to find a destination port in the UK that had the quarantine facilities for Danny Dog, and the only one was Southampton, so we began trekking up the coast to St Malo, Cherbourg and finally Le Harve. Here there appeared to be flaws in Danny's papers, and we made frantic phone calls to England to persuade someone to bring over copy documents from the Spanish Consulate. Ironically, of all the people we called, only Gypsy George volunteered to help us out, which was very good of him and typical of our rather volatile relationship. We were quite relieved until, on phoning to check, we found that although he had man- aged to get the correct papers, he had got on the wrong ferry, and we had to dash back to Cherbourg to meet him. We arrived just as the boat had cast off on its return trip with him shouting messages from the deck to us on the quay. He did not even wait till we got there, but gestured that he had left the papers in the P&0 office. Phew! What stress.

As we set sail the following day we were at first relieved to be on our way, but gradually the enormity of what we were doing to Danny Dog dawned on us, and it was a terrible moment when he was shoved into a cage at Southampton to be taken to the quarantine kennels. Then we drove to Devon in a chilling silence except for smart remarks from me about Danny Dog being in jail, while we were getting nearer home. It was NOT a good time for us. The kennels were somewhere near Taunton, so we moved

into a rented cottage to be near the quarantine station, but the manager
said that we should not visit for the first week because it might be unset-
tling for him. You have to remember that he was going to be in there for six
months. (A bloody long time in a dog's life.) We took a few doggy goodies
along and paid the bill, which worked out at something like £130 per
month.

We tried to settle but after the first week we realized that we could not
get anything going while Danny was in quarantine, so one night we
decided to go back to Europe and take our chances and made the arrangements to pick him up on the ferry back to France. It was a wonderful
moment to see him again at the dockside, as he bustled out of the wire cage
of the van and forced his way up to the car deck, dragging the handler
behind him. However he had to stay in a locked kennel until we cleared
British coastal waters, but finally on the morning of August 5th 1982 we
drove ashore at Cherbourg with absolutely no idea of where we were heading.

*   *   *   *   *   *

39

BRITTANY

THE EMERALD COAST

Sitting on a beach at Saint Jacut, roasting in the August sun.
Thinking what I should be doing, not caring if it ever gets done.
Ice cubes rattle in the Saumur jug, melon and shrimp taste fine.
Listening to the sound of a good guitar, floating on a tide of time.
I wonder what they're doing in Paris? Can't say that I really care.
Smelling the barbecued turkey floating on the sizzling air.
Sand feels like silk between my toes, the water's clear as a bell.
Another three kirs and I won't care if it's heaven or it's Hell.
Living it up on the Emerald Coast, having the time of my life.
Living it up on a pauper's pay, away from the trouble and strife.
Somehow we all find the money we need, somehow we get along fine.
If it's not going to be at your place, sure going to be at mine.
Ricard and Roquefort soften the blow of the winter
    that's just round the bend.
There'll be time enough to think about that when the Condors
    come to an end.
We're not the only ones living this way. It's the sea,
    it's the sun, and it's the air.
Reeling round the walls of St Malo, or swimming at La Passagaire.
A dapple of leaves on the banks of the Rance,
    these Brittany summers are fine.
The rest of the world is oceans away so just pass me
    that bottle of wine.

Frank Yonco. Jouvente. Aug 1986

I must make clear that this was not our first visit to France. We had first played here in 1966 but things had changed quite considerably in the intervening years. De Gaulle had come and gone, but during his time in office he had dragged the country kicking and screaming into modern Europe, like some recalcitrant infant. Not all the French approved and there were some violent protests, but after the debacle in Dien Bien Phu, and the ongoing volatile state of affairs in Algeria, the new Republic was rapidly loosing interest in the designs of Empire.

Metropolitan France itself had also improved beyond measure since our early trips, though one of Old Big Nose's first moves was to banish all the liberators of his country. by demanding the removal of U.S. Military bases. (A typically French government reaction—ask any Legionnaire.) Opinions vary as to the wisdom of this move. It certainly pandered to public opinion but perhaps the country's economic revival would not have been so long and painful, if like the Germans, they had retained American financial support and know how. Although in hindsight, the French do not have the drive, the discipline or the dedication of the Germans, so maybe De Gaulle's way was the only one that would work for them—but on with the story of St. Malo and a whole new French experience.

So here we were. Happy to be all back together again but with still really no clear idea where to go. We parked outside Le Harve and listed our options, not that there were many open to us. The next big town was Caen so we went there and after a good look round, booked in at a hotel on the riverbank called Les Cultivators, a typical small hotel obviously catering for French clients, as demonstrated by the toilet which had a sandpaper loo roll, two condom machines and no soap. But moving in did not prove to be simple, as there appeared to be some kind of range war going on between the recently deceased owner's daughter and his ex-mistress, about who actually had inherited the hotel. They were daggers drawn, and every time we came downstairs there was a flaming row going on behind the reception desk. In the end however things worked in our favor, as they were so distracted that they only charged us for two days, though we'd been there for almost a week. They even forgot to charge us for meals.

The next stop was at Bela Riva on the coast, and then we moved on to Avaranches, still wondering where to base ourselves. There was one place that came to mind, a small village in Brittany called Poubalay where we had stayed on our trip from Spain, so we headed back there. The thing I remembered most about this village was the local pub, called like so many village estaminets, "Le Café du Sports". It seemed your ordinary local French café with its hard floors and zinc topped bar, but behind was a honey comb of low rooms where some of the best French food I have ever tasted was served. From midday to three in the afternoon, the place was packed with punters of all kinds from blue clad farm laborers to smart suited sales reps. tucking into heaped platters of fruits–de–mer or succulent roasts, accompanied by crisp white bread and rough red peasant wine. The evenings were just as busy, so much so that it was necessary to book a table days in advance, even in winter. I tell you, that place made such a mark on me.

We called in at the little Hotel de la Post where we had stayed before. The proprietor remembered us and was delighted to give us a room overlooking the square at a special rate. The room was right opposite the village church, and the reason for that special rate soon became apparent. At 6am the very next morning the newly-installed church bells proudly boomed out to bring the faithful to prayer—and then continued to remind them of the time of day—BOINNNG! BOINNG!—every half hour till midday. We did not stay there long.

One of the punters in the bar told us about a hotel/club in the nearby village of Plessix Belisson, so we toddled off there only to find that it was a collection of decrepit buildings in a sea of shoulder high corn. The club, actually a disco, turned out to be closed until Easter but the caretaker, who like most French country folk can smell a dollar at fifty metres, noted our predicament and told us about a lady on the far side of the village who took in guests. It turned out to be his Auntie Rose. He must have phoned her because almost before the car stopped she jumped out and grabbed us before the neighbors could get a look in. She met us with a porcelain smile and a click of knitting needles. (Later experience led us to believe that she was actually a reincarnation of one of those shrieking tricoteuses who sat knitting beneath the scaffold as the guillotine blade lopped off aristocratic heads).

She hesitated a moment when she saw Danny Dog but that didn't stop her.

"Ah oui, pas problem," she grimaced and showed us up the uncarpeted stairs to the room she had to rent. It wasn't bad, but nothing to write home about, Only a lumpy bed, a few chairs and dresser, and when we asked for a pot of coffee she said that it was not possible and shut her kitchen door, so we all went to bed at nine o'clock. We could hear her muttering to herself and shuffling about downstairs, and could hear the hissing of a percolator and the clanking of pots but no coffee was forthcoming, so we decided to take matters into our own hands and brought out our little immersion heater and secret sachets of Brittany Ferry coffee, but the old cow must have been spying on us somehow, because as we collected a jug of water from the bathroom and plugged in our heater, she turned off the power. Pouff. That night we went to bed in the dark without our coffee, so naturally we did not stay there more than one night.

We spent the day wandering through this ocean of cornfields looking for somewhere to lay our weary heads. Hamlets and villages came and went, each one having the same blank look as they baked in the hot sun, deserted at this time of day with the occasional chug of a tractor behind some barn, or a stray dog sniffing at the shuttered butcher's door. Lamenais, Cobiniere, La Rouxiere—they all looked the same. We were going round in circles. Danny was panting and the weather was stifling, so we decided to head for the river at La Richardais where there was a quay and little launching ramp. This small port was about half a mile up river on the left bank from La Barrage (Usine Maremortrice), a combined dam and hydroelectric tidal generating plant across the mouth of the Rance.

In the garden of a small house on the quay an elegant middle–aged woman was trimming roses, and I asked her if she knew of anywhere to rent. She was a charming lady from Paris, who spoke good English and said that she was staying with her daughter who spent every summer in Brittany, and she was certain that she would know of somewhere. Apparently she was at the shops so we hung around bathing Danny in the cool water until she returned about half an hour later. She turned out to be an equally charming Parisienne who also spoke good English, and at her side was a large English sheep dog called Lola. Her name was Jacqueline Vintant and she operated an osteopathic clinic on the Parisian Left Bank. We all got on very well and over the years she became a good friend,

'Yes,' she said, "She did know of a place. How would we fancy living in a chateau on the river?" Well of course we jumped at the chance—at that stage we would have said yes to a beach hut.

The chateau turned out to be all that Jacqueline said it was. A wonderful turn of the century house beautifully restored and decorated with no expense spared. It stood on a high bank above the river, and was so placed that every guest room had a view of the Rance. The rooms were also superbly appointed, each one following a different theme, Breton, Belle Époque, Parisian, and 1930's Art Deco. Etc. The owner, Yvonne Jasselin, who also became a good friend of ours, was an elegant widow in her fifties, a retired hotel proprietor from Dinard, who made us very welcome. She showed us round the extensive gardens and orchards and pointed out below us the disused landing-stage and the building beside it, that would feature so strongly in our stay in France. This was a closed-up family restaurant that had served as a youth-hostel for several years, but had recently been purchased by an eccentric Jersey millionaire to create an English pub for his sailing club friends. He called it the Jersey Lily (More of this later).

We settled nicely into an annexe of Le Manoir de la Rance, but it was clear that we could not afford to stay for a long time. The rates were high not excessively so for such accommodation, but our money had still not come through from 'Perry Mason' in Mevagissey. Most days were spent flat hunting. We tried to rent a caravan, but it was the height of the season and mid August was really not a good time to find holiday flats in Brittany. The nearest small town was a couple of miles across the maize fields called Pleurtuit and it was from the post office here, that we made many fevered international phone calls trying to get our hands on our money which was tangled up somewhere in the French banking system. There was also a café called Le Relais that did a Plat de Jour for about thirty francs, that became our daily main meal. It was about all we could afford. Asking around we came across a room to rent, in a house on the road to Dinard Airport, where we could do a little self-catering again which would certainly make life easier, so we said goodbye to the beautiful chateau and moved in.

*   *   *   *   *   *

The Ramparts of St. Malo

Finally, we got some news of our money. It had been deposited in the St
Austell branch of the Nat. West Bank and been transferred by our diligent
bank manager (who I suspected was some relative of our Mevagissey
lawyer) to the BPB (Banque du Pays Bas) instead of the BNP. (Banque
National de Paris) and it had been sent back twice before the Mount
Charles manager got it right—so we took a trip to the branch in St Malo to
fix up a cheque account.

The effect of that visit was electric. We felt an immediate affinity to the
place, as we passed through the massive ramparts and wound our way
through the medieval streets and squares to the bank. For the first time
since leaving Cornwall we felt at home. This old walled city of St Malo
(Intra Muros) was fascinating. It was as though there was a permanent
carnival going on. Twisting cobbled lanes and steps with street singers,
sidewalk cafés, superb restaurants, knock out beaches, an old castle and
hundreds of happy visitors. 'Yeah,' we thought.' This'll do fine. Let's look
for a place here'—and Danny Dog woofed his approval. I suppose he was as
fed up with the travelling as we were. Even though it was high summer we
thought it was worth trolling round the estate agents to see if we could find
somewhere to rent. After an hour of blank faces, Gallic shrugs and insincere apologies we came across a small estate agent in the Post Office
square called Agence Dugay Trouin. (Named after the notorious pirate.
who with typical French pragmatism has gone down in history as a
national hero.) There were two people in the office, a strikingly beautiful
woman in her forties and a good–looking man about the same age. They
both spoke English very well and we did not experience the earlier blank
refusals, but instead a quite apologetic explanation about how difficult it
was to find holiday accommodation at this time of the year. I made it clear
that we were not seeking a vacation flat but a long lease of a year at least,
which appeared to spark a bit of interest. And they began to discuss a place
in Charlie's building, whoever he was.

The lady's name was Francette Jardin, a very interesting woman indeed.
She was the widow of a successful dentist and owned one of the finest
apartments in the city, which overlooked the bay. Apart from being a
partner in the agency, she was a fully qualified pilot with her own Piper
Cub plane at the Chateau Malo aero club. The man, who was the actual
estate agent, was Jean Paul Barthelemy and also became a close friend
during our time in Brittany. He spoke with a really great accent sounding
like Maurice Chevalier, and like the famous film star was full of charm and
bonhomie with a great appetite for the ladies and the booze. He asked me
what I did and as I wanted a change from the music game and writing was
beginning to interest me, I told him I was a writer. Then he made a few
phone calls, and told us that his friend Charlie had a small apartment that
would be available at the end of the month, and we could go and look at it

right away if we wished. The rent he quoted was very reasonable so off we went through the squares and along the walls above the vast beach.

The apartment was on the top floor of a seaside block overlooking the 'Bastion d' Holland, a green sward on the top of the wall where the cannons used to roar at the English ships chasing the Malouin Corsairs over two hundred years ago. It had a small living–room, a big bedroom, a well-appointed kitchen, a bathroom and another narrow room, which I used as an office and as an occasional bedroom if we had visitors. It was on the sixth floor but there was a lift to the fifth floor, and the beach was right opposite our front door. It was perfect. Thus began our long connection with St. Malo.

It was an idyllic summer. The weather was perfect and we enjoyed exploring the fascinating walled city. The afternoons were spent on the beach where I started to write a book called 'Angel Meadow'. We ate at home, but in the early evening strolled through the streets dropping in at one of the little bars for a drink. We got to know Jean Paul very well and finally met our landlord; the famous Charlie Hemar. He was the son of the great architect who oversaw the entire re–building of the city after its 85% destruction during the Second World War and he was a legend in St Malo as a bon viveur and ladies man without a peer. The Hemar family was comfortably off already, and the reconstruction contracts (to a 17th century plan and paid for mainly by America) made them very wealthy indeed.

Charlie was at college during the war and so escaped having to soldier but whether he ever qualified as an architect, I do not know. He certainly did not work as one. In fact he did not really have to work at anything. As a rich young man on the loose amongst all those Parisienne beauties on holiday in Brittany his time was fully occupied. He was a true gallant, a throwback to the days of the Belle Époque, who philandered shamelessly, but looked after his ladies.

Amongst the many properties he owned was the building we lived in. His own apartment covered most of the top floor and the roof cavity, and was crammed with valuable antiques and sailing artefacts. There were nautical pictures, oars, fishing rods, harpoons, models ships and cars, battle flags, guns, telescopes and some wonderful books. It was a breathtaking Aladdin's Cave, a rambling, bizarre collection of rooms on two levels. Charlie himself was about sixty–two years old, and his live–in mistress Monique twenty–nine, when she presented him with a baby daughter called Doris, which added more kudos to his reputation as the swinging 'Boulevardier de Paris'. He had been married about four times I think, and as a parting gift to his wives and consorts he usually gave them an apartment in one of his many properties. In our building alone his second wife, a Swede, had an apartment and five other relatives had flats there as well. His first wife lived in his country house on the river, and I think another lived in the Excelsior Hotel in Paris, which he also owned. Within a few short years however his wild and woolly ways caught up with him, and a summer cold turned quickly into the pneumonia that brought on his early demise at the relatively early age of sixty–six. In fact, quite a few of our hard living friends in St. Malo went that way,

One of first moves was to bring out our mothers for a holiday, and Kit's sister Ann flew with them to Jersey, and then took the Condor hydrofoil to St Malo. We moved them into a big apartment two floors below us over-looking the beach and. everybody had a good time. The weather was superb and the old town fascinated them. We took them to our favourite bars and restaurants, where they had difficulty accepting the slow French service, but all in all it was a great visit and they came back a few times while we were there

La Belle Epoque

We settled in very nicely on the Rue Guy Louvel. Now that our money had finally come through, taking the pressure off for a while, we began checking out the bars and cafés including one on the Rue de Dinan called the Belle Epoque, which was run by a chubby, happy faced middle–aged lady called Maria Queffilec and it became our 'Local'. Maria was a widow and had a worldly-wise kind of charm very much in the Edith Piaf mould. (There seemed to be an awful lot of widowed restaurant and hotel proprietors in Brittany, and many of them were caused by suicides. In Maria's case she finally traced her husband at his mistress's house one summer afternoon. He was hanging from the banisters.)

She ran it in the traditional French manner. There was a bar, about thirty tables and the cooking was done on an open chimney grill, and a grand piano completed the ambience. The tourists loved the place, particu-larly the Germans and Dutch. There was also a huge tank of live lobsters and crabs. You were sure of getting fresh seafood at the Belle Epoque. The punter pointed out the lobster he wanted and Maria would fish it out, bang a skewer into its head, cut it in half and throw it on the grill and in three minutes it was on the plate.

Her prices were outrageous but she got away with it. I clearly recall one incident. I was sitting at the bar sipping a beer when a young Belgian man and his mother arrived for lunch. Admittedly, it was a superb meal—Barbary duck breasts, orange sauce, lobster, brandy flambeed bananas, a couple of bottles of Sancerre topped off with coffee and liqueurs, but the bill came to f.1760. (App.£150). I thought that was a bit strong, but they paid up with a smile and even left a tip.

Oh yes, Maria took no prisoners.

Another afternoon I was walking by her estaminet when I heard some-one playing the piano so I called in and introduced myself as a fellow musician. The guy playing was a Moroccan, a tall thin Arab with the un-usual name of Manuel. He was brilliant both as a piano player and singer, specializing in the music of Jaques Briel, a cult avant–garde composer in France who, like my own hero Hank Williams, died young. (And, if rumor is to be believed, from the same compulsive self–destruction) He was booked that very evening to do a concert at the Belle Epoque so I went along. The place was packed to capacity and although I did not have to pay the £8 admission fee I did order a drink, a pint of lager for which Maria charged me four quid. At my shocked look she shrugged, saying, "C'est la Commerce,"—she'd done it again.

We got to know Manuel very well and jammed with him often at the café in the quiet afternoons. He had his wife Greta with him who was a very attractive South American girl who sang and played wonderful Mexican music, Songs like 'Vera Cruz' and 'Cielito Lindo'. My Country Music was alien to him but his favourite songs were Don Gibson's 'Sea of Heartbreak' and Hoyt Axton's 'Della & the Dealer'. Eventually they got a contract at La Louisiana, an Antilles Restaurant then run by Marc & Dominique Terragiani, another place which was also destined to play an important part in our lives. They were great times and great music.

However in the midst of all this good fortune tragedy struck. On Xmas Eve I was walking Danny round the block before turning in when he collapsed with a massive heart attack. I carried him back up to the flat, as he was panting for breath and his tongue turning blue, and phoned a doctor friend of ours, Bernard Lerich who was good enough to send round a vet colleague, who gave poor Danny an injection to stabilize him. But after that he was never the same and eventually died in our arms on the morning of February 1st.1983. It shattered us. He had been so much a part of our lives for almost fourteen years, through all the good times and the bad, and now he was gone. Terrible. To quote "Mr. Bojangles. "After fifteen years we still grieve". We buried him in the orchard of Madame Josselyn's Chateau at Jovente with his own carved headstone.

PICKER'S TIP 53

This is the defining difference between the true professional entertainer and the semi–pro. The committed believer will only take a day job when gigs become hard to find, while the semi–pro takes gigs to supplement his day job.

I'm not saying that there is anything wrong with this. I know part–timers who have been doing this for years. It is just a difference of attitude.

Dinard Casino

To take our minds off the grief, I began to reactivate our show business career and started looking round for gigs. My first target was the recently refurbished Casino de Dinard. It had been taken over by a charming middle-aged couple M.et Mdm. Quintin, and I'd heard they were looking for an attraction for their opening week of the summer season and what better than an authentic Country Rock act? That would make it just like Las Vegas, so I breezed in one spring morning, dressed in my best western suit and boots, toting a couple of our L.P.s, a publicity pack and a few tapes. It turned out to be what they were looking for and I left there with a two-week contract, which was fine except for one small snag. The fact that at that moment, I did not actually have a band. "You've done what?" demanded Kit when I got back home. She was more shocked when I told her that she was to be featured as a special attraction.

I put the word out and thought it would be dead easy with every musician in the UK clamouring to come to 'Le Continong'—but when I started phoning around I found that most of my aces turned out to be spades. Dave the Drummer, who was always nagging me to take him abroad, stalled until Kit phoned her friend Maureen who was married to him at the time, and said that we had to have an answer quickly. It turned out to be No. Bassist Alan Ross, another of my first choices also pleaded domestic pressure, and my favourite Irishman Denis, had dropped a girder on his playing hand (Surprise, surprise) but he did put me onto super picker Paul Henry. My old bassist Karl, as usual, had woman trouble and could only come out for a week, and several others did not want to miss their Giro cheques.

The opening of the cabaret room at Dinard Casino was getting closer all the time and already there were posters out across the coast advertising us. To aggravate the situation more, in a rash of over confidence I had offered to do a full season for Gerard Ballayer at the Café de l'Ouest in St. Malo. After a fevered weekend phoning to the UK. I did finally manage to cobble a band together, figuring that with a carefully selected program and a few days concentrated rehearsal, I could create a good show with the most basic musicians.

In the event I got some great talent and produced a superb and varied sound. Guitarist Paul Henry was a quintessential professional, and Terry Silver also proved to be a real gem on steel guitar, banjo and concertina, Jon Adkin was doing what he does best, playing great bass and singing harmony vocals, and he brought along a drummer who he had worked with before.

On Sunday, June 12th. Kit and I met them at the ferry and took them to a big mobile home we'd rented on a site near the causeway, across the Rance Estuary. I can't honestly say that they got on very well together socially, in fact, due to the differing personalities they just about tolerated each other, as often happens in pick–up bands, but we got stuck into rehearsals and after three days it was coming together.

The opening night at the Dinard Casino the following Saturday turned out to be a real winner, even if there was a smell of paint and some of the gaming tables had not yet arrived. We played in the beautiful Restaurant d'Or overlooking the beach, and the place was packed to the gills, with people sitting on the stairs up to the lavish roulette and blackjack rooms. I knew we were on a winner from the opening song and M. & Mdm. Quintin were beaming, as the happy crowd streamed upstairs afterwards to place their bets and crowd the bars. The timing too was just right as the glamorous US soap 'Dallas' had hit French TV, and so the press was there in force to hear some real Texas music, and Gerard and his family came to see what he had bought for the forthcoming twelve week season at his establishment in St Malo. He was very pleased too, and confirmed the booking right there. So after a successful and well–publicized two weeks in Dinard we moved across the barrage to the old walled city.

La Brasserie de l' Ouest

We found a big apartment for the boys behind the Place Chateaubriand, and we kicked off our gig for M. Bellayer, and now things really took off. The first week we played inside the restaurant, but due to the crowds, the stage was moved onto the terrace and the big glass doors opened up. Every seat was taken and as soon as one was vacated it was grabbed, while out in the square, crowds sang along and danced to our music till two in the morning.

The line–up proved to be good and by blending the multiple talents of Terry and Paul, we could do most kinds of Country Music including Rockabilly, Western Swing, Bluegrass, Tex Mex, or Cajun. It was great. Kit was superb and was a big favourite with the crowds, and Paul Henry almost became a cult figure with a generation of budding French guitar pickers. Jon and the drummer contributed some modern 'Urban Cowboy' items, and I did some of the great Country Classics. We had a dance rou-tine in a couple of numbers. The band looked great too. We had a few sets of fancy H bar C shirts left over from the shop and a few other Western bits and pieces, so we used them. It looked like we'd just rode in from Nashville.

The French didn't know what had hit them. It proved to be a hell of a season and the patron was overjoyed to have his restaurant full every night—so happy in fact, that he asked if we could do the Sunday night as well. Well I thought, why not?

There was one small hiccough though. With a view to cashing in on the current 'Dallas' fever, we went to great lengths to present an impressive arrangement of the soap's famous signature tune as an opener, but it got no reaction whatsoever from the crowd. We thought it would have knocked them out. Then a couple of nights into the gig Gerard told us that the French version of Dallas had a totally different signature tune. Gulp!

At first there was a little confusion about the band's accomodation, which actually consisted of a large room with two bedrooms off it. Paul claimed the back bedroom, saying that his lady was coming out to join him. (She turned up later but surprisingly, did not come to many shows). John and the drummer claimed the other bedroom, and Terry built himself a redoubt of wardrobes and other furniture in one corner of the big main room for privacy. We still had our old apartment across town, so we were spared all the squabbling, and soon everybody was settled and various life patterns evolved.

Often Kit and I would be up early and walk along the beautiful wide beach called the Sillon to Roteneuf, arriving back in time for lunch at the Petit Hermine* a small pizzeria where the cooking was out of this world. The lunch menu was about 36 francs and on offer were a superb Beuf Bourguignon, hand made pizzas, Escalope Milanese, divine chocolate gateaux and house wine at 12 francs a bottle, after which we would stagger round the corner to our apartment and sample a little 'Afternoon Delight' and take a siesta until it was time to get ready for the gig—perfect.

What did the great Jimmy Buffet sing in 'He went to Paris'?

Warm summer breezes and French wine and cheeses held his ambition at bay

Well, that's what happened to us. Except it was French wines and bubbly. At the end of the show everybody was on a high, and didn't want to go home to bed. So invariably we hung on with Gerard for a glass of champagne, or,in my case, that Norman moonshine, Calvados. Gerard's wife Yvonne, in true French style, cashed up and headed home with the loot, leaving her old man to get rid of the awkward punters and wind down with us. Around 2.30 every morning we could usually be found in one of the great all night bars, tucked away in the winding back streets under the high ramparts.

By far the best after–hours place was Les Chandelles off the Rue des Cordiers. It was a small bar, run by a couple of ex–showbiz pros. They had been an adagio dance act, and had worked some of the world's top cabaret venues before retiring in St Malo. She was an attractive middle–aged woman called Monique who still moved with the elegance of a dancer, while her husband Jean Pierre was a powerful man who had been a Parisian street fighter and circus strong man before meeting and marrying Monique. It was she who had taught him the act and they had been together over thirty years. I understand that after we left they sold up and moved to the Riviera.

We were big spenders and were always made welcome in the bars. The old walled town of St Malo was an intimate place, and we made such a

---

* Trans. The Little Stoat. This is not a reference to the Plat de Jour but the name of the boat of Jaques Cartier, the 17th century local hero and part–time pirate who discovered French Canada and founded Montreal. A place where time stands still and they're still burning witches.

mark that café owners and the local bourgeoisie were falling over themselves to buy us drinks, or inviting us to be seen eating at their cafés and
pizzerias. One importer of American clothing even paid for all our posters
and sponsored a couple of big concerts, while the manager of the big Le
Clerc Supermarket booked us for a number of Saturday afternoon open air
shows. It was a wonderful time and everybody was on Cloud Nine.

A couple of times there was a bit of trouble. The first was a gang of Rock
'n' Roll fanatics from Rennes who were run off by three plain–clothes flics,
a breed to be scrupulosity avoided and easily recognized by their dour
faces, leather jackets and shoulder holsters. You don't mess around with
these guys, who are indemnified against prosecution in the course of their
duties. Talk about a Police State. Another evening three rowdy sailors
dancing on the tables were ejected by Gerard himself with the aid of a
window cleaning spray filled with liquid CS gas.

But of course there was a down side. The drummer for instance appeared
to be completely out of his depth in this heady atmosphere, and took to
buying flick knives and booze with careless abandon. He kicked off a serious, (at least, serious on his side) love affair with a young woman married
to a French sea captain, and came close to me putting him on the ferry for
turning up late three times at the gig, almost off his head on booze and
dope. I had no objection to anything anyone did off stage, but show time
was different. In general though, the long season ran very well but cracks
did appear towards the end. Paul Henry was only contracted until the end
of August, as he was due to start touring with Lonnie Donegan in September, so I started seeking a lead guitarist for the last week of the engagement.

The Deauville Disaster

I remembered a guy I knew fairly well from a band on the circuit, who
had seemed so impressive when we were all working the US. Bases back in
the sixties. He could play great guitar, fiddle, banjo or anything else you
gave him, so I got in touch and offered him the job. At the same time Jon
decided to bring his wife Linda out for a holiday, so we had to do a bit of
juggling with the accommodation. Terry warned me that it was dangerous
to bring in a new musician, particularly a lead instrument for only one
week ,and said he could handle all the instrumental breaks we needed. But
I did not take any notice. And I should have done.

Because from the first moment he arrived, our new guitarist was full of
moans and complaints. "The ferry was crap, the French got on his nerves,
the food was expensive, and if he had his way he'd spend the rest of his life
in the Greek islands, not here with these poxy Frogs, etc, etc." And, after
the first run through, it was clear that in spite of his talent, his style of
playing did not fit with us. Terry had been right. I had made a *Big Mistake*.

With a lot of effort we struggled through the last week at St. Malo, but a
dangerous clique was developing. Jon and his wife connected very well
with our new arrival, and the drummer and his new love soon joined them

in a campaign of obstruction, orchestrated mainly by the new picker, whom I later found out had a reputation as a band breaker. There is nothing more insidious or destructive than outsiders putting pressures on disgruntled band members. It was looking like another Palace Insurrection, and I felt betrayed by Jon's decision to join the rebels. It came as quite a shock. The situation soon became very brittle with Terry, Kit and me on one side and them on the other, and things came to a head on that final week at the American Film Festival at Deauville Casino.

We travelled there with the equipment in a hired VW van while the others went by car, and when we arrived we found that they had already claimed two of the three rooms that had been booked, so I had to book an extra room for Terry. We produced a show of sorts but it was no sensation, mainly due to sloppy drumming, stuttering guitar work and non-existent vocal backing, so I did not feel that we could go on with the original plan of pursuing a long-term contract with the Lucien Barrier Group, a chain of top class hotels across Europe. Later this rebel group caused us much stress and embarrassment by abusing the hospitality and running up excessive room service, phone and bar bills, before making a quick getaway and leaving us to sort it all out. From an English speaking barman I also got a whisper of what was being planned when they got back to St. Malo, which was to grab their wages and run. So we moved to frustrate their plans by playing the bandleader's trump card, and I withheld everybody's end-of-contract money until the apartment had been fully cleaned up and all our gear accounted for, thus delaying the planned overnight flit. I'd seen radios, televisions, and microwave-ovens disappear from digs before, and as we had to put up a cash bond, we were doubly careful.

There was a lot of bluster and hidden threats, but they folded like a pack of cards when it came to the crunch. With long faces and lots of muttering they got the apartment back in shape, and then holed up at the drummer's girl friend's place for the last few days. Finally it was over, and they were on the ferry back to Blighty, all except the drummer, who hung on until news of his French girl friend's sailor husband's impending return put an end to their torrid affair.

The whole experience had a salutary effect on the drummer, and I understand that he quit the music business completely, got a haircut and became a sales rep. As for that stand-in guitar player, well, if I ever meet him again it'll be a year too soon. I hope that he has found his Shangri-La in Corfu, and met lots of Shirley Valentines. Back at the Brasserie de l' Ouest however Gerard was very pleased with the season, and offered me the same job next year. I accepted gratefully but vowed to be very careful about band personnel for 1984. That winter Kit and I went out to Australia.

*   *   *   *   *   *

40

WALTZING MATILDA

Gypsy George said he had been to Australia in 1980, for about a week I think, and he was very enthusiastic about it, apart from the fact that he had been let down by a big record producer out there. (Actually, he'd met a drunken Aussie back–packer at a Romford club one night, and they had hatched a scheme to corner the Far Eastern market with bootleg discs. So for George it was all kosher and he took off for Sydney at the first chance, but he never did find his partner). There was also a lot in the papers about the place and it seemed all right. They spoke a kind of English and the weather was good there, so at the end of the 1983 season in France we decided to give it a go.

We had a friend out there, well, at the time; we thought that he was a friend, who used to run a club in Cornwall (and for whom we had made a lot of money) He had sold up and followed his sons out there. Jim, the elder had married a very sexy and attractive Australian girl called Ramona (Wonder if that's the same Ramona in the old travelling musician's anthem?) and they were now running a hotel near Canberra. Our Cornish friends bought a house in the same area, and thought that it was ideal for their retirement. On one of our visits to Francis and his family in Bodmin, we met them and they were full of encouragement for us to come over and stay with them. There was plenty of work he assured us, and anyway he and his son now had a busy pub in the suburbs, so if it all went pear–shaped we could always work there. (Does that sound familiar? Remember our friends in Spain?)

I made the usual enquiries and the response I got from the agents, bookers and acts who had worked the club scene there, plus the apparent popularity of Country Music, all contributed to our decision to pay a visit Down Under. It seemed just the place to spend the winter instead of France. It proved to be yet another wrong move. We should have gone to the Riviera instead.

But let's get on with our Australian Saga.

Leaving the car in St. Malo we took the train to Paris, where we stayed for a couple of days with Jacqueline Vinton and took in the usual sights. We saw the Paris Marathon, and I had a meeting at Big Beat Records with promoters, Gilbert Rouit and Jacky Chalard, but nothing came out of the deal at that time. Checking out the airfares we found something very peculiar. The fare from Paris to Sydney was about F.9300. (Roughly £900) for a single one–way ticket (per person) but if we picked up the ticket from a 'Bucket Shop' in London we could get it for £875 each *return*. And   the peculiarity did not end there. When we did eventually leave London we were booked onto the airbus to Paris, where we were switched to UTA. (The French overseas airline) Paris to Sydney flight, the original flight that I had been quoted for in France. Who can explain it?

Looking back at our adventure 'Down Under', I think the luxurious flight out there was the best part of it. The service was superb on that big jet and we arrived fat and happy, full of good food and champagne at Sydney Airport, where before we were allowed off, a team of white coated Australian Health Service workers came aboard and sprayed us all with disinfectant. Cheeky sods.

"Welcome to Australia, you grimy peasants from the Old World."

Canberra

Our friends were waiting for us and on the long drive to their house at Queenbeyan they gave us the low down on the country, saying that we should consider settling there as there was plenty of work,, and if you couldn't make money in Australia you couldn't make it anywhere, especially in the leisure industry. The scenery was lush, almost tropical, but I found the tin roofs very incongruous. Even the big flash bungalows would have these green corrugated iron tops.

Queenbeyan turned out to be a small town on the outskirts of Canberra and their house was a spacious bungalow in a small, semi rural development, where we spent about ten days,a week before starting work. The former club owner however had somehow changed from his wild swinging days in Cornwall, and had become extremely Puritan in his attitudes. He did not like us drinking wine, and if Kit wanted a cigarette after dinner she had to go outside on the veranda. He was also tight lipped, and disapproved of his younger son's fiance. She was a lovely girl and they were obviously happy, but her sin was that she had been married before. Agh! The Devil's Spawn.

I think the parents were still looking for a virgin bride for their offspring, and they struck me now as the kind of peasants who might have a pond and ducking–stool handy for any passing witches. Welcome to Salem. There was also a teenage daughter who could apparently do no wrong and lived in a tumbledown old house, that was sadly in need of a dose of TLC, a complete renovation, or a good bulldozing. She was married to a postman, but I think in her case they had made some allowances.

It started to get a bit frosty there, both the weather and the welcome, and after a few days hints began to be casually dropped about a bit of rent.(the figure of $100 per week was casually hinted at). The mother was actually charging her errant younger son rent for living at home, although he was hardly ever there.

One evening they took us out to see the pub they had told us about, but it turned out that they didn't own it at all, they were just running it for somebody who was away on holiday, and when I mentioned in passing their promise of gigs at the pub we were met with blank stares and slowly shaking heads. So sniffing which way the wind was blowing we began to make arrangements to leave, and would spend the afternoons walking the dogs on the hills behind the house to get away from the atmosphere. It was on one of these walks that we came across our first wild kangaroos.

Grünhalle
Lager the Bavarian way

THE JERSEY LILLIE

Vue splendide sur Rance
"The Jersey Lillie"
(Authentique Pub Anglais)

Bières traditionelles de Jersey

35730 Pleurtuit   Tél. (99) 88-51-80

1987   PAUL YOUNG.   Louisiane Club. St-Male

11/83. Sydney Opera house & us.

HIV

1996

Frank Yonco's Bath Night

(left) On Wiltshire Boulevard, Beverley Hills.
December 1995

(above) Outside Capitol Building, Vine Street, Hollywood
December 1995

(above) Leaving Monte Carlo Casino ... BROKE!
September 1992

Mistress Bess Burdock & Cap'n Marryatt

.... And we got paid

A Change of role - Yonco the Thespian, filming Vanity Fair in Bath *2003*

We were making our way through an area of burnt out woodland, when the dogs suddenly took off towards the scorched logs. I tried to call them back but they had the scent of something, and disappeared into the under-brush yapping and howling. There was a loud rustling sound and the whole charred woodland suddenly came alive as a huge herd of big kangaroos broke cover, bounding from log to log and drumming on the hard–baked soil. I've never seen so many. It was amazing. When we got back to the house they told us that in herds they were very dangerous, and had been known to trap hunting dogs and kill them, raking their bellies with their powerful claws.

Our first jobs were actually in Canberra itself, at luxurious big social clubs like the 'Southern Star' and the 'Top of the Cross', where those con-stantly bickering writers of the theme music for 'Neighbours', Tony Hatch and Jackie Trent were headlining. We also played at a chain of specialized Country Music theme venues on the edge of town, which were modelled faithfully on the Stateside honky–tonks, with electronic shooting ranges and electronic bucking bulls. At the bigger cabaret clubs the standards were very high, the house bands and modern rock groups being particu-larly good. There were a lot of ex–pat acts on that circuit, singers and par-ticularly comics we had first met on the Northern Clubs at home.

With the prospect of perhaps moving to Australia, we began to note some facets of life in Digger Land. The rents seemed reasonable and there ap-peared to be plenty of accommodation available. Jobs were also not hard to find, particularly in our business, where a UK reputation was as good as a Nashville pedigree, but all in all it appeared a bit too bland and egalitarian for me. Everybody was 'Y' mate' and everything you asked for was 'No worries, Mate,' but by the same measure, if the promised service or item does not materialize, it was not done to complain or criticize the in-efficiency. After all you were all mates weren't you? It left me feeling a bit uneasy. Food, always of major importance to me, was another thing. Lamb of course was the cheapest meat available, but my real favourite, pork, was expensive and was considered somewhat a luxury, like veal in the UK—and I was rather suspicious of the garish butcher's shops with their bright pink lights over the meat display.

PICKER'S TIP 54

Record your successes and learn from your mistakes, then bury them.
In spite of our national tendency to applaud gallant failures,
You will find that. NOTHING SUCCEEDS LIKE SUCCESS.

The Pub with no Beer

The Country Music scene however, turned out to be very stuffy, with all the same elitist, small time attitudes we had found at home, complete with the usual self opinionated camp followers and petty officials, but this time the poor standards were complicated by the insistence on 'Pure Australian Country Music' (As if we did not already have enough problems with splinter groups still arguing about what American Country Music was.) Not real Australian music however, not the chants and honking didgeridoos of the Aboriginals but rather a melange of Irish ballads and imported American 'Singing Cowboy' songs from the Thirties, as portrayed by the likes of Ray Lindsay and Slim Dusty

I had the experience of catching one of Slim's shows at a rodeo outside Bathurst, and I regret to say that I was not impressed at all. The Digger Legend himself then came on to the sounds of his hit "On the Road to Gundagai', and rambled through his standard show consisting mainly of near the knuckle, macho 'Stockman' jokes, crude references to women and 'Queers', with a few ballads of life in the Outback. At one point he did an Outback version of some classic Hank Williams songs, changing the lyrics around, like,' Old, Cold Queer' and 'That Cheatin' Tart' etc. topped off by his thirty–year–old hit 'The Pub With No Beer'. But I must have been wrong because the crowd loved it and went wild, with the middle–aged men fighting, and the women screaming and shouting to the band. The press called his shows earthy and natural, but so is scratching your balls, but not on stage. I couldn't believe it.

I thought it was an Ozzie version of Lester Moron's the Caddilac Cowboys.

But there again, they even thought Tommy Trinder was funny out there, didn't they?

I know some of my friends will not agree with my view but that's the way it goes—

I know some people don't like Waylon—But I do.

Rocketing to Sydney.

Feeling acutely that we had worn out our welcome in Canberra, we decided it was time to move on to Sydney, where the Big Time was, or so everybody told us. One of the sons claimed he had contacts in the media, and had fixed a radio interview for me with a DJ called Nick Earby, and the first jobs were booked in at clubs in the suburbs, so we were off to the Capital of New South Wales. Our hosts insisted that we must take the new high–speed train service to Sydney so we decided to give it a go. (I think they would have been very happy to see us leave on a stagecoach or a mule train—or even walking.) At Queenbeyan Station we went through their State of the Art computerized booking system, where we reserved our seats on this super train. The tickets cost twice as much as the standard fare,

but we willingly forked out the forty odd dollars each required, to experience this much–touted 'Twenty First Century' travel,and at 7.30 the
following morning we watched admiringly as our space ship rolled
majestically round the bend from Canberra. This vision of orange and
silver slid silently into the station platform and with a hiss from the air
brakes, the doors slid open. Then it was fond waves of goodbye (and relief)
all round, and the train hummed its way smoothly along the shining new
tracks towards the Blue Mountains.

Then two miles out of the town it picked up the main line and slowed
down to a stately 40 mph and preceded to trundle its way over the warped,
rickety, seventy–year–old tracks to finally arrive in Sydney at lunchtime,
having taken over four hours to cover about two hundred miles. How's that
for high speed 21st Century commuting? Magnificent, though hardly a
French TGV. Of course, this antipodean Shinkansen picked up its skirts on
the approach to Kings Cross Station and thundered through the graffiti-
daubed districts of Enmore and Newtown, and on past the crumbling
ghettos as though it had been doing it all the way from Canberra. The
faster you got through there the better, because these were the rough districts where the city Aboriginals lived in primitive dwellings, often lacking
doors and windows.

Few people there seemed to have jobs and lived on their fortnightly
welfare cheque. Most of the families appeared to spend their lives on the
doorsteps, and only went inside to sleep or eat, and in the summer many of
them did that outside as well. There were a few old wrecks of pick–up
trucks around (Utes as they were called) some of them with truck tyres
loosely chained to the front bumpers, as a deterrent to theft. If you tried to
drive one off, the old tyre got caught under the car and the noise and
smoke (and sometimes the flames) gave the alarm. An effective if dangerous deterrent, with a good chance that the thief would get burned to death
in the process.

It's a dog's life

I think I've mentioned it before and surely I should have known better.
Don't ever stay with strangers if you are on the road, (check Picker's Tip
No 23) it might seem to be cheaper at the time, but the stress is not worth
it. But in a moment of weakness, compounded by being in a strange
country, we fell into the old trap and booked in at a guesthouse recommended by a friend from Cornwall who had visited Sydney. I don't want to
appear ungrateful, but after four days we couldn't get away quick enough—
and I think that the feeling was mutual on behalf our hosts.

I phoned the number that I had been given,, and a lady with a rather
starchy Sloane Ranger accent answered. After a lengthy pregnant pause,
she composed herself and confirmed that our mutual friend, Lord H. had
written to her and they had a double room available for a few days, but it
was the busy season and her sister was expected. In short, she did not

seem very enthusiastic about the idea, but as we came well recommended she would do her duty. An hour later she met us with her van at the Sydney railway station, and ran us to her boarding house in the trendy (Non Abo) side of the Enmore district. Her husband, I think his name was Colin, greeted us with in that traditionally British stiff upper lip manner that so many ex–pats from Essex adopt, and informed us loftily that he too was a musician, a genuine Trad Jazz clarinetist in fact, and he was doing about three or four gigs a week. They had emigrated from the U.K. in the seventies and most of their friends were also ex–pats, who talked longingly about Chris Barber or Kenny Ball and of wild nights with George Melly at the Marquee or on Eel Pie Island. The lady herself was also a bit of a poseur, especially about her Italian cooking and seemed a bit miffed about her spouse getting all the attention. They had a baby girl called Alicia and a dog they called Bluey—and there's a tale about Alicia and Bluey.

He was a nice old boy, an Australian Blue sheep dog who must have been around twelve years old and spent his time contentedly sleeping in the sun, except at Alicia's bedtime, when he would desperately try to get over the fence or hide in the pile of empty boxes at the bottom of the garden. Why? Well, listen to this.

One evening, they invited us to join them at dinner with a couple of their neighbours, and after consuming a full bottle of an Australian Chanti between six of us (Yeah, a Full Bottle) we ploughed through one of the hostess's Italian gooey specialties, a concoction of burnt cheese sauce, tomato paste and underdone veal mince. Old Blue was sitting placidly by my chair gratefully accepting the tit bits I was quietly dropping him. Opposite me, little three–and–a–bit year–old Alicia was in her high chair, gurgling loudly while treating herself to a rusk and pea soup shampoo, and generally banging everything in reach with her spoon and pusher. Mummy and Daddy, being very trendy and modern, did not attempt to chastise her but smiled indulgently at their late–arriving only child. Then it happened. As dinner slurped to an untidy end, Daddy announced that it was little Alicia's bedtime.

"But before she climbed the wooden hill she had to have her Music Lesson. Suddenly there was a frantic yelp at my feet as Old Blue realized what had been said, and scrambled madly for the kitchen door, but he had left his move too late and Daddy caught him by the tail.

Then we were all ushered into the front room to watch Alicia perform her nightly symphony. Daddy took out his clarinet, Mamma sat primly at the electronic organ, I was invited to join in on guitar and Alicia was given a tin drum to beat, the only flaw being that Old Blue had to join in the family fun as well. Little Alicia's tin drum was hung round his neck while she blasted away on it, belting drum, dog and nearby chairs with wild abandon as poor Bluey, his collar securely chained to a chair, wandered round in circles, wild–eyed and half deafened. What a bloody din. Bluey's frantic yelping and the crashing of furniture was accompanied by Daddy's squeaky liquorice stick and the out–of–tune Farfisa organ. Everybody was supposed to join in singing Cwmbaya and Puff the Magic Dragon. This was the regular evening ritual.

What a poor dog had to go through to get his dinner.

Bondi Beach

Two days later we thankfully departed Enmore with its decaying damp terraces and its canine Alcatraz, and moved to Bondi where I hired a car and drove over to North Sydney for the radio show that supposedly had been arranged by my Canberra Fixer. I got no farther than the answer phone on the door of the Australian Broadcasting Company, where my host's so–called friend refused to let me in. This was Nick Earby, a self opinionated, arrogant part time Country Music D.J. who proceeded to give me a lecture, (still over the security answer phone) on the great heritage of Australian Country Music etc., and how much better it was than the modern Nashville product.

I put up with it for about ten minutes, than told him that if they could not do better than Slim Dusty, Rolf Harris, Reg Lindsay and Chips Rafferty, they had better give it up and rang off. No wonder young Australian performers like Casey Chambers and Kieth Urban head for Nashville or London. It was quite obvious that there was going to be no radio career for me Down Under.

At the time I still had idealistic dreams of Australia, but felt I had missed out somewhere. Where were all the beach beauties, the superb seafood, the private swimming pools and all those riotous barbecues? Maybe we were in the wrong place. (Actually we were. We should have gone down to Melbourne and Adelaide) or maybe I was being too critical, because all I saw were rattling filthy commuter trains with armed guards, the blatantly obvious hookers in Kings Cross, and a preponderance of homosexual bars, the slums of Newtown and Enmore, and the rough working–class districts of Armadale and Paramatta.

The British influences were certainly receding. English was no longer required as necessary to obtain citizenship, and certain ethnic minorities seemed to have totally taken over the public services, such as the Lebanese who dominated the railways. On one occasion I had to take a bus from Sydney Harbour to Marubra and once out of the town centre, I saw nothing but blank oriental faces all the way there. True, there was an Anglo Saxon crust in the charming restored Victorian houses of Paddington, and the posh homes by Double Bay, but downtown Sydney was another big urban jungle complete with drug pushers, street crime and selective policing. There were three big scandals whilst we were there which involved some police corruption, and on one ludicrous occasion the Sydney version of the Special Branch, mounted a raid on a hotel in Manly, only to be disarmed and arrested by the two House Detectives. They were in the wrong hotel.

Checking out the responses that I had received from the agents I went to see what was on offer. My first call was to an agent in Marubra called Warren Smith. He was reputed to be the best. He booked most of the big Rugby League clubs and many of the popular R.S.L. (Returned Service-men's League) social clubs. He was as good as his reputation and put quite a few jobs our way, but on the other side of the coin was a cabaret agency in Ryde, called, would you believe, Kangaroo Promotions? It was a real rag tag outfit run by a disgruntled Yorkshire man, who claimed that it was he who had launched Jim Corrigan's Clubland Empire at Batley, but he had been conned out of his share. A couple of gigs for 'Kangaroo Promotions' led us to believe that he must have been dreaming. I doubt if he had ever met Jim Corrigan, but he did tell us about a cheap showbiz hotel in Bondi Junction, down the street from the cricket club, so we moved in there. It was rather basic but very clean, and there was a kitchen facility for self-catering so it suited us fine.

One of the residents in a ground–floor room was Ann Marie, the classic Happy Hooker, a very flamboyant thirty–something lady with flaming red hair, and a big chest. Her clientele were mostly Turkish immigrants who treated her with deference and respect, and brought her bottles of Tia Maria and nice presents. She and Kit became good friends, and often went shopping in the Junction shopping malls. She was very helpful and pre-vailed on her friends to run us to the airport when we left Australia.

One of the first gigs in the Sydney area was at the Bondi Digger's Club, which was great, and then some of the Eastern Rugby League Clubs. All of them magnificently appointed and very well run. The acts on this circuit were very good indeed and of an international flavour. There were smooth Italian crooners and Greek acrobats from Melbourne, Irish folkies from the outskirts of Sydney. Maoris from New Zealand and smattering of Yanks and British acts from the Northern cabaret clubs–it was usually presented like an old time variety show. Not 'Olde Tyme' as in the Victorian music hall, although the British ex–pat Bondi Bowling Club did often put on such shows. My old pal Clinton Ford would have turned 'em over here.

Before leaving Bondi however, we thought we would have a look at the famous beach itself. In the movies it always looked fantastic, with rolling breakers, beautiful bikini'd or topless girls and high–stepping macho surf rescue teams, wearing little red plastic hats tied under the chin and 1930's bathing suits. Well, forget it, because it looks like a bigger version of Per-ranporth in Cornwall, but not nearly as clean. Poorly kept, threadbare lawns and crumbling paths lead down to the grey gritty sand, in the middle of which was a big stagnant pool dotted with ice cream cartons and used condoms. The overlaying mood could be summed up in two words 'Gay Pride'—everywhere you looked, handsome, tanned young men jogged along the beach paths to Taramarra round the headland, or strolled hand in hand as they admired the body builders pumping iron in the bright sunshine.There seemed to be very few girls around, they were mostly around the bay at the next beach. Bondi was a place where a young man wouldn't know which way to turn. (As Slim Dusty might have put it.)

One hot afternoon we were sitting on a bench watching these antics, when we heard the hiss of air brakes and we turned to see a big Greyhound bus pull up on the beach road. The windows were blacked out and it was painted a deep Roman purple and along the side, in big gold script was scrolled "THE BITCH'. As it rolled to a stop the door was flung open, and the gays tumbled out in their colourful headbands, mini shorts, and the oiled, sculpted bronzed torsos began to cruise the water's edge for partners. We were definitely in the wrong place. So we got some fish and chips from the Cypriot café and walked home.

We also did shows at a chain of Country Music clubs that extended out to Bathurst and Tamworth. I think the clubs were called 'Spurs', and like the Canberra clubs had all the latest goodies such as a bucking electric bull, large video screens showing cowboy movies and a shooting gallery. However Country Music was not popular in Downtown Sydney itself, the entertainment there being mostly discos, with usual diehard Trad Jazz fans fighting a rearguard action around the harbour district around the famous Opera House which was a nice looking place, but unfortunately there was no car park there.

Some Country Music was played out in the suburban pubs around Enmore, Kingsford and Petersham. Also there was a smattering of folk music clubs with Irish overtones around Paddington. In one of these pubs I met an old friend of mine who used to run a band in London, and our paths would often cross on the Fuller' brewery circuit in West London the late 60's. Now he was working most of the year up on the Gold Coast, with a band of British ex–pats playing West Coast Country Rock. It was good to see him and to talk over old times.

Beachcomber Island

One afternoon, at a showcase set up by the Warren Smith Agency at a club near Randwick Racecourse, we met a very good Maori group called the Islanders. We got on very well with them and they invited us back for supper and also to see their show at the Beachcomber, a theatre club in Drumoyne on the Paramatta River. I think the best way to describe it would be as a theme club. Its full title was Beachcomber Island, and the whole idea was to imagine that you were on a South Pacific cruise liner visiting all the paradise islands. The interior was decorated as a ships saloon with mock portholes on the walls and pictures of old sailing ships. The nautical theme was continued behind the bars with varnished spars, old anchors, brass binnacles and massive sailing ship's steering wheels all round the place. All the staff were dressed in the same theme, the girls in mini skirts, white T–shirts and U.S. sailor hats while the boys were stripped to the waist with tight white jeans and red neckerchiefs.

On the night we visited, there must have been a thousand people there.

It was vast and the main hall was filled with long tables end on to a big stage, while at the side a series of smaller ones were piled high with tropical fruits and delicacies. The place was fully booked and it was only with the influence of our Maori friends that we managed to get seated. On the vast stage there was a big back–projection movie screen and of all things, a real swimming pool. Up to the right of this stage was a kind of minstrel's gallery with a six–piece band, the whole stage area being draped with tropical vegetation. A Polynesian meal was included in the ticket, which cost about twenty dollars per head, and as soon as everybody was seated the lights dimmed and candles on the tables were lit. Then the food arrived, huge bowls of barbecued spare ribs, large prawns, sliced roast pork, chicken pieces and deep–fried fish with bowls of spicy dips and real fishy poi. Everything had to be eaten by hand. There were no knives or forks, just oval wooden platters and a few wooden spoons for the various sauces, relishes and salads that came with the dishes. Obviously there were plenty of paper napkins around. Oh yes and a large jug of punch for each couple.

It was marvellous and the man who made it all happen was the Master of Ceremonies, Cap'n Jack. Dressed in a white uniform, he was a bouncy out-going character who seemed to know everybody by name. He sang a couple of songs while we were all at the trough and soon we were all in the mood for a good night out.

Suddenly there was the sound of a ship's siren, and a movie screen on stage came to life, as we appeared to float away from the quay of Sydney Harbour. Tugs hooted and crowds waved and led by the voice of Gracie Fields sang 'Now is the hour'. More whistles and sirens and engine telegraph bells and shouted commands: "Full ahead, Mr McIntyre,"—"Hard a port Helmsman,"—"Aye Aye Sir!"—then a voice came over the P.A. welcoming everybody aboard the cruise ship 'Southern Star', telling us the full itinerary of the tour. Mamouia, Samoa, Tahiti, the Gilberts and Hawaii etc. Then the band flowed into the sensuous 'South of Pago Pago' and six dusky grass skirted dancers undulated on stage. The effect was terrific. We were fascinated and ate our poi and spare ribs abstractedly, the juice dribbling down our chops, as the scenes changed and Cap'n Jack welcomed us to our new island, sternly warning us not to go ashore after dark, and to beware of the local home brew etc. At Mamouia the music had French overtones, as another group of beautiful dancers performed in bright sarongs and headdresses of exotic feathers. As the evening progressed and the ship approached the Hawaiian Islands, the music became 1940's American Swing and three dark beauties wearing khaki uniforms launched into an Andrews Sisters number with a boy singer, who did a very credible Bing Crosby imitation, followed by a native hula–hula troupe whose leader topped off his war dance with a spectacular dive into the swimming pool.

Off the Philippines the mood was Spanish. At Tahiti it was French again. In New Zealand, authentic Maori songs echoed round the hall, as blue-tongued tattooed hunks performed the Haka. In Java it was all Dyak masks and hideous witch–doctors waving shrunken heads to the thunder of jungle drums. Absolutely fascinating stuff.

All the time the bar was doing tremendous business, with the young servers rushing about madly and stuffing their tips in their jeans, and by the time the cruise ended with a wild disco at 2 a.m. most of us 'Tourists' were legless. Outside a fleet of buses, provided free by the management was waiting to shuttle us all back to Central Sydney. What a great night out.

Looking back at it now, I think that the trip to Australia would have been wonderful, if perhaps we had visited a few more different places, like Melbourne or Adelaide instead of only Sydney, Canberra and some more towns in New South Wales. There was plenty of work out there for UK acts, although you could run into a bit of criticism from the local per–formers. We came across this moody attitude at a big Country Music Festival at Bondi Beach. By this time quite a few promoters had begun to take notice of us so we were invited to appear as guest artistes on the show (i.e. not being paid) but the local Aussie singers didn't like it one little bit. They moaned that we were a bit too modern. Not quite their kind of Country. We were far too West Coast for them. I think that some of the British 'Old Tymey' semi–folk acts like the Natchez Trace, Bryan Golby or Brian Chalker, (Oh no. Not more Brians), would have fitted in better with the Aussie' Outback Cowboy/Irish Rebel' concept of the music. (G'wan Brian, try it.)

Bloated Capitalist Dog

It was time to leave. There was work to be done in Europe. A contract for the next American Film Festival at Deauville had arrived, (which I must admit was a surprise after our last appearance there), also there was some work to do in Paris, so it was time to get moving. The only flight that would get us back in time was on CSA (Czech Airlines) so we booked on that.

The first leg of the journey was all right as we were routed by Bali and Singapore on a big 747 Jumbo, but after that it all changed. After a frighteningly bad landing at Jakarta we had to leave the aircraft for some security search. All us 'Round Eyes' had to wait in the shabby airport lounge while sinister, evil looking Indonesian soldiers and police, all armed to the teeth, bullied and humiliated the other travellers as they demanded their papers and travel documents. It was over two hours before we were allowed back on board for the next stage of the journey to Malaysia.

Arriving at Singapore Airport we found the terminal magnificent; a beautiful H–shaped new building, more like a shopping mall than an airport, with dozens of bars, shops and restaurants. We landed at Gate 4 and checking our stubs, I found that our CSA flight to Prague was from Gate 26, so we set off through the beautifully carpeted and decorated cent–ral concourse. Through the smoked glass windows we could see the huge

Boeings and Douglas jets being loaded, and little passenger buses shuttling here and there, but as we progressed through the terminal things began to change. The shops became smaller and the Four Star Restaurants were changing into cafeterias or hot dog stands, while outside the planes appeared to be getting smaller, mostly older cargo aircraft and short haul planes.

By the time we'd reached Gate 26 it was obvious that we were at the bargain basement end of the airport. At the entrance two stoney–faced North Korean girls looked blankly at our tickets and ushered us into the waiting area which was filled with East Europeans and Oriental workers, muffled up in head scarves and turbans with bundles of plastic bags, and Japanese electronic goods in stringed–up paper bags and cardboard boxes. There was no muzak, no coffee and nobody spoke until one of the Koreans came in and gestured us to follow her to the bus. Unbelievably, the scarred and battered bus pulled up at the bottom of the steps to a Russian Tupelov jet. To me it did not seem much bigger than a Dakota,and inside it was like a tube train with rows of cinema seats. Was this it? Was this our non–stop flight to Prague? No cinema? No earphone music?—and what about refreshments? Then there was a message over the P.A. in Russian, and it was seat belts on and with a whoosh we were off like a rocket: An hour into the flight two big buxom Czech ladies came bustling down the aisle with bottles of Urquell Pilsner under their arms.

"You vant drink?" we were asked gruffly.

"Er. Yes please. Got any wine?" I enquired politely.

The big lady looked at me stonily. "No. Ees only beer. You vant? Food vill follow."

"Er, well, two beers please. How much is that?"

Obviously, this Bloated Capitalist Dog had said the wrong thing and frigidly she spat.

"There is no charge on State Airlines. All is free."

And flipping the tops off the bottles, she handed them to us with two paper cups.

Too cowed to reply, we slurped our beer until the food arrived. It was a cardboard tray with spicy sausage, fried fish, beetroot, sour cream, black bread and a big cake.

Yes. Very nice, very Slavic but all cold of course.

I woke up somewhere over the Carpathian Mountains and soon we were on the approach run to Prague Airport. When the plane rolled to a stop, armed police came on and ordered everybody off for a passport check and yet one more security inspection. As we shuffled down the steps onto the tarmac, I suddenly felt very cold, and then I realized it was *Bloody Snowing.*   And here we were. Kit in a T–shirt, shorts and sandals, and me in linen slacks and a thin short–sleeved tennis shirt. We were freezing. Militiamen toting AK 47s herded us with chattering teeth across the icy slush to a bare transit lounge. It took them over an hour to sort out all the

paperwork, by which time there were only five of us left for onward transport to London, so they put us aboard an Antonov with the London bound
mail.

It was a complete contrast, like a Lear Jet and we drank in the luxury of
it all. Three hours later we were touching down at Heathrow and we were
VIP'd through the terminal without a hint of Customs or Immigration.

The Land of Oz had been a great experience but not one I would be keen
to repeat, due in part to my desire to get back to the Old World in spite of
all its faults. Goodbye Digger.

PICKER'S TIP 55

When using an unfamiliar P.A. system, check the mike's response by
speaking before you start to sing. A simple 'Good Evening' will give you an
idea of the sound quality. Or better still get the band to do a song first.

41

BACK TO THE RAMPARTS

We got back from Australia towards Christmas 1983, which we spent in the north of England with our respective families, and after visiting some old friends in North Devon, we moved on to Cornwall to spend some time with Francis and his new family in Bodmin. It was good to see them all so contented, and it confirmed my early impression that Cornwall was a beautiful place to raise kids. The old values still held down there, and it was wonderful to see such gentleness and respect.

Francis' carpet business was doing well and Jill now worked full time at the local sports centre. I was never Francis' role model and he had no interest in the music business at all. I can only suppose it was some deep, perhaps sub-conscious resentment from his formative years when I was away on the road so much, a fact that undoubtedly contributed so much to the break up of my first marriage, but at least he did do one thing I had advocated, that he should work for himself and not a boss. So I guess we should be grateful for that and the fact that they had none of the traumas that haunt family life these days.

In St. Austell I bought an old SEAT car for £50. It had a rough body and on top of that, was a left hand drive. I only bought it as a runabout, intending to abandon it at the ferry port at Portsmouth but it proved such a flyer that we took it back to St Malo, which we now thought of as home more than England. In a couple of days we had found a nice modern apartment on the Rue de Toulouse and visiting all our friends was great. We got an international TV aerial fixed so that as well as French programs, we could see Coronation Street and all our old favorites.

The winter passed quickly in that snug apartment and as spring warmed into summer, M. Martial's promotional posters began to appear on the walls and in shop windows of the city, telling residents and tourists alike that on June1st.1984,

'THE FRANK YONCO SHOW, featuring MISS KIT CONNOR'

would be opening for a season at the Brasserie de l' Ouest, Place Chateaubriand, St. Malo and I got a regular twice-weekly Country Music show on Radio Force Sept. in St. Servan, a station that served the Emerald Coast region and included the Channel Islands.

In May we went across to Jersey to spend a few days with Kit's Mum and sister Ann, who were on holiday there, and while we were there I did a couple of shows at a country music venue called Wolf's Caves, with one of the top entertainers there called Simon Raverne. He was a good picker and a very impressive entertainer who could have built an international reputation, but preferred to remain in Jersey with his family. He also had another powerful string to his bow. Under the name of Geoffrey Glover Wright he was a well-established writer of thrillers.

In fact I'm reading a very good one at the moment called the Headhunter.

In St. Helier we met Kenny Gee, a great all round entertainer who we'd last seen in Germany back in 1967 with the Linda Leyton Show—he was now headlining in a show at the Theatre Royal, St Helier and we spent a couple of nice afternoons together talking about the old days and we also bought an H & H sound system from him. We must have been quite a sight, struggling aboard that Condor hydrofoil to St. Malo with it, speakers, cables and all. I felt like a sea–going Sherpa. On top of all that, I also bought a new guitar in a huge case, which also required carrying. It was a Fender Del Rio electro–acoustic, which looked very impressive, but had less than perfect electronics and was subject to spontaneous feedback, a major irritation to a singer like me who moved around a lot on stage. I never liked it and traded it for a Casio keyboard when we got back to the UK

Jersey was a very useful source of musical equipment for us. Most of the acts came from the UK for the summer season and a lot of them bought new gear because it was free of mainland taxes, VAT, etc. and as many of them traded equipment in, second hand amps and instruments were cheap. Conversely prices in France were horrendously high, so we did the same thing for our French colleagues, selling them our stuff when we left. On an earlier trip I had bought a Sanyo radio cassette with a high speed dubbing facility, which proved very useful indeed, as we had it running every possible minute of the day copying cassettes for sale on the gig. The quality was terrible but at 60 francs a time the punters snapped 'em up. So, who's complaining?

Conscious of the previous years problems, I selected the musicians very carefully as the season approached. I did not want any more of the trauma I had experienced the previous year. Finally I settled on a line up. Paul Henry picked up the lead guitar job again along with the multi–talented Terry Silver on pedal steel. The bass job I gave to a young French guy from Paris called Guy Mouffet, known to us all as Ziggy, and a Breton music–teacher called Dominic Le Botec came in on drums. Terry did a number of modern Bellamy Brother's songs and a nice bluegrass spot on banjo with Paul on mandolin. Kit and I did the main front line work, doing a Rock 'n' Roll dance–routine in numbers like 'One of those nights'. Even Dominic did a couple of numbers in French.

This bit about doing songs in French was strange. A number of French artistes did their own versions of Country Music, including Eddie Mitchell, who was by far the best Country singer in France and Johnny Halliday. who had tried his hand at every musical style from Rock 'n' Roll and Country to Heavy Metal in his quest to become an International Star. In spite of his frantic efforts, his trips to Nashville and the heavy publicity. He had shares in some of the glitzy gossip magazines, which ensured that his face was never off the front pages. He became a French equivalent of Cliff Richard, little known outside his own country. Even though he was not even French. He was born Johannes Smet in Belgium.

Strangely enough it was not the current Country standards, like Charlie Pride or Merle Haggard songs they copied, but more the obscure things, for example one of Eddie Mitchell cassettes contained the following numbers. Webb Pierce's 'Pick me up on your way down.' *J'attendrai le prochaine train* Chip Taylor's 'A hundred and one in Cashbox' *Ecoute Coco* Tom T. Hall's 'How I got to Memphis'. *La route de Memphis* Jerry Lee's 'She woke me up to say goodbye'.*Un sourire et au revoir* Chuck Berry's 'Promised Land' *Une Terre promise* There are several early Rockabilly hits as well as up beat versions of bluegrass standards like 'Sweet baby's arms' *Je ne sais faire que l'amour.* Even British born Petula Clarke was doing a version of the Elvis–Hank Snow hit 'Fool such as I.' in French. *Prends mon coeur* but in reality it was a specialized market and when I started singing the French lyrics, Gerard told me that most of the punters actually preferred songs in English—or maybe it was just my French.

That '84 season was better than the previous year. The venue was packed again and the weather was good. Remember, this was Brittany and the weather much like Cornwall, so the hot sunshine and warm nights were a bonus. I came across some original songs and arrangements from Nashville, most of them not yet published in Europe. The main source was a great, energetic studio singer called Ronnie Sessions. I adapted a lot of his material for the band and produced some feature numbers like 'Lucy Ain't Your Loser Looking Good 'and 'Victim Of Life's Circumstances' as well as our own Tex–Mex versions of Willie Nelson's 'Gone To Mexico' and that old pre–war British standard 'South of the Border'. The 'Commander Cody' albums also provided some impressive songs as well as a few of my own originals like 'Napa Valley Wine 'and 'The Emerald Coast'—padded out by the usual Country Standards. Kit did super versions of Lacy J. Dalton songs like 'Taking It Easy With You' and Willie Nelson's classic song 'Crazy'. The cassettes sold well and we got paid on time, so everything was fine.

There was a bit of trouble with visiting sailors and local idiots, but again Gerard dealt with it ruthlessly with his trusty CS gas spray–gun,and Paul ended up kicking shit out of a drunk who invaded the stage. It all came as a surprise. One moment he was playing a solo and the next he had handed his guitar to Kit, and was struggling in the shrub tubs behind the podium—but in general everybody seemed content to play and pick up the money, and there was no trouble or squabbling.

The season progressed as expected, with us playing or drinking the nights away, and spending the days on the superb beaches or walking along the sea walls, before flopping into the Petit Hermine pizzeria for the day's main meal. After the Ouest contract ended on the first of September, Paul went home to pick up another contract with Lonnie Donegan, and Terry moved on to Paris where he did some recording sessions with a pseudo–Russian street singer called Serge Lazar, but he was back in St

Malo two weeks later somewhat disillusioned with both Serge and the City of Light. He bought our old SEAT car and took his gear back to Cornwall, where I believe he formed a duo with a girl singer. He was a great musician and a good friend, who had had more than his fair share of life's difficulties. I don't know where he is these days but I wish him well.

Cote d'Azur

Determined not to make the same mistake as we had the previous year by scuttling off round the world, this time we did go to the South of France. An agent from Paris had caught our show whilst on holiday in St. Malo, and suggested I call a friend of his in Nice who was looking for an act like ours. As I mentioned earlier, the American soap 'Dallas' was making a big mark on French TV, (much to the annoyance of the Government who tried to get it banned) and music like ours was just what was needed, so I phoned the man who said that he did not want the band, as he already had a house group who could handle the backing, but he booked Kit and I into a big restaurant called the Mississippi on the Promenade des Anglais in Nice, for a couple of weeks and then for a further period at the Hotel Montelemar in Monaco. I sent down a tape of our programme, and the house band rehearsed it and provided very nice backings, without all the hassle and moodies I had come to expect with my own pickers. It was a method that I used thereafter for all my gigs abroad.

We found a nice apartment in Mount Boron, above the yacht basin at the eastern end of the sea front, within easy walking distance of the Mississippi and only a short drive to Monaco, where we passed a very pleasant Indian summer. If you are ever in Monaco and you fancy a bit of Country Music, drop into a bar called the Texan near the railway station. Great ambience. The weather was wonderful and the shops and restaurants superb.

Our favourite eating–place in Nice was a vast, open–air patio restaurant in the heart of the Old Town called Le Clair Fontaine, where they served such mouth–watering delicacies as peppered Beuf Daub and Escolpe Milanaise, with nice chilled bottle of Rose d'Anjou. What could be better on a warm summer's day? The region lived up to all our expectations and we had a wonderful time, leaving us more determined to return, which we have done time after time. (Especially these days with the superb rail connection from Bath via the Eurostar and the TGV). But now it was time to get back to St. Malo and review our options.

We bought 'a Jersey registered Volkswagen Golf from some Brit ex–pats, and also went back to England to visit relatives and friends. In Cornwall we saw our grandson Anthony Ross for the first time and stayed with our niece Barbara at her isolated house on the wild moor near Bugle, before going back to visit Kit's sister Frances in Bexleyheath. By this time I was fed up with being cramped up in the V.W. so on the way back to the ferry we traded it for a nice red Mercedes 250.

Throughout the early winter I continued writing 'Angel Meadow' in St Malo until December, when we moved back across the Channel to look after Dave and Jenny Parsons' house in Wadebridge while they were away in Africa. Whilst there we tentatively considered settling back again in Britain. We looked around for an apartment or house and we considered taking jobs, me doing a bit of high class chauffeuring, and Kit setting up a domestic cleaning agency, but on analysing things financially we decided that the required investment such as a new car, a mortgage etc. was just not on, so we began looking round for gigs again, but the show–biz situation in the U.K. proved to be almost worse than when we left, as the big Cabaret Clubs had all but disappeared and the discos were taking over. About the only sources left were the Country Music Clubs with their gunfighters and dance hall girls.

Then we were introduced to another lady from that era, that Channel Island beauty and mistress of King Edward 7th, Miss Lily Langtry.

The Famous Jersey Lily.

PICKER'S TIP 56

When learning a new song, tape yourself singing it without any backing until you are really comfortable with it, then play back the tape and find out what key you were in, making sure you sing the bridge (the middle-eight bars) as well, because this part often includes the highest part of the song. (eg. Kristoffeson's 'Help me make it through the night.')

It is much better than picking a key first and trying to fit the voice to it. This technique is particularly applicable when recording because studio conditions are quite different.

But, and this is important, when you do the song on a live show with the band behind you, go up half a tone to give your self more projection.

42

THE JERSEY LILY

We had first come across it a couple of years previously when we played at a wedding there for our friends Welsh Mags and David. At that time it was run by a young couple Judith, a Princess Di look–alike, who we later got to know very well, and her French husband, Alan. They had been working for a brewery in St Helier, Jersey, when they had been offered the job. They had a great time there, money being no object and surveillance limited to a fleeting once–a–month visit by the company accounts manager, who only had a smattering of schoolboy French. They were both in their twenties and as you can well imagine went wild, partying every night till dawn and opening when they felt like it, or just banging some regular customer behind the bar and going out on the town. From time to time we would call on them when we visited Danny's grave at the Manoir de la Rance above the place but apart from that, we did not take a great interest in it. On one such visit Kit mentioned, in passing, that if ever Judith and Alan left there we would not mind taking it over and thought nothing more of it.

It was not until some time later when we were in Manchester, house sitting while Kit's mother and sister were in Spain on holiday, that the subject of the Jersey Lily arose again. Things had slowed down in France, and we were considering a contract from Piero Massari to go out to Abu Dhabi. To be honest we were not wild about that idea. The prospect of five hours every night in some pseudo Western Bar as a duo seemed somewhat of a backward step, but as there was nothing worth while in the U.K. we decided to have a go at it, and were in the process of trying get Massari to let us bring Terry Silver along with us when, in March 1985, right out of the blue, a phone call came from Judith in France.

She said that she and Alan were splitting up and were leaving the Jersey Lil and she'd been trying to get in touch with us for a couple of weeks, so if we were still interested, we should phone the brewery boss to discuss the possibilities. This was a real coincidence, as I had already drafted out a letter to him asking if he had any management vacancies in his Jersey pubs, but before I could get round to sending it Judith's phone call had arrived. We called the Channel Isles right away, and after a brief discussion the brewery chief asked us to fly to Jersey at his expense for an interview.

There was a car to meet us at the airport and we were booked into a nice hotel, and told to present ourselves at the brewery the next day, where we met our new boss for the first time. It was a short but pleasant interview with a few drinks thrown in. He asked us some questions about our background and our experience. We told him about the club in Cornwall and the cafeˇ in St Malo, and he seemed satisfied. Then he got me to phone the pub and speak to Alan, to see if I really could speak French. And it was as simple as that. He offered us the place and a good salary as well and we were only too glad to take it. A date was fixed and a couple of weeks later on April 16th 1985 we were installed. Licenses were issued in my name, and it was made clear to us by a brewery official that our prime function was to make sure that everything ran smooth for the boss on his visits. As for the rest of the commercial enterprise it was up to us, buy what was required and keep the receipts, and once a month the accounts man would come over to sign the cheques. Then they left us.

Settling In

The Jersey Lily was an English pub on the banks of the River Rance in Brittany about four miles from the faded coastal resort of Dinard, which back in the 1920s & 30's was a favourite retirement place of officials and military men returning from Imperial Service East of Suez. A wealthy Jersey brewer owned it and its real function was as a base for his frequent continental trips.

Originally it had been a typical French family restaurant but some complication of the complex French inheritance laws had left it empty, and when a wealthy lawyer friend of his bought a riverside home up the lane from it, the brewer decided that he would create an authentic British Edwardian pub there, to show the Frogs how it should be done. It was a very nice conversion but certainly a cosmetic one because when we arrived you couldn't get in the back rooms for junk, but wait; I'm jumping the gun. Let me tell you all about the place.

The public side of things consisted of two large rooms, a saloon on the left as you entered and a bar room on the right. The main room had tall windows that overlooked the beautiful River Rance and was sumptuously fitted out with maroon velvet banquettes, and at one end was a superb open fireplace with an ornate and mirrored mantelpiece. On the ceiling there were two large Edwardian wicker fans and the room did look good with top–class carpets, Art Deco lampshades and Victorian military prints on the green baize covered walls.

There was a carved wooden bar, the front of which had once been part of an old Welsh chapel. It was all very impressive but there was one little flaw. After the bar fitters had put it in somebody noticed that there was no bar flap and for the first six weeks the only way you could get out of the bar was by walking all the way round the back through the kitchens. But all in all, it was a much better–appointed and welcoming than any French bistro.

I think at this point, I should clear up something that must puzzle many British visitors to France. Why do so many French bars look tatty compared with the average British pub? The main reason is that in France, generally speaking, the breweries do not own their retail outlets. Mostly they are privately owned and are not subsidized by the breweries. (Although, in parts of Alsace and Savoie there are certain exceptions). There are some arrangements made with loans provided by the brewers in return for a semi–exclusive deal to supply a certain brand of beer, but none of the great in–depth investment as happens in the U.K.

Obviously, the first thing to undertake was an inspection of our new home. The saloon bar as I've said looked marvellous, apart from a few stains and badly scarred table tops, and the ashes of some old furniture that had been burnt in the grate, but the rest of it was a mess. At the back, extending the full length of the building was a space of about four metres to a sheer cliff face filled with black plastic bags full of rubbish. There had been some dispute with the local council and the refuse trucks had not been calling, so in truly Gallic fashion, the previous tenants simply chucked rubbish out of the back doors. On inspecting the kitchen, we found piles of good equipment that had been allowed to rust, and the garage seemed to have been used as a scuba depot with inflatable boats, wet suits and outboard motors hanging from the walls. There were also two deep-freeze coffers in there stuffed with out of date foodstuffs. At the bottom we found some crabs in a plastic bag with a Monoprix label dated 1981, after which we dumped the lot.

The living accommodation upstairs wasn't too bad and, while we were inspecting this bit, we came across our lodgers—Lodgers? They were in two of the end rooms. It was a guy from Martinique, his wife with two kids. They'd been there for six weeks waiting for his yacht to be repaired at the boatyard down river. As tactfully as possible I explained that their occupancy must cease as soon as possible, and he replied belligerently that Alan had said that they could stay there as long as they wanted. I pointed out that Alan's writ no longer ran at the Jersey Lily and that I'd like to see the back of them by weekend. By the next morning they were gone—well, not quite gone exactly because they moored their boat on our pontoon and still sent the kids ashore to use our toilets. Cheeky bastards. But that presumption was nothing to what we had to discourage as time passed. It was one of the first indications of the French social attitudes. Give 'em an inch and they'll take a metre.

In spite of this, things were looking rosy, because as well as food, drink, salary and somewhere to live, we had a nice car that went with the job. It was a big diesel Peugeot 505 estate car; however right at that moment nobody could find it. It surfaced ten days later in Dinan where it was being used to move Alan's new family into their apartment. He arranged to deliver it to the Jersey Lily the next day, after phoning to make sure that Judith wasn't waiting there for him with a carving knife. Kit and I made a start at cleaning the place up but there was so much to do that we appealed for help, and our friend at the Manoir found us a cleaner who came in every week.

Work wise there was not much to do because at the change of the liquor license, French law required us to close for three weeks and all previous suppliers had to be paid off before new credit facilities could be granted. The license fee was a bit of shock too. I think the local stamp duty came to about £160 and it had to be paid in cash at Pleurtuit Town Hall. There was quite obviously no money left in the pot, and the bar float had been swallowed up in some obscure expenses, so the first thing was to get some money over from Jersey to replace what we were paying out for with our own account. A phone call to St. Helier soon sorted that out, and the next day I drove to Dinard Airport to pick up a cheque. The rest of the week was spent trying to get the place sorted out. Judith and her new baby got a small house in Poubalay and even though she was no longer in charge she continued to be a regular punter at our bar.

On the Friday of the second week the accountant flew over from Jersey to answer all our queries and what a joke that was. To almost every question we asked him, he said that we should do what we thought best and simply make sure that things ran smoothly when the boss arrived in his galleon.

"Opening hours?"—"Oh, Whatever suits you"

"Heating Fuel?"—"Just order what you need."

"Can we sell food?"—"Well, that's up to you."

We headed to the French comptable's (accountant's) office in Dinard to pay the month's bills. The accountant turned out to be a young lady with a gray–green smile and a bad case of B.O, masked in the classic French manner with clouds of sinus–blocking perfume. It was quite a show, with the accountant explaining everything in rapid Breton French, and our man nodding his bald head and understanding one word in twelve.

In the end she presented the month's bills and he signed a cheque and off we went to the Restaurant de la Paix for a celebration lunch. God knows what there was to celebrate. Perhaps, it was his safe fifteen–minute flight from Jersey? Then it was back to the Lily for a few more scoops before I drove him to the airport for the six o'clock flight and poured him through customs. This performance was to be repeated monthly for the next two years. He was so off–hand (or confused) about everything that I would spend days wandering about St Malo and Dinard buying tools and things we didn't need, and charging it to the accountant. As long as there was an invoice it was paid.

Mind you, I suspect the whole set up, including us, was some kind of tax loss ploy anyway. Though why the boss should have bothered I don't know. He owned a highly successful brewery and thirty pubs, but I suppose being careful with money was how he got them. His biography itself is a wonderful tale that one day I would like to write. He was a great adventurer in the Victorian tradition of British Empire builders, racing ocean-going yachts, hunting and generally living life to the full.

Our liquor license was granted and new credit facilities established, so off we went shopping for supplies and equipment. A brewery in nearby Dinard supplied all the liquor and another vintner down in Dinan sold us the wine, but the beer, our principal item, was shipped over from Jersey every second week. And of course, if it was rough weather, the boat often arrived three or four days late and we'd have no beer to sell. We worried about that but I think we were the only ones who did. The office in Jersey did not seem to care at all. In fact, as I found out later, everybody over there thought that the Lily was a joke, and if it had not been for it being the MD's private indulgence they would have gladly sold it on, which they did on his demise some years later. It was quite obvious from the very outset that the place would never make any money but that was not what we were there for.

Checking further, we found that two windows in the lounge were broken, and the cleaner's husband, who also happened to be the local policeman, said that his brother was a shop–fitter and would be only too glad to replace them. I gave him the o.k. and the glazier turned up one afternoon, three sheets to the wind to measure up the job. The next day he turned up in a similar condition with the glass. The panes were about four feet square so there was no way he could manage single–handed, and asked me to help him get them into position.

Well, the first one went in fine, but the next one was a little too large, and after wiggling this way and that he tried to force it in with a hammer. Kit and I were standing by the mirror above the fireplace and we heard the sound of a crisp nick at which the bleary–eyed artisan shot a swift glance at our backs and flipped the curtain across the corner before getting on with his puttying. Unluckily for him we could see behind the curtain from our view in the mirror, and the crack across the corner showed quite clearly, but instead of making a big deal out of it there and then we invited him over to the bar for a drink, and then pointed it out in the mirror

"Ah no, Monsieur Franck. C'est pas vrai!" He exclaimed. The mark that we thought was a crack was just a mark on the outside, he insisted, at which we invited him over to the inside of the window and suggested that he run his finger along the mark. Of course at this he admitted that it was his fault, but begged us not to tell his brother or he'd never hear the last of it. Well, we felt so sorry for him that we told him not to worry about it and had another drink, then stuck a plastic Guinness advert over it because by that time we too were in no condition to go through the process again.

We were awakened one morning by a loud rattling on our front door, and looked out of the bedroom window to see a small Frenchman in a fisherman's jersey and dirty jeans, unloading beer barrels off the back of his battered Citroen Maharis pick–up truck. "Bonjour Chef "He shouted "Voila les vides."

Empties? What empties? I thought, dragging on my pants and hurrying down.

I opened the garage doors where we stored the beer, and he proceeded to roll the empty kegs inside and pile them up in the corner as though he had been doing it for ages, then he looked round and started rolling out a full one.

"Eh, hold on!" I shouted "Whatcha doing?"

He stopped and lit another cigarette before spitting on the floor and barking at me.

"Its the tenth of the month, non? I always call for my beer on the tenth—ask the boss."

"I am the boss" I yelled. "The new boss, gottit? So, Marcel, you'd better get your hand down if you intend to load that keg on your tin donkey"

Voluble curses in raw Breton came hurting out of his mouth.

'Never been so insulted in his life', he spluttered.' What did I mean asking him for money? He had an arrangement with his friend and just wait until he told him about my insults. I'd be out of a job before I knew it'

He rattled on for a few minutes and then suddenly stopped, went a bit pale and asked if I was from Jersey, and started glancing nervously up and down river to see if there was a big motor cruiser lurking somewhere. I told him no and asked him how long he had had this 'Arrangement' with the Jersey Lily, but now realizing that something had definitely gone wrong, he puffed out his cheeks, jumped into his camionette and drove off in a huff calling me a 'Rosbif Pig.

This kind of thing happened regularly over the time we were there, but we never found out exactly what had been going on—although now and then empty kegs would appear at our door overnight with notes stuck to them detailing the following month's requirements, which we studiously ignored

V.I.P. visitors

Ah yes, I forgot to tell you about the pontoon. You see one of the things that had attracted the wealthy Jersey owner had been the discovery that there was a floating pontoon there, where he could moor his huge Riva motor cruiser. At first, I believe it had been a rather primitive affair, but before we arrived the boss had it improved and updated, and now it was a two metre wide floating pier of perforated aluminum sheeting, about twenty five metres long with a cross piece at the end providing moorings for about six big boats or a lot of little ones.

Even though it was for the use of the pub customers, there was some confusion as to who actually owned it, with the result that everybody used the bloody thing, whether they were pub patrons or not. It was a fine point in law, that while the pontoon belonged to the Jersey Lily, the bank and the river were in the public domain. Meaning that the public could wreck it but we had to repair it—and if anybody fell off it, it was our fault for putting it there. A bit like the Turkish Taxi Accident Theory, which said that if you had not hired the cab in the first place it would not have been involved in the accident—Ergo—You Are To Blame—and it used to get up our noses. I remember one afternoon when I counted sixteen cars in our car park and on the road outside and we had four punters in the bar. All the other sods were having picnics on our pontoon. I can still hear the rattling of the pontoon sheeting at five or six in the morning as the local boaties loaded their boats with beer and liquor, all bought from the local super-market.

Although the place looked nice, it was not in a fit state to operate properly, in fact the kitchen was primitive, and littered with worn out equipment and old pans, but we were settling in very nicely, thank you. In fact we were becoming quite smug until about two weeks into our new venture, when we got a shock phone call from the brewery in St Helier.

"They're coming over—and they want to eat," I yelped, "What are we going to do?"

The kitchen was absolutely useless. Nothing worked and here was our boss coming over in his monster motorboat for his dinner.

"What do they eat?" asked Kit. "You'd better phone them back and find out."

I got on the blower to Jersey and spoke to the boss' secretary, a vague woman with a strong Birmingham accent and asked her what they usually ate?

"Ooh, Oi dewnt know, do Oi?" she whined "'E niver tykes me euwt fer dinner but Oi did 'ear as 'e loikes a bit o' feesh, y'know, ayke or plyce. If Oi waz yew, Oi'd jus' give 'im wot you've gorr in."

"Well, we haven't got anything in."

"Oo, well, enee rewd oop, yew'd berra gerrout an' get sumpthink, double queek—they left 'ere about ten minutes ago—Good luck, me ol'duck."

"Fish?" yelped Kitty. "We don't know anything about fish and that old electric stove up in our apartment has only got one plate that works. What'll we do? The kitchen is a shambles. Nothing works. I mean, what do they expect us to do with a kitchen set–up that hasn't operated since the Liberation?

For the next hour we rushed about feverishly, getting a table set, charging down to Dinard fish market and storming through the local supermarkets.

Sure enough about 1o'clock the boss's big cruiser came nosing up the river and with a "Honk, Honk," turned and headed for our pontoon. I went down to greet the visitors while Kitty struggled with the primitive cooker. On the pontoon it was all indulgent smiles and false bonhomie, as I led the way up the swaying aluminum planking with the boss clumping behind me in his thick soled brogues, followed by his lady dressed like a Breton sailor, dreamily floating along on a cloud of gin fumes. Behind us, Bob the skipper tied up the monster Riva, and clambered back on board to continue his attack on the bar. I heard the clink of glasses, and I remember wondering if you could get breathalyzed when driving a boat?

The V.I.P.s nosed round the Jersey Lily nodding approvingly at all our spit and polish and the impressive table we had laid. Kitty came down to greet them sweat trickling down her neck, but suddenly had to rush back upstairs as a wisp of fishy smoke drifted down the stairwell. I got them seated and opened a good bottle of claret, which the boss pushed across the table saying that he would prefer a pint of his own bitter and his Lady would like a drop of gin.

"Yes, a double would be fine. Oh yes, and no ice," chimed Her Grace.

Time crawled by as they picked at their hastily constructed prawn cocktails, and I talked about everything under the sun, his boat, his car, the French, the weather, anything to keep their minds off the bloody fish.

Briefly I excused myself and shot upstairs to where Kit was fighting gamely with the uncontrollable single hotplate glowing bright red through the masses of smoke and fish fumes. Her eyes wet with frustration and her fingers blistered by the spluttering frying pan and finally she produced the lemon soles. They were an interesting blackish brown and crispy at the edges and completely raw inside—but they did look nice on the silver platter all dressed up with sprigs of parsley—even if I had forgotten to gut them before we started cooking the bloody things. Well, as I said, we didn't know a lot about fish. We thought it usually came from the chip shop.

The Boss took it very well. His upper crust breeding forbade him saying exactly what he thought about our presentation, tho' he did mention that on the next visit he might prefer it cooked a little bit more, and I must admit it did look a bit red when he stabbed it and all that grayish fluid seeped out. Her Grace had shunted her little fishy round the plate, and requested another double gin before they headed off to their apartment at the other end of the building for a siesta, which we kept in pristine condition for their visits.

They did not come back in that evening (they had probably gone to get something to eat) which was a bit disappointing because we had the place looking spick and span, the log fire roaring, the mirrors gleaming, the bar top polished and a few Frogs trying to make their kirs last an hour. However, about half past nine Captain Bob, the boss's one man boat crew came in for a beer, but trying to get anything out of him was like pulling teeth. He was totally incapable of giving an opinion about anything at all without reference to his employer.

"Evenin' Bob. Everything okay?

"Er—yes. Er no. I think so—is the boss coming in tonight?

"Don't know. Is it raining outside?"

"Er, I'm not sure'er. I'll ask the Gov'nor if he comes in."

And so on all night until he rattled off back down the pontoon to his lonely bunk aboard the Bounty.'

The following morning at 7 a.m. we heard His Lordship scuffing down to the quay in his flip flops and striped toweling bathrobe for his daily dip in the river, while his lady lay in bed trying to remember where she had left her head—eccentric? Ah, yes, but very charming with it. An hour later they were in for breakfast. This time it was easier. We had the table dressed like a pukka Five Star Hotel with a crisp white cloth, steaming coffee, fresh bread and croissants, a nice selection of cooked meats and the best fruit preserves, plus the boss's favourite sardines which he insisted on being left in the open tin. Her Grace had two bits of toast, three fags and her morning gin. (Pink, this time.)

After breakfast they took a drive round the Cotes du Nord in the souped up luxury Peugeot he kept in the pub's garage, and took us to lunch at one of the area's top restaurants, Chez Tirel at La Gousiniere, picking up the usual on the spot fine for speeding, from the local police on the way back. By three o'clock they were back on board the Riva and were nosing through the locks of the Barrage de la Rance and heading for Jersey and for us, our baptism of fire was over. The following day we got a phone call from the brewery authorizing us to carry out any kitchen improvements we thought necessary. And what an experience that turned out to be.

Through our regular adviser, the village policeman, we contacted a plumber in Minhic to put things right. He was a bit better than the glazier but not much. I remember him calling us into the huge kitchen and saying.

"Voila. M. Franck. Bonne Noel"

'Christmas?' I thought.' What's this loony talking about? Its only spring. Still grinning inanely at his own joke, he lit a wax taper and ran it round the thick gas pipes lining the room, leaving little blue lights every few feet. Yeah, I agreed, it did look like Christmas and no wonder we felt queasy after we had been in there a while. Up to that point I thought that it had something to do with the booze. I was surprised that the bloody place had not blown up years ago. Well, with that added motivation we headed off to the Leclerc hypermarket near Dinard and bought a full commercial kitchen set up. Two ovens, one conventional and one 850–watt industrial microwave plus loads of cooking utensils

We got everything looking good with the bar top shining like glass, all the furniture polished, and snow white linen on the tables. Dressed in our best we felt good and on bright autumn afternoons, with a bright log fire roaring in the vast chimney and the sweet sounds of ABBA on the stereo, we would open a bottle of Bollinger and sit and gaze at the panorama of passing boats beyond our pontoon. It was perfection.

And then the bloody customers would arrive and spoil everything.

PICKER'S TIP 57

Some dull, boring or dangerous places to avoid.
Turkey, Vietnam, Norway, Finland, Estonia, Belgium, Portugal, Austria, Corsica, New Zealand, Bosnia, Israel, Iraq, Albania—and Stalybridge.

La Cuisine Brittanique

About two weeks later when all the new installation was complete, we launched the business of providing good English pub grub to our Frog clients. And they loved it. English sausage and mash, steak and chips, roast pork and stuffing, but their real favourite on many a chilly evening was that good old Lancashire Hot Pot, well laced with HP sauce and under a thick crust, which we called Beuf et Carrottes a la Kitty. Sometimes we Brits have a misconception of some facets of French life. I suppose we are still influenced by tradition, thinking that Paris is still naughty and that everybody drinks champagne for lunch and spends half the year on the Riviera. But in truth it's not a bit like that, though the Frogs like to pretend it is, to wind up the foreigners and keep 'em spending their money.

Breakfast was another thing. The French don't know what it is. They start the day with Le petit dejuener (literally, a little lunch), which is only a cup of coffee and a croissant—and then a mad dash off to work. So we decided to play 'em at there own game and introduce 'em to that Great British Victorian invention, the classic English Gentleman's Breakfast. We also let it be known to any of the Jersey boaties coming across could have a free bed for the night if they came ashore with ten pounds of good British middle cut smoked bacon or sausages, and two Mothers Pride sliced loaves, such things being almost impossible to get in France at that time. It was slow at first but as the word got around the Jersey Marina, things picked up and a month later we were knee deep in pork products and sliced bread. All at the cost of increased laundry bills for the sheets.

The launch day was one Sunday in May and we primed it by giving away a few strategically placed freebies. You know the sort of thing. Invites went out to the local newspaper, the postman, the gendarmes and the small town bank staff, who returned the following week to introduce their families to these crazy 'Rosbifs 'who were putting on this amazing meal at such low prices. They thought it was dead cheap but we thought it a bit expensive. We soaked 'em for about five quid a shot when a trucker in the UK would expect to pay around £1.50; but after all, this was spring time and as they were sitting by the river and they could have a drink if they wanted, so we didn't think we were going too strong.

Well, they could not get enough and we were at it all Sunday until we decided to stop serving at 4 p.m. The terrace was crowded with Frogs and Jersey boaties stuffing themselves with bacon, Walls sausages, mushrooms and runny eggs. We did a brisk take–away trade in bacon butties at £3.50 each. The cooking was not up to Kit's usual Cordon Bleu standards, as I did a lot of it and by 3 p.m. we'd all got plenty of the old Bolly down our necks. So there were quite a few eggs missed the pan but it was all taken in good part, and if I dropped a few slices of bread, a quick wipe round the frying pan gave it that authentic 'Fried Slice' look and nobody knew the difference anyway.

Usually if it had been a good day we wouldn't open in the evenings, and stuck a 'Closed Because of Gas Leak' notice on the door, while we shot across to St. Malo to eat at Marc's and play a bit of guitar with him in the jazz cellar.

We got quite a few visitors from the UK.in that first year. Our nieces Barbara and Michelle came over with Tim Collingwood and his wife Janis and Barbara's boy friend Alan. Later on our ex–bank manager Fred and his wife came over, as did many others, and I was particularly pleased to welcome my old friend Karl Denver on a day trip from Jersey. Sadly it proved to be our last meeting.

Les Fruits de Mer

Now, most of the visitors to Brittany indulge themselves in the magnificent seafood available there. At all the markets there are superb lobsters and crabs to be had at almost unbelievable prices. But then you have the messy business of cooking them, and it is here that the ugly head of commerce appears.

My first inkling of this commercialism came about by accident. My friend Marc who ran a restaurant in St Malo introduced me to his Cash and Carry warehouse so that I could buy supplies for our bar meals, and while I was there I couldn't help noticing him loading quite a few slabs of Dutch processed cheese on his trolley. A bit of a liberty I thought, in this land so famed for its dairy products. But this was nothing compared to the shock that awaited me at the checkout, where from underneath the big cans of beans and pickles Marc produced four 2 kilo polythene covered blocks of frozen crab meat. All of them imported from the Far East. What? Korean crabmeat? Here on the Emerald Coast, the seafood centre of France? What next?

On the way back to town I commented on this and, with typical French pragmatism, he said that very few of the restaurants in town took more than a token amount of local seafood. It was easier to buy it all at the Cash and Carry and that the tourists knew nothing about it anyway—so now I knew what the frozen crab meat was for—Marc's celebrated Crab Farcie and Coquilles St Jacques—"just chop up a few shallots and bang in some scallops," he said, "And you can use the crab shells over and over again as long as you don't burn 'em". "

His enterprise made such an impression on me that I decided that we might put seafood on the menu at the Lily. I mentioned it to Kit on my return but she wasn't wild about the idea.

"We don't know anything about cooking seafood. We don't know a crevette from a sea snail", she said, "What do you do with 'em, boil em or what?"

"No. No," I said. "Marc told me what to do. He's got a mate at the docks who sells fish. He's called Stefan and he does it all there, cooks 'em and prepares 'em as well. Let's try it this weekend"

We worked it all out and decided that we would offer the punters a Plateau Fruits de Mer for two, and a bottle of Muscadet sur Lie, all for F250. Quite a good deal actually as we were only paying 70f per platter but to reduce the risk factor, we made a clear stipulation that orders were only taken in advance. I announced that the 'Special Offer' would be available all day Saturday and by Friday we had orders for fifteen plateaux. We were up and running

Saturday morning we were up early and while Kit got the tables ready, I was off in the Peugeot to the 'Criee' at St. Servan docks. Stefan was waiting for me in the big kitchen above the shop where it looked like the inside of a Turkish baths as he stirred the four massive vats of boiling shellfish.

"C'est tout pret. Franck," he yelled. "En bas avec Freddie. Je passerai chez vous demain. Pas problem, okay?"

In a room at the back of the shop my seafood platters were all ready to go on metal foil covered polystyrene trays. All I had to do was to load them carefully into the Peugeot and scoot off to the Lily. I also loaded up a bag of spider crab claws, which were being thrown out. When I got there Kit had the bar neat and tidy and some of the punters had already arrived and were sharpening their appetites with shots of Pastis. I backed quietly into the garage with my precious cargo and unloaded the platters into the kitchen and tidied them up, putting the pile of seafood and shells straight , and provided a sprig or two of parsley and slices of lemon here and there.

To add to the nautical ambience we got a big pan of water boiling, and dropped the inedible crab claws into it. And soon the tantalizing smell of cooking crustaceans was wafting through the bar. The punters were over-joyed and as we had supposed, apart from the original fifteen ordered, another five coughed up F250 each for the extra platters. Thereafter the Fruits de Mer became a great twice-weekly special at the Jersey Lily.That season the whole town was buzzing with crowds who were determined to sample the famous seafood—and late one night as we sat waiting for the last drinkers to leave Marc told me this story.

Ah, Yes, Sir. The Seafood Special

It appears that one of the top restaurants in St. Malo kept a very special lobster called Henri who spent a charmed life in a big fish tank at the back of the kitchen.

Henri was about six years old and was a real 'Chippendale' of a crustacean, broad of head with feelers nine inches long. He had claws that could free Land-Rover wheel nuts, and a tail like a Florida alligator. A Champion Specimen indeed. The Mike Tyson of Cancale Bay.

His duties were simple. From time to time a rich tourist in the restaurant would order Lobster Thermidor and Henri would be fished out of his tank; thick elastic bands slipped over his bone-crushing claws and be presented wriggling and waving to the gourmet diner, accompanied by gasps of wonder from his table guests and other patrons. He would then be ceremonially marched back to the kitchen and, instead of going into the oven, have his claws freed and be returned to his tank, until the next order of 'Homard' was required. A smaller and less impressive brother would then be cooked and dressed before being presented to the delighted guest as his own particular choice. Henri in the meantime would be tucking into a nice dish of kitchen scraps and putting on more weight. Oh yes, it was a great life for Henri until one unfortunate day in July.

It was a warm evening and the town was crowded. All along the Rue de la Soif the restaurants were full, and at the corner, Le Restaurant Gargantua was also crowded with diners, the terrace was overflowing. Into this wild carnival atmosphere there came four tourists who were greeted effusively by Luic the proprietor, and shown to a prominent table on the terrace under the envious gaze of the strolling evening strollers. They were Americans and their reservations had been made by the Hotel Universe, St Malo's premier hotel, so they were considered 'Star Guests' at the Gargantua. Luic spoke a little English, and feeling that he had found a mark with more money than sense, a not unknown presumption by the French when meeting US citizens, he enthusiastically recommended the 'Specialty of the House—the Chef's famous Lobster Thermidor.

Le Patron's choice being approved, Henri was duly plopped into his bucket and brought out to be presented to his prospective consumer with the usual oohs and aahs. Henri did his bit, waving his antenna around and clanking his claws and the Americans were very impressed at his stature.

"Waal, Vernon, ain't he a beauty," gasped the wife.

"He sure is, Lois," replied her spouse.

Turning wide-eyed to Luic, she asked innocently "You mean, this one is for us?"

Luic lowered his eyelids and answered patronizingly. "Ah Oui, Certaine-ment Madame. Ee eez ze Keeng and ever' tin' 'ere is fresh from de sea. We are renowned for 'aving zee best Fruits de Mer on the coast. Even Mini-sters of the Government eat here when they come to St Malo."

Vernon looked very impressed and glanced across the table to his friend.

"Well, Norman, you're from Maine. You ever see anythin' that big afore?"

"Nope Vernon, can't say that I have," Norman replied, and turning to the obsequious Patron he asked. "Can I pick him up?"

Luic reluctantly handed the squirming body to him and stood back pre-ening as more patrons stopped eating to admire the American's choice.

"Say! He really is heavy. He's jes' 'bout the biggest I've seen, an' I bet he's sure gonna taste good. So, to make sure he don't get lost in the cookin', I'll put my mark on him."

Before the astounded Luic could object Vernon brought out an indelible marker pen, and wrote his initials on Henri's broad tail, his back and both claws before splashing him back into the bucket.

A sickly smile transfixed Luic's face as he stumbled blindly back to the kitchen, where his wife was waiting to give him a good nagging and the kitchen staff were having hysterics. A wild argument ensued, but the deed had to be done because as his fuming virago of a wife pointed out, if 'Les Sales Yanquis' didn't get what they'd ordered, they were sure to report it to the Hotel Universe and then, Pouf! No more wealthy clients from them. So on this occasion, for the first (and last) time in three years, Henri did end up in the oven but the celebrated Lobster Thermidor Gargantua was taken off the menu for the foreseeable future.

'Goodbye Lily, we must leave you'

Yeah, life was rolling along very nicely, and it could have gone on forever because nobody cared what we got up to. But then we began to think about the situation a bit deeper and decided it was time for a change. We had lots of visitors from home. Jon & Linda came for a few days as did some showbiz pals like Paul Young and Karl Denver, but two and a half years at the Lily were more than enough. Our dream ticket was going sour rapidly. I think it was the weather that put the final nail in the coffin. The wild storms that could spring up anytime and are never mentioned on the brochures that advertise idyllic family holidays on the Cote Emeraud. We had snow regularly, and several violent tempests that often deposited wrecked fishing boats on our foreshore, but we were fed up with the punters as well.

The Brits were in the main Hooray Henrys from Jersey, coming across for a wild time in France. Not that they were in anyway adventurous or interesting. For them it was a modern version of the Victorian Eng-lishman's visit to the risque society of Belle Epoque Paris. All they did was to come ashore from their Princesses and Riva cruisers, stagger up the pontoon into the pub and stay there quaffing ale until they were legless or book a taxi into Dinard for a meal, then come back to the pub, and be sick on the carpet. Not the nicest of people. All money but no style. And that in-cludes their women folk who were mostly boating groupies or company wives with plastic noses and hard tucked smiles. I thought them as typical of those jellyfish tax exiles that had moved to the islands. They did not have the guts to live abroad so they had paid for the privilege of living amongst the Jersey Beans.

Our French clients were not much better. The locals, out of season, could only be described as river rats who would come in covered in mud, toting shotguns and fishing gear: When they had had a few, anything could hap-pen and often did. These nights usually ended with the neighbours calling the gendarmes and there is no arguing with those guys. They can even do you for 'Outrage' (Disrespect) so things quickly cooled down.

The other French punters were holidaymakers from Paris, Lyons or other big cities who considered that anyone who lived west of Chartres as peasants, and English as visitors from Mars. In my out–going manner I once innocently introduced two families from Paris to each other, but after formal acknowledgments both parties drank up and left. Apparently Les

Parigots from the 16th Arrondissement do not normally speak to those from the 7th—and *never* on vacation.

But this aloofness was nothing new. As far back as 1812 the French writer Stendahl wrote that the Parisians were 'A surly, envious people in a perpetual state of dissatisfaction and even pretty girls wore wrinkles of envy.'

It gave us an insight into the real character of the French and I was reminded of this story that the Belgians tell.

"When God had almost finished making the world, a deputation of Angels came to see him complaining that he was not being fair. Why, they asked him, had he given France so much? The wild coastal beauty of Brittany, the lush pastures of Normandy, the charm of the Loire Valley, the beaches and wines of Bordeaux, the rolling hills of Champagne, the snow covered Alps, the glorious Cote d'Azure and the magic light of Paris? They considered it most unfair to the rest of Europe—God listened carefully to their complaints for a moment and finally said—" Ah, yes, I know it's beautiful but I have not quite finished yet. Just wait to see what a bunch of unpleasant, quarrelsome, malcontents I populate it with."

So that was it. One morning sipping our morning coffee in bed, and listening to the unending slapping of wire ropes on the masts of boats moored outside our window, we decided that we had had enough of this toper's paradise, and phoned the brewery's accountant in Jersey and told him we wanted out. At first he did not believe us—why should anybody want to give up a dream ticket like the Lily? However when he realized that we were serious he came over with the boss, and tried to persuade us to stay by doubling our pay and offering a very generous package of bene-fits. But it was all to no avail and we insisted on leaving.

There was a guy in Jersey who had been hankering after the Jersey Lily for years, and came across visiting as often as possible. He had been born in the islands and had some tenuous connection with the brewery; I think he had a bar in Gorey. So we contacted him and told him that we were leaving and here was the opportunity he had been looking for. Predictably he jumped at the chance and within three weeks we were gone, and he was installed and also predictably, managed to booze himself to oblivion within a few short years.

On an autumn visit some time later we were sitting in the car at La Passagiere, the old ferryman's house directly across the Rance from the Jersey Lily, watching him standing alone at an upstairs window staring moodily at the deserted pontoon and the dark river, slugging whiskey from the bottle, waiting for something, anything to happen, and I remember thinking that that could have been us if we had not got away.

*   *   *   *   *   *

La Louisiane

Paul Young, the Pogues, Larry Coryell, Serge Lazard.

In March '87 we moved back inside the walls of St. Malo and luckily got our old apartment back overlooking the Gare Maritime. I started playing three nights a week in the jazz cellar of the Louisiane restaurant, and Kitty got her old job back with Georgette and Michel at the Petit Hermine pizzeria so things were fine. We got lots of guest performers including pop stars like Paul Young and top Nashville guitarist Larry Coryell, (or Cordell, if you wish) who later wrote the cynical hit 'Murder on Music Row' plus a fair smattering of French cabaret artistes. For three nights we had the Irish punk rockers the Pogues. The restaurant became a very popular place, one of the most successful late night venues in town—in fact it was too popular for me some nights. The jazz club was in the cellars which being in that small part of the town that survived General Omar Bradley's bombardment in 1944, were over two hundred years old and made of solid granite. However once the restaurant above had been closed and locked up,the only way in or out was by a rickety wooden staircase up to a single side door. It was very good for controlling access but at two in the morning with people attracted by our music and the prospect of late night booze and drug deals with the resident Senegalese pushers, the staircase became jam-packed. It came as quite a shock to me one night when after a particularly hectic rocking Jerry Lee Lewis set, I thought I'd grab a breath of fresh air and found the stairway crammed with yelling punters—it took me about five minutes to work my way into the street as the panic grew inside me—and I made a vow to get out earlier in future. God knows how the building's owner had got a fire certificate—any serious trouble and people would have been trapped down there.

Bastille Day

In November '85 I was invited to play at a huge Country Music festival at the Eldorado Theatre in Paris. There were bands and singers from all over Europe and some very impressive bluegrass groups from the Toulouse area. The first twenty rows of seats had been removed for dancing and the audience got into the swing of things, mostly dressed in expensive Western outfits of denim, fur, and leather, dripping with Navajo turquoise trinkets and crowding the sidewalks outside the venue with customized Harleys, Jeeps, Blazers and hot-rod dragsters.

My French back-up band was the Canyon Riders led by Lionel Pujol, who was a good Buck Owens type telecaster picker and the rest of the band also knew their stuff. They were all young and into both the classics and Country Rock, so my spot was right on the button with songs like 'Six days on the road and 'The Race is On' mixed in with modern numbers like the Maynes Brothers', 'The Wheel', and my Johnny Cash tribute went down very well. All in all I had a great time. I did the gig again the following

year as part of the Bastille Day celebrations, 'though thi.
was a big hall in the La Defense complex and while I was
magnificent military parade along the Champs Elysees.

It truly was a superb spectacle with every branch of the F.
forces represented. Magnificent cuirassiers wearing plumed he
drawn sabres, mounted on huge gleaming horses, escorted the F.
open carriage to the saluting base, and battalions of infantry, n.
troops, officer cadets, naval detachments marched by to the stirring
of massed bands. Modern jets flew low in salute streaming out red,
and blue smoke. The Foreign Legion in their white kepis plodded by sto
faced with sinister menace to their slow march Le Boudin. Bringing up t.
rear were 'Les Blindes', the tanks and armoured vehicles, each one with it.
commander standing proudly in the turret holding the horse hair plumed
standard of the ancient Gaul amid the fluttering regimental pennants.
Onward they rumbled, each one bearing on their side in bold white letters
old battle honours; Valmy, Austerlitz, Marengo, Lodi, Ulm, and many
others.

But then I noticed something peculiar, there were no tanks called
Poitiers, Agincourt, Blenhiem, Waterloo, Sedan or Dien Bien Phu.

Wonder why that was?

* * * * * *

43

BEAUTIFUL BATH

was obvious that the time in St Malo was coming to an end. Another ge was turning. The Jersey Lily was behind us and there were now nister rumblings behind the scenes at La Louisane. The St. Malo police vere now beginning to take notice of the goings–on at the packed late night music sessions. The final crunch came when one of their senior officers moved into an apartment behind the club. He clocked one or two local villains and several suspected Senegalese drug dealers who doubled as souvenir sellers popping in and out in the early hours of the morning. Marc and Dominique were getting close to their target figure and were preparing ttheir final move, so it was time for us to make a move also.

When we had been at the Jersey Lily on the River Rance our neighbour had been a charming Englishman called Richard Hann, who lived in a superb converted Breton farmhouse with his Danish/Canadian wife Karen and two young daughters. They came from Bath where his family had owned one of the premier hotels and it was on his suggestion that we decided to visit it.

At the time both Kit and I had family health problems in Manchester. My mother was not well and getting on a bit. She had been born at the turn of the century, the years were taking their toll, and Kit's mother was also getting frail. The constant travelling between St Malo and the North of England was getting very difficult. Particularly so in the winter, when connections between Jersey and Brittany closed down. The offer of a mini-tour of Cornwall enabled us to visit Bath on the way back to the Portsmouth ferry and we found that we liked the place and decided to set–tle there, even if it was only temporary. On our return to St Malo our suspicions of Marc and Dominique's move was confirmed. They had sold their flat and were living with Marc's relatives until the end of the month when they were off to Miami. Marc and I came to a mutual settlement about the club and we made plans to leave France too.

Our first stop was at Weybridge in Surrey, where we had agreed to house–sit again for our friends Jenny and Dave Parsons and look after their two dogs, Steve and Honey, while they were on holiday in America. Fortunately we got there the day after they flew out, because if they had seen us arrive they would have had a fit. Our red Mercedes 250 was loaded to the gills. The wide rear seat was packed to the roof with cases and household gear, the boot was full to bursting and on the roof rack were more cases and bags. I remember the suspension grounding on the ramp as we waddled off the ferry praying that some conscientious officer from HM Customs would not make us unload everything. Luckily our inspector took one look at our–burdened camel and with the condescending smirk he reserved for returning ex–pats waved us through.

Arriving at Jenny's house, we groaned up the drive and round the back and started unloading and stacking our worldly goods in every hiding place we could find before our hosts returned. There was stuff in the garden shed, in the garage, in our bedroom; in the loft—in fact anywhere it wouldn't be seen.

Three weeks later, Jenny, David, the nanny, and baby Carly returned and joined in the game by pretending not to notice anything different, which was very nice of them. It was a big house with plenty of space, (Well, not quite as much as there was before we started squirrelling our goods away), and as we acted as part–time housekeepers for our high–flying friends, they let us stay for a while.

For a month we tested the water in the Home Counties and juggled with several ideas and projects that ranged from house minding in America and Europe, to a top class chauffeur service we had briefly considered on our last trip but calculations confirmed that our earlier estimates were right. It was not practical. Obviously something else and somewhere else would have to be found—so it was back to the old six strings.

And as for the somewhere else, well, how about having another look at Bath?

The Georgian Gem

It was a late October afternoon when we arrived outside the Fearnley Hotel and parked. The street in front was York Street, so we called in at the first estate agency we came to and they offered us a six–month lease on a nice flat in Catherine Place. "Ok," We said. "Let's have a look at it."

The agent sent one of his colleagues with us and as we walked through the elegant town I was fascinated by it all. It was beautiful. The lush parks, the clean streets lined with the glowing golden stone–faced build-ings and well–dressed, stylish inhabitants. Open–topped buses cruised the elegant Regency squares and crescents, while groups of foreign and domestic tourists were shepherded round by verbose city guides. When the evening closed in, the haloed streetlights gave a timeless quality to the elegant town houses. As we walked through the streets, I thought we were going by car and was surprised when we turned off a street connecting the Circus and the Royal Crescent and he stopped at a house in Catherine Place

"Here we are," he chirruped, "Nice part of town, this is. (It all looked nice to us.)

This was our first home in Bath and I will never forget the atmosphere of complete peace that we felt there. Kit got a job running a bar and I joined the Hospital Car Service at the Royal United Hospital, which got us through that hiatus that always occurs when an entertainer relocates.

I took space in the Stage and the Country Music press to announce that I was back in the UK and informed some of the agents I used to work for that I was seeking gigs, Considering that I had been out of the country for some time, the response was good, but the work offered was months away, so I realized that I would have to get back on the road as soon as possible.

Kelvin Henderson, an old friend from Bristol, was now an influential figure in the New Country scene and he put a few jobs my way and a radio interview with Lee Williams in Wiltshire helped considerably. I contacted that most cautious of managers, John Mills, but it a was a pointless move because, as Shag Connors warned me, Old Pussy–Foot John only took on well–established mainstream West Country acts like the Wurzels or the Cornish comedian Jethro, so he would not be interested.

I found that Bath bursting with entertainers and musicians, and live music was featured every night of the week as well as Saturday and Sunday lunchtimes. It was more like the 60's than the 90's, almost a time–warp, where nearly everyone you met sang or played something. One of the best gigs was every Sunday lunch time at the Hat and Feather pub in Walcott, where the stylish guitarist–singer Johnny Gee, presented a bunch of talented musicians to keep the riotous post–hippy crowd rocking and boozing from noon till the late afternoon with a mélange of Jazz, Folk, Soul and—after my arrival—Country. It was absolutely great, with lots of visiting pickers and singers doing their thing and plenty of everything else. Forget your Karaoke and backing tapes. This was live music. Magic!

The same thing was happening every night of the week at busy pubs like the Kings Head, the Hop Pole Inn, the Golden Fleece, the Royal Oak and White Hart but most of all, at the famous Bell Inn on Walcott Street. This was one of the oldest pubs in the city, with a licence dating back to the 1660's, where you could hear superb bands like the Beer Brothers, the Daily Planet, an Irish folk/rock band featuring harmonica virtuoso Jamie Matthews, Johnny Gee's Walcott Symphonia, the Three Caballeros and many others. In fact I was so impressed by Johnny Gee and Jamie Matthews that I used them both in my band on the big festival shows at Skegness and Chelmsford.

There was also a thriving Country Music scene with artistes like Kelvin Henderson, Johnny Spencer, Felicity Haze, West & Elliot, Bill Smarm, Mike Ryder, Rockabilly Brian Streicher, and great duos like Pat Mallon and Sara. Pete, and Jean Gordon's Ponchartrain group added an authentic Cajun dimension. Some very good Bluegrass pickers operated from pubs in the Widcome area. All in all, it was a very vibrant cultural atmosphere. Many great musicians and performers settled in the area and several celebrities had homes there including the reclusive Van Morrison, Frank Ifield, Peter Gabriel, and Tony Robinson.

It took a couple of months before the work–flow began again but when the agents did begin to call I was more than ready to hit the bricks with some of my old sidemen, filled out with local musicians. The first shows were up in the Forest of Dean, where I shared the bill with Eddy Black–stone, an impressive singer–comedian whom I later discovered had written some good songs. In the early 90's Eddie abandoned his single act and teamed up with a very talented lady called Tejay Martin, who at one time had fronted her own band in the West Midlands, called in true 70's fashion,

Southern Sunshine. The duo took the title T.J. and the Bear and spent many successful years playing to the ex–pats in the Arab Emirates.

One of the first people I met in Bath was Bryan Chalker, who had formed a duo with the glamorous cabaret singer Felicity Haze and, having finished a season in Guernsey, they were off to the Muscat Intercontinental Hotel in Oman for what turned out to be, for Felicity at least, a long–running engagement.

We had known Felicity from shows we had done at Frys Club at Keynsham in the early '80s and Bryan for the best part of twenty years. He was a bit prickly at first, but he relaxed more when it finally dawned on him that I was not interested in stealing his gigs and after that we got on very well. Like me he was a Classic Car nut and we went to a few car shows and we often had dinner together, either at our place or Felicity's flat in Monkton Coomb.

Once more the heavy travelling schedule began and I found myself doing concerts and one–nighters in places as far apart as Rivington Pike in Lancashire and Southsea, Hampshire. It was not too hard because I had a nucleus of old sidemen who knew most of my stuff and specialists like Jamie Matthews and session steelie Ken Byng available for the bigger venues. Various radio interviews and a call from former club owner turned agent Roy Cooper, re–established me on the Country Music Festival Circuit with shows at Ayr, Skegness, Felixstowe, Clacton and Par, but there was not much personal satisfaction or creative pleasure with the constant change of musicians. For some gigs I pulled in some of my old musoes from Cornwall, Dave Fidler, Karl Benson, and Graham Walker, but the wild living and the booze over the past years had not been kind to them and we had, to say the least, an image problem. As everybody now had grey hair I thought of calling the act the Singing Badgers.

But that was not the only thing that had changed. The roads were crowded, the digs expensive and drugs featured much more than they used to do. I became more selective, playing clubs within reach of home whenever possible, and doing the occasional Country Festival, but preferred to spend my time on my second passion, writing.

Then a couple of years on, events happened that changed things dramatically.

*   *   *   *   *   *

L'Annee Triste

Caught up in the euphoria of our new home, we failed to notice the black cloud on the horizon heading our way which was to make 1989 a very sad year with three deaths in the family in close succession.

The first was my mother Louise. She was as old as the century and apart from emphysema (which she appeared to be handling well) and failing eyesight, was in reasonable health but the shock of a sudden fall at home put her in hospital which and triggered a fast decline. It became obvious that she could no longer look after herself properly and moved into a care home where, sadly and to everybody's surprise, she died on February 22nd.

In early February Kit's mother Elizabeth, who was also in her eighties, had a stroke, and was rushed into Oldham General Hospital and after the crisis came home to be nursed by her family until she was re-admitted with further complications. Then Kit's fifty-five year old sister Win became ill with a bowel blockage and she too was admitted to the same hospital. After an operation she came home but her condition worsened and she went back to Oldham General where she died on May 28th.

The Grim Reaper seemed to be striking us from all directions, but he was not finished yet—because only three weeks later Elizabeth too had a relapse and also passed away on June 19th. It was a terrible time.

The following months were spent shuttling backwards and forwards between Bath and Manchester trying to sort things out and we did not seriously get back on track until September, when we took another trip to St Malo to settle our affairs and say goodbye to our old friends. We were finally settled in Bath and I started gigging regularly but mostly within range of home, and I did some work as a consultant for estate agents selling property in France.

*   *   *   *   *   *

44

FLORIDA, WE LOVE IT

It was September 24th 1990 and we were off to Florida. The drizzly haze of Manchester faded as our Boeing 747 lifted off the Ringway runway westbound at 11.45 am. We headed across the West Lancashire flatlands split by the now defunct Manchester Ship Canal,which had brought such prosperity to the region almost a hundred years previously. Crossing the broad Atlantic, we touched down on the hot tarmac of Orlando International Airport, Central Florida, at 4.20 p.m. local time. There was the usual performance at the hire car firm but finally we were ensconced at the Marriott Hotel and strolling along International Drive checking out the shops and restaurants.

After breakfast at the Ramada Hotel, we took a drive up to Charles St. Station, an old railroad depot, now redeveloped as an entertainment complex., but we got lost on the way with the result that we ended up in the slums on the outskirts which had definitely not been redeveloped. It was very sinister indeed, I can tell you and brought back unpleasant memories of Bilbao in Spain. Sleazy bars on every corner were overflowing with Black, Hispanic and White Trash boozers covetously eyeing our hire car plates and hoping that we would stall the engine or worse still stop to ask directions. The much-hyped Florida Success Story had somehow passed them by and tourists were considered fair game for these disenchanted locals, even in daylight it was very scary.

Charles Street Station was in the old part of Orlando or to put a finer point on it, the station and its freight yards were the main reason for the town's existence, because what is now one of the world's holiday playgrounds, was once a declining citrus fruit growing area and this South Florida Railroad depot was its lifeline. About the only travellers who saw it, (as late as the mid 1960's) were breakfasting, affluent northern 'Snowbirds' on the last leg of their hibernation to the warmer climate of Miami but the New Conquistadors from the Disney Corporation had changed all that. In twenty short years Central Florida had expanded to provide diversion and sustenance for millions of visitors every year and Charles Street Station centre had become a focal point of that development.

This entertainment complex was vast but very well organized, catering for every taste both musical and gastronomic. There was the Orchid Garden, which recalled the golden days of Hollywood in the 40's and 50's, and Capt. Ragtime's, a fast food coffee shop with video games and roller skating waitresses. Across the street was the Exchange a big shopping mall, next to that was the Planter's Punch that featured circus acts and several more specialized eateries, including a seafood and Cajun joint called Crackers. Rosie O' Grady's was themed as the Old New York Bowery with cafés and shows featuring traditional jazz hosted by a large flamboyant lady in the Mae West mould

Probably the biggest and most atmospheric venue was the Country Music venue called the Cheyenne Saloon and Opera House, with its balustrade balconies and resident line dancers, leading the customers in the latest routines on the hardwood floor. I was booked as a guest artiste with Jerry Seymour's Raiders, the house band, and it was there I came across George Jones again. He was headlining but turned up late halfway through the second set as usual. (Well, they don't call him 'No Show Jones' for nothing). I also met my old friend Bobby Bare. Both of them looking a little older of course, as I was.

It had been the best part of twenty five years since I'd first met Bobby back in Wiesbaden and considering all the tough times he had gone through emotionally he did not look too bad: but the Possum seemed to be down to the canvas. He looked lined and much smaller than I remembered him and he seemed a bit confused with it all. His said that he had now given up drinking completely but he still carried a bottle of Four Roses bourbon in his bag, just in case he had a change of heart. Gone was his spiky crew cut and his hair was now a silky silver pageboy bob but when they finally got him on the high stage the old magic was still there. As Waylon put it,

"If we all could sing like we wanted to, we'd all sound like George Jones"

My mind went back to the first time I ever heard him, back in 1959 singing his Xmas Number One 'She thinks I still care'. (Yes, folks it really is that long ago.). He made a few jokes about his lifestyle and references to his ex–wife Tammy Wynette. They were at the start of the final, fraught on–off relationship that would storm on until Tammy's tragic early death. I last saw them together on the Country Music Awards show in the 90's, by which time George's long hair was completely white, and he came on stage wearing thick black framed spectacles to join the heavily made–up and very frail Tammy, They did a few of their old hits and the sound was good, but a British friend of mine who did not know who they were, remarked that it looked like 'Barbara Cartland meets Arthur Askey'

At another show I did, the guest band contained a couple of sidemen who claimed to be from Emmy Lou Harris' old backing group, the famous Hot Band but I did not know any of them. The venue was out in the sticks, this time up Highway 4 and a local driver from the agency took us there. Some six miles out of Altamonte Springs we picked up a two–lane blacktop to a small town where we came across the gig. It was a big barn with a huge parking lot, floodlit and patrolled by armed guards with dogs, and sur-rounded by a high double wire fence.

We were waved in and, after our documents were checked, we were welcomed warmly and shuffled round the back to the stage door, which was next door to the men's toilets and smelled terrible. As soon as we got inside the noise hit us. The place was heaving and the house band was having a hard time being heard above the yelling men and shrieking women shuff-ling round the hardwood floor. There was a three man fight raging in one corner accompanied by shouts and screams but generally not getting in the way of everybody's enjoyment.

The house band finished its first set and, looking frightened to death, scrambled off stage to a patter of applause and cat calls, and the jukebox was turned up loud until a sweating semi–inebriated, compere shuffled on. He introduced the 'World Famous Hot Band', who immediately got every-body's backs up by going right into a deafening bit of heavy rock, and by the third number they were being pilloried as West Coast druggies and worse. But the crowd kept boozing and dancing as they thundered on. As I peeped round the edge of the stage, a drunk reeled up to my elbow and yelled. "They's frum Califownya, y'know. the Land of Fruit and Nuts. Yew goes one way or t'other out there. Hee! hee!"

This was the kind of scene that Johnny Russel encapsulated so well in his great hit 'Red necks, White socks and Blue Ribbon beer'. He'd got it dead right.

Finally the ex–Hot Band cooled things down with a ragged attempt at Jim Reeves' hit 'He'll have to go' which brought a little peace to the tense atmosphere. (Even if it was the Roy Cooder version)—and before you know it, I was on stage belting out Six Days on the Road—which proved to be just what they wanted. So it was an easy night for me, with Merle Haggard standards and a few Brooks and Dunn numbers, plus some Lynard Skyn-yard stompers (Sweet Home Alabama hit the spot all right) and of course, some Waylon and Willie for the cognoscenti. At one point, in the middle of a guitar solo, I had enough time to reflect that times had not changed all that much from the wild days of Galveston Bay—or the Seaham Working Men's club, come to that. But at least up in Tyne and Wear you didn't need armed guards and dogs. Well, not back then anyway. This wild bacchanal was still going strong when we left at around 2.30 am. The armed guards threw the gates wide and feverishly gesticulated as we roared off into the hot night. It was like a re–run of the Mekong Delta in '68.

PICKER'S TIP 58

Publicity pictures are essential and 8 x 10 Black and White are the best. They have more dramatic effect than colour. Good copies are cheap but there is no point without displaying your name and contact number. How else can potential bookers get in touch?

Time-Share Tension

One could not visit Orlando without checking out the various Disney World theme parks, which we did. But before that let me recount how we got there and tell any prospective visitors this cautionary tale.

I'm sure that most of you will be familiar with the antics of those pushy timeshare touts on the Spanish Costas, well, here it was just as bad, except that the ploy was different. Young men and women would approach you offering a ticket for all the big attractions for five dollars. All one had to do was attend a seminar at a timeshare development and let them show you the apartments and villas available, no obligation of course. Being fairly streetwise, we easily put these hustlers off a few times but, after finding out the normal entrance price to Disney World (a day ticket worked out around $150 per family) we decided to take a chance and took a couple of vouchers that would be exchanged for tickets at the timeshare promotion. I think the development was on the Kissimmee Road about three miles from our hotel and we tooled down there in our hired Pontiac two mornings later. As we turned in at the main gate I expressed mild surprise at the two armed guards and another high wire fence surrounding the place but, hitching their pistol holsters and rolling their shoulders, they assured us that it was an extremely secure environment.

Oh yeah? I thought, so is San Quentin.

We followed the given direction and found a spot in the vast car park crowded with shiny new cars, pick–up trucks and massive, beautifully equipped Winnebago's, many with Out of State plates. When we nosed into our space on the edge of the lot, we noticed something that was distinctly out of place. About three rows over, standing forlornly in the midst of this sparkling sea of chrome and polished glass was an ex–US Army command truck that had suffered badly from an amateur conversion into a camper van. It was hand–painted a dull maroon with dirty streaks of black along the sides and rust–edged wheel arches. The roof was cluttered with ropes, buckets, plastic beer crates, and a sagging orange inflatable dinghy, while on a rack hanging off the back were two muddy Yamaha trail bikes. There was a Dixie flag drooping on a small mast on the front wing and the side door was open, hanging crookedly from its sliding frame while Travis Tritt and Joe Diffy were roaring out of the stereo speakers with raw Stone Country rock. Three scruffy kids were running around, shouting at two mangy–looking hounds and a couple of young fat women sat on sagging canvas chairs slugging Budweiser's, and a sullen looking teenager was lolling on the back fender oiling up a sinister Remington 12 Gauge shotgun. Somehow I knew that this was going to be trouble. And it was.

However, jealously guarding our tickets and looking back nervously, we made our way to the main hall where several other couples were milling around, partaking of the buffet breakfast provided and wondering, like us, what happened next. Then the double doors at the far end were thrown open and in trooped our 'Councilors' in their bright blue blazers. We were then herded into groups of about eight and told to follow our guides for a tour of the vast estate, which I must say was very impressive. The landscaped pastel stucco villas were superb, beautifully furnished and appointed with state of the art amenities and fittings. They were very spacious and some of the small blocks of apartments had their own pools and to be honest, were not that expensive by European standards. All the time the sales pitch was coming from these highly trained specialists about the easy terms available and the wonderful climate, and the convenience of having a holiday home of your own for life, and the possibility of passing the real estate onto your kids. You know how it goes, but we fixed bayonets and kept asking questions about our promised Disney World tickets, which were fended off with well–rehearsed moves.

The tour over, we were taken back to another vast hall filled with round tables where, after a lavish promotional film, we sat with our guides as they expertly fielded our questions and plied us with coffee and donuts and craftily tried to get us to hand over our credit card numbers. Ten minutes into this charade, there was a loud whistle and at a far table a yellow–jacketed supervisor stood up and announced

"Ladies and Gentlemen. Let's hear it for these great people. Mr. and Mrs. Kalowski from Detroit, Michigan. (Cheers from all the other Polaks present) who have decided to take villa number 686 on the Sunset Park development in May for week's number 38 thro' 41. Give 'em a big round of applause, folks."

We all clapped as ordered and our counsellor got back to his spiel until the supervisor's whistle shrilled again to announce that another mesmerized couple had signed their holidays away for the foreseeable future.

But still we held on. And by now, realizing that we were rather tougher nuts to crack they brought in the next echelon of hustlers. This time it is a big guy in a red jacket with a lapel badge.

"Oh, so y'all from England eh? Yeah. Ah been there. London sure is one great city. Where y'all from then? Bath, eh? Yeah, I heard about it, on the South Coast near the lake, aint it? (What lake?). Now, 'bout this villa of yours? (Ours? Oh!) Waal, it sure looks like yuh picked out a good 'un. Now, all ya gotta do is gimme your Visa card number and I'll see to all the confusin' details for yuh, an' yuh jes' select what time of year suits you best. We got full privilege status with Florida Air and can get you special rates on their flights. What d'y say now? Jes' think what them folks back in Wales are gonna think when yuh git back an' tell 'em 'bout yo' place in the sun."

Wales? Lakes? The South Coast? Well, his selling technique was good, but his grasp of British geography a little sketchy. But still we hung on, demanding our free Disney tickets. At one point we bluntly told him that it was the only reason we were there. But he still kept on socking it to us.

And we weren't the only ones putting up a fight either. At the next whistle from the supervisor, who rose to congratulate the Jack Stanton family from Akron, Ohio, on signing their pensions away, I noticed a party going on three tables down from us, where two burly tattooed hillbillies wearing worn jeans, boots and battered straw Stetsons were laughing with two 'Country Boy' reps, slugging from a brown bag as they blindly scratched their names on the various bits of paper on the table. Just behind us, a black couple were nervously trying to repel the sales pitch of some fast-talking college boy. Obviously he was getting nowhere, so the top brass bought in their heavies in the form of another black couple, who socked it to their 'Brother and Sister' victims with pure Soul talk and street jive rap, telling them that it was as much their Right to have a timeshare in Florida as them *White Honkies.*

Jesus! These people would stop at nothing to make a sale.

Finally realizing that they had hit bedrock with us, they gave up and sent us on rigmarole from one office to another to get our free Disney World tickets. At each stop a trained team were deployed to try to persuade us to accept their generous offers, and each time the price dropped until we could have had a villa for life for the outlay of less than £800, but still we wouldn't fall for it and, reluctantly, after two hours of this hard sell persuasion they gave up and went looking for softer targets.

Clutching our hard-won tickets we made our way back to our car and as we were about to get in we heard a shotgun blast from the direction of the DIY camper van and a screeching female Alabama yell split the hot afternoon air.

"Yew fuckin' done what wot? Jesus!   Yew've signed us up fer how long? Ah'll fuckin' kill ya."

We looked over and saw one of the fat women we had seen near the camper van holding the smoking Remington as she shrieked at the two rolling straw-hatted drunks, who hunkered down behind a waste bin grinning vacantly as they proudly waved the documents giving them title to their very own ground floor apartment every year for three weeks in July. The kids stopped playing and the other woman started throwing beer cans at the drunks, who by now were laughing hysterically as the women screamed at them. We cowered behind the cars as the Remington went off again and sirens wailed through the uproar as the security SWAT team came storming into the parking lot.

It seemed to be a good time to leave, so we seized the moment and took off, but in our rear view mirror I could see a situation develop as black combat-suited figures spilled from vehicles toting guns, gas canisters and handcuffs. Oh yes, as the gateman said, it was a very secure environment indeed.

I often wonder what happened next.

We decided to have a look round Central Florida while we were there and thought that Kissimmee was a nice area with some magnificent homes for sale but ,after our time–share experience, we did not stop the car in case a couple of touts were hiding in the bushes.

Disney World, of course was magnificent, and as it was October there were no big queues for the attractions. The organization was superb and the weather was balmy, ideal for strolling around. I was most impressed by the Epcott centre which was a moving museum of history and space, with all sorts of exhibits and demonstrations. The most charming attraction of them all was Sea World, where sea lions, dolphins, porpoises, seals, and killer whales, performed a pantomime in the huge pool, sometimes drenching the ringside audiences and then joyfully scooting off with a sea creature version of the giggles, even Sam the Walrus joined in. I loved those big lazy manatees that floated around munching the cabbages thrown to them by the crowd. Absolute Magic.

Gigolos at Breakfast

From Orlando we moved to the Gulf Coast to stay a few days at the fabulous Don Cesar Hotel in St. Petersburg Beach, certainly one of the best hotels I have ever stayed in. It was a beautiful, massive, rose–pink gothic building right on the beach, with exotic gardens and a big open air swimming pool beside the shimmering white sand. It looked like a film set; which at one time it was; being the location for the 1959 Marilyn Monroe, Jack Lemmon, Tony Curtis epic 'Some like it hot' These days though, hardly anybody came by train. Air travel was now dominant and it was a bizarre co–incidence that the first commercial passenger airline was born here back in 1914, when the Tampa–St. Petersburg Airboat Line was founded with a French Benoist sea–plane making two flights a day between the two cities. Although the company went out of business after about six months, it was a first and it set the pattern for the future.

December was no longer the high season it had once been, when the wealthy Canadians and New Englanders who could afford it, would winter down here. These days the big package tours from Europe were the main source of income, together with the retirees who sought a warm climate. These pensioners were a strange breed indeed, and one would encounter them at breakfast in the coffee shop, the men groomed to perfection, wearing their razor–sharp pressed pants and foulard cravats, while the women would appear as though going to some society function, in full coiffure with every wrinkle and facial flaw meticulously disguised, courtesy of Max Factor, wearing high heels and shiny frocks or expensive trouser suits, dripping with chunky jewellery with their scarlet tipped fingers loaded with huge rings—and this was at 8am.

I did a couple of guest spots at the Ocean Room in the Holiday Inn on the beach with a great act called Sam Maxim & Friends. They were simply a trio, two guys who played bass and guitar and a girl playing keyboards, but their presentation and imitations were superb. I did some rocking things like Chuck Berry's Promised Land and a few 'New Country' Al Ketchum and Clint Black numbers, in fact it was the first time I did one of my new favorites 'Leaving here a better Man.'

Sam Maxim was a great cabaret act on his own. In one number he did 'For all the girls I've loved before' as Willie Nelson and Julio Eglisias would have done it. Not only the voices either, because the whole left side of his body was dressed like Willie with a grand–dad vest, half a bandana (stuck on) one blue jean leg and one tennis shoe, while the other side of him was in half a tuxedo complete with floppy bow tie. And as each voice took over he would turn on stage—it was terrific. We got to talk after the show and I asked why he had never brought his act to Europe and he explained his reasons. It turned out that this was his 9th season at the hotel and that the seasons down here ran for eight months a year. He had only come down to Florida to take a rest from one of those grinding mid–West tours that I knew only too well and by chance the booked cabaret act had got stoned in Miami and failed to show, so he stood in. The manager had liked his act, so much so, that he got the job instead and he had been there ever since. Did he miss the travelling life? Not on your life. Now he owned his own condo on Boca Ciega Bay a '65 Mustang and Chris Kraft 27 foot motor cruiser.

So it was goodbye Carolina, so long Tennessee. That's show biz, Folks.

From the Affluent to the Effluent

Looking due south from the beach terrace of the Pink Palace (which was a lot different than the last one we visited in the Central Highlands of Vietnam) I was intrigued by what looked like a tall spindly tower in the distance and, checking the map, I found it was actually a long bridge called the Sunshine Skyway that traversed Tampa bay. So we had to try it. There was a toll booth at the entrance and we seemed to be on a causeway for the first two miles, before climbing steadily to the bridge itself, where we cruised in the bright sunlit silence. After another few miles we began to descend to the toll booth at Terra Ceia Island. It was terrific to be soaring high above the bay and seeing the coastal shipping sloughing up the Gulf of Mexico on one side and the green vegetation and dangerous urban sprawl of Tampa on the other. If you ever get to St. Petersburg try it.

From there we headed south through Sarasota and Port Charlotte to the beautiful developments of Fort Myers, Coral Cape, and the Naples region where we found a totally different breed of Florida Fugitive. These were the successful business men who had retired early and moved down there to a life of luxury with magnificent shopping malls, superb houses, excel–lent golf clubs and some of the finest marinas in the world and all protected by the tightest civilian security I have ever seen.

As we crossed the bridge into Fort Myers, a police cruiser picked us up and trailed us discreetly until we stopped at a coffee shop, when we were politely approached and asked our business in their town. We were told that they operated a 24 hour day Zero Tolerance policy in Collier and Lee counties and then, satisfied that we were British tourists, they smiled and wished us the classic 'Have a nice day' and gave us a town map before leaving

We had another three days to do in Florida and the next show was a Country–Rock festival at Daytona on the Atlantic Coast, which proved to be the complete opposite from the scene we had left. We could not believe it. It was as bad as anything I had seen in the most impoverished areas of Eastern Europe. Filthy, shabby buildings, pot–holed streets and derelict buildings, with graffiti everywhere across the empty and shuttered shops. A kind of Buffalo of the South. It seemed that about the only reason for the town's existence was the huge motor racing track a few streets inland from the long flat beach, where several world land speed record attempts used to be made. (That was before they discovered better conditions at Utah's Salt Lake). Nowadays it was infamous for its thriving drug scene and its outrageous homosexual community where every fetish and depravity was catered for.

It was unusual to find a gay town that was such a complete dung heap. Down on the Keys or up north at Martha's Vineyard, the public areas were always immaculate, but in Daytona there were drunks sleeping in doorways and drugs being pedalled openly in the bars and fast food joints. I saw a vendor on the beach just wearing a thong with a display tray round his neck coolly advertising his wares to the never ending parade of golden tanned poseurs and pimps, who paraded the foreshore in customized pick–up trucks and foreign sports cars, while in a couple of police cruisers, the crews munched on hamburgers and watched it all with boredom.

The show was on the beach and began at midnight with a succession of third–rate bands with the featured acts going on around 2am. Luckily I met a band I knew from Kissimmee and arranged for them to back me, so luckily everything went fine, but I was glad to take the money and run. The digs on offer at a beachside motel were so bad that we decided to drive all the way back to the Orlando Marriott to spend the last two days in the Sunshine State at the side of the swimming pool topping up our tans.

*   *   *   *   *   *

Yibbish Arrives Early

We arrived back at Manchester Airport in autumn and spent a few days in the north, staying with Kit's sister Agnes and her husband Eric before heading home to Bath where Kit took a job managing a city centre restaurant and I picked up a few gigs, but the big surprise came in late October.

Our niece Barbara and her sea–captain partner Alan had been living out on the Goss Moor near Roche in Central Cornwall but, as the house was a bit isolated, particularly so when Alan had to go back to sea on long trips, they had moved to a beautiful old stone house in the ancient village of Tyardreath in Par and they both appeared to be happy there. Barbara however was having great difficulty coming to terms with her mother's tragic early demise, and we were happy when she told us that she was pregnant as we thought that a child might ease her mind a little. The baby was expected around Christmas time but started kicking the walls early and Barbara was rushed into Trelisk Hospital where a healthy, blonde and beautiful little girl was delivered at noon on October 30th 1990. We drove down to see them the next day and I can remember clearly his new daughter held snug in the palm of his hand. In honour of the matriarch of the family who we all loved, they christened her Elizabeth. Gwen, which was quite a mouthful for a little toddler that came out as 'Yibbish'

She was destined to play a big part in our lives in the years to come and often stayed with us and went on holiday too. In fact until she became a teenager—and we all know what happens then. This poem I wrote about her arrival.

*　*　*　*　*　*

ODE TO ELIZABETH GWEN

You fooled us all in the Halloween rain.
When you arrived on an early train.
We planned to greet you with Christmas song,
But you decided not to wait that long.
  So now you're here to light our lives
  with a reason for the future years.
  smiles instead of tears.
When Dad was gone, time dragged away.
Now you keep us busy night and day.
Rushing around like leaves in a gale,
just grab 40 winks, then 'Top and Tail'
and make the cot, and make the feed.
You leave no doubt 'bout what you need,
'Cos if its not there, you make a fuss to let us
  know you're now one of us.
So welcome little Halloween Sprite
  with feather and hands and eyes so bright.
Whatever did we do before you came.
To share our life and bear our name?

Frank Yonco — Bath 1990.

*   *   *   *   *   *

45

LITTLE ENGLAND BEYOND WALES

When we got back from the Florida warmth and excitement, I felt charged up and began gigging again with enthusiasm but it was not very rewarding playing the shadows of the old Country Music Clubs that I had played in their heyday but it was the only source of work for a Stone Country entertainer like me—Then one morning I received a letter which launched me off in another direction

International talent on the Soap Market

British–born international country music star Frank Yonco must be wondering what it is about him; perhaps he has a naturally Gallic shrug? He is featured in the Welsh soap Pris y Farchnad (Market price) playing the part of Monsieur Diderot, the French Ambassador

The multimillion pound television series is produced by Cardiff–based independent company Penadur and stars veteran welsh actor David Lynn. The first of the nine, one–hour episodes is due to be screened on S4C on November 8.

Meanwhile Yonco who has a home in St. Malo, France may also be appearing as a senior detective in a French re–make of the great seventies hit Paris Precinct.

Cutting from 'Stage and Television', November 5th 1992

"What does that mean?" asked Kit.

I checked the letter that had arrived from a casting agency in Cardiff.

"Er, it says here that it is the title of big soap series on S4C the Welsh TV channel and roughly translated it means "The Price Is Right". It's all about a family of auctioneers. A sort of Welsh 'Coronation Street.'"

"Oh yes, and what do they want you to do? How did they get on to you?"

"They saw me on 'Casualty' (I'd worked as an extra on a couple of episodes) and got my CV from them. My part is M. Diderot, a European Union official—and it's in French. I'll give them a ring for more info."

A week later found me booking into a small hotel at Carmarthen on the beautiful river Towy with all the other actors. The filming was to be at the West Wales Showground, where a big agricultural event was being staged. It was not yet open to the public and all the film crew were busy setting up. I was quite surprised at the scale of the operation as there must have been about ten or twelve principal actors plus about thirty extras, and full catering facilities and changing rooms, with a couple of big buses fitted out as dining rooms.

Somehow, probably because it was being filmed in a distant rural area, I had expected it to be a bit primitive, but it was not like that at all. It was much more like 'Dynasty' or 'Dallas' than 'Coronation Street'. The strong story line was well delivered by the principal actors, who were mainly, young, good looking, well–dressed men and beautifully groomed women. The very experienced Welsh legend David Lynn was the central character and handled the direction as well. All in all it was a very good quality production.

The filming went well, but often the heavy rain delayed the outdoor shooting and the gig was extended to three weeks, but it was fun. As you can imagine, for me concentration was order of the day, as most of the action was in Welsh with the odd word of English, and my part was in French, so I had to keep a sharp ear out for my cues,

At the end of the day I would usually go back to the hotel or, if we had a day off, drive home to Bath. One day however we were rained off but shooting was due to start at 7 a.m. next morning, so I took a run down to Pembroke and on to Milford Haven, one the most important west coast ports in Tudor times. It was a strange but beautiful region and lived up to its name of Little England beyond Wales.

It was as though an imaginary line had been drawn from Fishguard, on the west coast, (the site of the only foreign invasion of the British soil since 1066, a small incursion by the French in the 1790s) to Tenby in the south and that everything west of this line was English. Here the people had none of the lilting Welsh accents of the valleys or the Cardiff coast, but spoke the same clear, careful, English you hear in the Scottish Highlands and the place names were not even Celtic. For example, instead of Llantrisant or Merthyr, we had Pembroke, Castlemartin, West William, Manor Newton and Rosemarket. It was a truly unique place, from the in-land mountains to the beautiful Cardigan Coast. Visit it if you get chance. You will find it quite amazing,

But back at the film location things were hotting up and it was only towards the end of the last week that I discovered the wild night–life going on after hours that made quiet laid back Carmarthen more like the Klondike, The combination of a visiting film crew and those West Wales farmers was dynamite, As the show went out on S4C, I never got to see any of the series but friends of ours in North Wales said that it was very good

Sylvia Clegg 1928-1993

More tragedy struck soon after though, when my first wife Sylvia died after a botched operation in Truro. It was a terrible tragedy, more so because they were on the threshold of a new life. She and my ex–bass player and truck driving partner Derek had married in September 1975 but, becoming disenchanted with the social conditions and the escalating violent crime in Manchester, had sold up and moved down to Cornwall for a gentler life and to be nearer our son Francis and his family.

They bought a nice house in Bodmin and were settling in nicely when Sylvia was booked into Trelisk Hospital for a normal hysterectomy. The operation was botched by the surgeon, who unfortunately nicked the bowel and septicemia set in. At the time a bitter range war was raging between two doctors there and they were both involved in Sylvia's subsequent treatments which proved ineffective, each one altering the other's instruc-tions, with the sad result that she passed away on October 20th 1993—It was her 65th birthday.

We were all devastated, because old wounds had faded and over the years we had all become good friends She was a charming, capable, very funny woman, and we still chuckle when we read some of her letters. It was a truly terrible time,

Oh the Bells, the Bells

One morning we were sitting having breakfast in the café of Jolly's store in Bath, when Kit remarked that my chin was wet and I was dribbling my coffee every time I took a drink. I had not felt a thing so I looked into a nearby mirror and found that my face looked strange and the whole left side was frozen. The corner of my mouth was dipping and I could not close it properly, Gradually, as we walked home the whole of my face slipped until I could not speak clearly and obviously I could not sing either. I began to get worried. I looked like Quasimodo, the Hunchback of Notre Dame, or somebody who had had a stroke, but I did not feel ill in any way and apart from an ache in my left ear, any pain or discomfort. So what was happening?

We spent an anxious night and the next day, I was off to the doctor but I did not get past the dour Scots lady in the receptionist's sentry box, who was well trained in dealing with time–wasting, hypochondriac, middle aged Bathonians.

"I know what's wrong with you," she said in her snooty Morningside accent.

"You've got Bell's Palsy. Och, I've seen it before. It's not very serious, I'll tell the doctor. Just you sit there,"

A few minutes later she came back into the musty waiting room which doubled as an archive for antique lady's magazines and handed me a piece of paper.

"That's a prescription for pain killers," she sniffed. "just keep your face warm when you go out and take a couple of these when you go to bed."

"Nothing else?" I asked anxiously, "Just pain killers? Is there nothing you can do? Don't I need an X ray or a blood test or something? How long will it take to get better? I will get better won't I? I'm a singer,"

"Och!" she sniffed, "You can forget about all that nonsense for quite a while. There'll be no singing for you for at least two months. And that's only if you keep your face warm. Let it get too cold and you might take a year or longer to get right. Singer indeed. Humpf!"

Her estimate was not far out because though I kept my face warm as I could and avoided draughts through that cold spring, it was August before my face returned to normal and the nagging pain in my neck and ear went away. Finally that damaged seventh aural nerve repaired itself and I could relax a little, but I could not control the side of my mouth properly. In truth it was the end of my time on the road. I could still play guitar and sing quite well, but I could no longer do a full forty–minute set without my chin dripping. So at times on stage I looked like Louis Armstrong, who used to carry a handkerchief in one hand while he played, although in my case it was not just to wipe away perspiration.

Some more bells. Wedding Bells.

At home in Bath the summer of 1994 was very warm and pleasant. In fact, it was ideal weather for a wedding. So we decided to have one of our own. After an extended courtship of over twenty–five years it somehow seemed the right thing to do; and as I said, the weather was fine. So we did it on Monday June 13th.

At first we considered a grand affair, with all our friends and relatives from Cornwall and the North but thinking deeper about it we began to have doubts. It would be expensive, and the closest people to us would probably cry off anyway and others had a track record of missing special occasions. So we booked a ceremony at the Bath Registry Office and a champagne lunch at the Francis Hotel with our guests,. Jon and Linda Adkin, and Flis Haze and Bryan Chalker, and it was a very nice day in– deed. Kit looked superb in her pink suit and flowered decorated straw hat. After that, we all adjourned to Flis' sun terrace for a few drinks. Around four p.m. Bryan left to go home to Claverton Down, where he was looking after his aged father, but we continued to chug–a–lug until the sun went down. Jon and Linda stayed over at our place and two days later Kit and I left on our honeymoon and drove to Portsmouth for the cross channel ferry: Which we missed.

So, we postponed the trip for a week. Well, after all there was no real hurry. We had already been waiting twenty–five years for this day. The following Monday we got the time right and took off for a nice few days in France, visiting La Baule and seeing old friends. So far we seem to be get– ting on all right and as we have recently celebrated our Tin Wedding (Ten years) there is a good chance it might last.

That's just me trying to be Mr Cool. This is a song I wrote sums up how I really feel.

*   *   *   *   *   *

KIT'S SONG

Well you told me once I never wrote a song for you.
And writing songs and singing them is what I do.
So here's a song for someone that I know.
I 've just got to think of her and the words begin to flow.
I call it Kit's song, 'cause I love you.
It may not be a hit song; it's the best that I could do.
The years we've spent together seem so short my dear.
But when you're not here each day's a long and lonely year.
You're the reason for the things I say and do.
I built my world around you and my universe is you.
I call it Kit's song, 'cause I love you.
It's not a hit song but I wrote it just for you,
There were times I know you must have doubted me.
When I thought that freedom was a prize.
But like the poet said "No man's an island."
And freedom is just lonely in disguise.
So I'll spend my days beside you darling, come what may,
And thank the Lord for each and every passing day.
You're the reason for the things I say and do.
I built my world around you and my universe is you.
I call it Kit's song 'cause I love you.
It may not be a hit song but I wrote it just for you.

Frank Yonco. KRA Bath.

*   *   *   *   *   *

46

OH NO! NOT SPAIN AGAIN?

A year or so later our American friends, Ron and Mary–Lou Rhoades, came to visit us and we were having dinner at the Beaujolais Restaurant in Bath with them when I happened to bring up the subject of Spain. It was not well received.

"Oh no. Not Spain again," spluttered Kitty. "You must be a sucker for punishment. What is the matter with you? Don't you remember the last trip?"

"Ah, but it's different this time," I smarmed. "This time it's all happening down on the Costa del Sol—y'know, where Frank Feeney said we should have gone instead of Calpe. There are people down there that I know."

Ron & Mary–Lou sensing a family row brewing, developed sudden interest in their Cote de Boeuf and kept their heads down as Kit snorted her response.

"Oh Yes? Well, that Calpe trip was fifteen years ago. And anyway, who do you know there?"

By now I had the bit between my teeth and blustered on, "Well, er, there's Cliff Leger for one and Lonnie Donegan, and that Welsh singer, Ivor Emmanuel, and quite a few Americans like Sonny Bono, and that guy who used to be in the Eagles. Oh, there are lots of people I know down there, dozens of 'em."

"Oh really?" she hedged. "And what, may I ask, has that got to do with you? Haven't you had enough yet? Do you want to become known as Yonco–saurus Rex, the Singing Dinosaur? You've already done everything you set out to do. Give it a rest."

"No, no," I persisted "It sounds like a good scene to me. There's lots of Brits out there and the weathers brilliant. C'mon. Wotcha think?"

Ron and Marylou munched on in silence with ears cocked for the next outburst, but Kitty had been down this road before and had heard it all.

Finally she looked up from the table, took a sip of her Cote de Rhone and resignedly sighed. "Well, give it a try then. But on your own. Leave me out of it until you've seen it for yourself. Okay?"

Mary–Lou put her fork down with a sigh and said as though nothing had happened "What a lovely piece of beef," and the subject changed to the consideration of what we would have for dessert.

But I'd got the message and two weeks later I took a plane from Bristol Airport and landed at Malaga in the late afternoon with no idea of where I was going. All I had was the address of a bar in Fuengirola, so I bummed a lift from a fellow passenger who was heading for Marbella with his Swedish girl friend, and they dropped me off in the district of Los Boliches where there is a massive tin silhouette of a bull marking the eastern limits of the town.

* * * * * *

Fuengerola

The first thing to do was to find some digs, so I headed to the seafront with my bag and guitar and dropped into a local bar. It was packed with Spaniards having a few vinos after work, not a tourist in sight and, in response to my basic Catalan they shook their heads, and pointed across the street to a big hotel called the Jabega, so I booked in there for the night. It wasn't too expensive by British standards, about twenty quid I think, but too heavy for an extended stay and I decided to look around the following day. That Spanish 'Manana' feeling was getting to me already. But the next thing was nosebags and then to find where all the action was. The evening was warm so I strolled along the wide promenade to check out the eating–houses. There were plenty of them and very cheap as well but there were not many people about, so with all the panache and style of the true international gourmet I selected sausage and chips at £2.50.from a greasy spoon café run by two middle–aged Welsh gays with orange tans and matching yellow nylon shell suits. They "Oooo'd" and "Ahhh'd" and rolled their eyes when I asked directions to Linda's Bar: It turned out to be on the next corner and looked like two empty shops, but in the curtained windows on the door were the usual photos of the coming attractions.

| WELCOME TO LINDA'S KAREOKI. BAR |
| Mon. LANCE EAGER (Guitar) The Elvis from Essex. |
| Tues. SHEENA BLUE. (Lady Comic) Blue's the name, be ready. |
| Wed. SANDRA and SARAH. (Top of the Pops) Abba & Spice Girls. |
| Thur. SIDE BY SIDE. Top Country & Irish duo. Cliff and Dee. |

And there it was. A colored poster featuring Cliff and his missus Delores.

Well, that was a surprise for a start, because I had never thought of Delores as a cabaret artiste. I knew that Cliff had been training his daughters to be part of the family act, but to me Delores had always been the lady who ran some very good showbiz digs in Redcar—but here she was, looking very glamorous indeed behind a big Yamaha keyboard. Cliff himself looked much the same except for a little weight , sporting a ponytail and what looked suspiciously like an earring.

I breezed in and ordered a beer to look the place over. There was a low stage at one end where a middle–aged slim blond guy was busy setting up his keyboard and speakers, and a small dance space in front with well–worn banquettes lining the walls. It all looked a bit tatty but it was still early evening. Perhaps it would look better after midnight with a bellyful of San Miguel. I asked the barman about Cliff and was told that he was away in the UK on holiday. 'Oh great.' I thought and asked when he would be back. The barman nodded over to the stage and told me to ask the man on the stage, as he was a pal of Cliff's.

Well, to my surprise this blond guy turned out to be someone I had worked with years ago in Scotland. His stage name was Ricky Scot and

when I knew him he was in the pop group Marmalade. Now he was working as a self-contained keyboard singer and he certainly was very good. We
got on very well and when he'd finished setting up, we sat around talking
about the old days in the Clyde Valley and the cabaret scene here on the
Costa del Sol.

I stayed on to watch his show and met his wife, a big lady from the Midlands with a strong Birmingham accent, who had a chronic arthritis problem and needed the heat of the Spanish summers to keep her mobile. She
was also looking forward to her retirement in the small flat in Fuengerola
from her divorce settlement. However her serious health problems did not
deter her or Ricky (who had already had a triple heart bypass operation)
from smoking heavily or drinking, which they did almost non-stop. They
were quite appalled at the price I was paying for my room and insisted that
I stay with them, so the next morning Ricky picked me up and moved me
into their spare room for the duration of my stay, which was very nice of
them. In return, I invited them out to dinner at a good restaurant but Anne
also brought along her son and his friend who were on holiday there so in
real terms I might have been better off staying at the Jabega Hotel. (Check
Picker's Tip No 23)

Ricky and I spent quite a few late nights on their balcony reminiscing
about the Scottish club scene in the 70's, when Sydney Devine was the top
earner, and comic Billy Connolly was beginning to make his mark. He also
proudly told me about his son, who was a chef with his own restaurant in
London and had won several Michelin Stars. I suspected that it might have
been the booze talking, but later I found out that his son was the famous
Gordon Ramsey, proprietor of l'Auberge in London's West End and alleged
TV profane bully-boy.

During the day they showed me around the Costa del Sol, and I did some
local gigs with Ricky that blended so well that we got around to thinking
about forming a duo. With our differing styles of music, we could appeal to
a broader audience and hit the bigger venues. We finally settled on the
name Crossfire and I got down to writing some publicity and sorting out
stage outfits.

A week later Cliff and Delores came back and we went to catch their
show at Linda's Bar. They were both surprised to see me and the reminiscing started all over again, although Cliff was at great pains to tell me that
there was not much cash around on the coast. I got the distinct impression
that he was not wild about the prospect of another Country singer on his
patch, old friend or not.

At this juncture I quite liked the town and it did seem to have a lot of
clubs and bars but, when Ann and Ricky introduced me to their crowd, I
began to have some doubts about the scene in general. They were late middle-aged ex-pats who, while insisting that life on the swinging Costa
Geriatrica was great, were covertly seeking ways of getting back to the UK
if they could do it without compromising their lifestyle or losing face. The

usual excuse was some fictitious family crisis or other event, that required their presence. If ever you want to put this to the test, let it slip that you are looking for an apartment or a business and you will be surprised how many of these people come knocking at your door. It's a buyers' market. Forget about those glossy overseas property magazines. Just take a trip and you'll find what you are looking for at almost half the price. I think I mentioned this when we were in Calpe, in 1980—and I found it was still the same fifteen years later.

It was at one of these soirées that I came across Honest Irene, a big brash Walsall hag who, after a few gins, had no qualms whatever on forcing her opinions down the throats of anyone in earshot, threatening anybody who tried to shut her up that she would tell her gangster ex–husband who would fly in and duff them up. They should have called her Obnoxious Olive. Ricky told me later that she did once invoke this sanction, claiming that somebody had insulted her gay son. The ex–husband came over with a mate to sort things out and seeing all the money around, decided to put the arm on a few clubs to cover their expenses, only to find that they were well out of their depth. They were both found unconscious on a quiet Marbella beach early the next morning in a bad way, Irene's ex with his leg impaled on a broken deck chair and his mate with a cracked skull. Oh no, it's not called the Costa del Crime for nothing.

Ricky and I got down to the serious business and did a couple of rehearsed shows which seemed to gel and so, armed with publicity packs and tapes of our act, we went to test the waters. When the club managers realized that there was a strong Country Music content they were very enthusiastic, saying it was the just thing that their affluent German, Dutch, and Nordic clientele were always requesting. I began to think that something was about to happen, so we ventured to some of the better class restaurants and clubs around Mijas and Benadalmena and found that they were willing to pay good money for our polished professional act. It looked as if my hunch was going to pay off and we began to lay plans for the 1996 season. At the time Ann seemed also very enthusiastic and offered to be our manager and handle bookings. Everything seemed be dropping coming together.

When I got home I sent off some of my publicity ideas to Ricky and in fact Ricky and Ann stayed with us in Bath on their next trip to the UK. At the time we all seemed to get on very well but something must have gone wrong when they got back to Coventry, because we completely lost touch with them. We had a sketchy contact through the winter and in May '96 I took Kit out to Fuengerola for two weeks to show her the place, hoping to get a definite time for launching the new act, but things did not feel the same somehow and I suspected that the brainwashing he had been subjected to, had taken root.

The trip got off to a bad start, as neither Kit or I are at ease in large groups of people and we were getting fed up as we were herded like sheep aboard a coach from Malaga Airport to our hotel in Fuengerola, dropping off other holiday makers en route. The distance from Malaga to Fuengerola is about eight miles but with all the detours and drop–offs if took us almost two hours—and some poor sods had to go on to Marbella and Puerta Banus. It must have taken them another two hours to get to their digs.To add to the frustration it rained for the first week and, on one of the rare hot days, I managed to get severely sunburned by stubbornly lying in the sun all afternoon on the beach, which meant that I had to spend the next day in our room uncomfortably wrapped in damp towels.

"Que gilipollas intregale," commented the hotel manager as I thanked him for his sympathy. I later found out that this was Spanish for 'What a complete dickhead.'

We did the rounds but this time the bars seemed to be much seedier than they had on my first visit. I still thought that there was money to be made out there and started to think seriously about renting a place for a few months to allow time for our act to become established and build up a reputation on the top class venues but it didn't work out that way. On meeting Ann and Ricky again, my earlier suspicions were confirmed and it was quite clear that there had been a sea–change in their attitude. It became even more apparent later that evening when she had got a few drinks down her neck. Because I wouldn't go along with her ratty criticism of Cliff and Delores, she turned on us viciously and accused us of being snobs and trying to wreck their marriage, and more or less told us to go home and leave them alone. Ricky smiled sickly and stuck his nose deeper into his glass of tinto.

So that was that. It was an opportunity missed but on the other hand the UK television show was beginning to shape up, so it did not bother me too much and I think that Kit was quite relieved. After that incident in Linda's Bar there was no point in staying on the Costa Del Sol and we tried to get back to the UK early but this proved so complicated and expensive we decided to stick it out till the end of the fortnight, filling the time with visits to Malaga, Marbella, and the huge open air markets at Torremolinos and Arroyo de la Miel, where most of the population seemed to have come from West Yorkshire. It was like Huddersfield with sunshine. I suppose that is the reason they were all there. But it's not my idea of paradise.

There is a sad postscript to the Ricky Scott Saga because early in January 1999 Ann phoned to tell us that Ricky had died of a heart attack on New Year's Day at their Margate home. Must have been all those ciggies. In fact it was a bad period for losing old friends as both Karl Denver and Marion Ryan passed away around the same time.

* * * * * *

47

CALIFORNIA HERE WE COME
B.B. King

Late in 1995 we decided to take a trip to Los Angeles and Las Vegas. Neither of us had ever been to the fabulous West Coast, so we decided to get a few brochures, call in a few favours and set up a working holiday. At the back of my mind was another idea, but more of that later. A lot of sorting out had to be done. Matching up hotels in Los Angeles with hotels in Las Vegas, turned out to be the Holiday Inn Hollywood and the Las Vegas Hilton. A travel agent in Bath fixed up the trip and generally it was a fair deal but we felt that we had been a bit ripped off on the travel insurance. To eliminate as much stress as possible, we also booked a night at the Heathrow Sheraton which cost approximately £100 but included 14 days parking for the car. (Actually this proved to be a complete waste because a week before we left the car broke down and we had to go by train.)

We made the connection with the airport coach at Reading and as darkness fell we arrived at Heathrow Terminal Two where we picked up the shuttle bus for the Sheraton. On the way there we checked the roadside for a nice chippy or curry house but we didn't see any. The first shock was after we had booked in at the hotel and decided to have dinner there. But one look at the prices soon changed that idea. A sandwich was £4.75, a bottle of beer was the same and the prices in the dining room were equally off the wall, the main courses running anything from £17 to £21 a plate. Obviously other plans had to be made and Terminal Two beckoned. So we boarded the shuttle bus back to the airport on the pretext of seeing off friends and spent a nice evening cruising the shops bars and restaurants. The services and refreshment were very good but there was one overriding question in my mind. Why were the majority of these cafés, bars and souvenir shops operated by Asians?

The following morning we were off early and boarded a Boeing 747 around midday just as it started snowing. We were in a bank of three seats, me at the window, Kit in the middle and a stocky guy in the aisle seat. I offered him the window seat but he declined it and we all settled down as the Jumbo became airborne. A conversation sprang up and it turned out that our fellow passenger was from Cornwall. Not just Cornwall, but from Tywardreath, the next village to Par where we used to live, and he knew quite a few people we did. So we passed a pleasant hour talking about old times, Kit wasn't very happy in the middle seat, so she changed to an empty bank across the aisle and tried to sleep. The flight was uneventful and we had plenty of drinks and about enough food and dozed or watched the chair–back television, or walked round the massive plane.

About eleven hours later we landed in Los Angeles. It was three thirty in the afternoon local time and we felt a bit shaky. It took about an hour to clear the airport and a Virgin rep. met us at the Arrival Lounge and hustled us aboard a shuttle bus to pick up our hire car. It was here that we experienced the American Hard Sell again, as the Filipino receptionist tried to bang up the bill by pushing extra insurance cover (£155) over and above the obligatory Crash Damage Waiver (£135) and enthusiastically trying to persuade us to take a bigger car.

"Only another $25 dollars a day Sir. And look what you are getting etc."

Suffering from jet lag and lack of sleep. (To us it was about three in the morning) we about managed to fend off his blandishments but we did see more than one harassed British family getting the treatment and ending up loading their crying tired kids into a Chevrolet nine seat people carrier. Poor confused sods. So much for the' Free Car Hire' option in the brochures.

Eventually, with the help of the Virgin rep. we climbed aboard our little Chrysler Neon and then more trouble hit. How did we get to the Holiday Inn? It was in Hollywood. Where the hell was it? And just where were we?

"Wassamatta?" Grunted our slant–eyed guide. "Ya gotta a map on page six of the Virgin Traveler's book. Just follow the instructions—no sweat."

And with that curt advice he rushed off to nail some more dog tired Brits.

We checked the map and the instructions in the book and I managed to get an overview picture of the place in my mind, noting ominously that if we made a wrong turn we'd end up in the South Central area. where the race riots had been, so we'd better be careful, right? It was like a scene from Bonfire of Vanities. Anyway off we went. Now what was it? Let's check the map on page six—oh yes, there it was at the top of the page about two inches square. Now—turn right—second right and right again at the third light onto La Brea Boulevard etc, etc. But first let's get out of this hire car depot.

'WOW! Watch it Yonk! Remember DRIVE ON THE RIGHT.'

Then we hit the rush hour. Yes! The LOS ANGELES RUSH HOUR. And by now it's going dark and we can't find the interior light to see the map. Oh, Great! I'm driving in this manic traffic stream and Kit's holding the instructions up to the window trying to read by the street lamps. Tempers are fraying and our eyes bugging out like organ stops, but somehow we find Hollywood Holiday Inn and book in. Still somewhat shell–shocked, we arrive at our room only to find ourselves on the 23rd. Floor. As Kit doesn't like being that high up so we moved down to the 12th. which wasn't so bad?

* * * * * *

Hooray for Hollywood

Ok, so, now let's check out Hollywood. We'll freshen up and grab a coffee and pizza in the foyer café and head out to see all the places we had heard so much about.

The famous Hollywood Boulevard was lit up like Blackpool's Golden Mile and had very much the same coarse charisma. It was crowded with garish souvenir shops, each one with its own security guard armed with a nightstick and a can of Mace. Fast food outlets and cafés were jammed between such epic buildings as Mann's (formally Grauman's) Chinese theatre with hand impressions of famous stars in the concrete forecourt and the huge Galaxy cinema complex. We went into Baron's Hamburger café for dinner but hardly managed to munch halfway through the massive portions before the fatigue hit us and we staggered back to our hotel and bed.

The following morning we stood at our window and looked out over the area, and the first thing that struck us was the layer of yellow smog that hung like a low cloud around the tall buildings. Beneath it in the streets of Hollywood there were many empty building plots and a lot of construction going on. We met the Virgin rep in the coffee shop and she told us where to eat and what to see and where the biggest shopping malls were. One of the best eateries was Jack's a small deli on La Brea run by a Thai couple where we took breakfast most mornings

Leaving the car, we set off sightseeing on foot. We followed in the 'Footsteps of the Stars' which was a trail of almost 200 special red star inserts in the sidewalk each bearing the name of a famous entertainer. There was Charlie Chaplin, Greta Garbo, Clint East wood, Bob Hope, etc., including my own favourite Jerry Lee Lewis, and it led along Hollywood Boulevard all the way from La Brea to Vine St. The sidewalk star was reputed to be the highest honor Hollywood could bestow on an artiste, a presumption that a jury of his fellow entertainers had elected the person, like a Grammy or an Oscar. The truth however is a bit more prosaic as explained by David Gritten and Stafford Hildred, biographers to the Stars. A management will propose a celebrity who, if accepted by the Hollywood Chamber of Commerce, gets a star by paying the sum of $3,500.

Turning left up Vine Street we came to the famous Capitol Tower, now sadly hedged in by garbage–strewn vacant lots and crumbling, boarded up shops. On the pavement, snuggled up against the razor–wire topped security fence we came across a hippy young man sitting on the pavement beside the star of John Lennon. It was the 15th anniversary of Lennon's death and this fan had built a small shrine with flowers and candles. A very touching and sincere tribute. Further down, at one of the world's most famous locations, that evocative junction of Sunset Boulevard and Vine St. that featured in so many movies, we came across a shabby shop cashing food stamps and 'Out of Town Welfare Checks' (No I.D. required) crowded with poor people, drunks and derelicts. It was a dangerous location. At one point we were window–shopping along Hollywood Boulevard when we noticed people in front of us moving rapidly into the shops and some café owners locking their doors. We were checking out a Western wear shop when the owner urgently beckoned us inside and locked the door. Then he pointed out a tattooed and combat–booted street gang as they passed by, menacingly swinging chains and baseball bats. Thanking him as we left I checked my watch. It was just 11.30 a m

Opposite the Galaxy Cinema Complex was the often–filmed Roosevelt Hotel, one of Marilyn Monroe's favourite hang–outs and, in spite of its un–impressive front entrance, the hotel was probably the classiest place on the street and still seemed to live up to its '50's reputation. Sybil Shepherd was doing the cabaret there along with the comic impressionist Rich Little, but the rest of the famous buildings of the Golden Era of Hollywood had sadly faded, most of them smothered with garish day–glo posters advertising strip shows or had been converted to cut price novelty shops. Fredrick's of Hollywood was still there, with its flashy lingerie, and behind on Sunset Boulevard was the Hollywood Athletic Club where Errol Flynn, Douglas Fairbanks and others used to work out back in the 1940's and discus their latest starlet conquests. That night we ate at a terrible Italian restaurant, where we were served absolute crap, but plenty of it by a wrinkled old crone in a crimpoline frock and scuffed trainers. She told us she was the owner's mother–in–law and accompanied every visit to our table with moans and complaints about him in a hard Brooklyn accent.Then it was back to the hotel and some TV because we had already been warned against walking away from the brightly lit strip at night. Mind you, it was not much better in daylight.

Feeling a bit more confident, the following day we took the car out and visited the massive Beverley Mall on Santa Monica Boulevard, but did not see anything that was not available for the same price in Europe. Somehow we had imagined that things would be cheaper there but it was not so. Most of the tourist souvenir merchandise seemed to be the same Pacific Rim trash available in cheap shops the world over. The weather was pleasant, so we drove the whole length of Sunset Boulevard through Bel Air and past the homes of film and TV Stars to the coast at Will Roger's Beach and on to Venice Beach. It was quiet, but that was due to the time of the year. I can imagine how busy it would be in summer. As we attempted to park on the street a local traffic warden came over and warned us that as we were so obviously tourists we should take shelter in one of the fenced and guarded parking lots. Venice beach was definitely not somewhere to wander aimlessly around.

Later that week we visited Beverley Hills, where we met Billy Connolly and his kids in a car park on the way to Planet Hollywood for burgers and fries. The shops on Rodeo Drive were fantastic and we spotted quite a few more celebrities. We ate in a bistro on Beverley Boulevard called El

Cucuroo with Bruce Willis in the next booth. Beverley Hills was full of beautiful homes but they seemed crowded together and each one carried a large sobering notice in the front garden announcing the protection and immediate response from armed security patrols.

Beverley Hills abuts onto West Hollywood, which in the sixties was probably the most creative music scene in America. Where the two areas meet on the corner of Doheney Drive is Doug Weston's famous Troubadour Café, where it all began for the likes of of the Byrds, the Flying Burrito Bros, Emmy Lou Harris, Crosby Still & Nash, and as it was the true birthplace of West Coast Country Rock so I HAD to go there. However, like many other icons, it failed to live up to its hallowed status, and had a sad neglected look about it. There were a few old faded posters of Emmy Lou and Janis Joplin and the Eagles on the stained walls, but most of the young boozers and sniffers in there dismissed them as ancient history. I did meet a few old soaks in the back room bar who claimed to have been there in the glory days and had known legends like Don Henley, and Roger M'Guinn, but closer examination proved their claims to be bogus. It was a bit like visiting a pub in Liverpool where everybody claimed to have known John Lennon personally. You must have met 'em.

"Oh yiss, Wack. 'im an Paul too. Sold 'im 'is ferst gitaar, I did. Made up, 'e woz."

But it was time to do a bit of work, so I contacted an agent I'd worked for in Vancouver who had moved to California and he fixed up a couple of guest spots with legendary blues giant B.B.King at his club at Universal Studios. His band was made up of top class blues men like bassist Tommy Besson and the grey haired New Orleans bottleneck legend Mat Corbeau playing a Gibson 335 tuned to an open G.

I was in virtuoso company, but I got through by pulling on my early folk club days and classics like 'Boogie Blues', 'Dirt dishin' Daisy' and 'Outskirts of town'. These classic blues howls were so old everybody thought they were new.

Another night we went to a place called 'The House of the Blues' in the scruffy end of West Hollywood where authentic ethnic Delta Blues were about the last sounds you'll hear from the DJs as they clubbed the sweat-ing mass on the dance floor with thundering Hip–Hop Garage and Porno–Gansta Rap. But hey! That's Hollywood.

What LA writer Julia Phillips called the Clone Capital of the Third World.

*   *   *   *   *   *

48

VIVA! LAS VEGAS

We were glad to leave the smog and violence of Los Angeles for Las Vegas, and the drive across the Mojave Desert was fantastic, with the sky colours constantly changing and every detail of the distant mountains visible in the clear air. You got some idea of the vastness the early pioneers must have felt. Once clear of San Bernardino and its dirty barren hills, the flat desert stretched endlessly before us with only the snow–tipped mountains in the distance and the sparse traffic on Route 43, mostly massive semi-trucks, battered four–wheel drive pick–ups, or the occasional sinister dark windowed, stretched limo streaking to the distant money mines.

We pulled in for a break at Barstow Freight Depot, roughly halfway to Las Vegas and found ourselves surrounded by dozens of complaining senior citizens, who had arrived in a fleet of coaches from the Lake Mead vacation area on a US version of Saga Holidays. It is not often you find bad cafés in the States, but the rambling collection of old railroad cars that served the travellers, was about the worst we came across. No wonder those retirees were moaning. Barstow itself seemed to be on a barren ridge with a cold wind constantly blowing up the fine dust. It was a most strange place for a major railroad junction, though it was also a major staging post on the old Route 66 from Chicago to Los Angeles.

We didn't stay long and as the dusk closed in we saw the bright lights of a casino and hotel complex at El Fontera on the Nevada border and soon the glow in the sky that showed that we were almost at the Gambling Capital of the World. The arrival at the Strip was breathtaking with lights, crowds and music everywhere. Eventually we found the Las Vegas Hilton and moved into our room, and then down to the Casino and started honking the tables and pulling the handles. Great. But we never did win that brand new Cadillac North Star.

Gordie Meltzer, a local agent, called at the Hilton to inform me that he had fixed me up with a few evenings with a very progressive New Country band called JUMPING BOOTS at the Excalibur Hotel. They were very good musicians and deeply into electronic aids. The drummer was fully mike'd and used synchronized electronic rhythm boxes, but was surrounded by a five–foot tall Perspex screen to avoid overtones. All three guitars had radio pick–ups, and the keyboard also went through a direct injection desk controlled from the back of the room by an audio technician. I felt a bit strange in this space–age set up, but the results were very impressive, with a mix of pre–recorded and live sounds coming over the P.A. It was great and the novelty of a "Limey" country singer was well received by the big, mainly Southern crowd. Apart from the current hits of Garth Brooks, Hal Ketchum, and Willie Nelson, they were delighted that I could do all those old country standards of Haggard, Jennings, and Cash, which changed the attitude of the resident band, who now treated me with great respect. Particularly when I shared out the tips.

When you are working in Las Vegas you work hard. The hours on this gig ran from 9.30 p.m. to 2.30am with three twenty–minute breaks, six nights a week. The money of course was great, but you had to know your stuff because, for every band job there were a dozen hungry Southern Country–West Coast Rock sharks waiting to grab your gig. Every karaoke bar and live band honky–tonk had its Garth Brooks clone eyeing the microphone.

Speaking of clones I must tell you about one the most bizarre things I saw in that ultra bizarre town. I had finished my third night at the Excalibur and on the way back to our hotel we decided to drop in to see the Mavericks, who were headlining at the Desert Inn, only to find that there was a $20 cover charge to go into the cabaret lounge. I tried the old stage door ploy, giving them the classic 'We're in the business' routine but they apparently had heard that before, and I got no change from the hard–nosed doormen, so, stuck for something to do, we headed to the Imperial Palace where they were featuring the Star tribute show.

'LEGENDS IN CONCERT'
Advertised on TV as 'just like the real thing.'

No problems here. The floor managers had caught me at the Excalibur so we were slipped in quietly. The show, like all Vegas shows, was superbly produced and presented, and the impressionist talent was certainly of very high standard. Dolly Parton came on, followed by Elton John, Roy Orbison, Elvis, and Tina Turner, et al., all using their own voices to do superb copies of their favourite stars. No pre–recorded vocal tracks here. It was a very entertaining tribute indeed, but the big surprise came after the show, when a crowd of excited starry–eyed vacationers lined up for the autographs of their favorites, which the look–alikes signed (in the name of the star) at five dollars a throw. (Ten bucks with a photo). Unbelievable.

Country Music was booming out there. In fact. in the summer of 1996 one of the biggest Country venues in the world was finished on the Strip. 'Home in the Country' is a huge complex with a thirty metre open air apron onto Sunset Strip itself. with line dancers and live bands performing every afternoon and evening, and shows featuring major New Country stars in the main room each night. Wonderful for any visiting fan, don't miss it.

Three other places made a big impression on me. The first concerns a private passion of mine, classic cars. It was an exhibition which covered the whole top floor of the Imperial Palace Hotel complex and, amongst the hundreds of vehicles on show, including the massive bulletproof Grosse Mercedes of Adolf Hitler and the Alfa Romeo used by Mussolini, was the full range of Duesenberg convertibles from the 1930's. I have seen classic car museums all over the word, but I've seen nothing as good or as varied as that Las Vegas show. It was better than the exhibition at La Defense in Paris or the one in Monaco and that's saying something.

The next breathtaking spectacle was outside Treasure Island. Yes, actually outside, on a water–filled moat at the side of the Strip. Part of the facade had been converted to an authentic Caribbean pirate cove, with ramshackle cottages and lantern lit taverns, complete with pirates and their women singing and carousing in the narrow streets. At the quayside a fully rigged galleon flying the Jolly Roger was moored with the crew un-loading barrels and stowing the sails. Background music came over the speakers and the atmosphere captivated the whole sidewalk audience. Suddenly, there was a loud banging of cannon fire and round the bend in the creek came a British man o' war, guns thundering and drums beating, with bewigged officers shouting orders and the red–coated marines loosed volley after volley of musket shots. The smoke, the noise, and the wounded pirates falling from the rigging into the moat got your blood racing. It was very, very impressive. Eventually an intrepid buccaneer rowed to the Brit-ish ship with a powder barrel and blew it up in a vast explosion and cloud of smoke—and then IT SANK. Yes, Blub, blub, blub, down it went until only the tip of the mast was left with the Captain clinging to it. Then the lights all went off, the music stopped and the preparations began again for the next show an hour later.

The third event was also in the nature of an illusion, which we came across by accident. I was booked to do a guest spot with the Fantastics at Caesar's Palace shopping mall. The back–up band was great, one of those real West Coast Country Rock combos, socking out songs like 'Memphis Tennessee, Margaritaville, C'est la Vie, and Promised land.' etc. They did the original version of 'Willing'. Great! I was almost out of my head. The Fantastics, like me, were older, grayer, and fatter, but they still had that old magic, and had the whole place dancing and clapping. There were two of the original members from the group, I had worked with in Germany back in 1979. They said they remembered me, but I think they were only being polite.

In one of the breaks we wandered round the shopping mall, which was laid out like a Roman street under a domed canopy that looked like the sky, which changed colour from light blue with drifting white clouds to night with twinkling stars. The road twisted round corners and at one point we came across a square with a huge ornate fountain with statues of Roman Gods in pale fawn marble as the water gushed and gentle music played. It was all very impressive but there was more to come.

Soon crowds began to gather round and uniformed security guards moved people back from the edge of the fountain. Then the music changed and a rumble of thunder echoed round the square and the statues began to move. There was a gasp from the crowd as the belly of the main statue began to quiver and his head turned to review the scene. Then his voice boomed out that it was time for drinking to begin and he raised his goblet. At this all the other statues began to move as well. The warrior raised his spear and the girls their harps and drinking jugs as the music swelled to a crescendo. For some three minutes the figures turned and gestured and appeared to sing, as the figure of Zeus roared drunken toasts and then just as suddenly it was over. The music faded and the statues return to their positions. Incredible. I went over and when the guard wasn't looking, touched a statue. It was hard and cold as real marble and I could find no seams or joints anywhere. The band told me that the novelty had cost four hundred thousand dollars—auto–tronics, they called it.

Las Vegas certainly lived up to its reputation. The show never stopped 24 hours a day. In fact to preserve the illusion, there are no clocks any–where in the public rooms. One night, it must have been about four in the morning, out of curiosity I slipped on a pair of pants and a sweater and took the elevator six floors down to the main gaming room of the casino. It was just like ten in the evening, still packed with punters, although there were many more high rollers around, mostly wealthy Orientals or Latinos with gorgeous women in tow. Slot machines clanked away, and on stages in the side rooms, comedians, showgirls, and singers were doing their best to keep the customers coughing up their hard–earned dollars. And remember, at that moment the same scene was probably being re–enacted at every big hotel casino in the town. It happened every night

Sometimes, however, even the enterprising Las Vegas kitsch narrowly misses its target, for instance, at the Las Vegas Hilton where we stayed, there is a life–sized gold–plated statue of Elvis Presley in the main foyer. He is playing his guitar and this is where it goes wrong, because the sculptor has portrayed him playing a gut–stringed Spanish guitar instead of his favourite Martin D18 or Gibson 200. It's the thing only an Elvis fan or a guitar player would notice, but you would have thought that for such a Las Vegas icon they would have got the details right.

Before leaving the Hilton, I was told by a regular visitor of a scam that enabled him and his wife to drink for free in every casino in Vegas. It worked like this. You hit the casino with a bunch of five–dollar bills and head for one of the bars. Here you ask for change and the bartender will hand you a roll of coins, which also entitles you to a free drink. So you take the Jack Daniels and move away to the machines before going to another bar and working the same ploy and getting another free drink. And so on, until you have a big plastic bucket full of unused coins, which you then take to the cashier's cage where it was exchanged for crisp dollar bills. And if you wanted any more to drink you simply moved on to another casino. We tried it once. And it really did work.

*   *   *   *   *   *

Oh No. Not the California Zephyr

By mid–week we realized that there was no way that we could leave Las Vegas in the morning and drive all the way to Los Angeles to catch our flight back to London at four the same afternoon. So we decided to leave a day earlier and spend the last night at the Los Angeles Hilton next to the airport. The desk was very co–operative and said that they would arrange for a room with their sister hotel. So on departure day we light–heartedly checked out and headed back across the desert, cruising very nicely until we reached the outskirts of San Bernardino and then we hit the traffic. We were in time for the afternoon rush AGAIN. Would you believe it?

Six lanes a side and all packed with traffic thundering along at 80mph.

What about this blanket 55 mph limit I'd read about? Nobody seemed to take a blind bit of notice of it. And there was not a traffic cop in sight. Where was the famous California Highway Patrol? (They were all busy making TV movies, I suppose.)

Eventually we left the Interstate 15 to pick up Highway I–10 only to find that it was bumper to bumper, with us stuck in the outside lane feverishly seeking out the exit to the Los Angeles airport (LAX). Utmost in our minds was the warning they had given us when we picked up the hire car, that one wrong turn in that sprawling South Central district and we could end up in one of the very dangerous downtown ghettos, or one of those districts shaded grey on our map indicating places to be avoided. I was still worrying about all this when, to top it all, Kit said, quite calmly:

"Ooh Look. There's a train."

"A what? Wotcha mean?" I stammered in shock. "A train? Nah! Where?"

I started scanning the roadside verge.

"No. Not there," she said. "Just check your mirror."

And at that moment a huge white double–decked train came thundering down the central reservation. At the time I was doing about 75 mph and it passed us like we were standing still. Yes, a BLOODY TRAIN. What next?

By this time my nerves were like shredded wheat as I bounced from lane to lane through this manic traffic, seeking the exit lane for Manchester Bvd. and the signs for the LAX Hilton. I finally managed to squeeze off the highway in front of a honking school bus, shot up the ramp, and somehow picked up the right road to the airport hotel. This was a scabby looking pot–holed highway lined with boarded up shops and neglected bungalows, guarded by razor wire fences where menacing Latino and black gangs lounged on every corner. There was nobody more relieved than me when we shot through the security gate at the Hilton.

One night was enough there. It was like a penitentiary with long window–less concrete passages and, apart from the central foyer, no staff to be seen anywhere. We explained our situation and produced our Virgin vouchers, but they said that we would have to pay for the room ($90) and get the refund from London. Oh yes, and there would be 12 dollars for overnight parking. Reluctant to incur any more expense in the CFTT (Café for Trapped Tourists) we risked a visit to a nearby eatery for a chicken burger, and hurried back to the security of the Hilton to watch TV

Early the following day we were up early to drop off our car at Dollar Rental where the same crew was still pressuring more jet–lagged, arriving Brits to hire bigger cars.

A day later we landed bumpily at Heathrow where it was still snowing.

*   *   *   *   *   *

49

THE CHERRY ON THE CAKE

Now for something I mentioned earlier. For some time now, I had been nurturing the idea of a series of TV shows called YONCO's EUROPE, that would combine, music, food, and travel and be made in a selection of venues across Europe and where better than Hollywood California to launch such an idea? Crazy? Well maybe, but read on.

A few years earlier, despairing of finding capable representation, I had joined a promotional organization called Kelston Ross Associates and, prior to my leaving the UK, they spent some considerable time putting together a dozen publicity packages. Each one contained a biography, photographs, and a CD, along with an outline of the idea, pointing out that although each one of these subjects, food, travel, and music, had all been done separately, never before had they been combined in one program.

Each package was addressed to one of the main regional ITV and BBC television companies in the UK, including some independent programmers like Carlton, Granada and Central etc. and, as soon as we were settled in our hotel, one of the first things I did was to head for the main post office off Sunset Boulevard and bang 'em off, covered with colourful US Mail stamps and that all important Hollywood post mark. If that didn't make somebody sit up and take notice then nothing would. This is the gist of the letter.

YONCO'S EUROPE

The basic concept is that a film crew follows THE FRANK YONCO SHOW around a series of venues in Europe combined with recipes and a mini travelogue of the featured town or area. But not to the usual venues. For instance.

No 1. A gig inside the walled city of St. Malo, Brittany with Breton cooking.
No.2 A concert at the Munich Bierfest, with Bavarian Cuisine.
No.3 The American Film festival at Deauville Casino, with Normandy food.
No.4 An open air concert with fireworks in the Piazza San Marco Venice.
No.5 A beach show at Marbella, complete with sangria & paella.
No.6 A floodlit concert in the castle grounds at Estoril, Portugal.

Other exotic venues could be at Montreux, Switzerland, Majorca, Paris, and Dublin, and at some of the UK's top tourist spots. Scheduled for 30 to 45 minutes, each show would follow the same format with a featured Star guest, etc.

I am currently touring on the West Coast but will be back in the UK in January if you would like to discuss the project in more depth.

Sincere Regards.
Frank Yonco. K.R.A. Hollywood, California.

Well, as you can imagine, when we got back we anxiously sorted through the mail to check on any response to our proposal. To be honest, TV production in Britain at that time was in a state of flux with mergers and financial reconstructing going on everywhere. The result was that the few visionary producers available were too busy watching their backs, and did not feel confident enough to take a chance on new ideas. Safety first was the motto of the day, so many programme controllers opted for the soft option of reality TV, nostalgia, or audience participation game shows. A few stations replied but they did not offer much hope, although Yorkshire and Anglia were cautiously interested, but in the main it was "Not today. Thanks" with varying degrees of courtesy. However, near the bottom of the pile was a letter from HTV. West. It was signed by the Program Controller, Jeremy Payne, and cautiously suggested that I call him on my return from California. He wasn't actually promising anything, but he would like to hear more about my idea. So one freezing day in late January '96 I made my way to the HTV Studios in Bristol. And to an appointment with destiny again.

Jeremy Payne proved to be a tall charming man, who looked to me to be in his early forties, very sharply dressed, and obviously very aware of the TV world and we hit it off right from the start. He said he liked my idea and asked me to outline what I had in mind. We discussed the project item by item, the music, the tourism and the food contents, and in the end he decided to commission a pilot show to be made in Bath. He asked for a few ideas on that and during the following discussion, he was the one who suggested doing the show on a boat. My original idea had been for the show on the sluice gate platform near Pultney Bridge but his boat idea was better and I promised to research it. Jeremy said that he would allocate a staff producer and that someone would be in touch. I could hardly believe it, we were up and running.

He suggested next that I should send videos of earlier TV Shows I had done, so I sent an edited version of the Country Style series I had done for Westward TV and a video from the Welsh SC4 channel of a soap called 'Prys y Farchnad'. I was leaving nothing to chance at this early juncture. All I had was a flimsy promise from Jeremy, but nothing on paper. In fact all through this project I never did get anything on paper. No contract or anything at all, except a photocopy of HTV 's letter to the production company and I knew from past experience that these kinds of plans can easily flounder on the smallest whim of the boardroom or the accountants; not to mention the all too often personality clashes.

Kit was over the moon at the idea, but made it very clear from the outset that she did not want to be involved in the show on camera, but would get right behind me on the production and research. Over dinner we talked it through. Surely, this was going to be the last bite of the apple. The cherry on the cake you might say, so we did not want to miss it. If nothing else, it would be a great way to finish off a career, so we decided to say nothing to anyone until the thing was firmly on the way and, believe me, it was not easy for me to keep my mouth shut (it never was) but somehow I managed to keep schtumm most of the time.

*   *   *   *   *   *

Pre-Production

Early in February, I got a phone call from the HTV producer assigned by Jeremy to the show suggesting that we meet the following day at the Podium in Bath. He turned out to be what I expected; very much like Paul Bernard, who had produced my TV series at Westward Television in Plymouth, a typical regional TV producer in early middle age. He was tall, of medium build with big tired eyes, and a lion's mane of white hair and quite friendly. He was not aware of what he was supposed to do with my project, and he obviously had no idea of my relationship with Jeremy. He asked a few tentative questions on this last point, and I gave him some suitably vague answers as we sized each other up.

My overall impression was that he was not wild about the project and, in spite of his self proclaimed status as a senior producer at HTV, musical shows were not his forte, particularly Country Music. And I knew we were in for a few problems when I showed him a script that referred to Waylon Jennings and he asked, "Who's that?"—although he did say he had heard of Johnny Cash. I realized there and then that he didn't know a Dobro from a doughnut and somehow I did not feel that our association was destined to be a long one, but you never knew. To him this was just another job he had been assigned, while to me it was a most important project. In the event he never used that Waylon bit anyway.

However I pushed ahead with my plans. I had already outlined the show and got stuck into the necessary research. Originally, I had planned for a helicopter taking opening shots of the river and then thought a Sony blimp I had seen cruising over the city one evening would be better, so I got in touch with the operator, Virgin Airships in Eindhoven, but as we could not give them a fixed date for filming, the idea was stillborn.

I checked out the boats available and chose the biggest boat on the River Avon, a pleasure cruiser called the Pride of Bath, which was well equipped for these kinds of functions. The producer and I had another meeting a few days later when budgets and salaries and the hire fee for the boat were agreed. As the filming of the music segment of the show was scheduled for the evening, availability proved no problem.

I put together a nicely–balanced package of tourism, food and music. The food input was from Sue Stiling a food demonstrator from Jolly's Store in Bath. She was good at her job, photogenic and in my opinion showed good potential, so I asked if she was interested in coming on the show and she agreed. It came out later that she thought it was some pick–up line. As for the tourist items, I was seeking the offbeat side of Bath, trying to avoid the well–worn 'Beau Nash–Jane Austin' theme. I felt that the overall effect should present the other facets of the city.

Georgian Bath was in fact the Las Vegas of its day, a gambling town where fortunes were won and lost at all–night card games, held either in private chambers or at the new Assembly Rooms. Today it is the Museum of Costume, but in those Regency times it was known as the Upper Rooms and featured dancing and cabaret as well as the green baize Bezique and Hazard card tables. It was here that the major pop musicians of their day like Hadyn and Paganini attracted huge crowds. The big society play–boys flocked to the city for their wild hell–raising, telling their starchy families they were off to take the waters. It was the same at all the fashionable spa towns across Europe. In Germany, Wiesbaden, Bad Homburg, and Baden–Baden were the stamping grounds of dukes and princes. The spas of southern France had been notorious since the days of Queen Eleanor of Aquitaine, and Georgian Bath copied their example and out–did them all. This was where the best London 'ladies of the night' headed to get some real action. Vicious protection rackets and white slavery flourished, and stolen goods regularly changed hands in the damp slums of Dolmeads and Kingsmead. People caroused all night and sobered up in the hot baths the next day. The steep hilly streets were the province of the burly sedan chairmen, who would often hold their wealthy customers to ransom and extortion, by locking them in the chairs and opening the roof to the cold and rain until they paid up.

Top–flight actresses like Sarah Siddons held court here, while on Gay Street a friend of the famous Doctor Johnson, Mrs. Piozzi, (the former Mrs Thale, who had elbowed her first husband, and married her children's piano teacher while on a tour of Italy). She kept a house of pleasing young ladies, who provided alternative diversions for the spa's visiting gentry, while setting the pace. Lording over all of it, was the dandy Beau Nash and his mistress Mrs. Popjoy. It must have been one hell of a place.

The Victorians did their best to bury this legacy, or to put a finer point on it Prince Albert did, but even the old Queen herself, on a visit to Bristol, insisted that while passing through Bath the blinds of her railway carriage should be drawn, so that she would not see the site of her family's philandering or that the depraved people of this riverside Gomorrah should not offend the royal presence with their rough gazes. It seems rather ironic that her son, who became King Edward VII, should have been so addicted to excesses of la Belle Epoque in Paris. You can see that Bath was a city rich in tradition and eccentric characters. What else do you need for a TV prog? But it wasn't as simple as that.

Mind you, if the target audience had been teenagers, it would have been easy. A famous Hollywood film director once said that to make a good teenage movie you needed only three ingredients. The defiance of authority, the destruction of property, and people taking their clothes off. But that wouldn't work in this case, so I kept looking for novel items.

On the wall of Phillips Auctioneers behind Jolly's store I found a huge mural of the text of the Magna Carta in gothic script. (The result of a competition by the Bath College of Art) and a little known beautiful late Georgian style square called Partis College at Newbridge that had been built in 1836 to house war widows and distressed gentlefolk. It was in fact, the first sheltered housing project ever built in England, and still fulfils that purpose to this very day. Then there was Beckford's tower at Lansdown, the Bath racecourse, the refurbished Avon & Kennet canal, and the beautiful buildings of the city itself. It was a cornucopia of nostalgia and scandal. Great, just what I needed.

There then began a one–way correspondence with me submitting ideas by mail and the producer responding with the occasional phone call. In fact during the whole eight months of the production, I only had one note from him. Even my final payment cheque came with only a printed compliment slip. I think he suffered from graphophobia. (You know, a reluctance to put anything on paper.)

It turned out, although unknown to me at that stage, that he was going through a traumic time; all the internal changes within commercial television resulted in his being made redundant. The outcome was that he decided to form his own production company and, as a parting gesture, HTV had given him this Bath project as an independent production, which rather changed the financial and contractual situation. Not that I would have said anything about it,as I was anxious to get this show on the screen, but I made a vow to look into things much more closely if further programs were to be made. To be honest I was quite surprised and pleased that the project had got this far, so I held my tongue and got on with my research, although I must admit to a few nights of pillow–punching frustration at the lack of enthusiasm by the producer.

Still without any confirmation other than Jeremy's verbal promise, I pushed on with the musical side of the show. The first thing to do was to get a rough idea of the running order and then select the people to be involved, particularly the guest star. I chose an old friend from our Cornwall days, Sarah Jory, who was making a big mark on the New Country scene. I say old friend, in spite of the fact that she was still in her early twenties, because we had first met her over twelve years previously as a child prodigy on the steel guitar. How well I remember her father bringing this little girl to our shows and her perching on a stool doing her thing aboard a Sho–bud 10 string steel guitar in the intervals. But now she was a singer— and what singer. And what a metamorphosis. Talk about the ugly duckling and the swan. Gone was the shy Cornish dumpling and in her place was a beautiful, vibrant, power–house singer with attitude, Very much a 90's New Country Girl out of Nashville. Ideal for the function I had in mind. I also flew in Felicity Haze from the Muscat Intercontinental Hotel to join the show. She was another glamorous singer and superb guitarist, with a vast experience of top class cabaret and who had worked in major venues in Nashville, so no problems there.

Next came the musicians and the recording of the music and, of course, the line dancers. I was undecided how to handle this. There were two options, either to use a ready–made band or to put together a group of session musicians specifically for this show. Taking the first option. I contacted Bristol–based bandleader Alan Brittan, whom I had known back in the days of the Shag Connors Show. He was a superb guitarist and had shared the stage with the great Chet Atkins. I liked the sound of the band very much. It was pure New Country and I went up with steelie Colin Scott to do a couple of songs with them at their regular gig. I found that they lacked flexibility, and were only there to support the leader, who both sang and played lead guitar. I must say he did the job very well, but how he would have handled playing in a pure backing situation I was not sure. I once had the same problem in the 70's with a contemporary from the Thames Valley who, in spite of the large fee, could not bring himself to back another British singer. It was an ego thing, so I had my doubts.

On the surface, the Bristol musician appeared to have everything going for him. He had a recording studio and good production skills and his wife was a good businesswoman, but the option fell apart when she submitted a budget to me for recording time, live music, and line dancing sessions that was totally unrealistic. In fact, it was almost four times higher than my allotted budget. So I had to find another way, and moved to the second option for the band, but there was still the line dancing problem. The answer came quite by chance a week later at a meeting with steel player, Bob Dixon, when he suggested I get in touch with Jackie Weymouth in Bristol, who also ran a team of line dancers, so I did and she jumped at the chance. Another problem solved—but it still left the music to sort out.

I called in the services of Pete Lamb and decided to use his Music Work–shop in Devizes and some of his musicians. In the event I used Pete himself on bass and second guitar, Kevin Romang on keyboards and accordion, Bob Dixon on steel, adding two top session men, the incomparable Paul Henry picking guitar and Peter Haige on drums. They had both worked with me in France and, apart from being the best men at their craft, they were a bunch of nice guys with none of the hang–ups that soured so many sidemen. But people like these and top quality recording studios don't come cheap, so I was still sweating about the paperwork from HTV—if it all went pear shaped then the bills would be down to me.

Flis Haze and Kevin volunteered to do the back–up vocals, which they did superbly. Then came the tedious part; selecting and timing the types and sequence of the songs, as well as selecting the background music. The dance items also needed timing and arranging, but it had to be done, and I spent many boring hours with a tape recorder and a stopwatch before the balanced program came together.

Early in June I finally did get some paperwork, though it was only a photocopy of a letter from HTV to the producer, commissioning the produc–tion of the FRANK YONCO SHOW as a 60–minute light entertainment show. I never did see the original, which was not addressed to me anyway, but I could now forge ahead with more confidence. It was definitely on.

However, there was a shock waiting for us when we had a meeting with the producer at Sue Stiling's house to finalize her cooking segment of the show. I had expected that we were going to have an experienced floor manager from HTV to provide the important link between the director and the performers, but our producer arrived with his lady who was also his business partner, and she bluntly announced that she would be co–producing the show. She did not give me the impression of having a lot of TV production experience but I was not in a position to object. Apparently she had been a watercolor artist of some note and was now writing novels, but I could not see a reason for her inclusion in the show.

She was a nice lady though, very much in the mould of a mature and faded left–wing hippy, all flowing skirts and folksy scarves, with a gentle voice that hid a steely determination. Petticoat power indeed. Quite naturally we did not see eye to eye on everything. There was no doubt a personality clash, but both of us managed to keep it under wraps—she wanted to pursue the standard Bath tourist approach, while I wanted to be more radical, but eventually we achieved a compromise in the script and a guarded mutual respect, although my doubts about her lack of floor management experience were justified at the show on board the boat later.

In July we got the musicians into the recording studio and laid down the show tracks, all of them very good. Sarah's DAT guide tape arrived and was patched into the show after which we did three days of arranging and playing and then left Pete Lamb to do the final mix. Pete ran copies off for the musicians so everybody was familiar with their parts. Felicity flew back to gigs in Oman and Ibiza, the line dancers got on with their rehearsals and I continued my research and writing and timing the show.

The producer was now also deeply immersed in a series of shows in Plymouth so we were only loosely in touch at this time. When we did meet again he was quite impressed with the work I had put in, and said that he had never expected such in–depth planning, which I found easy to believe as we differed greatly in approach. I have always liked to prepare the ground well beforehand, covering as many possible eventualities as I can, while he flew by the seat of his pants, firmly subscribing to the principal that 'It would be alright on the night.' And anyone who has seen Denis Norden's TV show knows what that can lead to. But it was going to be my face on that screen, so I wasn't going to take any chances.

When the show was first proposed to HTV it was envisaged as a thirty-minute feature, but somehow it was extended to one hour and we had to find an extra item. Something connected with rugby seemed to be a natural for the City of Bath but how to include it? Then, one afternoon while visiting Sue in Jollys I got the answer.

She was doing an exotic meats promotion and the specialty that afternoon was stir–fried locusts, also on the menu were crocodile kebabs, ostrich steaks. marinated goat and wild boar fillet—Mm.Yummy! (Well, interesting anyway). I thought 'What if I could challenge some of our macho Bath rugby heroes to feast on these delicacies and see how they reacted?' So, bursting with enthusiasm, I put the idea forward but, predictably, the budget–conscious producer and his assistant considered it being a bit too controversial—Jane Austen would not have approved. In the end we compromised once again by having Sue prepare a wild boar dish, and I spent a sweltering day in deepest Somerset filming a ramshackle cider brandy distillery. Although we did not get a drink, the generous owner offered to sell us some of his sub–standard distillate at a discount. After that it was on to a stinking wild boar farm. Ugh! They must be the smelliest, animals on earth.

The Cameras Roll

It was August 5th. The big multi–camera, filming days had arrived and the weather could not have been kinder, with the sun beating down making the fawn stone buildings of the city glow. We made an early start and by 8.30am we were setting up in Jollys store for the food item. Then, it was out into the city, shopping and doing commentaries at the Costume Museum, Sydney Gardens, and Beckford's Tower, after which there was the rather watered–down celebration meal in Jolly's sweltering Gold Card Room followed by the line dancing in the Abbey Courtyard, with its inevitable confrontation with the scruffy drunks and drifters.

Then we were off to the 'Pride of Bath'. Sarah and all the musicians had arrived in the afternoon and had set up on the deck. Fortunately Kit was on hand to organize things on stage. The audience turned up around 6.30 p.m. and piled aboard, all set to have a good time. Ollie Farnese, our host opened up the bar below decks and the drinks began to flow. There was only one moment of anxiety when suddenly the sky became cloudy just before we cast off, but the threatened summer rain did not materialize.

Luckily, the show sequence had been well worked out and everybody had a written idiot sheet, which was fortunate, as the producer had not allowed any time for rehearsal or stage positioning. The lack of a competent floor manager left everybody hanging around unsure of what they should be doing or exactly what positions to be in, until Kit took over the function and sorted it all out, including Sarah and Felicity's changing arrangements. At one point I asked the producer's PA to provide a big mirror below decks but she put on a pained expression and pleaded that she was much to busy for things like that. I wonder to this day what she was doing there.

Meanwhile our own 'W.D. Griffith' the producer–director was with the camera monitor at the prow of the boat behind the audience, while we were 80 feet away in front of them, with no contact with him except for a few frantic hand signals, with his loyal assistant standing closely at his side, looking dazed. So much for 'It'll be all right on the night' However the end result was very good as we cruised the river while the evening closed in and the floodlit weir and Pultney Bridge provided a sensational background as people clapped and waved from the bridges in the twilight. So we all ended up very pleased with the final show and we all got paid. So maybe I am being a bit picky.

The Screening

I asked to be involved in the editing, if only on the music side, but my request was tacitly ignored and due to his Plymouth commitments the producer and I did not have much contact. In fact the first knowledge I had that the program had been edited was when the manager of Jolly's store stopped me and said she'd seen the "Video" and that it was great. Apparently Sue Stiling had been given a copy to take with her on holiday to Australia but I never did get to see the film until the night of the first transmission and obviously I did not get to do any editing.

However, on the evening of November 22nd we unplugged the phone and settled down with a bottle of Bollinger, a platter of lemon sole gougeons and French bread, and at 10.45 p.m., *the Show came on.*

WELCOME
TO FRANK YONCO'S BATH NIGHT

Well, it was terrific! Everything about it was great and in spite of my earlier misgivings, I thought that the producer had done a superb job. I looked comfortable and both Felicity and Sarah performed magnificently. The planned balance worked out well with Felicity's songs interlaced with line dancing shots from the Abbey square and Sarah socking it to them on the boat. We did a couple of costume changes and I used both my 30-year-old Fender Newporter and the Telecaster guitars. The editing was good, as was the sound and the camera work. There were some small flaws in the musical editing, but in general it was a superb show. The response by the public was terrific. Lots of people wrote in to HTV asking when we were doing some more, and people stopped us in the street when we went down town to the shops, saying how much they enjoyed it. Even some of our rather reserved neighbours in Cavendish Crescent congratulated us. Flis was delighted with it when we showed it to her on her return from Oman, as were most of our friends and relatives.

Oh yes. I finally got a contract from the producer five months after we'd made the show and later, in January 1997, I got a nice letter from Jeremy Payne, who said that he had enjoyed the show and thanked me for the energy and enthusiasm I had put in. So it did turn out to be the Cherry on the Cake.

The projected series did not come to fruition due mainly to the boardroom changes at HTV. The new management had its own ideas of the company's future function, which apparently did not include the in-house production of light entertainment. However a couple of years later we made a very nice CD of the music from the show, plus a few nice original songs, including the haunting and nostalgic tribute to Cornwall, 'Red Rocks and White Waters.' and the emotive 'Kit's Song', which I wrote to thank her for our adventures and wonderful life together!

THE END (or is it?)

EPILOGUE

See? I told you it might not be the end.

We moved apartments to one of the most elegant streets in Europe, a wide boulevard called Great Pulteney Street, right in the heart of the city and friends could not see why we left one of the famous Bath Crescents. To be honest, I was having a knee problem and getting fed up with the steep hill. In town it was flat and the shops were conveniently to hand, our corner shop was the Waitrose Supermarket. Great. Actually, we had intended to return to Nice after leaving the Crescent, but we liked being in town and settled down very well. We still took our regular trips to the South of France, usually by the superb Eurostar and French TGV trains, so the idea of living abroad was put on the back–burner for a while.

What was not good though, was the discovery that Kit had breast cancer. She had felt a lump in the previous summer, and went for a biopsy in October 2001 that turned out positive. We were naturally shocked but stayed calm and determined to get it sorted out together. A month later Kit went to the special unit at the Royal United Hospital in Bath, and on December 6th she had surgery and came home, bright and cheerful six days later. She had to return on January 18th for a small clean–up operation and then started the debilitating process of radiotherapy.

This treatment required daily sessions at the R.U.H. for six weeks. I think by the end of this course the car knew its own way there and we were on first name terms with most of the nurses. This part of recuperation process was followed by a course of the anti–recurrence drug tamoxifen. Oh, yes, that winter was a very stressful time for us but, as the spring came we perked up like the sprouting daffodils, Kit started voluntary work and I got back to writing.

In June 2003 a Hollywood production company came to Great Pulteney Street to film Thackeray's Vanity Fair. It was of course a costume drama and the Georgian buildings were an ideal setting. Some of us residents were roped in as extras and support actors: I became Cap'n Marriyat, a rake and a gambler, and they cast Kitty as Becky Burdock, a poor working woman. Aw! How about that for type casting?

By the time of Waylon Jennings's death in February 2002, I had given up serious playing. The popular music scene had changed. Original talent was rare and appeared to be unwanted, as the back pages of the music magazines and even the prestigious 'Stage' proliferated with so–called tribute acts. Finally, the passing of Johnny Cash made me realize, for me too, the times were a–changing.

It struck me forcibly that the two dominant musical influences in my life, Hank Williams and Johnny Cash died almost exactly fifty years apart; Hank in 1953 and Johnny in 2003 and that those dates neatly encapsulated my own musical career.

So it was time to hang the guitars on the cabin wall, but I will say something. It's been a Hell of a Ride.

And this really is the End!

I can still hear those Pioneers

*   *   *   *   *   *